The Social History of Crime and Punishment in America

The Social History of Crime and Punishment in America
AN ENCYCLOPEDIA

4

Wilbur R. Miller ■ EDITOR

State University of New York at Stony Brook

$SAGE reference

Los Angeles | London | New Delhi
Singapore | Washington DC

SAGE

Los Angeles | London | New Delhi
Singapore | Washington DC

FOR INFORMATION:

SAGE Publications, Inc.
2455 Teller Road
Thousand Oaks, California 91320
E-mail: order@sagepub.com

SAGE Publications India Pvt. Ltd.
B 1/I 1 Mohan Cooperative Industrial Area
Mathura Road, New Delhi 110 044
India

SAGE Publications Ltd.
1 Oliver's Yard
55 City Road
London EC1Y 1SP
United Kingdom

SAGE Publications Asia-Pacific Pte. Ltd.
3 Church Street
#10-04 Samsung Hub
Singapore 049483

Vice President and Publisher: Rolf A. Janke
Senior Editor: Jim Brace-Thompson
Project Editor: Tracy Buyan
Cover Designer: Bryan Fishman
Editorial Assistant: Michele Thompson
Reference Systems Manager: Leticia Gutierrez
Reference Systems Coordinators: Laura Notton,
    Anna Villasenor
Marketing Manager: Kristi Ward

Golson Media
President and Editor: J. Geoffrey Golson
Director, Author Management: Susan Moskowitz
Production Director: Mary Jo Scibetta
Layout Editors: Kenneth Heller, Stephanie Larson,
    Oona Patrick, Lois Rainwater
Copy Editors: Mary Le Rouge, Holli Fort
Proofreader: Barbara Paris
Indexer: J S Editorial

Copyright © 2012 by SAGE Publications, Inc.

All rights reserved. No part of this book may be reproduced or utilized in any form or by any means, electronic or mechanical, including photocopying, recording, or by any information storage and retrieval system, without permission in writing from the publisher.

Library of Congress Cataloging-in-Publication Data

The social history of crime and punishment in America : an encyclopedia /
Wilbur R. Miller, general editor.
    v. cm.
 Includes bibliographical references and index.
 ISBN 978-1-4129-8876-6 (cloth)
    1. Crime--United States--History--Encyclopedias. 2. Punishment--United
States--History--Encyclopedias. I. Miller, Wilbur R., 1944-
 HV6779.S63 2012
 364.97303--dc23
                                2012012418

SFI Certified Sourcing
www.sfiprogram.org
SFI-00453

12 13 14 15 16 10 9 8 7 6 5 4 3 2 1

Contents

Volume 4

List of Articles *vii*

Articles

R	*1479*	W	*1899*
S	*1595*	X	*1979*
T	*1745*	Y	*1983*
U	*1835*	Z	*1987*
V	*1857*		

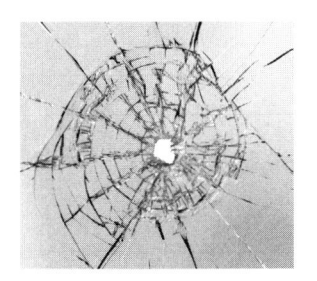

List of Articles

A
Ableman v. Booth
Abortion
Abrams v. United States
Adair v. United States
Adams, John (Administration of)
Adams, John Quincy (Administration of)
Adultery
Adversarial Justice
African Americans
Alabama
Alaska
Alcatraz Island Prison
Alien and Sedition Acts of 1798
American Bar Association
American Civil Liberties Union
American Law Institute
American Revolution and Criminal Justice
An American Tragedy
Anarchists
Anti-Federalist Papers
Antitrust Law
Appeals
Appellate Courts
Arizona
Arkansas
Arpaio, Joseph M.
Arraignment
Arthur, Chester (Administration of)
Articles of Confederation

Atlanta, Georgia
Attica
Auburn State Prison
Augustus, John
Autobiographies, Criminals'
Automobile and the Police
Aviation and Transportation Security Act of 2001

B
Bail and Bond
Bail Reform Act
Bailey, F. Lee
Bakker, Jim
Ballistics
Baltimore, Maryland
Barron v. Mayor of Baltimore
Beaumont, Gustave de
Bedford Hills Correctional Facility
Berkowitz, David
Bertillon System
Bible
Bigamy/Polygamy
Bill of Rights
Billy the Kid
Birmingham, Alabama
Black Panthers
Blackstone, William
Blood Sports
Blue Laws. *See* State Blue Laws
Bodie of Liberties

Bodine, Polly
Boles, Charles
Bonnie and Clyde
Book of the General Lawes & Libertyes
Booth, John Wilkes
Bootlegging
Borden, Lizzie
Border Patrol
Boston, Massachusetts
Bounty Hunters
Bowers v. Hardwick
Brandenburg v. Ohio
Brennan, William J., Jr.
Brocius, William
Brockway, Zebulon
Brown v. Board of Education
Brown v. Mississippi
Buchanan, James (Administration of)
Buck v. Bell
Bundy, Ted
Buntline, Ned
Bureau of Alcohol, Tobacco, Firearms and Explosives
Buren, Martin Van (Administration of)
Burger, Warren
Burglary, Contemporary
Burglary, History of
Burglary, Sociology of
Bush, George H. W. (Administration of)
Bush, George W. (Administration of)
Byrnes, Thomas

C

California
Camden, New Jersey
Caminetti v. United States
Capital Punishment
Capone, Al
Carter, Jimmy (Administration of)
Chain Gangs and Prison Labor
Chandler v. Florida
Chapman, Mark David
Chicago, Illinois
Chicago Seven/Democratic National Convention of 1968
Child Abuse, Contemporary
Child Abuse, History of
Child Abuse, Sociology of
Child Murderers, History of
Children, Abandoned

Children's Rights
Chillicothe Correctional Institution
Chinese Americans
Chinese Exclusion Act of 1882
Chisholm v. Georgia
Christie, Agatha
Cincinnati, Ohio
Citizen Participation on Juries
Civil Disobedience
Civil Rights Act of 1866
Civil Rights Act of 1875
Civil Rights Laws
Clayton Anti-Trust Act of 1914
Clemency
Cleveland, Grover (Administration of)
Cleveland, Ohio
Clinton, William (Administration of)
Clinton Correctional Facility
Code of Silence
Codification of Laws
Cohens v. Virginia
Coker v. Georgia
Colonial Charters and Grants
Colonial Courts
Colorado
Common Law Origins of Criminal Law
Community Policing and Relations
Community Service
Compton, California
Computer Crime
Comstock Law
Confession
Confidence Games and Frauds
Connecticut
Constitution of the United States of America
Convention on the Rights of the Child
Convict Lease System
Coolidge, Calvin (Administration of)
Corporal Punishment
Corrections
Corruption, Contemporary
Corruption, History of
Corruption, Sociology of
Counterfeiting
Court of Common Pleas
Court of Oyer and Terminer
Court of Quarter Sessions
Courts
Courts of Indian Offenses
Coverture, Doctrine of

Crabtree v. State
Crime and Arrest Statistics Analysis
Crime in America, Causes
Crime in America, Distribution
Crime in America, Types
Crime Prevention
Crime Rates
Crime Scene Investigation
Criminalization and Decriminalization
Criminology
Critical Legal Studies Movement
Cruel and Unusual Punishment
Cruelty to Animals
Cummings, Homer
Cunningham, Emma
Customs Service as Police
Czolgosz, Leon

D
Dahmer, Jeffrey
Darrow, Clarence
Davis v. State
Dayton, Ohio
Death Row
Declaration of Independence
Defendant's Rights
Delaware
Democratic National Convention of 1968. *See* Chicago Seven/Democratic National Convention of 1968
Dennis v. United States
Deportation
DeSalvo, Albert
Detection and Detectives
Deterrence, Theory of
Detroit, Michigan
Devery, William
Dewey, Thomas E.
Dillard v. the State of Georgia
Dillinger, John
Dime Novels, Pulps, Thrillers
Discretionary Decision Making
District Attorney
Domestic Violence, Contemporary
Domestic Violence, History of
Domestic Violence, Sociology of
Douglas, William O.
Dred Scott v. Sandford
Drinking and Crime
Drug Abuse and Addiction, Contemporary

Drug Abuse and Addiction, History of
Drug Abuse and Addiction, Sociology of
Drug Enforcement Administration
Due Process
Duren v. Missouri
Dyer Act

E
Earp, Wyatt
Eastern State Penitentiary
Eddy, Thomas
Eisenhower, Dwight D. (Administration of)
Eisenstadt v. Baird
Electric Chair, History of
Electronic Surveillance
Elkins Act of 1903
Elmira Prison
Embezzlement
Emergency Quota Act of 1921
Enforcement Acts of 1870–1871
English Charter of Liberties of 1100
Enron
Entrapment
Environmental Crimes
Equality, Concept of
Espionage
Espionage Act of 1917
Estes v. Texas
Ethics in Government Act of 1978
Everleigh Sisters
Executions

F
Famous Trials
Fear of Crime
Federal Bureau of Investigation
Federal Common Law of Crime
Federal Policing
Federal Prisons
Federal Rules of Criminal Procedure
Federalist Papers
Felonies
Ferguson, Colin
Fillmore, Millard (Administration of)
Film, Crime in
Film, Police in
Film, Punishment in
Fingerprinting
Fish and Game Laws
Fletcher v. Peck

Florida
Floyd, Charles Arthur
Ford, Gerald (Administration of)
Forensic Science
Fornication Laws
Fraud
Freedom of Information Act of 1966
Frontier Crime
Frontiero v. Richardson
Fugitive Slave Act of 1793
Fugitive Slave Act of 1850
Furman v. Georgia

G

Gacy, John Wayne
Gambling
Gangs, Contemporary
Gangs, History of
Gangs, Sociology of
Gardner, Erle Stanley
Garfield, James (Administration of)
Gates v. Collier
Gender and Criminal Law
Genovese, Vito
Georgia
German Americans
Gibbons v. Ogden
Gideon v. Wainwright
Giuliani, Rudolph
Glidewell v. State
Gotti, John
Grafton, Sue
Grant, Ulysses S. (Administration of)
Great Depression
Green, Anna K.
Gregg v. Georgia
Griffin v. California
Griswold v. Connecticut
Grutter v. Bollinger
Guiteau, Charles
Gun Control
Guns and Violent Crime

H

Habeas Corpus, Writ of
Habeas Corpus Act of 1679
Habeas Corpus Act of 1863
Hamilton, Alexander
Hammett, Dashiell
Hanging
Harding, Warren G. (Administration of)
Harris, Eric. *See* Klebold, Dylan and Eric Harris
Harrison, Benjamin (Administration of)
Harrison Act of 1914
Hauptmann, Bruno
Hawai'i
Hayes, Rutherford B. (Administration of)
Hays, Jacob
Hereditary Crime
Hillerman, Tony
Hispanic Americans
History of Crime and Punishment in America: Colonial
History of Crime and Punishment in America: 1783–1850
History of Crime and Punishment in America: 1850–1900
History of Crime and Punishment in America: 1900–1950
History of Crime and Punishment in America: 1950–1970
History of Crime and Punishment in America: 1970–Present
Holden v. Hardy
Holmes, Oliver Wendell, Jr.
Holt v. Sarver
Homeland Security
Homestead Act of 1862
Hoover, Herbert (Administration of)
Hoover, J. Edgar
Hurtado v. California

I

Idaho
Identity Theft
Illinois
Immigration Crimes
Incapacitation, Theory of
Incest
Indecent Exposure
Independent Treasury Act
Indian Civil Rights Act
Indian Removal Act
Indiana
Infanticide
Insanity Defense
Internal Revenue Service
Internal Security Act of 1950
International Association of Chiefs of Police
Internment

Interrogation Practices
Interstate Commerce Act of 1887
Intolerable Acts of 1774
Iowa
Irish Americans
Italian Americans

J

Jackson, Andrew (Administration of)
Jackson, Mississippi
James, Jesse
Japanese Americans
Jefferson, Thomas
Jefferson, Thomas (Administration of)
Jewish Americans
Johnson, Andrew (Administration of)
Johnson, Lyndon B. (Administration of)
Johnson v. Avery
Judges and Magistrates
Judiciary Act of 1789
Juries
Jurisdiction
Justice, Department of
Juvenile Corrections, Contemporary
Juvenile Corrections, History of
Juvenile Corrections, Sociology of
Juvenile Courts, Contemporary
Juvenile Courts, History of
Juvenile Delinquency, History of
Juvenile Delinquency, Sociology of
Juvenile Justice, History of
Juvenile Offenders, Prevention and Education
Juvenile Offenders in Adult Courts

K

Kaczynski, Ted
Kansas
Kansas City, Missouri
Katz v. United States
Katzenbach v. McClung
Kennedy, John F. (Administration of)
Kennedy, Robert F.
Kent State Massacre
Kentucky
Kevorkian, Jack
Kidnapping
King, Martin Luther, Jr.
King, Rodney
Klebold, Dylan, and Eric Harris
Knapp Commission

Korematsu v. United States
Ku Klux Klan
Kunstler, William

L

La Guardia, Fiorello
Landrum-Griffin Act of 1859
Larceny
Las Vegas, Nevada
Law Enforcement Assistance Act
Law Enforcement Assistance Administration
Lawrence v. Texas
Laws and Liberties of Massachusetts
Lawyers Guild
Leavenworth Federal Penitentiary
Legal Counsel
Leopold and Loeb
Libertarianism
Lincoln, Abraham (Administration of)
Lindbergh Law
Lindsey, Ben
Literature and Theater, Crime in
Literature and Theater, Police in
Literature and Theater, Punishment in
Livestock and Cattle Crimes
Livingston, Edward
Lochner v. New York
Los Angeles, California
Louisiana
Loving v. Virginia
Luciano, "Lucky"
Lynchings

M

Macdonald, Ross
Madison, James (Administration of)
Madoff, Bernard
Magna Carta
Maine
Malcolm X
Mandatory Minimum Sentencing
Mann Act
Manson, Charles
Mapp v. Ohio
Marbury v. Madison
Marshall, John
Martin v. Hunter's Lessee
Maryland
Maryland Toleration Act of 1649
Massachusetts

Matteawan State Hospital
Mayflower Compact
McCarthy, Joseph
McCleskey v. Kemp
McCulloch v. Maryland
McKinley, William (Administration of)
McNabb v. United States
McVeigh, Timothy
Memoirs, Police and Prosecutors
Memphis, Tennessee
Menendez, Lyle and Erik
Miami, Florida
Michigan
Military Courts
Military Police
Minnesota
Minor v. Happersett
Miranda v. Arizona
Miranda Warnings. *See Miranda v. Arizona*
Mississippi
Mississippi v. Johnson
Missouri
M'Naghten Test
Mollen Commission
Monroe, James (Administration of)
Montana
Moonshine
Morality
MOVE
Mudgett, Herman
Mug Shots
Muhammad, John Allen
Muller v. Oregon
Munn v. Illinois
Murder, Contemporary
Murder, History of
Murder, Sociology of
Murders, Unsolved
Music and Crime

N

Narcotics Laws
National Association for the Advancement of Colored People
National Commission on Law Observance and Enforcement
National Congress on Penitentiary and Reformatory Discipline
National Organization for Women
National Police Gazette

National Prison Association
National Security Act of 1947
Native American Tribal Police
Native Americans
Nebraska
Nelson, "Baby Face"
Ness, Eliot
Neutrality Enforcement in 1793–1794
Nevada
New Hampshire
New Jersey
New Mexico
New Orleans, Louisiana
"New Punitiveness"
New York
New York City
Newark, New Jersey
News Media, Crime in
News Media, Police in
News Media, Punishment in
Nitti, Frank
Nixon, Richard (Administration of)
North Carolina
North Dakota
Northwest Ordinance of 1787

O

Oakland, California
Obama, Barack (Administration of)
Obscenity
Obscenity Laws
Ohio
Oklahoma
Oklahoma City Bombing
Olmstead v. United States
Omnibus Crime Control and Safe Streets Act of 1968
Oregon
Organized Crime, Contemporary
Organized Crime, History of
Organized Crime, Sociology of
Oswald, Lee Harvey

P

Padilla v. Kentucky
Paine, Thomas
Paretsky, Sara
Parker, Isaac
Parker, William
Parole

Peltier, Leonard
Pendleton Act of 1883
Penitentiaries
Penitentiary Study Commission
Penn, William
Pennsylvania
Pennsylvania System of Reform
People v. Pinnell
People v. Superior Court of Santa Clara County
Percival, Robert V.
Peterson, Scott
Petty Courts
Philadelphia, Pennsylvania
Pickpockets
Pierce, Franklin (Administration of)
Pittsburgh, Pennsylvania
Plea
Plessy v. Ferguson
Poe, Edgar Allen
Police, Contemporary
Police, History of
Police, Sociology of
Police, Women as
Police Abuse
Political Crimes, Contemporary
Political Crimes, History of
Political Crimes, Sociology of
Political Dissidents
Political Policing
Polk, James K. (Administration of)
Pornography
Posses
Presidential Proclamations
President's Commission on Law Enforcement and the Administration of Justice
Prison Privatization
Prison Riots
Prisoner's Rights
Private Detectives
Private Police
Private Security Services
Probation
Proclamation for Suppressing Rebellion and Sedition of 1775
Procunier v. Martinez
Professionalization of Police
Prohibition
Prostitution, Contemporary
Prostitution, History of
Prostitution, Sociology of

Punishment of Crimes Act, 1790
Punishment Within Prison
Pure Food and Drug Act of 1906
Puritans

Q
Quakers

R
Race, Class, and Criminal Law
Race-Based Crimes
Racism
Rader, Dennis
Ragen, Joseph
Ramirez, Richard
Rape, Contemporary
Rape, History of
Rape, Sociology of
Ray, James Earl
Reagan, Ronald (Administration of)
Reform, Police and Enforcement
Reform Movements in Justice
Rehabilitation
Religion and Crime, Contemporary
Religion and Crime, History of
Religion and Crime, Sociology of
Reports on Prison Conditions
Retributivism
Reynolds v. United States
Rhode Island
Ricci v. DeStefano
Riots
Robbery, Contemporary
Robbery, History of
Robbery, Sociology of
Roberts v. Louisiana
Rockefeller, Nelson
Roe v. Wade
Romer v. Evans
Roosevelt, Franklin D. (Administration of)
Roosevelt, Theodore (Administration of)
Roth v. United States
Rothstein, Arnold
Ruby Ridge Standoff
Rule of Law
Rural Police

S
Sacco and Vanzetti
Salem Witch Trials

xiv List of Articles

San Francisco, California
San Quentin State Prison
Santobello v. New York
Schenck v. United States
School Shootings
Schultz, "Dutch"
Scopes Monkey Trial
Scottsboro Boys Cases
Secret Service
Securities and Exchange Commission
Sedition Act of 1918
Segregation Laws
Selective Service Act of 1967
Sentencing
Sentencing: Indeterminate Versus Fixed
Serial and Mass Killers
Sex Offender Laws
Sex Offenders
Sexual Harassment
Shaming and Shunning
Sheppard, Sam
Sheppard v. Maxwell
Sheriffs
Sherman Anti-Trust Act of 1890
Simpson, O. J.
Sin
Sing Sing Correctional Facility
Sirhan Sirhan
Slave Patrols
Slavery
Slavery, Law of
Smith, Susan
Smith Act
Smuggling
Snyder, Ruth
Sodomy
South Carolina
South Dakota
Spillane, Mickey
St. Louis, Missouri
Stamp Act of 1765
Standard Oil Co. of New Jersey v. United States
State Blue Laws
State Police
State Slave Codes
State v. Heitman
Steenburgh, Sam
Strauder v. West Virginia
Strikes

Students for a Democratic Society and the Weathermen
Supermax Prisons
Supreme Court, U.S.
Suspect's Rights
Sutherland, Edwin

T
Taft, William Howard (Administration of)
Tax Crimes
Taylor, Zachary (Administration of)
Taylor v. State
Tea Act of 1773
Technology, Police
Television, Crime in
Television, Police in
Television, Punishment in
Tennessee
Terrorism
Terry v. Ohio
Texas
Texas Rangers
Texas v. White
Thaw, Harry K.
Theories of Crime
Thoreau, Henry David
Three Strikes Law
To Kill a Mockingbird
Tocqueville, Alexis de
Torrio, John
Torture
Townshend Acts of 1767
Traffic Crimes
Training Police
Trials
Truman, Harry S. (Administration of)
Twining v. New Jersey
Tyler, John (Administration of)

U
Uniform Crime Reporting Program
United States Attorneys
United States v. Ballard
United States v. E. C. Knight Company
United States v. Hudson and Goodwin
United States v. Nixon
United States v. One Book Called Ulysses
Urbanization
USA PATRIOT Act of 2001
Utah

V

Vagrancy
Vermont
Vice Commission
Vice Reformers
Victim Rights and Restitution
Victimless Crime
Victorian Compromise
Vigilantism
Violence Against Women Act of 1994
Violent Crimes
Virginia
Vollmer, August
Volstead Act

W

Waco Siege
Walling, George
Walnut Street Jail
Wambaugh, Joseph
Warren, Earl
Washington
Washington, D.C.
Washington, George (Administration of)
Watergate
Weathermen, The. *See* Students for a Democratic Society and the Weathermen
Webb v. United States
Weeks v. United States
West Virginia
White-Collar Crime, Contemporary
White-Collar Crime, History of
White-Collar Crime, Sociology of
Whitney v. California
Wickersham, George
Wickersham Commission
Wilson, James Q.
Wilson, O. W.
Wilson, Woodrow (Administration of)
Wisconsin
Witness Testimony
Wolf v. Colorado
Women Criminals, Contemporary
Women Criminals, History of
Women Criminals, Sociology of
Women in Prison
Wuornos, Aileen
Wyoming

X

Xenophobia

Y

Yates, Andrea
Yates v. United States

Z

Zeisel, Hans
Zodiac Killer

Race, Class, and Criminal Law

While criminal law in the colonies and, later, in the United States has always been raced and classed, the specific relationships between race, class, and criminal law have fluctuated across time and place. Criminal codes were explicitly raced from the colonial period until shortly after emancipation. In these codes, whether a behavior was a crime and what the prescribed punishment for that crime was depended on the race of the alleged offender. Since the fall of Black Codes in the 1860s, states have adopted implicitly raced criminal codes.

Similarly, 18th- and 19th-century criminal codes were often explicitly classed; for example, codes included vagrancy laws that criminalized the status of being homeless or unemployed rather than a particular behavior. Since the U.S. Supreme Court found vagrancy and, later, most loitering statutes unconstitutional, criminal codes have become more implicitly classed. Criminal codes that are implicitly raced and classed criminalize activities in which poor people, blacks, and other people of color are disproportionately likely to engage or for which they are likely to be arrested, but nonetheless prescribe the same punishment for anyone convicted of a given crime.

Race and Criminal Law in U.S. History

Each colony—and after the Revolutionary War, each slave state—enacted slave codes, statutes that defined the status of slaves and the rights of slave owners. During this period, the "general" criminal codes applied only to whites and free blacks. The slave codes governed most blacks as well as the behaviors of whites in relation to blacks. As such, criminal law was explicitly raced along a number of dimensions, including what behaviors states criminalized, the mechanisms through which an individual's guilt was determined, and, what the prescribed punishment for a given criminalized act was. Slave codes criminalized speaking in any African tongue, reading and writing, owning or carrying a firearm, running away, and many other acts that were not criminal when engaged in by whites. Moreover, slave owners and overseers could punish slaves not only for the crimes enumerated in these codes but also for any act that opposed their wishes or whims. As such, slave codes gave slave owners nearly unlimited power to punish slaves, with some states failing to criminalize even the killing of slaves. Finally, slave codes prescribed some punishments, like hobbling and castration, to which whites were never subjected, regardless of the crime for which they were convicted. The codes also criminalized some behaviors only when whites engaged in them with blacks; for example, slave codes made it a crime for whites to teach blacks to read or write, to provide blacks with alcohol, or to aid a runaway slave. Although slave codes protected slave owners' near exclusive rights to determine when and how slaves were punished, the codes did provide for exceptions. When blacks were accused of crimes that affected an entire community rather than just an individual owner, local courts or magistrates would try blacks and set their punishment. However, the criminal processing of blacks, whether free or slave, did not mirror that of whites. Blacks accused of crimes were not entitled to juries and, in many states, blacks were prohibited from testifying or serving on juries.

Wilson Chinn, a branded slave from Louisiana in 1863, stands alongside some of the instruments of torture used to punish slaves. Each U.S. colony had its own slave code, defining slave status and slave owners rights.

Every former slave state enacted Black Codes in 1865, within months of the confederacy's defeat in the Civil War. Like slave codes, Black Codes criminalized many behaviors if, and only if, blacks engaged in them. These behaviors included being out past set curfews; using "foul" or "suggestive" language near white women, having sexual relations with white women, or marrying white women; being unemployed, not having proof of employment, or leaving the employ of a particular proprietor without his consent; and possessing a weapon. These codes sanctioned racially differentiated legal treatment.

The passage of the Thirteenth, Fourteenth, and Fifteenth Amendments to the U.S. Constitution and the Civil Rights Act of 1866 ended slavery except as punishment for a crime, and granted citizenship and equal protection to all people born in the country, and voting and all other civil rights to each adult man who was a U.S. citizen. Taken together, these laws enabled former slaves and poor whites to vote in new governments; each of these new governments abolished their state's Black Codes. For the next 20 years, southern blacks experienced a period of relative freedom and power. In the 1880s, the northern troops abandoned the south and the federal courts began to turn their backs on claims made by black plaintiffs. This allowed former Confederate states to enact new statutes, which became known as Jim Crow laws, limiting the rights of blacks. Convict lease systems, wherein states "leased" prisoners to private individuals or companies, flourished under these new regimes.

When leased, prisoners labored in a variety of highly exploitative contexts, from plantations to mines. Many scholars have argued that this system, while being less all-encompassing in its scope, was even more profitable for plantation and mine owners and even more deadly for blacks than was slavery. The system of convict leasing completely transformed the criminal legal system in the south. In 1850, for example, Alabama's state prison held 167 white men, three white women, and four "free colored people"; by 1888, 85 percent of prisoners in the state were black. While counties generally left white convicts in prisons and jails where they were taught a trade or used on chain gangs to make and maintain roads, black convicts were leased to mining companies.

Nine percent, or nearly one in 10, of leased prisoners died each year. The convict leasing system relied on the pairing of the enactment of vacuous laws—such as those against dead falls, or selling goods after sunset—purportedly applicable to all, selective arrest wherein only blacks were arrested for the new crimes, a system of fees and fines, and a (racialized and gendered) selective process that determined to whom inmates were leased. Notable is that the clearly racialized practice of convict lease could exist in the absence of explicitly racialized laws. Thus, the period of convict lease represents a turning point in the relationship of race and criminal law.

Class and Criminal Law in U.S. History

Each colony and later each state enacted vagrancy laws, criminalizing homelessness and unemployment and, in some instances, criminalizing leaving a job without the employer's permission. In colonial America, if a person wandered into a town and did not find work, he was told to leave town or be prosecuted. In the states, vagrancy laws were often replaced with laws criminalizing more specific behavior, such as loitering, sex work, and public drunkenness, although some states retained vagrancy statutes on the books. In the southeast, counties often arrested and summarily convicted homeless, unemployed black Americans as vagrants. While convict leasing ended in the late 1920s, vagrancy laws remained on the books until 1972, when the U.S. Supreme Court, in *Papachristou v. Jacksonville*, ruled that a Florida vagrancy law was unconstitutional because it was too vague to be understood. Since this time, cities and states have enacted new laws criminalizing behaviors associated with vagrancy, such as panhandling or sitting or lying on sidewalks.

Historically, loitering, or remaining in a particular public place for a protracted period of time, was often a crime in itself. More recently, however, loitering constitutes a crime only when one does so "in order to" solicit for prostitution, beg, consume alcoholic beverages, or engage in gang-related activities. Even when loitering statutes mandate that police only arrest people loitering with criminal intent, however, these statutes ultimately empower police to arrest anyone who is spending time in any public place—since intent is rarely incontestable. Because poor people, and especially homeless people, spend much of their time in public places, these laws allow police to arrest poor people with little or no cause. Acknowledging this, in 1999, the Supreme Court found Chicago's loitering statute, like Jacksonville's vagrancy statute, to be unacceptably vague and thus unconstitutional. Since that time, however, Chicago has enacted a revised loitering statute that attempts to address the court's concerns.

Race and Class in Contemporary Criminal Law

While contemporary sentencing policies are formally race and class neutral, they nonetheless punish noncriminal behaviors and traits, like being in or near public housing or being in a gang, that correlate closely with both race and class.

Drug use is widely distributed throughout the population. However, drug markets are concentrated in poor, urban areas. Street-level distribution, the type of drug trafficking that is most heavily policed, is an occupation dominated by young black, and in some regions, Latino boys and men. Moreover, because the drug market is highly resistant to criminalization, every time a young black or Latino man is arrested, convicted, and sent to prison, another young black or Latino man takes his place. This guarantees a nearly inexhaustible supply of poor, young men to fill U.S. prisons. Because laws stipulate that having drugs in your apartment or car makes you guilty of possession, young women of color are often charged for drug crimes along with their boyfriends and husbands. They are less likely to have "substantial assistance" to offer a prosecutor and, thus, prosecutors are less likely to offer women plea bargains that help them avoid mandatory terms. As such, the war on drugs, which increased funding for policing as well as increasing the sentences for almost every drug crime, has predictably increased the incarceration rates of poor men and women of color.

Sex work is an occupation disproportionately engaged in by poor women of color. Laws that criminalize sex work, therefore, necessarily target these women. Recognizing this, some states have sought to switch the focus of criminalization from sex workers to those who manage sex workers and those who buy sex, so-called pimps and johns. However, many sex worker organizations argue that even laws that view sex workers as victims and focus criminalization on johns and pimps lead to increased criminalization of sex workers and their communities. This is because these laws, like those enacted in Illinois in 2005, still respond to sex work with the blunt instrument of criminalization. For example, under the "End Demand" laws enacted in Illinois in 2005, a person who let her friend, who was a sex worker, stay the night at her house could be charged as a pimp or trafficker.

In addition to criminalizing behaviors associated with the poor, many states enacted dozens of sentencing enhancements in the last quarter of the 20th century. These laws prescribe that additional time be added to a convicted person's sentence if she committed the crime while engaging in other noncriminal behaviors (like being in or near public housing) or having other noncriminal traits. In Alabama, for example, people convicted of engaging in drug trafficking while within a three-mile radius of a public housing facility are subject to a sentence enhancement of five years without the possibility of parole. Noncriminal traits that can trigger sentencing enhancements include having been previously convicted of a crime. In California, for example, having been previously convicted of a single "serious felony" subjects anyone convicted of a new "serious felony" to a five-year sentencing enhancement.

Controversial Practices

Sentencing enhancements for gang affiliation are particularly controversial. While varying in their particulars, anti-gang ordinances rely on police creating a registry of people suspected of being in gangs. Civil gang injunctions require only a preponderance of evidence. Once police serve an individual with an injunction, that person may be prohibited from being outside after a given curfew; from socializing with other people, even if they are family members, whom police have categorized as being in the same gang; from consuming alcohol even in his/her own home; and from many other noncriminal behaviors. If an individual breaks any of the stringent rules placed upon him/her by the injunction, he/she can then be charged with a crime, even though the activity would not be a crime if he/she had not been categorized as "in a gang." In another variation of these policies, cities build up registries of suspected gang members. If anyone in the gang registry is convicted of a crime, he/she faces a sentencing enhancement simply for being on the registry. Because police can decide that people are in a gang on the basis of how they dress, their tattoos, and who they spend time with, racialized enforcement is rampant. In some cities, more than 95 percent of people served with gang injunctions or listed on gang registries are black or Latino.

Sentencing enhancements allow states to prescribe punishments for these behaviors and traits, which poor people of color are more likely to engage in or have, without criminalizing them per se. In the 2004 case *United States v. Booker*, the Supreme Court ruled that only facts admitted by a defendant or proven beyond a reasonable doubt to a jury may be used to calculate a sentence. While there was some speculation that this ruling would render sentencing enhancements unconstitutional, its reach has been considerably less broad.

Similarly, while many states have abolished parole, most still have some form of post-release supervision. Moreover, supervision strategies have increasingly emphasized surveillance and control. When a person is released from prison, he/she must follow a number of rules well beyond not committing a new crime. It is perhaps in these rules for the newly released that the class bias of the criminal legal system is most transparent. In New Jersey, for example, it is standard to require newly released people to have a permanent address and, eventually, a job. While people can often stay in homeless shelters when they are first released—although people marked as sex offenders, transpeople, women with boy children, and many others are excluded from most shelters—nearly all shelters limit the amount of time a person can stay. Once a person has stayed in the shelter for a certain amount of time, often 30 days, he/she must find a room to rent or other accommodations. Failing to do so is a violation of parole, and the newly released person's parole officer can choose to revoke his/her parole and send him/her back to prison for the remainder of his/her original sentence based on this "violation." In times and places when jobs are scarce and rents are high, states regularly send people to prison for failing to find work or shelter. The predictable effect of greater restrictions and closer surveillance has been an increase in the number of people admitted to prison not for new criminal convictions but rather for technical parole violations. In 2001, in fact, nearly 40 percent of all prison admissions were for parole violations. Parole revocations sustain large prison populations, even in the face of declining felony convictions, by creating a large group of quasi-permanent prisoners.

Traci Schlesinger
DePaul University

See Also: Convict Lease System; Gangs, Contemporary; Gender and Criminal Law; Prostitution, Contemporary; State Slave Codes.

Further Readings
Clear, Todd. *Imprisoning Communities: How Mass Incarceration Makes Disadvantaged Neighborhoods Worse.* New York: Oxford University Press, 2009.
Curtin, Mary Ellen. *Black Prisoners and Their World, Alabama 1865–1900.* Charlottesville: University Press of Virginia, 2000.
Gilmore, Ruth Wilson. *Golden Gulag: Prisons, Surplus, Crisis, and Opposition in Globalizing California.* Berkeley: University of California Press, 2007.
Mauer, Marc. *Race to Incarcerate.* New York: New Press, 1999.
Schlesinger, Traci. *The Limits of Equality: Sentencing Policies and Colorblind Racism.* Germany: VDM Publishers, 2011.
Sellin, Thorsen. *Slavery and the Penal System.* New York: Elsevier, 1976.

Race-Based Crimes

Race-based crimes occur when an offender targets a victim because of his/her racial group. Perpetrators of such crimes are motivated by bias against particular racial groups. Race-based crimes are often referred to as "hate crimes." The level of severity of these types of offenses can range from physical aggression to harassment. In the United States, both the Federal Bureau of Investigation (FBI) and the National Crime Victimization Survey (NCVS) keep track of hate crimes. There are

A Klansman watches a cross burning with his children standing in front of him in 1987 in Oak Hill, Ohio. The Klan was founded by six former Confederate officers in 1866. The group expanded rapidly and its members have committed untold acts of violence.

numerous examples throughout history that show ethnic conflict.

Early America
Anti-black violence was common throughout America in the 19th century. Lynching—murder by mob violence—peaked during the late 19th century and into the early 20th century. This was a common occurrence in the United States, particularly in the south.

The north also saw its share of antiblack riots in the slavery era. Cincinnati was home to recurring riots against blacks (some of whom arrived in the city after fleeing slave states), most notably in 1829, 1836, and 1841. Anti-abolition riots also broke out in northern cities, In 1838, a riot targeting both blacks and white abolitionists destroyed Philadelphia's Pennsylvania Hall after a speech by abolitionist Angelina Grimke. The New

York City Draft Riots (July 13–16, 1863) were motivated principally by anger over draft laws, but targeted blacks as scapegoats, and at least 100 blacks were killed in the violence.

New forms of white supremacy emerged in the south after the Civil War. The Ku Klux Klan was founded during Reconstruction as a paramilitary group targeting blacks, northerners, and their supporters. They practiced harassment, violence, and even murder. During this period of time, African Americans became scapegoats for the hardships, economic distress, and loss of social status of whites. White supremacy is an institutional system of oppression and exploitation against people who are nonwhite. It is used to maintain the privilege, wealth, and power of those who are white. White supremacy manipulates all aspects of relations in society, including housing markets and politics.

After the end of slavery, whites campaigned to disenfranchise African Americans through other means. These included segregation in housing, transportation, and public facilities, and changing laws in order to keep blacks from voting. Nonwhites were also controlled through the enactment of discriminatory Jim Crow laws at both the state and local levels from the 19th century through the 20th century.

These laws enforced the doctrine of "separate but equal," which legally enforced the unequal treatment of nonwhites. These laws mandated the legal exclusion of nonwhites from particular career opportunities, housing, educational institutions, and other social institutions.

Post–World War II

The Great Migration by African Americans from the south to the north brought with it major demographic changes in some regions. Social tensions increased among whites and blacks who competed in the labor market. Competition for limited resources between different groups resulted in racial conflict. One of the cities that experienced episodes of violence and chaos because of racial tensions between blacks and whites was Chicago. Tensions reached a boiling point and resulted in what is now commonly referred to as the Chicago race riots of 1919.

Al Sharpton (center, right) leads the first of dozens of protest marches after 40 white teenagers murdered Yusuf Hawkins, a 16-year-old black youth, in what was then the predominantly white neighborhood of Bensonhurst in Brooklyn, New York, in 1989. Sharpton led marchers through the area for over a year, despite verbal and physical threats to his life.

World War II also marked a significant shift in community demographics and social demands. African Americans began demanding equal rights and argued for the elimination of racial segregation. They became vocal about wanting social, economic, and political inclusion, particularly after having made a number of contributions during World War I and World War II. Demographic shifts were brought about in part because of economic and job opportunities in the north. This influx of black migrants caused strain on public facilities, which led to increased public tension over housing, public transportation, and use of recreational facilities. In spite of civil rights statutes, segregation of public facilities caused a rift between blacks and whites. Tensions between black and white residents of Detroit escalated in 1943, culminating in an outbreak of violence.

During the early 1940s, there were public outbreaks and disturbances across the United States caused by racial conflicts. The Detroit riot of 1943 marked one of the nation's most divisive moments based on racial conflict between blacks and whites. On June 20, 1943, chaos erupted in Detroit. The public clash started at an amusement park on Bell Island. On that day, there were minor quarrels between black and white youths at the amusement park. Rumors began to circulate about blacks murdering and raping whites, and whites doing the same to blacks. These rumors lead to race riots, looting of stores, and property damage. Whites attacked blacks who were out in public. Both groups took part in violence and looting over a three-day period. President Franklin Roosevelt dispatched federal troops to Detroit in order to quell the riot and restore peace. By June 23, when all of the damage was considered, 34 people had been murdered, the majority of whom were black. Approximately 700 individuals were injured, and more than 1,000 were arrested for their part in the riot. The riot caused an estimated $200 million worth of property damage.

The civil rights movement was one of the events that emphasized racial minority rights. Legislation like the Civil Rights Act of 1964 and the Voting Rights Act of 1965 were steps toward promoting equality for those who had historically been suppressed. Jim Crow laws were overruled by both the Civil Rights Act of 1964 and the Voting Rights Act of 1965. The Supreme Court in *Brown v. Board of Education* in 1954 ruled against segregation and ended the "separate but equal" doctrine. The U.S. government enacted legislation that recognizes the rights of all Americans, regardless of race. Increasing equality through legislation made it easier for nonwhites to fight against unequal treatment. Special dispensation has been given to law enforcement and the courts in order to arrest and prosecute those who commit hate crimes.

Pushback against the civil rights movement was unrepentantly violent. The 16th Street Baptist Church in Birmingham, Alabama, was one of several black churches bombed by white supremacists after the legal end of segregation. In Mississippi, three civil rights workers were lynched in 1964. In 1968, Martin Luther King, Jr., the most prominent civil rights leader, was assassinated by James Earl Ray.

Crimes Against Chinese and Mexican Americans

African Americans have not been the only racial or ethnic group targeted by race-based crimes; immigrant groups have also historically been targeted. In recent times, Chinese and Latino immigrants have been the victims of racially motivated crimes. The first wave of Chinese immigrants began arriving in the United States in 1848. Chinese immigrants were allowed into the United States to fill a labor shortage around the time of the 1849 gold rush. This wave of immigration was followed by another period of Chinese immigration to the United States later in the 1800s. Chinese immigrants worked on the railroad at a low-paying wage in dangerous conditions. As Chinese immigration increased, so did racial tension and violence against Chinese immigrants. During the 1870s, the Chinese immigrant population was one of the largest immigrant groups in California. During this time, Chinese Americans began to experience backlash from the public and politicians alike.

This group was met with violence and race-based discrimination, including prominent massacres in 1871 Los Angeles and 1880s Washington and Oregon. Often, this violence was supported, implicitly or explicitly, by labor unions concerned with the effect of the Chinese on American wages. In 1882, the U.S. Congress passed the Chinese Exclusion Act, which essentially froze immigration from China. This piece of legislation marked an important transition in U.S. immigration policy. This was the first time that a group of immigrants was intentionally excluded from the United States. One of the consequences of this act was that it created a shortage of cheap low-skilled laborers.

As a response to the demand for cheap labor, the U.S. government began looking for other alternatives. The United States set up a program in agreement with the Mexican government to fill this gap. The Bracero Program (1942–64) was set up as a temporary guest worker program to supply the much-needed laborers. During this time, illegal immigration also increased. In response to the increase of the Hispanic population, the public and politicians began demanding controlled immigration. In 1943, the "Zoot Suit Riots" (named for the suits worn by young Latino men) broke out when white sailors stationed in Los Angeles targeted Mexican Americans who they considered unpatriotic because their suits did not follow clothing rationing guidelines.

One of the methods used to control illegal immigration was through widespread deportation that targeted the Hispanic population. In 1954, the U.S. government set up Operation Wetback to deport over 1 million Mexican immigrants. There were cases in which undocumented immigrants along with their U.S. born children were deported. Agents interrogated and stopped those who were "Mexican-looking."

Since then, Hispanic immigrant groups continue to be victimized because of their ethnic background and have been the targets of violence and harassment solely because of their ethnicity. Some states, notably Arizona, have taken action to question and interrogate anyone who "looks" like an undocumented immigrant. This is simply a code for stopping anyone who looks Hispanic. Multiple states have taken legal action against immigrants and have adopted legislation that targets undocumented immigrants and their U.S.-born children.

Mercedes Valadez
Arizona State University

See Also: 1851 to 1900 Primary Documents; 1901 to 1920 Primary Documents; 1941 to 1960 Primary Documents; African Americans; Chinese Americans; Hispanic Americans; Xenophobia.

Further Readings
Arnold, C. L. "Racial Profiling in Immigration Enforcement: State and Local Agreements to Enforce Federal Immigration Law." *Arizona Law Review,* v.49 (2007).
Cornelius, W. A. "Controlling 'Unwanted' Immigration: Lessons From the United States." *Journal of Ethnic and Migration Studies,* v.31 (2005).
King, R. D. and D. Wheelock. "Group Threat and Social Control." *Social Forces,* v.85/3 (2007).

Racism

Race is a social construction or multidimensional process of competing race projects, as explained by Howard Winant and Michael Omi in their landmark text *Racial Formation in the United States* (1986). Race as a concept is often produced in social relations, as shaped by cultural, economic, and political systems of power. Race is also understood as a subjective phenomenon articulated in racial identities. Racial "identities" are shaped by perceptions about the physical body (phenotype) and cultural practices. Race as a marker of human difference evolved during the era of the Atlantic slave trade to justify the subjugation of Africans in the American plantation economy. Many scholars have recognized that race continues to operate at the social level in U.S. society though it is no longer understood as a fixed biological reality. Racism is based on false perceptions about physical types attached to human "races." The unequal policies and discriminatory practices used against groups or individuals erroneously designated as "naturally" inferior is defined as racism.

The U.S. criminal justice system has exhibited a long history of racism. This is evidenced historically in the unequal treatment of major ethno-racial communities in the United States such as African Americans, Latinos, and Native Americans under the U.S. penal system. The social history of crime, punishment, and criminal justice has been significantly marred by racism. This has been exhibited in the history of all-white juries, courtrooms, and the use of the harshest punishment reserved for nonwhites who victimize whites. Some whites involved in the administration of justice actively participated in or incited mob violence and riots against African Americans after slavery. People of color are overrepresented in nearly all aspects of criminal justice, including offending, victimization, and delinquency, and in all stages, including arrest, pretrial detention, sentencing, and confinement. Racism in the history of the U.S. criminal justice system is illustrated in police surveillance, sentencing, incarceration rates, and the juvenile justice system.

The framing of the U.S. Constitution in 1789, which counted each enslaved African as three-fifths of a person for the purpose of census taking, prohibited the end of the Atlantic slave trade until 1808 and allowed the recapture of fugitive slaves. These measures in the U.S. Constitution helped to anchor a system of racial slavery predicated upon white supremacy. The 1790 U.S. census defined citizens as "free white persons." Racial slavery and racism were entrenched in U.S. society through the 19th century. Crucial legal decisions such as the Supreme Court decision in *Dred Scott v. Sandford* (1857), in which black slaves and their descendants were declared "non-citizens," helped to illustrate racism in the administration of justice in a slave republic. Following the Civil War (1861–65) and the ratification of the Thirteenth Amendment to the U.S. Constitution, which abolished slavery, vigilante violence against African Americans soared as thousands were lynched across the American south and west through the early 20th century. At this same time, Native Americans had their land holdings vastly reduced through a series of unequal treaties with the U.S. government. Native Americans were ultimately forced onto 160-acre reservation plots by the late 19th century. The increased numbers of Latin Americans coming into the country illegally have also made them the target of the penal system in large numbers. Thus, people of color continue to serve as the chief recipients of racial discrimination in the U.S. criminal justice system. This is evidenced with an examination of racism in police surveillance, sentencing, incarceration rates, and the juvenile justice system.

Racism and Police Surveillance

The surveillance of people of color in U.S. society has a long history. Concerns about the control and surveillance of African Americans began with the slave codes first implemented in the mid- to late 17th century. These codes, although they varied across the colonies, and later the states, in most cases prohibited slaves from leaving the plantation. Slaves could not assemble without a white person present; they were not permitted to read, write, or marry, and they were subject to harsh punishment if these laws were broken. Punishments ranged from lashing and whipping to branding, imprisonment, and death. The slave codes were followed by the Black Codes with emancipation in 1865. The Black Codes were designed to limit the labor, mobility, and

As of 2008, 70 percent of prisoners in the United States are people of color, leading some to believe that racism is largely responsible for the overrepresentation of non-whites in all stages of the criminal justice system.

employment of the former slaves while severely restricting their rights and civil liberties. White southerners faced the dilemma of how to control postslavery black labor and behavior, which was once regulated by slave owners. Jim Crow laws (segregation) helped to solidify the domination of African Americans in southern society by separating the "races" and criminalizing interracial contact in nearly every social setting. The Black Codes were soon followed by the convict lease system and later the by infamous chain gang through the 20th century. Black labor resources in the convict lease system were used to till fields, build levees, railroads, and dig mines across the south. Black labor played an important role in the economic development of the region through the early 20th century.

Racial minorities continue to serve as the primary victims of police surveillance. African Americans and Hispanics are stopped most frequently by police and are more likely to be made subject to search and arrested, according to national statistics. In 1998, African Americans comprised 11.6 percent of drivers stopped by police but represented 19.9 percent of the drivers arrested, while Hispanics were 8.4 percent of drivers stopped by police but made up 11.7 percent of those arrested. Many individuals of Arab descent have complained of increased police surveillance and racial profiling since 9/11. The increased surveillance of Arab Muslims in the post-9/11 world has led to a greater number of detainments, interrogations, and arrests among Arab Muslims. Native Americans are also disproportionately made the subject of police surveillance, particularly in the states of the Great Plains (where they make up a disproportionate number of the prison population compared to their actual population). The prison industrial complex in the United States is disproportionately populated by people of color as a result of targeted surveillance and unequal sentencing.

Racism and Sentencing
African American men have a 32 percent chance of serving time in prison at some point in their lifetime, and Hispanics have a 17 percent chance; white men have a 6 percent chance of serving time in prison over the course of a lifetime. These numbers help to reflect racism in the sentencing of racial minorities. Women of color sentenced for drug crimes were the highest-growing segment of the U.S. prison population from 1998 to 2008. Some statistics suggest that as many as 33 percent of African Americans would receive less prison time if they were treated "equally" to whites in the criminal justice system. Hispanics and African Americans with no prison records are more likely to serve time on a first offense compared to whites with a similar history. Hispanics are twice as likely as whites to serve prison time as opposed to probation or a fine. African Americans, at roughly 14 percent of the U.S. population, are disproportionately sentenced to death in cases involving capital crimes. African American men make up 43 percent of the current death row prison population.

Native Americans have increasingly lost control of their sovereignty to the U.S. federal government. This has impacted issues of crime and punishment for the Native American community. In the past century, the jurisdiction over an expanding number of crimes has been removed from tribal authorities. The power to punish has been slowly appropriated by states. The U.S. Congress passed Public Law 280 in 1953, which offered states opportunities to assume jurisdiction over reservations within state borders. In 1968, the law was amended, but it continues to afford unequal punishment to Native Americans compared to crimes committed by their white counterparts against Native Americans. Tribal affiliations that do not have the economic resources to support law and order or to regulate crime and punishment are forced to rely on local, state, or federal authorities to provide law enforcement, courts, and jails. Native American communities with the resources and jurisdiction over law enforcement have limited powers in terms of sentencing. In fact, the Supreme Court ruling in *Oliphant v. Suquamish* (1978) determined that non–Native Americans are immune from criminal and tribal prosecution in the Native American judicial system. This illustrates the limited control or protections that Native Americans have in regard to matters of law enforcement.

The war on drugs has helped to fuel racism in sentencing. In 1988, the U.S. Congress passed a law that created a 100:1 quantity ratio between the amount of crack and powder cocaine required to produce a mandatory minimum sentence for trafficking and created mandatory minimums for simple possession. In other words, the possession of 5 grams of crack would receive a five-year sentence while a person would need to be caught with 500 grams of cocaine to receive a five-year sentence. Crack, a drug commonly associated with African American communities—as opposed to the more expensive cocaine associated with whites—is the only drug with a mandatory prison sentence for a first simple possession offense. Despite the fact that the majority of crack users are white or Hispanic, in 1994, African Americans made up 84.5 percent of the defendants convicted of crack possession (10.3 percent were white, and 5.2 percent were Hispanic). African Americans have routinely made up the majority of persons charged with trafficking crack, with estimates as high as 88 percent or more by 2001. The disproportionate number of African Americans incarcerated today (at roughly 50 percent of the total prison population) is caused in part by the increased number of arrests for drug offenses that disproportionately target African Americans. By 2000, African Americans made up 53 percent of those convicted by state courts for drug offenses.

Racism and Incarceration Rates

People of color are overrepresented in U.S. rates of incarceration. The U.S. prison population was less than 200,000 in 1973, but by 2004, it was calculated at more than 2.2 million. The United States leads the world in rates of incarceration with 700 inmates per 100,000. Between 1980 and 1996, incarceration rates in state and federal institutions increased by 200 percent. The number of people incarcerated in the United States has now reached 2.3 million, and more than 64 percent of those in prison are racial minorities. In 1910, African Americans made up 11 percent of the U.S. population and 31 percent of the prison population. African Americans now comprise 50 percent of adults in federal, state, and local prisons and jails. Hispanics currently constitute 18.6 percent of the U.S. prison population. The 43 percent of African Americans on death row is three times the percentage of the African American population in the United States (at roughly 14 percent). In 2003, whites were imprisoned at a rate of 376 per every 100, 000, compared to 2,526 African Americans per every 100,000. In the states where Native Americans comprise a significant minority, rates of incarceration for Native Americans are relatively high. Native Americans make up 6 percent of the population in Montana but make up 16 percent of the prison population, while in North Dakota, Native Americans make up 5 percent of the population but 19 percent of the prison population.

The high rates of incarceration of racial minorities may be influenced by a series of contributing social, environmental, economic, and educational attainment factors. Most statistics indicate that social environment and poverty serve as factors that may contribute to one's future incarceration. Many have noted that the African American high school dropout rate mirrors the African American prison rate at 50 percent. The rate of recidivism is also extraordinarily high for those who have served time in prison. The move away from rehabilitative prisons to those with greater emphasis on incapacitation in the U.S. prison system has had a serious impact on prison rates. This has been coupled with more aggressive drug enforcement practices.

Racism and the Juvenile Justice System

The school to prison pipeline is fueled by racial bias, particularly toward African American and Hispanic youth. African American youths are six times more likely to be held in a youth detention center than their white counterparts. Hispanic youths are three times more likely to be detained. In the 1980s, African American and white rates for juvenile drug arrests were similar, but by 1993, African American rates were more than four times the rate of white arrests; 46 percent of all juvenile arrests by 1993 were arrests of African American youths. In 1994, one in three young African American men between the ages of 20 and 29 was under correctional supervision, compared to one in four in 1990.

At the end of 2004, 8.4 percent of black males ages 25 to 29 were in prison compared to 2.5 percent of Hispanic males and 1.2 percent of white males. Racism in the juvenile justice system engenders distrust, suspicion, and hostility among youths of color along with a profound sense of alienation from mainstream society, which in turn shapes perceptions of fairness. The essence of a democratic

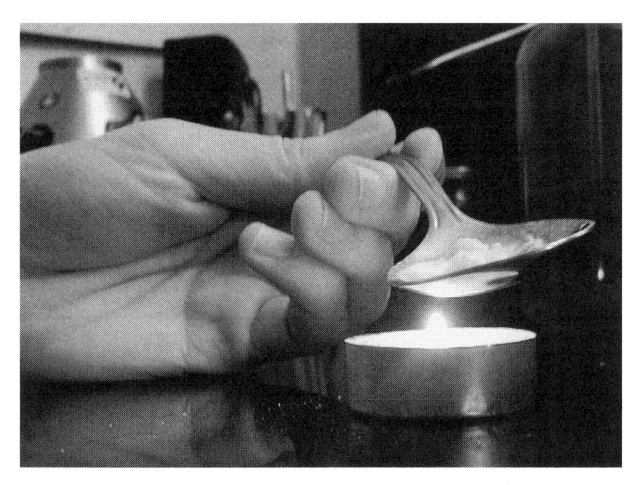

African Americans comprise 84.5 percent of all defendants convicted of crack possession and trafficking despite the fact that the majority of users are white or Hispanic.

society is voluntary obedience to laws, and this becomes compromised with perceptions of unfairness. Many scholars suggest that racism in the juvenile justice system is more profound than at any other level in the criminal justice system overall.

Racism continues to permeate the social history of crime and punishment in U.S. society. Racism causes tremendous damage to communities of color disproportionately affected by the unfair practices in surveillance, sentencing, and incarceration, as well as in the juvenile justice system. Felony convictions lead to the forfeiture of civil liberties such as voting. An estimated one in seven African American men have been disenfranchised because of felony convictions. Racism in the criminal justice system helps to impact the economic development of individuals and communities. Individuals with arrest records suffer an estimated 7 percent decline in income as a result of having a prison record.

The racism evidenced in the social history of crime and punishment in the United States is a reflection of the larger racial bias that remains present in the society as a whole despite attempts at remedy that have been made. Native Americans represent less than 2 percent of the U.S. population but make up roughly 4 percent of the total prison population. Hispanics are routinely and explicitly singled out by the Immigration and Naturalization Service (INS) for immigration enforcement, making up 96.2 percent of illegal immigrants arrested by the INS, though they make up only 54 percent of the total number of illegal immigrants in the United States.

Social scientists have argued that racism symbolizes a deeper racial divide, though the Supreme Court since the Warren era has done much to minimize the racial disparities in the U.S. criminal justice system. The recognition of such a divide has also opened a dialogue on potential remedies that are in progress.

Hettie V. Williams
Monmouth University

See Also: 1801 to 1850 Primary Documents; 1851 to 1900 Primary Documents; 1901 to 1920 Primary Documents; 1921 to 1940 Primary Documents; 1941 to 1960 Primary Documents; Capital Punishment; Juvenile Justice, History of; Sentencing.

Further Readings
Alexander, Michelle. *The New Jim Crow: Mass Incarceration in the Age of Colorblindness.* New York: New Press, 2010.
Blackmon, Douglas A. *Slavery by Another Name: The Re-Enslavement of Black Americans From the Civil War to World War II.* New York: Anchor Books, 2009.
Kennedy, Randall. *Race, Crime, and the Law.* New York: Vintage, 1998.
Loury, Glenn C. *Race, Incarceration, and American Values.* Cambridge, MA: MIT Press, 2008.
Mauer, Marc. *Race to Incarcerate.* New York: New Press, 2006.
Oshinsky, David M. *Worse Than Slavery: Parchman Farm and the Ordeal of Jim Crow Justice.* New York: Free Press, 1997.
Perkinson, R. *Texas Tough: The Rise of America's Prison Empire.* New York: Picador, 2010.
Wideman, John Edgar. "Dong Time, Marking Race." *The Nation* (October 30, 1995).

Rader, Dennis

On March 9, 1945, Dennis was the first of four sons born to William and Dorothea Rader. The Raders moved to Wichita, Kansas, where young

Dennis participated in the Boy Scouts and even church group activities and was an average student. However, by his own admission, Rader was already strangling animals while developing fantasies about control, bondage, and torture. His college career was comprised of mediocre grades and a severe lack of socialization, so Rader joined the U.S. Air Force in 1966. After an unremarkable five years with the military, he returned home to Wichita, Kansas, in 1971, where he immediately married Paula Dietz. By 1974, unemployed and depressed, Rader was fantasizing about actually committing murder by strangulation when he chanced upon Julie Otero. The Oteros were a Hispanic family who had recently moved to Wichita, and they were to be the first victims of the BTK.

After observing the family for several days to get an idea of their routine, Rader gathered his "hit kit," consisting of a gun, ropes, knives, and various tools for breaking and entering. Around 8:00 A.M. on January 15, 1974, he cut the phone lines and entered through the back door, expecting only Julie and the children (Josephine, 11, and Joey, 9) to be present. Unexpectedly, her husband Joe was also there, as well as the Oteros' vicious dog. However, using the gun, Rader managed to subdue and then systematically bind and strangle all four of the Oteros, even with their extensive training in the art of judo. Part of this may have been the story that he concocted: He was a wanted criminal and simply needed money, food, and a car to escape. It was with this same ruse that Rader managed to fatally wound another Wichita woman named Kathryn Bright. Later that same year, Rader wrote to a local newspaper after discovering that the murders of the Otero family were going to possibly be blamed on someone else. The newspaper directed the journalist to look inside a book at the local library. Inside the book, the police found a hand-written letter from Rader, who professed his guilt for the murders of the Otero family in extreme detail and proudly proclaimed that "the code words for me will be Bind Them, Torture Them, Kill Them ... BTK." It would be this same need for credit that would later lead to his downfall.

Rader continued to kill and to write the media sarcastic poems and letters through 1979, by which time he was employed by the ADT alarm system company and had two children with his wife Paula. Then, his murders became more sporadic, with self-proclaimed kills occurring in 1985, 1986, 1987, and 1991. Eventually, he stopped killing and did not contact the media again until 2004. On March 17, he mailed an envelope to the *Wichita Eagle*; it contained three photocopied pictures of his own photos of the dying Vicki Wegerle taken in 1986, as well as a photocopy of her missing driver's license. He signed it with the BTK symbol he had used in his previous letters in the 1970s. Over the next 11 months, Rader sent nine more packages to the police and to television and radio stations. Some were merely letters confessing past deeds, whereas others were sketches, photos, and dolls grotesquely posed like previous victims. On February 16, 2005, Rader sent the police, among other things, a diskette. Technical analysts uncovered Rader's name, as well as reference to Christ Lutheran Church, where he had officially been made president the month before. He was immediately placed under surveillance while his daughter's DNA was matched to semen he had left at various crime scenes.

On February 25, Rader was arrested and provided a 30-hour confession of all his crimes, in detail. After he was formally charged with 10 counts of murder, the media began leaking information about Rader and interviewing his friends and family, who swore that they never could have imagined such heinous crimes being committed by the man. On June 27, Rader pled guilty to all charges and began describing, in detail, every murder he had committed. At the end of the proceeding on August 18, Judge Gregory Waller sentenced Dennis Rader to a minimum of 175 years to life in prison.

Brandy B. Henderson
University of South Florida

See Also: Murder, History of; Serial and Mass Killers.

Further Readings
Crime Library. "The BTK Story." http://www.trutv.com/library/crime/serial_killers/unsolved/btk/index_1.html (Accessed December 2010).
Hickey, Eric. *Serial Murderers and Their Victims*. Belmont, CA: Wadsworth, 2010.

Ragen, Joseph

Joseph Ragen is best known for serving as the long-standing warden of the Illinois State Penitentiary at Joliet. He served as warden at Joliet-Stateville for 25 years from 1936 to 1961. Joseph E. Ragen was born in 1896 in Trenton, Illinois. His father was the county sheriff. He served in the U.S. Navy during World War I. In 1922, he began serving as deputy sheriff for Clinton County, Illinois, working under his father. In 1926, Joseph Ragen was elected sheriff of Clinton County. In 1930, he was elected county treasurer of Clinton County.

In 1933, Ragen was appointed aswarden at the Illinois State Penitentiary at Merard, Illinois. He was also appointed superintendent of prisons for the state of Illinois, a position that required him to inspect all of the state prisons, including the Joliet-Stateville complex, which consisted of two maximum-security prisons designed to hold about 3,500 prisoners, but which commonly swelled to over 5,000 inmates, as well as a prison farm. In 1936, there was a series of escapes and major disturbances at Joliet-Stateville and the governor demanded the resignation of the warden and appointed Ragen in his place. Thus, in 1936, Ragen became warden and superintendent of all prisons at Joliet-Stateville, Illinois. From 1941 to 1942, Ragen served briefly with the U.S. Department of Justice. In 1942, he returned as warden at Joliet-Stateville.

Ragen established an autocratic leadership style at the Joliet-Stateville prison complex. He made all the rules and frequently hired and fired employees at will. No one could enter the Joliet-Stateville complex without Ragen's personal approval, including journalists, whom he may have regarded as being unfriendly to his administration. Inmates were not permitted to organize clubs or other associations. All inmate mail was diligently censored. For many years, inmates at Joliet-Stateville were forbidden to write or send writs to the courts. Ragen is credited with keeping partisan politics out of the operations and personnel decisions at Joliet-Stateville. This was a time when there were no prison unions, no central prison authorities in the state, and when federal courts took little interest in prison conditions.

During Ragen's 25-year tenure as warden at the Joliet-Stateville prison complex, there were no reported or acknowledged escapes from Stateville; there were no major disturbances or riots, and there were very few deaths. This included the 1950s, a time when prison riots were sweeping the United States. Ragen kept a firm grip on affairs at Joliet-Stateville, controlling the penal environment while also maintaining a profitable flow of food and manufactured goods from the prison factory and its 2,200-acre prison farm. This calm and orderly state of affairs won Ragen international acclaim and he played host to a series of international visits by foreign corrections officials. In 1950, he became president of the American Prison Association.

Ragen kept a rigid and orderly system of operations in place at the Joliet-Stateville prison complex. He advocated maintaining a clean,

Joliet Correctional Center in Joliet, Illinois, was part of the Joliet-Stateville complex that housed from 3,500 to 5,000 inmates. Joseph Ragen was appointed warden and superintendent of the complex in 1936 and established tight control over inmates, visitors, and the press. Ragen served as warden for a total of 25 years, and Joliet Correctional Center was decommissioned in 2002.

safe, and secure environment. Inmates marched in tight formation through formal gardens. He could place unruly prisoners in disciplinary segregation for several years at a time. Corrections officers were not allowed to beat inmates. Ragen regularly walked the prison walls and personally inspected all aspects of prison operations. He insisted that the inmates must work while incarcerated. Initially, this work mostly involved maintaining cleanliness within the prisons. In the mid-1950s, Ragen established a large correctional cannery that reached an annual production level of 300,000 gallons of fruits and vegetables. He also established a prison furniture factory, clothing factory, textile mill, and sheet-metal plant.

Ragen was well known for hosting lavish meals at his warden's residence in Stateville. He regularly entertained legislators and other politicians to ensure that they did not endeavor to exercise any political or other authority over him and his operation. When one Illinois governor attempted to use his position to award patronage jobs to potential corrections officers, Ragen and his key administrative staff resigned. Serious troubles began brewing at Joliet-Stateville, and within six months, the governor conceded defeat and Ragen returned as warden. Ragen tended to hire rural, uneducated white males as corrections officers, which created some tensions as the inmate population became more African American and urban. After Ragen retired, subsequent wardens had difficulty maintaining order as racations worsened. In 1961, Ragen resigned as warden of Joliet-Stateville and was appointed director of the Illinois Department of Public Safety. He served as public safety director until 1965, when he began serving as vice president for the Louis Joliet Bank. Ragen died on September 22, 1971.

Victor B. Stolberg
Essex County College

See Also: Chain Gangs and Prison Labor; Corrections; Illinois.

Further Readings

Erickson, Gladys A. *Warden Ragen of Joliet: Famous Warden of One of the World's Toughest Prisons.* New York: E. P. Dutton, 1957.

Jacobs, James B. *Stateville: The Penitentiary in Mass Society.* Chicago: University of Chicago Press, 1977.

Ragen, Joseph E. and Charles Finston. *Inside the World's Toughest Prison.* Springfield, IL: Charles C Thomas, 1962.

Ramirez, Richard

Richard was the youngest of five children raised by Mexican immigrants Julian and Mercedes Ramirez. He was born on February 29, 1960, in El Paso, Texas, and like his siblings before him, had medical disabilities throughout childhood. In particular, he suffered from epilepsy, which resulted in grand mal seizures. The children were all physically beaten, and although Richard had four older siblings to turn to, it was his cousin Michael who held the most influence over him. Michael had served in the Vietnam War and came back emotionally hardened and physically violent. He would call Richard over and show him photographs of himself raping and murdering Vietnamese women, or they would go hunting for animals with knives. One day, in the midst of a fight with his wife, Michael calmly drew his gun and shot her in the head. Richard was right beside him when this happened, and Michael told him to go home and tell no one what he had seen.

Michael also introduced Ramirez to marijuana, and he eventually dropped out of high school to pursue his various drug habits. In 1978, he moved to southern California, where he began stealing cars to burglarize houses so that he could support his various drug addictions. Along with the drugs, Ramirez's diet consisted primarily of convenience store food: items so laden with sugar that his teeth started to rot, giving his breath a distinctive odor.

It was also at this time that he began practicing his worship of Satan, which later became part of his signature. Eventually, burglary was no longer enough for Ramirez. On June 28, 1984, he murdered Jennie Vincow, 79. Her son discovered her body sprawled out on the bed; she had been stabbed repeatedly, and her throat was slashed so savagely she was nearly decapitated. Her valuables had been stolen, fingerprints were recovered from the windowsill, and the autopsy revealed signs of sexual assault.

Ramirez did not kill again until March 17, 1985, but became so enraged that he began a full-blown murderous rampage that would span from San Francisco to Mission Viejo and last until he was captured on August 31, 1985. Although in the beginning he was sloppy and would just shoot the victim and steal their belongings, eventually he developed a pattern: sneak in during the middle of the night, dispatch the husband first with a gunshot directly to the temple, then restrain the woman so he could have his way with her after casing the house. He sometimes carved an inverted pentagram into the walls or even the flesh of his victims. He did not discriminate either; he raped and killed females and males from the ages of 6 to 83. His last successful attack, on August 24, 1985, resulted in the identification of his vehicle due to the fact that he left the female victim alive, as he had in several other incidences. A few days later, a young boy saw the same bright orange Toyota truck driving through his neighborhood in the early hours of the morning and called the license plate in to the police. The forensics team was able to identify a fingerprint from the steering wheel of the vehicle as belonging to Ricardo Leyva Ramirez. Immediately, the police put out a bulletin with his name and photograph, and within 24 hours, Richard Ramirez had been captured by several Hispanics who refused to become further victims of the Night Stalker.

Upon his arrest, Ramirez, 26, was charged with 14 murders and 31 other felonies. Throughout his trials he added to his demonic persona: dressing in all black, wearing sunglasses, showing off the inverted pentagram carved in his palm and shouting "Hail Satan!" intermittently. After nearly a year, the jury finally started deliberations with 8,000 pages of trial transcripts and 655 exhibits to consider. On September 20, 1986, almost two months after they had begun, the jury announced that they had reached a unanimous decision: On each of the 43 counts, the jury had voted guilty. "Dying doesn't scare me," Ramirez later responded. "I'll be in hell. With Satan." Despite his conviction, several females remained convinced of his innocence and, on October 3, 1996, Doreen Lioy, the most outspoken of them all, married him in the main visiting area of San Quentin State Prison. Ramirez's appeal against his conviction and sentence continues.

Brandy B. Henderson
University of South Florida

See Also: Murder, History of; San Quentin State Prison; Serial and Mass Killers.

Further Readings
Crime Library. "The Night Stalker: Serial Killer Richard Ramirez." http://www.trutv.com/library/crime/serial_killers/notorious/ramirez/terror_1.html (Accessed December 2010).
Hickey, Eric. *Serial Murderers and Their Victims.* Belmont, CA: Wadsworth, 2010.

Rape, Contemporary

Rape is defined as a form of nonconsensual sexual contact in which the bodily integrity of the victim is violated vaginally, orally, or anally, using either the body of the perpetrator or an object. Both males and females may be victims of rape.

Mistaken Notions About Rape

Although rape has been defined as a crime throughout American history, its definition has evolved as the social understanding of the issue has developed, especially in light of the work of feminist activists and scholars in the late 20th century. Traditionally, rape was considered more a crime against the father or the husband than against the victim herself. Reflecting the dependent status of women in a patriarchal society, the law viewed a sexual assault as either an offense against a father in whose care she was presumed to be or an insult to a husband, who was assumed to have the only sexual access to his wife. Based on those assumptions, rape was a grave insult to a husband or father's honor and to his status as head of the household. In addition, until well into the 20th century, accusations of rape were regarded with a great deal of skepticism—unless the accused was African American and the victim

According to the results of the 2000 National Violence Against Women Survey, 40 percent of rapes were likely to include physical assault along with sexual assault.

was white. Victims often felt that dealing with the criminal justice system was like a "second rape." Their privacy was invaded as they were asked about prior sexual contacts and they were often treated without dignity or respect, as if they were responsible for provoking an attack. Much of the legal framework surrounding rape law implied that the woman who claimed assault was not to be believed. Many of the definitions and evidentiary rules in rape cases derived more from men's fear of false charges than from the experience of the victim. For example, when rape was defined as "carnal knowledge without consent, of a woman not [one's] wife," the notion of consent focused on the victim's behavior rather than on that of the assailant. How could it be proved that a woman did not consent? Typically, nonconsent required resistance, preferably physical resistance. The expectation seemed to be that a woman, usually taught all her life to avoid violence, would prove her unwillingness to be raped by fighting like a man. If a woman failed to demonstrate enough opposition, the courts were likely to conclude that she had acquiesced. Thus, using enough physical force to break down a woman's resistance often sufficed to indicate that she had consented, and that therefore no crime had occurred.

Other assumptions indicating a lack of trust in women victims included rules of evidence that required that a charge of rape be corroborated. Although witnesses to rape were unlikely to come forward, torn clothing, bruises, or other injuries might serve to substantiate the victim's story. Courts were also permitted to use information about someone's past sexual history to inquire into her good character and presumably her truthfulness. Such a line of questioning might imply that if she had sexual relationships with other men, the victim was not respectable, and that she might lie. Past sexual history might also be used to suggest that a woman who would have sex with one man would have it with anyone. Charges of rape were also expected to be based on a "fresh complaint," coming immediately after the incident occurred. Here, the implication was that if time had passed, a woman might concoct a story. Until the late 20th century, rape laws reflected several other false and unflattering myths. A persistent belief that no woman can actually be raped against her will bolsters the notion that women provoke rape by their dress, by flirting, by drinking alcohol, by living alone, or by going home with a man. Another pervasive myth is that women are more likely to be raped by crazed, psychopathic strangers who jump out from behind bushes than by acquaintances, dates, or intimate partners. In fact, the reverse is true, because in nine out of 10 rapes, the perpetrator is known to the victim. A number of major feminist works in the late 20th century challenged these mistaken notions.

Rape and Women's Civil Rights

Susan Brownmiller argued that rape was the original method by which men subdued women and kept them in a position of dependence. She theorized that rape and the fear of sexual assault disadvantaged women as a group by intimidating them and by limiting their options to move freely through society. Significantly, Brownmiller's work is credited with spreading the argument that rape is not about sex but about violence and power. She claimed that rape is essentially a deliberate hostile act of degradation, stemming from the concept of male privilege, the myth that men have a "right" to women's bodies. Susan Estrich expanded the understanding of the crime of rape by explaining how the criminal justice responses to any rape are related to the appropriateness of the relationship between the victim and the rapist. The more conventional the liaison, the more likely the behavior will be excused. However, if the assailant is a member of a minority group, greatly older or younger than the victim, or a stranger, it is more likely that the assault will be seen as a crime. Estrich advocated treating nonconsensual sex, no matter how appropriate the man involved, as "real rape." Much of the feminist scholarship on rape also raised the point that too often rape was defined from a male perspective and focused on women's sexuality. Instead, they called for considering rape from the point of view of the victim and using her experience as the yardstick for determining what constitutes a crime.

Scholars writing about rape produced the theoretical foundation for an anti-rape movement. In addition, women meeting in consciousness-raising groups often found they had a common experience of nonconsensual sex. Starting from the premise that "the personal is political," and arguing that violence against women is a form of patriarchal control, many women began to see rape as a feminist and women's rights issue. Groups created task forces to monitor how the criminal justice system treated rape victims and publicized the practice of blaming the victim. They started community education efforts such as "Take Back the Night" marches and they helped to organize rape hotlines and counseling services for victims, often in association with domestic violence survivors' services. Throughout the late 20th century, the idea took hold that violence against women was not just individual criminal behavior but was part of a larger social structure that kept women in a persistently inferior position.

Statistics on Rape
Patterns of violence against women were also highlighted in two major studies from the National Institutes of Justice (NIJ). In 2000, the National Violence Against Women Survey questioned 8,000 women and 8,000 men and demonstrated that victimization was linked to the sex of the victim and the offender. Among other things, the survey showed that women were 10 times more likely than men to be raped and that rape was likely to be accompanied by physical assault in more than 40 percent of cases. Only 10 percent of women who were raped were the victims of strangers; the other 90 percent were victimized by current partners, acquaintances, or relatives. More than 54 percent of victims were raped before the age of 18 and those women were twice as likely to be raped again as adults. The same year, NIJ released a second study, "The Sexual Victimization of College Women." That report found that between 20 and 25 percent of college women experience a rape during their college years. The investigators did not begin by asking the respondents "Have you been raped?" Instead, they described behaviors that meet the definition of rape and asked the subjects whether they had those experiences. More than 40 percent of those who had experienced the behavior that met the definition of rape did not realize they had been raped. The study revealed a contradiction between the terms the victims used and their actual experience. A sizable minority seemed unable or unwilling to name what happened to them as the crime of rape. Perhaps they feared reprisals from the assailant or perhaps they blamed themselves. As 90 percent of college rapes are by persons known to the victims, the latter may be unwilling to label a boyfriend or classmate as a rapist. The college survey also indicated that only 5 percent of victims report their rape to law enforcement, although two-thirds tell someone, usually a friend. The findings support the belief that campus rapes are seriously underreported and that, therefore, they go unpunished and the survivors do not receive necessary services. Another consequence is that young women going off to college are often not made aware that the real threats of sexual assault are from men they know, in familiar places, with alcohol involved.

Major Legislation
Women's groups and their allies have had a significant impact on the way the criminal justice system deals with rape, even if the response is still often inadequate. Most jurisdictions have broadened their definitions of rape to include all forms

of sexual assault, oral and anal as well as vaginal, and those in which an object is used. They also define marital rape as a crime and recognize that it often accompanies other forms of domestic violence. There seems to be greater understanding that rape involves not just sexual contact but also forced subjugation of a victim to a violent act. Rape shield laws are designed to protect victims from having their prior sexual history used against them. Prosecutors today are more likely to be pro-victim and tougher on assailants, although courts still often seem unwilling to convict otherwise upstanding young men.

The 1994 Violence Against Women Act (VAWA) reflected the theory that crimes against women are civil rights violations, that women have a constitutional right to be free from violence directed against them because of gender. The supporters of the act argued that the states had failed to adequately address violence against women, whether it took the form of rape, domestic abuse, stalking, or sexual harassment, although the Fourteenth Amendment to the Constitution promised "equal protection of the law." Therefore, VAWA allowed victims of gender-based violence to sue their assailants in federal court and to claim monetary damages. Christy Brzonkala, a freshman at Virginia Tech, was raped by two male students in 1994. When the university failed to provide an appropriate disciplinary response, she sued the rapists in federal court. Her case made it all the way to the Supreme Court, which in 2000 found VAWA to be unconstitutional. The majority of the justices ignored the evidence that crimes against women were not treated as seriously as crimes against men. They failed to grasp the argument that violence against women perpetuated gender inequality. By ruling against VAWA, the court missed a historic opportunity to address structural barriers to women's full citizenship. They preferred to consider rape as a crime by individuals and not as a violation of women's civil right to be free from violence based on gender.

Mary Welek Atwell
Radford University

See Also: 2001 to 2012 Primary Documents; *Coker v. Georgia*; Rape, History of; Rape, Sociology of; Violence Against Women Act of 1994.

Further Readings
Bevacqua, Maria. *Rape on the Public Agenda: Feminism and the Politics of Sexual Assault*. Lebanon, NH: Northeastern University, 2000.
Brownmiller, Susan. *Against Our Wills: Men, Women, and Rape*. New York: Simon & Schuster, 1975.
Estrich, Susan. *Real Rape*. Cambridge, MA: Harvard University Press, 1987.
Tjaden, Patricia and Nancy Thoennes. *Full Report of the Prevalence, Incidence, and Consequences of Violence Against Women*. Washington, DC: National Institutes of Justice, 2000.

Rape, History of

Rape has always been a gendered victimization throughout the world. This means that the victims are overwhelmingly one gender—female. While many rapes are committed by strangers, researchers have found that most rapes are committed by acquaintances. These acquaintances may be individuals familiar to the victim, including current or former dating intimates and spouses or relatives. However, U.S. culture has historically defined rape as stranger-on-stranger crime, and the American legal system has addressed this crime using this myth. Reliance on this rape myth has denied justice for many victims of all races and economic statuses and has left many rapists unpunished. Throughout American history, however, social definitions, also known as social constructions, of rape have changed. With social change, society has experienced legal change.

Historical Context
Rape, as distinct from sexual assault, has historically been limited to penal-vaginal penetration in which, by law, the male was defined as the aggressor and the female as the victim. This definition excluded all other forms of sexual violence against females as well as all sexual violence against males. Since females have historically been defined as weak, submissive victims, these legal definitions fit well within existing social constructs. Furthermore, social definitions of males as aggressive and strong fit well within legal definitions of males as rapists.

Just as rape is a gendered victimization, the legal system is also a gendered institution. This means that the legal system is a male-dominated institution that enacts law through a male perspective. Social constructions of rape also influence legal definitions. As women did not have a voice in the political system, their interests were not recognized. The history of rape reflects the history of women's position within the larger society.

Until the passage of the Nineteenth Amendment in 1920 giving women the right to vote, women were legally defined as the property of their fathers or their husbands. In colonial America, marriage was a contract in which the husband would provide for the necessities of the wife (and children) but upon marriage, the wife would become the property of the husband. As a result, the rape of a woman was a violation of the property of the husband, or father. Further, rape within marriage was not illegal as the husband had the legal right to access his property. Adding to this acceptance was the court's recognition that a husband had a right to physically punish his wife if she misbehaved (*Bradley v. State of Mississippi*, 1824). Thus, women often experienced legally acceptable domestic violence and rape.

Extending the male's rights within the marriage contract to other male suitors, rape was more likely to be defined as stranger-on-stranger behavior. As such, females who were raped by men who were courting them were viewed to have consented in order to secure a marriage proposal. As courtship was the first stage leading to the marriage, men were given a level of power that required that the woman prove that she did not consent. An unchaste woman was not marriageable and, as such, when she had intercourse, consensual or otherwise, she lost her value.

All of these ideas are based on what scholars have identified as rape myths. Rape myths are commonly held notions, stereotypes, prejudices, or false beliefs about rape, rape victims, and rapists. Rape myths are supported by cultural ideologies of family, gender, and decency. As the male is defined to be naturally aggressive and the female naturally submissive, scholars have uncovered a rape myth that blurs the lines between date rape and seduction.

Criminal seduction laws in the 1840s demonstrate the blurred lines between date rape and seduction. Common within colonial America, fathers were able to sue a rapist for loss of chastity, and thus income. Seduction laws of the 1840s were designed to protect family reproduction, male property rights, and the class status of unstained women. These laws focused on men and criminalized consensual premarital sex with a chaste female under the promise of marriage. In Ohio, for example, a man found guilty under the seduction law may have received up to 10 years in prison. However, following rape myths regarding resistance, it was often difficult for the victim to prove seduction or rape.

Under rape and seduction laws, victims were required to undergo a resistance test. The resistance test required that the victim provide evidence to show that she engaged in the "utmost reluctance and utmost resistance" to the sexual act. Following further rape myths, resistance

Titian's 1571 painting The Rape of Lucretia. *Rape victims are overwhelmingly female and researchers have found that 90 percent of women are raped by partners or acquaintances.*

was demonstrated through the evidence of violence and injury. Hence, without the evidence of extreme physical abuse (utmost resistance), the victim was unable to convince family members and justice officials that she resisted. The rape myths that men are naturally aggressive and women are naturally submissive were ingrained within culture; this allowed society to reject the woman as a rape victim and did not punish the rapist for his crime.

Unfortunately, resistance and consent were only believed if the woman was chaste. While prosecutors focused on resistance, defense attorneys focused on chastity. A rape myth used here was the belief that good women are raped; in other words, they resist. On the other hand, bad women do not resist; they want the sexual interaction. Chastity refers to the goodness of character and of body. However, while a chaste body (never having had sexual relations in the past) was a requirement in showing the possibility of resistance, defense attorneys focused on chaste character. A woman who had sexual relations in the past or who did not behave like a "good woman" was easily believed to be an unchaste woman who would not resist.

Adding to rape myths of consent and chastity was the myth that women lie about rape in order to secure marriage or to protect a chaste reputation. As a result, corroboration laws were enacted. It was not enough for a woman to claim that she was raped; she had to have other evidence, often another witness, as testimony to the rape. This could be an individual who witnessed the violence or who provided aid in the aftermath of the violence that resulted. In 1974, New York became one of the first states to repeal the corroboration law. By the early 1980s, most states followed suit.

Changing Social Definitions and Legal Responses

Social constructions of property, consent, resistance, and other forms of rape myths historically have also been vital to the arrest, prosecution, and conviction of rapists. During the 1970s, the nation underwent an anti-rape movement in which victims and other advocates fought for the right to say "no" and for equal protection under the law (the Fourteenth Amendment to the U.S. Constitution). The legal pattern of the day was to discount all claims of rape unless they were committed by men against chaste women in an overly violent manner. Advocates, however, lobbied for a legal redefinition of rape to recognize sexual assault. In the 1970s, states added sexual assault laws that defied rape myths and recognized as sex crimes any sexual assault by a male or female on another male or female against his or her will. These laws recognized attempted rapes, sodomy, and other unwanted sexual violence.

Along with legal redefinitions of rape and the repeal of corroboration laws in the 1970s and 1980s, society saw a change in social constructs of resistance and resistance laws. A common rape myth held for so long has been that rape involves physical violence. Physical violence is the nonsexual violence that subdues the victim to the rape. However, in the 1980s, society and justice officials started to recognize the existence of psychological coercion. The terror of the sexual assault often subdues the victim for fear of serious injury. In fact, almost three-quarters of all completed rapes involve psychological coercion. As such, resistance as demonstrated by injuries to the victim is often absent. This was the most common form of resistance and corroboration required by the courts. When the justice system came to acknowledge that no injury may be present on a rape victim, resistance standards began to change. Laws moved from an "utmost resistance" standard to an "earnest resistance" standard in the 1980s.

Today, these legal corroboration and resistance standards no longer exist. However, rape myths persist and as a result, the practice of applying standards that have been legally repealed persists. These are especially applicable to more than 60 percent of sexual assault cases, those involving non-strangers. Of particular concern to rape reform are marital rape and date rape.

As identified earlier, husbands had a legal right to take sex from their wives—property. This was dictated by the legal interpretation of the marriage contract. It was not until the mid-1970s that the idea of marital rape was socially constructed. The notion of marital rape was first addressed in the 1975 case of Judy Hartwell. Hartwell killed her abusive husband after he raped her. The Michigan court judge presiding over the case argued that a wife had the right to say "no" and to defend herself against violence. In 1977, Oregon was the first state to criminalize rape by a husband. Before this time, states included a marital exemption to rape. This meant that an act was not rape if the act was committed by a husband. By the late 1990s, all 50 states criminalized marital rape. Some states removed the language from law that specified the relationship to the offender; other states legislated that marriage is not a defense, while others created a separate spousal rape category.

In the 1980s, date rape was first recognized as a punishable sexual assault. The focus of research was mostly on campus rape, and colleges brought awareness to their students through workshops and orientations. However, persistent rape myths continued to hinder the arrest, prosecution, and convictions of rapists. In order to subvert the negative effects of rape myths, rape shield laws were passed beginning in the mid-1970s. By the 1980s, most states had some form of rape shield law. The rape shield laws were intended to eliminate victim blaming and the assumption that chasteness dictates rapist behaviors. The laws prohibited defense attorneys from using a victim's past sexual history as proof of consent. These laws recognized that expectations of chaste character and body did not provide for women's equal protection under the law.

Evolving Debates and Solutions

As with all changes in social definitions, debate continues as to who is considered to be a rape victim and who is considered a rapist. While society has maintained its belief that rape also included many other forms of sexual assault, social constructs of specific rape circumstances, victims, and offenders continue to persist. The social constructions of wives as property of males, resistance, and consent persist within legal definitions. Currently, only 17 states do not include exemptions to marital rape laws. Some exemptions to marital rape laws include a statute of limitation that is shorter than non-spousal rape. This means that the victim has a shorter time to report the crime. Other states require that force or the threat of force must have been present. Still other states require that the married couple be legally separated for the offense to be considered a sexual assault. These laws bring to the forefront the continued use of earlier legal definitions. The wife is still defined as the property of the husband when legal separation is mandated, and shorter reporting windows are thrown up. Furthermore, evidence of force supports the long-standing myth that all rapes are physically violent.

As in earlier seduction laws, a degree of ownership is given to the dating rapist. Rape shield laws have great potential; however, exemptions to these laws tend to leave many victims exposed and unprotected to the dangers of rape. Many rape shield laws exempt victims who were previously sexually intimate with the rapist. Further, evidence of prostitution and other promiscuity is often exempted. In other words, if the victim was sexually active with the rapist, even through marriage, then she may have her sexual history brought before the court as evidence of consent and unchaste character. Additionally, a sexually promiscuous victim is one who is unchaste and is considered to be a liar if she claims to have been raped.

As society moves forward in reconstructing ideas of rape and sexual assault, debilitating rape myths persist. Advocates claim that further reform needs to be made. They argue that while the victim must have a right to equal protection, so too must the defendant be given due process of the law. As a result, it has been proposed that evidence of sexual contact of the crime in question must be admissible in court; however, evidence of sexual conduct prior to the act in question must be inadmissible.

As society moves through history and into the contemporary approach to rape and sexual assault, scholars have uncovered consistent evidence of rape myths and victim blaming. Beliefs that the victim shares some responsibility for the sexual assault tend to minimize the seriousness of rape and sexual assault in the eyes of society and especially the criminal justice system. The use of rape myths, however, has further-reaching effects. Specifically, rape myth acceptance and victim blaming by society often result in the victim's inability to understand that he or she has been sexually assaulted. This is known as the unacknowledged rape victim.

As many as 50 percent or more of rape victims do not know that aggression against them is legally defined as rape. Often, it is the female who has been raped by her dating partner and has engaged in previous sexual contact with him. If a victim has been intoxicated, acting flirty, or dressed promiscuously, she may blame herself for the rape and may not understand that the act was a crime punishable by law. These victims have accepted rape myths and are unlikely to report these crimes to the police.

Sexual assault is the most underreported violent crime in the United States. It is also least likely to result in an arrest, prosecution, or conviction. Currently, 74 percent of women who experience attempted rapes and 65 percent of women who experience completed rapes do not report these crimes to the police. Only 14 percent to 18 percent of all reported cases are prosecuted in criminal court. More than half (53 percent) of rape defendants are released before the case disposition is determined. Only 62 percent of all rape cases prosecuted result in a conviction. This is the lowest conviction rate following assault cases (54 percent). Following this knowledge, 21 percent of all convicted rapists are given probation.

Until society can shed its rape myths and extend the citizenship to all women by providing equal protection under the law, society will remain ignorant. Historically, rape was defined as a crime of sexual perversion. This myth allowed the justice system to neglect these violent offenders. Today, rape is moving toward being defined as a crime of power and control. This means that the rapist is asserting his or her power over the victim through sexual domination.

Venessa Garcia
Kean University

See Also: 1851 to 1900 Primary Documents; 1921 to 1940 Primary Documents; Domestic Violence, Contemporary; Gender and Criminal Law; Rape, Contemporary; Rape, Sociology of.

Further Readings
Donovan, Brian. "Gender Inequality and Criminal Seduction: Prosecuting Sexual Coercion in the Early 20th Century." *Law and Social Inquiry*, v.30/1 (2005).
Estrich, Susan. *Real Rape*. Cambridge, MA: Harvard University Press, 1987.
Fry, Melissa S. "Becoming Victims, Becoming Citizens: A Brief History of Gender-Motivated Violence in U.S. Law. In *Female Victims of Crime: Reality Reconsidered*, V. Garcia and J. E. Clifford, eds. Upper River Saddle, NJ: Prentice Hall, 2010.
LaFree, Gary D. *Rape and Criminal Justice: The Social Construction of Sexual Assault*. Belmont, CA: Wadsworth, 1989.
Peterson, Zoe D. and Charlene L. Muehlenhard. "Was It Rape? The Function of Women's Rape Myth Acceptance and Definition of Sex in Labeling Their Own Experiences." *Sex Roles*, v.51/3–4 (2004).

Rape, Sociology of

At its simplest, rape is forced sexual action, particularly referring to sexual penetration. While the Federal Bureau of Investigation's (FBI's) Uniform Crime Reporting (UCR) Program designates forcible rape as that perpetrated by men onto women, both males and females may be victims, as males and females may also be perpetrators. Sexual attacks on males are counted by the UCR Report as aggravated assaults or sex offenses, depending on the circumstances and the extent of any injuries. In 2009, the number of forcible rapes of women by men was estimated at 88,097. During this same time, only 21,407 arrests for forcible rapes were made.

While rape is legally defined as a nonconsensual sexual action, sociologists argue that the violation is not about sex per se. Rather, rape is an issue of social power (or lack thereof). Therefore, sex is merely a weapon used by one individual to establish power over another. As such, characteristics commonly associated with sexuality, such as perceived attractiveness of the victim and/or the perpetrator, social standing, or occupation, do not factor into the likelihood of becoming a victim or a perpetrator.

No one deserves to be raped. Rape is perpetrated by an individual who has social (and often physical) power over another. Contrary to popular belief, being sexually appealing to others does not mean an individual is "above" rape—if rape is an issue of power rather than biology, access to legitimate means to obtain sexual gratification becomes irrelevant. Further, being viewed as either "too available" (e.g., a prostitute, or a woman dressed provocatively) or as sexually undesirable and unable to utilize conventional channels to achieve sexual contact does not preclude one from becoming a victim. The sociological understanding of why rape occurs may be explained by the three sociological perspectives: functionalist, conflict, and symbolic interactionist.

Functionalist Perspective

According to Emile Durkheim's view of functionalism, some crime is necessary for the continuation of social life. While excessive deviance is deemed pathological, some degree of deviance, such as rape, contributes to the social order through manifest and latent functions. Functionalists view deviance as a social good, not necessarily as a moral good. A social good is an action or occurrence that serves some purpose in the functioning of society as evidenced by its reoccurrence over time. According to functionalist theorists, behaviors that do not benefit society or social members will eventually become extinct. Manifest or apparent functions of deviance include boundary setting, group solidarity, adaptive innovation, and tension reduction.

When rape occurs in a society and is punished appropriately, boundaries are set for societal members. Through the action of sanctioning, social norms are established so that cultural members are reminded of which behaviors are sanctioned as opposed to condoned. If the action were not committed and condemned, cultural members would have no verification of the boundaries of society. Further, when a culture member violates the social norms, the community tends to bond together, creating a band of support for either the victim or the accused. Rather than a society of individuals, group cohesion is created.

Because of the need for hard evidence, new technologies have been created to verify the guilt or innocence of perpetrators and victims. For example, rape kits that enable professionals to determine whether DNA evidence is available. In terms of tension reduction, rather than focusing on social ills such as structural breakdowns contributing to a violent culture, being able to focus on the prosecution of a deviant such as a rapist permits society to redirect its focus from a systemic problem to that of an individual problem with a ready solution.

Latent function is the social good that is less apparent and clearly defined than manifest function. While rape is a heinous deviant action, the deviance does serve a purpose in that it justifies the need for social services to reduce such crimes. For example, because of deviants such as rapists, there is a need to employ people to fill a variety of roles within the criminal justice system, among others. Examples include the patrol officer, lawyers, judges, prison guards, and parole officers. According to the application of the functionalist perspective on deviance, if society were able to rid itself of all deviance, a large segment of the population would become unemployed.

Robert Merton's strain theory elaborates that deviance is the result of a discrepancy between socially engendered goals and the legitimate means to achieve those goals. Nondeviants, termed *conformists*, both accept the social goal and have at their disposal legitimate means to achieve those goals. Merton's typology contains four types of deviants, including the innovator, retreatist, ritualist, and rebel. A rapist would be an example of an innovator, such as a male accepting the socially engendered goal of social power over females or effeminate males. If this power is unable to be achieved in a legitimate way, such as through success in the workplace, the individual may resort to illegitimate means such as rape to ensure social power over another.

While crime generally, and rape specifically, are not moral goods for society, according to the functionalist perspective, their existence does provide a social good and is necessary for the maintenance of society and social order. So, while rape is predominantly considered dysfunctional and there are overwhelming negative attributes to the action for the individual, the occurrence of deviance does retain some redeeming qualities for the continuation of society.

Conflict Perspective

According to the conflict perspective, deviance occurs as a result of an unequal society. Rape is the manifestation of the struggle between the powerful and the powerless. The specific application of the conflict perspective to the deviant act of rape varies between pluralistic conflict theorists, who view the battle of power as being a conflict over scarce resources, and radical Marxist

Sailors stationed at Naval Air Station Jacksonville listen to a presentation given by Men Against Violence Against Women, an organization focused on effecting social change by making men aware of the prevalence of violence against women, stressing that it is aslo a man's issue, since the majority of violent crimes against women are perpetrated by men.

conflict theorists, who view the struggle as a structural issue resulting from the inequality inherent in a capitalist system.

Pluralistic conflict theorists propose that deviance, such as rape, is a cultural response to particular situations or events that bring to light competition for social or economic advantage. Thus, conflict is the inevitable result of distinctions between those in authority and those subject to authority. Richard Quinney's *Social Reality of Crime* (1970) articulates the following five propositions, with a sixth proposition being a composite statement, resulting in the social reality of crime:

1. *Crime is a definition of human conduct that is created by authorized agents in a politically organized society.* Rape is itself a definition of behavior that is projected on some persons by others. That the UCR report defines rape as an action conducted by men to women is constructed by political agents.
2. *Criminal definitions describe behaviors that conflict with the interests of the segments of society that have the power to shape public policy.* Those who have the power to have their interests represented in public policy, generally white upper-class males, regulate the definition of rape and victimization.
3. *Criminal definitions are applied by the segments of society that have the power to shape the enforcement and administration of criminal law.* Those who have the power to determine the definitions of rape and victimization, generally white upper-class males, also have the power to enforce the definitions (or not).

4. *Behavior patterns are structured in segmentally organized society in relation to criminal definitions, and within this context persons engage in actions that have relative probabilities of being defined as criminal.* The acceptance and continuation of rape culture is learned in social and cultural settings. If a perpetrator is socialized such that rapists are not prosecuted, then the perpetrator is not likely to perceive the behavior as criminal.

5. *Conceptions of crime are constructed and diffused in the segments of society by various means of communication.* Definitions of who should be labeled as rapists and victims are socially constructed. As such, anecdotal evidence suggests that certain segments of the population, such as prostitutes, the obese, and the feeble-minded, are categorically denied protection due to their social ostracization and status as social pariahs.

Radical (Marxist) conflict theorists view social conflict in terms of a struggle between social classes as a result of the structural inequalities inherent in capitalist societies. Conflict is the result of ongoing social struggle between those who profit and those who suffer to the benefit of others. There are two predominant conditions of conflict. First, the more significant the behavioral difference between authorities and subjects, the more significant the conflict. Second, subject(s) are organized to the degree that authorities can be resisted. Conflict increases when legal norms reflect the cultural norms. When the culture and laws coincide, there is a greater likelihood that a rape will be prosecuted. If, on the other hand, there is little sympathy for the victim, there is less likelihood that the rapist will be prosecuted. Conflict also increases when subjects have little power; if the definition and enforcement is likely to meet with little resistance, prosecution is more likely. If the accused is perceived as a person of importance, the likelihood of prosecution decreases.

Whether the inequality exists between groups over perceived scarcity of resources or between classes over structural inequality, conflict theorists would concur that rape occurs when there is an imbalance. When the individual with power seeks to maintain or gain more power, the most effective way to do this is to subjugate the other. When a female is raped by a male, the patriarchal social order is reinforced.

Rape is more likely to be reported in egalitarian cultures than in more traditional, patriarchal cultures. Egalitarian cultures, such as the United States, are those in which males and females hold relatively equal power and responsibility. There is little clear division between the sexes in terms of the separate spheres of labor: both sexes are participating in the workforce outside the home (public sphere) as well as engaging in the domestic-based, private sphere. Because of this blending of responsibility and a lack of clear gender division in either the workplace or, increasingly, in the home in egalitarian societies, sexual violence may occur in an attempt to maintain patriarchal control in a nonpatriarchal society.

Conversely, in patriarchal cultures, such as India, where there is a clear delineation between men's and women's work and places in society, women are less likely to report being victims of sexual violence. Sexual violence committed against women is often viewed more as an affront to the family than to the violated female. Under Islamic law, women are required to provide four witnesses to rape. Those who are unable to do so are often revictimized by being charged with adultery. Violence against women in developing countries often goes unreported and may be used systemically as a way of maintaining social control, such as the widespread rape of women and children in the republic of Bosnia-Herzegovina by Serbian men from 1992 to 1995 in an attempt to force Muslims into fleeing their villages.

Symbolic Interactionist Perspective

Symbolic interactionists view deviance as a matter of labeling and social construction. J. L. Simmons noted that deviance, like beauty, is in the eye of the beholder. Specifically, rape is only deviant and criminal where and when it is so labeled. While this may seem contrary when considering the personal devastation of rape, consider the issue of marital rape, also known as spousal rape and conjugal rape, whereby a husband rapes his wife. Until the late 1970s, most states in the United States did not consider marital rape a crime, traceable to a 17th-century decree that a husband cannot be guilty of rape of his wife "for by their mutual matrimonial consent and contract the wife hath given up herself in this kind unto the husband which she cannot retract." Thus, as part of the marital contract, the wife did not have the power or right to refuse sexual advances by her husband. As recently as 1993, a North Carolina law stated, "a person may not be prosecuted under this article if the victim is the person's legal spouse at the time of the commission of the alleged rape or sexual offense unless the parties are living separate and apart."

While conjugal rape is currently deemed criminal in the United States, not all states prosecute to the same extent as stranger rape. A person convicted of spousal rape will typically receive much more lenient sentencing than a person convicted of stranger or date rape. Further, the same rules of circumstance often do not apply. For example, in Ohio, if a perpetrator uses a drug or intoxicant to influence consent, a charge of rape is not considered a viable charge for spouses who live together. In many other countries, such as the Bahamas, marital rape is not illegal.

Howard Becker suggests that labels are created as a result of powerful "moral entrepreneurs." This labeling occurs in an orderly process: initial recruitment, role imprisonment, and entrance into sustaining subcultures. Initial recruitment into the behavior in question, such as rape, might include coercion by peers to commit an offense. Role imprisonment occurs as the perpetrator takes on the label of rapist, meaning that society has labeled the offender and the perpetrator accepts and embraces the label, unable to free himself or herself of the stigma of sexual offender. Finally, due to the social ostracization of the rapist, the perpetrator enters into sustaining subcultures that are accepting of the perpetrator in spite of, or because of, their label and status as social pariah. However, norms precede labels and the progression occurs only as the labels are applied and accepted. In cases where perpetrators are not considered deviant, such as when a Bahamian husband rapes his wife, role imprisonment will not occur.

Conclusion
The job of the sociologist is not to pass judgment on the quality of social acts and actors but rather to offer an objective, generalizable explanation for social behavior. Toward that end, the sociology of rape offers three explanations for rape as a social behavior that has occurred throughout time. The action of rape contributes to social stability, maintains power differentials in society, and serves as an indication of the relativity of perception of action across time and place.

Leslie Elrod
University of Cincinnati

See Also: 1851 to 1900 Primary Documents; 2001 to 2012 Primary Documents; Gender and Criminal Law; Rape, Contemporary; Rape, History of.

Further Readings
Becker, Howard S. *Outsiders: Studies in the Sociology of Deviance*. New York: Free Press, 1963.
Durkheim, Emile. *The Rules of the Sociological Method*. New York: Macmillan, 1964.
Federal Bureau of Investigation. "Crime in the United States." http://www2.fbi.gov/ucr/cius2009/index.html (Accessed January 2011).
History Place. "Genocide in the 20th Century: Bosnia-Herzegovina." http://www.historyplace.com/worldhistory/genocide/bosnia.htm (Accessed February 2011).
National Center for Victims of Crime. "Spousal Rape Laws: 20 Years Later." http://www.ncvc.org/ncvc/main.aspx?dbName=DocumentViewer&DocumentID=32701 (Accessed January 2011).
Quinney, Richard. *Social Reality of Crime*. Boston: Little, Brown, 1970.
Simmons, J. L. *Deviants*. San Francisco: Boyd & Fraser, 1969.
Turk, Austin. *Criminality and the Legal Order*. Chicago: Rand McNally, 1969.

Ray, James Earl

James Earl Ray (March 10, 1928–April 23, 1998) was a career criminal convicted of the assassination of American civil rights leader Dr. Martin Luther King, Jr. He was convicted on March 10, 1969, after agreeing to a plea bargain by which, in exchange for a guilty plea, he was sentenced to 99 years in prison. He later recanted his confession and tried unsuccessfully to gain a trial.

James Earl Ray was born in Alton, Illinois. He dropped out of 10th grade at the age of 15. He worked for a while at a shoe company, but was laid off at the end of 1945 and joined the army. After two years of service in the infantry and the military police, mostly in Germany, he received a less-than-honorable general discharge in December 1948 for "ineptness and lack of adaptability to military service."

In 1952 he served two years for armed robbery of a taxi driver in Illinois. In 1955, he was convicted of mail fraud. After an armed robbery in Missouri in 1959, Ray was sentenced to 20 years in prison. He escaped from the Missouri State Penitentiary in Jefferson.

Ray spent the next year as a fugitive, living for a time in Mexico and then in Los Angeles. He was briefly a volunteer in George Wallace's presidential campaign and considered migrating to Rhodesia, which was governed by a white-minority government. Ray, using the alias Eric Starvo Galt, eventually made his way to Atlanta, King's hometown. Ray, who had purchased a rifle in Birmingham, Alabama, on March 30, 1968, using another alias, Harvey Lowmeyer, then went to Memphis, where Martin Luther King, Jr., was lending his support to black sanitation workers who were on strike for higher wages and better treatment. King was shot and killed by a sniper on April 4, 1968, while standing on the second-floor balcony of the Lorraine Motel in Memphis, Tennessee.

Captured in London

On June 8, 1968, Ray was captured at London's Heathrow Airport while traveling on a false Canadian passport under the name of Ramon George Sneyd. He was extradited to Tennessee, where he was charged with King's murder. He confessed to the crime on March 10, 1969, and was sentenced to 99 years in prison. Within days, Ray attempted to withdraw his guilty plea, which was rejected by the courts. For the rest of his life, Ray would claim that he had not shot King, but that he was part of a conspiracy with a man named Raoul.

On June 10, 1977, Ray and six other inmates escaped from the Brushy Mountain State Penitentiary in Petros, Tennessee. Ray was recaptured three days later. Ray continued asserting his innocence. The United States House of Representatives Select Committee on Assassinations (1976–79) reviewed the matter and concluded in its report that Ray killed King, although "there is a likelihood" that there was a conspiracy. Ray took a polygraph test as part of a 1977 interview with *Playboy*. The magazine said that the test results showed "that Ray did, in fact, kill Martin Luther King, Jr., and that he did so alone."

In 1992, Ray's book, *Who Killed Martin Luther King?: The True Story by the Alleged Assassin*, appeared. In December 1993, Loyd Jowers appeared on the ABC-TV program, *Prime Time Live*, where he claimed that Ray was not involved in the King assassination. Instead, he asserted that King had been killed by an Earl Clark, a Memphis police officer, and that the killing was the work of a conspiracy involving the Mafia and the U.S. government. In 1998, the King family filed a wrongful death suit against Jowers and other un-named co-conspirators. In December 1999, the jury found Jowers responsible. An investigation by the U.S. Department of Justice of Jowers's claims that was completed in 2000 found they could not be substantiated. King's family supported Ray's request for a trial, believing that it would reveal the existence of a conspiracy to murder the civil rights leader.

Ray died on April 23, 1998, while in custody of Tennessee authorities at the Columbia Nashville Memorial Hospital; his body was cremated and his ashes were scattered in Ireland.

Jeffrey Kraus
Wagner College

See Also: 1961 to 1980 Primary Documents; Civil Rights Laws; King, Martin Luther, Jr.; Racism.

Further Readings
Huie, William Bradford. *Did the F.B.I. Kill Martin Luther King?* Nashville, TN: T. Nelson, 1977.
McMillan, George. *The Making of an Assassin.* Boston: Little, Brown, 1976.
Posner, Gerald. *Killing the Dream: James Earl Ray and the Assassination of Martin Luther King, Jr.* New York: Harcourt Brace, 1998.
Ray, James Earl. *Who Killed Martin Luther King?: The True Story by the Alleged Assassin.* Washington, DC: National Press Books, 1992.
Sides, Hampton. *Hellhound on His Trail: The Stalking of Martin Luther King Jr. and the International Hunt for His Assassin.* New York: Doubleday, 2010.

Reagan, Ronald (Administration of)

Ronald Reagan (1911–2004), the 40th president of the United States, was an actor and a politician. Both professions are noted for having members whose words and actions are sometimes inconsistent, if not contradictory, while being routinely pleasing to the constituent's ear. Unlike many politicians, however, Reagan also had a rare willingness to adjust to circumstances. His law-and-order rhetoric was usually but not always matched by tough action against criminals. Still, he was tough rhetorically, allowing those who admired him to misconstrue him as consistently tough on crime and to cite him as the model for their tough actions.

As president (1981–89), Reagan often talked of the list he kept on his desk as governor. The list named a dozen murderers who had completed their sentences or been paroled and then added another 22 victims to their original 12. He noted that capital punishment would have kept that total at 12. Despite the tough rhetoric, during eight years as governor of California, Reagan executed only one person, in 1967, and granted clemency in a second capital case because the man had brain damage. He later said the 1967 execution decision was one of the hardest he ever had to make. Still, he was disappointed that a judge he appointed was the one to throw out the California capital punishment law after Reagan left office.

As president, Reagan enjoyed high approval ratings and favorable relations with Congress, which enabled him to enact much of what he wanted. Tougher laws against crime were easy to pass because they matched the mood of the country as well as congressional Republicans and southern Democrats.

Stance on Crime

Between 1960 and 1975, the number of violent crimes nationwide rose from 288,000 to 1.04 million, and the number of murders more than doubled from 9,000 to 20,000. In the late 1960s, conservatives—first Richard Nixon and later Ronald Reagan—decried the breakdown of law and order as a means of destroying the already unraveling liberal consensus. "Law and order" is a label for the broad issues including a stricter criminal justice system for violent and property crimes, harsher penalties including mandatory sentencing, longer sentences, and even capital punishment. Politicians use law and order to tar their opponents as weak against crime, and it can also be a cover for police abuse.

As liberals took control of the Democratic Party, millions of Democrats fled what they saw as excessive pandering to minorities and lack of commitment to law and order. Many became "Reagan Democrats," while others shifted to the Republican Party. For Reagan, the underlying cause of crime was not environment but moral failure. The same breakdown in values that led to increased crime led also to government growth and economic decline. He regarded as mistaken the 1950s and 1960s intellectuals who treated crime as a problem of impoverished childhood environment and called for government intervention to correct the environment that promoted criminal behavior. Reagan believed that good and evil were not changed by improvement in material environment. Federal government merely exacerbated social problems.

Reagan contended that victory in the war on crime would come only with a change in American attitudes, when once again right and wrong mattered, when individuals took responsibility for their actions, and when retribution was swift and sure. The legal system was the moral voice of society, and, given that the values were sound, their expression in punishment was nothing to feel guilty about. Theft and murder were not political statements, matters of relativity, but absolute crimes.

Crime Legislation

Crime and criminal law became politicized. One legacy of this state of affairs was the Comprehensive Crime Control Act of 1984, which reformed sentencing, bail, and forfeiture laws and made procedural changes. The Sentencing Reform Act set guidelines to standardize punishments for classes of crime, eliminating judicial discretion. This had been a goal of others, including Edward Kennedy, since the 1970s. The act was good in theory because it eliminated the wide disparity in sentences that had plagued the courts for years It came under fire quickly, however, because in

At 3.1 million square feet, the Ronald Reagan Building and International Trade Center is the largest building in Washington, D.C. Congress mandated that the center provide a setting where the best public and private resources could create a national forum for trade advancement. The building also houses a conference and events center and office space.

practice the guidelines were much narrower than liberal reformers anticipated, and both jurists and convicts sought relief, throwing the system into chaos for several years before it stabilized. Criticisms continue that the guidelines are unduly rigid and harsh. The law left no room for compassion for congenital criminals.

The Bail Reform Act of 1984 changed the traditional rule that only genuine flight risks were denied bail. While claiming to preserve the presumption of innocence, the act allows a judge to incarcerate a defendant believed to be dangerous. It authorized preventive detention for the first time during peace, incorporating the discredited notion that past behavior is an accurate predictor of future conduct. Twenty years later, federal prisons overflowed with pretrial detainees, among them low-level drug dealers, and pretrial detentions of a year were not unusual.

The Reagan administration also weakened the insanity defense, made forfeiture more oppressive, abolished parole in many cases, and established mandatory minimum sentences for cases involving drugs or weapons. Reagan continued and increased the war on drugs and established the Office of National Drug Control Policy. The war on drugs targeted not only traffickers and dealers but users as well, criminalizing a social issue.

War on Crime
Ronald Reagan was not the first to promise to get tough on crime—law and order has been a favorite excuse used against antilynching advocates, civil rights sympathizers, and politicians who supported the right to demonstrate, among others. Richard Nixon blamed civil unrest and crime on the civil rights movement, and he was frustrated that there was no federal law allowing him to enter the cities and take on street crime. After Nixon's term, crime faded as an issue until Ronald Reagan vowed to use federal law enforcement to take back the streets and strongly encouraged his agencies to shift from white-collar to street crime.

He could have been harsher. For instance, in 1982, Reagan approved a middle path when given three options by budget director David Stockman. The extreme was a 14 percent real growth and construction of seven more prisons. The low end was a reduction of 5 percent in real growth and no new prisons. Reagan's choice was 6 percent real growth and the building of three new prisons. His advisers, Stockman and Attorney General William French Smith, indicated their preference for the high end.

Ronald Reagan regarded the war on crime as black and white, a battle of good versus evil. He left a legacy of being tough on crime. The 1980s and 1990s were a time of excess and soaring crime; Reagan sought to rebalance the system to restore the edge to law against the forces of lawlessness. He led an unprecedented campaign against greed, corruption, and crime. His legacy included "three strikes" laws, the war on drugs, and conservative talk radio demanding even more changes. New crimes meant new criminals in new prisons, and soon, the United States led the world in share of citizens per capita incarcerated even as the crime surge of the 1980s abated and the violent crime rates dropped consistently over the next 30 years.

John H. Barnhill
Independent Scholar

See Also: 1981 to 2000 Primary Documents; Bail Reform Act; Capital Punishment; Crime in America, Causes; Federal Rules of Criminal Procedure; Nixon, Richard (Administration of).

Further Readings
Cannon, Lou. *President Reagan: The Role of a Lifetime.* New York: Simon & Schuster, 1991.
Farrell, Steve. "Reagan's Common Sense on Capital Punishment, Crime, and Moral Absolutes." http://archive.newsmax.com/archives/articles/2006/6/28/170302.shtml (Accessed September 2011).
On The Issues. "Ronald Reagan on Crime." http://www.ontheissues.org/Celeb/Ronald_Reagan_Crime.htm (Accessed September 2011).
Shargel, Gerald. "No Mercy: Ronald Reagan's Tough Legal Legacy." Slate. http://www.slate.com/id/2102352 (Accessed September 2011).

Reform, Police and Enforcement

There are two broad categories of police reform: performance and enforcement. Performance reform efforts are aimed at improving how the police conduct business and began with the professionalization movement in the early 1900s. This effort focused on training and educating police so they would provide better service to citizens. Other performance reforms have focused on the relationship between the police and the public, such as community-oriented policing. The second category of reform efforts emphasizes which laws the police enforce and how they do so. This includes focusing on specific types of crimes per political or public desire, and policies and case law, which guide enforcement activities. Performance and enforcement reform are not mutually exclusive; they are related, and often the reform efforts in performance impact enforcement and vice versa.

Professionalization of the Police
Modern police did not appear in the United States until the 1830s and 1840s. As cities grew on the east coast, the need for organized policing became apparent. There were more people, more businesses, and more opportunities for crime and disorder. Despite the clear need for a formalized police force, the organization effort was difficult. There was resistance from citizens who feared the police would become a military presence in their cities. As a result, the first police officers did not wear uniforms or carry guns until several years after they were organized. Eventually, the police were required to wear uniforms and badges and were permitted to carry firearms. Training for these first police officers was nonexistent. Men were often hired off the street and sent to work immediately. Departments did not have regulations, and most officers were not knowledgeable of the law. Performance standards were minimal, and enforcement was largely driven by the desires of political officials. Most men were hired as officers because of the politicians they knew and enforced the law according to what those politicians wanted. Advancement within the ranks was not based on skill, experience, or aptitude;

it was based upon political affiliation. The result was unskilled police officers improperly enforcing laws against citizens who had little legal recourse in those days of brutality and corruption.

The first reform movement in the early 1900s largely focused on police performance. The Progressives wanted to professionalize the police by removing control from the politicians and requiring that officers be educated and trained. Some police officers supported this reform effort. August Vollmer and O. W. Wilson advocated what were, at the time, radical changes in policing. Vollmer, the chief of the Berkeley, California, police department, believed that police officers should have college educations and formal training on how to be a police officer. Partly as a result of this early effort, many departments now require at least some college education, and some require four-year degrees to be hired as an entry-level patrol officer. Vollmer was an advocate for using technology to improve performance and enforcement capabilities and believed in patrolling communities to prevent crime. Wilson served as an officer under Vollmer and also supported police reform. He was regarded by police administrators as the leading authority on police leadership. His influence is still recognizable in police agencies as demonstrated by their bureaucratic and paramilitary structure and procedures.

Other police reformers of the Progressive Era were William Gaynor and "Golden Rule" Jones. Gaynor was the mayor of New York City from 1910 to 1913. He required the police to abandon the enforcement of liquor violations and the use of warrantless searches to raid bars serving alcohol during Prohibition, thus promoting the constitutional rights of citizens. Jones believed the poor were disenfranchised from proper legal representation and dismissed the cases brought before him. The effect was reduced police harassment and eventual changes in the New York criminal code. The Progressive Era also introduced women into policing. Although their role was limited to handling cases involving women and children, females had a solid role in police departments as the moral arm of justice.

Despite these efforts, the Wickersham Commission report of 1931 presented evidence that police performance needed improvement. The report revealed that corruption among police and local politicians was widespread as they capitalized on Prohibition. The police were as much a part of organized crime as they were the vehicle that was supposed to stop it. The report detailed police practices and found that officers were often brutal toward suspects, frequently giving them the "third degree." The third degree was a physical beating suspects were subjected to until they confessed to a crime or provided information. The third degree was also administered to punish a disrespectful suspect or citizen. These revelations put pressure on police administrators to professionalize their officers and eradicate corruption and abuse.

Technology

Several technological changes occurred in the late 1800s and early 1900s that changed police performance and law enforcement—and that continue to impact American policing. The invention of the telephone allowed citizens to call the police for help directly from their homes—and led to the police being invited to enter private dwellings on a regular basis. Private problems increasingly became police business, including domestic violence and other family-related issues. The public was now also able to call the

A New York Police Department security camera keeps watch over midtown Manhattan. With technological advances like these cameras, critics fear a huge surveillance infrastructure without adequate public oversight or outside regulation.

police for nonlegal matters as well, broadening the scope of policing duties.

A related technological advancement was the portable police radio. Prior to the radios, police relied on emergency whistles to call for assistance, thus limiting the distance an officer could walk on patrol without placing him in danger. Officers also had limited contact with their supervisors while on patrol. The radio allowed officers to safely expand their patrol areas and to communicate with each other. Officers also had more supervision than they did previously, making it easier for supervisors to be sure that any policies and procedures that did exist were being followed.

Automobiles and motorcycles also changed police performance and enforcement. Officers no longer were confined to a few blocks on foot—they could cover several miles of jurisdiction and move quickly from place to place. It was possible for them to respond to crimes soon after they occurred and for them to vigorously pursue suspects, who also were acquiring vehicles. The use of vehicles did, however, put a barrier between the police and the public, who previously could speak to officers freely as they walked down the same streets. As officers and the public grew farther apart physically, the image of the police as aloof crime fighters was enhanced. This was not entirely unplanned, as the professional reform effort sought to remove the police from public and political influence to reduce the opportunity for corruption and unfair enforcement.

Other technology rapidly developed and changed the way the police investigated crimes and thus enforced some laws. In an early form of crime mapping, detailed record-keeping systems were implemented so that the police could track crimes based upon locations and possible suspects. Fingerprint analysis revolutionized criminal investigations, allowing suspects to be identified based upon evidence left at a crime scene. Now crimes that once might not have been given much attention could be investigated with relative ease when compared to the effort that would have previously been expended.

Court Rulings

A series of state and federal court rulings have dramatically changed the way the police conduct business. These rulings were largely concerned with police violation of citizens' constitutional rights. *Weeks v. United States* (1914) set the stage for search and seizure case law, requiring that federal law enforcement agencies have warrants to seize a person's property. The Warren Court heard the case of *Mapp v. Ohio* (1961) and extended the search warrant requirement to state law enforcement agencies. The Warren Court ruled in the case of *Miranda v. Arizona* (1966) that a suspect has the right to counsel and is not required to speak to the police until counsel is obtained. *Tennessee v. Garner* (1985) prohibited police officers from shooting at fleeing felons, contributing to a dramatic change in when officers were permitted to discharge their firearms to apprehend suspects. Case law continues to impact police performance and enforcement of laws.

The 1960s to the Present

The President's Commission on Law Enforcement and Criminal Justice report was published in 1969 and included recommendations for reform. Among the recommendations was that the police strive to become closer to the public, and that drug enforcement be increased. Following the report's recommendations, some departments attempted to change their image by adopting team policing in the 1970s. The goal was to improve police-public relations by promoting a less military atmosphere surrounding the police and by encouraging officers to have more direct contact with community members outside law enforcement duties. A group of officers was permanently assigned to the same patrol area and wore business attire to avoid the military stigma of the police uniform. These efforts were met with resistance from officers and the public. Officers were ridiculed by the public and by other police agencies, and the idea was eventually abandoned.

In the 1980s, police departments began experimenting with community-oriented policing (COP) as a way to improve police-community relations and encourage citizens to take an active role in improving their communities. The philosophy of COP is that policing will be more successful if community members have a voice in how policing is conducted where they live. Police departments began assigning officers to permanent shifts and beats (similar to team policing) to encourage more

Delaware Senator Tom Carper (left) and the Laurel's Police Department announce a community-oriented policing (COP) hiring program grant. Community policing supports partnerships and problem-solving techniques to proactively address crime. A main component of the strategy is to place more officers on the street to fight crime and to build trust in the police force.

interaction with citizens. It was hoped that officers would be able to determine which solutions to crime and disorder would work based upon community needs, in addition to building trust so that citizens would provide information about criminal activity. The police engage the community by hosting town meetings and citizen police academies, by using foot patrols in business areas, and by establishing substations to encourage citizens to come to them for assistance.

COP has also been used as a vehicle to improve the relationship between the police and minorities. The police have historically had a negative relationship with racial and ethnic minorities that has created much controversy. The push for drug enforcement in the 1980s put the police at odds with minorities living in the inner cities. The highly publicized police assault on Rodney King in Los Angeles in 1992 fueled tensions, and there was outcry from the black community about how the police treated black suspects, particularly males.

Racial tension continued as police departments across the country were accused of targeting minorities (largely blacks) during traffic stops. The U.S. Department of Justice investigated several departments and instituted oversight efforts to reduce the targeting of minorities, leading to reform in police record keeping and how traffic stops are conducted. Some police departments have initiated COP efforts in areas heavily populated by minorities in an attempt to improve relations by familiarizing the police and citizens with each other and jointly addressing community problems.

Problem-oriented policing (POP) is a reform focusing on both performance and enforcement. POP requires that the police gather and analyze information to determine the best course of action when a problem presents itself. This method requires that the police think "outside of the box," and consider other options besides enforcing the law to solve a problem. POP differs from COP in that it does not require community participation to be effective—the police can identify which problems to solve on their own accord. Using POP necessitates that officers be given latitude in decision making and be permitted to do what is reasonable to resolve issues. This directly opposes the paramilitary decision-making structure proposed by early reformers and still used by many departments. POP does not necessarily require enforcement of law to be successful; however, when the law is enforced to solve a problem, it is done based upon information that has determined enforcement is the best option.

CompStat is a method of law enforcement and accountability designed to reduce crime while holding police officers responsible their enforcement efforts. First initiated in New York City, CompStat uses crime mapping to determine problem areas in the various jurisdictions. Zero-tolerance policing is used as the primary means of reducing instances of crime. Zero-tolerance policing occurs when the police make arrests for all offenses in their districts, regardless of how minor they are. Routine meetings are held between police leadership and patrol supervision, which must provide explanations for any failure to achieve a reduction in crime.

Police Discretion and Reform

Controlling discretion is one way to institute reform among police. Police have always had latitude in how they perform their duties. The policies and procedures that are in place are designed to guide officers, not dictate their every move. Some policies and procedures allow more discretion than others. However, some areas of controversy have been the focus of changing policies, procedures, and laws designed to change the way the police respond to these situations. Two such areas are domestic violence enforcement and vehicle pursuits.

In the 1980s and 1990s, several events occurred that reformed the way police responded to domestic violence. The battered women's movement gained national and local support and encouraged lawmakers to create laws making it easier for the police to arrest in cases of domestic violence. There were also several lawsuits against the police for failing to protect victims of domestic violence. Many states and some departments adopted preferred or mandatory arrest policies, and police departments responded by providing more education about domestic violence and its impact on victims to their officers.

Vehicle pursuits have always been a source of controversy for the police because of the danger involved. When a suspect leads police on a vehicle chase, there is always the chance that the pursuit will end in the loss of life of the suspect, the officer, or an innocent bystander. Since the 1990s, there has been a push for the police to limit, or completely eliminate, police pursuit of suspects. Some police departments have no-pursuit policies, while others provide stringent guidelines for when a pursuit should or should not be initiated.

Police reform will continue to occur as problems with the police are identified and as the needs of the public and the police change. Members of the police community, lawmakers, or the general public may lead future reform efforts. These reforms may come in the form of case law, policies and procedures, and new ways of enforcing the law.

Wendy Perkins Gilbert
Urbana University

See Also: Law Enforcement Assistance Administration; Police, Women as; Police Abuse; President's Commission on Law Enforcement and the Administration of Justice; *Weeks v. United States*.

Further Readings
Center for Problem-Oriented Policing. http://www.popcenter.org (Accessed November 2011).
Community-Oriented Policing Services. http://www.cops.usdoj.gov/Default.asp?Item=34 (Accessed November 2011).
Mapp v. Ohio, 367 U.S. 643 (1961).
Miller, W. R. *Cops and Bobbies*. Chicago: University of Chicago Press, 1977.
Miranda v. Arizona, 384 U.S. 436 (1966).
Tennessee v. Garner, 471 U.S. 1 (1985).
Weeks v. United States, 232 U. S. 383 (1914).
Willis, J. J., S. D. Mastrofski, and D. Weisburd. *CompStat in Practice: An In-Depth Analysis of Three Cities*. Washington, DC: Police Foundation, 2003. http://www.policefoundation.org/pdf/compstatinpractice.pdf (Accessed November 2011).

Reform Movements in Justice

The American criminal justice system is intended to uphold fundamental positive values: community safety, fairness and consistency in the law, accountability for harm, and boundaries of acceptable behavior. Reform movements in justice attempt to remedy perceived abuses against these values. Reformers seek to amend, or in some cases transform, the processes by which we apprehend, prosecute, defend, sentence, punish, and supervise those charged with criminal offenses. But reforms almost always fall short of expectations. Some sociologists theorize that reform movements fail because of the incompatibility of conscience with convenience, that is, the reformers' idealism, or conscience, must confront the pragmatic expediency of the complex penal field. Additionally, reformers typically function outside the criminal justice system and hold ideals and expectations incompatible with the actual workings of judicial and correctional processes. Finally, reform efforts fail because of competing ideologies. Some advocate treatment-oriented incarceration, state benevolence, decriminalization, and decarceration to reform the system. Others promote increased state deterrence through more punitive incarceration, or "swift and certain punishment." Ultimately, reformers must negotiate the fraught dialectic between social control and social reform. This entry traces these patterns of reform, in their social and legal contexts, from the colonial period to the 21st century.

Early Reforms

The colonists, while primarily deriving their penal codes from English law, began the first reform efforts by deemphasizing public displays of corporal and capital punishment, which had been the standard means of punishment in England. They preferred confinement. Up to this point, jails were deplorable facilities, primarily used to hold people for relatively short periods before they were publicly beaten or executed. Instead of individual cells, they featured large, disorderly rooms that simply functioned as temporary holding areas. But early reformers like William Penn, James Wilson, Thomas Jefferson, Benjamin Franklin, William Bradford, and Benjamin Rush advocated abolition of the public death penalty and torture in favor of the prison as a way to reform offenders. Penn lobbied that the purpose of punishment should be "to reclaim, rather than destroy," and Rush argued that "all public punishments tend to make bad men worse, and to increase crimes, by their influence on society."

Their ideas reflected the influences of Enlightenment thought, evangelical Christianity (especially the Quaker commitments), and the earlier reform philosophy by punishment theorists like Cesare Beccaria. Although their efforts to completely abolish the death penalty never succeeded, states drastically reduced capital crimes, and the Pennsylvania legislature even divided murder charges into two "degrees" in 1794, resulting in manslaughter as punishable only by imprisonment, not death. Most states quickly adopted this practice. Additionally, almost all states eliminated the death penalty for property crimes and sodomy. In this shift away from English reliance on public and physical punishment, the early reformers consistently asked: What kind of punishments befit a democracy? How can offenders be rehabilitated?

The prison system seemed to answer these questions. After visiting American prisons, Alexis de Tocqueville observed that our social reformers seemed obsessed with incarceration, excessively concentrating on prisons as the panacea to crime: "They have the monomania of the penitentiary system, which seems to them the remedy applicable to all of ills of society," he wrote to a friend. Indeed, incarceration has remained ubiquitous as America's primary response to crime for the past 250 years.

As the new states formed their penal codes, reformers optimistically experimented with the burgeoning concepts of the penitentiary, with its implicit religious connotation of penitence, and the correctional institution, which carries the reformers' optimism that incarceration can be a curative experience for offenders. Pennsylvania continued to lead innovative reform efforts with the Eastern State Penitentiary, which featured separate confinement for every inmate. New York also experimented and developed the Auburn system, which housed inmates in their own cells at night but used a congregant system during the workday. Inmates and guards participated in a

Colorado State Penitentiary prisoners circa 1898 walking in "lock-step"—marching men as closely together as possible, in which the leg of each man moves at the same time with the corresponding leg of the person before him.

military-style discipline, including the famous "lockstep," and factory-style industry. Also known as the "big house" prison model, variations of the Auburn system have prevailed in American criminal justice. But the criminal population rapidly outgrew Auburn, and both recidivism and prison violence revealed the current system's failures, so the convicts themselves labored to build another experimental prison, the Elmira Reformatory, in 1876. Under the direction of the venerated penologist Zebulon Brockway, the Elmira system deemphasized punitive and humiliating treatment of prisoners in favor of vocational and religious instruction, "good-time" credits, and post-release supervision. Although Brockway envisioned his prison as a college, transforming the dangerous classes into "Christian gentlemen" who embraced the Protestant work ethic, mismanagement, overcrowding, and the fundamental problems of rehabilitative penology led to Elmira's failure. In the early 19th century, Edward Livingston, by turns a member of the House of Representatives, an attorney, and the mayor of New York, led another significant reform movement. Also opposed to the death penalty and retributive punishment, Livingston was confident in social reform as a way to reduce crime. He committed to a serious emphasis on rehabilitation, which included proactive social programs such as "houses of refuge" and "houses of industry" that provided structured living conditions and work for those who could not find them elsewhere. Livingston spent the last 12 years of his life on his most significant contribution, the Livingston Code (1833), in which he recodified criminal procedure to be more reformatory, humane, and simple. Although states didn't officially adopt the Livingston Code, it significantly influenced subsequent reform efforts, especially in the Progressive Era.

Parole, Probation, Indeterminate Sentencing, and the Juvenile Court

The Progressive Era (1890s to 1920s) abounded in reform efforts in many social and political arenas, from immigration policy to women's suffrage to the child labor laws. The Progressive Era reformers contributed substantial changes to criminal justice: the innovative concepts of parole and probation, indeterminate sentencing, and the juvenile court. Both parole and probation represent a shift away from the big house prisons as a way to reform offenders to an understanding that offenders could rehabilitate more substantially by interacting in their communities, under supervision. Between 1900 and 1925, all 48 states initiated probationary sentencing practices. In 1925, under the Federal Probation Act, even federal judges could opt for probation over incarceration, if they deemed that "the ends of justice and the best interest of the public as well as the defendant [would] be served thereby." Similarly, indeterminate sentencing would incite prisoners to seek their own reform, motivated by the understanding that they had "the key to the prison in their own pocket." The juvenile court reflects the Progressive Era's interest in child welfare. Juveniles always held special protections under the law; from the house of refuge movement to the early 19th-century pre-delinquency efforts to reform schools, criminal law sought to distinguish minor offenders from adults. But the newly formed juvenile court, first established in Chicago in 1899, then reproduced in 45 states by 1920, formally codified a less adversarial process for juvenile offenders, treating them less as "criminals" and more as children in need of correction and guidance.

Progressive Era reformers assumed these changes made the criminal justice system more fair and humane; they believed they were creating individual justice, as opposed to previous generic concepts of a criminal class. They attempted not only to make the punishment fit the crime but to make the punishment fit the criminal. Their optimism rested in their unmitigated belief that humans could be perfected if only the right method were discovered and that state mechanisms could mete out the reforms in fair and just ways. But as historians and sociologists have traced, the Progressive Era reforms usually resulted in increased state control and actually subjected offenders to prolonged incarceration and arbitrary sentencing practices. Their attempts to correct the failures and abuses of the prison system never materialized as they intended.

Model Penal Code

In 1931, 100 years after the Livingston Code, the American Law Institute and the American Bar Association proposed a Model Penal Code, which served as an archetype for states to clarify, streamline, and reconcile the competing theories behind criminal law: progressivism's perfectibility ideal, emphasizing treatment and rehabilitation, and new concerns for the mid-20th-century rising crime rates, deterrence, and culpability. Under the direction of Columbia law professor Herbert Wechsler, the Model Penal Code was completed in 1962 and served as a prototype for state reform of the existing patchwork penal codes: Within 20 years, 34 states enacted new penal codes, and others were substantially revised.

Racial Justice

Generations of civil rights reformers have advanced the criminal justice system from the legal institution of slavery in the 18th century to eventual abolition, the Emancipation Proclamation, the Thirteenth, Fourteenth, and Fifteenth Amendments (banning slavery, granting citizenship and due process, and protecting voting rights), and eventually the Civil Rights Acts outlawing discriminatory legal and social practices. Civil rights reformers advocate equitable legal treatment for racial minorities, primarily through a liberal equality paradigm. Formal institutions like the American Civil Liberties Union (ACLU) and the National Association for the Advancement of Colored People (NAACP), as well as hundreds of grassroots racial justice organizations, continue to initiate reform of racially biased practices in American criminal justice. Most recently, these reforms have addressed police brutality, racial disparities in arrests and convictions, drug offense policies, and the wide disparities in incarceration rates. But while their broad aims coincide, civil rights reformers differ widely philosophically and politically. Some of these discrepancies have led to a rejection of the principles behind civil rights by critical race activists, who work outside traditional liberalism.

Critical race theory, initiated in the late 1970s by Derrick Bell and others, is an academic and activist movement by legal scholars to address

Attorney General Robert F. Kennedy speaking in June 1963 to a civil rights crowd and reporters in front of the U.S. Justice Department, with a sign for the Washington Congress of Racial Equality prominently displayed.

how racism is a deeply embedded structure in the legal system and the penal field. Although dominated by minorities in the legal profession, critical race theory is in many ways a countermovement to civil rights reforms. Critical race theory critiques the beliefs that racism can be defeated through education and an eventual "colorblind" society. Instead, critical race theorists merge racial issues in law, sociology, economics, literature, and psychology to show how the law constructs and maintains social domination and subjugation. While civil rights (and most reform movements) are affirmative, seeking to restructure the existing systems to be more fair, critical race theory is often criticized for being too negative: Primarily, its contribution involves illustrating the failures of racial justice. But the empirical research behind critical race realism provides a framework for understanding how, almost four decades after the Civil Rights Act, eight black and Hispanic males are incarcerated for every one white male in the United States.

From the Correctional Institution to Mass Incarceration

The 19th-century "big house" prisons led to the rise once again of the correctional institution movement, also known as rehabilitative penology (1950s to 1980s). This reform movement initiated treatment-oriented prisons, with more professional staffing, psychotherapy, addiction counseling, and a heavy emphasis on education. Even the most punitive level of incarceration, solitary confinement, was labeled the "adjustment center," illustrating how reformers attempted to ameliorate every aspect of incarceration. This was a period when convicts like Malcolm X, George Jackson, and John Irwin went to prison uneducated and emerged as important political and social theorists. This era of prison reform correlated the prison to a hospital: Inmates were treated almost as patients in need of care. But rising crime rates, empirical failures of reform, and increasing politicization of crime legislation led to the failure of the correctional institution and the rise of the warehouse prison.

As a result of disillusionment with rehabilitation programs that did not seem to work, in the mid-1980s, a new era began, one of "sending a message" to criminals. Subsequently, the war on crime and the war on drugs (with resulting "three strikes and you're out" sentencing procedures) quadrupled the prison population between 1980 and 2010. In the 21st century, the United States incarcerates a higher per capita rate of its population than any other country, with about 3 percent of the population in prison, on parole, or under probationary supervision. Former emphases on rehabilitation and treatment shifted to punitive, control-oriented prison systems and longer sentences that function almost solely to "warehouse" offenders, or to remove them and store them away from communities. One example is the 1994 retraction of Pell Grant funding for inmates, which illustrated legislators' "tough on crime" stand to the public but effectively ended the only program that statistically lowered recidivism rates.

Reformers decry mass incarceration as exorbitantly expensive, socially deteriorating, racially unjust, and insufficient to deter crime or to fully satisfy victims. They claim it diametrically opposes what the original reformers sought as "befitting a democracy." But after 200 years of reform efforts, sociologists observe that the United States has failed to create a system capable of sufficiently deterring crime, making communities safer, fully satisfying victims, eliminating racial bias from the justice system, or empirically reforming offenders. Many reformers are turning to a paradigm shift, restorative justice, with promising social, legal, and moral dimensions to correct abuses in the criminal justice system.

Restorative Justice

Reformers in the 21st century believe that restorative justice functions as a viable corrective to the failed paradigms of criminal justice reform. It gained extraordinary momentum in Europe, South Africa, New Zealand, and Australia, particularly after Desmond Tutu's Truth and Reconciliation Commission (which he explicitly understood as restorative justice). First a grassroots and academic movement, restorative justice has steadily achieved workable credibility: The National Institute of Corrections researched, then piloted a restorative justice program, and the U.S. Department of Justice has integrated restorative justice principles into the Office of Juvenile Justice and Delinquency Prevention and into drug courts. Most states use some form of restorative justice mediation for juveniles and are increasingly incorporating it into their state correctional institutes. In addition to government adoption, restorative justice has attracted media attention, sparked the development of nongovernmental organizations, and been the focus of extensive academic scholarship in the fields of law, sociology, and criminal justice.

Restorative justice shifts the criminal justice process away from punishment and control, and toward meeting the goals of all stakeholders in the offense: victims, defendants, those impacted in the community, mediators, and community safety advocates. It focuses on the harm caused by criminal behavior rather than on guilt against the state; in this way, restorative justice seems to meet the divergent ends of both retributive justice and welfare justice models.

The practices of restorative justice involve identifying the harm caused by criminal behavior, determining the steps to repair that harm, then facilitating a process through which the harm can be remedied. This can include group conferences, victim/offender mediation, restitution options, victim assistance, community service, and ex-offender assistance. The key values are "encounter," which creates opportunities for victims, offenders, and community members to meet and discuss the harm of the offense; "amends," which facilitates the offender's repair of the harm; "reintegration," which seeks to restore the offender as a productive member of the community; and "inclusion," which provides all people with a stake in the crime to participate in the resolution.

Conclusion

While history illustrates persistent oscillation between competing theories of reform, generally understood as retribution and rehabilitation, restorative justice offers a new lens through which to consider crime and punishment. Instead of focusing on the criminal act as a violation of a specific penal statute, with a punishment to be exacted, restorative justice focuses on who has been hurt and what society's role should be to repair that harm. In a shift away from conceiving of crime as a felony against the state, and toward handling the offense in a more socially egalitarian way, restorative justice responds to the original reformers' question: What kind of punishment befits a democracy?

Sarah Higinbotham
Georgia State University

See Also: Prisoner's Rights; Rehabilitation; Retributivism; Suspect's Rights; Vice Reformers; Victim Rights and Restitution.

Further Readings

Berman, Greg and Aubrey Fox. *Trial & Error in Criminal Justice Reform: Learning From Failure.* Washington, DC: Urban Institute Press, 2010.

Braithwaite, John. *Restorative Justice and Responsive Regulation.* Oxford: Oxford University Press, 2002.

Garland, David. *Punishment and Modern Society: A Study in Social Theory.* Chicago: University of Chicago Press, 1990.

Haney, Craig. *Reforming Punishment: Psychological Limits to the Pains of Imprisonment.* Washington, DC: American Psychological Association, 2006.

Monkkonen, Eric, ed. "Reform." In *Crime & Justice in American History: Historical Articles on the Origins and Evolution of American Criminal Justice.* Munich: K. G. Saur, 1992.

Rothman, David J. *Conscience and Convenience: The Asylum and Its Alternatives in Progressive America.* New York: Aldine de Gruyter, 2002.

Simon, Jonathan. *Governing Through Crime: How the War on Crime Transformed American Democracy and Created a Culture of Fear.* Oxford: Oxford University Press, 2007.

Rehabilitation

Rehabilitation is one of four philosophies governing systems of punishment (along with deterrence, incapacitation, and retribution) and is often used to justify penal programs such as in-prison drug addiction programs, in-prison employment programs, and community corrections such as parole and probation. The use of rehabilitation as the main philosophy of punishment, however, has changed over time. Rehabilitation has moved from dominating the criminal justice system for roughly 70 years in the 1900s to being viewed as not possible in the 1980s and 1990s to regaining popularity in the 2000s. Furthermore, it is unclear what is meant by rehabilitation, especially as a goal of correctional systems.

Early History

Rehabilitation as a guiding philosophy of the correctional system first took hold in the early 1800s. At this time, America's criminal justice system was moving away from the gallows and toward penitentiaries. The first penitentiaries were designed to reform the offender by isolating him from negative influences and reclaiming his soul through hard work and religious instruction. Although the goals were the same, two competing models developed. Under the Pennsylvania system, reformation was achieved through silent mediation and solitary confinement. Under the Auburn system, reformation was achieved through group labor during the day and silent meditation at night.

At this time, however, inmates were released upon the expiration of their sentences, making it difficult to ensure that a released offender was truly reformed. This began to change in the 1870s when Zebulon Brockway, a penologist and warden at various U.S. institutions, suggested the United States adopt an earned-release method similar to Ireland's and described the usefulness of an indeterminate sentencing structure and a parole system at the very first meeting of the American Prison Association. His suggestion was formally adopted in 1876 in New York's Elmira Reformatory, where Brockway implemented a mark system in which inmates were required to earn a specified number of marks before earning release on parole. Brockway's system was the first to base rehabilitation on in-prison behavior rather than religious conversion.

It was not until the early 1900s, however, that the belief grew that the rehabilitative process was different for different people. Under the Progressive movement, correctional systems began adopting the idea that crime was caused by biological, psychological, or social deficiencies. It was also during this time that many states shifted to an indeterminate sentencing structure that allowed release based on rehabilitative progress rather than the passing of time. Indeterminate sentencing allowed for the development of programs based on an individual offender's background and needs. It also permitted judges, wardens, and probation or parole officers to have complete discretion in determining when an individual was reformed and ready for release.

The implementation of indeterminate sentencing also paved the way for an increase in the use of parole supervision. The first formalized parole system, in which specialized agents supervised parolees, was established in New York in 1907. By 1942, all states and the federal government had formally established parole systems. The implementation of formalized parole systems enabled parole boards to determine when a convict was ready for release from prison and enabled parole agents to determine when an ex-convict was ready for release from supervision. In this way, rehabilitation was formally linked to a person's behavior and progress while under supervision rather than on time. The linking of prisons and parole and indeterminate sentencing also provided a means by which to return a parolee to prison if it was determined that the individual had was not truly rehabilitated.

Medical Model of Rehabilitation

Although rehabilitation had been used almost from the inception of correctional systems, the

In the 1800s, U.S. criminal justice was moving from severe punishment and the gallows toward imprisonment. At the Colorado State Penitentiary, the "Old Gray Mare" was a structure used to punish inmates with beatings.

use of the rehabilitative ideal in America gained strength during the clinical or medical model of the 1950s and 1960s. The medical model argued that biological, psychological, and social deficiencies indicated that offenders were sick and in need of treatment or a cure to prevent further recidivism. This treatment involved in-prison programming such as employment, education, and drug addiction programs. This version of the rehabilitative ideal is different from earlier versions for several reasons. First, disciplines concerned with human behavior (e.g., psychology and criminology) emerged. Second, the rehabilitative ideal dominated scholarship to such an extent that the treatment and reform of offenders were viewed by some as the only questions worth asking within the field of corrections. Third, it was not necessary to prove complete rehabilitation prior to release from prison. Rather, inmates needed to show that they were on the road to rehabilitation and could maintain their treatment in the community. This belief created a rehabilitative process that began in prison and continued with parole. Fourth, treatment of offenders was based on scientifically designed programs and various treatment modalities were tested to determine which worked best. Finally, such programs were to be designed around the individual's needs and were not to be a one-size-fits-all model. In order to accomplish this individualization, many correctional systems began classifying offenders based on their needs and deficiencies.

The medical model also resulted in greater reliance on parole systems to facilitate reintegration of offenders into society and continue their rehabilitative treatment in the community. Parole boards were granted broad discretionary powers in determining who could be released from prison and when. Parole boards were to release those individuals who had received as much treatment as possible while in prison and who were able to continue their treatment in the community. Parole agents were then responsible for ensuring inmates continued their treatment in the community and returning those who still required in-prison treatment.

Decline in Popularity

Although rehabilitation was viewed as the ultimate goal of the corrections system, not all offenders had access to rehabilitative programs. Indeed, some legislation prohibited offenders with multiple felonies from accessing their services. For instance, the Narcotic Addict Rehabilitation Act (NARA) of 1966 prohibited those who were convicted of three or more felonies from a rehabilitative commitment and required that they be sentenced to prison. Although prisoners challenged these barriers in *Marshall v. United States* (1974), the Supreme Court found that the NARA, and by extension similar exclusionary rules, did not violate an offender's due process or equal protection rights because the state could reasonably assume that a repeat offender would not benefit from such treatment.

As such, there is reason to believe that not all inmates were able to participate in rehabilitative programs even if they wanted to. Additionally, questions arose as to the effectiveness of penal-based therapy: specifically, who decided what constituted rehabilitation and who decided what constituted a cure. Questions also arose as to the effectiveness of treatment carried out in artificial, and sometimes hostile, environments.

As a result, the attachment to the rehabilitative ideal did not last long. Throughout the 1950s, 1960s, and 1970s, multiple studies analyzed the effectiveness of existing rehabilitative programs and found that few, if any, achieved the desired effects. Possibly the most damaging study was Robert Martinson's report on the effectiveness of correctional programs nationwide. Although the study found that some programs were promising, the general conclusion was that nothing worked to reduce recidivism. This report confirmed the growing belief that the rehabilitative ideal was a failure and resulted in a lack of faith in the correctional system and loss of legitimacy among those authorizing rehabilitation.

Changes within the larger social structure also impacted faith in the rehabilitative ideal. For instance, some scholars argue that the decline of the rehabilitative ideal can be summarized as a loss of faith in the malleability of human beings and a loss of consensus about the goals of rehabilitation. The lack of belief in the malleability of people was related to several culture shifts, including a loss of faith in social institutions—such as schools and families—once believed to play a large role in shaping one's moral character. Additionally, there was a drop in legitimacy of those participating in the rehabilitation programs, where those in the programs were viewed as different from those not in the programs, and thus incapable of change.

Additional criticism of rehabilitation included critiques of the methods used in the name of rehabilitation and a view that rehabilitation was detrimental to a fair correctional system. As Edgardo Rotman notes, treatments such as shock therapy were carried out in the name of rehabilitation. As these treatments fell out of favor because of their abusiveness and intrusiveness, the idea of rehabilitation was held responsible for such harsh treatment, leading many to critique the rehabilitative approach. Furthermore, legislators on both sides of the political spectrum were calling for changes in sentencing schemes. Liberals argued that indeterminate sentencing led to abuses of power by sentencing and correctional officials and that the rehabilitative ideal helped justify longer sentences; conservatives argued that indeterminate sentencing led to increased leniency and that rehabilitation took the bite out of the prison systems. While liberals and conservatives had differing views on the failure of indeterminate sentencing, the result was a decline in the support of rehabilitative policies and a shift away from discretionary release.

Additionally, radical criminologists argued that individual treatment was ineffective without first implementing structural changes of society and that the rehabilitative ideal was an excuse to avoid such changes. They argued that without these structural changes, former prisoners would return to unchanged conditions—the same conditions that propelled them into crime to begin with. Radical criminologists also critiqued the discretionary power associated with indeterminate sentencing and the ineffectiveness of correctional institutions. They argued that rehabilitation was masking the ways in which prisons were perpetuating unequal power structures.

As a result of these criticisms, many states moved away from the indeterminate sentencing structure and abandoned rehabilitation as the main goal of the correctional system. A new system was put in place that emphasized incapacitation and retribution as justification for the prison system. Determinate sentencing structures were put in place, and by the 1980s, many states eliminated their parole boards. Sentencing guidelines, mandatory minimums, and truth-in-sentencing laws were used to determine when someone would be released, and release dates were dependent on the crime, not the individual. Where programs were available, they focused on risk management. According to the risk management model, branded by Malcolm Feely and Jonathan Simon as the "new penology," correctional systems utilize actuarial tools to determine who should be released, who should be in programs, and whom to be most concerned about. Rather than focusing on individuals, the new penology focuses on minimizing the risk of groups of people. Such attempts have led to an increase in the surveillance of parolees to minimize the risk they pose to the community and greater reliance on drug testing and statistical risk analyses.

Even at this time, however, rehabilitation programs were still utilized within the corrections system in America. Indeed, numerous rehabilitative programs were developed and utilized well after Robert Martinson's report was released. For instance, hundreds of sex offender programs were implemented during the 1980s and continue to be used today. Furthermore, programs aimed at addressing and reducing alcohol and drug addictions were used even after faith in the rehabilitative ideal waned. The late 1990s also saw a resurgence of faith-based prison programs aimed at reforming inmates, though the effectiveness and constitutionality of such programs are unclear. This has led to criticism of the notion that nothing works. Many scholars are now arguing that it is not that programs do not work; rather, it is that existing programs are poorly designed or implemented.

Rehabilitation Revival

Today, there seems to be a reemergence of rehabilitation within the correctional system. For instance, in 2005, California added the word *rehabilitation* to the title of its Department of Corrections and established a new mission statement that emphasized rehabilitation. In 2009, the U.S. Congress passed the Second Chance Act, which provides a way for qualified nonviolent offenders to have their criminal records expunged. There has also been a push in several states to utilize evidence-based practices, develop intermediate and alternative sanctions for nonviolent offenders, and develop alternatives to reincarceration for parolees and probationers who violate their conditions of release.

Additionally, several recent studies have shown that rehabilitative programs implemented correctly not only reduced recidivism but saved states money. Indeed, Steve Aos, Polly Phipps, Robert Barnowski, and Roxanne Lieb reviewed hundreds of programs that target different groups and found that many of these programs significantly reduced recidivism rates. For instance, in a review of programs aimed at juvenile offenders, they found that programs such as Multisystemic Therapy and Multidimensional Treatment Foster Care not only reduced juvenile recidivism rates but also saved at least $28 for every $1 spent. In a review of programs aimed at adult offenders, they found that programs such as drug treatment programs, cognitive-behavioral therapies, and educational and vocational programs all reduce adult recidivism rates and either save money for every $1 invested or break even. The authors also found that programs aimed at certain types of criminals such as sex offender therapy also reduce future crimes. Extreme overcrowding and lack of state funds, however, have prevented many states from effectively implementing such programs. A lack of funding and resources in the communities also prevents probationers and parolees from accessing programs.

Studies have shown that effective rehabilitation programs share several guiding principles. First, effective programs should focus on scientifically known predictors of criminal behavior and recidivism reduction. These factors include static factors that do not change over time (e.g., gender and criminal conviction offense) and dynamic factors that can change over time (e.g., educational attainment and antisocial behavior). Second, the programs should focus on both thought processes and behavior patterns of offenders (also known as cognitive-behavioral therapies). Third, rehabilitative programs are most effective when working

Inmates listen to a social worker explain their rehabilitation options. Modern rehabilitation theories include the principles of correctional rehabilitation (attempting to eliminate criminal behavior and its causes), legal rehabilitation (eliminating a criminal record and restoring legal rights), and generic rehabilitation (the use of psychological and physical therapies).

with offenders with the highest risk of recidivating. Fourth, programs should address a range of additional factors (e.g., community-based interventions and utilization of well-trained and specialized program providers) whenever possible. Finally, effective programs are those that have been independently evaluated to ensure that the desired outcomes are actually achieved.

Although the use of rehabilitation has ebbed and flowed, some scholars argue that even at times when punishment and risk management are the main focus, the notion of rehabilitation is present in some way. For instance, in a study on parole agents and their role in the correctional system, Mona Lynch finds that, in practice, parole agents function as more than risk managers and that the practice of punishment does not fall in line with all of the theoretical tenets of the new penology. Steven Hutchinson argues that punishment and rehabilitation are braided together. In other words, the notions of punishment and rehabilitation cannot be separated, though one may be more prominent than the other. Indeed, some scholars speculate that while the use of rehabilitation declined during the late 1900s, its use may not have disappeared entirely and likely shifted from a central role to a peripheral role. This notion is further supported by the continued use of rehabilitative programs in the 1980s and 1990s.

Furthering this idea, Gwen Robinson argues that the concept of rehabilitation in the United Kingdom and Wales did not disappear, then reappear; rather, it evolved over time. In the 1950s and 1960s, rehabilitation was viewed as a form of welfare and was understood as designed to benefit the lives of former inmates. During the "nothing works" period of U.S. corrections in the 1970s through the 1990s, Robinson notes that rehabilitation evolved into a risk management tool. Treatment programs were viewed as a way of maintaining an individual's criminogenic risks and assisting in preventing future crimes. Today, rehabilitation is reframed as a tool for the improvement of society, for risk management, and as a form of punishment. Thus, rehabilitation is used as a means of providing the greatest good to the greatest number of people by managing and maintaining risk, reducing recidivism, and providing alternatives to incarceration (e.g., community sanctions).

Although a similar analysis has not been conducted for the United States, the historical use of rehabilitation in America seems to echo the pattern described by Robinson.

Modern Rehabilitation Theory

Several theories abound as to what rehabilitation means. The three prominent theories are (1) correctional rehabilitation, (2) legal rehabilitation, and (3) generic rehabilitation.

Correctional rehabilitation seeks to eliminate criminal behavior or to eliminate the causes of criminal behavior. Some argue that factors important to achieving recidivism reduction include repairing relationships, restoring one's status in the community, and establishing stable employment. While many rehabilitative programs aim to reduce recidivism, they often accomplish this goal by addressing noncriminal factors such as increasing educational attainment and improving jobs skills. Two current models exist to assist with the elimination of criminal behavior or causes of criminal behavior: the risk, needs and responsivity model and the good lives model.

The risk, needs and responsivity model (RNR) was first developed in Canada and offers a mix of the risk management methods described by the new penology and the rehabilitative methods adopted in the 1950s and 1960s. This model focuses on three key ideas: the amount of risk posed by the offender, the needs of the offender, and the ability to adjust the program to be responsive to the offender. The model argues that in order to minimize the harm, or risk, one may cause, it is necessary to address the offender's criminogenic risks such as antisocial behavior and poor problem-solving skills, and that treatment delivery must be adjusted in a way that maximizes change.

Building on the risk, needs and responsivity model, the good lives model (GLM) argues for a human-centered, holistic approach to rehabilitation. Specifically, the GLM is based on the idea of helping the offender find pro-social ways of achieving the benefits gained through criminogenic behaviors. Rather than focusing on managing the risk to society, GLM argues that focusing on what is best for the individual will result in positive outcomes for society as a whole. In other words, helping individuals achieve specific goods or goals in socially accepted ways will automatically eliminate criminological behavior.

Legal rehabilitation implies an undoing of the criminal conviction. In other words, legal rehabilitation focuses on eliminating the criminal past and restoring legal rights and standing after a period of punishment. Such a restoration includes a return to full citizenship status (including a return of full voting rights) for recently released prisoners. Indeed, some scholars argue that the reinstatement of full citizenship is an important step in reintegrating former prisoners into the community and could potentially reduce recidivism. Some states and the federal government now have legislation in place that effectively removes a criminal history from one's past (e.g., Second Chance Act of 2009; California's Certificate of Rehabilitation; various state systems of pardon), though the process is often difficult to navigate and can take decades to finish.

Finally, generic rehabilitation is based on rehabilitative methods utilized in psychological and physical therapies, many of which are now used in prison- and community-based correctional programs. This view argues that rehabilitation is an ongoing effort that may be achieved in numerous ways and encompasses four principles: (1) it is a process; (2) it is viewed as a change for the better; (3) it implies a return to a former state (e.g., a mobile state after an accident; in this case, a return to the community); and (4) it implies the intervention of some other party. Even for those who may not seek official forms of intervention (e.g., therapists, support groups, drug rehabilitation programs, education or job skills classes), some assistance exists through the support of friends, family, and community members. For criminological purposes, the process of rehabilitation may mean "the restoration of a former state ... [or] the acquisition of skills, and the establishment of rank, rights and responsibilities previously denied."

These theories of rehabilitation are not necessarily mutually exclusive. It would be easy to see rehabilitation as a mixture of several of the theories, if not all of them. For instance, rehabilitation could be an elimination of criminal behavior or the causes of criminal behavior as well as a restoration of civil and legal rights. Furthermore, correctional and legal rehabilitations may be accomplished by utilizing the four principles found in generic rehabilitation. The common theme throughout these theories is that rehabilitation is, in some way and regardless of the role rehabilitation plays in corrections, enacted by the state.

In order for rehabilitation to be truly effective, however, some scholars argue that rehabilitation must be viewed as a right that is provided by the state. The argument made by scholars working in this vein is not that all offenders should receive rehabilitation but that all offenders have the right to an opportunity to rehabilitation and that rehabilitation is what the state owes the offender in exchange for future adherence to the law. Advocates of rehabilitation as a right argue that this view requires an overarching change in the penal system, focusing more on individual outcomes and less on overall effectiveness. Finally, rehabilitation advocates also argue that this shift to a rights-based focus is necessary to maintain the rehabilitative ideal. Sam Lewis argues that without this view, rehabilitation could be abandoned in favor of more politically accepted policies.

Rita Shah
University of California, Irvine

See Also: Auburn State Prison; Corrections; Deterrence, Theory of; Incapacitation, Theory of; Parole; Penitentiaries; Pennsylvania System of Reform; Retributivism; Sentencing, Indeterminate Versus Fixed.

Further Readings
Aos, Steve, Polly Phipps, Robert Barnowski, and Roxanne Lieb. *The Comparative Costs and Benefits of Programs to Reduce Crime.* Olympia: Washington State Institute for Public Policy, 2001.
Cullen, Francis T. and Paul Gendreau. "Assessing Correctional Rehabilitation: Policy, Practice, and Prospects." *Criminal Justice,* v.3 (2000).
Farabee, David. *Rethinking Rehabilitation: Why Can't We Reform Our Criminals?* Washington, DC: AEI Press, 2005.
Hutchinson, Steven. "Countering Catastrophic Criminology Reform: Punishment and the Modern Liberal Compromise." *Punishment and Society,* v.8/4 (2006).
Lewis, Sam. "Rehabilitation: Headline or Footnote in the New Penal Policy." *Probation Journal,* v.52/2 (2005).

Marshall v. United States, 414 U.S. 417 (1974).
Raynor, Peter and Gwen Robinson. *Rehabilitation, Crime and Justice*. New York: Palgrave Macmillan, 2005.
Robinson, Gwen. "Late-Modern Rehabilitation: The Evolution of Penal Strategy." *Punishment and Society*, v.10/4 (2008).

Religion and Crime, Contemporary

Some of the earliest efforts to explain criminal behavior involved supernatural phenomena like religion. During the earliest times, human inquiry regarding the causes of deviant or criminal behavior led many to believe that witchcraft, spells, or demon possession were among the root causes of aberrant social behavior.

These ideas are reflected in the resulting public responses to criminal behavior. For example, trial by ordeal became a common practice in many parts of the world. In essence, trial by ordeal involved subjecting a suspected individual to a harsh physical task that could either injure or kill the accused in an attempt to see if some sort of divine intervention would occur. If the accused was not seriously harmed or killed by the assigned task, it was thought to be proof of innocence and divine vindication of guilt. If the accused was injured or killed by the assigned task, it was thought to be evidence of divine retribution and proof of the individual's guilt. During later times, trials by combat became more common and pitted two individuals against each other in battle. The underlying belief behind tests of this nature was that God would aid the most righteous combatant, thereby providing them with evidence of absolution. During this period, religious beliefs provided both a basis for understanding deviant behavior and a process through which justice could be administered and dispensed.

Historically, the church was much more actively involved in the provision of law and social control and had a great impact on the way in which society understood and related to crime. This may help explain the existence of beliefs regarding the causal nature of the religion and crime relationship. The greater involvement of the church in this regard may have been inevitable given that a more formalized system of law and justice was largely lacking. This greater involvement is underscored by the role that the church played in helping define criminal behavior, investigating allegations of deviant behavior, and punishing those individuals thought to have violated established standards of behavior. Remnants of this influence are reflected today in certain laws that prohibit some types of sexual, recreational, and social practices. Over time, however, the direct involvement of the church in the control and punishment of criminal offenders became less significant. As organized systems of justice evolved, there were fewer duties for the church and practices such as trial by ordeal and trial by combat were largely abandoned. Beliefs positing a direct causal relationship between supernatural phenomena and crime began to fade with the advent of the classical and positivist schools and the first tentative steps toward the scientific study of crime. However, the debate regarding the correlation between religion and criminal behavior has continued unabated ever since.

Effect of Religion on Behavior

Much of the discussion regarding religion and crime in contemporary times has focused on whether religion has a mitigating or limiting effect on criminal behavior. However, questions have also arisen in regard to the degree to which religion might contribute to or precipitate violence toward others. Throughout history, there are numerous examples of deviant or violent behavior that have, at least in part, been attributable to the religious motivations, ideologies, or divisions of those involved. Events such as these tend to resonate with the public imagination and have an especially significant social impact when they involve religious leaders who occupy positions of public trust. High-profile examples of this nature may influence societal attitudes toward religion and undermine public trust in religious institutions. Additionally, these types of incidents may solidify social attitudes regarding the nature of the religion and crime relationship and mask the degree to which religious beliefs may have an insular effect on criminal propensity.

Discussions concerning how religion influences criminal propensity tend to center around a number of different issues. First, questions have arisen regarding the degree to which the divisions between religions have created animosity, inflamed tensions, and ultimately contributed to violence between rival religious groups. There are numerous examples, both historical and contemporary, of religion contributing to conflicts of varying severity in widely disparate geographic regions around the world. The Armenian genocide serves as one of the most graphic historical examples of events in which religion was thought to be one of many precipitating factors that contributed to both the origination and continuation of extreme violence. Second, questions regarding how religious principles might be related to individual criminal propensity have surfaced and been addressed. There are numerous examples of individuals who claim to have been influenced to commit criminal acts as a result of their adherence to the principles of their religion, at least to the degree that they are capable of understanding those principles. Recent investigations of polygamist sect leaders and polygamist sect members regarding allegations of sexually based criminal offenses provide a disturbing example. Third, evaluations regarding how religious beliefs have contributed to a culture that may be more conducive to the occurrence of certain types of criminal behavior have been undertaken. For example, attitudes regarding the desirability of male-dominated households and the need for females to be subservient to their husbands have been associated with religious teachings. These beliefs have also been linked to an increase in both the frequency and the severity of domestic violence.

Research regarding the way in which religion contributes to criminal propensity has not been overlooked, but research regarding the degree to which religion and religious beliefs inhibit criminal propensity has been far more robust. Many have speculated that religious beliefs should be inversely related to criminal involvement. If this were the case, individuals with greater religious attachment would be expected to be less likely to engage in criminal behavior. Beliefs of this nature are based upon the assumption that religions advocate characteristics such as honesty, piety, compassion, and benevolence that are not conducive to criminal involvement. These principles are communicated through religious teachings and texts, and it is believed that once they are internalized, they will influence an individual's personality and outlook. In turn, these changes are thought to influence a wide variety of human behaviors. For example, religion's influence on prejudicial beliefs, political identity, and attitudes toward child rearing and sexual practices have been examined. When directly applied to criminal behavior, many have assumed that religious principles would influence adherents in such a manner that they would become less willing to view the attitudes and behaviors that are associated with deviant or criminal behavior as desirable or acceptable.

Portrait of Mormon polygamists imprisoned at the Utah Penitentiary in 1889. Polygamy is an example of committing criminal acts as a result of adherence to religious principles.

Investigations regarding the degree to which religion inhibits criminal propensity have reached vastly different conclusions. Some findings have seemed to indicate that religion has little if any prohibitive influence on criminal involvement. Other findings seem to indicate that religion does have a significant influence on reducing criminal activity. As a result of the very divergent conclusions that have been reached, there is no universal consensus regarding the degree to which religion is related to reductions in criminal activity. Some more recent examinations have focused on attempting to explain the divergent conclusions that have been reached rather than the underlying nature of the relationship itself. One potential explanation for the divergent conclusions that have been obtained in this regard pertains to the way in which certain key terms and concepts associated with the religion and crime relationship have been operationalized, defined, and measured. Religion is a malleable and flexible concept that can be difficult to precisely define and understand. As a result, the concept has been viewed through a number of different theoretical lenses across time. If religion is viewed as the observance of a set of practices, such as church attendance, a less definitive relationship might be observed. However, if religion is viewed in relation to the extent to which it alters an adherent's underlying beliefs, a more substantive relationship might be found. Given the importance of differences of this nature, the concept of religious orientation or religiosity has become increasingly important.

Religiosity

Briefly stated, religious orientation or religiosity focuses on the degree to which an individual's religious attitudes and attachments alter his/her beliefs, attitudes, and method of understanding the social world. When viewed in this manner, religion is a more complicated concept and one that cannot be fully understood through an individual's adherence to religious practices and rituals. Instead, the concept of religion is best understood through the degree to which the principles associated with a given religion have been internalized and the extent to which they have in turn altered the behaviors and understandings of a given follower. Typically, individuals are roughly divided into one of several categories when viewed through the lens of religious orientation. One category includes those who have a very limited or superficial attachment to religious principles and beliefs. These extrinsically oriented individuals may have an ulterior motive for their religious involvement, which does necessarily generate any type of sincere commitment. A second category includes those individuals with a very intense and meaningful attachment to their religious beliefs. For these intrinsically oriented individuals, religious principles have become part of their lived experience and are viewed as guiding principles that influence the way in which they live their lives and relate to the world around them. The identification of these more subtle distinctions between larger "religious" populations allows the religious orientation concept to provide for a more detailed and meticulous examination of the role that religion might play in regard to criminal propensity. In doing so, the religious orientation concept may well be able to overcome some of the discord that has resulted from past overgeneralizations of the religion concept. If so, future investigations might be able to provide greater clarity regarding the degree to which religion influences deviant and criminal propensity.

Conclusion

A thorough evaluation of the nature of the relationship between religion and crime proves both the enduring and the contentious nature of these concepts. Individuals have been attempting to examine what type of relationship exists between religion and crime from a variety of different perspectives since the very earliest of times. Today, there are many individuals in society who strongly believe that religion exerts either a causal or an inhibitive effect on human deviance. At the same time, there are many individuals in contemporary society who remain convinced that religion has little, if any, influence on the darker side of human behavior. In the end, it is likely that disagreements of this nature will continue and may not ever be fully and completely resolved. Despite disagreements of this nature, religion has almost certainly influenced how society views the concepts of crime and deviance to at least a certain extent. It also appears likely that public interest in the individual concepts of crime and religion will persist and that the relationship of these concepts to each other will continue to capture the public imagination for the foreseeable future.

Jason R. Jolicoeur
Cincinnati State Technical and Community College

See Also: 1961 to 1980 Primary Documents; 2001 to 2012 Primary Documents; Bakker, Jim; Bible; Bigamy/Polygamy; Religion and Crime, History of; Religion and Crime, Sociology of.

Further Readings

Allport, Gordon. "The Religious Context of Prejudice." *Journal for the Scientific Study of Religion,* v.5/4 (1966).

Baier, Colin and Bradley Wright. "If You Love Me, Keep My Commandments: A Meta-Analysis of the Effect of Religion on Crime." *Journal of Research on Crime and Delinquency*, v.38/1 (2001).

Burkett, Steven and Mervin White. "Hellfire and Delinquency: Another Look." *Journal for the Scientific Study of Religion*, v.13/4 (1974).

Hirschi, Travis and Rodney Stark. "Hellfire and Delinquency." *Social Problems*, v.12 (1969).

Morgenthau, Henry. *Ambassador Morgenthau's Story: A Personal Account of the Armenian Genocide*. New York: Cosimo Classics, 2010.

O'Connor, T., et al. "Criminology and Religion." *Criminology and Public Policy*, v.5/3 (2006).

Stark, Rodney and William Bainbridge. *Religion, Deviance, and Social Control*. New York: Routledge, 1996.

Religion and Crime, History of

Contemporary Western societies have grown so accustomed to the formal separation of religion and the state that it may come as a surprise that the distinction between sin and crime did not even enter into Western consciousness until early in the second millennium, and then only incrementally; and in many parts of the world, the idea that religion and the exercise of criminal justice exist on two different planes has only recently been considered, if at all. One can thus conclude that the common historical experience of the human species has favored the idea that religion and governance, heterodoxy and treason, and sin and crime are by no means antithetical and are in many ways synonymous.

This entry gives a brief overview of the period in which the boundaries between religious codes of conduct and social delinquency were far more fluid than today. It then discusses the development of secular legal systems and their institutions of punishment that borrowed liberally from religious law and penal practice, yet have largely existed independent of the religious domain. It concludes with some observations on the history of American corrections, its resonance with early penal history, and how, in America, the relationship of religion and crime is once again recovering some of its ancient cooperative roots.

The Early Experience of Religion and Crime

Social scientific literature claims that the origin of society lies in the symbols emanating from totemic worship. Emile Durkheim's early work points to the mechanical nature of such primitive groupings in which individual self-consciousness was inseparable from communal identity and shared standards of conduct. In his later work, he demonstrates how these "sacred" beliefs fueled the moral commitment that each member felt for the clan. Any infringement of the ritual elements related to totemic worship or of the moral requirements of mutual care was a serious threat to the religious underpinnings of the clan and, by virtue of that fact, to its very existence. Violations not only were decisively punished, they reinforced for all the need to reproduce constantly the religiously driven ethical norms.

This same dynamic is found repeatedly in ancient societies. For Confucius and for the Chinese dynasties influenced by his thought, shame, as opposed to the Christian concept of guilt, was the dominant moral and spiritual concept. One was categorically defined by one's external actions, not internal modes of thought or perception. To disregard any of the Confucian ethical teachings was perceived as an attack upon the entire society. Chinese criminal codes were unambiguous in their attempts to quell any wayward conduct and the emperor was the figurehead embodying both spiritual fulfillment and criminal enforcement.

In Egypt, documents from the Middle Kingdom (2050–1786 B.C.E.) reveal that preservation of public peace was a religious duty. Any harm inflicted upon a fellow Egyptian threatened the sacred order and, by extension, the pharaoh, who was obligated to preserve it.

The prologue to the Code of Hammurabi announces that Marduk has been given dominion over earthly creatures and that Hammurabi, as a god-fearing ruler, undertakes the task of providing a law based upon divine righteousness in which the evil and violent are destroyed, lest they bring harm upon the weak and the innocent.

Throughout the ancient Middle East, the divinity ruled the land; the legitimacy of the monarch was understood to derive from the favor bestowed by God. Because of this divine blessing, the ruler often received the honor befitting a God. A fortiori, violations of legal statutes were not only attacks upon the sovereign and the people, but also upon the divine legislator. The experience of the Hebrew people is a long meditation on these themes. The isomorphism of religion and society was revealed in the intensity of God's repeated insistence that all forms of idolatry be eliminated from Israel, by violence if necessary, as well as in the punishments endured during times of exile when the captive Israelites were repeatedly confronted with the choice to either conform to the religion of the conqueror, or die.

In the Christian West, the experience was similar in many ways. Although the Romans were sagacious in tolerating the practice of the native religion of subjugated peoples, they were often fierce in their suppression of alternative religious practice within Rome. The virulent waves of persecution against the early Christians are a case in point. When Constantine converted to Christianity in the early 4th century, the content of criminal activity was altered, but little changed regarding the relationship between religion and crime. Those who did not honor Christian belief and cultic activity often became the objects of judicial reprisal. When the influential legal code of Emperor Justinian was promulgated in the 6th century, an entire section was devoted to the comportment required of all with regard to the Christian faith and to the penalties and the general sentence of "infamy" attending their violation.

The fall of Rome in the 5th century also led to the collapse of the Roman legal system. The task of governance and the adjudication of conflict often fell upon the clergy, who were, for the most part, the only educated members of the local community and respected figures because of their religious vocation. As a result, religious sins such as adultery and blasphemy came to be viewed in the same species as crimes, such as theft or murder.

There was one area in the Christian West where there was some distinction between the church and the civil realm in regard to crime: that was the shedding of blood. Early church councils forbade the clergy either to sentence the guilty party to sanguinary punishment or to participate in such punishments. Thus, the persistence of the ancient practice of the vendetta, for instance, would have existed outside the domain of religious sanction, as would most other forms of violent reprisal.

In summary, throughout ancient history and into the 2nd millennium of Christian civilization, there was, except in isolated instances, little difference between religion and society in the understanding and treatment of crime.

Canon Law and the Birth of Secularization

When Pope Gregory VII declared in 1075 that the Roman Catholic Church was a distinct social and legal entity, independent in all ways from the interference of earthly princes, the age-old alliance between secular and ecclesiastical law was

The title page from a late-16th-century edition of the Digesta, *part of Emperor Justinian's 534 C.E. Corpus Juris Civilis, or Code of Justinian. The emperor's legal codes were produced in three parts and were intended to be the sole source of law.*

decisively fractured by a stroke of the pen. This momentous decision inaugurated two great and lasting legal developments: The church began to promulgate the world's first "modern" legal system, canon law, and the newly developing states of Europe had to draft their own legal and criminal codes.

Another outcome of this decisive change, was an unprecedented understanding of law and the concept of crime. With canon law, there developed a separation between what was termed the internal forum (the private domain of conscience adjudicated between priest and penitent) and the external forum. The latter addressed public breaches of morality that were called "criminal sins." As a result, not only were sin and crime now separate areas of punitive attention, but also actions meriting punishment no longer consisted simply of offenses against God and the victim; one was culpable for violations against the law itself.

Since the church had already developed within its own penitential system the basic foundation of the Western understanding of punishment—sentencing the offender to a penance measured in segments of time—and since it had also developed within the monasteries the basic model of the prison (recalcitrant monks confined in a cell for a specific temporal period), there was abundant precedent for Boniface VIII to declare in the late 13th century that every diocese in the Catholic Church had to erect at least one prison to confine clerics convicted in ecclesiastical courts of criminal sins.

At the same time, secular authorities began to imitate the Catholic Church in the inauguration of imprisonment as the basic form of social reprisal in the West. Finally, secular polities also mirrored the ecclesiastical understanding of law as an independent moral and social fact, the violation of which signaled the need of and justification for punishment.

Consequently, the initial period of separation between church and state was more an amicable separation than a complete divorce. Not only did the church use the state for its own ends in criminal matters (the execution of heretics, for instance), but the state also imitated the church in the formation of its criminal codes and penal arrangements. The shifting contours of the relationship between religion and crime are also revealed in the American context.

Religion and Crime in the American Context

As with ancient civilizations, the early history of America reveals a reciprocal relationship between religion and crime. The Puritans established a holy commonwealth in which every element of life, including the method of addressing social delinquency, was derived from biblical sources. God was, in effect, both the legislator of law and the dispenser of justice. Thus, Thomas Hooker could cry out to the disobedient, "It is not arguments you gainsay, not the counsel of a minister you reject, the command of a magistrate you oppose, evidence of the rule of reason you resist, but be it known to you, you fly in the very face of the Almighty."

Similarly, in Pennsylvania, under the leadership of William Penn, the Quakers sought to develop a "Holy Experiment," the aim of which was to magnify "the Glory of Almighty God and the Good of Mankind." Unlike the Puritans, however, whose Calvinism took a disparaging view of human nature, the Quakers believed that each person was endowed, in Penn's words, with "Native Goodness." In consequence, their penal philosophy was noticeably more mild. They endorsed the death penalty only in the case of homicide done with "malice or premeditation." In lieu of formal legal procedure, they instituted an early form of community corrections with the appointment of arbitrators known as "peacemakers," whose task it was to mediate disputes between citizens and achieve a form of what is now termed restorative justice without the need of formal judicial prosecution.

After the American Revolution, constitutional provisions formally separated law from religion, but with the rise of the penitentiaries in the early 19th century, religion and crime became related in a new and powerful way. The evangelical revival known as the Second Great Awakening was predicated not only upon the Puritan belief that America was the "new Israel," but also upon the conviction that America must show the world the way to redeem those lost to sin and bound for perdition.

The two prototypical penitentiaries at Philadelphia and Auburn, New York, revealing Quaker and New England Calvinist influences, respectively, both claimed to accomplish with their penal methodology the necessary means for the conquest of sin within the errant individual. Whether their regimens fulfilled their stated purposes is a matter for debate, but it cannot be denied that

Pope Saint Gregory VII is depicted saying mass. The pope's 1075 reforms, declaring that the Roman Catholic Church was a separate legal entity, independent of the laws of "earthly princes," were the basis of modern seculariztion.

these experiments influenced the development of the modern prison in the United States and around the world.

The initial religious tenor of American penal institutions remained strong, with some demonstrative exceptions, until after the Civil War. Then, with the advent of the social sciences, the influence of Italian criminologists such as Cesar Lombroso and Enrico Ferri, and the impact of Darwinism, a distinctly secular, rational, and therapeutic approach to corrections ensued.

Religion came to be viewed in the contemporary way that many have experienced it in relation to the issue of crime: on the one hand, a peripheral and voluntary choice for inmates, judges, and correctional staff unrelated to the practice of law and the imposition and execution of sentence; on the other hand, a frequent catalyst for exclusionary extremism as witnessed in the violent reaction to Catholics and Mormons in the 19th century and, to a lesser but still significant degree, Muslims in the present day.

The "desacralization" of corrections remains by and large the case, but there have been several developments that signal not so much new developments in the correctional milieu as a recovery and refashioning of concepts tracing back in some instances several millennia. Two cases in point are the growing phenomena of faith-based prisons and the concerted worldwide attention given to the practice of restorative justice.

Charles Colson, one of the Watergate conspirators, had a powerful spiritual conversion during his period of incarceration. After his release from confinement, he devoted his life to prison reform. One of his most noteworthy innovations grew from a visit he made to a prison in Brazil, run by three Catholic laypersons. All of the procedural guidelines for the facility were based upon biblical, and especially New Testament directives, in which no violence would ever be sanctioned and a daily regimen of prayer, work, and mutual respect would be fostered. Colson was able to import that concept to the United States and other countries of the world where it has been instituted in a number of jurisdictions. While the methodology may not exactly duplicate the monastic prison of an earlier age, the idea that the criminal offender often requires something more morally substantive than vocational and educational programs, and/or psychological and medical treatment, and something far less morally problematic than idleness and an atmosphere of retribution, has apparently struck a chord with a growing number of judges, prosecutors, and political officials.

In the same way, restorative justice reproduces penitential practices tracing back to the New Testament, the early history of the church, and the use of peacemakers in colonial Pennsylvania. In simple form, this practice seeks to return to the era before the development of modern systems of law in which an offense was primarily understood not as a statutory violation, but as an act of harm brought by one person upon another. It seeks to bring the victim and offender together into a mediated conference in which each can express his or her feelings and a mutually agreeable solution can be worked out independently of the criminal court and the penal system.

The fact that each of these methods has stimulated such widespread national and global interest reveals that the early conflation of religion and crime is once again revealing itself in the contemporary practice of criminal justice.

Andrew Skotnicki
Manhattan College

See Also: 1600 to 1776 Primary Documents; 1801 to 1850 Primary Documents; 1921 to 1940 Primary Documents; 1961 to 1980 Primary Documents; 2001 to 2012 Primary Documents; Bible; Morality; Religion and Crime, Contemporary; Religion and Crime, Sociology of.

Further Readings

Dunbabin, Jean. *Captivity and Imprisonment in Medieval Europe.* Houndmills, UK: Palgrave Macmillan, 2002.

Fingarette, Herbert. *Confucius: The Secular as Sacred.* New York: Harper & Row, 1972.

Lewis, W. David. *From Newgate to Dannemora.* Ithaca, NY: Cornell University Press, 1965.

Peters, Edward. "Prison Before the Prison." In *The Oxford History of the Prison*, Norval Morris and David Rothman, eds. New York: Oxford University Press, 1995.

Teeters, Negley and John Shearer. *The Prison at Philadelphia Cherry Hill.* New York: Columbia University Press, 1957.

Zehr, Howard. *Changing Lenses.* Scottdale, PA: Herald Press, 1990.

Religion and Crime, Sociology of

The sociological perspective of the relationship between religion and crime is focused on several key areas. In addition to the basic application of the major theoretical perspectives in sociology to the nature of the relationship between religion and crime, this focus includes substantive examinations of social issues and processes such as religious fundamentalism and religiously motivated violence and criminality, religion and terrorism, religion as a protective factor against criminal behavior, the role of religious organizations and their response to crime, religion and morality, and types of religious criminality. Sociologists consider the context of the relationship of religion with the broader culture and with the other social institutions of society in which it is embedded as they seek to investigate the more specific connection between religion and criminal behavior.

Sociological Frameworks for Understanding Religion and Crime

Each of the three major theoretical perspectives in sociology—structural functionalism, conflict theory, and symbolic interactionism—offers a generic framework for understanding and analyzing the relationship between religion and crime. The structural functionalist approach, which originated with the work of Emile Durkheim, views religion as a central social process, one that has the function of maintaining the basic moral order of a society. Through its myths, rituals, and symbols, religious behavior produces social solidarity and allows social groups to function and survive with relative health and stability. Relative, because in this understanding, some amount of deviant and criminal behavior is actually necessary for the smooth functioning of society. This is because behaviors defined as "criminal" create, sharpen, and reinforce social boundaries, reminding members of social groups and the culture at large which behaviors are acceptable and unacceptable. In this view, whatever the social causes of criminality, its function—in appropriate amounts—is to provide and define the normative set of behavioral guidelines individuals are to follow. When the normative rules of society are violated through criminal actions, social sanctions of varying kinds are imposed in order to both highlight the boundaries of what is acceptable and unacceptable and to bring the individual back into the normative order.

Conflict theory, in contrast, argues that crime in society is ultimately a product of the unequal relationship between those in positions of power and those who are subject to this power. Religion becomes a part of the ideological structure that ultimately reproduces this inequality and helps to maintain the status quo. Importantly, criminality is not simply a given set of behaviors with a corresponding set of essential qualities. Rather, it is those in power who have the social, political, and material resources to define what is criminal and what is not; when a behavior works against the interests of those in power, it is more likely to be defined as criminal or considered immoral. Conservative Christian groups in the United States (which have been a powerful political force in the last decade) have sometimes acted as moral entrepreneurs; that is, they have been very influential in asserting and defining, sometimes explicitly through legislation, what is moral and what should be legal and illegal in society. The political actions of these groups regarding social issues such as abortion and gay rights are strongly connected with the specific religious beliefs and worldviews of religious groups. Other instances where a conflict perspective can be useful in understanding the relationship between religion and crime involve cases of specific religious beliefs and their conflict with the broader secular society and the law. Examples include court cases when parents have refused medical care for their children because of their religious views. Gary and Margaret Hall, of Faith Assembly, a church that believes in and practices faith healings, were sentenced in 1986 to five years in prison for reckless homicide after their infant son died from pneumonia, which doctors testified could have been prevented with basic medical care. Conflicts such as these raise questions about religious freedom, the role of the state, definitions of criminality, and the relationship, and differences between religious and secular authority and power.

The final major sociological approach, symbolic interactionism, with its focus on social process and the social psychological and micro interactions of small groups, contrasts with the macro perspectives of both structural functionalism and conflict theory. A core principle of symbolic interaction is that people act toward objects (whether physical or abstract) based on the meaning those objects have for them. It highlights the socially constructed nature of religious meaning. That is, religious beliefs, values, and ideas—in short, religious worldviews—are the products of meaningful interactions and ongoing human relationships.

The actions of individuals are strongly influenced by the religious worldviews to which they subscribe and which are constructed in the context of group dynamics and social interactions. The symbolic interactionist thus investigates the substantive meaning of religion for individuals, their personal religious identities, and how this connects to the behavioral choices they make in the context of their associations. To understand criminality, a person investigates the subjective interpretations, self-understanding, and religious identities of individuals as they have undertaken criminal actions based on the meaning and purpose those actions have had for them.

Substantive Issues in Religion and Crime

The relationship between religion and crime is complex and sometimes controversial, as the sociological work in this area indicates. One way in which this is most evident is that the beliefs and values central to different religions in the United States can be viewed in very different ways—as either protections against criminal behavior or motivators of criminal behavior. The first is usually referred to as religion as a deterrent. That is, religion serves as an important aspect of social control, and one of its functions is to inhibit criminal behavior. This view seems to be consistent with the American public's general assumptions about the connection between religion and morality—that crime itself, and the potential "moral decay" of a society are best resisted with a strong religious foundation.

Crime, defined as any behavior that is considered an offense against the state and that is punishable according to the law of that state, is an ongoing social issue. Sociologists who argue religion is a deterrent to crime do so based on substantial research on the subject. For instance, as Robert Wuthnow observes, a review of close to 60 studies from the 1970s through the 1990s concluded that there is a positive correlation between religiosity—measured primarily through religious participation—and compliance with social conventions and the law. There has since then been general agreement among scholars that religion can act as a deterrent to crime. However, the same research has also led scholars to not overstate this relationship, as the cumulative findings suggest that the relationship is moderate and may not hold across all conditions or for all types of criminality and delinquency. For example, with regard to normative views concerning crimes against individuals (such as murder and theft), specific religious convictions are not particularly relevant, and the secular institutional sphere alone appears adequate in effectively conveying proscriptions against these types of crimes. Further, not all research has been consistent with the conclusion that religion has a deterrent effect on crime (see Travis Hirschi's study of religion and delinquency) and not all sociological perspectives share the assumptions about human motivations and inhibitions toward criminal behavior that the research on religion and social control seem to take for granted (one notable theory is the rational choice model).

Deterrence to crime is just one of the effects that religion has on other aspects of social life. It has frequently been observed that religion can motivate altruistic behavior and can also be a vehicle for positive social change. Moreover, this change can be brought about through what may be viewed—especially at the time—as deviant or unlawful means. An oft-cited example in the United States is the influence of Christianity—its symbols, values, moral guidelines, narratives, and language—and how it was taken up by various religious leaders and activists during the civil rights movement of the 1950s and 1960s in order to push for greater equality and social justice. Acts of civil disobedience, boycotts, and other means were used to bring about this change, and the movement was suffused with religious meaning and justification.

Religious values and attitudes also have implications for criminal justice. Religious organizations have historically been involved, even if indirectly, in the making of criminal law, and religion has continued to strongly influence public opinion about a host of social, moral, and political issues. Concern over abortion, gay marriage, stem cell research, pornography, drugs, and other issues have prompted religious individuals and groups to become involved in the political sphere and advocate their specific views on these topics. Thus, religion motivates particular responses to criminality and ultimately helps shape social policy and the ways in which the criminal justice system handles criminal offenders. For instance, as Harold Grasmick argues, evidence suggests that conservative Christians are more likely to hold retributive attitudes concerning punishment for criminal offenses than their secular or less religious counterparts. That is, violations of social rules of all kinds (from misdemeanor-level juvenile delinquency to adult criminality) are met with more stringent and punitive attitudes

A U.S. Navy serviceman photographed the American flag on display on September 15, 2001, at the site of the terrorist attack on the World Trade Center four days earlier. The attacks provide an example of both the effect of the perception of the West as a threat to traditional religions and their worldviews and the way that religion is at times used to justify violent acts.

toward punishment for offenders, especially if the offenses are seen as violations of religious or moral codes. Criminality not only violates the law of the land but is also an inherent violation of God's law. This is one sense—consistent with the conflict perspective—in which religion can function to sacralize the social order and legitimate certain, even controversial, responses to criminal actions, such as the death penalty. A good portion of the response of religion to crime, however, takes the more implicit form of informal social sanctions. As a primary agent of socialization, religion imparts codes of conduct that mostly discourage violations of the law. Religious values and attitudes are closely connected with how individuals think about and respond to crime. Religion is also unique as a form of social control in that its adherents often are motivated not just to obey the law but also to respond more enthusiastically to violations of the law by others, because of the view that ethics and morality are rooted in, and ultimately justified by, a supernatural source.

In addition to religion as a form of social control and deterrent to crime, it can also motivate and justify criminal behavior. Some acts of terrorism and violence are impelled by religious impulse, and religious beliefs and views can provide the rational basis for committing criminal acts that individuals or groups might otherwise not consider. This religious extremism can lead to terrorist acts that are often the most striking instances of the connection between religion and crime, and it is these actions that seem to offer the best evidence of religion being a core cause of criminality—although based on the evidence and arguments of scholars in this area, using religion as a justification for crime after the fact is much less difficult to establish.

Mark Juergensmeyer observes that at the macro level, the processes of modernization, globalization, and the general influence of the West are perceived by some religious communities around the globe as threats to their traditions and the religious worldviews that undergird these traditions. The attacks of September 11, 2001, are an example of both this kind of conflict and the ways in which religion can be used as a justification for acts of violence. Domestic acts of violence also demonstrate how specific religious views can come into conflict within the broader society. The perception by some religious groups that American society is in moral decline, caused by secular forces, gives similar motivation and justification for acts of violence. The string of abortion clinic bombings across the country over the last several decades have been not so much about modernization and Western power but about upholding specific conservative religious views against the threat of secular culture.

Typology of Religion-Related Crime

It is useful to differentiate religion-related crime from other types of criminality. Karel Kurst-Swanger defines religion-related crime as "any illegal or socially injurious act which is committed within the auspices of religious practice or as a result of a particular religious belief." It is important, when applying this definition, to also distinguish types of religion and religious organizations, as they have varying relationships with the broader society and will be connected with criminality in different ways and to different degrees.

Kurst-Swanger suggests three descriptive and distinct—though also occasionally overlapping—types of religion-related crime: theologically based crimes, reactive/defensive crimes, and abuse-of-religious-authority crimes. Theologically based crimes are those that follow from basic religious attitudes or viewpoints, or specific religious beliefs. Crimes against women that draw upon the reinforcing and legitimating aspects of religion's role in patriarchy are an example. Likewise, and more concretely, an individual who feels ordered by God through a literal interpretation of a religious text to carry out a violent act against another would be categorized as a theologically based crime. Reactive/defensive crimes involve a religious person or group feeling threatened by some external social or political force and engaging in crime as a response to this threat. Resisting secular—or even competing and conflicting religious—forces through violent means is a common form of this type of crime. Terrorist acts and abortion bombings fit within this category. The final type, abuse of religious authority, has received heightened attention in the last few decades. This occurs when individuals or groups in positions of religious leadership abuse their power and status. Unlike the previous two types, this type has little to do with the content of religious ideas motivating crime. Rather, it is the institutional structure of religion that provides the context for the exploitation of crime, a context wherein offenders can gain protection from the institution and/or from appealing to their status as a religious authority in order to avoid the consequences of criminal behavior. The sexual abuse of children by priests who received protection within the Catholic Church provides the clearest example of this type of religion-related crime.

Jesse M. Smith
University of Colorado Boulder

See Also: 1600 to 1776 Primary Documents; 1801 to 1850 Primary Documents; 1851 to 1900 Primary Documents; 1961 to 1980 Primary Documents; Crime in America, Types; Criminology; Religion and Crime, Contemporary; Religion and Crime, History of; Terrorism.

Further Readings
Hirschi, Travis. *Causes of Delinquency*. Berkeley: University of California Press, 1969.
Juergensmeyer, Mark. *Terror in the Mind of God: The Global Rise of Religious Violence*. Berkeley: University of California Press. 2003.
Kurst-Swanger, Karel. *Worship and Sin: An Exploration of Religion-Related Crime in the United States*. New York: Peter Lang, 2008.
Roberts, Keith A. *Religion in Sociological Perspective*, 4th ed. Belmont, CA: Thomson/Wadsworth. 2004.
Wuthnow, Robert. *Encyclopedia of Politics and Religion*. Washington, DC: Congressional Quarterly, 1998.

Reports on Prison Conditions

Reports on prison conditions have been compiled since the late 18th century, and many of them have triggered prison reform. Since 1980, the U.S. prison population has increased dramatically, reaching approximately 2.3 million by 2009—the highest documented incarceration rate in the world. During the same time, the average sentence length of inmates more than doubled. The rapid growth in prison population has been accompanied by numerous reports on prison conditions compiled and published by a diverse range of stakeholders.

Early Prison Reports
Written by John Howard in 1777, *The State of the Prisons in England and Wales* attracted public attention because of its meticulous description of prisons' poor sanitation, high rates of starvation, and chronic overcrowding. In search of best prison practice, Howard traveled the European continent extensively. His advocacy for prison reform was influential when William Blackstone and William Eden drew up the Penitentiary Act 1779; the act contained features that Howard admired in foreign countries' prison systems, including individual cells, a prison labor regime, improved sanitary conditions, elimination of the sale of alcohol, religious instruction, prison uniforms, and a policy that rewarded good conduct with remission of part of the prisoner's sentence.

In the 1820s, U.S. prisons adopted either the Auburn system, which required inmates to work and eat together in silence, or the Pennsylvania system, which kept inmates in solitary confinement for both work and meals. As a result of longer sentences and an influx of new immigrants, overcrowding became problematic by the 1860s. The New York Prison Association commissioned Enoch Wines and Theodore Dwight's *Report on the Prisons and Reformatories of the United States and Canada* (1867). Wines and Dwight called for reform of the entire prison system because, according to their investigation, not a single institution was pursuing the reformation of its inmates. They criticized the use of cruel and degrading corporal punishment as a disciplinary measure, the lack of staff training, and the lack of centralized prison supervision. Recommendations included training of guards, establishment of educational programs and vocational training for inmates, and purposeful inmate preparation for release. The resulting prison reform emphasized rewards for positive inmate behavior, abolished corporal punishment as a disciplinary measure, and established indeterminate sentences that allowed for early release on parole compared to previously immutable sentences.

Despite various reform efforts, a report compiled by the President's Commission on Law Enforcement and Administration of Justice 100 years later (1967) was characterized by the same keywords as its predecessors: prison overcrowding, brutal and degrading treatment of inmates, and poor preparation for reintegration upon release. Since that time, the prison population has risen steadily. Incarcerating more offenders for longer periods, the United States faces the challenge of detaining an increasing number of inmates in constitutionally adequate conditions.

Constitutionally Adequate Prison Conditions

Constitutional standards for adequate prison conditions are framed through the Eighth Amendment to the U.S. Constitution, which prohibits the infliction of cruel and unusual punishment. State and federal courts have addressed several questions on which conditions of imprisonment constitute cruel and unusual punishment. Before 1970, courts only assessed specific acts committed against individuals. For example, the Supreme Court ruled in *Estelle v. Gamble* (1976) that staff's deliberate indifference to prisoners' serious medical needs violates the Eighth Amendment. In *Hudson v. McMillian* (1992), it held that using excessive physical force against an inmate may constitute cruel and unusual punishment even if the prisoner's injuries are minor.

Since *Holt v. Sarver* (1970), more complex cases have challenged the constitutionality of entire prison structures. Broad remedial orders have been imposed in more than 24 jurisdictions directing prison administrations to ameliorate prison life. For example, in *Plata v. Schwarzenegger* (2005), the Californian Prison Health Care System was found to be in violation of the Eighth Amendment and was put under receivership after the court determined that one inmate died every week as a result of medical maltreatment.

The basic standards applied by courts to the question of constitutionally adequate prison conditions have been summarized by William Danne as including (1) conditions that are of such inherent cruelty that no inmate conduct can warrant it, (2) conditions that are abhorrent to contemporary society, and/or (3) conditions where punishment for prison disciplinary purposes is excessive. These standards generally allow prison guards

A cellblock in the Philadelphia County Prison. The Philadelphia Prison System is the birthplace of modern corrections, beginning with the city's first jail, a seven-by-five-foot cage built in 1683 to detain "miscreants," expanding to houses of correction by 1721.

to use reasonable force in order to protect themselves or other inmates from attack or to enforce compliance with orders from staff. The standards prohibit the denial of essential medical care, shelter, clothing, bedding, basic hygiene implements, and nourishment. However, solitary confinement, forced labor, bodily searches, and failure to provide inmates with rehabilitative programs have not been considered to constitute cruel or unusual punishments unless they violate one of the basic standards discussed above.

The standards set forth by U.S. courts provide a point of reference for governmental agencies' reporting on prison conditions, as well as for state and federal court decisions in cases of inmate litigation. However, reports from nongovernmental agencies also frequently refer to the United

Nations Standard Minimum Rules for the Treatment of Prisoners (UN Minimum Rules). While these rules are not legally binding, and therefore are not applicable to U.S. courts, they nevertheless provide guidelines specifying what is generally accepted as good practice in the treatment of prisoners.

Reports on Conditions in Supermax Facilities

The first supermax prison was created at the Federal State Penitentiary in Marion, Illinois. Following a series of violent incidents, including the murder of two guards in separate incidents on the same day in 1983, the prison went on permanent lockdown—prisoners remained in their cells except for isolated exercise. As this reportedly resulted in a safer prison environment, other jurisdictions started adopting supermax facilities. By 2000, the Federal Bureau of Prisons and at least 40 states had built various forms of supermax prisons. Today, more than 20,000 prisoners are held in state or federal supermax facilities in the United States.

Labeling this process "Marionization," Human Rights Watch (HRW) published its *Report on Prison Conditions in the United States* in 1991. This report was based on interviews with inmates, former inmates, prison advocates, lawyers, relatives of current inmates, and correctional officials in more than 20 jails and prisons. Supermax facilities in particular were criticized in respect to human rights abuses. Violations of the UN Minimum Rules evidenced in the HRW report were numerous. The rules require at least one hour daily outdoor exercise, yet prisons such as the Florida State Prison at Starke had a windowless wing where inmates were confined 24 hours a day, some for several years. In the Disciplinary Segregation Unit at Oregon State Penitentiary in Salem, the use of so-called "strip status"—where prisoners are stripped of all clothing, cell items, and personal possessions and can only "earn" them back bit by bit demonstrating good behavior—was frequently imposed as a disciplinary measure. Strip status is seen as violating the UN Minimum Rules, which entitle prisoners to clothing and bedding and prohibit degrading punishment. In the same prison unit, observers reported witnessing the use of handcuffs as a disciplinary measure; collective punishment; and the ordering of undesirable, unpleasant work as a means of punishment, all of which are prohibited by the UN Minimum Rules.

The HRW report concluded with recommendations on how to address such violations. First, it suggested that supermax facilities should only be used under independent supervision from correctional administration. Second, the report proposed that physical restraints, collective punishment, and denial of access to reading material, a table and chair in prison cells, outdoor time, and contact visits should never be used as disciplinary measures. Third, the report proposed an end to the mixing of nonviolent offenders with dangerous criminals. Last, the report recommended that the U.S. Department of Justice publish an annual report on violence in prisons and jails to protect inmates against violence from other inmates and to examine the conduct of officials in institutions where repeated incidents of violence take place.

The *Report on Prison Conditions in the United States* was followed by other HRW reports on individual supermax facilities. The report *Cold Storage: Super-Maximum Security Confinement in Indiana* (1997) took a critical view of the use of solitary confinement for mentally ill inmates. The report *Red Onion State Prison: Super-Maximum Security Confinement in Virginia* (1999) detailed how the state of Virginia randomly subjected inmates with low security risk to the strict conditions of supermax facilities, primarily in order to utilize their excess capacity. In its 2011 annual report, Amnesty International condemned conditions in U.S. supermax facilities for reasons similar to those addressed by HRW, highlighting that these conditions are in some cases imposed for years on individuals awaiting trial, which may affect their health and ability to assist in their defense.

However, reports on prison conditions are not only gathered by nongovernmental organizations. Reports are also heard before courts through testimony of expert witnesses, whose observations are included in the courts' decisions and thus attain the status of factual evidence. Contrary to conventional reports, which can only offer recommendations for action, evidentiary reports can directly impact judicial decision making and render enforceable action. Expert witnesses' reports on prison conditions in the United States before the European Court on Human Rights have prevented the extradition of a number of people for whom a warrant existed and who were likely to face incarceration in supermax prisons. The European court argued that current prison conditions violate Article 3 of the Convention for the Protection of Human Rights and Fundamental Freedoms, which states that no one shall be subjected to torture or inhuman or degrading treatment or punishment.

Reports Addressing Prison Rape and Sexual Abuse

Prison rape has long been part of the prison mythology. It has become a common feature in the portrayal of prison life in popular media. Society has even tacitly condoned prison rape when incarceration is imposed on notorious offenders, particularly sex offenders. However, it has only been with the massive growth in prison populations that the problem of prison rape has become a public one, in part because of the rise in the rates of nonviolent offenders, and in part because of the increasing awareness that official rates of sexual assaults in prisons do not reflect the reality of this type of violence.

In 1996, HRW published *All Too Familiar: Sexual Abuse of Women in U.S. State Prisons*, a report focusing on sexual violations by male staff against female prisoners. The organization followed up with *Nowhere to Hide: Retaliation Against Women in Michigan State Prisons* (1998), a report documenting widespread sexual abuse of female inmates and exposing retaliatory punishment of prisoners who reported such abuse. In the same year, Amnesty International released its report *Not Part of My Sentence: Violations of the Human Rights of Women in Custody*, which confirmed that sexual abuse of female inmates by male staff is commonplace and uncovered that staff found guilty are often retained and transferred to other prisons. Arguably the most influential report, *No Escape: Male Rape in U.S. Prisons*, was released by HRW in 2001. Based on a survey of 34 prisons, including testimony of more than 200 victims, the report illustrates that rape and sexual slavery are commonplace in U.S. prisons. A culture of indifference and ignorance as well as the lack of empirical data on the subject were identified as the main causes for the persistence of prison rape. Through extensive media coverage of this report, the taboo subject of prison rape was introduced to the public.

Prison officials and the U.S. government, who had long described the problem as minimal, were obligated to formally address the issue. *No Escape: Male Rape in U.S. Prisons* was a primary driver in the passage of the Prison Rape Elimination Act of 2003. As called for in the legislation, the National Prison Rape Elimination Commission (NPREC) was established to study the causes and consequences of sexual abuse in U.S. prisons and to develop mandatory nationwide standards for correctional facilities in order to eliminate prison rape through prevention, detection, and punishment of sexual abuse in confinement.

The NPREC published its report in 2009. Conducting a survey of more than 63,000 inmates in more than 400 prisons and jails, the report found that an estimated 60,500 inmates were sexually abused annually. Notably, more inmates reported abuse by staff than by other prisoners. The NPREC found that some of the abuse prevalent in women's prisons was facilitated through prison policies on regular pat-down searches for weapons, drugs, and other contraband by staff of the opposite sex.

The NPREC suggested that every correctional facility should have a written zero tolerance policy for all forms of sexual abuse. It also recommended that staff receive extensive training on how to prevent sexual abuse and how to respond when it has occurred. Meanwhile, prisoners should be educated about their right to be safe. To prevent sexual abuse, the NPREC suggested offering competitive compensation packages to recruit and retain appropriate staff. It also recommended the supervision of staff and prisoners at all times (especially cross-gender supervision in women's prisons) and the improvement of reporting procedures. Acknowledging that some inmate groups have features that make them more vulnerable to sexual abuse than others (e.g., young people, women, homosexuals, transgendered individuals, and people with a mental disability or illness, a lack of experience in correctional facilities, or a history of sexual victimization), the NPREC proposed that such features be taken into account and be the nationwide driver for decisions about inmate housing and programming. In the event of sexual abuse, the NPREC recommended that investigations should be conducted thoroughly and competently, that perpetrators should be held accountable through administrative sanctions and criminal prosecution, that staff members who have engaged in sexual abuse not be hired or retained, and that victims receive immediate and ongoing medical and mental healthcare to minimize trauma.

The commission also regarded the lack of any empirical data collection that may reveal patterns of abuse and a lack of rigorous internal monitoring and external oversight as contributors to the persistence of prison rape. To this end, the report recommended standard audits by independent auditors on a three-year cycle. Finally, the NPREC report criticized the restrictions of the Prison Litigation Reform Act (PLRA). The PLRA was enacted in 1996 to reduce the strain on the judicial system by inmate litigation. Two requirements made it difficult for inmates to pursue lawsuits involving complaints about their treatment in prison. First, inmates are required to exhaust internal administrative remedies before their claims can proceed to court. Second, inmates are required to prove physical injury to receive compensation. The NPREC suggested amending the exhaustion requirement; however, it did not specify what these modifications should be. Furthermore, it recommended changing the second requirement as it fails to acknowledge emotional and psychological injuries caused by sexual abuse.

In its *World Report 2011*, HRW noted that even 17 months after the NPREC provided its report, the attorney general had not promulgated nationwide standards, although prison rape remains commonplace.

Reports on Prison Overcrowding

Every prison facility is built with a design capacity in mind, in particular, the number of beds and inmates it can accommodate. In an effort to house increasing numbers of inmates, however, many prisons now routinely fill their gymnasiums and classrooms with bunk beds—a trend commonly referred to as the "warehousing" of prisoners. Conservatively defined, overcrowding occurs when the prison population exceeds 100 percent of the facility's design capacity, but other factors like number of staff and available programs and services (operational capacity) also influence the overall capacity of a prison. In 2008, the Bureau of Justice Statistics found that federal facilities operated at 135 percent of capacity, and 18 states worked at or above 100 percent capacity. Applying the conservative design capacity above as a measure, some facilities were found to be operating at well over 200 percent capacity.

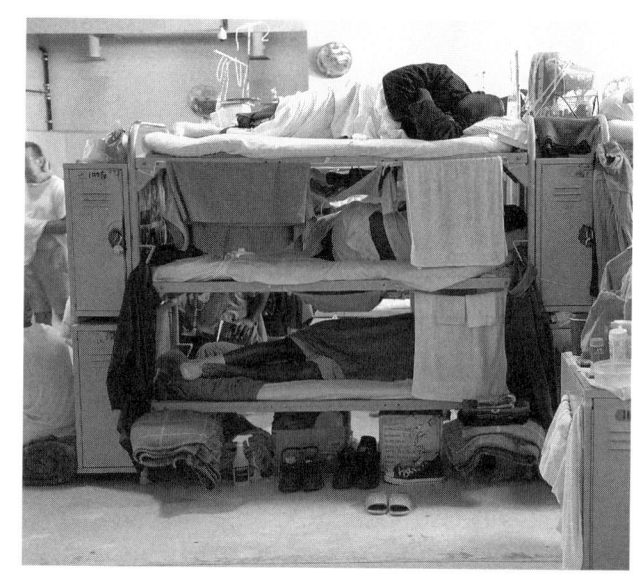

Twenty-first-century prison overcrowding in California, where prisoners are stacked three high on triple bunks in what was the gymnasium at Solano Prison in Vacaville, California.

In 2006, the privately organized Commission on Safety and Abuse in America's Prisons published its report *Confronting Confinement*. This report was not commissioned by a governmental agency but was initiated by the commission's co-chairs, former Attorney General Nicholas Katzenbach and former Federal Appeals Court judge John Gibbons. Overall, the report covered four areas of concern: (1) the dangerous conditions of confinement, including violence, poor healthcare, and inappropriate solitary confinement; (2) the challenges facing labor and management; (3) weak oversight of correctional facilities; and (4) serious flaws in the available data about violence and abuse. The report concluded with a number of recommendations; however, overcrowding was identified as the number one cause of prison violence, and therefore the report insisted that crowding must be reduced to a level that ensures safety for inmates and staff.

Reports on overcrowding have also been received by courts. Upholding a district court decision, the Supreme Court made a landmark decision in *Brown v. Plata* (2011). It ordered the state of California to reduce its overall prison population to 137.5 percent of design capacity within two years. To achieve the reduction and remedy the presently occurring Eighth Amendment violations, the court mandated that California either increase capacity via new prison construction or release prisoners through parole or sentencing reform. The Supreme Court based its decision on testimony by expert witnesses, who detailed major deficiencies in healthcare provision, including understaffing of medical personnel, inadequate housing for disabled and elderly inmates, lack of basic medical equipment and medications, and the general abysmal state of prison medical facilities. Witnesses also described the impact of overcrowding on the existing medical conditions. Overcrowding had increased inmate violence and the rate of infectious diseases. This situation put medical and correctional staff into a constant state of crisis, which made retaining—let alone hiring—staff extremely difficult. Increased inmate violence caused more lockdowns, which in turn impacted the provision of medical care. In consideration of these reports, the Supreme Court concluded that prison overcrowding promotes violence and results in significant and chronic understaffing of medical personnel with the effect of significant delays in treating prisoners. Thus, the Supreme Court stated that overcrowding is the primary cause of systemwide Eighth Amendment violations.

Conclusion
Contemporary reports on prison conditions have largely been initiated and published by nongovernmental organizations. Findings and recommendations of these reports have subsequently been validated through governmental reports, official statistics, and reports before the Supreme Court and the European Court on Human Rights. All reports stress the importance of reducing overcrowding, preventing sexual abuse, and limiting long-term solitary confinement. They also bring attention to the fact that the majority of inmates will be released at some point in the future, and that the treatment they have experienced in prison will have an effect on the communities they are returning to.

Antje Deckert
AUT University

See Also: Chain Gangs and Prison Labor; Federal Prisons; Prisoner's Rights; Punishment Within Prison; Supermax Prisons.

Further Readings
Amnesty International USA. *Not Part of My Sentence: Violations of the Human Rights Watch in Custody.* New York: Amnesty International, 1999.

Danne, William H. "Prison Conditions as Amounting to Cruel and Unusual Punishment." *American Law Reports*, v.51 (1973).

Dolovich, Sharon. "Cruelty, Prison Conditions, and the Eighth Amendment." *New York University Law Review*, v.84 (2009).

Human Rights Watch. *Prison Conditions in the United States.* New York: Human Rights Watch, 1991.

National Prison Rape Elimination Commission. *Report.* http://www.ncjrs.gov/pdffiles1/226680.pdf (Accessed June 2011).

Retributivism

Retributivism is a theory of justice that applies to the provision of rewards and punishments to someone based on their actions. A reward or punishment is retributively just if it is based on what the recipient deserves. People should receive their due, their "just deserts." Retributivism is not a comprehensive or exclusive theory of justice, because goods may be justly distributed on many other bases, such as one person one vote, to each according to his needs, and maximizing utility, and retributivists may well accept one or more of these principles as appropriate in many circumstances. But when the authority, whether a parent, employer, military commander, or criminal court, understands itself to be rewarding or punishing an individual for his conduct, retributivism insists that it be based on, and proportional to, the actor's desert. A retributivist might say that his theory is implicit in the very words *reward* and *punishment* and argue that the words are being misused if applied to distributions not based on just deserts.

Retributivism is best seen as a particular application of the deontological claim, which holds that some acts are themselves right or wrong, independent of whatever outcomes they produce; the ends do not always justify the means, because acting justly is more important. The best example of a deontological proscription is the celebrated transplant hypothetical: everyone agrees that it is immoral for a doctor to kill a healthy person in order to distribute his organs to five desperate transplant candidates, even though her act of killing would save five lives at the cost of one. The deontological view prohibiting undeserved punishment and mandating deserved punishment is more commonly known as retributivism. Although retributive justice may be applied to rewards and punishments generally, the theory is especially important, and most commonly invoked, in the context of a state's criminal punishment.

Retributivism as a Theory of Criminal Justice

Because criminal punishment constitutes the deliberate infliction of suffering on an individual, imposing a punishment must be justified, and according to retributivism, punishment is justified only if two elements are present. For any particular sentence to be deserved, and therefore retributively just, (1) the defendant must be blameworthy for his conduct, and (2) the sentence must be proportional to the degree of his blameworthiness. Therefore, despite its harsh colloquial connotation, retributivism serves to limit punishment as well as justify it: Under these two principles, punishment may not be inflicted on the innocent, or the guilty beyond their desert, even if doing so would achieve a greater good for others. The retributivist formula for criminal punishment is a matter of justice, not vengeance; revenge may be what a victim wants, but psychological satisfaction to the victim is merely incidental.

Utilitarianism provides the chief rival justification for criminal punishment, and what counts as utilitarian justification is opposed in almost every respect to the retributivist one. Where retributivism finds punishment justified because criminals deserve to suffer, utilitarians find punishment justified only by the societal benefits it will produce, particularly in the form of crime prevention through its deterrent, incapacitative, norm-reinforcing, or rehabilitative effects; therefore, retributivism will likely mandate the acquittal of an insane compulsive killer as not responsible for his actions, while utilitarianism will likely justify imprisonment to prevent further killings. Where retributive punishment looks backward to past wrongful conduct, utilitarian punishment looks forward to its effects. Where retributivism is concerned only with individual fairness and depends for its force on a normative assertion, utilitarianism is concerned only with collective benefits and depends for its force on empirical proof of efficacy.

But to remove desert from the punishment equation (as utilitarians do except to the extent that a desert-based system will increase future utility) leaves any criminal justice system unmoored from some of the most deep-seated moral convictions. Absent countervailing utilitarian considerations, utilitarianism would presumptively justify such blatantly unfair state actions as imprisoning individuals who have committed no crimes when their personal characteristics predict such activity, as may be the case with the class of unemployed, impoverished, and addicted male school dropouts; demolishing the family homes of suicide bombers because it might be one of the few ways to deter terrorists willing to kill themselves; and finally, the execution of an innocent person if it would deter more killings than the one it inflicts. Retributivism seems to be the only theory of criminal justice that can explain why such acts are unacceptably immoral.

In recent decades in the United States, retributivism seems to have gained ascendency over its utilitarian rival. In 2011, the influential 1962 Model Penal Code, a project of the American Law Institute (ALI) intended to influence and reform criminal codes, was the subject of an ALI reexamination designed to better reflect the retributive philosophy. Yet, despite its common-sense appeal, retributivism is notoriously difficult to apply in practice, whether that involves the judicial imposition of a sentence or the legislative drafting of a criminal statute. To do so, authorities must discern more precisely what it means for a person to be "blameworthy" and for a punishment to be "proportional" to his or her blameworthiness.

Blameworthiness

To be blameworthy is to commit some wrongful act, having freely chosen to do so with some level of ill intent. That the conduct be wrongful (harmful or threatening harm to others, or immoral albeit victimless) is a prerequisite to deserved punishment, arguably with the exception that violating a duly passed law, in itself, should not qualify as the kind of wrongful conduct that suffices. Otherwise, any criminal law regime would be self-justifying, so that criminalizing singing would justify punishing a yodeler, and the wrongfulness prerequisite for criminalization and punishment would be illusory. It is the requirement that the defendant have freely and intentionally chosen to commit the wrongful act that is much more difficult to apply. American criminal law generally requires that the defendant's act must be a product of his will (rather than, for example, a seizure or an act during sleepwalking) and was committed with some kind of ill intent. In American jurisprudence, both a willed act (*actus reus*) and guilty mind (*mens rea*) are generally required.

The problem is that it is perfectly possible for someone to choose to act, and to do so with ill intent but without the freedom of choice that is essential for blameworthiness. Imagine a drug addict who intentionally purchases heroin but whose addiction was itself acquired through medical treatment after a car accident. Many would characterize his choice to buy heroin and the intent accompanying it compelled, not free, the product of bad luck, of circumstances beyond his control. If so, the idea that this person deserves to be punished is undermined.

The U.S. Supreme Court was on the verge of finding a free will requirement in the Eighth Amendment to the Constitution in the 1962 case of *Robinson v. California*, 370 U.S. 660, but retreated soon afterward, concerned with the imponderables of free will. To philosophical determinists, every choice and state of mind is unchosen, however it

The retributivism theory holds that criminal punishment is justified only if the defendant is blameworthy for his or her conduct and that the sentence imposed must be proportional to the degree of the criminal's blameworthiness (having chosen to commit an act freely with ill intent). The retributivist formula stresses criminal justice over vengeance or revenge.

may seem to the actor, due to the prior unchosen causes that produced them. On this account, the free choice that seems necessary to deem someone blameworthy dissolves into a matter of bad luck, the antithesis of free choice. The solution in American jurisprudence is to carve out the most obvious cases of compulsion like insanity and duress, while presuming free will as the norm. But even if this kind of total determinism is rejected as false, science keeps discovering new unchosen antecedents for acts and thoughts, and thus where to draw a line between freedom to choose and its absence is always unstable and almost infinitely contestable. What, for example, should a retributivist make of the fact that the large majority of child abusers were themselves abused as children? Or of the oft-stated claim that poverty causes crime? It seems retributively unjust to blame an offender whose choices are thought to result not from his blameworthy choice but from such unchosen prior influences as poverty, psychological makeup, or genetic infirmities that led to that choice.

Moreover, while retributivism generally corresponds to intuitive moral convictions, in some instances it does not. Imagine two people, both driving home drunk but only one of whom kills a pedestrian. There appears to be no difference in their respective blameworthiness; the difference is a result of bad luck. Yet, most people would demand greater punishment for the one who kills, and most criminal codes adopt the position that results, even if fortuitous, count. Drunk driving is punished less severely than vehicular homicide, and attempted murder is typically punished less severely than a successful murder.

Proportionality

The second requirement and dilemma for retributively just punishment concerns not whether to punish but how much. "The punishment must fit the crime," which to a retributivist means it must be proportional to both the gravity of the crime and the degree of ill intent accompanying its commission. On this account, an armed robber should receive a more severe sentence than a pickpocket, and a purposeful killing deserves a more severe sentence than a reckless but unintended one. The U.S. Supreme Court has read a very modest proportionality requirement in the Eighth Amendment, ruling the death penalty unconstitutional for rape in *Coker v. Georgia*, 433 U.S. 584 (1977) and unconstitutional for juvenile killers in *Roper v. Simmons*, 543 U.S. 551 (2005), and proportionality is key to what lawmakers and judges typically aim to achieve in their fashioning of punishments.

But intractable and inherent difficulties plague this principle as well. Most people may agree that the most blameworthy crimes should receive the gravest punishments, which in most countries means the longest term of imprisonment. But this can't describe anything about where the schedule of imprisonments should begin or end or how large the range should be; authorities must give retributive sense to a system of rankings with no "anchoring points." The one retributive version that does have such touchstones is the *lex talionis*, which mandates that the criminal receive the precise suffering he inflicted on the victim, "an eye for an eye, a tooth for a tooth." But no one regards raping a rapist, or torturing a torturer, as appropriate punishment today.

Even with an objective way to discern the appropriate range of punishments, there would remain the problem of grading between the poles. How many more years should a premeditated killer receive compared to an impulsive killer, if any? Who is more blameworthy, the prosecutor who withholds evidence resulting in an unwarranted conviction or the armed robber? If a fraudulent broker has already suffered the loss of reputation and the revocation of his license, should that amount of suffering be deducted from the degree of punishment or not? The problems of application are endless; retributive theorists have debated for many years whether a defendant whose negligent acts cause unintended harm deserves any punishment, and if so, how much, without settling on any definitive answer to the question.

Why Retributivism Holds That Punishment Must Be Deserved

Retributivism holds that desert is necessary for punishment and in its pure form also holds that desert is wholly sufficient to require punishment. There is great intuitive appeal to this claim, and a retributivist might say that no more is required to support it, that his claim is self-evident. But is there anything more that a retributivist can say to support the theory? Many philosophers have tried, most notably Immanuel Kant. For Kantians, the retributive principle most centrally embodies respect for the right of autonomous individuals to determine their futures. An individual wills his own punishment by his own blameworthy act, and only by inflicting punishment can the state respect the defendant's own moral choices. Because this view is based on respect for the defendant's autonomous agency, proponents of this view sometimes speak of the right of the criminal to be punished. Another theory also posits that the defendant has a moral right to punishment but traces it to a defendant's right to atone for his crime and thereby restore his standing as an equal member of the community.

Some theories place more focus on the victim's right to justice. On one account, the state has an affirmative duty to punish a blameworthy wrongdoer because he has treated the victim as a mere object of no intrinsic worth, and the state is obligated to repudiate this subjugation by the infliction of punishment. If instead the state does nothing, it leaves the victim an outcast and unrecognized as part of the social compact, thereby reinforcing and joining in the criminal's debasement of his victim. Somewhat related is Herbert Morris's "free-rider" conception, holding that a criminal deserves and must receive punishment in order to redress the unjust advantage over law-abiding citizens he acquired by his crime. The criminal has benefited from the protection of the criminal law but hasn't suffered the burden of self-restraint that others have assumed. By forcing the defendant to suffer a theoretically equivalent burden, punishment restores equality between the criminal and the victim and the proper balance of benefits and burdens that attach to each.

A Variation: Retributivism Reduced to a Limit on Punishment

In its strictest Kantian version, retributivism both prohibits punishment of the innocent and demands punishment of the guilty. But a "softer" version of retributivism exists, which holds that punishment of the guilty is merely permissible, not mandatory; desert then becomes a necessary but not sufficient condition for punishment. How can this version be justified, and what is the criterion by which the state is supposed to decide whether to punish or not? This one-way retributivism may at first thought appear to be incoherent. If no one should be punished beyond what he deserves, how can someone who does deserve punishment need not receive it? To say A deserves B seems to mean that A should receive B, at least in the absence of a stronger countervailing reason. Yet, the soft retributive version has an appeal that neither strict retributivism nor strict utilitarianism has alone: it jettisons the most undesirable aspects of both the former (which mandates an offender's suffering even when useless) and the latter (which may authorize the scapegoating of an innocent if socially useful). What remains is an account that combines the overwhelming moral truth that it is unjust to punish the innocent and the humane directive to impose punishment only when something would be accomplished by doing so.

One might see soft retributivism as a kind of forfeiture theory in which a person who engages in blameworthy criminal conduct forfeits his liberty right in proportion to his blameworthiness. The state then chooses whether to impose the punishment it now has a right to inflict, and the yardstick by which the state makes this choice is almost certainly going to be the comparative social utility of each option. In that sense, soft retributivism constitutes a mixed theory combining two moral theories that in pure form are irreconcilable. It is the most prominent of several variations that attempt to reconcile retributivism and utilitarianism in the field of criminal punishment and responds to a common, almost universally perceived need: The Rosetta Stone of the substantive criminal law is to find a principled way to reach an accommodation between the preventive goals of punishment and the ethical considerations of fairness.

Eric Blumenson
Suffolk University Law School

See Also: Corrections; Criminalization and Decriminalization; Cruel and Unusual Punishment; Deterrence, Theory of; *Furman v. Georgia*; Incapacitation, Theory of; Rehabilitation; Sentencing; Three Strikes Law.

Further Readings

Blumenson, Eric. "The Challenge of a Global Standard of Justice: Peace, Pluralism and Punishment at the

International Criminal Court." *Columbia Journal of Transnational Law*, v.44 (2006).

Cottingham, John. "Varieties of Retribution." *Philosophical Quarterly*, v.29 (1979).

Davis, Michael. *To Make the Punishment Fit the Crime: Essays in the Theory of Criminal Justice.* Boulder, CO: Westview Press, 1992.

Feinberg, Joel. *Doing and Deserving: Essays in the Theory of Responsibility.* Princeton, NJ: Princeton University Press, 1970.

Feinberg, Joel. *The Moral Limits of the Criminal Law: Harm to Others.* New York: Oxford University Press, 1984.

Fletcher, George. *With Justice for Some.* New York: Addison-Wesley, 1995.

Hampton, Jean. "Correcting Harms Versus Righting Wrongs: The Goal of Retribution." *UCLA Law Review*, v.39 (1992).

Kant, Immanuel. *The Metaphysical Elements of Justice.* Trans. John Ladd. Indianapolis, IN: Bobbs-Merrill Co., 1965.

Klenig, John. *Punishment and Desert.* The Hague: Martinus Nijhoff, 1973.

Moore, Michael S. "The Moral Worth of Retribution." In *Responsibility, Character, and the Emotions: New Essays in Moral Psychology*, Ferdinand Schoeman, ed. Harvard, MA: Cambridge University Press, 1987.

Morris, Herbert. *On Guilt and Innocence.* Berkeley: University of California Press, 1976.

Morris, Herbert. "Persons and Punishment." *Monist*, v.52 (1968).

Packer, Herbert, *The Limits of the Criminal Sanction.* Stanford, CA: Stanford University Press, 1968.

Whitman, James. "A Plea Against Retributivism." *Buffalo Criminal Law Review*, v.7 (2003).

Reynolds v. United States

Reynolds v. United States, 98 U.S. 145 (1879), held that the practice of polygamy (plural marriage) for religious purposes is not protected by the First Amendment's free exercise of religion clause. *Reynolds* was also the first Supreme Court case to interpret the free exercise clause.

The Church of Jesus Christ of Latter-day Saints, commonly known as the Mormon church

Mormon emigrants traveling in covered wagons circa 1879. Members of the Mormon faith were driven out of the midwest and migrated to what is now Utah.

after the Book of Mormon, was founded by Joseph Smith in 1830. The church required the obedience of its members because it believed that God commissioned it to establish His kingdom on earth. Mormons voted as a bloc, formed their own militias, and conducted business only with fellow Mormons. Hostile residents ran Mormons out of Illinois and Missouri. Mormons finally migrated to the desert of what would become the Utah Territory. The Mormon church in the 19th century taught that it was a divine duty for a Mormon male to have more than one wife if he could afford it. About one-quarter of all Mormon families were polygamous. National outrage at the practice resulted in four federal laws challenging the practice. Six American presidents actively campaigned against polygamy. By the 1850s, tensions between the federal government and the Mormon establishment escalated into the Mormon War. President James Buchanan declared martial law and sent 3,000 troops to Utah to put down what he perceived as a rebellion. Mormon leader and territorial Governor Brigham Young called upon his followers to fight federal troops. About 150 people died during the year-long war. The Mormons eventually surrendered but continued to practice polygamy.

President Abraham Lincoln signed the Morrill Anti-Bigamy Act in 1862, making polygamy a federal crime. Enforcement of the law had to wait until after the Civil War. Confident that the act was unconstitutional, Mormon leaders asked George Reynolds, a devout Mormon married to two wives, to challenge the law. Reynolds contended that his plural marriage was sanctioned by his religious faith and that the law infringed on his constitutional right to freely exercise his religion. Moreover, plural marriage posed no threat to the public. The trial judge instructed the jury not to accept religious duty as a ground for acquitting Reynolds. The jury found him guilty and sentenced him to two years in prison and a $500 fine. The territorial supreme court affirmed his conviction. Chief Justice Morrison Waite, speaking for a unanimous U.S. Supreme Court with Justice Stephen Field concurring, asked whether a religious belief could justify an "act made criminal" in federal law. While conceding that the government has no authority over religious opinions, Waite held that Congress could regulate actions that violated community norms and threatened public order. Calling a behavior "religious" does not make it immune from government regulation. Reflecting beliefs of the time, Waite argued that not only did polygamy violate the law of every state, it was also an affront to democracy itself. Democracy depended on monogamy. Polygamy leads to patriarchy, and patriarchy threatens democracy.

Reynolds served 18 months in prison. At least another 1,000 Mormon men were convicted for polygamy during the decades following *Reynolds*. Mormons ignored the federal ban on polygamy until the federal government began to confiscate church property and ordered the church dissolved. The Mormon church renounced polygamy in 1890. Utah became a state in 1898. In 1984, federal courts reaffirmed *Reynolds*'s central holding that the First Amendment does not protect polygamy. However, Supreme Court decisions in cases such as *Cantwell v. Connecticut* (1940) and *Wisconsin v. Yoder* (1972) extended some protection to sincerely based religious conduct. These cases rejected *Reynolds*'s simple distinction between belief and action. The First Amendment protects not only religious beliefs but also "the free exercise [action]" of religious beliefs. Recent cases such as *Employment Division v. Smith* (1990) have held that so long as the law does not target religious groups, the government can burden religiously motivated conduct. The debate over the government's authority to outlaw plural marriages between consenting adults continues. As the portion of the Muslim population in America grows, there may be a second confrontation between the state's secular interest in prohibiting polygamy and the Muslim doctrine of plural marriages.

Timothy J. O'Neill
Southwestern University

See Also: Bigamy/Polygamy; Religion and Crime, History of; Utah.

Further Readings
Firmage, Edwin. *Zion in the Courts*. Urbana: University of Illinois Press, 1988.
Gordon, Sarah Barringer. *The Mormon Question*. Chapel Hill: University of North Carolina Press, 2001.

Rhode Island

One of the original thirteen colonies, Rhode Island is the smallest state but, thanks to the Providence metropolitan area, is the second most densely populated. It has the distinction of being the only predominantly Catholic state in the country, as well as having the highest percentage of Portuguese Americans.

Police and Punishment
The Rhode Island Sheriff's Department, a statewide law enforcement agency, is one of the oldest law enforcement agencies in the country, having been established in 1663. Organized by county, the sheriffs are responsible for judicial and courthouse security, the transport and custody of inmates and detainees, and the execution of writs

The Pettaquamscutt Historical Society in Rhode Island bought the Washington County Jail from the state to use as its headquarters in 1960. The current stone building, constructed in 1858, replaced a wooden structure with three-foot-wide outer walls buried three feet in the ground, stone ceilings, and cell doors and outside windows made of heavy iron. It was considered more humane than the previous wooden jails that had almost no ventilation and were infested with bugs and other vermin.

and civil processes. When initially established, their responsibilities were broader, until the organization of modern police forces in Rhode Island's cities and towns in 1864 and the creation of the Rhode Island State Police. The Rhode Island State Police was founded in 1925, earlier than that of many states, and was based on the Pennsylvania State Police. While many state police organizations originated as highway patrol units and were given broader powers around the time of World War II, Rhode Island's state police were—like Pennsylvania's—intended from the start to be a highly organized statewide law enforcement agency, with captains and lieutenants paid professional wages and a superintendant, serving a five-year term, given broad powers.

The Rhode Island State Police and the Rhode Island Sheriff's Department were both originally part of the Department of Administration. In 2008, a new bill reorganized Rhode Island law enforcement, creating the Department of Public Safety, consisting of six agencies: the Rhode Island State Police, the Division of the State Fire Marshal, the 911 Uniform Emergency Telephone System, the Capitol Police, the Municipal Police Training Academy, and the Public Safety Grants Administration Office. The state police superintendent became the commissioner of the new department, with his successors to be appointed by and to serve at the pleasure of the governor.

Because of its small size, Rhode Island did not build a state prison until 1838, relying for more than 200 years on town and county jails. In the colonial era, other forms of punishment were used to avoid the cost of incarceration to the colony whenever possible, including corporal punishment, the stocks, and fines. As corporal punishment began to be phased out, incarceration was necessary more and more often. The first building used as a prison proved to be unsuitable and was replaced in 1869 by the facility that came to be known as the State Farm, in the village of Howard. It was managed by the state until 1920 and included not only the State Workhouse and House of Corrections but the State Hospital for the Insane, the State Almshouse (which became the State Infirmary after 1917), the State Prison and Providence County Jail (managed with Providence County), and two juvenile facilities, the Sockanosset School for Boys and the Oaklawn School for Girls. The State Workhouse was a mixed-sex facility until 1924, when it became the State Reformatory for Women, eventually closing in 1968. The State Prison and Providence County Jail became the Adult Correctional Institution and remains in operation, occasionally housing federal inmates.

Rhode Island was one of the first states to abolish capital punishment. While 52 executions had been conducted from 1673 to 1845, most of them in the colonial era, the legislature voted to abolish capital punishment for all crimes except murder and arson in 1844. Rhode Islanders had spent several years considering abolishing capital punishment altogether, but Amasa Sprague, the brother of former Governor William Sprague, was murdered on New Year's Eve, 1843, in a dispute over the renewal of a liquor license.

The desire to see Sprague's death avenged influenced the legislature's preserving the use of the death penalty for murder, and John Gordon was executed on Valentine's Day, 1845. Arguments over Gordon's trial and the duo's involvement in the labor movement contrasted with the perception of Sprague as a powerful industrialist persisted for years, and eventually the legislature was persuaded to abolish capital punishment entirely in 1852.

An 1872 provision reintroduced the death penalty for murders committed while already serving a life sentence, but no one was ever executed under it. A century later, the law was broadened to make mandatory the death penalty for a murder committed by an incarcerated inmate, but the Rhode Island Supreme Court ruled it unconstitutional. After several suggestions for redrafting the law, in 1984, the legislature voted to simply remove it entirely. There have been many attempts since to reinstate the death penalty, but none have succeeded.

Crime

Rhode Island is home to what is, in the 21st century, the most active organized crime family outside New York City: the Patriarca crime family, named for its third and most successful leader, Raymond "Il Patrone" Patriarca. Originating in Boston in 1916 under the leadership of Gaspare Messina, the organization that became known as the Patriarca family relocated to Providence when Il Patrone inherited the reins after Messina's successor, Phil Buccola, retired to Sicily in 1954. Patriarca owned a vending and pinball machine distributorship in Providence, from which he ran his criminal operations; associates called it "The Office." He quickly established the family's exclusive claim on criminal activities in New England and formed alliances with New York crime families in order to help him preserve his territory. Underbosses were set up in major sites outside Rhode Island, most notably Boston; it is somewhat counterintuitive to think that Mafia interests in Boston, with a metropolitan population some four times that of the entire state of Rhode Island, were controlled from a small city an hour away.

The Patriarca interests in Boston were impacted by the 1960s ramp-up of federal investigation into organized crime, spearheaded by Attorney General Robert F. Kennedy, and by the increasing strength of non-Italian gangs, especially Irish American and foreign drug cartels. While the overall power of the Patriarcas declined, the syndicate's hold on Rhode Island never weakened. Il Patrone died of a heart attack in 1984, not long after being arrested for the murder of a suspected informant. Incarcerated Jerry Angiulo, Patriarca's Boston underboss, openly sought the leadership of the family, but Il Patrone's son Raymond Patriarca, Jr., was ultimately given the reins. His leadership proved to be weak and ended in 1990 when he and 20 family leaders and associates were arrested on a variety of racketeering and other charges; a series of trials included as evidence a video of a Mafia induction ceremony. Nicholas Bianco, the Providence underboss and a former Colombo family capo, succeeded Patriarca Jr. briefly before being incarcerated as part of the same investigation.

Boston underboss Frank Salemme took over after Bianco and moved the family to Boston amid internal warfare that continued throughout the 1990s. The Providence operations remain involved in gambling, narcotics, and other endeavors, and the family has broadened its crimes to include Internet scams, credit card fraud, and securities fraud.

The crime rate in Rhode Island is lower than that of the country as a whole, about 256.6 violent crimes per 100,000 inhabitants in 2010. Slightly higher now than before the financial crisis of 2008, the crime rate has otherwise been on a general decline since the peak of 462 in 1991, which was reached after decades of gradual increase. Aggravated assault makes up more than half of the violent crimes. The murder rate (2.8 in 2010) is roughly half of the national average (5), while the commonality of rape (28) is about the same.

Bill Kte'pi
Independent Scholar

See Also: Boston, Massachusetts; Organized Crime, Contemporary; Organized Crime, History of.

Further Readings
Cianci, Buddy. *Politics and Pasta: How I Prosecuted Mobsters, Rebuilt a Dying City, Dined With Sinatra, Spent Five Years in a Federally Funded Gated Community, and Lived to Tell the Tale.* New York: Thomas Dunne Books, 2011.
Stanton, Mike. *The Prince of Providence.* New York: Random House, 2004.

Ricci v. DeStefano

Ricci v. DeStefano is a U.S. Supreme Court decision involving claims of reverse discrimination against white firemen in New Haven, Connecticut, during the promotional process. The case garnered national attention during Supreme Court Justice Sonia Sotomayor's confirmation hearings in 2009. The Supreme Court ruled that statistical racial disparities in testing do not allow employers to use race-based criteria in employment decisions. Although provisions of both Title VII of the Civil Rights Act of 1964 (prohibiting employment discrimination based on race, color, religion, sex, or national origin) and the equal protection clause of the Fourteenth Amendment could be analyzed, the court exclusively examined the Title VII argument.

The Facts
The case was filed by firemen who stated that they were denied promotion within the fire department because of their race. The petitioners, mostly white firemen, took a promotional exam in late 2003 but were not certified because of the low passing rate of minority test takers. The controversy revolved around the validity of the promotional exam. The exam process consisted of two elements: a written and an oral examination. The written exam was produced by

The white firefighters in the Ricci v. DeStefano *suit claimed they were experiencing reverse discrimination for promotions due to statistical racial disparities during promotion exams.*

a company specializing in such exams, using both industry and departmental standards. To correct for potential bias, the exam was pretested on a nationwide sample of firemen, including a large number of minorities. Additionally, the racial composition of each oral examination panel consisted of one African American, one Hispanic, and one white examiner, again by design to minimize potential bias.

The respondents (i.e., the City of New Haven, Connecticut) stated that the exam results were not certified due to the disparate impact on minority test takers, citing evidence that pass rates for whites were more than twice those of minority firemen. Disparate passing rates in conjunction with a clause within the city's charter mandating open positions be filled by one of the top three scoring candidates would have likely resulted in the promotion of disproportionately few, if any, minority candidates. The respondents claimed this showed a disparate impact and that certification of the results was inconsistent with federal law.

The case was originally filed in federal court in 2006, resulting in summary judgment in favor of the city. The petitioners appealed the decision to the Second Circuit Court of Appeals, where in 2008, summary judgment in favor of the city was issued largely on the reasoning of the lower court. The decision was appealed to the Supreme Court, which granted certiorari, largely because the case was not heard before the entire appellate court in 2009.

The Decision

In late June 2009, the Supreme Court, in a 5–4 decision, ruled in favor of the petitioners. The ruling issued by the court contains two important holdings. First, the city's decision to not certify the exam results because whites performed better than minorities without additional reasons violated Title VII. Secondly, the court held that the actions of the city could be justifiable if strong evidence showed the action was taken to avoid disparate impact liability. The city had stated that certifying the results would violate the rights of minority firemen; however, this evidence was insufficient because the court believe any legal actions against the certification would have likely been unsuccessful. The court further reasoned that the city could have taken any steps to minimize disparate impact prior to administration of the promotional exam; however, after the exam was administered, the city was obligated to certify the results unless disparate impact could be shown.

This case provides little guidance to lower courts with similar cases. The Supreme Court established the standard of avoiding disparate impact liability; however, this standard was never clearly defined. Some courts have used this case to eliminate the use of voluntary affirmative action plans by employers. Although the Supreme Court did not consider the petitioners' equal protection claims, looming questions remain as to the constitutionality of Title VII under the Fourteenth Amendment. This point was raised in a concurring opinion and may force this issue to be revisited in the future.

Jon Maskaly
University of South Florida

See Also: Bill of Rights; Civil Rights Laws; Equality, Concept of.

Further Readings
DeAngelo, Kathy. "Recent Development: Title VII's Conflicting 'Twin Pillars' in *Ricci v. DeStefano*, 129 S. Ct. 2658." *Harvard Journal of Law and Public Policy* (Winter 2010).
Klein, Lauren. "*Ricci v. DeStefano*: 'Fanning the Flames' of Reverse Discrimination in Civil Service Selection." *Duke Journal of Constitutional Law and Public Policy Sidebar*, v.4 (2009).
Phillips, Edward G. "The Law at Work: Where There's Smoke But No Fire: *Ricci V. DeStefano* Holds Statistical Disparities Cannot Justify Race-Based Employment Decisions." *Tennessee Bar Journal* (October 2009).
Ricci v. DeStefano, 129 S. Ct. 2658 (2009).

Riots

Riots are inherently political, not only in the moment of their eruption but also in the social drama that follows as interested parties contest conflicting interpretations of the events. Some street battles that resemble riots superficially are not typically considered riots at all, in part because dominant narratives have assigned to them alternate political definitions, for example, as uprisings, insurrections, rebellions, revolts, or revolutions. Ordinarily, what comes to mind when thinking of riots in the United States are race riots from the time of Reconstruction through the civil rights era, although the history of riots show more diverse motivations. In the contemporary scene, riots have become hypermedia events, and their representations circulate around the world through mass communication outlets, saturating public attention.

Unlike crimes that are defined by a specific act, the legal definition of a riot requires that a general set of conditions met. One person cannot be a riot; commonly, the minimum required for a riot is three people, although that number has changed with time. As the Bill of Rights protects freedom of assembly and freedom of association, there has to be some violent or threatening quality in the collective behavior of the group, transforming its legal status to that of an "unlawful assembly." What makes a riot distinct from a peaceable assembly is that it is comprised of warring parties that are working in concert to achieve some objective. This is fundamentally different from a group, which by happenstance come to blows, resulting in the destruction of property. It also underscores the inherently political subtext to rioting. Rioters take sides with particular factions, an act that is in itself a public declaration of identity. All riots in American history, and even those violent conflicts given other labels and assigned other meanings are, in addition to destructive and dangerous, also performances of collective identity.

Rioting poses a real or perceived threat of bodily harm or loss of property. Further, throughout history, it has been interpreted as an explicitly moral threat with judgment rendered on riot participants in the public sphere. An etymology of the word *riot* reveals that the moral evaluative function of labeling rioters as such is rooted in the word's older uses. From this moralizing framework, rioters are considered the same as a mob—a seething mass of people and driven by a "mob mentality." The mob, in its behavior, acts to the detriment of others, but also against its own best interests morally. Included among these archaic meanings of *riot* is the sense of acting in an unrestrained and wanton manner, suggestive of individuals who have no self-control or compassion for the well being of others. Clamor, din, and brawl are all synonyms of this form of rioting. It is a state of reckless impulsiveness. In a similar vein, *to riot* has meant to indulge in an excess of luxury, bringing to mind a sinful display of gluttony. Carousal and excess are synonymous with this sense of *riot*; New Orleans during Mardi Gras is a modern day corollary. In both senses, rioters are perceived as deriving pleasure and personal gain from irresponsibility at the expense of others, and this is their principal moral flaw.

Not everyone perceives rioters as morally compromised; some who are sympathetic with the combatants may hold them in high esteem. A different terminology is used by this group who reject the label *riot* because of its stigma in favor of a positive moral evaluation of their actions conveyed by words such as *rebellion*. Objectively, the many violent conflicts not ordinarily considered riots—such as rebellions—do share many of the same characteristics as riots, both physically and legally, if not symbolically.

Early-American Riots

Many instances of protest and armed conflict against the state resemble rioting in important ways. Consider the many colonial uprisings against the British in the run-up to the Revolutionary War, such as the Stamp Act Protests of 1765, which included masses of people in the street, opposing groups taking sides, and the illegal destruction of property. However, these actions are now seen as patriotic acts of rebellion, not as illegal acts resulting in loss of property. From the point of view of the colonial British authorities, something like the Boston Tea Party of 1773, only one instance in a string of collective uprisings around Boston in the late 18th century, was illegal rioting, but from the American present, these events are seen as a formative moment for the nation and are positively evaluated. Similarly, from the colonial era through the Civil War, there were dozens of slave revolts, such as Nat Turner's Slave Rebellion in 1831, which present many of the same outward appearances of a riot. Slave revolts were illegal, resulting in severe retaliation by property owners

British authorities considered the Boston Tea Party, when colonists dumped British tea into the Boston Harbor in protest of that government's monopoly on tea and its tax on tea from other sources, an illegal riot, rather than a protest.

and the state against African slaves. Today, they are more likely to be read as righteous examples of the oppressed rising up against their oppressors.

The difference between a planned uprising or protest, and a seemingly spontaneous riot, are more apparent than real. A riot appears to be spontaneous primarily from the point of view of those in positions of authority, whereas for the riot participants, whatever event that may have incited their actions may be taken as only the latest event in a long line of grievances that precede the riot. Rebellions and riots are congruent in the ways that they produce meanings, contingent upon historical and cultural contexts, through collective violence.

On the theme of racial violence, some lynchings exhibited many of the same features as riots on the occasions when the lynching party turned against an entire minority community. Lynching was part of a regime of fear and retaliation against minority targets for real or imagined crimes of symbolic importance. These were extrajudicial executions carried out against African slaves from colonial times through the early republic, and against African Americans from Reconstruction through the civil rights era, although there are modern corollaries. Lynching and other acts of collective violence were also carried out against other racial minorities, most notably in the American west against the Chinese in the 19th century.

Some labor strikes that resulted in armed conflict against strikebreakers or police show some of the same qualities as riots. From miners in Colorado and West Virginia to the Teamsters and manufacturing unions of the midwest and east coast to the Industrial Workers of the World (IWW) protests along the west coast, there were numerous instances when peaceful protest broke down into violence, when hired goons with weapons took on the strikers, or where state authorities intervened with an excessive show of force. The Battle of Matewan in 1920 epitomizes this level of conflict with violent factions warring against the state over labor rights.

Returning now to what might be thought of as genuine riots, there are many different types of conflicts and motivations to consider. Some of the worst riots of the early republic fell along class lines as the exploited took to the streets, directing their anger against the rich. This was the case in the Baltimore Bank Riot of 1835, when thousands of citizens outraged by financial mismanagement at the Union Bank of Maryland ransacked the homes of the privileged and burned their possessions. The Anti-Rent War in 1839 was a similar case of the underclass revolting against the wealthy when tenant farmers in the Hudson Valley rose up against their landlords.

The Anti-Draft Riots of 1863 in New York City were part of widespread resistance to the Civil War in the northern states, but were far more violent and greater in scope than any other U.S. uprising before or since. As potential draftees into the Union Army, working-class men resented that the wealthy could opt out of the conscription lottery by paying a $300 commutation fee, and Irish immigrants, already in direct competition with blacks for the lowest-paying jobs in the city, were irate at being forced to go to war to fight to free the slaves. Shortly after the names of the draftees were drawn, angry citizens took to the streets—more than 50,000 individuals by some accounts—driving back the police and militias. Some blacks were lynched and Protestant churches were burned, while police stations and the mayor's residence, symbols of the state, were also targeted.

Vigilante mobs can be the perpetrators of rioting violence when citizens feel that the criminal justice system has failed and it is necessary to take matters into their own hands. Vigilantism may overlap with lynching in some contexts and there is a long and proud tradition of vigilante justice in the American west, but the Cincinnati Courthouse Riots of 1884 were an example of how this can turn into a citywide conflagration. Following the sentencing of a murder case that was seen as too lenient, an angry crowd attempted to steal the prisoner from his cell and ended up destroying the city courthouse.

There have been many anti-immigrant riots in American history, most notably against Germans, Irish, Catholics, and Chinese. A slew of anti-immigrant riots are attributed to the Know-Nothings, a splinter group of the Whig Party who advocated American nativism. From 1855 to 1858, there were riots in numerous cities, all attributed to the Know-Nothings. The Orange Riots, which took place in Manhattan in 1870 and 1871, pitted Protestant Irish against Catholic Irish. Along the west coast, a string of riots directed against Chinese immigrant communities commenced in 1871 with the Chinese Massacre in Los Angeles and continued sporadically through the Seattle riot of 1886.

Civil Rights Riots

Riots directed against blacks are a formative part of American history, and one of the most consequential was the Pulaski, Tennessee, riots in 1866, which marked the birth of the Ku Klux Klan. After the U.S. Supreme Court decided *Plessy v. Ferguson*, establishing the constitutionality of racial segregation, violence directed against African Americans continued. A cluster of incidents in 1919 are known as the Red Summer Riots, in which whites attacked black communities in dozens of cities across the United States. These riots were tied to labor disputes and black migration into industrializing areas during World War I. Perhaps the best-known race riot of this era took place in Tulsa, Oklahoma, in 1921, when whites burned more than 1,200 African American homes in what was characterized then as a "Negro uprising."

The Harlem Riots of 1935 signify a transformation of the structure of American racial violence. An otherwise ordinary encounter between an employee at a five-and-dime store and a would-be shoplifter proved the catalyst for a community protest outside the store after a rumor circulated that the shoplifter had been beaten. The predominantly black crowd did not turn its violence against white individuals per se, but rather they battled against the police and engaged in the destruction of white-owned property as businesses were looted and burned.

The different racial and ethnic composition of the American west led to different frictions between the dominant group and minorities. In Los Angeles, the Zoot Suit Riots occurred in 1943, in which white sailors and Marines targeted Mexican Americans, recognizable based on their distinctive choice of clothing. These riots took place over several days and were echoed by sympathetic attacks across the United States.

After the Supreme Court decided *Brown v. Board of Education* in 1954 and put an end to the era of "separate but equal," American society became embroiled in a long civil rights movement. During this time, mass protests led by African Americans, but comprised of people from all backgrounds, were, time and again, subject to extraordinary displays of force from state authorities. From 1966 to 1971, there were scores of riots in cities large and small across the nation that were either racially motivated or linked to protest of the war in Vietnam. A symbolic starting point for all this was the Watts Riots of 1965, which lasted six days and resulted in 34 deaths and more than 3,000 arrests. The assassination of Dr. Martin Luther King, Jr., on April 4, 1968, sparked riots in many American cities. In contrast to historical and continuing collective violence of whites against blacks, some of these events are, like the Harlem Riots of 1935, distinguished by black destruction of white property or symbols of the state.

Riots in the Late 20th Century

The late 1960s and early 1970s were also a time of widespread political protest and civil disobedience. The 1968 Democratic National Convention in Chicago is probably the best known of these riots. A political protest led in part by the Youth International Party escalated to six days of violence after the shooting death of a young man at the hands of Chicago police. The 1969 Stonewall Riot in Greenwich Village, New York, was a symbolic starting point for the gay rights movement. The Stonewall Inn, a bar that catered to the gay community, was frequently raided by police, who arrested any men dressed as women. The riot began one night when the 200 patrons of the establishment collectively resisted and repelled law enforcement. At Kent State University in Kent, Ohio, a student protest of the American invasion of Cambodia devolved into a melee in which the Ohio National Guard fired on the students, killing four. This resulted in a nationwide student strike and galvanized public sentiment among youth against the role of the United States in Vietnam.

The Attica prison riot took place in 1971, when prisoners seized control of the facility, demanding better conditions; 39 people died over the course of several days of fighting. The American Indian Movement took control of the town of Wounded Knee, South Dakota, in 1973, and fought U.S. marshals, the Federal Bureau of Investigation (FBI), and other law enforcement officials in a siege that lasted 71 days. This was one of many violent political protests associated with the Red Power movement. These and many other examples from the era illustrate the blurred boundaries separating planned protest from spontaneous riot, especially when state agents used excessive force against an assembly of citizens.

In 1992, Los Angeles erupted in riot once again, the worst conflict since the 1965 Watts Riots, this time sparked by the acquittal of four white police officers who were videotaped beating a black motorist, Rodney King. This situation was unique in that as soon as the riot broke out, local and national television news cameras were on the scene broadcasting events as they happened. Aerial

The 1964 fatal shooting of 15-year-old James Powell by a police officer who said the boy lunged at him with a knife spurred a riot through Harlem streets. Angry residents march while displaying photographs of the New York Police Department lieutenant. Civic action continued in New York City for five days: stores were looted and there were violent clashes between police and the public.

footage was provided by helicopter, and coverage of the six-day riot was continuous. The hyperreal nature of this media-saturated event lent the riots a cultural cachet, and representations of the Los Angeles riots soon permeated popular culture in music, film, and television.

In Seattle at the 1999 meeting of the World Trade Organization (WTO), planned antiglobalization protests captured national attention. Police quickly turned on the demonstrators, using tear gas, pepper spray, and rubber bullets to turn back the crowd. Some retaliated against this suppression by breaking store windows, burning dumpsters, and vandalizing property. This conflict set the tone for future WTO meetings, which are now well known for their tight security.

The Study of Riots
The political sensitivity of labeling an event a "riot" illustrates the degree to which the aftermath of the conflagration necessitates a public relations strategy on the part of governments. Accordingly, it is not unusual for persons in positions of authority to avoid the word *riot* altogether. There is a stigma attached to rioting that many communities may wish to avoid. For example, city leaders may be concerned that riots reflect poorly on the city's image and that negative perceptions could be detrimental to perceptions of their effectiveness as leaders, or that capital will flee the area, resulting in a loss of economic growth. Similar concerns may be reflected in local news coverage of riots when, either swayed by pressure from outside forces or similarly invested in maintaining a public front, the word is avoided. Euphemisms such as "disturbance" or "unrest" diminish the conflict and make it seem less substantial than it really is. Riots may also be described metonymically, as in "the fires" or "the violence," which lends a vivid description of the scene, but successfully ignores the political demands at the heart of the conflict and avoid the stigma of "riot." In all cases, riots may be viewed as social dramas. They illustrate the sudden emergence of a neglected population demanding visibility, and mainstream society, often caught off guard, must acknowledge their presence.

In terms of disciplinary considerations, the body of literature addressing riotous behavior is interdisciplinary, touching on history, sociology, psychology, political science, and journalism. A central debate in scholarly circles has been interpreting the meaning of collective violence, including riotous action. Gustave Le Bon's argument that crowds are essentially unthinking and directed only by a "mob mentality" dominated the literature in the early 20th century, until social historians such as George Rudé and others ushered in a new paradigm that rioting behavior of large groups could be read as rational. Paul Gilje's comprehensive work examines collective violence in the United States in context of its democratic political system, identifying rioting as a persistent cultural trait in America. Likewise, David Grimstead focuses on the question of the political consequences of collective violence in American society, specifically, the differing responses of governmental authorities in the north and south to abolitionist and antiabolitionist revolts. This theme of crowd action as having some larger political meaning or effect is continued in the work of Jack Tager, whose scope concerns patterns of social violence in Boston, Massachusetts, from the early Republic through the 1970s.

Sociological literature on riots in the United States was mostly written in the late 1960s and early 1970s, but there is also a significant amount written about the Los Angeles riot of 1992. A good deal of this material is applied research directed at municipal officials who are particularly concerned with managing a riot, so that the number of people injured and the amount of property damaged can be minimized quickly. Bruce Porter and Marvin Dunn, writing on the Liberty City riots of Miami in 1980, indentified three types of rioters who elected to participate in the riot at different times relative to different social factors.

Young males were most likely to be the earliest participants, risking arrest in exchange for the possibility of fun, or even profit. Experienced criminals tended to wait until they felt that police could not interfere with their plans to exploit the opportunity. The last to enter the fray, the most cautious group, were older, stable, and without criminal backgrounds. These participants proceeded only once looting appeared to be normal and police appeared to be unable to secure calm. Writing on the role of the state in the Los Angeles riots of 1992, Bert Useem argues that the actions of police during a riot are more complicated than it may seem. He describes two basic strategies available to state authorities. A diplomatic strategy relies on convincing participants that rioting is not in their best interest. A force-based strategy relies on authorities attempting to physically inhibit participant movements. Each strategy is limited in its own way. A massive show of force may antagonize rioters and undermine any future diplomatic efforts, while the use of diplomacy, should it prove ineffective, can delay the state's ability to respond with force in a timely manner.

Matthew D. Thompson
Old Dominion University

See Also: 1600 to 1776 Primary Documents; 1777 to 1800 Primary Documents; 1801 to 1850 Primary Documents; 1851 to 1900 Primary Documents; King, Rodney; Ku Klux Klan; Lynchings; Strikes.

Further Readings
Gilje, Paul. *Rioting in America*. Bloomington: Indiana University Press, 1996.
Grimsted, David. *American Mobbing, 1828–1861: Toward Civil War*. New York: Oxford University Press, 1998.
Le Bon, G. *The Crowd: A Study of the Popular Mind* [1895]. Mineola, NY: Dover Publications, 2002.
Porter, Bruce and Marvin Dunn. *The Miami Riot of 1980: Crossing the Bounds*. Lexington, MA: Lexington Books, 1984.
Rude, George. *The Crowd in the French Revolution*. New York: Oxford University Press, 1959.
Turner, Victor. *Dramas, Fields, and Metaphors*. Ithaca, NY: Cornell University Press, 1974.
Useem, Bert. "The State and Collective Disorders: The Los Angeles Riot/Protest of April 1992." *Social Forces*, v.76/2 (1997).

Robbery, Contemporary

Robbery has historically been deemed one of the basic common law felonies, punishable by death. The common law elements of robbery are (1) a person taking another's personal property of value, (2) from the person's possession or presence, (3) by force or by placing the person in fear, and (4) with the intent to permanently deprive the other person of that property. Many modern robbery statutes require proof of the same legal elements. Robbery is a crime throughout the United States and is subject to extensive punishment in prison. The Federal Bureau of Investigation (FBI) and the Uniform Crime Reporting (UCR) program have a short definition of robbery. The UCR defines robbery as "The taking or attempting to take anything of value from the care, custody, or control of a person or persons by force or threat of force or violence and/or putting the victim(s) in fear."

Robbery Patterns

Some common robbery patterns include bank robberies, carjacking, home invasions, taxicab robberies, automated teller machine robberies, convenience store robberies, and truck hijacking. The UCR's analysis of robbery types includes (1) street/highway: 42.8 percent, (2) bank: 2.2 percent, (3) gas or service station: 2.4 percent, (4) convenience store: 5.4 percent, (5) commercial house: 13.7 percent, (6) residence: 16.9 percent, and (7) miscellaneous: 16.6 percent.

A bank robber shouted, "Everyone down on the ground; this won't take long, folks!" His accomplices, wearing celebrity masks, jumped over kneeling bank tellers filling duffle bags with money. One robber, wearing a stopwatch around his neck, caught the attention of law enforcement investigators, thus earning them the nickname the Stopwatch Gang. The Stopwatch Gang committed their robberies in less than two minutes and in some cases in as little as 90 seconds. This is an example of a planned operation that is designed to produce maximum profits, avoid the use of force, and reduce the possibility of apprehension. Three team members executed their robberies with expert reconnaissance, planning, and timing. The Stopwatch Gang robbed more than 100 banks in Canada and the United States, for a total net of $15 million.

Typical armed robbers are not meticulous planners with high-profile targets. The Stopwatch Gang and the Tilley Bandit, who was known for his distinctive hat and was responsible for 17 bank robberies, represent special exceptions. The Tilley Bandit was an unemployed businessman with a master's degree who planned his robberies

A thief can break into a car using a thin strip of metal known as a Slim Jim within seconds. The overall rate of auto theft is reported to have dropped 7.2 percent during 2010, declining from a total of 794,616 vehicles stolen in 2009.

and surveillance for the approach of police patrol officers.

Opportunistic street robberies prevail because offenders have the motivation and opportunities to target victims. Street robberies persist because the robbers understand the terrain, neighborhood, and predictable victim patterns. This ambush style of robbery involves little planning and can occur because of the need for the money and victim vulnerability. The amount of money acquired is rather limited; therefore, street robberies require frequent scores to reap a financial return. A victim is more likely to encounter a single robber rather than a group of offenders. In most cases, the robber will be armed with weapons or will execute a physical attack; these strong-armed robberies are commonly referred to as "muggings." Robbers ambush rapidly, assault the victim to possible unconsciousness, then seize cash, jewelry, wallets, and credit cards.

Motivation and Violence Factor

Someone asked Willie Sutton, the famous bank robber and escape artist, "Why do you rob banks?" Sutton's response: "That's where the money is." Victims are subject to attack because of their vulnerability and their appearance of wealth. Robbers have a certain kind of victims in mind. These criminals target victims who carry a considerable amount of cash and those wearing expensive jewelry. Opportunistic robbers select victims or business targets based on a brief planning strategy. Individuals who appear to present a challenge are avoided. These robbers isolate their victim, thereby ensuring compliance. The exceptions to basic planning and strategies are drug and alcohol abusers, who are generally more careless and vulnerable to apprehension and prosecution.

Victims who frustrate the robber's monetary motivation are more likely to become the recipients of physical violence or death. However, in more than 80 percent of the robbery cases in which force takes place, the offender initiated the attack without victim resistance. In many cases, the victim will be beaten, disfigured, or killed simply because of the robber's need for violence. Assaults occur frequently if the robber is under the influence of alcohol or drugs. Drug use—especially of cocaine or amphetamines—can serve as a significant violence multiplier.

with expert precision. Professional bank robbers have distinctive patterns that include unique signature clues that differentiate their crimes. The more general robbery patterns comprise opportunists who prey on soft targets.

Even the infamous Bonnie and Clyde do not compare to these exceptional bank robbers; they were opportunist bank robbers. Opportunist-selected raid robberies transpire in rapid succession after token informal planning. The robbery locations are preselected; possible routes of approach and escape receive minimal planning. The financial return is low to moderate. For example, several team robberies might unfold in rapid succession. Occasionally, there may be a backup robber or additional team members who are responsible for covering the first offender

Robbery is a high-profile violent crime that instills considerable fear in the public and in the many victims of violence. The opportunity for violence is higher because of the use of force during victim/robber confrontations. The violence may include assault and battery with possible recovery, disabling injuries, or even death.

FBI Statistics

- Nationwide in 2009, there were an estimated 408,217 robberies.
- The estimated number of robberies decreased from the 2008 and the 2005 estimates—8 percent and 2.2 percent, respectively. However, the 2009 robbery estimate increased slightly from the 2000 number.
- The 2009 estimated robbery rate of 133 per 100,000 inhabitants reflected a decrease of 8.8 percent compared with the 2008 rate.
- An estimated $508 million in losses were attributed to robberies in 2009.
- The average dollar value of property stolen per reported robbery was $1,244. The highest average dollar loss was for banks, which lost $4,029 per offense.
- Firearms were used in 42.6 percent of the robberies for which the UCR received additional information in 2009. Strong-arm tactics were used in 41.1 percent of the total number of robberies; knives and cutting instruments were used in 7.7 percent; and other dangerous weapons were used in 8.7 percent of robberies in 2009.

Methods of Investigation

Strategic and tactical intelligence products strive for real-time intelligence. Crime and pattern analysis serve the purpose of trying to interrupt robbery offenses. The modus operandi (MO) system report serves as the foundation for robbery analysis. Behavioral science is an excellent tool of crime analysis. It allows investigators to plan for future intervention and prevention strategies. Crime analysis computer software and technology assist in the collection and statistical analysis of burglary data.

The MO report collects criminal intelligence and describes all known factors concerning the robbery that make up the sum total of the series. The basic master clue to every crime is the general theory or particular method pursued in the commission of the crime. The MO reporting system has two basic objectives: (1) the early identification of unknown offenders before arrest and (2) the clearing of all related cases after the arrest of the responsible offender. Crime analysis should assist in the assignment of preventive patrols and surveillance to detect robberies in progress.

MO information includes type of robbery, time (day and hour), method of attack (threatened or observable weapon), object or property sought, number of robberies, voice and words of the robber, and vehicle description. MO strategies include the robbery attack type, object of attack, and the special features of the method or trademark. For example, the robber pointed a chrome-plated, .45-caliber automatic at the victim. The trademark helps individualize and link related cases to a specific offender pattern.

Robberies may include a series of cases that are signature clue related and outside the necessary requirements to accomplish the crime. These represent psychological behaviors that the offender must complete to feel satisfied—the emotional and compulsive behaviors that link robbery cases to a particular robber. For example, the robber requires victims to undress to expose certain body parts for the purpose of humiliation or psychological gain. Robber hostility may serve as a trademark clue to identify and link certain cases. The force or assault may exceed the amount necessary to accomplish the robbery. Pistol whipping or shooting the victim after securing his/her valuables is a useful indicator of robber personality. Another case linkage trademark clue might move in the opposite direction. For example, thanking the bank teller for cooperation.

Law enforcement agencies maintain current information on known offenders. Known offender files and mug shot files are helpful in the investigative process. Offender files are divided into known active and inactive files. The files contain the suspect's description, MO, and summary of the suspect's criminal record. Mug shots, known offender files, and criminal suspect descriptions are the primary means for investigators to review potential robbery suspects. Computer programs like Inter-Quest and FACES may help develop the robber's physical and facial description for the victim identification of the suspect(s). This computer software is most helpful when the victim is not able to identify the existing mug shot photographs.

Conclusion

Professional bank robbers have distinctive patterns that include unique signature clues in their crimes. The Stopwatch Gang thought they planned the perfect crimes; however, their perfection became a unique modus operandi (MO) and trademark. Their three-person team's distinctive serial robbery pattern and trademark ultimately led to their detection and arrest. Professional robbers do not represent the typical robber case. They may be initially quite successful; however, their planned bank robbery forecasts eventually lead to imperfections and vulnerabilities. Their high-profile targets and robbery patterns are subject to crime analysis and law enforcement tactical strategies.

Crime analysis supports field operations through planning strategies and investigative personnel deployment. The general robbery pattern consists of opportunists who prey on soft targets. Many of these robberies are spontaneous, and limited contact between victim and robber often results in a low arrest clearance rate. The MO crime analysis system may help suppress robberies through early intervention based on corrective action through specific field countermeasures. Police surveillance and decoy operations offer some of the best strategies to prevent street robberies.

Thomas E. Baker
University of Scranton

See Also: 1921 to 1940 Primary Documents; 1941 to 1960 Primary Documents; 1961 to 1980 Primary Documents; 1981 to 2000 Primary Documents; Crime and Arrest Statistics Analysis; Crime in America, Distribution; Crime in America, Types; Guns and Violent Crime; Robbery, History of; Robbery, Sociology of.

Further Readings

Baker, Thomas, E. *Introductory Criminal Analysis: Crime Prevention and Intervention Strategies.* Upper Saddle River, NJ: Pearson/Prentice Hall, 2005.

Federal Bureau of Investigation. *Uniform Crime Reporting (UCR) Program, Crime in the United States.* Washington, DC: U.S. Department of Justice, 2010.

Swanson, Charles, R., Neil Chameleon, Leonard Territo, and Robert Taylor. *Criminal Investigation,* 10th ed. New York: McGraw-Hill, 2010.

Robbery, History of

Robbery involves illegally removing property from another person or organization, often using force or intimidation. Robbery has changed in nature throughout history because of the changing nature of goods that are available to be robbed, the rise in capacity of the state to deal with the robbery, and the motivations of the robber. Increasingly, robbery has become a small-scale but widespread issue fueled by the desire to obtain cash to meet an addiction. This kind of crime is associated with urban rather than rural or suburban areas, where social solidarity and higher levels of police coverage make the threat of robbery comparatively remote.

Bank Robberies

In the early days of American banks, deposits were protected by lock and key only, and the most likely means of gaining access was to get a replica key or to suborn the locksmith in one form or another. This was the case for the first such robbery, which took place in Philadelphia in 1798 at the Bank of Pennsylvania, as a result of which suspicion was wrongly placed on locksmith Patrick Lyon, who was victimized by a combination of bank executives and state authorities who banded together to provide the lesson that such crimes would not be tolerated. Lyon was eventually able to clear his name and identify the guilty parties, who had found an alternative means to obtain insider status. Even when dynamite and guns have replaced the insider access, ruling authorities have remained eager to procure arrests and imprisonment of perpetrators of crimes, and in some cases the burden of proof was scarcely satisfied. Still, notorious criminal gangs made careers from violent robberies, such as the Reno Brothers Gang (also active on the railroad), the James Brothers Gang (most active 1866–76) and Henry

Starr, who was the first man known to use a (stolen) car to make his getaway.

Bank robberies have also been used by radical groups as a means of gaining sensationalized coverage of their actions and causes, to obtain money to fund their further activities, and to strike a perhaps symbolic blow against the capitalist system. The most infamous of these robberies took place in 1974 at Hibernia Bank in San Francisco and was perpetrated by the Symbionese Liberation Army and included the kidnapped but machine gun–wielding heiress, Patty Hearst, who was a victim of Stockholm syndrome. Hearst was subsequently captured and in due course was pardoned.

Train Robberies

The development of the railroad system represented in a quite real sense the extension of capitalist control of the continental United States, and the trains that used them occasionally carried large amounts of cash or other valuable items. This made the train system an attractive target for robberies and also made the prevention of such crimes, or at least the tracking down and prosecution of perpetrators, a significantly important undertaking for the state to complete. One result of this is that high-profile robberies gave rise to very well-known criminals, including Jesse James and Butch Cassidy, who were pursued by not just the state authorities but by additional private detectives, including Pinkerton men, who might be hired. Police and private detectives were often hired on the basis that they could keep part of any loot recovered from suspected criminals, which intensified conflicts between them. Victims, whether individuals or organizations, might have to satisfy themselves with just a portion of what was recovered.

Since trains are large and powerful machines, it requires quite serious measures to make them

The engineer of a Kansas Pacific train, which held a Wells Fargo safe, being held at gunpoint in 1874 by the Jesse James gang. The gang only robbed train passengers two times because James was mainly interested in safes carried in express or baggage cars, giving his gang a type of "Robin Hood" perception, where only the wealthy were targeted.

stop and to force the crew to provide access. This might have been effected by creating a blockade on the track or by digging up a section of the track or using some other means to force the train to stop peremptorily. This involved considerable risk to the train drivers, crew, and any passengers, and, indeed, to the criminals who might get too close to a derailed engine or carriage. Since guards of money or valuable items were almost certainly armed, then the criminal gang (it is difficult to imagine one individual person holding up a train in the way that highwaymen would hold up horse-drawn carriages) would also necessarily be armed, and violence was that much more likely. These measures made the perception of the robbery a much more serious offense and so sentences and punishments were that much harsher. Nevertheless, stakes were often high as stagecoach robberies, beginning with "Tom Bell" (Thomas J. Hodges) in 1856, were often motivated by the discovery of gold or other precious minerals and their transportation in one direction with payroll payments moving in the opposite direction through mostly rough, partly mapped, and unpoliced territory. Stagecoach robberies continued into the 20th century.

Train robberies declined in importance because of the rise in importance of automobiles and airplanes in long-distance communication and the increased use of electronic transfers of money. The last reported train robbery took place in 1963, although acts of robbery on or around a train have continued.

Mugging

Mugging is a form of robbery that takes place in a public space, usually a city street but any public area may be used, and may involve the use of violence to disable the victim prior to removing her or his possessions. In other cases, a threat of violence is used or an item is simply snatched, and the mugger aims to make an immediate escape. An international fear of garroting erupted in the 1850s and 1860s, in the aftermath of the revolutionary war of 1848 and emergence of the bomb-wielding anarchist, and this sparked a street-level arms war of knuckle-dusters and belt buckle pistols. This helped cement in the public mind the connection between street robbery and possible deadly violence.

Mugging regularly involves vulnerable people unlikely or unwilling to be able to respond effectively. Women's handbags, for example, are a common item of theft in this way, since they are comparatively small, likely to contain valuable items, and the victims will be unlikely to challenge a male mugger. When mugging involves the use of cars, then it is termed *carjacking*. As people have generally become richer and, especially, as they are more likely to carry around small but expensive and relatively anonymous products such as mobile telephones and computers, the motivation to commit mugging for financial gain has increased. However, depending on the environment concerned, the definition of what represents a valuable item can vary considerably. There are numerous anecdotes, many no doubt apocryphal, of muggings that have taken place for the sake of a pair of basketball shoes, often derived from 1970s New York, described as the "mugging center of the world." It is no coincidence that mugging is so commonly associated with inner-city locations and with gang activities that are also correlated with young ethnic-minority men. This is not necessarily an example of straightforward racism but part of a wider attempt to portray the inner-city areas as dangerous and ungovernable and, hence, to justify the use of zero tolerance policies, three-strike sentencing policies, and other draconian approaches. Cities have become increasingly subject to this kind of law enforcement regime as the wealthier citizens have moved out to suburban areas or, as in the case of New Orleans, quite literally to the more desirable higher ground. In reality, of course, mugging has taken place throughout the history of human society.

Shoplifting

Shoplifting involves stealing items from shops and can be conducted by both staff and customers. When conducted by staff, shoplifting is usually motivated by financial gain or by some measure of disaffection with the job. When conducted by others, it might be simply motivated by desire to obtain something that could not otherwise be afforded or that could be exchanged for cash but might also be motivated by a form of rite of passage (or hazing) among young people or some other psychological need. There is a particular form of desire to commit shoplifting by wealthy women, of a variety of ages. This was referred to as "kleptomania" in the 19th century and was the preserve of wealthy middle-aged women and hence forgivable, although some professional thieves also played upon the issue. That this type of theft can stem from a psychological need is suggested by the fact that the women involved have little or no interest at all in the items that are in fact stolen. However, it has also been argued that the distinction in the ways and reasons in which people shoplift depends on the way they are described and perceived. Hence, if poor people are involved, it is because they are giving way to vicious inclinations, but if they are from the wealthier classes, then it is a case of teenaged high spirits or, as mentioned, psychological kleptomania among the wealthy. Sometimes, causes are impossible to know. Lizzie Borden, acquitted of axe murders, was accused of shoplifting in 1897, for example. Shopkeepers and security can differentiate between "boosters," who are career criminals, and "snitches," who act in the same manner as serial criminals but are otherwise law-abiding citizens.

Since a great deal of shoplifting appears to be undetected or unreported, to some extent because shop owners are reluctant to allow society to know too much of the reality of their trade, comprehensive evidence is not available.

Looting

Looting involves theft or robbery in the midst of a general outbreak of disorder, perhaps as a result of a riot or in the wake of a natural disaster. Widespread looting took place in Los Angeles as part of the so-called Rodney King riots (or uprising), which was sparked by a court decision exonerating white police officers of the beating of a black man (King), despite video evidence to the contrary. This sparked outrage among many minority groups who felt themselves to be unfairly treated by the state and who responded in part by stealing goods that they would not otherwise have been able to afford but that were flaunted in front of their eyes on a daily basis as evidence of their lack of economic empowerment. This kind of looting has been seen in numerous cities in U.S. history and represents rage and frustration with inequality as much as any desire to commit theft. Nevertheless, looting has been met with swift and violent response by the state as it represents a threat not just to public order but to the privileges of the property-owning classes. Some elements of the popular media were complicit in making the link in the public eye between black men and incipient desire for lawless rioting and theft. Consequently, after New Orleans was struck by Hurricane Katrina and thousands of people were desperately searching for food and water to survive, there were outbreaks of racially motivated shootings of black men.

Looting is a term that has also been used to describe the removal of Native American remains from their resting places for scientific analysis or for display elsewhere. This was previously considered acceptable behavior by scientists and archaeologists in what was considered effectively to be "empty land" prior to settlement and has now become seen as an aspect of colonization. The practice is now regulated by the 1990 Native American Graves Protection and Repatriation Act. However, some issues remain unresolved.

Computer Crime

In recent years, some elements of computer-mediated (or Internet) crime have become new forms of theft. Although most such crime is probably best described as fraud, in that it inspires people to part with money under false pretenses, the practice of identity theft and subsequent extraction of savings from banks accounts is certainly a case of robbery. Additionally, computer-based infrastructure conduits have also become increasingly popular for people wishing to steal electronically denominated assets from their rightful owners through hacking into the system. This kind of crime is new in that it can be conducted without respect for physical geography but from nearly any point on earth, and this not only makes finding the perpetrators more difficult but also raises issues of jurisdiction and the ability to commit policing actions on a transborder basis.

Perpetrators and Victims

The type of robbery involved determines the nature of the perpetrator to a certain extent. For example, train robbery or bank robbery almost certainly requires a considerable degree of planning and conspiring and the involvement of a number of people over the course of time. By contrast,

After Hurricane Katrina hit New Orleans in 2005, businesses tried to open as soon as possible to serve a desperate community but looting was rampant as residents sought food and water from any possible source. This food store on Magazine Street displayed a makeshift sign directing shoppers to their location while warning that "Looters Will Be Shot."

house burglary or shoplifting may be an entirely opportunistic form of crime. However, since more opportunities for robbery occur in an urban rather a rural environment, this type of crime tends to be more prevalent in urban settings. This in turn has an impact on the nature of victims and the ways in which this has changed over time.

Policing Robbery
Individual police forces had the reputation, with a basis of reality, of having little interest in dealing with robbery unless they were offered the opportunity to profit from recovery of property. Their reputation for incompetence and venality reached a peak with the cinematic portrayal of the *Keystone Cops*. Reformers and establishment figures such as August Vollmer (1876–1955) professionalized the police and revolutionized practices with respect to robbery and other crimes. Prevention was stressed in addition to detection, and victims could subsequently expect to have all of their belongings returned to them by right.

As the number of retail and service outlets has grown, the willingness and ability of the state police forces to patrol each one to deter robbery has declined. Indeed, those states internationally that tried to create a regime of total surveillance have ended up with police states hated by the citizens and, therefore, lack the social solidarity necessary to deter crime in the first place. As a result, retail outlet owners have turned to private police or security guards, technology, or armed response to try to prevent robberies. Security guards can be expensive and, like the early banks, susceptible to providing inside assistance in some cases. To reduce costs, modern businesses can join security schemes together, which provide some in-premises technology that detects unwanted activities and then provokes a response from the security team. The same service might be provided by the police but it is very expensive, and limited resources mean it is effectively limited to only very important or valuable locations that can be protected. Hence, market-based transactions have arisen to provide the necessary protection. Using technology on its own, whether it is closed-circuit television, shuttering, or post-theft modifications of a product, tends to be an acceptance of failure in that it is more useful in finding criminals after the event than deterring them in the first place. However, such technology can have a deterrent effect on theft by staff, which can also be a significant problem in some situations. Meanwhile, relying on an armed response is a very dangerous course of action.

John Walsh
Shinawatra University

See Also: 1851 to 1900 Primary Documents; 1921 to 1940 Primary Documents; 1941 to 1960 Primary Documents; Burglary, History of; James, Jesse; Private Detectives; Robbery, Contemporary; Robbery, Sociology of.

Further Readings
Hearst, Patricia C., with Alvin Moscow. *Patty Hearst: Her Own Story.* New York: Avon Books, 1998.
Jacobs, Ronald L. *Race, Media, and the Crisis of Civil Society: From Watts to Rodney King.* Cambridge: Cambridge University Press, 2000.
Mishra, Birendra K. and Ashutosh Prasad. "Minimizing Retail Shrinkage Due to Employee Theft." *International Journal of Retail and Distribution Management,* v.34/11 (2006).
Segrave, Kerry. *Shoplifting: A Social History.* Jefferson, NC: MacFarland, 2001.

Robbery, Sociology of

Robbery involves the theft of property from an individual or an organization, often but not always with the use of violence or the threat of violence or another form of intimidation. Insofar as robbery is inspired by the need for financial gain, it has been committed by people of all categories, especially if they believed that they would not be caught or that their actions were justified. However, there has been a difference in a number of cases between acts of robbery by the rich, which has been aimed at personal aggrandizement, and robbery to obtain food or other necessities, which is the preserve of the poor and vulnerable.

Theft, Property, and the State

From an early part of its history, U.S. federal and state governments have been willing to place property on the same level or higher than the rights of individuals. Property rights were enshrined while large numbers of people were categorized as slaves and were not only considered to be property themselves but also were considered unworthy of receiving the full rights of free people. The authorities, both through the official police and military and also through the use of private police and detectives, have been used to protect the assets of the rich and deny them to the poor. People have been unwilling to accept this situation when they believe that the asset accumulation has been conducted unfairly and at the expense of victims. In the early years of the nation, outlying areas were far from official scrutiny, and powerful individuals could use this opacity to create their own fiefdoms through the use of force or intimidation. The dispossessed in such situations often had the option of moving on to new open land but may not always have been willing to do so.

As late as the second half of the 19th century, the great capitalists who were developing the American west, laying railroads, and developing powerful institutions were commonly referred to as "Robber Barons," because of the way they had enriched themselves and impoverished others to achieve their goals. While the acts of which they were accused seem quite often to have taken place, the state was generally happy to turn a blind eye or even to collude in such activities because it was thought more important to develop national capacity in the age of imperialism, when aggregate, biddable economic power could be used to further the growth of American influence in the international realm. As has been seen internationally, state authorities around the world have shown themselves quite willing to give freedom of action to large capitalists if their goals may be construed as being broadly in line with national developmental goals.

Robbery and Poverty

The most common motivation for robbery is financial gain, and the people most in need of money are the poor. Academic studies concerning the links between poverty and crime find there is often but not always a direct correlation between the two and also suggest that crime rates are higher when society exhibits higher levels of inequality of income and of opportunity. Recent research indicates (although there have been a number of dissenting voices) that less inequality in the country or among the 50 states would lead to better outcomes in terms not just of crime but also of physical and mental health, levels of imprisonment, and marital breakdowns, teen pregnancies, and a range of other societal indicators. Insofar as this is true, then, it suggests that those who most commonly commit robbery are those who are or who feel most likely to be suffering from such inequality.

Given the low level of social security in the United States, the period of time in a family between the principal breadwinner losing a job and the onset of hunger can be very short, at least compared to European countries, for example. Other immediate threats include loss of housing or failure to meet house repayments or other loans. To some extent, the threat of social disorder and familial breakup that follows robbery or other crimes is mitigated through the use of state transfers, such as food stamp or soup kitchen programs, although these can be subject to stigma in practice to those using them. Additionally, America has a comparatively high number of religious institutions, and some of these offer help and assistance to people and families suffering from poverty and hunger. Inevitably, many of these institutions expect to be repaid in part by receiving attention to their religious messages or even conversion to their beliefs. People in vulnerable situations can indeed be persuaded to take actions that they might otherwise not make if they had more security and self-esteem.

Workers who are constantly aware of the flimsy nature of their income and food security can suffer from stress and attendant health problems such as heart diseases, while also forcing themselves to be quiescent and nonconfrontational in the case of problematic workplace issues for fear of job loss. Once the descent into crime is made, social stigma and prejudice against former convicts has in many cases been such that decent work can never again be found.

The descent into poverty is most rapid and the situation most insecure when the country is suffering economic recession. It is also more prevalent in those types of work that are seasonal, that are strongly affected by external environmental conditions, or in which barriers to hiring and firing practices are extremely low. These industries include fruit picking, meat packing, and the service sectors of the tourism industry. It is clear that in at least some of these cases, comparatively large numbers of ethnic minority migrants may be clustered together. Outbreaks of thefts following economic problems have tended to inspire harsh treatment from the state and from local people. It has been common, therefore, for authorities to justify their actions by ascribing to certain ethnic or racial groups a propensity to theft or other forms of crime. This attitude dates back to the time of slavery, of course, when many people

Broken glass is all that remains after the pictured vehicle theft. It has been suggested that robbery is committed by those who perceive a social and financial inequality with society.

found it necessary to try to justify their role in maintaining a slave-based industry by traducing the humanity of those involved. Harsh economic conditions also frequently inspire governments to turn against other scapegoats, as happened to the hundreds of thousands of Mexicans and many of their American-born children during the Great Depression, not to mention ethnic Japanese during World War II. At the same time, new historical studies have revealed the extent to which the slaves and other oppressed minorities should not be seen as passive chattel but as vigorous individuals, many of whom were involved in staging numerous acts of resistance against the slavers. Robbery was seen as one such justifiable response to unjust and barbaric treatment. A shadow of such actions may be seen in later history in the case of theft in the workplace.

Insofar as the motivation for robbery varies depending on economic factors, it will also necessarily have an uneven distribution over the geography of the country. Areas of rural poverty, for example, will be united with impoverished inner city areas as places where the crimes are more commonly seen on a per capita basis. However, police involvement is more likely to be found in urban areas, whereas rural victims may have wished to take matters into their own hands.

Although poverty and other economic factors certainly contribute to the likelihood of individuals committing robbery or other crimes, they do not explain why some individuals fall into this behavior and others do not. At the more immediate, individual level, people are also affected by such motivations as past experience, peer group pressure, social relationships with potential victims, and the effects of chance and opportunism. A much stronger disincentive to robbery is the likelihood of being caught rather than the nature of any future punishment. Similarly, anticrime measures such as security systems, spotlights, and CCTV, if they are credible, may deter a person who might commit a crime of opportunity, or at least transfer it elsewhere. Discouraging membership in peer groups that are more likely to encourage crime can also an effective strategy.

Deviant Behavior

An unknown but surely significant proportion of robbery, in common with many other types of crime, results from the voluntary adoption of deviant behavior by a wide range of individuals. Deviant behavior involves contradicting cultural or social norms in some way, and this can involve crime and, in this case, robbery. The interactions between deviant behavior and robbery can take several forms: Peer acceptance might be obtained by an act of robbery or shoplifting, especially when the prospective victim might be characterized as being inimical in some way; the robbery might be inspired by the desire for money to fuel a deviant addiction; or the act might itself be attractive from an ideological perspective, either to strike at an individual or organization or to demonstrate independence from conventional thinking. This last form of behavior might lead to occupation of a residence and marking out the act in some graphic way. The situation is similar to computer hackers who break into other peoples' systems and, instead of causing damage or theft, act to vandalize the system and leave marks of their acts in evidence.

To some extent, the introduction of the term *deviant behavior* into the discourse of crime and punishment has been, so it has been claimed, a means of reducing the culpability of the rich and powerful while criminalizing the poor. This has been the case with shoplifting or shop theft. When this is committed by the poor or by members of certain ethnic or racial groups, it is termed *theft* and the victims are deemed suitable for strong punishments. When it has been middle- or upper-class youth, the crime has been reclassified as one of social disorder and juvenile boundary testing: As a result, the punishments have been greatly diminished in severity. When it comes to well-known wealthy celebrities committing the same crime, albeit often in a different physical environment, then they are said to be suffering from some kind of psychological problem that causes aberrant attention-seeking behavior for which the culprit should be exonerated and pitied.

Robbery in the Workplace

Since the workplace can represent a place of conflict between employees and employer or between employees, it has been quite common for disaffection to strike at least some workers (and also some managers, of course). Managers tend to have more opportunities to commit acts of fraud or corruption to enrich themselves while punishing the company; ordinary workers tend to be restricted to acts of minor theft of workplace stock or office supplies, in addition to acts of sabotage or vandalism, which usually have different motivations.

There seems generally to be a difference in motivation between stealing from an employer and stealing from a fellow employee. While the latter tends to reflect personal hostility or antipathy to the individual victimized, the former reflects an organizational culture in which it is acceptable to steal from the employer or even justified because the employer lacks moral legitimacy. By committing acts against the employer, employees might be involved in acts of social bonding with their workmates or be performing an act of organizational or retributional justice. In other words, the items stolen may be of secondary importance to the fact that the act represents a blow against the organization.

Striking Against the Capitalist or Despotic State

In some cases, robbery may be considered an act that strikes against an unjust or improper state, and this justifies the illegal action. In the case of riots and looting, the theft of property from shops may be justified by perpetrators in that the victims are complicit in erecting and sustaining the unequal state. This is one reason why looted items are so often the high-value consumer goods that are symbols of personal success, in addition to items that are of direct personal use or utility. Acquiring high-ticket consumer goods from rioting is, of course, an irrational act because of the difficulty of hiding them from official scrutiny subsequently and the determination of the owner to regain them.

Riots have also provided the opportunity for some personal score settling. For example, if many Korean-owned grocery or other retail stores were attacked during a riot, it may appear that this was motivated by resentment that one set of ethnic minority people had been benefiting from the system that was held to be systematically preventing the rise of another group.

A similar situation has existed with regard to radical or terrorist groups, who often identify the possession of large amounts of apparently surplus capital as being representative of the ills of the capitalist state and its allies in banking, finance, and commerce. Consequently, a bank robbery may be seen to be a justified strike against injustice, although that justification would not generally extend to the use of violence against low-level employees committed in the conduct of the theft, since this would be an act of class treachery.

John Walsh
Shinawatra University

See Also: Political Dissidents; Slavery; Terrorism.

Further Readings

Clinard, Marshall B. and Robert F. Meier. *Sociology of Deviant Behavior*, 14th ed. Belmont, CA: Wadsworth Cengage Learning, 2011.

Hoffman, A. *Unwanted Mexican Americans in the Great Depression: Repatriation Pressures, 1929–39*. Tucson: University of Arizona Press, 1974.

Jarjoura, Roger G., et al. "Growing Up Poor: Explaining the Link Between Persistent Childhood Poverty and Delinquency." *Journal of Quantitative Criminology*, v.18/2 (June 2002).

Liechtenstein, Carl. "'That Disposition to Theft, With Which They Have Been Branded': Moral Economy, Slave Management, and the Law." *Journal of Social History*, v.21/3 (Spring 1988).

Messner, Stephen F. and Scott J. South. "Economic Deprivation, Opportunity Structure, and Robbery Victimization: Intra- and Interracial Patterns." *Social Forces*, v.64/4 (1986).

Pickett, Kate and Richard Wilkinson. *The Spirit Level: Why Greater Equality Makes Societies Stronger*. New York: Bloomsbury Press, 2011.

Roberts v. Louisiana

Roberts v. Louisiana (431 U.S. 643, 1977) asked and answered the question of whether the death penalty could be mandatorily given for first degree murder. In a 5–4 opinion, the Supreme Court of the United States decided on June 6, 1977, that Louisiana's death penalty law violated the Eighth and Fourteenth Amendments to the U.S. Constitution. The Louisiana statute that was declared

The hanging noose at the County Courthouse, a National Historical Landmark in Tombstone, Arizona. Historically, hanging was the most common method of execution. Following a conviction for first-degree murder and being sentenced to death, Harry Roberts challenged the constitutionality of Louisiana's death penalty statute, and the Supreme Court found that Louisiana's sentencing scheme does not allow juries the constitutionally required right to consider mitigating factors based on the circumstances of the crime or the offender's character.

unconstitutional imposed the death penalty for first-degree murder of a police officer. Jurors were not allowed to consider any evidence about intent or other mitigating factors.

Harry Roberts was arrested, tried, and convicted of murdering Dennis McInerney, an on-duty police officer in New Orleans, Louisiana. During Mardi Gras in 1974, Harry Roberts, then 19 years old, began shooting neighbors. The police were called to the scene and two officers, one Officer McInerney, responded to the call. McInerney and his partner, Officer George Tobin, arrived in a marked squad car and in uniform. They approached Roberts, who shot both officers before they could exit their vehicle, killing Officer McInerney, who died at the scene within minutes. Roberts was wounded in the leg by Officer Tobin and fled the scene. He was apprehended by additional officers called to the scene by Officer Tobin. Roberts was tried under a Louisiana statute that required a mandatory death sentence for individuals intentionally killing a police officer. He was found guilty and, under state law, received the death penalty without any discussion of factors that would work in Roberts's favor.

Upon appeal, Roberts raised the constitutionality of the Louisiana statute. The U.S. Supreme Court had recently litigated another portion of the Louisiana law in *Stanislaus Roberts v. Louisiana* in 1976 (428 U.S. 325). In this case, the Supreme Court struck the mandatory provision of the statute for the killing of a police officer in the course of an armed robbery. The court found the mandatory component in violation of the Eighth and Fourteenth Amendments to the Constitution. Both Harry Roberts and Stanislaus Roberts (no relation) were convicted under different, but similar, state provisions that both resulted in their automatic sentences of death. While *Harry Roberts v. Louisiana* was being appealed, the court's decision in *Stanislaus Roberts v. Louisiana* was handed down.

Roberts v. Louisiana is contextually important in terms of the post-*Furman* death penalty decisions. In *Furman v. Georgia*, 1972 (408 U.S. 238), the Supreme Court struck down the death penalty and imposed a national moratorium, forcing states to reconsider the random "wanton and capricious" nature of sentencing perpetrators to death. After several years, the states had rewritten their death penalty statutes, and in 1976, in a series of cases, *Gregg v. Georgia* (428 U.S. 153), *Jurek v. Texas* (428 U.S. 262), *Proffitt v. Florida* (428 U.S. 242), *(Stanislaus) Roberts v. Louisiana* (428 U.S. 325) and *Woodson v. North Carolina* (428 U.S. 280), the Supreme Court ruled that replacing mandatory sentencing structures with random ones still did not meet constitutional muster. While the per curiam opinion in *Roberts v. Louisiana* struck the Louisiana statute, the four dissenters—Chief Justice Warren Burger and Justices William Rehnquist, Louis Powell, and Bryon White—argued that all mandatory sentencing schemes were not unconstitutional and the state of Louisiana could differentiate the killing of a peace officer as a more egregious crime warranting the death penalty.

The majority reasoned that mandatory sentences solved the randomness problem of *Furman* but created other constitutional problems by not allowing juries to consider all factors that both encourage and discourage a sentence of death. *Gregg*, *Proffitt*, and *Jurek* held that the death penalty was not unconstitutional per se, but death penalty trials must be bifurcated. The remaining 1976 cases made clear that juries must take into account both aggravating and mitigating factors when imposing punishment in the second phase of the trial following the first guilt/innocence phase. *Woodson* and *Roberts* both focused on the punishment phase, stipulating that the consideration by the jury must be nuanced, accessing all factors that work in favor of the criminal (mitigating factors) and work against them (aggravating factors). Mandatory death sentences violate the Eighth Amendment as cruel and unusual because they deprive the jury of information, such as intent and extenuating circumstances. The court would later find that mandatory life sentences are not the same as mandatory death sentences and can be instituted for certain crimes.

Priscilla H. M. Zotti
United States Naval Academy

See Also: Cruel and Unusual Punishment; *Furman v. Georgia*; *Gregg v. Georgia*.

Further Readings
Banner, Stuart. *The Death Penalty: An American History*. Cambridge, MA: Harvard University Press, 2002.
Bedau, Hugo, ed. *The Death Penalty in America*, 3rd ed. New York: Oxford University Press, 1982.

Rockefeller, Nelson

Nelson Aldrich Rockefeller was the 41st vice president of the United States under Gerald Ford and the 49th governor of New York. As governor of New York, Rockefeller championed stringent laws against drug use, sale, and possession. He dealt with the siege at the Attica Correctional Facility during his term, which ended with an assault by State Police officers and National Guardsmen where 39 were killed, including 10 hostages held by rebellious inmates.

Early Life and Career
Rockefeller was born on July 8, 1908, in Bar Harbor, Maine. He was the son of John Davison Rockefeller, Jr., and Abby Aldrich Rockefeller. He was the grandson of Standard Oil founder and chairman John Davison Rockefeller, Sr., and U.S. Senator Nelson Wilmarth Aldrich, a Republican from Rhode Island. He attended the Lincoln School, an experimental elementary and secondary school run by Teachers College of Columbia University. In 1930, he graduated cum laude with an A.B. in economics from Dartmouth College. After graduation, he worked in a number of family-related businesses, including Chase National Bank (1931); Rockefeller Center Inc. (joining the board of directors in 1931, serving as president from 1938 to 1945 and 1948 to 1951, and as chairman from 1945 to 1953 and 1956 to 1958); and Creole Petroleum, the Venezuelan subsidiary of Standard Oil of New Jersey (1935–40). From 1932 to 1979 he was a trustee of the Museum of Modern Art (serving as tteasurer, 1935–39, and president 1939–41 and 1946–53). He and his four brothers established the Rockefeller Brothers Fund, a philanthropy, in 1940

In 1973, as governor of New York State, Nelson Rockefeller signed new drug laws that were the toughest in the United States. These included mandatory life sentences for drug users.

(he was a trustee from 1940–75 and 1977–79, and president in 1956).

Government Service

Rockefeller's first government service was as a member of the Westchester County Board of Health, (1933–53). In 1940, President Franklin D. Roosevelt appointed him coordinator of inter-American affairs. In 1944, Roosevelt appointed Rockefeller assistant secretary of state for American republic affairs, a position he held until August 1945. Rockefeller was a member of the U.S. delegation at the United Nations (UN) Conference on International Organization at San Francisco in 1945. He was instrumental in persuading the UN to establish its headquarters in New York City. His father donated the $8.5 million required to purchase the land for the UN.

In 1950, President Harry S. Truman appointed Rockefeller chairman of the International Development Advisory Board. In 1952, President-Elect Dwight D. Eisenhower asked Rockefeller to chair the President's Advisory Committee on Government Organization to recommend ways of improving efficiency and effectiveness of the executive branch of the federal government. Rockefeller joined the administration as undersecretary of the new Department of Health, Education and Welfare (HEW) in 1953. The following year, Eisenhower appointed him special assistant to the president for foreign affairs, a position he held until December 1955.

Rockefeller entered New York politics, chairing the Temporary State Commission on the Constitutional Convention (1956–58) and the Special Legislative Committee on the Revision and Simplification of the Constitution (1958). In 1958, he was elected governor by over 600,000 votes, defeating the incumbent, multimillionaire W. Averell Harriman (he was reelected in 1962, 1966, and 1970).

Governor

As governor, Rockefeller doubled the size of the State Police, established the New York State Police Academy, and signed legislation authorizing 228 additional state judgeships to reduce court backlogs. In 1963, Rockefeller signed legislation abolishing mandatory capital punishment, establishing a two-stage trial for murder cases with punishment determined in the second stage. Rockefeller oversaw 14 executions by electrocution as governor, including that of Eddie Mays (1963), the last execution in New York. While a supporter of capital punishment, Rockefeller signed the bill abolishing the death penalty in 1965, except in cases involving the murder of police officers.

What became known as the Rockefeller Drug Laws were his response to the rapid increase in narcotics addiction and related crime. In 1962, the state legislature enacted his proposal that offered rehabilitation to convicted drug addicts in lieu of prison time.

When this program proved unsuccessful, Rockefeller called for compulsory treatment, rehabilitation, and aftercare for three years in 1966. This did little to reduce the narcotics trade and associated crime. Rockefeller then offered a hardline approach. In 1973, new drug laws included mandatory life sentences for anyone convicted of selling two ounces or possessing four ounces of a "narcotic drug"; rewards for information leading to the conviction of drug pushers; and more severe penalties on youthful offenders. Once again, the laws failed because they did not lead more addicts to seek rehabilitation as hoped and ultimately did not solve the problem of drug trafficking. The drug laws were among the toughest in the United States when they were enacted. Mayor John Lindsay of New York City denounced the laws as "merely a deceptive gesture offering nothing beyond momentary satisfaction and inevitable disillusionment." To carry out the rehabilitation program, Rockefeller created the State Narcotics Addiction Control Commission, which administered the largest methadone maintenance program in the country.

The laws proved ineffective, as drug use did not decline, even as drug convictions increased. At the time the laws were enacted, 11 percent of inmates in the state's prisons were drug offenders; the proportion of drug offenders reached 35 percent in 1994. In 2004, Governor George E. Pataki signed legislation reducing the maximum mandatory sentence to 20 years. In 2009, mandatory sentences were eliminated for all offenders, except those convicted of being "major traffickers," who could be sentenced to 15 years to life.

On September 9, 1971, inmates at the state prison in Attica, New York, took control of a cell block and seized 39 guards as hostages. After four days of negotiations, Department of Correctional Services Commissioner Russell Oswald agreed to most of the inmates' demands for reform, but refused to grant complete amnesty to the rioters, with passage out of the country and removal of the prison's superintendent. When negotiations stalled and the hostages appeared to be in imminent danger, Rockefeller ordered New York State Police and National Guard troops to storm the prison on September 13. When the assault on the prison was over, 39 were dead, including 10 of the hostages. All but three of the deaths were attributed to the gunfire of the National Guard or State Police. The other three dead were inmates killed by other inmates at the start of the riot. Opponents blamed Rockefeller for these deaths, in part because of his refusal to go to the prison and talk with the inmates, while his supporters, including many conservatives who had often differed with him in the past, defended his actions as necessary to maintain law and order. "I was trying to do the best I could to save the hostages, save the prisoners, restore order, and preserve our system without undertaking actions which could set a precedent which would go across this country like wildfire," Rockefeller said.

In December 1973, Rockefeller resigned as governor to devote his attention to the Commission on Critical Choices for America, a privately funded group established to study the problems facing America. He served as chair until becoming vice president in December 1974. Rockefeller unsuccessfully sought the Republican presidential nomination in 1960, 1964, and 1968. After Gerald Ford became president following Richard Nixon's resignation (1974), Rockefeller was named vice president, taking office in December 1974. Opposed by conservatives within the Republican Party, Rockefeller announced that he would not be a candidate for vice president in 1976, allowing Ford to pick Robert Dole of Kansas as his running mate. Rockefeller died on January 26, 1979, at age 70 from a heart attack.

Jeffrey Kraus
Wagner College

See Also: Attica; Ford, Gerald (Administration of); New York; New York City; Roosevelt, Franklin D. (Administration of); Truman, Harry S. (Administration of).

Further Readings

Benjamin, G., et al. "Attica and Prison Reform." In *Governing New York State*, G. Benjamin, et al., eds. New York: Academy of Political Science, 1974.

Connery, Robert H., et al. *Rockefeller of New York: Executive Power in the Statehouse*. Ithaca, NY: Cornell University Press, 1979.

Gonnerman, Jennifer. "Addicted: The Myth of the Rockefeller Drug Laws Repeal." *New York Magazine* (April 6, 2009).

Gray, M. "A Brief History of New York's Rockefeller Drug Laws." *Time Magazine* (April 2, 2009). http://www.time.com/time/nation/article/0,8599,1888864-2,00.html (Accessed March 2012).

Kramer, M. S. *"I Never Wanted to Be Vice-President of Anything!" An Investigative Biography of Nelson Rockefeller*. New York: Basic Books, 1976.

Persico, Joseph E. *The Imperial Rockefeller: A Biography of Nelson A. Rockefeller*. New York: Simon & Schuster, 1982.

Reich, Cary. *The Life of Nelson A. Rockefeller*. New York: Doubleday, 1996.

Warth, Patricia, et al. *A Quick Guide to Rockefeller Drug Law Reform 2009*. Syracuse, NY: Center for Community Alternatives, 2009.

Wilson, Aaron D. *Rockefeller Drug Laws Information Sheet*. New York: Partnership for Responsible Drug Information, 2000.

Roe v. Wade

On January 22, 1973, the Supreme Court handed down a 7–2 decision in *Roe v. Wade*. The court declared unconstitutional a Texas law that considered an attempt to procure an abortion a criminal act unless done by a physician to save a woman's life. The court found the Texas statute interfered with a doctor's right to pursue the best medical treatment for patients.

A number of factors led to abortion reform. The thalidomide scare in 1962 resulted from a drug marketed in Europe as a cure for morning sickness; while the Food and Drug Administration did not approve it for distribution in the United States, some Americans traveling abroad brought home the pills. Reports confirmed that the drug caused severe birth defects, especially early in pregnancy. Similarly, German measles swept the nation between 1962 and 1965, posing a 50 percent chance of fetal deformity in pregnant women afflicted with the disease. Some doctors ignored state laws and performed abortions, bringing legal action against themselves as they endeavored to help their patients. The introduction of the European vacuum or suction aspiration in 1967 to replace the bloodier dilation and curettage procedure made abortion more acceptable to many physicians. Some physicians requested that the American Law Institute (ALI) investigate ambiguous state laws and devise a model reform law that would permit greater freedom to medical practitioners. The ALI's recommendation allowed abortion when a woman's physical or mental health was endangered, the fetus was physically or mentally defective, or pregnancy resulted from rape or incest.

Issues outside the medical realm also influenced pressure for change. This era witnessed an expansion of human rights with movements for civil, women's, and privacy rights. Apprehension regarding overpopulation meshed with concerns over mounting welfare expenditures, especially among recipients of Aid to Families with Dependent Children. Rhetoric regarding the cost-saving potential of abortion swayed many legislators prior to *Roe v. Wade* to begin decriminalizing abortion. California was the first state to liberalize its abortion law in 1967, followed by 11 other states by 1970; these laws modeled the ALI recommendation. Four states in 1970—New York, Alaska, Washington, and Hawai'i—passed laws that went beyond the ALI model, in effect legalizing abortion on demand.

In addition to legislative activity, there were more than 25 abortion cases pending before state courts when the Supreme Court decided to hear *Roe v. Wade*. Two years earlier, the court had heard its first case devoted solely to abortion in *United States v. Vuitch* (1971). The court overturned the 1901 anti-abortion statute in the District of Columbia as unconstitutionally vague because a doctor's decision to perform an abortion to protect the woman's health could later be second-guessed by a jury. The court declared abortion to be a surgical procedure and as such was left to doctors to decide its medical necessity. *Roe v. Wade* confirmed this medical jurisdiction.

Jane Roe's Case

Norma McCorvey, alias Jane Roe, lived in Dallas County, Texas. Her marriage had failed and her mother and stepfather were raising her 5-year-old daughter when she became pregnant at age 21 in 1969. She wanted an abortion because of the economic hardship of raising a child as a single mother and because of the social stigma attached to illegitimacy. McCorvey met attorneys Linda Coffey and Sarah Weddington, who represented her as Jane Roe; they challenged the Texas statute passed in 1854 and revised in 1857 that prohibited abortion unless the woman's life was at stake. They presented two main arguments. First, McCorvey could not secure an abortion because the pregnancy did not threaten her life; she did not possess funds to travel elsewhere to obtain a legal abortion. Second, the Texas law violated her privacy protected by the First, Fourth, Fifth, Ninth, and Fourteenth Amendments to the Constitution.

The case came before the federal court in Dallas in 1970. The court rejected the law because it denied Jane Roe her Ninth Amendment right of privacy to decide whether or not to procreate. While the court issued a declarative relief that the law was unconstitutional, it did not issue an injunctive relief mandating the law not be enforced against physicians, assuming the state would comply with the court's decision. District Attorney Henry Wade, however, decided to proceed with prosecutions, providing Weddington and Coffeey with the basis for a Supreme Court appeal.

John Tolle, Jay Floyd, and Robert Flowers from the Texas attorney general's office served as lawyers for the state. They argued that Jane Roe had no standing before the court because she was no longer pregnant by the time her case reached litigation. The court disagreed: if "termination makes a case moot, pregnancy litigation seldom will survive much beyond the trial stage.... Our law should not be that rigid." Jane Roe would represent pregnant women in a class-action suit. Tolle et al. also argued that the state had a compelling interest to protect the legal rights of the fetus.

Weddington, with help from Coffey, presented Roe's case twice. They argued in December 1971, but the retirements of Justices John Harlan and Hugo Black in September had left the court with only seven justices, who were hesitant to decide this case without a full bench. They reargued in October 1972 after President Richard Nixon appointed Justices Lewis Powell and William Rehnquist, two men Nixon assumed would reject abortion liberalization. Weddington's main argument was that privacy rights declared in *Griswold v. Connecticut* (1965) should extend to a woman's decision whether or not to bear a child. Amicus briefs supporting this claim came from the American College of Gynecologists and Obstetricians, the New York Academy of Medicine, and Planned Parenthood Federation of America.

Blackmun's Majority Opinion

Justice Harry Blackmun wrote the majority opinion. Drawing on history, Blackmun found that ancient codes and ancient religions did not proscribe abortion. Common law did not prohibit abortion prior to quickening (first sign of fetal movement). As he argued, "a woman enjoyed a substantially broader right to terminate a pregnancy" at common law, at the time of the drafting of the U.S. Constitution, and during much of the 19th century than she did in the 1970s. He located the legislative change in the latter half of the 19th century when states passed abortion statutes for three main reasons. The laws were part of a Victorian effort to curb illicit sex, but Texas did not advance this reason as part of the argument in *Roe*. The laws also attempted to protect women from dangerous abortions, but medical advancements had abrogated this reason. Lastly, Tolle argued the laws were there to protect prenatal life, but Blackmun could not find this assertion in the 19th-century legislation;

U.S. Supreme Court Justice Harry A. Blackmun's official 1976 portrait. Although Blackmun is best known as the author of Roe v. Wade, *he made great contributions in the fight against race discrimination and protecting disadvantaged citizens.*

the law claimed to protect the mother's life. The availability of abortion in the early 19th century confirmed his belief that a fetus is not a person under the Constitution.

In addition to history, Blackmun drew upon the privacy foundation laid in *Griswold*, *Loving v. Virginia* (1967), and *Eisenstadt v. Baird* (1972). Blackmun contended that "This right of privacy, whether it be found in the Fourteenth Amendment's concept of personal liberty and restrictions upon state action, as we feel it is, or, as the district courts determined, in the Ninth Amendment's reservation of rights to the people, is broad enough to encompass a woman's decision whether or not to terminate her pregnancy." This right to abortion was "fundamental" and could only be regulated if a "compelling" state interest exists.

Blackmun expanded on this notion of state interest when he introduced the trimester approach to abortion. During the first trimester, state interest in protecting maternal health is not compelling enough to interfere with the woman's decision to abort because mortality rates for abortion were as low as or lower than for childbirth. In the second trimester, the state may have a compelling interest to regulate but not prohibit abortion to protect maternal health because mortality rates were higher for abortion than childbirth. By the third trimester, the state has a compelling interest to protect a viable fetus and thus may prohibit abortions unless the mother's health or life is at stake. Blackmun acknowledged the arbitrary nature of his trimester framework: Neither side arguing before the court had introduced this concept. Blackmun maintained that it left states the right to set medical guidelines between the first and third trimesters.

Doe v. Bolton, the companion case to *Roe*, declared Georgia's abortion statute unconstitutional. The court struck down the approval of a hospital staff committee and two consulting physicians prior to an abortion; the attending physician's approval is sufficient. The court also rejected the residency requirement because no other medical procedure had such a prerequisite. The state could not interfere with the exercise of a woman's right to abortion by prohibiting or limiting access to it.

Justices Byron White and William Rehnquist dissented. White argued that no language existed in the Constitution to support the right to abortion. In his view, the court "simply" announced an unfounded right for pregnant women; he found the decisions to be "an improvident and extravagant exercise of the power of judicial review." Rehnquist agreed that the court had overstepped its boundary, breaking a long-standing tenet that the court should not "formulate a rule of constitutional law broader than is required by the precise facts to which it is to be applied." Privacy, in his opinion, did not apply to abortion because the procedure occurs with a medical professional in a hospital or clinic, not the privacy of one's home. He also took issue with Blackmun's historical analysis: The fact that most states for over a century had prohibited abortion unless to save the mother's life meant that a right to abortion was not "so rooted in the traditions and conscience of our people as to be ranked as fundamental."

Criticisms

Some legal scholars have critiqued the majority decisions in these cases. They believe abortion rights would have been on firmer ground had the court invoked sex equality considerations rather than due process and privacy. Justices could have looked to *Reed v. Reed* (1971) in which the court unanimously ruled that dissimilar treatment of men and women was unconstitutional based on the Fourteenth Amendment's equal protection clause, but the court did not pursue this track. The shaky grounding of *Roe* in privacy galvanized antichoice groups to propose overturning *Roe* by constitutional amendment and numerous state and federal laws to limit abortion. The trimester approach has set up a possible collision course as technology allows safer abortions later into pregnancy and moves back the point of viability earlier in pregnancy. It has led to state efforts to institute mandatory viability testing before performing an abortion. Some scholars believe the court should have struck down the Texas law and gone no further, allowing the battles to be played out in state legislatures that were already passing liberalized abortion statutes. By delineating the medical and trimester approach, the court sparked bitter debate on the issue for decades.

In sum, *Roe* and *Doe* invalidated state power to criminalize abortion. They struck down nearly all state abortion laws, including those that had been liberalized prior to 1973. The court ruled that abortion fell under the right to privacy recognized in *Griswold* and protected by the Fourteenth Amendment's due process. Yet the court did not remove all restrictions nor mandate access to abortion. The ultimate decision to abort rests not with the woman but with her physician, confirming the medical rather than feminist framework of the judgment. Since 1973, the court has upheld the right of public hospitals to refuse to perform abortions; parental consent laws as long as judicial bypass exists; and 24-hour waiting periods. Still, the basic ruling in *Roe* remains intact in 2010.

Simone M. Caron
Wake Forest University

See Also: 1851 to 1900 Primary Documents; Abortion; *Eisenstadt v. Baird*; *Griswold v. Connecticut*.

Further Readings
Garrow, David J. *Liberty and Sexuality: The Right to Privacy and the Making of* Roe v. Wade. New York: Macmillan, 1994.
Petchesky, Rosalind Pollack. *Abortion and Woman's Choice*. Lebanon, NH: Northeastern University Press, 1984.
Weddington, Sarah. *A Question of Choice*. New York: G. P. Putnam's Sons, 1992.

Romer v. Evans

In 1992, the citizens of Colorado adopted Amendment 2, which added the following to the Colorado Constitution:

> Neither the State of Colorado ... nor any of its ... political subdivisions ... shall enact, adopt or enforce any statute, regulation, ordinance or policy whereby homosexual, lesbian or bisexual orientation, conduct, practices or relationships shall constitute or otherwise be the basis of or entitle any person or class of persons to have or claim any minority status, quota preferences, protected status or claim of discrimination.

At the time Amendment 2 was adopted, several municipalities, including Aspen, Boulder, and Denver, had already enacted ordinances prohibiting discrimination on grounds of sexual orientation in areas such as employment, education, housing, health and welfare services, and public accommodations. Amendment 2, supported by 53 percent of voters, would not only have rescinded the existing antidiscrimination ordinances but would have prohibited any future legislative, executive, or judicial action, at any level of government, designed to protect people on the basis of sexual orientation.

The amendment, which had generated significant controversy even before its passage, was immediately challenged and a court-ordered injunction prevented it from taking effect. A trial was held to establish the facts in the case, and when the trial judge ruled in favor of challengers, the case was appealed to the Colorado Supreme Court. According to Keen and Goldberg (2000), those challenging the amendment made three primary arguments. First, because the amendment prohibited lesbian, gay, and bisexual people from obtaining governmental protection against discrimination, it infringed their fundamental right to participate in the political process. Second, challengers argued that Amendment 2 was discriminatory because it treated one class of citizens (gay people) differently from the rest of Coloradans without a legitimate purpose. Third, challengers argued that the amendment violated their First Amendment rights to free expression and association. The state offered several arguments in defense of the amendment, the principal ones being that it prevented factionalism by promoting legal uniformity across the state, it preserved resources to support existing civil rights laws, it prevented governmental interference with the personal, familial, and religious privacy of those opposed to homosexuality, it protected children from psychological harm, and that it was the will of the people.

In 1994, the Colorado Supreme Court affirmed the trial court decision, stating that Amendment 2 violated the fundamental right of lesbian, gay, and bisexual people to participate equally in the political process. Because Amendment 2 implicated a fundamental right, the court applied strict scrutiny, meaning not only that the law needed to have a legitimate government purpose but that it also had to be narrowly tailored to achieve that purpose. According to the Colorado Supreme Court, none of the state's arguments in favor of the amendment met this burden. Proponents then appealed to the U.S. Supreme Court, which granted a writ of certiorari.

In 1996, Justice Anthony Kennedy, joined by Justices John P. Stevens, Sandra Day O'Connor, David Souter, Ruth Bader Ginsburg, and Stephen Breyer, upheld the decision of the Colorado Supreme Court but adopted a different legal rationale. Adopting a less stringent form of legal analysis known as rational basis, the court found that Amendment 2 violated the equal protection clause of the Fourteenth Amendment. In his majority opinion, Justice Kennedy wrote, "A law declaring that in general it shall be more difficult for one group of citizens than for all others to seek aid from the government is itself a denial of equal protection of the laws in the most literal sense." Moreover, the court found that Amendment 2 did not bear a rational relationship to a legitimate government purpose. Consequently, Justice Kennedy states, "We must conclude that Amendment 2 classifies homosexuals not to further a proper legislative end, but to make them unequal to everyone else. This Colorado cannot do. A state cannot so deem a class of persons a stranger to its laws."

Jason J. Hopkins
University of California, Santa Barbara

See Also: *Bowers v. Hardwick*; Colorado; Due Process; Equality, Concept of; *Lawrence v. Texas*; Sodomy.

Further Readings
Anderson, Ellen Ann. *Out of the Closets and Into the Courts: Legal Opportunity Structure and Gay Rights Litigation*. Ann Arbor: University of Michigan Press, 2005.
Gerstmann, Evan. *The Constitutional Underclass: Gays, Lesbians, and the Failure of Class-Based Equal Protection*. Chicago: University of Chicago Press, 1999.
Keen, Lisa and Suzanne B. Goldberg. *Strangers to the Law: Gay People on Trial*. Ann Arbor: University of Michigan Press, 2000.
Koppelman, Andrew. "*Romer v. Evans* and Invidious Intent." *William & Mary Bill of Rights Journal*, v.6/89 (1997).

Powell, H. Jefferson. "The Lawfulness of *Romer v. Evans*." *North Carolina Law Review*, v.77/241 (1998).
Romer v. Evans, 517 U.S. 620 (1996).

Roosevelt, Franklin D. (Administration of)

Franklin Delano Roosevelt (1882–1945) was the 32nd president of the United States and the only president elected to more than two terms in office. First elected in 1932 against Republican Herbert Hoover, Roosevelt was re-elected three more times and ultimately passed away during his fourth term as president. Following his death, the Twenty-Second Amendment to the U.S. Constitution limited the number of terms a president can serve to two. Roosevelt's leadership during two of the country's greatest crises of the 20th century, the Great Depression and World War II, have consistently earned him a top-tier rating among scholars and historians of U.S. presidents.

Immediate Action
In 1932, the United States was in the midst of the Great Depression, and public sentiment had shifted from the Republican Party in favor of the New Deal promised by Roosevelt. Ultimately, Roosevelt accomplished the goal of providing for a more powerful federal government, including the establishment of a more powerful federal law enforcement organization that was widely supported by the public. In February 1933, before Roosevelt officially took office, Joseph Zangara attempted to assassinate him but instead ended up killing Mayor Anton Cermak of Chicago.

When Roosevelt first entered office, many suspected he would put into place an attorney general who would remove then director of the Bureau of Investigation (renamed the Federal Bureau of Investigation in 1935, hereafter FBI) J. Edgar Hoover. However, Roosevelt placed Homer Cummings into the position of attorney general. Cummings had similar views regarding crime as Hoover, most notably that a powerful federal law enforcement institution was necessary to engage

Franklin D. Roosevelt with his son and wife in Rhinebeck, New York, in 1932. Roosevelt was elected president at the height of the Great Depression: By March 1933, 13,000,000 Americans were unemployed and nearly all of the country's banks were closed. Among other accomplishments, Roosevelt created a more powerful federal government and federal law enforcement system, controls over banks and public utilities, Social Security, and a work relief program for the unemployed.

in effective crime control. To ensure states' rights advocates were in tune with a stronger federal institution, Cummings and Hoover campaigned for a force that would focus on interstate issues, as the regulation of interstate commerce was already in the purview of the federal government, and did not attempt to create a nationalized police force akin to Great Britain's Scotland Yard.

An early action taken by the Roosevelt administration regarding crime was to repeal the National Prohibition Act (Volstead Act). The first step was to transfer control of enforcement from the highly corrupt Prohibition unit within the Bureau of Internal Revenue located within the Department of Treasury to the Justice Department. Hoover, whose FBI was located within the Justice Department, did not approve, as he saw the corruption and lack of scientific policing techniques of Prohibition agents as detrimental to law enforcement. Hoover was able to maintain control over the management and hiring of the FBI, allowing the FBI to remain free of the public disdain associated with Prohibition agents.

Federal Law Enforcement

In 1933, Cummings declared that the Roosevelt administration was entering a war on crime, and he proposed a 12-point plan to be passed by Congress to expand federal law enforcement powers. Under the administration of President Herbert Hoover, there had been a rise in crimes involving kidnapping and bank robbing. It was during this time that Congress first started to expand federal law enforcement powers with the passage of the Federal Kidnapping Act (Lindbergh Law), named after 20-month-old kidnap victim Charles

Lindbergh, Jr., making it a federal crime to transport a kidnap victim across state lines. Although this expanded federal law enforcement powers somewhat, congressional focus was on social and economic policies proposed by the White House. Crime control was not yet a major factor for Congress.

On July 17, 1933, congressional concern with federal law enforcement was triggered by the killing of two federal agents and the bank robber Frank "Jelly" Nash outside Leavenworth penitentiary. The fact that federal agents at the time were not allowed under law to carry firearms sparked concern among members of the public and Congress. In his January 3, 1934, State of the Union address, Roosevelt stated that crime was a threat to the nation and in order to combat the crime wave involving kidnapping, bank robbing, and extortion, some type of federal enforcement was necessary, so Congress should pass the Cummings plan. In June 1934, Congress enacted six of the 12 points of the Cummings plan. The focus was on making criminal actions that crossed state lines federal crimes. Thus, interstate racketeering, bank robbing, and car theft, as well as killing a federal agent, were made federal crimes. This expanded the power of the FBI drastically and led the way to having a more centralized federal law enforcement agency.

The focus of the FBI was not on organized crime during these early years. In fact, it was largely ignored by federal law enforcement. Hoover avoided going after these types of vice crimes as he was known for disavowing the existence of syndicate crime. Rather, the focus was on bandit crimes such as bank robbing, automobile theft, and kidnapping, where clear public enemies could be established that Hoover could use for public relations purposes to promote the FBI. On July 22, 1933, the capture of bank robber and kidnapper George "Machine Gun" Kelly proved an excellent tool for Hoover when Kelly shouted "Don't shoot, G-men. Don't shoot!" This pushed the use of *G-man* (government man) into the public lexicon and promoted the image of the professional, efficient, incorruptible federal agent. This image was fueled by other notable events such as the killing of public enemy number one John Herbert Dillinger on July 22, 1934, and the 1935 capture/killing of the members of the Barker-Karpis gang. As the FBI became more prominent, congressional appropriations rose rapidly, doubling between 1932 and 1936.

International Relations

As the change in social and economic policy was coming to an end, Roosevelt faced other problems in his administration. In 1940, Roosevelt won an unprecedented third term for the office of president. Unlike in Roosevelt's first two terms in office when the economy was the main issue, he faced problems on the international front with the rise of Adolph Hitler in Germany and the beginning of World War II.

In the late 1930s, the United States was officially a neutral country. In 1935, Congress passed the Neutrality Act, which banned weapons shipments to fighting nations. While Roosevelt was opposed to the act, the public was not, thus he signed the legislation. In 1938, Roosevelt attempted to convince Congress that the United States should not maintain neutrality, but it was not until after World War II actually began that Roosevelt was able to make his concerns heard with the Congress and the United States at large. When Germany invaded and took control of Paris in 1940, congressional and public opinion in the United States shifted to support Roosevelt's positions, including a major increase in military and defense spending. Roosevelt believed that the United States should provide support to Great Britain, most notably by turning the United States into an "arsenal of democracy" wherein the United States would supply armaments and ammunition to the Allied forces. It was made clear during 1941 with the passage of the Lend-Lease Act by which the United States would lend weapons to Great Britain that the United States was clearly on the side of the Allied forces.

National Security Versus Individual Rights

In addition to syndicate and bandit crime, radical movements developed during the Great Depression that were associated with Nazism and Fascism. These were considered "fifth column" movements by the Roosevelt administration and spurred the development of further counterespionage and counterintelligence activities by the FBI. In 1935, the FBI uncovered a German espionage organization that had been operating in New York City since around 1927. In 1936, Hoover and Roosevelt met to discuss ways to counter espionage; one focus of Hoover's was to infiltrate certain types of organizations, most notably unions, in order to keep radical elements out of industry. Roosevelt's plan was much more minimal than Hoover's; however, the control and independence Hoover established for the FBI allowed him to take bigger actions and to inform the attorney general only after the fact. Congress officially expanded the FBI's powers in 1939 and 1940 after Germany invaded Poland and the crisis of World War II truly began. Over the next few years, special divisions were created for the purpose of counterespionage and intelligence such as the Special Intelligence Service and Office of Strategic Services. In 1940, Hoover established a detention program to go after enemy aliens that would hold and track persons of interest.

In 1937 and 1939, the U.S. Supreme Court had determined that forms of wiretapping were unconstitutional; however, Roosevelt in 1941 issued a secret directive that allowed the FBI to engage in wiretapping. Because of legal concerns, the attorney general informed Hoover that records should not be kept. This type of practice is considered one reason why the FBI was able to engage in other investigative activities of questionable legality in 1940, such as opening the mail of suspects. The fear of radical activism was not limited to the political and criminal arena, when, for example, the FBI instituted investigations of the motion picture industry under the 1942 COMPIC program.

World War II
In 1941, many in the United States believed the country would at some point enter the war but no one was prepared for the December 7, 1941, Japanese attack on Pearl Harbor. The next day, Roosevelt asked for a congressional declaration of war. As the United States mobilized for war, industrial production grew rapidly and unemployment decreased, allowing for the entrance of more women and minorities into the workforce. In 1941, Roosevelt signed Executive Order 8802, which forbade hiring discrimination based on race in defense industries. Roosevelt's strategy for war was to focus on going after Nazi Germany, the root of the problem. When Germany and Italy declared war on the United States on December 11, 1941, Roosevelt's strategy gained a stronghold, and the U.S. entrance into World War II fully began.

In 1941, Attorney General Francis Biddle established lists of German and Italian aliens who could be detained, and in 1942, Roosevelt issued Executive Order 9066, which relocated and placed in internment camps immigrants and dual-citizenship holders of Japanese descent. Hoover, for his part, argued that this latter executive order was without merit and thus did not support that particular internment. The U.S. Supreme Court upheld the constitutionality of the executive order in *Korematsu v. United States* (1944).

Roosevelt held a number of strategy meetings with prominent leaders of the Allied forces: Winston Churchill of Great Britain, Joseph Stalin of the Soviet Union, and others such as Chiang Kai-shek of China. These meetings laid the foundation for a future interventionist foreign policy by the United States. Throughout the war, Roosevelt maintained a positive view, despite those who thought otherwise, of Joseph Stalin. However, Roosevelt eventually realized that the fear others in the administration had that Stalin would prove to be a tyrannical leader were ringing true. This led to the eventual replacement of Roosevelt's vice president, Henry Wallace, who was considered pro-Soviet, with Harry Truman as a running mate in the 1944 election, an election that Roosevelt won to secure his fourth term as president.

In March 1945, Roosevelt spoke to Congress about the goal of creating an international organization that would bring together nations striving for peace. This organization, the United Nations, was something Roosevelt hoped to be directly involved in. However, before this could occur, Roosevelt suffered a stroke on April 12, 1945, and died that day. Not long after his death, the United States and the Allied forces defeated Germany and the rest of the Axis powers to win World War II.

Cindy Pressley
Stephen F. Austin State University

See Also: Great Depression; Hoover, Herbert (Administration of); Hoover, J. Edgar; Lindbergh Law.

Further Readings

McJimsey, George T. *The Presidency of Franklin Delano Roosevelt*. Lawrence: University Press of Kansas, 2000.

O'Reilly, Kenneth. "A New Deal for the FBI: The Roosevelt Administration, Crime Control, and National Security." *Journal of American History*, v.69/3 (1982).

Swisher, Carl Brent, ed. *Selected Papers of Homer Cummings: Attorney General of the United States 1933–1939*. New York: Da Capo Press, 1972.

Theoharis, Athan G. *The FBI & American Democracy: A Brief Critical History*. Lawrence: University Press of Kansas, 2004.

Roosevelt, Theodore (Administration of)

The 26th president of the United States (1901–09), Theodore "Teddy" Roosevelt is commonly referred to as the first modern American president for his role in momentously expanding the influence and power of the executive branch of the government. He is noted for his opposition to the ideas of limited government and individualism, and he advocated the use of government regulation to attain social and economic justice. Roosevelt was born in New York City, New York, on October 27, 1858, the second of four children of Theodore Roosevelt, Sr. (1831–78) and Martha Bulloch (1835–84). Born into a wealthy family as a sickly and asthmatic child, he was educated at home with the help of private tutors until he entered college. In 1876, Roosevelt entered Harvard College; he graduated in 1880. While at Harvard, he developed his lifelong political and historical interests, as well his study of the U.S. Navy role in the War of 1812.

Upon graduating, he married Alice Hathaway Lee (1861–84), with whom he had one daughter, and went on to study law at Columbia University. He withdrew from law school after one year to pursue politics when offered the opportunity to contest for New York Assemblyman in 1881, which he won in 1882. In the New York Assembly, he became the leader of the Republican Party's reform wing, during which time he gained a reputation for fighting against illegal or unethical political practices. The sudden deaths of Roosevelt's wife and mother in the same house on the same day in February 1884 were a discouraging double tragedy in his last term in the assembly.

Roosevelt retired to his ranch in the Badlands of the Dakota Territory and spent two years there in an endeavor to recover while he engaged in hunting, herding cattle as a rancher, and hunting down outlaws as a frontier deputy sheriff. He also spent his time there studying and writing about frontier life for eastern magazines. In 1886, he returned to New York with politics and a romantic interest in his childhood sweetheart, Edith Kermit Carow, on his mind. He went to London and married Edith (1861–1948) on December 2, 1886, resulting in his induction into the British Royal Society. They raised six children, Theodore, Kermit, Ethel

Known for its antitrust actions, Theodore Roosevelt's administration also created the formal Federal Bureau of Investigation (FBI) by executive order on July 26, 1908.

Carow, Archibald Bulloch, Quentin, and Alice Lee, Roosevelt's daughter from his first marriage.

Political Ascendancy
Roosevelt was appointed in 1889 by President Benjamin Harrison (1833–1901) to serve on the Civil Service Commission in Washington, D.C. Roosevelt's significant achievement was that he provided the leadership for the commission to become dedicated to opening equal opportunity access for all who where qualified to serve and work in government, particularly for African Americans, who were historically victims of oppression and discrimination. In 1895, he returned to New York to serve two years as president of the New York City Police Board. During his tenure in this post, he radically reformed the police department and enforced the law with relentless proficiency and rectitude. He succeeded in improving the force, raising personnel morale and reducing corruption. Roosevelt provided leadership that enabled him and his fellow commissioners to institute new disciplinary procedures, new recruitment policies based on physical and mental qualifications instead of political affiliation, and established meritorious service methods to combat corrupt police favoritism. Unfortunately, some of his achieved improvements were abandoned after he left.

In 1897, Roosevelt resigned from the position of president of the police board and was appointed by President William McKinley (1843-1901) to the post of assistant secretary of the Navy. As assistant secretary, he enthusiastically worked with senators to promote justification for war against Spain. He played a significant role in preparing the Navy for the Spanish–American War (1898), which resulted in moving control of Latin American colonies, including Philippine territories, from Spain to the United States. Upon the start of the war, Roosevelt resigned from the Department of the Navy in April 1898 and formed the First U.S. Volunteer Calvary regiment. Known as the Rough Riders, members of the cavalry consisted mostly of cowboys from the western region and Roosevelt's friends from the New York area. Under his command, the cavalry regiment became famous for leading dual charges up Kettle Hill and San Juan Hill in Cuba on July 1, 1898. He returned home as a distinguished war hero and was nominated for governor of New York.

In the fall of 1898, Roosevelt became governor of New York, a term that he began by pushing a profound body of new laws and regulations through the New York Assembly and Senate. Because of his Progressive policies, public opinion was favorable to him and showed him to be a master politician. In 1900, Roosevelt was selected as the Republican vice presidential running mate under the William McKinley presidency, which defeated William Jennings Bryan in a landslide. His time as vice president was short. On September 6, 1901, President McKinley was shot in Buffalo, New York, while attending the Pan-American Exposition; he died eight days later, making Roosevelt the president of the United States.

Presidency
Roosevelt's first major presidential achievements include his antitrust actions to curb the power of large corporations. He delivered a 20,000-word address to Congress, persuading it to control the activities of large corporations, referred to as trusts. Over his two terms as president, he maintained aggressive attacks on trusts and has been called a "trustbuster." His foreign policy was aimed at limiting European influence in the Western Hemisphere while expanding American influence globally. In 1904, Roosevelt was elected to a full presidential term in a landslide, making him the first president to be elected on his merits after gaining office because of the death of his predecessor. In the area of crime and criminal justice, Roosevelt's administration created the Bureau of Investigation (FBI after 1935) by executive order on July 26, 1908. Deriving its powers from the Interstate Commerce Act of 1887, the Bureau's first crime-fighting FBI comprised some transferred secret service men and specially appointed agents. The bureau's first crime-fighting task was to take surveys of prostitution houses in preparation for enforcement of crimes related to the White Slave Traffic Act.

As an environmentalist president, one of Roosevelt's major accomplishments in his second term was setting aside nearly 200 million acres for national public control, monuments, parks, and wildlife refuges. He continued his Progressive movement agenda, preaching the so-called Square Deal for people to earn a living wage. People still associate him with his famous saying: "Speak softly and carry a big stick, and you will go far." Theodore Roosevelt died on January 6, 1919, in Oyster Bay, New York.

Felix O. Chima
Prairie View A&M University

See Also: Federal Bureau of Investigation; New York City; Secret Service.

Further Readings

Hagedorn, Hermann. *Roosevelt in the Badlands.* Boston: Houghton-Mifflin, 1921.

Miller, Nathan. *Theodore Roosevelt: A Life.* New York: Quill/William Morrow, 1992.

Roth v. United States

In legal settings, the term *obscenity* is frequently used to describe expressions (e.g., actions, images, or words) of an explicitly sexual nature (e.g., pornography). Most often, the term *obscenity* is used around discussions of which type of content should be protected under the First Amendment of the Constitution. *Roth v. United States* (1957), along with another case, *Alberts v. California* (1957), was a landmark case presented before the U.S. Supreme Court that redefined the constitutional test for determining whether material is considered obscene and therefore unprotected by the First Amendment. In the case of *Roth*, the court defined obscenity more narrowly and adopted the "community standards" test, or "whether to the average person, applying contemporary community standards, the dominant theme taken as a whole, appeals to the prurient interest." Materials that appeal to the prurient interest are those "having a tendency to excite lustful thoughts." In addition, materials failing to meet this test could be banned as obscene. In *Roth*, the court reaffirmed its decision that obscenity was not protected under the First Amendment and, consequently, upheld the convictions of Samuel Roth and David Alberts for publishing and distributing obscene material through the mail.

Samuel Roth, who operated a literary business in New York City, was convicted for violating the federal statute (i.e., the Comstock Act) that criminalized sending "obscene, lewd, lascivious, or filthy" materials through the mail. David S. Alberts was convicted under California statute for selling lewd and obscene books, in addition to composing and publishing obscene advertisements for his products. The court combined the *Roth* and *Alberts* cases because they raised the same issue: Did either the federal or California's obscenity restrictions, prohibiting the sale and transfer of obscene materials through the mail, encroach upon the freedom of expression as guaranteed under the First Amendment?

In a 6–3 decision written by Justice William J. Brennan, Jr., the court held that obscenity was not "within the area of constitutionality protected under speech or press." The court noted that the First Amendment was not meant to protect every utterance or form of expression and stated that a published work is obscene if it (1) appeals predominantly to prurient interest, (2) is patently offensive by contemporary community standards; and, (c) is utterly without redeeming social value. Justice Brennan went on to state that such a definition of obscenity gave sufficient fair warning and satisfied the demands of the due process clause guaranteed under the Fourteen Amendment. As a result, the court ruled that because obscenity is not protected, constitutional guaranties were not violated in the cases of both defendants, Samuel Roth and David Alberts.

In his concurring opinion, Chief Justice Earl Warren expressed his concern that "broad language used here may eventually be applied to the arts and sciences and freedom of communication generally" and recommended that the court's decision in *Roth* be interpreted within a limited scope. In their dissenting opinion, Justices William O. Douglas and Hugo Black argued that the First Amendment protected obscene material. Justice John Marshall Harlan II dissented in *Roth*, but concurred in *Alberts*, because, he argued, that although the states have broad power to prosecute obscenity, the federal government did not have such authority to criminalize the possession and distribution of obscene materials.

In the case of *Roth*, despite its good intentions, the court failed to distinguish sex from obscenity. Because the court relied on vague language (e.g., "average person," "contemporary community standards," and "prurient interest") it spent decades addressing the shortcomings of the *Roth* decision (see *Jacobellis v. Ohio*, 1964; *Miller v. California*, 1973; *Reno v. ACLU*, 1997).

For example, in *Miller v. California* (1973), the court created a modern three-prong test for judging obscenity: (1) the proscribed material must depict or describe sexual conduct in an obviously offensive way, (2) the conduct must be specifically described in the law, and (3) the work must, when taken as a whole, lack serious value, and must appeal to a prurient interest in sex. Today, there continues to be much debate on how to best define obscenity, especially because perceptions of what is considered obscene differ from culture to culture. As the legal definition of obscenity continues to develop, censorship restrictions may present civil liberty issues for the court to consider in the near future.

Shane W. Kraus
Bowling Green State University

See Also: Brennan, William J., Jr.; Obscenity Laws; Pornography.

Further Readings

Miller v. California, 413 U.S. 15 (1973).
Moore, Roy and Michael Murray, eds. *Media Law and Ethnics*. New York: Lawrence Erlbaum Associates, 2008.

Rothstein, Arnold

American gambling figure Arnold Rothstein enjoyed a reputation as the nation's biggest high-stakes gambler during his lifetime and is today known for his connections to the 1919 Black Sox betting scandal. Rothstein's father, Abraham, was born in New York City to a Russian immigrant family. Called "Abe the Just" by New York Governor Alfred E. Smith for his rectitude, he prospered in the textile industry. His son Arnold was attracted to gambling in his teenage years. Progressive Era–New York had a thriving gambling subculture, with elaborate illegal casinos and street-corner dice games. Early on, Rothstein supplemented his gambling winnings with income derived from moneylending. As he grew older, he worked day jobs as a salesman but continued to hone his gambling ability, for a time under the tutelage of famous gamblers "Honest" John Kelly and Richard Canfield. After saving $2,000, he retired from sales and pledged himself to the life of a professional gambler.

New York gangster Arnold Rothstein is best remembered for financing the bribery of eight Chicago White Sox players (above) to throw the 1919 World Series by losing games.

Through the 1910s, Rothstein worked in bookmaking, taking and placing bets on both horse races and sporting events; bankrolled floating illegal dice games; and played cards and billiards for high stakes. He also owned clubs in which gambling was conducted, although this was ostensibly illegal in the state of New York. Tied to the city's political establishment (he was a protégé of Tammany leader Big Tim Sullivan), he did not fear the law. Usually, his operations continued without police harassment, and even when the police attempted to close him down, they inevitably failed. In early 1919, he was accused of firing shots at police officers during a raid of one of his dice games. The indictments were dismissed before trial, a testament to his political connections.

Rothstein's stamina was legendary—he once played pool for 32 hours straight and followed nights at the dice tables with days running his gambling establishments. He grew wealthy from his gambling interests and boasted that he never ran crooked games. Yet, he was involved in what is likely the largest gambling scandal in American professional sports history: the bribery of players for the purpose of throwing the 1919 World Series. With the Chicago White Sox heavily favored to beat the underdog Cincinnati Reds, smart operators understood that, should the Reds win, those who bet on them might make a fortune. The exact sequence of events that led to the cheating is unclear; those involved had good reason to obscure their roles. Most believe that a coterie of gamblers, led by Rothstein, offered to pay $10,000 to eight members of the Chicago White Sox to throw the series by deliberately losing games. Cincinnati won the series 5–3, and almost immediately allegations of a fix began circulating. A series of investigatory articles in the *New York World* led to public demands for a formal inquiry. Subsequent scandals during the 1920s fueled the fire. Testifying before a Chicago grand jury, Rothstein denied any role in the "fix" and escaped indictment.

Despite his protestations, Rothstein's name was thereafter linked with the World Series scandal. He publicly foreswore his gambling interests and announced his intentions to concentrate on his real estate investments; over the next decade, he built a large real estate empire that included two office buildings in midtown Manhattan, a New York City hotel, and 1,000 furnished apartments, which he rented. With the advent of Prohibition, Rothstein emerged as a mentor for a rising cohort of bootleggers and gangsters, including Frank Costello, Charles "Lucky" Luciano, and Meyer Lansky.

He reportedly bankrolled both massive bootlegging operators and hijacking ventures. In 1924, Rothstein was accused of income tax evasion; the case was never resolved. His personal fortune was estimated at between $2 and $10 million, a tremendous sum for the period. Rothstein remained, until he died, a gambler. On November 5, 1928, he was shot at Manhattan's Park Central hotel, reportedly after his failure to square a gambling debt. He died shortly afterward, steadfastly refusing to name his killer, who was never brought to justice.

David G. Schwartz
University of Nevada, Las Vegas

See Also: 1921 to 1940 Primary Documents; Genovese, Vito; Luciano, "Lucky"; Schultz, "Dutch."

Further Readings
Katcher, Leo. *The Big Bankroll: The Life and Times of Arnold Rothstein*. London: Victor Gollancz, 1959.
Peterson, Virgil. *The Mob: 200 Years of Organized Crime in New York*. Ottawa, IL: Green Hill Publishers, 1983.
"Rothstein a Power in Gambling World." *New York Times* (November 7, 1928).
Schwartz, David G. *Roll the Bones: The History of Gambling*. New York: Gotham Books, 2006.

Ruby Ridge Standoff

The Ruby Ridge Standoff is one of the most devastating indictments against law enforcement in the history of America. The Ruby Ridge Standoff resulted in the deaths of a U.S. marshal, a teenager who was shot in the back while running from law enforcement officials, and an unarmed mother who was shot dead while holding her infant child.

Randy Weaver has been described as a white supremacist, a religious fanatic, an ultraconservative religious fanatic, and an isolated survivalist. He was formerly a Green Beret. Weaver lived in a small isolated cabin made of plywood and a sheet-metal roof without electricity in a forested and mountainous area in northern Idaho with his wife, Vicki, and his teenage daughter, Sara, his younger teenage son, Sammy, and his subsequently born infant daughter, Elsabeth. It was common practice for people in this part of the state to carry weapons while walking or working in the forest. The family had little money and obtained much of their food from farming their small garden and hunting. In 1989, Weaver needed money. Weaver was enticed by an informant for the U.S. Bureau of Alcohol, Tobacco, and Firearms (BATF) to sell illegal sawed-off shotguns. There is a dispute as to whether the shotguns were ever delivered; however, Weaver's subsequent acquittal indicates that they were never, in fact, delivered.

A Warrant Is Issued

As a result of the entrapment by the BATF, in 1991, a warrant was issued by the U.S. District Court for the arrest of Weaver on the gun charges. After he was bailed, a court date of February 21 was set, which was reset for February 20 at the request of the BATF. However, the notice sent to Weaver's lawyer had March 30 for the hearing date. When Weaver failed to show at the February 20 hearing, a warrant was issued for his arrest for failing to appear before the court, even though the judge was notified of the clerical error. Subsequently, the U.S. Marshals Service prepared a threat assessment concerning Weaver that included numerous falsehoods, such as allegations that Weaver had been involved in a bank robbery, that Weaver's cabin was a fortified house with blackout curtains, that Weaver had vehicles in his "compound" that were mounted with heavy caliber guns, and that he would likely shoot officers on sight. By 1992, the U.S. Marshals Service began surveillance of Weaver's cabin.

On April 21, six marshals dressed in camouflage uniforms, black ski masks, and body armor while carrying submachine guns approached the Weaver cabin, ostensibly for a "reconnaissance" mission. When the marshals approached the Weaver cabin, they threw pebbles at the cabin to see if they could attract the attention of the Weavers' dogs. One of the dogs responded and began to approach the marshals. Weaver, a friend, and his teenage son, who carried a shotgun and rifles at the time, followed the dog. Weaver went in one direction and his son and his friend went in another direction.

As Weaver approached a stand of trees, a camouflaged marshal yelled at Weaver to freeze. Weaver refused and retreated back to the cabin. A short time later, as the dog approached the stand of trees where the marshals were hidden, one of them shot the dog. Weaver's son shot once into the forest and started to run back to the cabin. Weaver yelled to his son to hurry back to the cabin and fired several shots into the air to distract whoever it was who was shooting. At that time, the marshals opened fire and shot Weaver's son in the back, killing him. Weaver's friend returned fire in the direction of the marshals. One of the marshals was struck and killed, although there is some question whether he was killed by Weaver's friend or friendly fire from the other marshals. After taking shelter in the cabin, the Weavers later retrieved their son's body and placed him in a shed on their property. The siege then began. The log road that led to the Weaver's cabin was blockaded. Eventually, hundreds of law enforcement and military personnel were brought in, along with over 250 law enforcement and military vehicles, including armored personnel carriers. The FBI Hostage Rescue Team was brought in, along with specially trained sniper teams.

The Seige and Outcome

On April 22, later in the afternoon, the Weavers wanted to check on their son's body in the shed. Weaver, his friend, and his teenage daughter exited the cabin and went to the shed. When Weaver attempted to open the shed door, one of the snipers shot Weaver. Weaver, his friend, and his daughter fled back to the cabin. Weaver's wife, who was unarmed and holding her infant daughter, held the door open for them. At that time, a sniper shot Weaver's wife, killing her. The bullet went through her skull and struck Weaver's friend, who was seriously wounded. The siege lasted nine more days before the Weavers were eventually convinced to surrender. During the siege, the situation attracted national attention. Hundreds of people appeared at the scene but were prevented from approaching due to the blockade. During and after the siege, the government issued numerous press releases that were subsequently shown to be false, which only inflamed the public reaction.

Weaver and his friend were indicted for the crimes of conspiracy, the original gun charge, failing to appear, assaulting U.S. marshals, murder, resisting U.S. marshals, concealing a fugitive, receiving firearms, committing crimes while on bail, and carrying firearms. Weaver was represented by the famous trial attorney Gerry Spence. After a long trial that revealed numerous problems and inconsistencies concerning the evidence presented by the government, Weaver was acquitted of all the charges except for the minor crimes of failing to appear and violating bail. Weaver's friend was acquitted of all charges. The result brought a wave of public outrage at the conduct of the government.

Numerous calls were made for investigation into the conduct of the federal law enforcement agencies. Subsequently, a few of the law enforcement officials involved in the Ruby Ridge Standoff were given minor punishments such as a reprimand or a short suspension. Incredibly, one of the higher law enforcement officials who was so punished was simultaneously recommended for promotion. None of the federal law enforcement officials were ever criminally prosecuted for their actions. The government subsequently paid each of Weaver's daughters $1,000,000 and paid Weaver $100,000 in damages when they brought a civil suit for violations of their civil rights. Weaver's friend was awarded $380,000 in damages. The Ruby Ridge Standoff was a disaster for American law enforcement. It provided ammunition for many of the critics of government who had been continuously raising vociferous allegations of criminal misconduct. Its effects are still felt today, although the terrorist attack of 9/11 has caused much of such criticism to be muted.

Wm. C. Plouffe, Jr.
Independent Scholar

See Also: Civil Rights Laws; Famous Trials; Federal Bureau of Investigation; News Media, Police in.

Further Readings
Bock, Alan W. *Ambush at Ruby Ridge.* London: Dickens, 1995.
Spence, Gerry. *From Freedom to Slavery: The Rebirth of Tyranny in America.* New York: St. Martin's Press, 1996.
Walter, Jess. *Every Knee Shall Bow.* New York: ReganBooks, 1995.

Rule of Law

Today the concept of the rule of law as a government of laws and not a government of men is inherent in democracy. It has gone beyond the specialized realm of legal doctrine. In fact, the very conceptualization of the rule of law predates the emergence and establishment of democratic politics. Euro-American history traces the origin of the rule of law back to the ancient Greeks and later to the events and the illustrious figures that contributed to the foundation of British constitutionalism. Aristotle and Plato (400–300 B.C.E.) argued that "the rule of law is better than the law of any individual" meant that judges and governments should abide by the law in order to restrain despotism and to avoid discretionary power. However, until the medieval period, the general assumption was that the prince or the king would be above all law. During the Christian era of the late Roman Empire, the emperor was subordinated to the law of God but certainly not to the law of other men.

The Magna Carta, one of the most ancient written guarantees of English liberties, is traditionally regarded as the first step toward the emergence of the rule of law. It was drafted at Runnymede by the Thames and signed by King John in 1215 under pressure from his rebellious barons. The barons, exasperated by cutthroat royal taxation and supported by the archbishop of Canterbury, Stephen Langton, requested a solemn grant of their rights. While deeply revealing of the feudal system for limiting to nobles the newly acquired rights, the Magna Carta provided for equality before the law, right to property, and religious freedom, reforms of law and justice, and restrained the power of royal officials.

It was not until the 17th century in England that a specific limitation to the power of the king was formulated. Sir Edward Coke, one of the most authoritative common law lawyers of the time, argued that although the king had no superior on earth, he was not legitimated to act as judge because he lacked the specialized knowledge possessed by lawyers. Toward the end of the 17th century in England, the Bill of Rights (1689) provided the Parliament with the first recognition of the principle of exclusive privilege of legislative rights. This had immediate effect on the revenue system, for the king could not raise taxes without seeking legislative approval. Yet separation of powers and primacy of the rule of law in the society at large took a long time to be established. It was not until the 18th century that the judiciary was granted security on the basis of the Act of Settlement (1701), by which King

William III established tenure for judges unless the Parliament would remove them. Secrecy and independence of the jury would not, however, be a priority until the 18th century. The latter saw four main events taking place, all of which are considered to have substantially contributed to the consolidation of the rule of law: the U.S. Declaration of Independence in 1776, the U.S. Constitution in 1787, the French Declaration of the Rights of the Man in 1789, and the U.S. Bill of Rights in 1791 positing the freedom of religion, of person and property, and the right to due process and a fair trial (also the controversial right to bear arms). Many see the above sequence of events as a historical process of consensus progressively affirming the necessity for the primacy of the rule of law and the progressive abandonment of feudalism for the embracement of modernity and democratic institutions.

However, until the 19th century, civil service was still appointed on the basis of patronage, and political participation was still limited to the elite, and all of this was perfectly consistent with the classical liberal tradition theorized by Alexis de Tocqueville.

Contemporary Rule of Law

The current formulation of the rule of law is indebted to Albert Vann Dicey (1835–1922), professor of constitutional law in the United Kingdom. The essential characteristics of the rule of law, as originated from Dicey's ideas, should involve (1) supremacy of the law—all persons, irrespective of their rank and condition, and governments alike, are subject to the law; (2) interpersonal adjudication—law based on standards and on the importance of legal power; (3) restrictions on the exercise of discretionary power and

A crowd is allowed to view the heavily guarded ancient Magna Carta document after it is installed in the U.S. Congressional Library in Washington, D.C., by British Ambassador Lord Lothian in 1939 for the time span of World War II. The Magna Carta was a set of laws imposed on King John by a group of feudal barons attempting to limit his powers.

exclusion of arbitrary power; (4) the doctrine of judicial precedent; (5) the common law methodology; (6) that legislation should be prospective and not retrospective; and (7) separation of powers—the parliament has the exclusive right to the legislative power, restrictions apply on the exercise of legislative power by the executive, and the judiciary is independent.

Dicey's positivistic vision, which did nothing to hide some disregard for continental legal traditions, was limited by its inability to distinguish between arbitrary governments lacking formal rules and political regimes (such as apartheid in South Africa, colonial settlements in many areas of the world, and Nazi Germany) that had rules that were discriminatory and unjust. However, Dicey's original formulation of the rule of law, which he used for the first time in 1875 to describe a salient feature of the constitution, was reinterpreted and expanded by subsequent generations of scholars.

In the 20th century, following the growing legal consciousness regarding the perpetration of human rights abuses at the hands of governments, the concept of rule of law became increasingly interlinked with international human rights seen as focusing on the protection of ethnic minorities, women, and children, as well as on the achievement of international standards of labor. However, it was after World War II, with a shift from human rights as protection of minorities and specific social groups to a set of political, civil, economic, social, and cultural rights established as universal and applicable to everybody, that the notion of the rule of law acquired crucial importance: It was no longer about procedures and formal requirements but about substantive conditions in absence of which governments would be free to infringe upon human rights. The rule of law—it was argued by the United Nations—should meet international standards. Yet in the aftermath of World War II in Europe, imposing positive international laws on all states was perceived as likely to jeopardize the exclusivity of state sovereignty.

Formal and Substantive Rule of Law

North American legal theories know two main versions of the rule of law: formal and substantive. The first one, advocated by Joseph Raz, Lon Fullers, and Robert Summers, stresses procedural features; the second one, promoted by Ronald Dvorkin, Sir John Laws, and Trevor Allan, foresees the need for substantial requirements based on contents in addition to its formal requirements. As a result, a middle path has also been articulated as principled adjudication grounding on legal reasoning, transparency, and accountability. The oaths that all government officers, including the president, Supreme Court justices, and the members of the Congress in the United States must pledge on the Constitution, confirm the superiority of the rule of law over any human prerogative. However, both the judiciary and the executive are granted some degree of discretionary power that fuels scholarly debates on the interpretation of the rule of law, especially in relation to the ongoing absence of ratification by the United States of the Rome Statute of the International Criminal Court in 2000. In the 21st century, the universalistic framework of the rule of law was reasserted with renewed vigor by post-9/11 security precautions resulting in a reconfigured world order. Since then, although a certain consensus consolidated around the necessity to reach universal standards of the rule of law, the debate on how this is to be done is still open on the basis of the factual ground that careful scrutiny of the notion and implementation of the rule of law shows how this encompassing and powerful idea assumes different forms in different contexts.

Although the conceptual origin of the rule of law is considered to be indisputably Western, some scholars point out that similar ideas have been elaborated in the east as well. The most ancient example may be the Cyrus cylinder dated 539 B.C.E. It is a written declaration on a clay cylinder, which attests to a long tradition in Mesopotamia whereby kings used to begin their reigns with reforms. For a long time, the cylinder has been interpreted as an act of self-legitimacy by Cyrus seeking the loyalty of his new Babylonian subjects and promising in exchange respect for the religious and political traditions of Babylonia. However, in the early 1970s, the last shah of Iran adopted the Cyrus cylinder as a symbol of his reign, and while celebrating 2,500 years of Iranian monarchy, he defined the cylinder as "the first human rights charter in history," an interpretation that is still advocated by some, but criticized by others as "anachronistic, tendentious, and erroneous." Another example of non-Western ancient conceptualization on the rule of law is Ashoka's edicts: inscriptions on rocks and pillars disseminated at different location in Afghanistan, India, Nepal, and Pakistan. Made by the emperor Ashoka during his reign (269–231 B.C.E.), they promised reforms and policies and promulgated his advice to his subjects. The present formulation of these edicts, based on earlier and subsequent translations, provides some insights into the ruler's attempt to legitimize his empire by making the moral and spiritual welfare of his subjects the primary concern. Some scholars also trace the rule of law back to Chinese legal tradition that elaborated on the concept of the well-governed society as early as the 2nd century B.C.E. by founding it on the legitimacy of the ruler, the ability to exercise power, and on the exclusivity of the publicly proclaimed power. In fact, the Qin Code (Qin Lu) compiled by Emperor Qin Shihuangdi, who reigned between 246 and 210 B.C.E., is considered to be the first archived code of law in China for its attempt to depart from Confucian immunities related to social hierarchy and kinship.

Notwithstanding undeniable similarities of conceptualizations in the history of political thoughts and legal theories all over the world, it is also a fact that the rule of law sits oddly with the traditions that view good governance as the exclusive prerogative of the ruler and discourage litigation as potentially going against the interest of stability, efficiency of government, and social peace. Inferring, however, a polarization between countries governed by the rule of law and countries lacking the rule of law would not only be too simplistic but also risks discrimination against societies that have different conceptualizations of the rule of law.

Conclusion
Finally, the rule of law in its Western formulation and historical development has its own detractors: Leftist scholarship has denounced it as an ideological construction whose birth is rooted in the purpose of legitimizing the privileges of feudal landowners thanks to the alliance with the common law courts. Yet the criticism of the rule of law features substantial variants. Roberto Unger, Ugo Mattei, and Laura Nader, probably the most radical critics of the rule of law, have pointed out the discrepancy between the rhetoric of the rule of law and the actual practice of governance by colonial regimes first, and subsequently in the postcolonial market economy. The rule of law is, therefore, considered to be an instrument of oppression and plunder in the hands of Euro-American expansionism. However, among the scholars criticizing the overvaluation of rule of law for perpetuating the stereotypical image of Western legal superiority, some such as Edward Thompson and William Jenner have advanced moderate instances based on the consideration that even the ruling elite must at least partially abide by the rule of law if they do not want to risk losing their legitimacy. Eventually, the rule of law emerges as a concept historically linked with the political struggles for the establishment of democracy in the West but also as a powerful argument for legitimizing institutional settings and military interventions that have not necessarily supported democratic institutions.

Livia Holden
Lahore University of Management Sciences

See Also: Constitution of the United States of America; Convention on Rights of the Child; Juries; Magna Carta; Tocqueville, Alexis de.

Further Readings
Allan, Trevor R. S. *Law, Liberty and Justice: The Legal Foundations of British Constitutionalism.* New York: Oxford University Press, 1993.
De Tocqueville, Alexis. *The Old Regime and the French Revolution.* New York: Doubleday, 1955.
Dicey, Albert V. *Introduction to the Study of the Law of the Constitution.* London: Macmillan, 1959.
Dvorkin, Ronald. *Taking Rights Seriously.* Cambridge, MA: Harvard University Press, 1977.
Mattei, Ugo and Laura Nader. *Plunder When the Rule of Law Is Illegal.* Malden, MA: Blackwell, 2008.
Neal, David. *The Rule of Law in a Penal Colony: Law and Power in Early New South Wales.* Melbourne: Cambridge University Press, 1991.
Peerenboom, Randall, ed. *Asian Discourses of Rule of Law: Theories and Implementation of Rule of Law.* London: Routledge, 2004.

Rural Police

Rural policing is an often discussed but little understood concept within the criminal justice system. There are many different definitions of what constitutes a rural community and of what police do in the community. There is a common belief that is often backed up by the uniform crime report (UCR) of the Federal Bureau of Investigation (FBI) that crime is less common in rural than urban areas. However, rural police agencies are also less likely to report their data to the FBI. Some features of rural culture that affect policing are distrust of government; reluctance to share internal problems, which may lead to a failure to report crime among citizens; and informal social controls among citizens. Rural police may get calls that are out of the ordinary to urban agencies, including housing checks for citizens on vacation, animal problems, utilities, littering, acting as parade escorts, and many other duties that may take time out of the day.

More than 50 percent of law enforcement agencies in the United States are rural police agencies. However, rural police agencies have to deal with less funding on average than their urban counterparts, and the geographic regions that they have to reach are much larger, which leads to longer response times. Rural areas also tend to be more homogenous than urban areas. Many rural areas do not have the basic dispatch necessities that other areas may have, such as E-911, or even a clear dispatch system. Because of the limited funding, continuing education is not a service that rural officers receive, so they may fall behind in new ways of policing. Salary differences also give an added disadvantage to rural police agencies. Being unable to recruit the most qualified officers in a system where officers receive inadequate training furthers the problems of rural policing. With the problem of finding qualified officers comes the problem of using reserve officers who may be even less qualified than the officers already in place.

Rural policing in the United States is carried out by three distinct agencies: state law enforcement such as the highway patrol, county agencies such as the sheriff's department, and municipal or local police agencies. Oftentimes, municipal police agencies may have less than 10 sworn officers, and many of those are part-time employees. Municipal police agencies are often more reliant on cooperation with other agencies than in urban areas. The bureaucracy for rural police agencies is often less complex than that of their urban counterparts.

Because of funding and lack of police training, many rural agencies rely more heavily on state and federal law enforcement than their urban counterparts. Since many rural areas do not have crime labs, they may send evidence to a state crime lab or federal crime lab. Since some crimes in rural areas may involve wildlife or poaching, state and federal bureaus of wildlife may become involved more quickly in these cases. In many cases with fugitives who are on the run, there must be coordination between the state police, federal U.S. Marshalls, and local police agencies. Sometimes, a state police agency will take the lead in dealing with fugitives because they must track where the fugitive has been and where they are going.

While there may be a need for more state police agencies in rural areas due to lack of funding and training, the interaction between rural and state police may not be as forthcoming. This lack of interaction may also be multiplied by political officials who may feel an affront that their police cannot do the job that locals need. Despite these incidents, state bureaus of investigation routinely work with local officials in complex cases. State bureaus are often called in at the request of the sheriff or local officials, which helps to alleviate some concerns by political officials.

The California Highway Patrol in Bridgeport, California, uses the Dodge Durango in the rural area where the vehicle's handling capabilities allow for all-weather and off-road use.

Many state police agencies have had a history of working with rural areas. Probably the most famous of these police agencies were the Texas Rangers. Originally started in 1823, they were primarily known for fighting and chasing Native Americans, bank robbers, and gangsters. Until 1935, gaining entry to the rangers was primarily based on nepotism because rangers often favored certain candidates over others in political races; after the reforms of 1935, the favoritism ended.

The Office of the Sheriff
The office of the sheriff dates back to the 1000s in England. There are currently more than 3,100 sheriffs in the United States, with most sheriff positions elected. The duty of a sheriff differs in a rural area because he is often seen as the preeminent officer in the county. The sheriff is in charge of all administrative duties for the county police agency, including investigations that range from homicide to vagrancy. Because some rural areas lack a police department, the sheriff may be the sole provider of police coverage for a large area. Because the sheriff holds an elected position, he or she may face undue pressure that is not applicable in urban areas. Therefore, it is important for sheriffs to maintain a unique bond and close communication with members of the community. The duties of sheriffs and deputies are sometimes difficult because of the large geospatial distance that a single department covers. The problems become compounded in poorer rural regions because funds do not extend to adequate staffing or up-to-date equipment.

The sheriff also often runs the county jail. While jails in urban areas are often overcrowded, jails in rural areas tend to be under capacity. Similar to police agencies, jails in rural areas are often understaffed and have very few programs for prisoners. Many jails in rural areas are structurally deficient. Inmates in rural areas are less supervised and less often separated by age. This leads to a huge increase in homicide, suicide, and deaths from illness within the inmate population.

In many areas of the south, the sheriff has been viewed as one of the most influential, if not the most influential, figure in the county. This is because the sheriff is one of the few office holders in the county that runs nationwide. People in the rural south generally have a great deal of respect for the office of the sheriff. While the sheriff commands respect, sometimes the line between policeman and criminal becomes thin. During the 1960s, sheriffs were often called upon in the south to reinforce or promote violence against African Americans. One of the most famous cases of this was that of Lawrence Rainey in Neshoba County, Mississippi. He was accused of involvement in the deaths of three civil rights workers in Mississippi. While not convicted of either the murders or subsequent civil rights charges, many believed that he played a role in the cover-up. Another famous example was Gerald Hege in North Carolina. Hege came to office as a tough, hands-on enforcer of the law. He created a line of merchandise and ordered his police officers to wear paramilitary uniforms. As the years progressed, charges of corruption began to surface, and he became a convicted felon.

History of Rural Policing
In the past, rural policing has been popularized by TV shows like *The Andy Griffith Show* and others as having little, if any crime. However, throughout history, rural police have had to deal with a wide range of issues unique to the rural experience. In many rural areas in the south, bootlegging was a major problem that was dealt with primarily by federal and local police. Rural police agencies have also had to deal with the specter of race. Many lynch mobs were formed and were not controlled well by rural police agencies, either because of sympathies the police officers had with the local mob, or because of lack of resources. Since these early days, rural policing has advanced to looking for meth houses and marijuana crops through many advanced technologies; rural policing today is front and center in the battle against drugs.

While popular culture has historically portrayed rural areas as being low in crime, western films such as *Tombstone* have depicted lawlessness as rampant in rural western towns. Movies and popular culture have depicted many outlaws as heroes, including Billy the Kid and Jesse James, while the police were portrayed as outlaws. However, the days of the Old West are gone. There are no longer gunfights at high noon as popularized in movies. Today, rural police agencies in the west deal with immigration, drugs, and many other problems.

Rural policing in the United States is often seen as a public service, as well as a tool for crime prevention. Rural police are often asked to do things that in the big cities may be the responsibility of the fire department, emergency management, or animal control. Rural police have to deal with things that urban police do not, including organized theft of livestock, grain, and farm equipment.

Vigilantism has also been associated with rural areas. With lynchings occuring primarily in rural areas of the south by organizations such as the KKK and others, vigilantism has also had significant racial undertones. In southern Indiana, a group called the White Caps lynched several people who were either criminals or suspected of being criminals. They caused an international incident by lynching members of the Reno Gang in 1868, which caused Great Britain to threaten to pull their extradition treaty with the United States. While lasting to the early part of the 1900s, the White Caps lost much public support after an 1888 incident in which they lynched a man who was possibly innocent. Another vigilante group was the Anti Horse Thief Association, which was formed to protect against marauders invading the border and to stop horse thievery. The group was prominent in Oklahoma and other parts of the midwest but expanded into other areas.

Informal Control in Rural Areas

Because of strict gun laws in many urban areas and the conservative political nature of many rural areas, guns are more prevalent in rural areas. Many people in rural areas are avid hunters, and hunting even makes some rural areas tourist destinations. While gun ownership is higher in rural areas, commission of a crime with guns is higher in urban areas. However, there is some evidence that police in rural areas are more likely to have a gun pulled on them than police in urban areas. This could be because of the distrust of government by many people in rural areas.

Lyerly and Skipper have argued that there are informal social controls that lead to less delinquency in rural areas; many other studies have found that crimes such as shoplifting and other types of property theft are often handled informally between individuals. This informal control happens because many residents in rural areas know each other, newcomers to these areas and overall social mobility are also rare in these areas. While this informal control may seek to help police, it also may lead to problems. For example, many women are unwilling or fearful of having law enforcement intervene in domestic violence situations, possibly because the women do not want to be embarrassed and have people they know intervene in a domestic situation. Another reason is that the woman may be fearful that her husband may know the officer, and that the officer would side with him.

The very nature of crime is that people are more likely to commit crimes against people they know, rather than people they do not know. Rape, homicide, assault, and many other crimes may not be reported to the police in rural areas because of distrust of government or fear of reprisal. The social isolation of rural areas and the togetherness of the community is a central key to understanding the strengths and weaknesses of rural policing.

Derrick Shapley
Mississippi State University

See Also: Federal Bureau of Investigation; Sheriffs; State Police.

Further Readings
Liederbach, John and James Frank. "Policing Mayberry: The Work Routines of Small-Town and Rural Officers." *Journal of Criminal Justice*, v.28 (2003).
Lyerly, Robert R. and James K. Skipper. "Differential Rates of Rural-Urban Delinquency: A Social Control Approach." *Criminology*, v.19/3 (1981).
U.S. Department of Homeland Security. "Rural Policing Institute." http://www.fletc.gov/rpi (Accessed September 2011).
Weisheit, Ralph L., et al. "Crime and Policing in Rural and Small-Town America: An Overview of the Issues." http://www.ncjrs.gov/txtfiles/crimepol.txt (Accessed September 2011).
Weisheit, Ralph L., et al. "Rural Crime and Rural Policing." http://www.ncjrs.gov/pdffiles/rcrp.pdf (Accessed September 2011).

Sacco and Vanzetti

After the Russian Bolshevik Revolution in 1917, fears of communism quickly spread throughout the United States, and in 1919, a series of bombings heightened these suspicions. In April, the U.S. Postal Service intercepted several mail bombs, and in June, eight bombs—in eight cities—exploded within minutes of each other. Fears of conspiracy and communists at the national level further fed social hysterias. Attorney General A. Mitchell Palmer and his assistant J. Edgar Hoover led a series of raids throughout the country (known as the Palmer Raids), and in May 1920, two Italian immigrants in Braintree, Massachusetts, found themselves at the center of this national hysteria. Nicola Sacco and Bartolomeo Vanzetti were quickly accused, tried, and convicted of murder. Normally, a murder conviction would not make national and international headlines, but this case centered on the ethnicity of the accused, national origin, and political leanings. To this day, much controversy surrounds the Sacco-Vanzetti case, questioning if they really were anarchists.

On April 15, 1920, F. A. Parmenter and Alessandro Berardelli—a shoe factory paymaster and his guard—were shot in South Braintree, Massachusetts. Records note that about $15,000 in cash was taken, which was not an uncommon crime. Immediately, Sacco and Vanzetti were not suspects, but they fell into a police trap at Boda's Garage three weeks later. The duo, both carrying weapons, lied to the police about their whereabouts and weapons. They were arrested on the basis that they were carrying a weapon similar to that of the crime and the vehicle they were claiming was seen in the Braintree area at the time of the shooting.

On September 11, 1920, they were charged, and Vanzetti was also charged with a December 24, 1919, robbery in Bridgewater. In the summer of 1920, Vanzetti stood trial for the Bridgewater robbery, and he was subsequently found guilty, even though he had a sound alibi and witnesses to support him. He received a stiff sentence of 10 to 15 years for an attempted robbery with no injuries. After the harsh verdict, the recently formed American Civil Liberties Union hired Fred H. Moore, a well-known labor attorney on the west coast, to defend Sacco and Vanzetti. Moore used his own socialist beliefs to defend the duo, and throughout the trial he likened the Braintree police to the actions of the Palmer Raids. More so, he argued that the two were being wrongly prosecuted because they did not fit the American ideal, nor did they speak much English.

The trial lasted six weeks, and Moore used grassroots techniques to rally not only national public support but also that of the international community. He even enlisted the help of the

A group tries to draw support for an upcoming protest in London, England, in 1921 to support protest of the death sentences imposed on Nicola Sacco and Bartolomeo Vanzetti.

Italian government. On July 14, 1921, the jury found the duo guilty, even though the evidence was conflicting, evidence that the crime could have been committed by the Morelli Gang, and a confession from convicted bank robber Celestino Madeiros (given in 1925) came into play.

Several witnesses testified that Sacco and Vanzetti were in Boston at the time of the murders, but these accounts did not aid the defendants. In addition to base facts, the prosecutor—Frederick G. Katzman—used the defendants; political beliefs as motive for the murder. The two were known to converse with anarchists and socialists.

In addition to the conflicting testimonies, Judge Webster Thayer repeatedly threw out testimony from known political activists, in the retrial he refused to allow the testimony of Celestino Madeiros, and he presided over Vanzetti's trial for the attempted robbery in 1919. Thayer's actions reflect the rise of nativism in the United States, and they also mirror the amount of media attention the case received. Moore captivated his audience and he made frequent use of newspapers and other media outlets to argue that the defendants were being penalized for their political beliefs and not for their actions.

In 1924, while attempting to reverse the court's decision, Moore was replaced as defending council. William Thompson, a well-known Bostonian, took over the case. As the defense progressed, he stated that he did not care for the defendants political beliefs, but he did admire them for their dedication and determination. He attempted to downplay the political front, but it was to no avail. In 1926, the Massachusetts Supreme Court reviewed the case, but it did not see a different outcome (*Commonwealth v. Sacco and Vanzetti*, 255 Mass. 369, 151 N.E. 839 [1926]). Attempts to save the duo lasted until 1927.

The two faced their fate on April 23, 1927, as they died in the electric chair. Afterward, they received an elaborate funeral in Boston, as the trial had brought great attention to the city. At the time, comparisons were made between the Sacco-Vanzetti affair and the Boston Massacre.

Annessa A. Babic
New York Institute of Technology

See Also: Anarchists; Italian Americans; Political Dissidents.

Further Readings

Selmi, Patrick. "Social Work and the Campaign to Save Sacco and Vanzetti." *Social Service Review*, v.75/1 (2001).

Tejada, Susan. *In Search of Sacco and Vanzetti: Double Lives, Troubled Times, and the Massachusetts Murder Case That Shook the World*. Lebanon, NH: Northeastern University Press, 2012.

Topp, Michael M. *The Sacco and Vanzetti Case: A Brief History With Documents*. Bedford Series in History and Culture. New York: Palgrave Macmillan, 2005.

Young, William and David E. Kaiser. *Postmortem: New Evidence in the Case of Sacco and Vanzetti*. Amherst: University of Massachusetts Press, 1985.

Salem Witch Trials

In colonial Massachusetts, between 1692 and 1693, a series of infamous trials occurred where more than 150 people were arrested and 19 people were convicted and hanged. The crime these people were accused of committing was witchcraft. These trials, the Salem witch trials, have become so well known in America today that they are essentially as much a part of popular early American history as Captain John Smith and Pocahontas of Jamestown Colony or George Washington and the cherry tree. However, they are not representative of a positive part of early America. In fact, the Salem witch trials are a prime example of mass hysteria, social ignorance, and religious intolerance, which can have deadly results.

Massachusetts Bay Colony, as it came to be known after the Puritans landed at Plymouth in 1620, was heavily reliant on religious principles. The Puritans left England in search of freedom to practice their religion as they saw fit; however, the Puritans and their descendents were not the most receptive to people of other religious practices. The colonists were, generally, very strict in their observations of religious law and ritual. They did not approve of such common things as music, dancing, or toys for children. Those people who violated the religious norms were often subject to severe peer pressure and even criminal punishment, which included being placed in the stocks for people to gawk at and abuse. Even though the colonists did not have a theocratic form of government, it was generally accepted practice that government leaders were strong believers in their religion.

The time of the Salem witch trials was toward the end of the Inquisition the Catholic Church had conducted in Europe. During the time of the Inquisition, thousands of people were arrested, questioned, tortured, and executed for heresy, blasphemy, and other crimes. Witchcraft was also a crime investigated by the Inquisition, although it was not the primary goal. Death in the Inquisition usually meant being burned at the stake. Interestingly, in America, many people think that the people convicted of witchcraft in Salem were burned at the stake, but, in fact, they were hanged. The act of being burned for being a witch was apparently transferred in American lore from the stories of the Inquisition to the Salem witch trials. However, there is little doubt that the colonists were well aware of the religious zealotry in Europe that mandated that witches be found, tried, and executed, and that the colonists adopted this attitude and brought it with them to America. There were witch hunts in England as well.

The year 1692 was a year of change for the colonists in Massachusetts. A new charter for the Province of Massachusetts had been approved in 1691, and a new governor had been appointed. In 1692, one of the first concerns of the new governor was the creation of a Court of Oyer and Terminer to address the problem of the full jails. At the time of the Salem witch trials, there were two municipal entities involved: Salem Town and Salem Village. Salem Town was the larger of the two municipalities. Salem Village was generally considered a troublesome place, where the residents quarrelled with each other often. It is reported that there was a family feud in Salem Town, with the town being split between the two sides.

Mass Hysteria

The events leading to the Salem witch trials began in Salem Village when two young girls, Betty Parris, age 9, and Abigail Williams, age 11, began to experience strange fits of screaming and tantrums for which doctors could not find any medical cause. The girls would complain about being stuck with needles and pins. More accusations were brought by Ann Putnam, age 12, of Salem, although some historians hold the position that Putnam's accusations were a result of an ongoing family feud between the Putnam and Porter families.

Initially, three people were arrested: Sarah Good, who was a homeless woman with a dubious reputation; Sarah Osborne, who did not regularly attend church and was twice married; and Tituba, a slave of Indian or African heritage, who had been accused of telling the girls tales of sexual practices with demons. In March 1692, the women were arrested, interrogated, and held in jail. After these initial arrests, over the next few months, more accusations were made against other people, and more people were arrested and examined in Salem Village and Salem Town. Three women who had been arrested, Abigail Hobbs, Mary Warren, and Deliverance Hobbs, confessed to the charges and, as a result, more arrests were made.

By the end of May 1962, more than 60 people were in custody when the Court of Oyer and Terminer convened in Salem Town. Bridget Bishop, a woman who was described as not living according to the Puritan lifestyle, was the first person convicted and hanged on June 10, 1692.

A dramatic scene from a 17th-century witch trial with a woman conjuring up supernatural powers and a man passed out on the floor. The Salem Witch hunts and trials resulted in 19 women executed, at least four accused witches perishing in prison, and one man being pressed to death. About 100 to 200 others were arrested and imprisoned on witchcraft charges.

More accusations and arrests followed. On July 19, 1692, five more women were found guilty and hanged. On August 19, 1692, four men and another woman were convicted and hung. On September 22, 1692, eight more people were convicted and hanged. In October 1692, the Court of Oyer and Terminer was dismissed. Despite the dismissal, trials for witchcraft continued in other courts in 1693. Although some people were found guilty, the governor pardoned them before they were executed.

A few years after the conclusion of the Salem witch trials, public criticism of the trials began. Some of the participants in the Salem witch trials even expressed their regret over the events and asked for forgiveness. Starting in 1700, petitions began to be filed with Massachusetts courts, asking for reversal of the convictions and compensation. In 1711, some of the convictions were reversed by the General Court, and compensation was paid to survivors and relatives. In later years, several memorials were erected to the victims of the Salem witch trials. In 1957, the remaining convictions of the Salem witch trials that had not been reversed were reversed by the Massachusetts General Court.

A number of historians have speculated as to why the witch hunts occurred and why certain people were singled out. These proposed reasons have included personal vendettas, fear of strong women, and economic competition. Regardless, the Salem witch trials are a memorial and a warning to what hysteria, religious intolerance, and ignorance can cause in the criminal justice system. Unfortunately, American history shows that such events can and will happen again and again. The primary example of this repetition is the McCarthy hearings and the Red Scare in America during the 1950s, which destroyed the lives of numerous people. Indeed, the injustice of the Salem witch trials has entered into the American lexicon with the famous phrase *a witch hunt*, which is often used when people are being falsely charged.

Wm. C. Plouffe, Jr.
Independent Scholar

See Also: 1600 to 1776 Primary Documents; Court of Oyer and Terminer; Famous Trials; Religion and Crime, History of.

Further Readings
Aronson, Marc. *Witch-Hunt: Mysteries of the Salem Witch Trials*. New York: Atheneum, 2003.
Boyer, Paul S. and Stephen Nussbaum. *Salem Possessed: The Social Origins of Witchcraft*. Cambridge, MA: Harvard University Press, 1974.
Boyer, Paul S. and Stephen Nissenbaum, eds. *Salem-Village Witchcraft: A Documentary Record of Local Conflict in Colonial New England*. Evanston, IL: Northwestern University Press, 1972.
Breslaw, Elaine. *Tituba, Reluctant Witch of Salem*. New York: New York University Press, 1996.
Ericson, Kai. *Wayward Puritans: A Study in the Sociology of Deviance*. New York: Allyn & Bacon, 2005.
Jackson, Shirley. *The Witchcraft of Salem Village*. New York: Random House, 1956.

San Francisco, California

San Francisco was founded by the Spanish in 1776 and passed to Mexico in 1821. The Mexican state of which it was a part was seized by the United States in 1846. Shortly thereafter, the former quiet and undeveloped town grew 2,500 percent in one year: Gold had been discovered nearby. Ineffective military rule in the pre-statehood period and a weak criminal justice system thereafter led to serious crime and social unrest. Crime, prostitution, and political violence became endemic. In effect, self-styled vigilantes, with their own alternative control institutions and militia, overthrew democratic government. The city suffered a catastrophic earthquake and fire in 1906 but rose from the ashes, though its prominence as a vice center was finished. In the 1950s, the city became known as a haven for alternative lifestyles and in the 1960s presaged a new type of youth culture. Today, it enjoys a progressive, tolerant environment and city governance, perhaps a cultural survival of its free-wheeling past as a wide-open boomtown. It is known as a major tourist destination because of its picturesque neighborhoods, mild climate, and specific scenic attractions, one of which is the former Alcatraz prison, located on an island in the bay. The stately and beautiful Golden Gate Bridge, a place with a dubious distinction of popularity for suicide, overlooks the area.

Gold Rush and Vigilante Days

The first committee of vigilance in San Francisco was constituted in 1851. It was concerned with the problem of arson and an alleged gang of Irish Australian provenance, the Sydney Ducks. Nativism was rising as a political force in the United States, and crime was used as a pretext to deport and otherwise expel undesirables, particularly Australians. The committee also took on policing powers and hanged four reputed criminals.

In 1856, several political duels so inflamed the business community that the vigilance committee was reconstituted. It should be noted that civic warfare and reaction broke out in Baltimore, New Orleans, and New York in the same era. Vigilantes in San Francisco were backed by their own militias and even seized arms from the U.S. government. This apparent anarchy was supported by local newspapers and many historians, all of whom cited "corruption" as a rationale. However, it is quite apparent that much of the struggle involved control of municipal government. The "People's Party" of the vigilantes seized control from the Democratic administration and then merged with the Republican Party.

Prostitution and other forms of vice were endemic from the gold rush period through the early 1900s. Especially prominent in that regard were the Tenderloin area and Chinatown. An area closer to the waterfront called "the Barbary Coast" was an internationally known brothel district. Women flocked to the city from points east in the United States and from many foreign countries to get in on this secondary gold rush. Unwary and drunk customers were often drugged in the area's many saloons and robbed or even shanghaied—knocked out and dragooned into involuntary service on a merchant vessel. It is notable that the vigilantes made no effort to thwart the profitable trade of women, drugs, and spirits. Drug trafficking, chiefly of opium, was an issue that related to Chinese immigration; opium dens were closed in 1878, chiefly as an anti-Chinese measure. But other vice continued to flourish, almost untrammeled, until the early 1900s when moral crusaders led by the clergy closed down the various venues. Thereafter, prostitution continued on a much more subdued basis, but saloons, with a few notable exceptions, faded from the scene.

San Francisco Renaissance
In the early 1950s, a small group of East coast and west coast intellectuals began to coalesce in several urban American locales. New York's Greenwich Village was one pole in the world of the Beats, but North Beach is where some of the critical events leading to the San Francisco Renaissance and the subsequent Summer of Love and hippie movement occurred. San Francisco was known as a tolerant small city with a lively cultural life. Numerous coffeehouses and jazz clubs, low rents, cheap food, mild climate, and bookstores were among the attractions of the North Beach area that appealed to this group of disaffected intellectuals. Drugs such as cannabis and various hallucinogens were popular among this group as they sought to find truth outside the normal parameters of mundane experience. Jazz, with its combination of improvisation, artistry, and insistent beat, contributed to that desire to transmute the quotidian reality. Beat writers, after "beat down," or, alternately, "beatific," included Jack Kerouac, Allen Ginsberg, Gary Snyder, Neal Cassady, and bookstore proprietor and poet Lawrence Ferlinghetti.

Ginsberg's reading of his prophetic and jeremiad-style poem "Howl" at City Lights Bookstore in 1956 ignited a cultural revolution. The published poem itself was seized by the police, and the ensuing court battle eventually set a legal precedent protecting artistic freedom. The attendant publicity and the success of Kerouac's *On the Road* ignited a minor influx of the like-minded into the North Beach area, which became notorious as a "beatnik" locale. Beats were known for a slang derived from black and underworld argot, for example, "dig," "daddio," "pad," and "chick"; most men wore beards, and most women had long hair and were attired in dancing tights. A few beats like Allen Ginsberg were "out" and openly homosexual. Beats were tolerant of experimentation, be it with drugs or sexuality. This was a huge departure from the middle-class norm of Eisenhower-era American. Media fixated on Beat imagery, and the beatnik became a familiar stereotype in film and television by the early 1960s.

Summer of Love and Aftermath
As rents rose in the North Beach area and it became more of a tourist destination, Beats and other bohemians moved into nearby neighborhoods. By the mid-1960s, the formerly working-class Haight-Ashbury neighborhood became a student and Beat quarter. A vibrant and exciting series of events transformed the neighborhood into a tolerant, musically and artistically innovative destination. Cannabis and hallucinogens were easily attainable and drew some repressive tactics from police such as mass arrests in neighborhood sweeps. By the summer of 1967, the youth revolution that had swept the country found its focal point in that neighborhood, and thousands of young people literally mobbed the streets. Many of these young people were exploited by predatory criminals who were also drawn to the area. Hard drugs and hallucinogens of dangerous potency and unknown provenance contributed to the downfall of the neighborhood. This led to a general disaffection with the entire urban "hippie scene" and a resultant "back to the earth" movement in which many young people moved to rural areas where some formed communes.

In a return to the city's vice-begotten roots, the adult entertainment industry began its national rise to prominence in the 1960s and 1970s in the city's North Beach area. The Condor Club housed the first topless dancers and gave rise to a host of imitators in the same district, which, incidentally, was very near the old vice haunts of the 1800s. Adult bookstores and cinemas prospered in North Beach and in the Tenderloin district. Many old Beat haunts were displaced by the growing number of clubs boasting risqué entertainment. Today, both the Tenderloin and the sex district of North Beach attract tourists and locals looking for a night on the town.

The generally tolerant atmosphere that drew the Beats and hippies to the area also appealed to many gay Americans. In the early 1970s as gays "came out" all over the United States, this community was especially prominent and vocal. San Francisco, particularly the Castro district, became a gay mecca and was the setting for gay novels, movies, and, increasingly, politics. San Franciscan Harvey Milk became the first avowed gay city councilman in the United States in 1978 and was murdered that same year. Another tragedy followed close on the heels of this incident: human immunodeficiency virus and acquired immune deficiency syndrome (HIV/AIDS), which was initially known as the "gay plague," killed thousands of young men in the city. As a consequence, many places of gay assignation such as baths and certain clubs were closed. Today, the "Castro" is known as a largely gay neighborhood and retains a lively cultural and social life.

Crime Today

Not surprisingly, much of the area's crime is centered in the old Tenderloin district and the area directly south. This area is known for assaults, larceny with contact (pickpocketing, purse snatching), public intoxication, and drug- and sex-related crime. Tourists and conventioneers straying from their meeting venues are frequent victims. Police actions over decades have had little impact on this historic skid row. Other high-crime areas are the North Beach area—a tourist destination and secondary sex industry locale—the Haight, and the touristy Embarcadero. The city, particularly in the Tenderloin and the Haight, has a large homeless population who account for a disproportionate amount of police and social services. Western residential areas of the city, such as the Richmond district, enjoy much lower crime rates. Most crime in these areas involves property offenses.

The city and county are completely coterminous today but the sheriff handles the jails (there are seven, including a hospital ward), protects courts and civic buildings, deals with taxes and emergency communications, and is considered a significant public official. All routine law enforcement is handled by the San Francisco Police Department (SFPD). The SFPD began operations in 1849, at the beginning of the gold rush, with Malachi Fallon as captain. Fallon had a force of some 35 officers, and the department, like many municipal police organizations of its time, was reputed to be corrupt and politically dominated by a Tammany-like Democratic machine. It was a focus of vigilante frustration. The first jail was built in this period: Prisoners were lodged in a beached ship in Yerba Buena Cove. In 1856, a

The Chez Paree in 1991 in San Francisco's sex district known as the Tenderloin. In the 1800s, the area also housed many of the city's vices, including gambling halls and speakeasies.

member of the vigilance committee was made chief. In the early 1900s, the SFPD was one of the first departments on the west coast to embrace police modernization and technical innovations. It developed a reputation for efficient riot control when dealing with labor issues in the 1930s and continued to sharpen those tactics during the unrest of the 1960s and 1970s. The SFPD enjoys a reputation of being somewhat lenient and tolerant of minor and vice-related offenses today, a significant change in public perception since the 1960s. In the mid-1990s, the SFPD created a Crime Response Unit to Suppress Homicides (CRUSH) to deal with a large number of drug-related homicides. This unit purported to have solved more than half of the homicides to which it was assigned but was reputed to have used questionable methods and to have arrested innocent people. City police are called upon to deal with protecting hundreds of thousands of tourists and conventioneers yearly, as well as to handle the problems emanating from the city's skid row, the Tenderloin.

The city has also been the locale for several police and crime movies; the *Dirty Harry* franchise and both *Bullitt* productions were filmed there. Hitchcock's *Rear Window* was set in the city as well. Also, *The Streets of San Francisco,* a popular television series of the 1970s, was based on the interaction of a young criminal investigator and an old veteran of the SFPD.

Francis Frederick Hawley
Western Carolina University

See Also: 1851 to 1900 Primary Documents; Alcatraz Island Prison; Oakland, California; Pornography; Vigilantism.

Further Readings
Brown, Richard M. *Strain of Violence: Historical Studies of American Violence and Vigilantism.* New York: Oxford University Press, 1975.
Coblenz, S. *Villains and Vigilantes.* New York: Thomas Yolseloff, 1936.
Courtwright, D. T. *Violent Land: Single Men and Social Disorder From the Frontier to the Inner City.* Cambridge, MA: Harvard University Press, 1998.
Richards, Leonard. *The California Gold Rush and the Coming of the Civil War.* New York: Knopf, 2007.

Stewart, G. *Committee of Vigilance: Revolution in San Francisco, 1851.* Boston: Houghton Mifflin, 1964.

San Quentin State Prison

San Quentin is California's oldest state prison and houses California's death row for male inmates (the largest in the nation). Prior to 1848, the California Territory was sparsely populated and required little in the way of law enforcement. However, the discovery of gold that year set off a growth boom known as the California gold rush; the territory's population increased by more than 100 percent in just three years, and sleepy towns like San Francisco were transformed overnight into bustling cities. Not surprisingly, the massive population growth strained California's meager infrastructure and led to a substantial increase in crime. When California became a state in 1850, the newly elected legislature began making moves to regularize the territory's criminal justice system and to establish a state prison to house the burgeoning criminal population.

Initially, the new state incarcerated state inmates on a wooden ship known as *The Waban,* which was anchored in San Francisco harbor. Beginning in 1852, the ship's inmates were put to work building the new prison, located near the San Francisco Bay on a strip of land known as Point San Quentin, which is how the prison got its name. San Quentin opened in 1854, and almost immediately became a magnet for scandals, including brutal guards, lax oversight, and frequent escapes.

Undoubtedly, this was because of the fact that, at least initially, the prison was a for-profit venture. Originally, the state of California had "leased" San Quentin's convict labor to two speculators, Mariano G. Vallejo and James M. Estell, both former military men. From the state's perspective, leasing the convict labor was a great deal: The speculators were responsible for feeding, clothing, and securing the prisoners, and paid the cash-strapped state $100,000. In order to make a profit, Estell forced the inmates to work seven days a week from sunrise to sunset

An aerial view of San Quentin State Prison in Marin County (the north San Francisco Bay area) in California. The facility houses the only gas chamber and death row for condemned male inmates in the state. San Quentin is the oldest correctional institution in California and a dungeon built there in 1854 is believed to be the state's oldest surviving public structure.

quarrying clay for the prison brickworks or gathering wood to heat San Quentin's kilns. As early as 1855, the legislature was forced to investigate the prison's operation because of the notoriously questionable management, finances, and discipline procedures that Estell employed, and by the Civil War, the lease (which by this point had been sold to John F. McCauley) was voided and the prison officially came under state control. Since that time, the prison has developed a fearsome reputation reinforced by its role in such films as *San Quentin* (1937), *San Quentin* (1946), *Dark Passage* (1947), *Duffy of San Quentin* (1954), *Want to Live!* (1958), and *Take the Money and Run* (1968).

In the 20th century, a new generation of reformers tried to end some of the worst abuses at San Quentin. Most notable is Clinton Duffy, who served as the prison's warden between 1940 and 1952 (the prison's second-longest-serving warden up to that point). Duffy eliminated corporal punishment, instituted an Alcoholics Anonymous chapter at the prison, desegregated San Quentin's dining hall, and established vocational and recreational programs, including an inmate-produced newspaper and an inmate-staffed radio station. Yet San Quentin remained a dangerous, violent place, a fact symbolized by the prison's most infamous riot. In August 1971, a riot broke out following an escape attempt by George Jackson, author of *Soledad Brother* and cofounder of the Black Guerrilla Family prison gang; Jackson was shot to death during the uprising, an event that galvanized African American inmates across the country and contributed to the infamous Attica prison riot the following month.

Since 1893, San Quentin has housed California's death row for male inmates, and in 2001, it was awarded the dubious distinction of the largest death row in the Western Hemisphere.

Between 1893 and 1937, San Quentin hanged inmates who were condemned to death; the prison then moved to lethal gas for executions. When this method of execution was ruled unconstitutional by the 9th Circuit Court of Appeals, California adopted lethal injection as its official method of executing inmates.

Paul Kahan
Montgomery County Community College

See Also: Alcatraz Island Prison; Attica; Capital Punishment; Penitentiaries; Riots.

Further Readings
Duffy, Clinton T. *The San Quentin Story*. New York: Doubleday Press, 1950.
Lamott, Keith. *Chronicle of San Quentin: California's Oldest and Most Famous Prison, 1852–1972*. New York: Ballantine Books, 1972.
Petry, Bonnie L. and Michael Burgess, eds. *San Quentin: The Evolution of a California State Prison*. San Bernardino, CA: Borgo Press, 2005.

Santobello v. New York

In *Santobello v. New York* (404 U.S. 257), Rudolph Santobello's case was remanded for reconsideration to the trial court by the U.S. Supreme Court in 1971. The issue in question was whether a new trial is warranted if there is a breach of promise by the prosecution with regard to a negotiated plea resulting in a significant material effect on the disposition of the defendant's case, even if the breach of promise by the prosecution was inadvertent or unintentional.

In June 1969, Santobello was originally charged with two felony counts related to gambling. The charges were promoting gambling in the first degree and possession of gambling records in the first degree, N.Y. Penal Law §§ 225.10, 225.20. Under the advice of his attorney, Santobello agreed to plead guilty to the lesser included charge of possession of gambling records in the second degree, N.Y. Penal Law § 225.15. In addition to dismissing the two more serious charges, the prosecutor agreed not to make any sentencing recommendations. The court accepted the plea bargain and set a date for sentencing. However, upon sentencing, a different prosecutor, having reviewed Santobello's lengthy criminal history from his pre-sentence report and unfamiliar with the previously established negotiated plea, recommended that Santobello be given the maximum sentence. The judge concurred and followed the prosecutor's recommendation. Santobello then filed a motion to withdraw his plea of guilty, re-enter his plea of not guilty, and have the case go to trial. His motion was denied by New York's court of appeals. The U.S. Supreme Court granted certiorari in this case. Upon review, the court sided with Santobello, vacated his guilty plea, and allowed him to resume his plea of not guilty and regain his right to a trial.

The Supreme Court found fault with the prosecution reneging on its promise to abstain from making any sentencing recommendations to the judge. The original prosecutor of the case had been replaced by another prosecutor who had no knowledge or official record of the original plea bargain. Like the judge, acting on the pre-sentence evaluation, the second prosecutor inadvertently violated the agreement by recommending that Santobello receive the maximum sentence.

According to the Supreme Court, this prosecutorial mistake had a significant impact on the voluntariness of Santobello to enter into such an agreement. The importance of questions on voluntariness and what constitutes coercion had long been addressed prior to *Santobello*. It was this issue of fundamental fairness, involving one's right to a trial by jury or judge, which was the basis for the decision to remand the case. In so doing, the Supreme Court again was balancing the need for plea bargaining against the most fundamental due process rights of an individual. In the majority opinion of the Supreme Court, it was decided that when a prosecutor did not honor a plea negotiation, the sentence must be vacated and the state court decide if (a) the plea bargain must be honored or if (b) the defendant be given the opportunity to go to trial on the original charges, with the preference of the defendant being given consideration. The dissenting court agreed with the majority decision, but suggested that the petitioner also be able to replead the original charges on the indictment.

It is estimated that approximately 90 percent of criminal sentences are the result of plea bargains, which is critical to the efficient functioning of the courts. However, the court also recognized the importance of the office of the prosecution to honor negotiated pleas with defendants. Thus, the Supreme Court obligated trial courts to make record of any plea agreement and the sentence to be vacated if the plea agreement was not honored. Congruent with other Supreme Court decisions, it was not decided exactly how a sentencing court must rectify any such error made by the prosecutor's office. These types of decisions, according to the Supreme Court, should be the venue of the state courts.

Marilyn Simon
University of Cincinnati, Blue Ash

See Also: Courts; District Attorney; Judges and Magistrates; Mandatory Minimum Sentencing; New York City; Plea.

Further Readings
Brady v. *United States*, 397 U.S. 742, 751-752 (1970).
Kercheval v. United States, 274 U.S. 220 (1927).
Lynch v. Overholser, 369 U.S. 705. 719 (1962).
North Carolina v. Alford, 400 U.S. 25. 37-38 (1970).
Powell v. Alabama, 287 U.S. 45 (1932).
Santobello v. New York, 404 U.S. 257-No 70-98. Supreme Court (1971).

Schenck v. United States

The late 1800s and the early 1900s were a time of great political unrest in the United States. There were a number of political movements, including anarchism, socialism, and communism. Strongly linked with the socialist and communist movements was the labor movement. With the end of World War I and the success of the Bolshevik Revolution in Russia, a fear of communism coalesced into the Red Scare of 1919–20. Little distinction was made between socialists and communists, and all social activists were generally considered to be part of the threat.

During World War I, a number of socialist organizations actively opposed the entry of the United States into World War I. Charles Schenck, who was the secretary for the Socialist Party of America, was actively involved in opposing the war. The records of the Socialist Party of America showed that a resolution had been passed by the party authorizing the printing of 15,000 leaflets to be mailed and distributed and authorizing the expenditure of $125 for Schenck to accomplish the task. On one side of the leaflets was a comparison of conscription to slavery, in violation of the Thirteenth Amendment to the U.S. Constitution. The other side of the leaflets contained statements encouraging the reader to assert his or her rights to oppose the draft of men into the military and to not submit to intimidation. Schenck and various members of the party then engaged in the production and distribution of the leaflets. After a search warrant was executed on the Socialist Party of America's headquarters with the concurrent seizure of the party's records, Schenck was indicted and arrested and brought to trial for violation of the Sedition Act of 1917 and illegal use of the U.S. mail service.

At his trial, Schenck was convicted of conspiracy to cause insubordination in the military and to obstruct recruiting and enlistment in the military. He was also convicted of conspiracy to illegally use the U.S. mail and the actual illegal use of the U.S. mail. He appealed to the Supreme Court on the grounds that the convictions violated his rights to freedom of speech and freedom of the press under the First Amendment of the U.S. Constitution.

The Supreme Court agreed to hear the appeal in 1919. The Supreme Court acknowledged that in ordinary times, the words and ideas expressed in the leaflet would have been constitutionally protected. However, the Supreme Court recognized that the right of free speech is not absolute and the circumstances of particular speech might cause the speech to be outside the protection of the First Amendment. It is at this point that Justice Oliver Wendell Holmes, Jr., coined the famous phrases that: "[t]he most stringent protection of free speech would not protect a man from falsely shouting fire in a theater and causing a panic." Accordingly, the Supreme Court affirmed Schenck's conviction on the grounds that the state of war existing between the United States and the German Empire was a circumstance that placed Schenck's attempts to interfere in the draft outside the protections of the free speech clause of the First Amendment. Justice Holmes expressed this prohibition on certain speech when there is a clear and present danger that the words will bring about the evils prohibited by Congress.

The *Schenck* case is extremely important in the history of the American criminal justice system. It is one of the first cases of the Supreme Court to address the applicability of the First Amendment to the interpretation and application of the criminal laws. Its importance to the criminal laws is that the *Schenck* decision recognized that the protections of the First Amendment and the Bill of Rights are not absolute and are, occasionally, subordinated to criminal laws. The *Schenck* decision is also very important for its application of criminal law during wartime to limit the constitutional rights of individuals. This position during wartime has been followed in a number of subsequent Supreme Court decisions. It is also important in that the *Schenck* decision affirmed the use of the criminal law to address what might otherwise be considered political speech, which appears to raise a serious issue in the United States of America, which ostensibly recognizes political freedom. Some critics of *Schenck* have suggested that the affirmation of Schenck's convictions was due, in part, to the Red Scare that was occurring in the United States and that, in another time, Schenck's convictions might have been reversed.

Wm. C. Plouffe, Jr.
Independent Scholar

See Also: Civil Rights Laws; Political Crimes, History of; Political Dissidents; Political Policing.

Further Readings
Levin, Murray B. *Political Hysteria in America: The Democratic Capacity for Repression.* New York: Basic Books, 1971.
Murray, Robert K. *Red Scare: A Study in National Hysteria 1919–1920.* New York: McGraw-Hill, 1964.
Rabban, David. "The Emergence of Modern First Amendment Doctrine." *University of Chicago Law Review*, v.50 (1983).

School Shootings

The decade of the 1990s was traumatic for parents, students, and public schools as 10 school shootings left 43 people dead and more than 60 wounded. The shootings led to extensive media-engendered speculation about the nation having a culture of violence. In the locales impacted—suburbs, bedroom communities, and rural areas—the question reporters and researches continually encountered from bewildered residents was "Why here?" Those who lived in the school districts were completely flummoxed by apparently random rampage violence inflicted in areas that had previously known almost no violent crime or student victimization whatsoever.

The national focus suddenly shifted from inner-city, minority-based gangsters to the angry, maladjusted kids next door. Parents became obsessed with safety, driving their children to school, insisting that their children have cell phones in class, and demanding that schools institute tough policies to identify, label, and deal with potential offenders. This tendency manifested itself in predictably reactive and draconian ways, typically with new rules such as zero tolerance policies, which expelled offenders for even trivial technical violations of drug or weapons policies. A new concern with bullying was in evidence, and schools tried to find ways of dealing with that issue. The media continued to obsess about the United States having a "gun culture," but new gun control legislation was not passed. Gun availability, though a factor in these incidents, played only a small part in these tragedies.

Shooter Characteristics
The most dominant characteristic of the school shooter in this period was his marginal status. Almost all school shooters were white, male, middle class, and socially isolated. Some were clinically depressed, and many showed other symptoms of mental illness. Their schoolwork, computer postings, and artistic works frequently displayed morbid, violent, and suicidal themes and content. Additionally, some were obsessed with violent cinema, television, and video games. It is not incidental to note that some experts have indicted violently themed video games with increasing desensitization to violent behavior in

general. Specifically, it is alleged that the U.S. Armed Forces use such role-playing shooting games to overcome the socially ingrained aversion to killing noted among enlistees. Therefore, students voluntarily and frequently using such games would be less reluctant to use deadly force in a stressful situation. Indeed, one scores in such games by accumulating victims.

School shooters frequently report being the victim of bullies. It has been suggested that the shootings are attempts to get even with those who bullied them— rejecting females, queen bees, obnoxious jocks—the "popular kids." However, anecdotal evidence suggests that the shooters themselves occasionally took on the role of bully. One of the Westside Middle School shooters was alleged to be a bully. The role of getting even with "popular kids" in the process of motivating a school shooter is important but is considerably more complex than has been suggested by media. As a marginal student, not really belonging to an "in group" or even an "out group" of any kind, the typical shooter is in limbo among his peers and within the system. Ignored by school administrators and, more importantly, held in scant regard by peers, including desirable females, he clumsily struggles to get attention and a place in the sun. Usually meeting frustration in areas athletic, scholastic, and social, he grimly soldiers on. Finally, his almost total rejection by adolescent peer culture becomes intolerable. At last, the shooter wants to demonstrate masculine power and mastery over something within his reach; his real and symbolic tormentors become the objects of his dramaturgical action. Thus, the shooting event is less an attempt to assassinate individual tormentors than a symbolically charged endeavor to show the school and community at large that he is as worthy of their attention and regard as are jocks, cheerleaders, and other types who are valued and celebrated by conventional others.

Before the fact, school shooters fantasize about avenging the manifold indignities and ostracism that they have encountered from their peers. As

A memorial located in Clement Park in Littleton, Colorado, to honor victims of the Colombine High School massacre. The tragic incident, using an intricately planned attack involving propane bombs and firearms, was carried out by two alienated students in April 1999. After 12 students and one teacher were killed and 23 were wounded, the shooters committed suicide.

in the case of the Columbine shooters, the ostracized students often plan detailed attempts to wreak havoc on all and sundry in the school and share this with their friends, sometimes online. In the case of Columbine, Dylan Klebold and Eric Harris actually planned to blow up the school with compressed gas and were only prevented from doing so by technical problems. This, too, was known to some cohorts. But because the youth subculture is characterized by a code of silence, this information was seldom vouchsafed to adults. Those shooters whose plans manifested more specificity, for example, " I am going to kill Vice Principal Jones on Thursday," were more likely to follow through. This was probably to maintain the articulated fantasy of being a "man of action."

Media attention focused on school shooters being drug users or members of a Goth-like subculture. Neither stereotype has much basis in reality. Most shooters were so marginal that even low-status groups like Goths and dopers were leery of them and their motivations. They were often seen as "wannabees" even by marginal groups. Surprisingly few used recreational drugs for fun or to self-medicate, but several, including one of the Columbine killers, had taken or were taking antidepressants at the time of the shootings. The use of such prescription drugs (which have been linked in media to suicide) by these youth suggested to some that they perpetrated the school shootings in order to be shot by police, that is, to commit "suicide by cop." It is extremely unlikely that these drugs had any causal impact. If the school shooters were suicidal, as some demonstrably were, it was because they were depressed and the medication was not working, and not because of the medication used to treat them.

Many of these shooters had experienced a traumatic event or events in their lives immediately prior to the shooting event. One of the Columbine shooters had been turned down for military service because of his depression and use of drugs. Kip Kinkel, a shooter in Oregon, had endured one rejection and indignity after another because of his hyperactivity and learning disorders. Another shooter feared being forced to move to another state as punishment for a phone sex–related offense. Yet another, a middle school student in Arkansas, had been specifically rejected by a girlfriend. Coupled with systemic indifference, parental inattention, and the omnipresent undercurrent of peer judgment and concomitant rejection, these traumas seemed to precipitate the shooting events.

Though guns themselves possess no evil agency, their presence and or easy accessibility in the parental home or in the homes of others provided the mechanism for the commission of the act. Some guns used in shootings were low-quality, low-caliber revolvers and pistols, but some shooters used expensive imported Glock and Taurus pistols. Only a few used sniper-like tactics and deer rifles. One boy's parents bought him a police-quality Glock pistol to use in father-son shooting activities. The boy, Kip Kinkel, shot both parents dead, then took the gun with other weapons to school and continued his shooting spree at that location.

School Factors

Large, impersonal public schools received substantial criticism from media and concerned citizens as a result of these events. That students could easily get lost within such institutions was axiomatic. Such schools routinely honored and rewarded athletes and other favored groups but did almost nothing to engage or celebrate the achievements of others, let alone marginal students. The continuing overemphasis on athletics (e.g., weekly pep rallies where athletes received the collective adoration of the student body) specifically rankled and further alienated school shooters and other students who were less than engaged. There were more systemic issues, as well. Marginal students frequently make the claim, and not without some justification, that not only do teachers ignore them and their concerns but that they systematically ignore bullying and culturally oriented ostracism.

It is alleged that the victimized student is used as a "negative social resource," that is, as an example of what not to be. As a stigmatized loser, he is a walking boundary-maintenance device. That such students have little intrinsic value to the system, except as a negative resource, is a fact that is not lost on the students themselves; they come to resent it deeply. And some are moved to act radically to affirm selfhood in an adolescent world that demeans, disconfirms, and devalues them to the core. That their actions are also aimed at the adult would, which ignores the evident injuries and injustices they experience, seems manifestly obvious.

Almost all teachers and administrators are unaware of what is really going on in their institutions. Dealing with bureaucratic reality and system-dictated necessities, they are happily oblivious to the authentic hunger, alienation, and increasingly unquiet desperation that haunt their halls. In all fairness, some of this ignorance stems from the adolescent code of silence, which ensures that little of interest or importance is passed to school, police, or social service agents. That being said, schools continue to celebrate athletics, the high-profile province of a tiny minority, while underfunding other avenues for expression such as art, drama, dance, and music that might appeal to a much wider spectrum of students.

Social Reaction

It was foreseeable that much of the reaction to school shootings would promote ill-conceived programs. Experts on juvenile delinquency are almost uniform in their critique of zero tolerance policies. Such policies punish all drug possession (even of prescribed drugs), firearm or ammunition possession, and fighting with expulsion. Some schools deal with those caught with drugs or firearms or fighting by having the student arrested and taken to juvenile court, as well as having them expelled. Whether these policies deter shooters is beside the point; they trample on the notion of basic fairness and evade and avoid any form of due process. No extenuation is possible. An empty shotgun shell rolling on the car floor is as culpable as a loaded AK-47 and will lead to expulsion. A girl discreetly taking an over-the-counter remedy for a headache is as blameworthy as a drug dealer. Students allege that preferential treatment is routinely granted to favored classes of students.

School resource officer (SRO) programs, much beloved by administrators, have not proven effective in fighting or averting school shootings. In schools in which they were employed prior to shooting incidents, they played no part in curtailing the events. SRO programs are simply a way for police departments to gather intelligence, often of a sort peripheral to the school, such as gang intelligence. School administrators support SRO programs because they purport to deter crime on campus and because the programs allow them a zero tolerance way to deal with routine troublemakers. There is no evidence that they provide any protection for students. On the contrary, there are numerous examples of SRO officers taking advantage of suggestible young students.

Even more ominous has been the fortification of public education. At many schools, students are forced to file through metal detectors, use clear backpacks, and work under prison-like conditions. This includes razor wire–enhanced fencing, stone walls, and video cameras in all areas. Urinalysis is also routinely used in some school systems, though its relationship to school programs and effectiveness in deterring violence seems incidental. Although none of these safeguards would deter any but the most minimally motivated of potential offenders, it would seem that in the name of safety, no program, no matter how intrusive or transparently unfair, would be deemed excessive by the public at large.

Francis Frederick Hawley
Western Carolina University

See Also: 1981 to 2000 Primary Documents; Child Murderers, History of; Colorado; Klebold, Dylan, and Eric Harris.

Further Readings

Critical Incident Response Group. *The School Shooter: A Threat Assessment Perspective.* Quantico, VA: National Center for the Analysis of Violent Crime, 2000.

Cullen, Dave. *Columbine.* New York: Hatchett Book Group, 2009.

Frymer, Benjamin. "The Media Spectacle of Columbine: Alienated Youth as an Object of Fear." *American Behavioral Scientist,* v.52 (2009).

Grossman, Dave and Gloria DeGaetano. *Stop Teaching Our Kids to Kill.* New York: Crown Publishing, 1999.

Newman, K., C. Fox, D. Harding, J. Mehta, and W. Roth. *Rampage: The Social Roots of School Shootings.* New York: Basic Books, 2004.

Vossekuil, Bryan, Marisa Reddy, and Robert Fein. *Safe School Initiative: An Interim Report on the Prevention of Targeted Violence in Schools.* Washington, DC: U.S. Secret Service National Threat Assessment Center, 2000.

Schultz, "Dutch"

Born Arthur Flegenheimer in the Bronx to Herman and Emma Flegenheimer, Schultz drifted into criminal activity after his father, a saloon keeper, abandoned the family in 1916. Schultz went on to become one of the pre-eminent bootleggers and gambling entrepreneurs of the 1930s, and his violent death sealed his place in the pantheon of organized crime. Apprenticed to a roofer, then a printer, as a teenager, Schultz found the street life of Bronx petty criminals more attractive than regular work and took to crime; at the age of 17, he was arrested for burglary. After a 15-month stint in prison (the only jail time of his career, despite many arrests), Schultz returned to the Bronx with the sobriquet "Dutch" Schultz," borrowed from a well-known local boxer. This was in 1920, after the gold rush of national Prohibition had started. But Schultz, then only 18 and relatively inexperienced at organized criminal activity, did not immediately rise to prominence. Instead, those slightly older than he, who had a few years of serious racketeering under their belts but who retained ambition, took the lead.

Schultz, meanwhile, started at the bottom, working on trucks that delivered beer in the Bronx. In 1928, he opened a speakeasy in partnership with fellow gangster Joe Noe; they parlayed Schultz's experience in trucking into their own beer distribution network. The speakeasy was so successful that Schultz took over a larger rival. By 1931, he was working in partnership with the larger operators like Frank Costello, "Lucky" Luciano, Meyer Lansky, and others, and had expanded his operations to include Manhattan as well as the Bronx. Yet, it was not always friendly. It was alleged that Schultz was behind the nonfatal shooting of Jack "Legs" Diamond, in retaliation for Diamond's supposed complicity in the murder of Joe Noe. Some believe that Schultz engineered the murder of Arnold Rothstein, Diamond's mentor, as well.

In 1931, Schultz survived an attempt by the insurgent Coll brothers to take over his bootlegging organization. Around this time, he diversified into both gambling and union rackets. His gambling interests were chiefly in policy, an illegal lottery game that was virulently popular in the slums of New York City and other urban centers. Though the bets were small, often pennies,

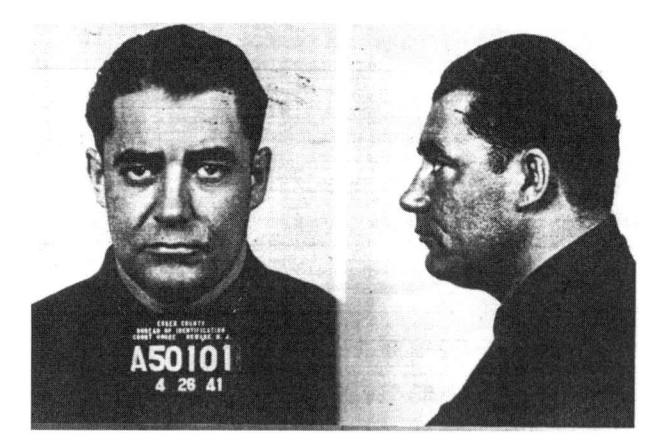

One of "Dutch" Schultz's many mug shots, having started his criminal career at age 17. The Jewish American gangster made his fortune in bootlegging and gambling.

cumulatively, they represented big business. To succeed, an operator needed a sense for organization and protection from political/police harassment and the depredations of other gangs. With his beer fortune and an army of strong-arm men at his command, Schultz had both. He effectively forced his partnership on the chiefly African American entrepreneurs who had been running policy games in Harlem. Adding his own organizational genius, he turned policy into a large source of income.

Schultz also ventured into labor extortion, unionizing restaurant workers and then demanding protection money from both employees and business owners. His brutal tactics made this a successful line of business. But while he didn't fear rivals or those he strong-armed, he was forced into hiding after being indicted for federal income tax evasion. Finally surrendering in 1934, he was tried for tax evasion in Syracuse, New York, in the following year. Schultz freely spread money throughout the city, and, after a hung jury (amid charges of tampering), the case was moved to Malone for a retrial. Despite being acquitted by the jury, Schultz was not welcome to return to New York City; agents were ready to arrest him on an outstanding indictment. He attempted to resume control over his criminal empire by remote control, first from Connecticut, then from New Jersey.

On October 23, 1935, gunmen burst into Newark's Palace Chophouse, which Schultz had been using as a temporary meeting place, and gunned down Schultz and three of his associates. A fourth Schultz lieutenant was also gunned down in New York City. As his wounds were being tended to, Schultz denied any knowledge of his assailants. Following the shooting, Schultz alternated between refusing to answer questions and speaking incoherently before succumbing to his wounds the day after his shooting.

David G. Schwartz
University of Nevada, Las Vegas

See Also: Corruption, History of; Gambling; Genovese, Vito; Luciano, "Lucky"; Rothstein, Arnold.

Further Readings

Haller, Mark. "The Changing Structure of American Gambling in the Twentieth Century." *Journal of Social Issues*, v.35 (1979).

Peterson, Virgil. *The Mob: 200 Years of Organized Crime in New York*. Ottawa, IL: Green Hill Publishers, 1983.

"Schultz Dies of Wounds Without Naming Slayers," *New York Times* (October 25, 1935).

"Schultz Reigned on Discreet Lines." *New York Times* (October 25, 1935).

Scopes Monkey Trial

In the United States, and especially in education, the issue of evolution and creation has been a continuing problem. The fundamental religious/conservative part of the population believes that the biblical account of creation is true and wants only that account taught in schools, or wants it to be taught with equal emphasis as given to evolution. In opposition, the liberal/scientific portion of the population wants the theory of evolution, which was formulated by Charles Darwin in his book *The Origin of Species*, to be taught in schools, and want creation to be limited to courses in religion.

Because this controversy involved what was being taught in school, and because there are numerous public schools in America, the propriety of teaching evolution and/or creation became a serious political issue. In the early part of the 20th century, there were many efforts undertaken by religious fundamentalists to make the teaching of creation in public schools mandatory and to criminalize the teaching of evolution. This effort was successful in Tennessee, which passed the Butler Act on March 21, 1925, making it a crime to teach evolution in school. In Tennessee, the American Civil Liberties Union (ACLU) offered to defend anyone accused of teaching evolution in violation of the Butler Act. A group of businessmen in the town of Dayton, Tennessee, thought that such a trial would be good publicity for the town. Subsequently, a young high school biology teacher in Clark County, John T. Scopes, agreed to be the test case and he proceeded to teach evolution in his classes.

In May 1925, Scopes was indicted for violating the Butler Act. The indictment became national news with the press descending upon Dayton. Over 200 reporters came to Dayton from all across the nation. For the length of the trial, newspapers across the nation were focused on "the Monkey Trial" (coined by famous commentator and author H. L. Mencken). The trial was the first in America to be nationally broadcast on radio. The nation was enthralled. A number of attorneys were considered to represent both sides. Ultimately, Williams Jennings Bryan was selected to assist as a special prosecutor for the state to prosecute Scopes. Bryan was a nationally known politician and a religious Presbyterian. Clarence Darrow, the famous defense attorney, was selected to be the lead counsel for Scopes. Darrow was an agnostic.

At trial, Darrow and the trial judge, John T. Raulston, had a number of disputes. The trial judge quoted from Genesis in the Bible and the Butler Act, which which revealed Raulston's bias. The ACLU originally became involved in the issue because of the potential violation of the First Amendment. However, Darrow had other ideas. Darrow attempted to introduce testimony from various experts on evolution, but Raulston refused to allow them to be presented to the jury. At trial, the prosecution attempted to focus the jury on the legal issue, which was whether Scopes had taught evolution, the crime he had been charged with violating. The defense concentrated on the literal interpretation of the story of creation in the Bible and that it was not inconsistent with evolution. One of the defense attorneys, Dudley F. Malone, gave an inspiring argument, raising fears of an "inquisition" if evolution were contained by the discipline of theology, and that evolution belonged in the discipline of science. The courtroom exploded in support.

Finally, in a most unusual request, Darrow asked for Bryan to be examined as an expert witness on the Bible, as the trial judge had refused to allow any of the defense's expert witnesses. Bryan agreed to take the stand, even though he was an attorney for the prosecution. After a few exchanges between Darrow and Bryan, the trial judge closed the proceedings. Neither the prosecution nor the defense made any closing arguments. The matter was placed before the jury, which found Scopes guilty after only a few minutes deliberation. Scopes appealed. The Tennessee Supreme Court found that the Butler Act was constitutional under free speech because the state had a right to regulate Scopes's conduct. Further, it found that the Butler Act did not violate the religious preference clause of the Tennessee constitution because the law did not establish a state religion. However, the court reversed the conviction on a legal technicality. The state of Tennessee declined to retry the case.

The effect of the trial across the United States was significant. Initially, many textbooks stopped including evolution. Numerous states began to consider enacting antievolutionary statutes. Most of these efforts, however, failed. This did not stop the antievolution movement. In the last half of the 20th century, the antievolution movement morphed into the intelligent design movement, which posits that there is an intelligent being that designed and created the universe and that intelligent being is God. With the advent of the modern scientific age in the 1950s and the 1960s, with America focusing more on science and education in fear of falling behind the Soviet Union after the launch of Sputnik, the teaching of evolution became widespread, as it is considered one of the fundamental principles of biology. There are still calls from religious fundamentalists attacking the teaching of evolution and advocating more attention to intelligent design, but it appears that evolution will stay in the science books.

The Scopes Monkey Trial was immortalized in the famous play and movie *Inherit the Wind*. It is frequently used today, whether correctly or not, as an example of how a closed-minded perspective can inhibit the advance of science and knowledge.

Wm. C. Plouffe, Jr.
Independent Scholar

John Scopes, a month before the Tennessee v. John T. Scopes trial. Scopes violated the Butler Act, passed in 1925 making it a crime to teach evolution in school in Tennessee.

See Also: 1921 to 1940 Primary Documents; Darrow, Clarence; News Media, Crime in; Trials.

Further Readings
De Camp, L. Sprague. *The Great Monkey Trial*. New York: Doubleday, 1968.
Larsen, Edward J. *Summer for the Gods: The Scopes Trial and America's Continuing Debate Over Science and Religion*. New York: Basic, 1997.
Lienesch, Michael. *In the Beginning: Fundamentalism, the Scopes Trial, and the Making of the Antievolution Movement*. Chapel Hill: North Carolina University Press, 2007.

Scottsboro Boys Cases

On March 25, 1931, a small town in Alabama was changed forever. A group of hoboes accused black youths who were on a train bound for Memphis of assault and throwing the hoboes off the train. The train was stopped in Paint Rock, Alabama, and the sheriff deputized a posse that was ordered to capture all the black men on the train. Later, two women, Victoria Price and Ruby Bates, accused the men of rape. Nine men were arrested: Olen Montgomery, Clarence Norris, Haywood Patterson, Ozie Powell, Willie Roberson, Charlie Weems, Eugene Williams, and brothers Andy and Roy Wright. All men were teenagers. As word began to grow in the small community of Scottsboro where the men were jailed, a lynch mob developed, and the governor had to order the National Guard to protect the jail. In the Jim Crow south, these men were not allowed to consult a lawyer and most were illiterate.

The trial brought national and international attention, with the Communist Party, National Association for the Advancement of Colored People (NAACP), and International Labor Defense (ILD) vying to represent the defendants. The ILD won the rights. The first trial began on April 6, 1931, before Judge A. E. Hawkins. On April 9, 1931, eight defendants were convicted and sentenced to death, with only 12-year-old Roy Wright not receiving the death penalty. On June 22, 1931, all executions were stayed pending appeal to the Alabama Supreme Court. On January 5, in a letter to Earl Streetman, Ruby Bates denied she was raped. However, the Alabama Supreme Court, in a 6–1 ruling, affirmed seven of the eight convictions, granting only Eugene Williams a new trial on the grounds that he was a juvenile. In May 1932, the U.S. Supreme Court announced that it would review the Scottsboro boys case; in a 7–2 ruling in November 1932, *Powell v. Alabama* reversed the convictions and ordered a new trial on the grounds of inadequate counsel in a decision written by Charles Evans Hughes.

Due to the press coverage of the original trials, the next trials were set in Decatur, 50 miles from the birthplace of the Ku Klux Klan in northern Alabama. For the Decatur trials, Samuel S. Liebowitz was retained by the ILD to be the attorney for the Scottsboro boys. The case was assigned to District Judge James Edward Horton. The first case to be retried was that of Haywood Patterson on March 27, 1933. Patterson was once again found guilty and sentenced to death on April 9, 1933. Due to increasing local tensions and the fact that the other defendants could not get a fair trial, Judge Horton ordered the other trials postponed. During this postponement, there were many marches across the nation, including one in Washington, D.C., that protested the Alabama trials. On June 22, 1933, Judge Horton, in a move that he knew would cost him re-election, granted a new trial for Haywood Patterson. The Scottsboro cases were removed from Judge Horton's jurisdiction and transferred to Judge William Callahan.

During the Callahan trials, from 1933 to 1937, the judge banned photographers and typewriters from the courtroom to try and get the trial off the front pages. Judge Callahan excluded evidence that Judge Horton allowed. Often, Callahan would interrupt the defense in cross-examining, especially during Victoria Price's testimony. The cases went to the Alabama Supreme Court, which once again affirmed the conviction, and back before the U.S. Supreme Court, which once again overturned the convictions of Norris and Patterson in *Norris v. Alabama* due to African Americans being excluded from the jury.

The final round of trials were significant because Creed Conyers became the first black to serve on a grand jury post-Reconstruction. Local attorney Charles Watts was the lead attorney for the defendants with Samuel S. Liebowitz assisting the case. Haywood Patterson was once again convicted and sentenced to 75 years in prison, becoming the first black man to avoid the death sentence for raping a white woman in Alabama. Clarence Norris was once again convicted of rape and sentenced to death. Andrew Wright was convicted of rape and sentenced to 99 years. Charlie Weems was convicted of rape and sentenced to 105 years in prison. Charges were dropped against Willie Roberson, Olen Montgomery, Eugene Williams, and Roy Wright. Many of the ones who were convicted were later paroled, or in the case of Haywood Patterson, escaped from prison. Clarence Norris was pardoned in 1976 by Governor George Wallace.

Derrick Shapley
Mississippi State University

See Also: African Americans; Alabama; Civil Rights Laws; Juries.

Further Readings

Carter, Dan T. *Scottsboro: A Tragedy of the American South.* Baton Rouge: Lousiana State University Press, 1979.

Kwando, Kinshasa. *The Man From Scottsboro: Clarence Norris in His Own Words.* Jefferson, NC: MacFarland and Co., 1997.

Patterson, Haywood and Earl Conrad. *Scottsboro Boy.* Garden City, NY: Doubleday, 1950.

Secret Service

Established in 1865, the Secret Service is a federal law enforcement agency of the U.S. government. It was the Federal government's first detective force. The agency was previously under the auspices of the Department of the Treasury until March 2003, when it was transferred to the newly created Department of Homeland Security, which was established by the federal reshuffling following 9/11. Otherwise referred to as the "USSS" or simply the "Service," sworn members of the Secret Service are divided into two categories—special agents and the uniformed division—and perform one of two responsibilities in accordance with their mission: "To safeguard the nation's financial infrastructure and payment systems to preserve the integrity of the economy, and to protect national leaders, visiting heads of state and government, designated sites and National Special Security Events."

While the Secret Service agency initially held a treasury role with primary investigative responsibilities to suppress currency counterfeiting, the agency has evolved considerably over the years. Consequently, some responsibilities were transferred to other agencies—namely, the Federal Bureau of Investigation (FBI), Internal Revenue Service, Immigration and Customs Enforcement, and Bureau of Alcohol, Tobacco, and Firearms. Today, the agency holds a dual protective role for the safety and protection of current and former national leaders and their families, such as the president, and the provision of diplomatic security for visiting foreign leaders, a service for which the agency is more commonly known. Both roles are reflected in the Secret Service's motto—"worthy of trust and confidence." Recently, the Secret Service inherited a third responsibility—the investigation of crimes committed electronically—which is shared through concurrent jurisdiction with the FBI. Based in New York City until 1874, the Secret Service is currently headquartered at 245 Murray Drive in Washington, D.C. Operating on $1.43 billion annually as of 2010, the agency includes more than 4,400 sworn members working in 150 offices in the United States and abroad under the command of Mark J. Sullivan—the 22nd director of the Secret Service, who was appointed on May 31, 2006.

Evolution

The Secret Service can be traced back to the early 19th century, when the surge of counterfeits and forgeries plaguing the country required the creation of a federal agency specifically tasked to tackle these growing crimes. As such, on October 25, 1860, the U.S. Treasury allocated $10,000, and on July 5, 1865, Chief William P. Wood was officially sworn in by Secretary of the Treasury Hugh McCullough to command a new agency. Only two years after inception, responsibilities of the Secret Service were greatly expanded to include any person committing frauds against federal law, such as smugglers, illegal distillers, mail robbers, land frauds, and a range of other criminals, until other federal agencies were formed to take over these duties. In order to arm the Secret Service with the necessary investigatory powers, Congress enacted a plethora of new laws before the 20th century, for example, prohibiting the counterfeiting of any coin—gold or silver—in 1877 and outlawing counterfeiting and possessing forged stamps in 1865.

Finally, on August 5, 1882, an act was passed by Congress to officially recognize the agency as a division of the Treasury Department. In 1894, the Secret Service informally began to provide protection to presidents, starting with Grover Cleveland, and was officially assigned in 1902 to provide full-time protective services following the 1901 assassination of President William McKinley. Congress in 1907 enacted the Sundry Civil Expenses Act in order to supply the necessary funds for this new dual responsibility of the Secret

Flanked by Secret Service agents, President George W. Bush along the inaugural parade route inside an armored limousine headed toward the White House after his re-election.

Service, budgeting $125,000 to cover 56 agents stationed in 31 offices. In 1908, nine Secret Service agents resigned from the Department of Justice in order to help establish the Federal Bureau of Investigation. In 1922, the Secret Service created the White House Police.

Much of the expansion of the Secret Service between the early 1900s and the 1980s involved the protective diplomatic role. In the 1980s, the emergence and growth of credit and debit card usage was complemented by a rise in electronic fraud, which prompted Congress in 1984 to pass legislation making this a federal offense. In turn, this granted authority to the Secret Service to investigate these crimes, including federal-interest computer fraud and false identification documents. In 1990, the Secret Service began to share jurisdiction concurrently with the FBI in order to civilly and criminally investigate any cases related to federally insured financial institutions. During this decade, Congress enacted two key laws—the 1994 Crime Bill Public Law, which prohibited the manufacturing, trafficking in, or possession of American currency counterfeited abroad, making this an offense punishable as if committed in the United States.

In 1998, Congress enacted the Telemarketing Fraud Prevention Act, which allowed the Secret Service to confiscate fraud proceeds in convicted cases, including conspiracy to perpetuate such an offense if done through telemarketing. In the same year, the Identity Theft and Assumption Deterrence Act was also enacted, thereby creating the crime of identity theft with penalties for anyone knowingly and illicitly using another person's identity for the purpose of committing unlawful activity.

The new millennium saw many changes and some high-profile cases for the Secret Service. Shortly after September 11, 2001, the USA PATRIOT Act armed the agency with the necessary legal artillery to rapidly expand operations, for example, with increased investigative powers to deal with fraud and other crimes involving computers. In addition to increasing penalties for counterfeiting violations and forgeries and vesting the agency with more power to respond to transnational terrorist financing, this legislation provided former director of the Secret Service Brian Stafford with the authority to establish an extensive nationwide network of electronic crime task forces for purposes of detecting, preventing, and investigating electronic financial crime and similar activities, such as cyber attacks, committed through computers against financial infrastructures, government agencies, private industry, and academic institutions in the United States. In 2006, this database greatly expanded from 15 to 24 nationwide task forces, in cities around the United States, because of productive public-private partnerships.

During this decade, the Secret Service was also involved in many high-profile cases, for example, Operation Firewall in 2004, leading to the arrests of 28 American and foreign suspects in six countries for identity theft, electronic fraud, and conspiracy charges; in 2008, 11 American and foreign individuals were charged with the theft of more than 40 million credit cards. Since 2003, these efforts have resulted in more than 29,000 arrests with a 98 percent conviction rate and have led to the seizure of $295 million in counterfeited currency. Since this time, the Secret Service has also closed cases with losses amounting to $3.7 billion and has helped thwart more than $12 billion in potential losses.

Michael J. Puniskis
Middlesex University

See Also: Computer Crime; Counterfeiting; Federal Bureau of Investigation; Federal Policing; Identity Theft; Terrorism; USA PATRIOT Act of 2001; Washington, DC.

Further Readings
Ansley, N. "The United States Secret Service: An Administrative History." *Journal of Criminal Law, Criminology, and Police Science*, v.47/1 (1956).
Baker, L. C. *A History of the United States Secret Service*. Middlesex, UK: Wildhern Press, 2009.
Johnson, David R. *Illegal Tender: Counterfeiting and the Secret Service in Nineteenth-Century America*. Washington, DC: Smithsonian Institution Press, 1995.
U.S. Secret Service. "Fiscal Year 2009 Annual Report." http://www.secretservice.gov/FY09 _SecretService_Annual%20Report-Web.pdf (Accessed February 2001).
U.S. Secret Service. http://www.secretservice.gov (Accessed January 2011).

Securities and Exchange Commission

The Securities and Exchange Commission (SEC) is a federal government agency established by the Securities Exchange Act of 1934. The primary role of this agency is to regulate all business related to the sale and purchase of securities in the United States. What we know today as the SEC began in 1933 with the passage of the Securities Act during the early months of the presidency of Franklin D. Roosevelt. The purpose of this act was to clean up the securities industry by requiring that all information about securities sold to the public be made available to investors and to prohibit actions considered to be fraudulent and illegal as defined by the act. Congress took this course of action toward regulating the securities industry because false information, sales lower than market prices, and other illegal practices contributed to the stock market crash in 1929. Prior to this point, the securities industry did not come under government regulation.

The Securities Act of 1933 was a good start but it failed to create a mechanism to oversee and regulate the securities industry. Congress created the SEC as an independent government agency under the president to oversee the regulation and practices of companies selling securities to the public. Under the law, the SEC has the power to require the registration of brokerage firms, transfer agents, and self-regulatory organizations (SROs) in the United States. The agency also has the power to determine which activities related to securities are considered illegal and to enforce disciplinary actions on the individuals and firms with which they are associated. In accordance with these areas of regulation, the various firms and persons regulated by the SEC are required to submit a report on a regular basis fulfilling the requirement of public information.

Structure and Organization
The SEC's organizational structure includes five commissioners appointed by the president who serve five-year terms that are staggered so all five seats are not vacant at once. One of these commissioners is named chair by the president. The agency currently has five divisions and 18 offices in Washington with 11 regional offices all over the country and a working staff of more than 3,500 people. The first of the five divisions of the SEC is the Division of Corporation Finance, which is responsible for meeting the public information requirement of corporate finance. The division reviews the documents that companies must submit to the SEC such as filings, annual shareholder reports, and filings related to mergers and acquisitions. In the Division of Trading and Markets, the SEC reviews proposed changes to regulations and practices submitted by the self-regulatory organizations, thus

watching over NASDAQ and the New York Stock Exchange, and also offers advice for new regulations and changes within the agency.

Another SEC division is the Division of Investment Management, which has the responsibility of oversight of U.S. capital markets such as mutual funds. This division regulates the information provided to investors, monitors fees paid, and reviews the information provided to consumers about the funds. The fourth division of the SEC is the Division of Enforcement, which takes its name from its primary responsibility. Within this division, investigations are initiated and information is collected about possible illegal activities from informers, consumer tips, and review of reports and other agency documents. Investigations are informal, and findings are first presented to the commission. In most cases, investigations are settled out of court, although the commission can require a trial in the district courts or another form of administrative action. The final division is the Division of Risk, Strategy and Financial Innovation, which was created in 2009 in response to the economic crisis and the need for more detailed information regarding risks and trends in the markets. This division researches strategic developments, financial innovations, and risk and economic analysis to help the SEC predict trends and anticipate changes in the financial markets.

Function

The SEC tracks the securities industry and requires that companies disclose their information. Companies that have assets greater than $10 million and that also have more than 500 members holding securities are required to file quarterly and annual statements, which can be viewed by anyone via the EDGAR database. Other related laws require the disclosure and monitoring of how stockholder votes are obtained, particularly in the case of proxy settings and tender offers in the case of one person trying to gain control of a company.

The SEC monitors investors for prohibited activities such as insider trading. Recent high-profile cases related to insider trading include the cases brought against E. F. Hutton, Martha Stewart, Enron, and Bernard Madoff, who created a Ponzi scheme that collapsed in 2008, along with the fortunes of countless investors. Investigations resulted in not only Madoff's conviction but in further changes to how the SEC regulates the securities industry.

The influence and activity of the SEC has varied over time since its 1934 inception. During the presidency of Dwight Eisenhower, for example, the SEC maintained a low profile, which continued during subsequent administrations until the election of Ronald Reagan, when the agency began to regulate the industry more heavily. During subsequent administrations, regulation of the financial sector became increasingly lax; banks and mortgage companies made increasingly complex and risky trades that were allowed under these lax regulations and led directly to the financial crisis that began in 2008. With the election of Barack Obama and a Democratic-controlled Congress in 2008, steps have been taken to rein in bank fees and credit card fees and to monitor financial institutions to protect consumers.

Conclusion

The SEC can trace its roots back to the post–World War I financial boom that resulted in businesses selling securities for a fraction of what they cost and individuals borrowing money to purchase them.

The U.S. Securities and Exchange Commission (SEC) headquarters is located in of Washington, D.C. The SEC was created by section 4 of the Securities Exchange Act of 1934.

When this practice ultimately led to the stock market crash of 1929, it became very clear that federal regulation of the securities industry was necessary. Congress then passed laws in 1933 and 1934 that created the SEC and provided the agency its mandate. As a regulatory agency, it not only provides oversight for securities and related businesses, but it also sets regulatory policy. Today, the SEC works in combination with the Federal Reserve Board, the U.S. Department of Treasury, and the Commodity Futures Trading Commission to advise the president on economic matters. Since the 1930s, only two major legislative updates have modified the SEC: the Investment Company Act of 1940 and the Sarbanes-Oxley Act of 2002.

Theresa S. Hefner-Babb
Lamar University

See Also: Great Depression; Reagan, Ronald (Administration of); Roosevelt, Franklin D. (Administration of).

Further Readings
Hafer, R. W. and Scott E. Hein. *The Stock Market*. Westport, CT: Greenwood Press, 2007.
Securities Act of 1933. http://www.sec.gov/about/laws/sa33.pdf (Accessed September 2011).
Securities Exchange Act of 1934. http://www.sec.gov/about/laws/sea34.pdf (Accessed September 2011).

Sedition Act of 1918

The Sedition Act of 1918 was a law that forbade the use of "disloyal, profane, scurrilous, or abusive language" about the U.S. government, its flag, or its armed forces from its signature by President Woodrow Wilson on May 16, 1918, through its repeal on March 3, 1921. The law also allowed the U.S. Postmaster General to refuse to deliver mail that met the same standards. It applied only during times when the United States was at war; in 1918, the United States was actively engaged in the combat of World War I. The law was actually part of a set of amendments to the Espionage Act of 1917, so many scholars report on both acts simultaneously as the Espionage and Sedition Acts.

When it was enacted in 1917, the Espionage Act made it a crime to aid enemies of the United States or to interfere with World War I efforts or military requirements. The Sedition Act of 1918 expanded these provisions to include a broader range of offenses possibly subverting the war effort, including speech and the expression of opinions that cast the U.S. government in a negative light, or interference with the sale of government bonds. Offenders convicted under the act typically received prison sentences lasting from 10 to 20 years.

During congressional debate, one argument made in the law's favor was that the country was witnessing instances of mob or vigilante behaviors from members of the public punishing unpopular speech. The Sedition Act, thus, would help to preserve a rule of law by preventing mobs from doing what the government was unable to do. Critics of the law, including former president Theodore Roosevelt, argued that the law attacked the U.S. Constitution's guarantees of free speech and expression. Senator Hiram Johnson accused the Wilson administration of failing to use laws already in place to prosecute offensive speech or actions. The final vote for passage of the act was 48–26 in the Senate and 293–1 in the House of Representatives.

Approximately 2,000 people were prosecuted under the Espionage and Sedition Acts. Perhaps the most famous prosecution was that of Socialist Party leader Eugene Debs. Debs was arrested after giving a speech that jurors believed was meant to obstruct the military draft. He was sentenced to 10 years in prison but was released after two, following commutation by President Warren Harding. Similar prosecutions occurred for less conspicuous offenses. Peter Holzmacher of Illinois was sentenced to five years for calling the American flag "a dirty rag." Women made up approximately 10 percent of the prosecutions. They included labor activist Helen Gurley Flynn, as well as the frustrated Amanda Murphy, who was arrested after denouncing the war, President Wilson, and the Red Cross following too many solicitations for donations.

The U.S. Supreme Court upheld the constitutionality of the Sedition Act in *Abrams v. United States* in 1919. In a famous dissenting opinion that shaped First Amendment law for the rest of the 20th century, however, Justice Oliver Wendell

Holmes encouraged scrutiny of sedition prosecutions to ensure that only individuals whose activities constituted a clear and present danger to society were convicted.

Approximately 800 people were convicted on sedition charges during the life of the act. The law was rendered void with the end of World War I, though some leaders advocated a peacetime version of the law. Attorney General A. Mitchell Palmer, who was also seeking the Democratic Party nomination for president, proposed a peacetime Sedition Act, citing dangerous foreign-language presses and growing civil rights unrest among African American communities. J. Edgar Hoover, then head of the General Intelligence Division of the Bureau of Investigation at the Department of Justice, also supported the peacetime law. At one point, Congress reviewed 70 versions of the proposed peacetime Sedition Act but chose not to act upon any. Congress formally repealed the Sedition Act in 1921. The act has been described by historians as the nation's most extreme anti–free speech legislation.

Tiffany Middleton
Independent Scholar

The St. Louis, Missouri, National Association for the Advancement of Colored People (NAACP) holds a 1960s protest march against the segregation of U.S. schools.

See Also: 1941 to 1960 Primary Documents; *Abrams v. United States*; Alien and Sedition Acts of 1798; Espionage Act of 1917; *Schenck v. United States*.

Further Readings
Kohn, Stephen. *American Political Prisoners*. Westport, CT: Praeger, 1994.
Stone, Geoffrey. *Perilous Times: Free Speech in Wartime From the Sedition Act of 1798 to the War on Terrorism*. New York: W. W. Norton, 2004.
Thomas, William. *Unsafe for Democracy: World War I and the U.S. Justice Department's Covert Campaign to Suppress Dissent*. Madison: University of Wisconsin Press, 2008.

Segregation Laws

Segregation constitutes a policy of physically separating socially designated "races" in residential, educational, recreational, and public facilities. Segregation may be defined as either *de jure* (sanctioned by law) or de facto (segregation in "fact," persisting in varying degrees) and can exist within institutions such the U.S. military, which employed the policy until 1947. Segregation laws in U.S. history are often referred to as Jim Crow laws. The phrase *Jim Crow* originated in the 1830s and is believed to have been first associated with the minstrel show performances of Thomas "Daddy" Rice. Rice (a white American) blackened his face with burnt cork and danced a jig while singing the tune *Jump Jim Crow* as based on his observation of an African American man while traveling through the south. By the 1850s, the Jim Crow character created by Rice had become a main feature in the 19th-century minstrel show while the term *Jim Crow* became an adjective utilized by writers in the late 19th century. Some historians have argued that "Crow" was actually the surname of the owner of the slave that Rice witnessed singing a similar tune. The term *Jim Crow law* was first listed in the *Dictionary of American English* in 1904. Segregation laws or Jim Crow laws dominated U.S. social relations from the 19th century through the 1960s and ended as a result of the activism of African Americans during the civil rights movement.

The policy of segregating the races began before the end of slavery in the northern section of the United States. Segregation laws began to appear in the southern section of the United States following the Civil War and Reconstruction through 1877. These laws, as they appeared in the south, were based on the pro-slavery argument that claimed the inferiority of African Americans. The segregation laws that appeared in the north were largely characteristically de jure forms of segregation after Reconstruction while the laws that emerged in the south were also a manifestation of de jure forms of segregation. As segregation laws became less noticeable in the north, through the first few decades of the 20th century, the segregation laws in the south became increasingly visible and more rigid. Segregation laws in the south divided whites from blacks in nearly every social setting, including hospitals, schools, hotels, churches, recreational facilities, and forms of public transportation. The history of segregation laws and practices, north and south, through the 21st century signifies an important aspect of the social history of crime and punishment in U.S. society.

Segregation Laws in the North

Segregation laws appeared in the northern U.S. states before becoming an integral feature of social relations in the southern states. In fact, segregation laws governed nearly every interaction between whites and blacks in northern states through 1860. These laws were grounded in white supremacist beliefs that African Americans were inferior and must be regulated. African Americans were systematically separated from whites on stagecoaches and railcars, and in theaters, restaurants, churches, hospitals, prisons, and lecture halls. States such as Indiana, Illinois, and Oregon had provisions in their constitutions prohibiting the admission of African Americans into the borders of these states. South Boston did not have one African American family among its various neighborhoods in 1847, and this was not unusual for the time. In Cincinnati, African Americans were segregated into "Little Africa," while in Boston, "New Guinea" became the dwelling of African Americans in the city. Only five northern states (Massachusetts, New Hampshire, Vermont, Maine, and Rhode Island) permitted African Americans the right to vote before the Civil War. African Americans were excluded from serving on juries in northern states until Massachusetts allowed the practice in 1855. Some northern states prohibited African Americans from testifying in court. There were bans on African Americans serving in positions as jurors, witnesses, and judges throughout northern states before the Civil War.

Segregation laws and practices continued to be present in northern states through the 20th century. African Americans were separated from whites in residential housing, schools, employment, and other public facilities. States such as Illinois, Ohio, Pennsylvania, and New Jersey maintained segregation laws in the public school system through the modern civil rights era. The Great Migration north of African Americans from the south after 1919 compelled many northern cities and locales to uphold segregation in jobs, trade unions, neighborhoods, and public facilities. In fact, one of the preeminent civil rights organizations created in the 1940s, the Congress of Racial Equality (CORE), practiced "sit-downs" in downtown Chicago to protest segregation in public facilities long before the mass movement for civil rights began in 1955. The growing black northern population through the 1920s became increasingly isolated into ghettos through the 1930s and 1940s as a result of restrictive residential covenants that barred African Americans from securing housing in specific neighborhoods, coupled with the policies of redlining and blockbusting. Despite the persistence of segregation laws and policies in northern states through the 20th century, the term *Jim Crow law* is often more routinely associated with the southern section of the United States and with a particular historical period, from roughly the era of Reconstruction through 1954; specifically, in the years between the Supreme Court decisions in *Plessy v. Ferguson* (1896) and *Brown v. Board of Education* (1954).

Segregation Laws in the South

Segregation laws emerged across the south upon the end of the Civil War. These laws began as early as 1865. In slavery, African Americans were heavily regulated by white slaveholders; thus, the south

A young boy drinks from a segregated water fountain designated for "colored" people on the county courthouse lawn in Halifax, North Carolina, in 1938. Segregation laws existed in the United States from the 19th century through the 1960s and also required African Americans to be separate from whites in stagecoaches, trains, restaurants, public toilets, and schools.

did not require comprehensive segregation laws to regulate the civil liberties of African Americans before the Civil War and emancipation. In fact, the physical proximity between blacks and whites during the slave era was far greater than it was after emancipation. The first major postwar legal restrictions on African American civil liberties in the south came in the form of Black Codes during the presidency of Andrew Johnson in 1865. These codes were reminiscent of the slave codes that were first developed in the late 17th century to restrict African American autonomy in servitude. Three states adopted laws that allowed discrimination on railroads between 1865 and 1866. Mississippi did not allow African Americans to ride in any first-class passenger cars set aside for whites, the Florida legislature forbade whites to use cars set apart for use by black passengers, and a Texas law required all railroad companies to attach to passenger trains one car for African American accommodation. In the 1870s, a series of Supreme Court cases helped to undermine African American civil rights despite the passage of the Civil Rights Act of 1866 and the ratification of the Fourteenth Amendment, which guaranteed citizenship to the freed slaves.

The *Slaughter House Cases* (1873) and the Supreme Court decision in *United States v. Cruikshank* (1876) both weakened the federal ability to protect African American citizens. In 1883, the Supreme Court declared the Civil Rights Act of 1875, a law that guaranteed the freed slaves equal access to public places, unconstitutional, stating that Congress had no power to prevent acts of discrimination. The series of decisions by the Supreme Court helped to anchor a system of segregation in the American south as various states and locales began to pass laws requiring the separation of the races. In 1890, Mississippi wrote a disenfranchisement provision into its state constitution; that same year, in Louisiana, African Americans were required to ride in separate rail cars. The Louisiana law was challenged by people of color in Louisiana such as Homer Plessy, who boarded a Louisiana railcar in defiance of the law and was arrested. The Supreme Court decision in *Plessy v. Ferguson* (1896) declaring the doctrine of "separate but equal" constitutional sanctioned the separation of the races from the late 19th century through 1954.

By 1910, every state of the former Confederacy had Jim Crow laws on the books. Segregation laws were taken to the extreme in some locales throughout the southern section of the United States. Louisiana required separate entrances for blacks and whites by 1914; in 1915, Oklahoma segregated telephone booths. Mississippi made it a crime to publish notions of equal rights as applied to African Americans in textbooks in 1920. Texas prohibited integrated boxing matches, while Georgia barred black ministers from performing marriage ceremonies for whites. New Orleans segregated its prostitutes, and most southern states banned interracial marriage, African American voting rights, and civil rights in general through the laws of segregation. Southern states implemented the poll tax, literary test, and grandfather clause to prevent African Americans from exercising their voting rights. The system of segregation was kept in place by vigilante violence exercised by whites determined to maintain segregation through extreme measures. Thousands of African Americans were lynched by white mobs between 1890 and 1954. African Americans responded by creating such groups as the National Association for the Advancement of Colored People (NAACP), organized in 1909, and the National Urban League, developed in 1911, among other agencies.

The NAACP, through its Legal Defense Fund, began to fight segregation laws in the first decade of the 20th century, securing a series of legal victories against all-white primaries and the grandfather clause. In these years, the NAACP developed a strategy of legal gradualism (fighting segregation through the courts) as evidenced in its support of *Guinn v. United States* (1915), a case that challenged the grandfather clause in Oklahoma; *Buchanan v. Warley* (1917), in which the Supreme Court stated that residential segregation may not be required; and other landmark decisions such as the 1944 Supreme Court decision in *Smith v. Allwright* that declared all-white primaries unconstitutional. The legal assault against segregation laws advanced by the NAACP led to the emergence of the modern civil rights movement, particularly in terms of the NAACP challenges to segregation in schools. As a result of this legal campaign waged by the NAACP, the Supreme Court was compelled to declare the doctrine of "separate but equal" to be unconstitutional in the historic case *Brown v. Board of Education* (1954), thereby effectively clearing the way for the dismantling of segregation laws throughout the American south. The Civil Rights Act of 1964 allowed all citizens equal access to public facilities and equal employment opportunities. The Voting Rights Act of 1965 gave African Americans access to the ballot without restrictions. Fair housing practices were implemented in the Fair Housing Act of 1968. Jim Crow laws began to disappear across the American south through the decades following the civil rights movement. Patterns of de facto segregation continue to exist in U.S. society, particularly in terms of housing, education, and employment, while segregation laws or *de jure* segregation once sanctioned by state and local governments are no longer on the books.

Conclusion

Segregation laws have been an important facet in the social history of crime and punishment in U.S. society. Interracial social relations were criminalized on nearly every level in the American south. African American men were lynched across the American south and southwest, by the hundreds, at the mere hint of any contact with white women through 1955. The crime of interracial association, voluntary or not, sanctioned the punishment of lynching with or without trials. Race relations between blacks and whites were anchored in the laws of segregation for decades following the Civil War. Indeed, southerners in support of segregation often made the argument that to maintain law and order, the "races" must be separated as a measure of public safety through the police powers of the state. The Supreme Court's support of segregation laws in the late 19th century was shaped by the accepted notions of the majority about African American inferiority. Stereotypical ideas about nonwhite ethno-racial groups continue to shape governmental policies related to law, order, crime, and punishment in U.S. society. This is evidenced in the high rates of arrests, incarceration, and punishment experienced by African American communities. The racial attitudes that influenced segregation laws in regard to the supposed "inferiority" of nonwhites must be dispensed with completely before all forms of segregation can disappear.

Hettie V. Williams
Monmouth University

See Also: 1851 to 1900 Primary Documents; *Brown v. Board of Education*; Lynchings; *Plessy v. Ferguson*; Racism.

Further Readings
Ayers, Edward L. *The Promise of the New South*. New York: Oxford University Press, 1992.
Brundage, W. Fitzhugh, ed. *Under Sentence of Death: Lynching in the South*. Chapel Hill: University of North Carolina Press, 1997.
Hale, Grace Elizabeth. *Making Whiteness: The Culture of Segregation in the South, 1890–1940*. New York: Pantheon Books, 1998.
Litwack, Leon. *Trouble in Mind: Black Southerners in the Age of Jim Crow*. New York: Knopf, 1998.
Perlaman, Michael. *Struggle for Mastery: Disfranchisement in the South, 1888–1908*. Chapel Hill: University of North Carolina Press, 2001.
Williamson, Joel. *The Crucible of Race: Black-White Relations in the American South Since Emancipation*. New York: Oxford University Press, 1984.
Woodward, C. Vann. *The Strange Career of Jim Crow*, 3rd ed. New York: Oxford University Press, 1974.

Selective Service Act of 1967

The United States began conscription during the American Civil War in 1863, and it proved unpopular, culminating in draft riots. During World War I, the Selective Service Act passed in May 1917 established the Selective Service system. Originally, the act gave the president the power to draft men for military service. Males 21 to 30 were required to register for a service period of one year, and in 1918, the age was raised to

Draft-age Americans being counseled by Mark Satin (far left) at the Anti-Draft Programme office on Spadina Avenue in Toronto, Canada, in August 1967. About 30,000 deserters and draft dodgers fled to Mexico and Canada while the mandatory draft was in effect in the United States during the Vietnam War. A volunteer armed service replaced the U.S. draft in 1974.

45. In 1920, the draft was discontinued, but in 1940, the Selective Training and Service Act of 1940 established the first peacetime draft in U.S. history. This version stated that all males 18 and older must register, with those between 19 and 26 viable for service of 21 months. With the outbreak of the Korean War, the Universal Military Training Service Act (1951) extended service to 24 months and the minimum age to 18.5 years. Then, after the outbreak of the Vietnam War, President John F. Kennedy signed Executive Order 11119 giving exemption to married men aged 19 to 26. President Lyndon Johnson revoked the married clause, to exempt only those with dependent children, with Executive Order 11241.

During the height of the Vietnam War, and at the beginning of the Tet Offensive, the Military Selective Service Act of 1967 again altered the conscription law. It stated that all men from 18 to 35 must register for selective service, with exemptions for dependent children and education. Student deferments ended upon graduation or the student's 24th birthday, whichever came first. Coinciding with the unpopular war, the education exemption set off further social discontent. Critics claimed that deferments for education discriminated against the working class and the poor, since the majority of those eligible for school deferments were males from middle- and upper-class backgrounds.

Critics also began arguing that a disproportionate amount of nonwhites were being drafted, and, in an effort to counter the perceived discrimination, the lottery system was instituted. President Johnson signed this as an amendment to the Military Selective Service Act of 1967 in November 1969. The voices of critics and the public acts of draft protesters forced this change. Beginning in 1965, resistant males began publicly burning their draft cards, and draft dodgers began fleeing to Mexico and Canada (predominantly) to avoid service. The first draft lottery occurred in December 1969 with random numbers being called; those whose draft ID numbers fell within the parameters were required to report for service. This new system of blindly calling individuals into service was thought to ease the tensions of those who were conscripted, but the unpopularity of Vietnam did not die. By 1973, the draft was revoked, in favor of an all-volunteer army, and President Gerald Ford gave many draft dodgers and draft-card burners clemency in 1974.

Annessa A. Babic
New York Institute of Technology

See Also: Johnson, Lyndon B. (Administration of); Military Courts; Military Police.

Further Readings
Kusch, Frank. *All American Boys: Draft Dodgers in Canada From the Vietnam War*. Westport, CT: Praeger, 2001.
Segal, David R. *Recruiting for Uncle Sam: Citizenship and Military Manpower Policy*. Lawrence: University Press of Kansas, 2002.
Todd, Jack. *Desertion: In the Time of Vietnam*. Boston: Houghton-Mifflin Harcourt, 2001.

Sentencing

Sentencing is the imposition of a punishment by a court for a violation of the criminal law. Sentencing takes place after the defendant has been found guilty or has confessed to a crime. Although sentencing occurs post-conviction, it is deemed an essential phase within the criminal justice process, and defendants are entitled to legal counsel during these proceedings. While sentences are usually imposed by trial judges, they may also be imposed by juries or sentencing councils. Sentences are crafted to achieve multiple philosophical goals, including deterrence, incapacitation, rehabilitation, and retribution. Fines, incarceration, or community supervision are all common sentences. In some jurisdictions, under more elaborate sentencing procedures, the death penalty is still imposed.

Goals of Sentencing
Commentators have identified a number of sentencing objectives, but four goals comprise the cornerstones of sentencing: deterrence, incapacitation, rehabilitation, and retribution. The first three (deterrence, incapacitation, and rehabilitation) are consequentialist theories of punishment, focusing on the prospective reduction of future crimes; retribution is a nonconsequentialist and

retrospective theory of punishment, focusing on the punishment that is deserved for previous conduct. These four goals of punishment sometimes harmonize, such as incarcerating a dangerous offender to prevent him from injuring others (incapacitation) and to discourage others from committing comparable crimes (deterrence). Sometimes, however, the goals of punishment are more difficult to reconcile. Playwright George Bernard Shaw described the tension between retribution and rehabilitation, noting that if we are to punish defendants retributively, we must injure them; conversely, if we are to rehabilitate them, we must improve them; but we cannot do both simultaneously, for men are not improved by injuries.

Deterrence is based on the view that humans maximize their pleasure and minimize their pain. In order to induce people to forgo the pleasures of crime (e.g., the taking of goods or services without payment or the euphoria of illegal drugs), the state must establish penalties for crimes. The threat of punishment is enough to deter people from committing crimes. The theory of deterrence comes in two forms: specific deterrence and general deterrence. Specific deterrence suggests that if an offender commits a crime and is punished for it, that offender will be less likely to reoffend. General deterrence is based upon the fact that people learn vicariously (not only from punishments imposed on them directly). General deterrence suggests that punishment imposed upon an offender may deter future crime not just for him, but for others.

Incapacitation is a straightforward theory: Punishment can make it difficult (or impossible) for an offender to commit further crimes. Offenders can be incapacitated by spatially removing them from society (e.g., imprisonment or banishment) or by physically eliminating the capacity to offend (e.g., cutting off the hand of a thief or chemically castrating sex offenders). Capital punishment is the ultimate incapacitating punishment: Executed offenders never reoffend.

Rehabilitation is rooted in the idea of crime as disease. If people commit crimes because of inherent defects, one obvious way to reduce future crime is to simply correct the defect, regardless of whether the defect is physical (e.g., a chemical imbalance), psychological (e.g., criminal thinking patterns), or social (e.g., association with criminal peers). During the 1960s, there was great interest in the United States in rehabilitation. In the 1970s, however, catalyzed by Robert Martinson's 1974 article that dismissed rehabilitation programs as ineffective, public opinion shifted, and rehabilitation was rejected as a legitimate basis of punishment. Only recently has interest in rehabilitation re-emerged within mainstream policy circles.

Retribution (sometimes called "just deserts" or simply "desert") is a nonconsequentialist theory of punishment, suggesting that criminals should be punished because they deserve it. Retribution, it is suggested, redresses the unfair advantage of society that the criminal has taken. Georg Hegel explained that when the criminal violates the law, his crime is the negation of the right of society. Punishment is the negation of this negation and thus an affirmation of right, brought upon the criminal by himself. Retribution takes two forms: negative and positive. Negative retribution requires that only the guilty may be punished and then only to the extent they deserve, but it does not require that punishments must be imposed. Positive retribution, on the other hand, requires that the guilty must be punished to the full extent of their desert. The view of positive retribution was articulated by Immanuel Kant, who argued that even if an island society was about to disband, the last murderers lying in its prisons should be put to death. Society not only has a right to punish them, but it has a duty to do so.

While deterrence, incapacitation, rehabilitation, and retribution operate as the principal goals of sentencing, there are other goals that inform sentencing decisions. For example, Joel Feinberg's expressive theory of punishment suggests that criminal sentences communicate moral opprobrium to offenders, relating social attitudes about criminal behavior. In this vein, just sentences can reinforce legal norms, enhance respect for the law, and provide catharsis for crime victims. Sentences that include restitution may help to ameliorate the financial, physical, emotional, and/or social harms to victims of crimes by requiring the criminal to compensate the victim (usually financially).

Types of Sentences

Historically, a variety of penalties have been imposed at sentencing, including financial penalties

The night before the execution of Ronnie Lee Gardner in June 2010, a protest against the death penalty was held at the Utah State Capitol. Gardner was serving a life sentence for murdering a man during a robbery and killing another man in an escape attempt while being transported to a court hearing. He received the death penalty for the second killing. Gardner threatened to sue to force the state of Utah to execute him by firing squad, which he claimed to prefer because of his Mormon background.

(fines, forfeiture, and restitution), corporal punishment, capital punishment, carceral punishment (jail and prison), community supervision (probation and parole), and intermediate sanctions (intermittent confinement, electronic monitoring, and community service orders). Judges might impose multiple types of penalties to accomplish the goals of sentencing. For minor offenses, defendants might be fined and/or assigned community service. For more serious offenses, defendants might be placed on probation or be incarcerated. Very serious crimes might result in a sentence of death.

The sentences imposed by courts have changed throughout history. In the American colonies, serious crimes were punished by execution (usually hanging) and less serious crimes were punished with nonlethal physical penalties (e.g., branding or whipping). Jails existed, but they served principally as places of detention for those who could not post bail or pay their fines. Between about 1750 and 1850, however, punishment underwent a transformation. Prompted by humanitarian reformers, the prison was reinvented from a place where criminals awaited punishment to the vehicle of their punishment. In *Discipline and Punish*, Michel Foucault traces this evolution from a system of corporal punishments to one of carceral punishments, using the prison as a metaphor for society at large.

Financial penalties are common at sentencing. Like taxes, criminal fines may be used to deter undesired conduct, but fines differ from taxes in that they express moral opprobrium. Fines may involve modest sums of money (e.g., for parking violations or speeding) or millions of dollars (e.g., for corporate antitrust or environmental violations). Some jurisdictions have experimented with day fines, penalties that are adjusted to income levels. The forfeiture of assets involved in criminal activity (including high-ticket items such as real estate, automobiles, aircraft, and boats, as well as cash) is another means of deterring criminal conduct. Restitution, the defendant's compensation of crime victims for their losses, is often part of a criminal sentence.

Corporal punishment, as such, is no longer part of U.S. sentencing. Whippings and canings are no longer imposed. Indeed, after the 1968 case *Jackson v. Bishop*, the practice of imposing physical punishments all but disappeared. Still, for some crimes, some jurisdictions do impose physical penalties on offenders. For example, several states chemically castrate recidivating child molesters with a birth-control drug. Federal courts and the majority of state courts may also impose the death penalty, which, by definition, punishes offenders physically. In the United States, most executions are conducted via lethal injection, although four other methods are still authorized: electrocution, gas chamber, hanging, and firing squad.

Carceral punishments are also common at sentencing. Approximately 2 million U.S. citizens are incarcerated in jails or prisons. For misdemeanors, crimes punishable by one year of incarceration or less, confinement usually takes place in a jail; for felonies, crimes punished by more than one year, confinement usually takes place in a prison.

Community supervision is less restrictive than incarceration. Offenders might be supervised by a probation officer, as an alternative to jail or prison, and offenders who have been deemed ready might be released from prison on parole and be supervised in the community by a parole officer. Offenders on probation or parole may be required to meet with their supervising officer on a regular basis, to maintain employment and residence, and to submit to drug tests. Community supervision is even more common than incarceration: Approximately 5 million U.S. citizens are on probation or parole.

When a sentence combines aspects of incarceration and community supervision, it is called an intermediate sanction. Intermediate sanctions fall between probation and incarceration in terms of severity. Other varieties include house arrest, electronic monitoring, intensive supervision probation, and boot camp programs.

Occasionally, courts impose other types of punishment. Modern courts do not sentence offenders to confinement in stocks or pillories, but they do occasionally impose shaming punishments, such as requiring men who solicit prostitutes to advertise their convictions in a newspaper or requiring shoplifters to wear placards that read, "I steal things." Although sentences of banishment are no longer imposed by federal or state courts, the penalty is sometimes imposed by tribal courts on Indian reservations. In some jurisdictions, sex offender residency restrictions functionally banish offenders from their communities.

Determinate Versus Indeterminate Sentencing
There is great variation among states in terms of how sentencing authority is allocated. At root, sentencing authority lies with the legislature, but other actors in the criminal justice system—judges, jurors, prison officials, sentencing commissions, release authorities, even executives such as state governors and the president of the United States—often play key roles. Which individuals are involved in sentencing decisions and how much discretion they wield depends in large part upon whether the structure in a given jurisdiction is determinate or indeterminate in nature.

In a jurisdiction with determinate sentencing, the sentence imposed by the court is the sentence that the defendant will actually serve. The judge considers the range of sentences authorized by the legislature (penal codes usually establish maximum, and sometimes minimum, terms of incarceration for crimes). The judge then considers the goals of sentencing and imposes a sentence (say, five years in prison). This defendant then serves five years in prison (less any "good time" subtracted from his sentence for good behavior at the discretion of prison authorities). There is truth in sentencing. Unless the sentence is reversed upon appeal or the executive branch modifies the sentence through amnesty, pardon, or commutation (both of these events are relatively rare), the defendant knows the length of his upcoming prison sentence on the very day he leaves the sentencing proceeding. Determinate sentencing is closely linked to the sentencing goals of desert and retribution.

In a jurisdiction with indeterminate sentencing, the legislature creates a release authority (usually known as a parole board) that has the discretion to grant early release to offenders. In an indeterminate jurisdiction, a judge might impose a statutory sentencing range for the offense (say, for example, five to 10 years). Under such an indeterminate sentence, the defendant goes to prison for a term of at least five years but no more than 10 years. The actual time of release depends upon the decision of the parole board, which considers the defendant's conduct in prison, rehabilitative progress, and other relevant factors. Indeterminate sentencing is closely linked to utilitarian goals of sentencing, especially rehabilitation.

Colonial sentencing was almost entirely determinate, and early U.S. judges had little or no authority to modify the punishments imposed by law. But during the late 19th and early 20th centuries, indeterminate sentencing became increasingly widespread. Associated with reformers such as physician Benjamin Rush, indeterminate sentencing promised a more humane system of punishment. Instead of incarcerating prisoners for fixed periods of months and years, sentences might operate as maximums, but in practice, offenders could be incarcerated until they were rehabilitated (and no longer). Indeterminate sentencing also became popular for pragmatic reasons: It provided an effective means for prison administrators to control prison crowding. Between the early 1930s and 1970, U.S. sentencing was dominated by the indeterminate model. Indeed, in California, one of the states most committed to the indeterminate and rehabilitative punishment, almost all serious offenders were sentenced to a term of between one year and life in prison. The actual sentence was determined by California parole authorities. During the late 1970s (around the time Robert Martinson published his "nothing works" article), however, many U.S. jurisdictions denounced indeterminate sentencing (and rehabilitation) and asserted new determinate sentencing regimes based upon nonconsequentialist principles of retribution and desert.

Sentencing Disparity

It is easy to see that in an indeterminate sentencing system, sentencing disparity may be commonplace. Identical defendants, with equivalent criminal histories and backgrounds, guilty of identical crimes, might be required to serve very different sentences. One offender, saying the right things to a parole board, might be released after just five years; another offender, less eloquent but no more blameworthy, might be incarcerated for 10 years. Disparity also can affect determinate systems. Identical defendants, appearing before different judges with different sentencing philosophies, might receive wildly different sentences. One judge, guided by rehabilitative philosophies, might sentence an offender to probation; another judge, guided by philosophies of retribution, might impose a lengthy prison sentence. Neither would be "wrong," and because historically, sentences that fell within the legislatively prescribed range were virtually unreviewable, defendants had no recourse to challenge disparately imposed sentences.

Judge Marvin Frankel condemned this kind of disparity as "judicial lawlessness." He noted that many federal statutes imposed absolute judicial discretion (rape committed within federal jurisdiction was punishable by death or imprisonment for any term of years or life) and warned against the potential abuses inherent in any sentencing system that conferred such broad discretion. Sentencing disparities between racial, gender, and class groupings plague many jurisdictions. Eliminating judicial disparity, however, is difficult and sometimes creates other sentencing inequities.

Mandatory Minimum Sentences

One approach to limiting judicial discretion is to impose mandatory minimum sentences. Cesare Beccaria and Jeremy Bentham both advocated such an approach, suggesting that once the penal law is written, the role of the judge should be limited, so as not to be swayed by personal prejudices. In practice, mandatory minimum sentences operate as sentencing "floors." Judges still have discretion to impose higher sentences (up to the limits authorized by law), but cannot impose a sentence below the mandatory minimum, no matter which considerations might lead them to do so. If, for example, the law requires that all those trafficking five grams or more of crack cocaine are punished by at least five years in prison, it does not matter whether it is the defendant's first offense or whether he sold crack to support his own drug habit. The goals of sentencing, which

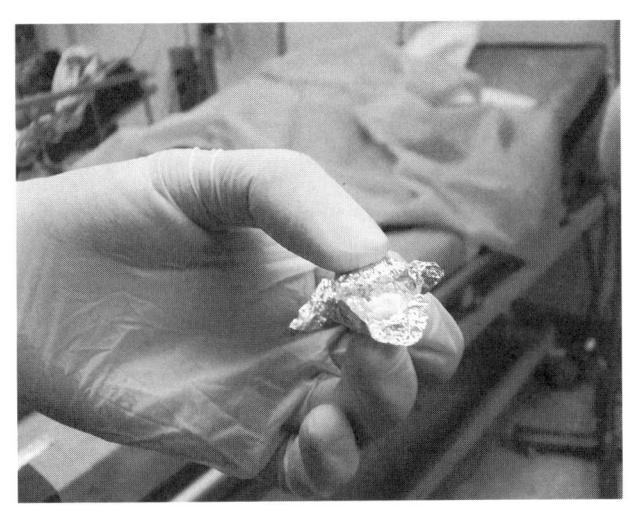

A tin foil package of crack cocaine found on a patient who survived a gunshot wound to the head. Under mandatory minimum sentencing laws, a first offense of possession of 25 grams of crack will trigger a five-year sentence.

might determine the judge's sentence in other cases, are trumped by the law.

Although mandatory minimum sentences are popular with politicians and useful to prosecutors, they are criticized by many academics and judges as being blunt and inflexible tools, often using just one aggravating factor (such as drug weight or possession of a firearm) as a basis for the penalty. Mandatory minimum sentences also create sentencing "cliffs," disparities created by the mandatory nature of the sentence. For example, the first offender convicted of trafficking 4.98 grams of crack might receive a sentence of probation, but an identical offender convicted of trafficking 5.01 grams must serve five years in prison—a great disparity in sentence—even though their crimes are virtually indistinguishable.

Three Strikes Laws

Three strikes laws are another form of mandatory minimum sentences. Instead of focusing upon drug weight or firearm possession, they focus on criminal history. Habitual felon laws (enhancing sentences for recidivists) have a long history, extending at least as far back as 1797 in New York, but they became politically popular in the 1990s as "three strikes laws." Washington State passed the first modern three strikes law in 1993, California in 1994, and then more than 20 states followed during 1994 and 1995. Today, half of the states have three strikes laws, although California's infamous three strikes law accounts for more than 90 percent of the three strikes cases in the United States.

California's three strikes law requires that any defendant who has committed an enumerated serious or violent felony and then commits another felony (the second strike) must serve twice the term otherwise required by law, and that any defendant with two or more serious or violent predicate offenses who then commits another felony (the third strike) must serve 25 years to life for that felony. Defendants can receive multiple third strikes (which must be served consecutively, not concurrently), and "good time" is reduced: Whereas most California prisoners can reduce their sentences by 50 percent, those convicted of a second or third strike can reduce their sentences, at most, by 20 percent. The California three strikes law is unquestionably strict but was upheld by the Supreme Court in 2003 in the cases *Ewing v. California* and *Lockyer v. Andrade*.

Sentencing Guidelines

Sentencing guidelines are one mechanism to channel sentencing discretion without resorting to mandatory penalties. Formulated by the U.S. Parole Board as a means of improving transparency and predictability in parole decisions during the 1970s, guidelines were adapted to the sentencing context in Minnesota in the early 1980s.

Sentencing guidelines typically assume the form of a two-dimensional grid. One axis identifies the range of offenses, from least serious to most serious; the other axis identifies criminal history, from those with no criminal record to those with extensive criminal records. At the intersection of the appropriate row and column, judges will find the expected sentencing range. Judges may choose to depart upward or downward from the specified sentence when special circumstances are present (and may be expected to do so), but as a general matter, the guideline range is considered to be the correct sentence for the offender, given the offense and the criminal history.

Guidelines-based sentencing has been successful in many jurisdictions that implemented it, but it has been criticized. It has been noted, for example, that guidelines are not very different from mandatory minimum sentences; whereas mandatory minimum penalties are imposed on the basis of one variable (e.g., drug weight or criminal history), guidelines use two (offense severity and criminal history). All of the other factors that might lead a judge to impose a severe or lenient sentence are subordinated to these two factors; what should be a solemn exchange between the government's criminal justice authority and the convicted defendant is reduced to a desiccated exercise in accounting.

Guidelines-based sentencing also faces legal limitations. Systems in which sentences are imposed based upon judge-found facts may violate the Constitution. In 2004, in *Blakely v. Washington*, the Supreme Court held that the Sixth Amendment prohibits judges from enhancing sentences based on facts other than those admitted by the defendant or found by a jury beyond a reasonable doubt. In 2005, in *United States v. Booker*, this holding was applied to the federal sentencing guidelines, which, deemed unconstitutional, were made advisory. In 2007, in *Cunningham v. California*, the Supreme Court held that California's determinate sentencing law (allowing judges to impose a low, middle, or high term for offenses) was subject to the holding in *Blakely*.

Evidence-Based Sentencing

Some courts are beginning to explore the possibility of evidence-based sentencing, an actuarial approach that uses risk prediction instruments to guide the imposition of sentences. Since the 1970s, risk assessment instruments have become ubiquitous in community corrections and are frequently used to determine the appropriate conditions of probation or parole. Some judges have asked if these risk instruments can also be used at sentencing. Research indicates that statistical assessments outperform the clinical judgment of even trained experts (like judges). If actuarial assessment instruments can distinguish recidivists from those who will not reoffend, then law enforcement resources can be reallocated to minimize crime. Individuals who are likely to commit future crimes can be incapacitated for longer periods (selective incapacitation), while low-risk defendants could receive noncustodial or alternative punishments. Virginia has adopted this approach, and it may prove to be attractive to other jurisdictions struggling with swelling prison populations and dwindling corrections budgets.

Capital Sentencing

Sentencing in death penalty cases is different from noncapital sentencing, perhaps because as the Supreme Court frequently notes in its opinions related to capital punishment, "death is different." The same tension that exists in noncapital sentencing exists in capital cases: On the one hand, sentencing discretion must be channeled to ensure that resulting sentences are just and not imposed upon arbitrary or impermissible grounds; on the other hand, defendants must be afforded individualized consideration. But in capital cases, the stakes are literally life and death, which has resulted in a kind of super due process.

In 1972, in the watershed case *Furman v. Georgia*, the Supreme Court held that imposition of the death penalty (as then applied) constituted cruel and unusual punishment under the Eighth Amendment of the U.S. Constitution, resulting in *de facto* abolition of capital punishment. Four years later, however, with the court's decisions in *Gregg v. Georgia* and *Proffitt v. Florida*, capital punishment was reinstated in the United States. Capital sentencing proceedings differ from noncapital proceedings in at least three ways. First, capital cases provide for an automatic appeal. Second, capital proceedings employ bifurcated trials, consisting of guilt and penalty phases. The question of whether a defendant should be put to death is not raised unless and until the defendant is found guilty of an offense punishable by death. Third, capital defendants are free to introduce a variety of mitigating evidence during the penalty phase in order to rebut the prosecution's evidence of aggravating factors. In 2002, in *Ring v. Arizona*, the Supreme Court held that the jury—not the judge—must determine whether statutory aggravating circumstances have been proven.

Other restrictions apply to capital cases that do not apply in noncapital sentencing proceedings. For example, the death penalty equivalent of mandatory minimum sentencing—the mandatory imposition of the death penalty upon a finding of first-degree murder—was struck down as unconstitutional in *Woodson v. North Carolina*. In noncapital cases, legislatures enjoy broad discretion in setting the penalties for various crimes, but the death penalty has been limited to the most serious of crimes. While upheld in cases of first-degree murder where aggravating circumstances distinguish the crime as especially egregious, capital punishment has been struck down as unconstitutional in cases of the rape of an adult woman (*Coker v. Georgia*) and the rape of a child (*Kennedy v. Louisiana*).

Whereas juveniles or mentally handicapped individuals can be punished, including the imposition of life imprisonment without the possibility of parole, the Constitution bars their execution (juveniles in *Roper v. Simmons* and the mentally handicapped in *Atkins v. Virginia*). While offenders who go insane in prison can be kept in prison, in *Ford v. Wainwright*, the Supreme Court held that death row prisoners who go insane in custody cannot be executed.

James C. Oleson
University of Auckland

See Also: Capital Punishment; Corporal Punishment; Cruel and Unusual Punishment; Deterrence, Theory of; Incapacitation, Theory of; Rehabilitation; Retributivism; Sentencing, Indeterminate Versus Fixed; Three Strikes Law.

Further Readings

Foucault, Michel. *Discipline and Punish*. New York: Pantheon Books, 1977.

Friedman, Lawrence M. *Crime and Punishment in American History*. New York: Basic Books, 1993.

Luna, Erik. "Gridland: An Allegorical Critique of Federal Sentencing." *Journal of Criminal Law and Criminology*, v.96 (2005).

Martinson, Robert. "What Works? Questions and Answers About Prison Reform." *The Public Interest*, v.35 (1974).

Reitz, Kevin R. "Sentencing." In *The Handbook of Crime and Punishment*, Michael Tonry, ed. New York: Oxford University Press, 1998.

Stith, Kate and José A. Cabranes. *Fear of Judging: Sentencing Guidelines in the Federal Courts*. Chicago: University of Chicago Press, 1998.

Tonry, Michael. *Sentencing Matters*. New York: Oxford University Press, 1996.

Ulmer, Jeffrey. *Social Worlds of Sentencing: Court Communities Under Sentencing Guidelines*. Albany: State University of New York Press, 1997.

von Hirsch, Andrew and Andrew Ashworth, eds. *Principled Sentencing*. Lebanon, NH: Northeastern University Press, 1992.

Zimring, Franklin E., et al. *Punishment and Democracy: Three Strikes and You're Out in California*. New York: Oxford University Press, 2001.

Sentencing: Indeterminate Versus Fixed

Indeterminate sentencing refers to sentencing practices where judges incarcerate offenders for statutory ranges of time, generally later determined by a release authority (often known as a parole board). Fixed sentencing refers to sentencing practices where offenders are incarcerated for a legislated fixed length of time and whose release is nonconditional; this may include determinate sentencing, mandatory minimum sentencing, and three strikes law sentencing.

Indeterminate Sentencing

Colonial American punishments were often corporal in nature, ranging from the death penalty for serious crimes to nonlethal forms of corporal punishment (e.g., flogging or branding) for less serious crimes. Fines were also common for those who could pay. Jail was primarily used to confine offenders to await trial if they could not post bail or if they could not pay any accrued fines. However, between 1750 and 1850, the system of punishment in the United States (particularly in northern states) moved toward an increased use of imprisonment, as opposed to corporal punishment, largely in response to calls for humanitarian reforms and in the growing belief that criminals could be rehabilitated. During the 19th century, prison became the primary form of punishment for more serious offenders.

In 19th-century American prisons, the use of indeterminate sentences became common in response to a number of factors. Such sentences were seen as a way of providing relief for convicts in acknowledgement of rehabilitation and good behavior. In effect, convicts were given to correctional facilities for an indeterminate period of time until rehabilitated. Another factor was the economic pressures caused by incarcerating increasing numbers of offenders. Overcrowding and expense of maintaining offenders in prison often forced states to pardon or release convicts early on in their sentences. Due to the possibility of bribery and corruption in the use of pardons, new systems were required to achieve these reductions in prison populations and expense. This can be seen in the advent of "good time" provisions that allowed sentences to be shortened due to convict cooperation and good behavior. New York introduced these provisions as early as 1817, the federal government in 1867.

The basis for the use of indeterminate sentencing was the belief that criminal activity was in part a result of poor environment and in part a result of poor heredity. This understanding of criminal activity assumed that, given enough time, many offenders could be taught how to lead productive lives and rehabilitated back into society. The term *correctional facility* reflects the idea that convicts might be corrected of their criminality through exposure to hard work, religious reflection, and separation from corrupting influences. Further underlying the logic of indeterminate sentencing was a utilitarian goal. While strict utilitarian approaches such as that proposed by Cesare Beccaria in his work *On Crimes and Punishments* (1764) had argued for fixed sentences as a means of both general and specific deterrence, the rehabilitative logic of indeterminate sentencing retained the aim of specific deterrence insofar as it required that offenders be kept in confinement only for the time required for them to desist from committing further crimes. There was also a belief that indeterminate sentences would actively promote convicts' good behavior in prisons, because their release would be conditional on their rehabilitation. The expectation that as a convict one could be held for an indefinite amount

President Barack Obama talks with members of Congress after signing the Fair Sentencing Act in August 2010. It reversed the Anti-Drug Abuse Act of 1986, which held that crack cocaine was more dangerous and harmful than powder cocaine and required a five-year mandatory minimum sentence for possession of five grams of crack cocaine.

of time, for perhaps even a small crime, would ensure that convicts complied with the rules and actively worked toward rehabilitation.

Fixed Sentencing

Indeterminate sentencing was the predominant form of sentencing throughout the United States until the late 1960s and early 1970s. Beginning in the late 1960s, however, the United States had begun to experience a marked increase in violent crimes, as well as widespread social unrest linked to civil rights and other social protest movements. This led to public and political impressions, particularly within white and middle-class America, that crime was out of control and that the government was doing an inadequate job in maintaining law and order. However, between conservatives and liberals there was a marked split as to the specific ways that the government was in fact failing to address these issues. Conservatives generally saw the criminal justice system as too lenient and too accommodating to the needs of criminal offenders, while liberals generally saw the criminal justice system as racially biased and not rehabilitative enough. However, both positions held the same opinion that use of indeterminate sentencing was problematic. For conservative critics, indeterminate sentencing was too soft on violent or habitual offenders, while for liberal critics indeterminate sentencing was seen as resulting in widely varying punishments between white and minority offenders for similar offenses. Questions were raised about indeterminate sentencing's fairness in other ways as well. Similar offenders displaying similar criminal histories were often at the mercy of parole boards for release, and not infrequently the decisions of such boards varied widely from one offender to the next.

A primary catalyst in the debate over the merits of indeterminate sentencing emerged in Robert Martinson's report in 1974 of 231 correctional rehabilitation programs, where Martinson suggested that there was little empirical evidence to support the idea that such programs effectively rehabilitated offenders. This study, commonly called the "nothing works" study, had wide-ranging political impact. Even though Martinson was primarily concerned with addressing what he saw as gross failures in the potential of rehabilitative programs, as well as gross racial discrepancies in the use of indeterminate sentencing, his report coincided with a growing and influential body of conservative criminological literature that advocated punishment, not rehabilitation, as the primary legitimate function of the criminal justice system. Criminologists such as James Q. Wilson and Charles Murray argued that punishment, not rehabilitation, was a more effective means of deterring offenders and reducing crime. At the same time, other scholars such as Andrew von Hirsch argued that criminal offenders should be held accountable for the social harms of their offenses, and that the primary function of the criminal justice system should be to ensure that criminals received their "just deserts" for the harms they caused.

In this regard, even for the differences between conservatives and liberals, as well as differences within these groups, they agreed that indeterminate sentencing was not working. The work of Marvin Frankel in particular provided the shape and form of a solution to the problems of indeterminate sentencing. Frankel's 1973 work *Criminal Sentences: Law Without Order* argued that the combination of indeterminate sentencing and the wide judicial discretion afforded to judges constituted a type of "judicial lawlessness," which had resulted in a failure to reduce crime and to administer justice equitably. Frankel proposed that sentencing discretion should be removed from individual judges and invested rather in expert commissions that could set binding and uniform recommendations on sentencing regulations. Frankel argued that such a move would provide more uniform application of sentencing and less arbitrary and capricious uses of incarceration.

As a result of the work of Frankel and others, in the late 1970s and early 1980s, a number of states and the federal government moved to implement laws and policies that restricted judicial discretion in sentencing in favor of legislatively mandated sentences. In 1984, Congress passed the Sentencing Reform Act to provide "truth in sentencing" by requiring all convicted offenders to serve at least 85 percent of their sentence, and to help mitigate the wide disparities in federal sentencing. The act also abolished the use of parole in the federal prison system and established the U.S. Sentencing Commission. By 1987, the commission had produced and implemented a set of mandatory sentencing guidelines for all federal felony and Class A misdemeanor crimes. The guidelines consisted of 43 variants of offense level, which could be cross-matched with six differing levels of criminal history. The intent was to produce a system that would deliver a standardized sentence for each possible combination of offense and history.

The use of mandatory sentencing guidelines is commonly referred to as determinate sentencing, where the range of sentences for specific offenses is determined by legislative action or by sentencing commissions. Aside from determinate sentencing, however, two other types of fixed sentencing used by many U.S. states and the federal government are mandatory minimum sentencing and three strikes laws. Mandatory minimum sentences have been used to a lesser degree for decades, particularly for drug offenses. They differ from determinate sentencing in two ways, namely, they usually have a lower fixed range of punishment before an offender can be eligible for release, and they are often targeted at specific types of crimes. Beginning in the late 1980s and early 1990s, mandatory minimum sentences began to replace determinate sentences for several reasons, most directly because determinate sentences were increasingly seen by policy makers as a cumbersome and blunt instrument of sentencing reform. On the other hand, mandatory minimums faced fewer legal challenges, were easier to legislate, and were increasingly seen as able to more precisely target specific types of offenses or offenders.

Three strike laws are aimed at habitual offenders and impose gradated penalties for each serious conviction. As the offender commits repeat offenses that are deemed strike eligible, the mandatory sentences for criminal activity increase in duration until a minimum predetermined threshold, frequently 25 years or more is reached. Habitual offender laws date back to at least the 19th century, but three strike laws differ in the important respect that they are usually mandatory. Washington State passed a three strikes law in 1993 and California in 1994. Today, at least 24 states have some form of habitual-offender laws.

Debates and Directions in Sentencing

Today, mandatory minimum sentencing and three strike laws have largely taken the place of earlier determinate sentencing guidelines in terms of fixed sentences. While determinate sentencing was already waning in popularity, a series of Supreme Court decisions, including *Blakely v. Washington* (2004), *United States v. Booker* (2005), and *Cunningham v. California* (2007), effectively gutted the mandatory aspect of determinate sentencing laws.

Mandatory minimum sentences are not without their own problems, however. While popular with legislators and policymakers, they have been criticized by judges and academics for their inflexibility. Sentencing is often apportioned on the strength of one aggravating factor alone, rather than taking into account all the factors of a criminal activity. Mandatory minimum sentences also tend to produce sentencing disparities due to severe gradients between similar offenses, particularly in the case of drug crimes, where a very minor difference in the amount of drugs possessed by an offender can lead to widely different sentencing outcomes. Similarly, three strikes laws are criticized as being inflexible and arbitrarily punitive. The most widely used three strikes laws are the California statutes. Offenders are increasingly subject to longer periods of incarceration depending on their criminal history. Little account is made of time between offenses or the nature of the offenses that count toward criminal history as a strike. Also, strikes are accrued off single charges, not single cases, so one case might accrue multiple strikes. Perhaps the largest criticism is that life sentences can be imposed for nonviolent felony convictions. This length of sentence does not accurately reflect the seriousness of the criminal activity or the actual risk of the offender.

In the face of these criticisms, new approaches to dealing with sentencing have been investigated to better match sentence type and duration with offender nature and risk. One approach discussed is the use of evidence-based sentencing. Evidence-based sentencing calls for actuarial risk assessment tools to be applied to convicted offenders in sentencing. This allows the sentence to be proportionate to the offender's likelihood of further criminal activity and chances of being rehabilitated. High-risk assessed offenders can be incarcerated for longer periods (selective incapacitation), while low-risk assessed offenders can be shifted into noncustodial or alternate punishment schemes. Such actuarial sentencing is neither indeterminate in the traditional sense nor fixed in a manner similar to mandatory minimums or three strikes, but rather it is ideally fixed according to the relative risk and likelihood of rehabilitation for individual offenders. Currently, Missouri, Pennsylvania, and Virginia have adopted some form of actuarial sentencing, and it is likely that other jurisdictions will follow.

Robert W. Fleet
William R. Wood
University of Auckland

See Also: Corporal Punishment; Corrections; Discretionary Decision Making; History of Crime and Punishment in America: 1970–Present; Incapacitation, Theory of; Judges and Magistrates; Mandatory Minimum Sentencing; New Punitiveness; Parole; Penitentiaries; Probation; Rehabilitation; Retributivism; Sentencing; Three Strikes Law; Wilson, James Q.

Further Readings

Frankel, M. *Criminal Sentences: Law Without Order.* New York: Hill & Wang, 1973.

Griset, P. *Determinate Sentencing: The Promise and the Reality of Retributive Justice.* Albany: State University of New York Press, 1991.

Martinson, Robert. "What Works? Questions and Answers About Prison Reform." *The Public Interest*, v.35 (1974).

von Hirsch, Andrew and Andrew Ashworth, eds. *Principled Sentencing.* Lebanon, NH: Northeastern University Press, 1992.

Serial and Mass Killers

Society is deeply intrigued by serial killers and mass murderers, who are considered to be some of the most dangerous, callous, and capricious criminals known to man. Stories of sadistic individuals who inflict torture on their victims and stories of psychologically disturbed individuals who "go berserk" have spread fear and trepidation about unpredictable violence committed by strangers. Further, numerous novels, television series, and movies have helped to increase this anxiety as well as heighten fascination with these extreme killers. However, disinformation and hysteria have long inhibited a true understanding of these criminal events. Social scientists and practitioners alike have studied serial killers and mass murderers in an effort to better understand these individuals. Social research offer some insights about serial killers and mass murderers, in addition to a framework for discussing commonalities found in their crimes. It is useful to examine each form of extreme murder (i.e., serial killings, mass murder) and discuss the characteristics and typologies of offenders. While examples of extreme murderers are provided, this entry does not intend to provide a comprehensive listing of these killers. Rather, it examines the commonalities of these crimes and perpetrators, then touches upon responses and emerging initiatives to the phenomenon of extreme killings.

Defining serial and mass murder is not always an easy task; definitions vary from study to study. Serial killers and mass murderers are alike in that they both engage in the unlawful, purposeful, and unjustifiable killing of multiple persons. Nonetheless, they differ in many aspects. In general, serial murder has been described as the intentional killing of multiple victims in multiple events. Typically, it involves the killing of three or more victims in three or more events. However, according to the Federal Bureau of Investigation's (FBI's) criteria, it can involve as little as two victims in two events. Mass murder, on the other hand, has been defined as the intentional killing of multiple victims, typically four or more, in a single event or events that last a short period of time. Another distinction between serial killers and mass murderers is that serial killers often revert back to ostensibly normal lives in-between killings, whereas mass murderers usually do not; serial killers also are more likely to attempt to evade law enforcement.

A Little History

As long as mankind has existed, so too has murder. Many historical accounts focus on members of the upper class, as no mind was paid to the lower class because they were deemed insignificant to society. These accounts have been questioned and debated but nonetheless exist. One of the earliest accounts of a serial murder dates back to 144 B.C.E. Liu Penli, cousin of the emperor of China during that period in time, was said to have murdered more than 100 people and taken their belongings for sport. He was later banished from the area, as the emperor could not bear to kill his kin. Gilles de Rais was also a historical serial killer dating back to the 1400s. This wealthy man, a leader in the French army and comrade to Joan of Arc, was said to have been a pedophile who gruesomely murdered hundreds of children as part of an occult ritual to appease demonic forces. He was condemned to death and was hanged in 1440.

Elizabeth Bathory (Blood Countess, or Blood Queen) and Thug Behram have been dubbed the most prolific serial killers in history. Born into Hungarian nobility, Bathory was a legendary countess said to have killed as many as 650 young female peasants so that she could bathe in their blood in an attempt to preserve her youthfulness. She was also said to have committed numerous other unspeakable atrocities prior to their deaths. Bathory was arrested in 1610 and was imprisoned in a castle, where she later died. Thug Behram, a member of the Thugee Cult in India, was said to have murdered nearly 1,000 individuals by strangulation with a ceremonial cloth during a 40-year reign of terror from the 1790s through the late 1830s. His fellow cult members are likely to have been responsible for some of these murders as well. The violent behavior of this group eventually gave way to the English term *thug* (although this term today is used in a different context). Besides being classified as serial killers, Behram and his cult members could also be classified as mass murderers, since they would kill a group of individuals in one setting.

Herman Webster Mudgett, aka Dr. Henry Howard Holmes, was the first known serial killer in American history, at least according to historical records. Dr. Holmes committed more than 20 murders during Chicago's World Fair in 1893. He designed, built, and opened a hotel with the intent to murder his victims, many of whom were employees who named him as the beneficiary of their life insurance policies as a condition of employment. Dr. Holmes used his "murder castle" as a place to suffocate, torture, and mutilate his victims; he was arrested for his crimes in 1894. Known as the Mad Butcher of Kingsbury Run, the Cleveland Torso Murderer was another early

Nineteenth-century mugshots of Herman Webster Mudgett, aka Dr. Henry Howard Holmes. The first documented serial killer in the United States confessed to killing 27 people but may have killed hundreds at his Chicago World's Fair hotel.

infamous serial killer who murdered at least 12 victims from 1935 to 1938 by decapitating them, cutting their torsos in half, and inflicting other heinous acts. His identity remains unknown, as do the identities of many victims, since their heads were never found.

Although extreme killers have been present throughout the course of history and all over the world, many people in U.S. society are aware of only a few; namely, American serial killers who have received media attention in the past few decades like Ed Gein (the Butcher of Plainfield), the Zodiac Killer, Charles Manson, Ted Bundy, David Berkowitz (Son of Sam), John Wayne Gacy, Jeffrey Dahmer, and Gary Ridgeway (the Green River Killer), to name a few. Nevertheless, there have been countless others who are less well-known or well-researched killers.

Beyond Race, Gender, and Nationality
Although there are many listings of killers, the actual acts of serial killing and mass murder are rare in comparison to other crimes. Yet much attention has been drawn to such extreme events. Movies, television series, and the media have sensationalized these killings and used the killers as inspiration for a myriad of novels (*The Devil in the White City, American Psycho, Red Dragon, Manhunter*) as well as movies (*Texas Chainsaw Massacre, Hannibal, Along Came a Spider, Kiss the Girls, Copycat, Silence of the Lambs, The*

Deliberate Stranger) and television shows (*Dexter, CSI, Criminal Minds, Deadly Women, California Hillside Strangler*). These novels, movies, and shows are often based on rare and shocking events involving heinous crimes against strangers rather than violent acts against family members, loved ones, or acquaintances. The media influences public fear of such events by casting stories about random acts of violence, creating alarm and feelings of defenselessness when it comes to going outdoors. Consequently, there is an increasing belief that these crimes are more commonplace than they are. In reality, rates of homicide are declining, and these extreme events represent only a minute portion of all homicides. Yet people fear these killers the most. Public perception of these events is also fueled by unique cases. People are shocked and infatuated by the reality of what the killers have done and how they have done it, as it challenges them to think about the evil that exists in this world.

In general, serial killers and mass murderers have been stereotyped as mentally ill, middle-aged white men. Although many of these extreme killers have mental disorders, have experienced some form of psychological stress, and/or are disconnected from society at large, such factors do not always pervade them. Extreme killers have also ranged in age from very young to very old. They have come from diverse racial and ethnic groups. For instance, Luis Garavito (La Bestia) was a Colombian serial killer who raped and murdered approximately 140 boys; John Floyd Thomas, Jr. (the Westside Rapist), was an African American serial killer who raped, choked, and killed numerous elderly women in California during the 1970s and 1980s; Yang Xinhai was a Chinese serial killer who confessed to 65 murders between 1999 and 2003; Mohammed Bijeh (the Tehran Desert Vampire) was an Iranian serial killer who raped and killed 16 boys in 2004; and Anders Behring Breivik is the Norwegian right-wing extremist responsible for the 2011 Norway attacks that killed eight people in government offices and 69 others at a youth camp. The list goes on and on. These murderers come from all social classes and commonly live and work in the very same neighborhoods where they strike.

In some cases, females and males co-offend, although women do represent a portion of extreme killers, albeit a small one. For instance, Miyuki Ishikawa was a female serial killer responsible for an estimated 100 infant deaths in the 1940s. Aileen Wuornos was also a female serial killer. Wuornos worked as a prostitute and killed seven men in Florida from 1989 to 1990 after they had sexually assaulted her or attempted to do so. Most of her victims were truck drivers and/or "johns" (patrons of prostitutes). She was sentenced to death and was executed via lethal injection in 2007. Jennifer San Marco was a female mass murderer who shot and killed her neighbor and six others at a postal facility in California. She then took her own life.

In an effort to understand extreme murderers, multiple methods have been used, including academic research, crime reports, databases, diaries, autobiographies, and personal interviews when possible. Although the validity of some of these methods has been questioned because of recording errors, exaggeration of events, and other issues, they help to provide a more precise understanding of these killers than their portrayals on television and in movies. They have also assisted in understanding the motivation underlying the killings.

Similarities Between Serial Killers and Mass Murderers

In earlier times, serial killers and mass murderers were thought to be individuals possessed by some form of evil or those who had undergone some unexplainable transformation (e.g., werewolves, vampires, monsters, or other creatures of the night); now, much more is known about these killers. The epistemology of serial and mass killers has been interdisciplinary, involving biology, psychology, criminology, sociology, and even political science, among other branches of study.

These areas of study have aimed to find answers as to the prevalence of extreme murderers, why people engage in such heinous crimes, and how law enforcement and other personnel should respond to it. For instance, biology examines the role of genetics in influencing one's behavior; psychology studies the mental state of offenders and conditions at the time of killing; criminology gives insight into the extent of the problem, risk factors for the crimes, and how to respond to the problem; sociology assists in understanding the social meaning behind killings; and political science helps provide an understanding of how actions guide public policy. In short, all of these fields have been relevant in understanding extreme killers.

Serial killers and mass murderers are alike in that they have engaged in extremely violent behavior. Their actions have been facilitated by the availability of handguns, semiautomatic guns, and rifles, though other methods of violence have been used. It has been thought that alcohol consumption, having an extra Y chromosome, and even observing behavior on television, in the movies, or in games influence the use of such violence; yet many people who drink, have the hereditary trait, or watch violent video games, films, or pornography do not engage in such behavior. Also, it is commonly thought that killers start off with early disturbing behaviors such as animal torture, although this has not always been the case. Thus, caution should be used when interpreting the actual influence and strength of these factors.

Although no single factor can explain extreme murder, numerous theories have been proposed to explain such behavior. One grouping of theories that has commonly been used is that of social process. According to social process theories, behavior is the product of our interactions with others. When one's interactions are negative, it can be very detrimental to one's well-being. Research has supported this notion and found that rejection is a key element present in serial killings and mass murders.

This may include rejection by the family, peers, or society at large. Family violence in the forms of physical, sexual, and/or emotional abuse, neglect, or abandonment, as well as family characteristics like the death of parents, divorce, and corporal punishment have often disproportionately been found in the lives of killers. It may be possible that negative consequences of these experiences (e.g., psychological disorders, mental illness, or brain injury) are heightened by social and environmental issues that trigger the events. Perceived victimization by others (e.g., by classmates in the form of bullying or dismissal frp, employment) has also been thought to relate to killings and to contribute to feelings of inadequacy and low self-worth, which are often characteristic among extreme killers.

Characteristics of Serial Killers
Serial killers are cyclical in their behavior: They kill, have a "cooling off" period, then kill again. During the cooling off period, they return to their normal daily lives, where they tend to blend in with mainstream society. They may work, have families of their own, and seem to be otherwise law-abiding. When they engage in killings, most are alone, but it is estimated that about one out of every five cases involves team killers. They vary in their relationships from lovers who offend to siblings who offend to friends who offend, just to name a few. While men represent the vast majority

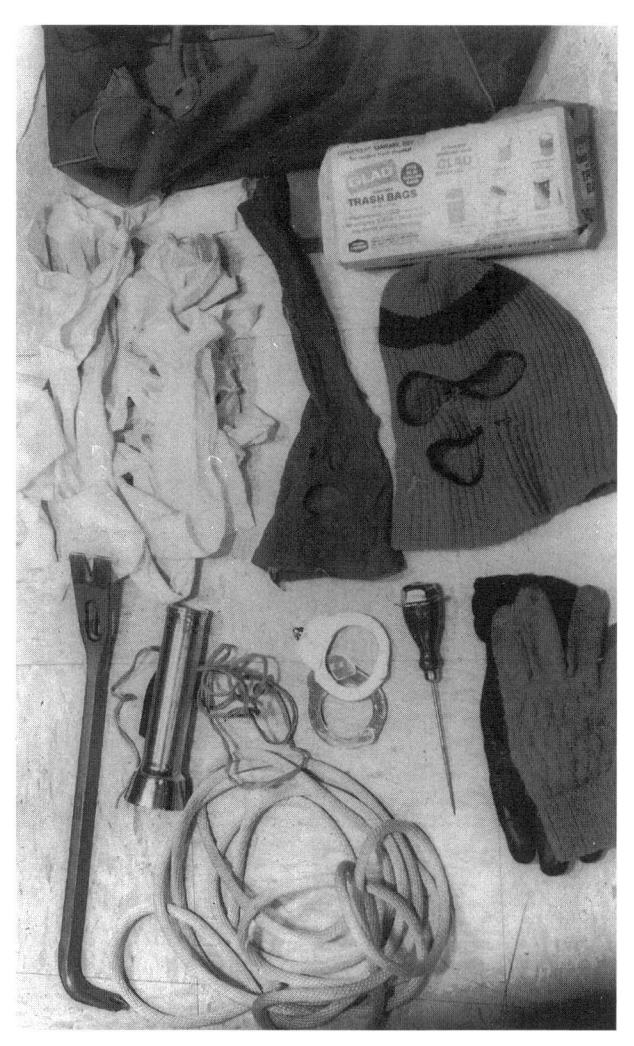

In 1975, serial killer Ted Bundy was stopped for a traffic violation. Police searched the car and found an ice pick, handcuffs, a crowbar, a ski mask, and gloves, and believed he was a burglar.

of serial killers, women make up approximately one out of every six offenders. However, this may be an underestimate given the less obvious methods of killing females typically use that may go undetected and therefore, overlooked. Males are much more likely to use extremely violent tactics (e.g., handguns, knives, mutilation, torture, or beatings), while females use more covert methods (e.g., poison or suffocation).

Yet there are always exceptions. Females may use extreme methods like guns but have generally been found to be more likely to aim for parts of the body other than the head. Other important gender differences in serial murderers also exist. Females are more likely to kill someone close to them than are males and oftentimes lure their victim in. Males, on the other hand, are more likely than females to kill acquaintances or strangers and often stalk their victims prior to the killings. Females also tend to be older, are more likely to use drugs/alcohol, and have mental diagnosable disorders in comparison to their male counterparts, who are more likely to have personality disorders. Yet there are always exceptions.

Serial Killer Typologies
Researchers have developed numerous classifications of serial killers that assist in understanding serial murderers and why they take lives. These typologies vary from study to study, but nonetheless hold underlying themes. Classifications exist according to mental state as well as patterns in the nature of the offense and motive underlying the crimes. When attempting to understand what drives people to kill, two of the main classifications focusing on mental state include psychotic killers and psychopathic killers. Psychotic killers are those individuals who cannot tell right from wrong. They may experience auditory and/or visual hallucinations that have compelled them to engage in lethal violence.

These killers can be considered legally insane. For example, Ed Gein was one of the most bizarre and mentally disturbed thrill killers in U.S. history. A grave robber, necrophiliac, and cannibal, Gein engaged in abnormal behavior. He exhumed corpses from graveyards and turned the decomposing parts into souvenirs; lampshades and bodysuits were made from skin. He later killed two victims in Wisconsin in the 1950s. Although some may not consider Gein to be a serial killer, he meets the criteria for a serial killer according to some standards. He has also been thought to have killed his brother as well as several others. Gein ultimately served as the source of inspiration for characters in numerous movies and novels, including *Psycho, The Texas Chainsaw Massacre,* and *The Silence of the Lambs.* Conversely, psychopathic killers do not suffer these symptoms. These killers are in touch with reality but lack empathy and remorse for their victims and actions.

Classifications of killers based on patterns include thrill, visionary, mission, and expedience. Thrill killers are the most commonly portrayed killers. They kill for excitement, power, and lust, all of which provide killers with psychological gratification. Thrill killers can derive excitement from simply killing victims. The Zodiac Killer is another thrill killer who killed at least five victims between 1968 and 1969 and stated that killing "is so much fun." The Zodiac Killer was particularly well known for the cryptic letters he sent to the police and claimed to have killed many more victims. Thrill killers also kill because they wish to establish control in their lives. They look for vulnerable victims to dominate (e.g., women with low social status, or children) and may enjoy watching their victims suffer/die. By engaging in such behavior, they gain a sense of power. These perpetrators may also fantasize about dehumanizing victims and obtain a high by engaging in sexual assaults, mutilations, and/or torture, among other behavior. Dennis Lynn Rader, known as the BTK Killer (for "bind, torture, kill"), fits into this classification. Rader killed 10 individuals in Kansas between 1974 and 1991. Like the Zodiac Killer, Rader sent taunting letters in an attempt to gain media attention and even sent various items symbolizing his bizarre killings to police. He was a sadistic killer who engaged in paraphilia (i.e., abnormal sexual behavior) by stealing lingerie from his victims and wearing it himself.

John Wayne Gacy, known as the Clown Killer, is another example of a thrill killer who strangled, sexually abused, and killed 33 young males from 1972 to 1978. He later buried the bodies of his victims under his house and property. Another infamous example is that of Jeffrey Dahmer. Between 1978 and 1999, he killed and dismembered 17 men and boys, saved some of their body parts, and engaged in necrophilia.

While some serial killers are sadistic in their offenses, numerous other classifications exist outside this typecast. Visionary killers are psychotic killers who engage in murder because of severe psychological disturbances. These murderers may kill in response to commands from voices or visions. For example, individuals may claim to hear voices from a higher power that trigger their violence. David Berkowitz, known as the Son of Sam, was a visionary killer who killed six victims and shot several others from 1976 to 1977. He claimed to have heard voices from his neighbor's dog, which he said was possessed by a demon. Berkowitz could also fit into a mission killer typology, if the killings occurred as part of a satanic cult ritual, as some claim. Mission killers kill for a sense of purpose. They may have a strong desire to rid the world of a group of people. Gary Ridgway, known as the Green River Killer, was notorious for killing approximately 50 prostitutes during the period spanning 1982 to the early 1990s. He had stated that they were easy to pick up and he hated them. Jack the Ripper could also fit this typology. This unidentified killer operated in the late 1800s, killing an estimated 11 prostitutes and performing graphic mutilations on their bodies.

Mission killers may also kill to end suffering among those who are in pain. Typical examples of this are employees at hospitals and nursing homes who kill patients. These killers are often referred to as "angels of death." Some have also been noted to murder individuals for ideological reasons.

Expedience is another classification for killers who kill for financial gain or profit. This may involve individuals who kill while committing other crimes (e.g., a gang member who killed multiple victims during multiple street robberies) or those who kill for insurance money (e.g., a woman who has killed several husbands, commonly known as a "black widow"). Serial killers in one classification may permeate into other classifications as well. Nevertheless, the classifications help to understand the perpetrators and may help in their apprehension.

Characteristics of Mass Murders

Mass murderers engage in behavior commonly labeled by society as "random acts of violence," although these acts are not truly as random as they seem. High rates of mental illness, especially depression, paranoia, and personality disorders, are prevalent among these killers. These psychological dysfunctions are often the result of chronic or acute stress, and the source of this stress is often targeted by perpetrators of mass murders. This enables the killer to gain a sense of power and control. Mass murderers can attack in homes, schools, workplaces, places of worship, restaurants, malls, subways, streets, or just about anywhere. These include the deranged lovers, school shooters, disgruntled employees, terrorist bombers, mentally ill offenders, and violent criminals whom society constantly fears. Examining characteristics of mass murderers, virtually all mass murderers to date have been male.

Unlike serial killers, these individuals are typically unemployed males, some of whom have had military training (e.g., the Fort Hood shooter) and they do not have a cooling-off period. Further, they differ in that their crimes are rarely, if ever, sexual in nature. Rather than having one victim at each event like serial killers do, the perpetrator takes action against a group in a single outburst. Firearms are the most common weapon of choice, although bombings and other methods have been used. Many mass murderers commit suicide directly after their massacre, while others are arrested or killed at the scene by law enforcement.

Mass Murderer Typologies

Mass murderers have been classified according to their motives: love, revenge, profit, and mission. Love murderers are typically people who annihilate their immediate families and then kill themselves. An example of this occurred in 2009 when Curt Wheat killed his wife and three children before killing himself. Similar cases are often covered in the news. However, love mass murderers have also been known to kill their children and not their partners, families of intimate partners, or other persons, and they do not always kill themselves. Their actions may be the result of mental illness, relational stress, financial strain, or feelings of "saving" loved ones because no one

A candlelight vigil was held on April 17, 2007, after Seung-Hui Cho opened fire and shot 57 people, killing 32 at Virginia Tech, the deadliest U.S. massacre by a single gunman.

can take care of them. Andrea Yates is an example of a love mass murderer who gained great media attention by drowning all five of her children in a bathtub in 2001. Yates had suffered severe depression and psychosis. She thought that by killing her children, God would "take them" since she was an unfit mother; if she didn't, they would go to hell. After she committed the murders, she called the police and phoned her husband, repeatedly saying "It's time."

Seung-Hui Cho, who shot 57 people resulting in 32 deaths in the 2007 Virginia Tech massacre before taking his own life, could also be classified as a love murderer. It is believed that he was infatuated with a fellow female student, who turned him down. Cho also fits the revenge murderer typology. Revenge murderers are a classification of mass murderers involving those who commit a mass murder out of anger, making it an expressive crime. Cho wrote notes that signified that his actions were payback to the "rich kids" and all those who mocked him. His actions resulted in the deadliest school shooting (and shooting by a single gunman) ever documented. In addition to school shooters and those rejected by their peers, revenge mass murders may involve disgruntled employees or any persons whose actions were perpetrated with vengeance in mind. Examples of revenge killers include Jiverly Wong, a paranoid man who killed 13 people at a New York immigration center in 2009 before killing himself (he believed the police were trying to ruin his life); Eric Harris and Dylan Klebold, bullied "outsiders" who killed 12 students and one teacher in 1999 before killing themselves in the Columbine High School massacre; Gang Lu, who killed five people at the University of Iowa when he was not nominated for a prestigious award for his dissertation in 1991; Patrick Sherrill, a U.S. Postal Service employee, who shot and killed 14 employees in a post office in 1986 after being reprimanded for his performance, a mass murder that led to the phrase *going postal*; and Richard Farley, who shot and killed seven coworkers in 1988 after being fired for stalking a coworker.

Unlike love and revenge killers, profit murderers kill for an instrumental purpose. They pursue their self-interest and want to achieve financial gain. This type of killer may engage in a mass murder when, for instance, he or she is involved in the commission of another felony (e.g., a bank robber who kills multiple people at the scene). By killing any witnesses to a crime, the offender hopes to avoid detection. Mission murderers are another typology whose purpose may be instrumental or expressive. These killers wish to change society by ridding the world of a certain group of people or achieving a certain purpose. Targets may be selected based on religious beliefs, sexual orientation, belonging to a certain racial or ethnic group, or for some other ideological reason.

For instance, the 16th Street Baptist Church bombing in 1963 was committed by a Ku Klux Klan group, resulting in the death of four young African American girls. Terroristic murderers, or those who engage in killings due to politically or socially motivated reasons, can also fit into the mission category. Among the most notorious mass murders are the Oklahoma City bombing by Timothy McVeigh in 1995, where more than 500 were injured and 168 were killed as a result of hatred for the government, and the September 11 attack on the World Trade Center in 2001 that produced immense terror among the public. The impact of this event caused widespread sorrow and panic about where violence would strike next. Finally, cult suicides may also be classified as mission mass murders when leaders of these esoteric groups persuade individuals to take their own lives. For instance, Marshall Applewhite convinced members of Heaven's Gate in 1997 that by taking their lives, they would be able to leave Earth in a spaceship that would take them to the comet Hale-Bopp to live a better life.

Responses to Extreme Murder

Because of the extreme and horrific nature of serial killings and mass murders, an enormous amount of pressure has been placed on police personnel as well as researchers to identify who will become involved in these acts. However, recognizing and catching extreme killers can be a difficult task. Their victims are often unknown strangers, and their targets and actions can be unpredictable. Further, there may be a lack of warning signs, or little evidence may exist at the crime scene(s). For serial killings, different methods of killing can also hinder investigation. In the case of the organized crime member Richard Kuklinski (the Iceman), police were unable to link the murders given the assortment of tactics used to kill. Such matters increase the complexity of the cases, and if personnel are not trained well, they may fail to make the link. Many police departments lack training in the detection of these criminals. They are also ill equipped and lack investigative tools, and many do not communicate effectively with other departments. However, preparing investigators to identify risk factors and to know how to properly search, identify, collect, and record information from crime scenes is advantageous. This can assist law enforcement in obtaining evidence and in understanding how to locate information on motives and signatures left at crime scenes. Training law enforcement in interviewing individuals can also provide invaluable information.

Police departments have been interdisciplinary in collaborating with others in regard to examining evidence and linking offenders to their crimes. They have worked with criminologists, who analyze DNA, hair and fiber evidence, toxicology reports, ballistics, and other evidence gathered at crime scenes. The Combined DNA Index System (CODIS) and the National DNA Index System (NDIS) along with the Automated Fingerprint Identification System (AFIS) are examples of databases containing the results of such analyses that can be used by law enforcement. These tools integrate data at the local, state, and federal levels and assist in investigations. The analysis of such evidence and the sharing of information are crucial in arrest, securing prosecution, and ensuring the conviction of these individuals.

In addition, law enforcement officers have teamed up with criminologists and psychologists in what is referred to as "offender profiling." This is a behavioral and investigative technique involving the creation of criminal portraits to help assist law enforcement and other personnel in understanding criminals and their crimes. It provides a social and psychological assessment of an offender as well as evidence or clues about the crime. Offender profiling focuses on the victims chosen, the method(s) used to kill the victims, and the motivation underlying the crime to generate a profile. The FBI uses offender profiling to gather as much information as possible about offenders and subsequently classifies them into "organized" or "disorganized" murderers. Organized murderers are seen as intelligent and gregarious individuals who meticulously plan out their murders while disorganized murderers are of average or lower intelligence, may be socially immature, and spontaneously carry out their killings. Organized murderers are often driven by thrill; they have been found to return to the crime scene, interact with police, and sometimes seek attention for their crimes. Disorganized killers may return to the scene, but they tend to be much more anxious and act in a more erratic manner. These classifications may overlap in some cases, but they generally help to determine if patterns are present.

Local, state, and federal agencies have collaborated in investigations via information sharing, resource maximization, and apprehension of offenders. The Investigations and Operations Support Section (IOSS) in the Federal Bureau of Investigation's (FBI's) Critical Incident Response Group, located in Quantico, Virginia, is a prime example. It encompasses the National Center for the Analysis of Violent Crime (NCAVC), which consists of the Behavioral Analysis Unit (BAU) and the Violent Criminal Apprehension Program (ViCAP), which assist in investigations of serial killings and mass murders, among other serious crimes. The NCAVC focuses on repeat offenders and is a clearinghouse for unusual and vicious or repetitive crimes. Its four units include three in the Behavioral Analysis Unit (i.e., BAU for terrorism, BAU for crimes against adults, and BAU for crimes against children) and one in ViCAP, a repository of cases that contains information about solved and unsolved homicides, attempted homicides, missing persons information, and other violent crimes involving unidentified victims. These units assist in numerous ways and can be accessed by law enforcement personnel through Law Enforcement Online (LEO), a database that serves as an information-sharing system for law enforcement personnel.

Other efforts have also been made in an effort to prevent extreme murders. For instance, numerous school systems have begun to employ school resource officers (SROs), who are police who operate in the school to prevent what is considered to be increasing violence within schools. Surveillance systems, metal detectors, and numerous other forms of situational crime prevention measures have also been used in various settings to deter potential offenders from engaging in their crimes. In short, many advances have been made in the criminal investigation of serial killers and mass murderers and the way they are responded to. Specialized programs have also been developed in the treatment of some offenders, but there is still a long way to go in eliminating these crimes.

Alison Marganski
Virginia Wesleyan College

See Also: 1961 to 1980 Primary Documents; 1981 to 2000 Primary Documents; Autobiographies, Criminals; Ballistics; Berkowitz, David; Billy the Kid; Bundy, Ted; Child Murderers, History of; Crime Scene Investigation; Dahmer, Jeffrey; Kaczynski, Ted; Kevorkian, Jack; Ku Klux Klan; Manson, Charles; McVeigh, Timothy; Yates, Andrea; Zodiac Killer.

Further Readings
Cawthorne, Nigel. *Serial Killers and Mass Murderers: Profiles of the World's Most Barbaric Killers.* Berkeley, CA: Ulysses Press, 2007.

Douglas, John and Mark Olshaker. *Mind Hunter: Inside the FBI's Elite Serial Crime Unit.* New York: Pocket Books, 1995.

Federal Bureau of Investigation. "Critical Incident Response Group." http://www.fbi.gov/about-us/cirg (Accessed May 2011).

Fox, James and Jack Levin. *The Will to Kill: Making Sense of Senseless Murder.* Needham Heights, MA: Allyn and Bacon, 2001.

Hickey, Eric. *Serial Murderers and Their Victims.* Belmont, CA: Wadsworth, 2010.

Keppel, Robert and William Birnes. *The Psychology of Serial Killer Investigations: The Grisly Business Unit.* San Diego, CA: Academic Press, 2003.

Newton, Michael. *The Encyclopedia of Serial Killers: A Study of the Chilling Criminal Phenomenon, From the "Angels of Death" to the "Zodiac" Killer.* New York: Checkmark Books, 2000.

Vronsky, Peter. *Female Serial Killers: How and Why Women Become Monsters.* New York: Berkley Publishing Group, 2007.

Sex Offender Laws

Sex offender laws represent the societal response to sexually based crimes such as rape, sexual assault, child molestation, and child pornography. Crimes of this nature are typically considered to be among the most heinous acts an offender can perpetrate against a victim. Although sex offender laws are often portrayed as a new response to societal dangers, the United States has had sex offender laws since the establishment of the original thirteen colonies. Borrowing from the tradition of English common law, all the colonies established laws that made sodomy punishable by death. Each new state that joined the union either codified a law against sodomy or accepted existing common law regarding this act. The punishment for sodomy slowly decreased as the nation moved toward a more secular rather than religious system; however, by 1960, all states had laws prohibiting sodomy. Rape was also considered a crime in the early colonies, but it was considered a criminal trespass by one man against another man's property. The punishment for this crime was extremely harsh corporal punishment. It was not until the 1970s that rape laws reflected a woman's right to refuse sexual relations with any man—including her husband—with imprisonment resulting in those convicted of felony rape.

Clearly, there has always been some form of sex offender laws—against rape, sodomy, or other acts—but modern legislation is particularly detailed and focused, taking sex offenses out of the realm of ordinary felonies and misdemeanors. The current legal response to rape, sexual assault, child molestation, and other sexually based offenses has increased significantly since 1994, when a series of legislation intended to increase the punishment and monitoring of sex offenders began to be passed throughout the United States at the state and national level. Many of these laws involve limiting where a convicted sex offender may live and work and requiring him/her to report his/her work and home addresses on sex offender registries available for public review. Sex offender laws often prohibit sex offenders from living near a school, park, day care, or playground and are intended to reduce the opportunity for sex offenders to reoffend. These requirements vary by state, but in some jurisdictions, convicted sex offenders are required to report their whereabouts and remain on the sex offender registry for life. While most sex offender laws and registry requirements target felony offenders, some states also require registration for sexually based misdemeanors such as public indecency and sexual misconduct. The continued introduction of new or expanded sex offender laws reflects the categorization of sex offenders as the most stigmatized group of criminal offenders in the United States.

Origin of Sex Offender Laws

The 1990s are recognized as a significant period in the development of sex offender laws and the sex offender registry, but such laws existed far earlier in the country's history. In 1931, in anticipation of organized crime activities expanding to California, Los Angeles County passed a convict registry that required offenders convicted of any felony, and some drug and weapons charges, to register with the sheriff. This requirement was adopted in other jurisdictions throughout California and in other states as well. Eventually, these laws were used to target those involved in consensual sexual acts that offended the common moral sensibility, such as homosexuality; thus, even consensual acts between legal adults were considered felony. Many states practiced indefinite civil commitment following an offender's release from prison for a sex offense, thereby keeping a person in prison for several years or for life after serving a sentence for a sex offense. The Los Angeles Police Department extended its focus on sex offenders by developing a Bureau of Sex Offenses in 1938 focused upon maintaining fingerprints, photographs, and other records of those convicted of sex crimes. California subsequently became the first state to develop an official state sex offender registry in 1947, and by the early 1990s, 12 additional states adopted similar registries.

A mural painted by artist Symeon Shimin titled Contemporary Justice in Relation to the Child *is displayed at the Department of Justice Building in Washington, D.C.*

Sex Offender Legislation

Although states were beginning to require sex offender registries on their own, in 1994, legislation passed by the federal government required all states to develop a registry within three years or face a financial penalty. The Jacob Wetterling Crimes Against Children and Sexually Violent Offender Registration Act, which was enacted as a part of the Omnibus Crime Bill of 1994, mandated states to confirm the place of residence of persons required to register as sex offenders for a period of 10 years; offenders convicted of violent sex crimes have their place of residence confirmed on a quarterly basis for the rest of their lives. This law was enacted after the stranger abduction of 11-year-old Jacob Wetterling, whose whereabouts were never discovered. Following the passage of this act, the remaining 38 states developed sex offender registries by August 1996, the same year that a national registry was established.

Within two years of the new registration requirements, the Wetterling Act was amended in 1996 by Megan's Law. Megan's Law was named in honor of 7-year-old Megan Kanka, who was raped and murdered by a convicted sex offender just 30 yards from her home. This law provides for the public dissemination of information from state sex offender registries, and that any information collected under state registration programs can be disclosed for any purpose permitted under a state law. The law also requires state and local law enforcement agencies to release relevant information necessary to protect the public about persons registered under a state registration program established under the Wetterling Act.

The Jacob Wetterling Act was amended again by the Pam Lychner Sexual Offender Tracking and Identification Act of 1996. This law was named after Pam Lychner, who survived a brutal assault in 1990 by a convicted felon. Following her assault, Lychner went on to develop a victims' rights advocacy group lobbying for a national database to track sex offenders. Congress named the new act after Lychner, who died in the TWA Flight 800 explosion in July 1996, in recognition of her extensive advocacy efforts for victims' rights. The Lychner Act amended the Jacob Wetterling Act by requiring the attorney general to establish a national database (the National Sex Offender Registry, or NSOR) to enable the Federal Bureau of Investigation (FBI) to track certain sex offenders. The law also required sex offenders living in a state without a sufficient sex offender registry to register with the FBI and required the FBI to confirm the addresses of those sex offenders under the act's jurisdiction. The Lychner Act also permitted the release of information collected by the FBI to federal, state, and local officials responsible for law enforcement activities considered necessary to protect the public or for running background checks pursuant to the National Child Protection Act. The act also provided for the notification of the FBI and state agencies when a sex offender moved to another state.

In 1997, Congress passed the Jacob Wetterling Improvements Act as part of the Appropriations Act of 1998 and amended several provisions of the Jacob Wetterling Crimes Against Children and Sexually Violent Offender Registration Act, the Pam Lychner Sex Offender Tracking and Identification Act, and other federal statutes. The Improvements Act expanded the manner in which state courts determine whether a sex offender should be considered a sexually violent offender to include the opinions of victims' rights advocates and law enforcement officials in addition to treatment experts on sex offender behavior. The act also gave states the right to assign the responsibility of notification and registration, including FBI notification, to a state agency not affiliated with each state's law enforcement agency. Under the Improvements Act, offenders who move to a new state must register under the provisions of their new state, and offenders are required to register in states where they work or attend school if those states are different from the offender's state of residency. In addition to other administrative changes involving registration and notification, the Improvements Act provides states with the discretion to register offenders whose committing offenses do not include Wetterling's definition of registerable offenses.

Between 1998 and 2003, several smaller sex offender acts were passed, including the 1998 Protection of Children From Sexual Predators Act, which directs the Bureau of Justice Assistance to carry out the Sex Offender Management Assistance program to assist eligible states in complying with registration requirements. This act also prohibits federal funding to programs found to give federal prisoners Internet access without appropriate supervision.

In 2000, the Campus Sex Crimes Prevention Act, passed as part of the Victims of Trafficking and Violence Protection Act, required any person who is required to register under a state's sex offender registry to alert his/her institution of higher education, whether the sex offender be a student or employee, and to notify the institution of any changes in enrollment or employment status. Included in the Campus Sex Crimes Prevention Act is the provision that all information collected under this act be reported to local law enforcement immediately and entered into the state's registry and recording system. This act also amends the Higher Education Act of 1965 to require institutions of higher education to report campus security policy and crime statistics and to provide notice of how information about registered sex offenders on the campus can be obtained. The Prosecutorial Remedies and Other Tools to End the Exploitation of Children Today (PROTECT) Act of 2003 requires states to maintain a Website containing registry information and requires the Department of Justice to maintain a Website with links to each state Website. This act also provided appropriations to assist states with defraying the costs of complying with new sex offender registration requirements.

The final significant piece of sex offender legislation in recent years is the 2006 Adam Walsh Child Protection and Safety Act. This act includes the Sex Offender Registration and Notification Act. This act established new baselines for jurisdictions to adhere to regarding sex offender registration and notification, with the definition of "jurisdiction" expanded to include 212 federally recognized Indian tribes. This act expanded the sex offenses that must be contained in a jurisdiction's registry to include all state, territory, tribal, federal, and Uniform Code of Military Justice (UCMJ) sex offense convictions, as well as certain foreign convictions. The act also created the Office of Sex Offender Sentencing, Monitoring, Apprehending, Registering, and Tracking, a division of the Department of Justice, Office of Justice Programs, to coordinate training and technical assistance and administer sex offender and notification standards. The act also established a Sex Offender Management Assistance (SOMA) program within the Department of Justice.

The culmination of the progression of sex offender laws has resulted in requirements that sex offenders register their whereabouts in jurisdictions where they reside, work, and attend school. They are also required to report in person to verify their existing information on file or to update their information; the committed offense controls how often offenders have to check in to verify their information. Sex offender legislation has also created a national registration database that is uniform across jurisdictions and requires the inclusion of certain information about offenders who are required to register that must be made available on the Internet. The registration and notification requirements apply to states, the District of Columbia, territories, and federally recognized Indian tribes.

In addition to laws requiring registration and notification, laws limiting where registered sex offenders may live have become increasingly popular during the 2000s. By 2007, 27 states passed laws that prohibited sex offenders from living near schools, parks, playgrounds, or day care centers. These laws have been accused of interfering with reentry and reintegration and limiting an offender's chances of being successful after release from prison. The same argument has been made about many of the provisions in the extensive sex offender registration and notification laws. Some of the unanticipated consequences include limiting housing options for sex offenders so severely that they report false addresses or don't report at all, which makes it almost impossible for law enforcement and community corrections staff to monitor sex offenders' whereabouts.

Constitutional Challenges

Sex offender registration laws have been challenged at the state and federal level. The U.S. Supreme Court has made rulings on two constitutional issues regarding sex offender registration laws. Two noteworthy cases, both decided in 2003, are *Smith v. Doe* and *Connecticut Dept. of Public Safety v. Doe*. In *Smith v. Doe*, at issue was whether an Alaska state law violated the constitutional guarantee against ex post facto, or punishment after the fact. In this case, the court upheld the constitutionality of the law,

Assemblyman Todd Spitzer with Governor Arnold Schwarzenegger (right) as the governor signed California's Assembly Bill 488 to provide the public with Internet access to detailed information on registered sex offenders.

stating that the Alaska legislature intended the law to be regulatory, not punitive, in nature. The next case, *Connecticut Dept. of Public Safety v. Doe*, involved a challenge to Connecticut's sex offender registration law as a violation of due process because offenders were not allowed hearings to determine if they continued to pose a danger to society. The court ruled that even if an offender could prove he/she is no longer dangerous, the state retains the right to disclose public information about all offenders.

Conclusion
Supporters of sex offender registration and notification laws argue that these convictions are already public record, and therefore, states are only disclosing information that the public already has access to. In addition, the argument has been made that the public has a right to know when a violent or sexual predator is living or working in their vicinity. Others argue that these laws only serve to continue punishing offenders who have fulfilled the terms of their criminal sentence, and that sex offender laws only extend the stigma of persons committed for sexual offenses. Public opinion surveys consistently demonstrate support for sex offender registration laws, and it is not anticipated that public sentiment in the current political climate of getting tough on crime is going to result in a reversal of these provisions anytime in the near future. What makes modern sex offender laws unique, however, is the depiction of these acts as distinctly different from other felonies and misdemeanors, with increasingly harsher punishments and limitations placed upon those who commit sex offenses. Although the United States has always had laws against sex offenders, current trends in legislation reveal a distinct focus upon shaming and labeling in addition to punishing those who commit sex crimes.

Jennifer N. Grimes
Indiana State University

See Also: Rape, Contemporary; Rape, History of; Rape, Sociology of; Sex Offenders; Sodomy.

Further Readings
Rogers, Laura L. *Sex Offender Registry Laws: From Jacob Wetterling to Adam Walsh*. Washington, DC: U.S. Department of Justice, Office of Justice Programs, 2007.

Tewksbury, Richard. "Collateral Consequences of Sex Offender Registration." *Journal of Contemporary Criminal Justice*, v.21/1 (February 2005).

Tofte, Sarah. "No Easy Answers: Sex Offender Laws in the U.S." *Human Rights Watch* (September 12, 2007).

Sex Offenders

Society's concept of and attitude toward sex offenders have evolved from those based primarily on religious tenets to those based, in large part, on psychological theories, scientific research, and public safety concerns. This change reflects the lessened authority of organized religion in modern society and the concomitant increase in reliance on science to solve problems, including ones on the societal level. Psychology and psychiatry played leading roles in the use of science to understand sex offenders, especially those who commit multiple offenses, and the use of this knowledge to design interventions to prevent sex offenders from committing further offenses. This scientific approach found itself in competition with a public safety approach that focused primarily on incapacitating sex offenders through incarceration, open-ended institutionalization, and strict monitoring of offenders upon their release. The increased emphasis on public safety was a response to several highly publicized incidents in which known sex offenders committed atrocious crimes. This evolution continues, as society struggles with how best to prevent sex offenders from committing further offenses.

History of Sex Offenders

The historical view of sex offenders found in the holy books of the three major religions—Judaism, Christianity, and Islam—calls for the punishment of sex offenders based on the degree that the offense lessened the value of the victim of the sexual assault, the woman. Women were viewed as property, their value dependent upon whether a woman was a virgin. Raping a woman decreased her value, so the punishment given the rapist varied as a function of whether the woman was a virgin. The purpose of the sanction was to punish the offender for damaging another man's property, not retribution for harming the woman as an individual. Rapists were not considered deviant or unfit for society. They were viewed in the same way as other criminals who damaged the property of another, or anyone who failed to adhere to the tenets of their society's religion. This view was consistent with the fact that rape was condoned or promoted as a legitimate part of war.

The belief that rapists are pathological became widespread with the development and increasing acceptance of Sigmund Freud's psychoanalytic theory. Freud theorized that there were three major components of the human personality the id, ego, and superego. In Freud's model, the id is the repository of instinctual needs and desires. It is guided by the pleasure principle, demanding immediate gratification of all desires. It is home to both sexual desire and the instinct for aggression and destruction. The id is amoral; it has no concept of right or wrong. The superego, the part of personality that serves as the conscience, is the last part of the personality to develop. It counterbalances the demands of the id for immediate gratification. The superego develops as the individual matures. It represents the internalization of social mores. Its development depends in large part on the extent that parents have been able to instill a sense of morality and social responsibility in the child.

The remaining component of Freud's theory is the ego. It seeks to fulfill the instinctual needs of the id for the immediate gratification for all desires within the constraints set by the superego and external reality. The ego is guided by the reality principle. It understands that not all desires can be gratified immediately or in ways that are harmful to the individual or violate the limits set by the superego and society regarding acceptable behavior.

Healthy development of the ego and the superego depend on the child successfully completing each stage of psychosexual development. In Freud's theory, men rape because of insufficient ego and superego development. The person lacks the conscience, constraint, and sense of morality that is part of a healthy superego. The rapist also has an underdeveloped ego, as the rapist seeks immediate gratification of his desire for sex and aggression without benefit of the constraints that would prevent the person from acting in ways that ultimately are self-destructive. These deficiencies are attributed to pathological parenting, with most of the blame being given to the mother, as parents have the responsibility of instilling a sense of morality in the child. In this perspective, the rapist is, at least in part, a victim in need of treatment.

Although Freud made a valuable contribution to psychiatry and psychology, his theories have not been supported by research. Despite this, psychoanalysis, and the theoretical orientations it spawned, continues to have many adherents. It has had a profound and long-lasting impact on society, as is evident from its influence on movies, literature, and language. Freud's theory implies that rapists can be treated successfully through psychoanalysis. The belief that sex offenders suffered from a mental illness that could be treated led many states, beginning in 1937, to pass statutes for the civil commitment of sex offenders to treatment programs.

The scientific study of sex offenders did not end with Freud. As psychology matured, it developed into a scientific discipline based on empirical evidence derived from increasingly rigorous research. Current research on sex offenders uses the biopsychosocial model, examining the biological, psychological, and social factors that distinguish sex offenders from other offenders to predict the likelihood of recidivism and the offender's amenability to treatment.

Sex Offender Characteristics

The scientific and public safety approaches to sex offenders share a common goal, that is, to prevent sex offenders from reoffending. In response to the public outcry following several highly publicized crimes committed by known sex offenders, most states passed laws requiring the registration of sex offenders, notification of the community in which the offender lives, and laws authorizing the civil commitment of sex offenders after the offender has served his or her criminal sentence. These laws are designed to protect the public by reducing sex offender recidivism. Research has focused on determining the factors that identify the offenders who are at highest risk to reoffend. These predictive factors are discussed in detail below.

Although the likelihood of a specific sex offender reoffending cannot be determined with absolute certainty, a determination, to a reasonable degree of certainty, can be made of the relative risk that the offender will commit another sex offense. This determination is made using the multiple factors research has shown to be the best predictors of sex offender recidivism. These factors can be divided into three major categories: predisposing, disinhibiting, and inhibiting. Within each category, factors can be divided into static or historical factors and fluid or dynamic factors. This is important in efforts to minimize recidivism risk as these efforts address those factors that can be changed, that is, those factors that are fluid or dynamic.

Predisposing factors are traits, characteristics, or experiences that result in the proclivity or inclination to engage in nonconsensual or otherwise illegal sexual activity. Predisposing factors tend to be static and related to past behavior or events rather than malleable, as with dynamic factors, and may be biological, psychological, social, or cognitive. Disinhibiting/destabilizing factors serve to trigger the offender to commit an offense. Even individuals who are predisposed to engage in a certain form of inappropriate behavior do not engage in this behavior constantly. Some factor "triggers" them to engage in the inappropriate behavior. Disinhibiting factors tend to be dynamic or fluid factors, that is, factors that can change as a function of variables such as time and situation. Inhibiting factors act to prevent the individual from engaging in sexual misconduct. Inhibiting factors include static and dynamic factors.

Predisposing, disinhibiting, and inhibiting factors work in concert. Behavior is thus multiply determined. For example, if an individual's predisposition is sufficiently strong, only a slight disinhibiting factor or trigger is necessary. Alternatively, if the predisposition is weak, a stronger trigger will be necessary. A similar type of analysis is applicable to inhibiting factors. An evaluation

Acceptance of Sigmund Freud's psychoanalytic theory of human personality led to a belief that rapists are pathological and are seeking immediate gratification of sexual desire.

of sexual dangerousness is designed to determine whether and to what extent the offender possesses the predisposing, disinhibiting, and inhibiting factors that have been found to be characteristic of offenders at high risk for reoffending. The relevant evidence is best obtained using multiple data-gathering methods (interviews of the offender and collateral sources; observation of behavior; review of educational, mental health, medical, and criminal records; and psychological testing) and multiple sources of information about the offender's life.

Predisposing Factors
Research has shown that the following predisposing factors are the best predictors of a sex offender's recidivism risk. A deviant sexual arousal pattern, a stable pattern of sexual arousal to inappropriate stimuli (e.g., children, rape, sadism, animals, or inanimate objects), is an exceedingly powerful predisposing factor. Individuals with deviant sexual arousal patterns tend to commit sexual offenses consistent with their sexually arousing fantasies. Thus, individuals with a stable and exclusive pattern of sexual arousal from thoughts or acts of rape are predisposed toward committing this sex offense. It is important to note that many rapists do not show this pattern. Rape is complex; a rapist's primary motivation may be nonsexual, such as anger, power, revenge, or humiliation.

Some deviant sexual arousal patterns have formally been recognized as paraphilias, or mental disorders. The paraphilias of greatest concern are pedophilia and sexual sadism. In pedophilia, the individual's primary sexual interest is in children. Treatment to change the sexual orientation of pedophiles has not been shown to be successful. However, pedophiles can be taught coping strategies to minimize the likelihood that they will act on their sexual urges and molest a child. The effectiveness of this approach depends on the motivation and commitment of the individual.

Sexual sadists are sexually aroused, often exclusively, by inflicting pain and suffering on nonconsenting victims. Victims may be severely injured or killed by the sexual sadist, since the degree of sexual satisfaction depends on the degree of pain inflicted. Death at the hands of a sexual sadist may be unintentional; for many sadists, the death of the victim means the loss of their source of sexual gratification. For others, the death of the victim after being tortured results in the ultimate sexual satisfaction.

A common assumption about sex offenders is that they are mentally ill. The validity of this assumption depends on what is meant by mental illness. If mental illness is defined as a psychosis, one of the disorders that significantly impair an individual's capacity for rational thought and reality testing, then sex offenders, as a group, are not mentally ill. Although some individuals diagnosed with a psychotic disorder may commit a sex offense, most do not. Similarly, most sex offenders are not psychotic. This also is true for neurological disorders such as mental retardation, dementia, tumors, and brain damage caused by a traumatic brain injury or infection. While these disorders may result in impaired judgment and poor impulse control, they account for a very small proportion of sex offenses.

Certain mental disorders have been found to predispose the individual to engage in antisocial behavior, including sex offenses. One such disorder is psychopathy. Interpersonally, psychopaths are characteristically grandiose, manipulative, domineering, and cold-hearted. Emotionally, they are shallow, lack empathy, and are unable to form long-lasting bonds to people. Behaviorally, they are impulsive and thrill seeking. Psychopathy and deviant sexual arousal are two of the most potent predisposing factors. Individuals with both factors are at extremely high risk of committing future sex offenses.

Cognitive distortions, as used in research on sex offender recidivism, are an individual's attitudes or beliefs that support or condone his or her sex offenses. Although the research literature is mixed, there is evidence that attitudes or beliefs that support or condone sex offenses increase the likelihood that an individual will commit a sex offense. Typically, cognitive distortions are thoughts or beliefs that place blame for the offense on the victim, relieving the perpetrator of any responsibility for the offense. They are more than convenient rationalizations, as they accurately reflect the offender's mind-set.

A history of incidents in which the sex offender is the aggressor and a pattern of engaging in violence are risk factors, especially for sex offenses in which violence plays a prominent role. The inability to develop and maintain close interpersonal relationships has also been found to be a risk factor. Other predisposing factors include a history of supervision failure, which refers to violations of parole, probation, or other legally imposed restrictions; a high density of sex offense, as in the commission of several sex offenses close together in time; and multiple sex offense types. Rapists who have committed multiple types of sex offenses are at increased risk for recidivistic sexual violence. Multiple sex offense types refers to whether the perpetrator's sexual offenses have varied in nature of offense and/or victim selection.

Physically harming a victim of a sex offense is suggestive of the presence of a deviant sexual arousal pattern, as in sexual sadism, cognitive distortions that support or condone sexual violence, and poor impulse control. Other related predisposing factors include the use of weapons of threats of death in sex offenses and escalation in frequency or severity of sex offenses.

Research has shown that a history of childhood physical or sexual abuse is a general risk factor for criminality, nonsexual violence, and sexual violence. It is important to note that while most sex offenders report that they were abused physically or sexually, most people who have been abused do not become sex offenders or commit other violent crimes. However, this knowledge is useful in treatment planning, thus playing a role in minimizing the likelihood of a re-offense.

A history of difficulty sustaining employment, unless accounted for by a physical or mental disability or other valid external cause, can be a predisposing factor for antisocial behavior, as can extreme minimization or denial of sex offenses.

Disinhibiting and Inhibiting Factors

The next major category includes factors that serve a disinhibiting or triggering function. Intoxication is one of the most common disinhibiting factors in all offenses, including sex offenses. Psychological stress and availability of victims can also serve as triggers for sex offenders.

The final major category includes factors that act to inhibit or stabilize an offender and thus reduce the likelihood of a re-offense. The absence of inhibiting factors increases the likelihood of a re-offense. These factors include employment; social support from family, friends, mental health and social service professionals, and community organizations; active religious involvement; personal growth and maturation; treatment; and fear of reincarceration.

Given the high stakes of making an incorrect determination of sexual dangerousness, sex offender evaluations must be thorough. Among the methods typically used for this purpose are clinical interviews and psychological testing. The best psychological tests for this purpose aiding in the diagnosis of relevant mental disorders include the Minnesota Multiphasic Personality Inventory, Second Edition (MMPI-2), the Personality Assessment Inventory (PAI), the Millon Personality Inventory, and the Hare Psychopathy Checklist, Revised (PCL-R). These tests are supported by decades of research. In addition, each include validity indicators, measures to determine whether the person taking the test is "faking good," falsely denying symptoms of a psychological disorder or maladaptive traits, as is often seen in evaluations of sex offenders, or "faking bad," falsely reporting such symptoms and traits, usually for some personal gain.

A thorough assessment of sexual dangerousness includes one or more of the following sex offender specific tests: the Violence Risk Appraisal Guide (VRAG), Sex Offender Risk Appraisal Guide (SORAG), Rapid Risk Assessment for Sex Offender Recidivism (RRASOR), Static-99, and the Sexual Violence Risk-20 (SVR-20).

Conclusion

Society's understanding of and attitudes toward sex offenders have evolved from those primarily based on fundamentalist religious beliefs to, in large part, those based on science and public safety concerns. Sigmund Freud's theory on the structure of the personality and psychosexual development opened the door for the scientific examination of sex offenders. Current research has focused on determining the biological, psychological, and societal factors that predict an offender's recidivism risk and identifying and refining sex offender treatment approaches. Sex offenders are a heterogeneous population, most of whom do not fit the common stereotypes of rapists and child molesters. Research has identified multiple factors that, taken together, allow sex offenders to be classified as to their risk of re-offending. This ability is central to the success of sex offender registration and notification laws, as well as to laws that provide for the indeterminate civil commitment of sex offenders until they are no longer at high risk for committing additional offenses.

Allen J. Brown
Anna Maria College

See Also: Rape, Contemporary; Rape, History of; Rape, Sociology of; Sex Offender Laws; Sexual Harassment.

Further Readings

American Psychiatric Association. *Diagnostic and Statistical Manual of Mental Disorders-IV-TR*. Washington, DC: American Psychiatric Association, 2000.

Hare, R. D. *Without Conscience: The Disturbing World of the Psychopaths Among Us*. New York: Guilford Press, 1993.

Holmes, S. T. and R. M. Holmes. *Sex Crimes: Patterns and Behavior*, 3rd ed. Thousand Oaks, CA: Sage, 2009.

Huss, M. T. *Forensic Psychology: Research, Clinical Practice, and Applications*. West Sussex, UK: Wiley-Blackwell, 2009.

Lalumiere, M. L., G. T. Harris, V. L. Quinsey, and M. E. Rice. *The Causes of Rape: Understanding Individual Differences in Male Propensity for Sexual Aggression*. Washington, DC: American Psychological Association, 2005.

Quinsey, V. L., G. T. Harris, M. E. Rice, and C. A. Cormier. *Violent Offenders: Appraising and Managing Risk*, 2nd ed. Washington, DC: American Psychological Association, 2006.

Sexual Harassment

The term *sexual harassment* was first used in the early 1970s. Sexual harassment is considered a form of sex discrimination that violates Title VII of the Civil Rights Act of 1964. Under Title VII, employers may not discriminate against employees on the basis of race, color, religion, sex, or national origin. The U.S. Equal Employment Opportunity Commission (EEOC) Fact Sheet on Sexual Harassment states, "Title VII applies to employers with 15 or more employees and includes state and local governments. It also applies to employment agencies and to labor organizations, as well as to the federal government." In addition to these employers, most universities and colleges have detailed sexual harassment policies to which all members of the university community must adhere. Under Title IX of the Education Amendments of 1972, sex discrimination is prohibited under any educational program or activity that receives federal funding. The coverage of sexual harassment policies at universities often extends to faculty, researchers, staff, students, vendors, contractors, and visitors to a university.

Concomitant to the formation of laws to protect individuals from sexual harassment was a change in society's attitude toward and tolerance of sexually harassing behaviors that occur in a professional setting. The feminist movement in the late 1960s and the 1970s brought to light how girls and women were objectified in society and called for equal rights for women. Specifically, the women's movement demanded that women, like men, enjoy an environment free of harassment, sexual and otherwise, in the workplace. Before this time, what is now considered sexually harassing behaviors, such as comments about a woman's attractiveness, touching, telling sexually charged jokes, and even asking for sexual favors in return for favors at work, were more commonplace, and even considered "part of the job." Sexual harassment in the workplace did not violate legal standards or behavioral norms. The women's movement brought the current heightened awareness of the issue of sexual harassment and consequently much less tolerance of sexually harassing behavior in the professional sphere. The feminist movement in essence influenced a marked change in social values, which led to laws that criminalized sexual harassment, behavior that prior to this movement victims had no legal recourse to fight.

Types of Sexual Harassment

Sexual harassment claims fall into two categories: quid pro quo and hostile environment. Quid pro quo, meaning "this for that," describes situations in which a supervisor makes unwelcome sexual

A protest was formed at Arnold Schwarzenegger's gubernatorial inauguration on November 17, 2003, protesting the fact that several women had made allegations of sexual harassment against the governor. The Equal Employment Opportunity Commission defines sexual harassment as "unwelcome sexual advances, requests for sexual favors, and other verbal or physical harassment of a sexual nature ... which can include offensive remarks about a person's sex."

advances, requests or demands sexual favors, or explicitly or implicitly communicates to the victim that his or her employment or conditions of employment (for example, getting a raise or promotion) is contingent on submitting to those advances. In the university setting, a classic example would be a professor who promises an "A" to a student if she has sexual relations with him. A power relationship is an important element in a quid pro quo sexual harassment complaint.

The form of sexual harassment termed *hostile environment* involves unwelcome verbal, written, or physical conduct of a sexual nature that is severe and is considered to interfere unreasonably in the victim's work setting or academic environment or that creates an intimidating, hostile, or offensive atmosphere at work or in the context of one's access to education. A power differential is not required to prove that the complainant is a victim of sexual harassment involving a hostile environment situation. At work, employees of the same status may be perpetrators or victims of the hostile environment form of sexual harassment. A supervisor may be a victim of sexual harassment if his or her subordinate continually makes unwelcome jokes of a sexual nature, for example. Likewise, in an educational setting, fellow students and academic colleagues may be either offenders or victims of sexual harassment involving a hostile environment.

Complaints of either quid pro quo or hostile environment may be claimed by both males and females against both males and females. In other words, the protections against sexual harassment in the workplace and at universities cover both same-sex and opposite-sex situations of unwelcome sexual advances, requests for sexual favors, and other forms of unwelcome conduct, behavior, and writings of a sexual nature that create a hostile environment.

For both quid pro quo or hostile environment situations of sexual harassment, it must be determined that the behavior of the accused was unwelcome. Sexual harassment policies generally distinguish between welcome and unwelcome sexual advances. Some employers and universities have separate policies that outline rules for consensual sexual relationships between supervisors and employees, employees who work together, and professors and students. Whereas these policies vary widely from one company to another and differ across universities and colleges, most sexual harassment policies are relatively consistent, as they draw on Title VII of the Civil Rights Act of 1964. Title VII also makes it unlawful for the accused to retaliate against the complainant for making an allegation of sexual harassment and going through the employer's complaint procedures.

Employers and universities often distribute information about sexual harassment prevention to the institution's members in an effort to take a proactive approach to avoiding situations that may be considered sexual harassment. These may include requiring training that defines what sexual harassment is, what situations may or may not constitute sexual harassment, proper grievance procedures, and the steps that should be taken if an allegation of sexual harassment is made.

Complaints of Sexual Harassment

Employers should provide information about complaint procedures to all employees. In the case of universities, these complaint procedures are made public to the entire university community. These procedures direct the person who believes that he or she is a victim of sexual harassment to report the conduct to his or her supervisor and/or to an office of affirmative action within the organization. The complainant is also often directed to tell the harasser that the conduct is unwelcome and that it must stop. If the complaint is found to be legitimate, the harasser will face penalties outlined by the organization, which may include suspension or dismissal.

It is important to understand that the victim's perspective is key to understanding how sexual harassment complaints are handled. Whether the perpetrator *meant* to create a hostile and intimidating environment through discussions about sex, for example, is usually irrelevant to findings that sexual harassment occurred.

In some respects, quid pro quo situations involving sexual harassment are more obvious than hostile environment situations. Arguments may be made that people vary in their tolerance and sensitivity to talk regarding sexual subjects and that it is harder to establish that the alleged offender has created a hostile working environment. The same discussion or comments that offend one woman, for example, may not offend another. In *The Morning After: Sex, Fear and Feminism*, Katie Roiphe suggests that sexual attention is a part of nature, and that for sexual attention to be wanted and reciprocated, people sometimes have to risk offering what she characterizes as unsolicited sexual attention. Otherwise, she suggests, we would all be alone. Indeed, some would argue that the line between flirtation and harassment is thin.

American Association of University Women Study

The American Association of University Women (AAUW) published *Drawing the Line: Sexual Harassment on Campus* in 2005. It reported findings from a nationally representative survey of undergraduate students at colleges and universities. This study shows that almost two-thirds of students attending colleges and universities in the United States experience some form of sexual harassment. More than one-third of college students indicated that they were sexually harassed during their first year in college. The nature of the harassment varied in seriousness from unwelcome remarks concerning sex to forced sexual contact. Most of the students who reported sexual harassment described incidents without contact, which included hearing sexual remarks, having sexual messages posted about them on the Internet, being the target of sexual rumors, and being called a homophobic name. Approximately one-third encountered incidents of physical harassment, such as having someone pull off their clothing, being forced to kiss someone, or being forced to do something sexual.

The results of this survey research showed that the probability of being sexually harassed on campus was similar for males and females, but that the nature of the harassment differed. Females were more likely to be victims of unwanted sexual looks, gestures, comments, and recipients of unwanted sexual jokes. Males who were harassed most often were called gay or homophobic names. Lesbian, gay, bisexual, and transgender students were more likely to be harassed, compared to straight students. Both male and female students who are victims of sexual harassment are more likely to be victimized by a male. Most students identify the harasser as another student. About one-third of female and one-half of male students admitted to sexually harassing someone on campus.

The AAUW concludes that the experience of being a victim of sexual harassment can affect one's emotional health and one's academic well-being. The impact of being sexually harassed on female students was more pronounced, compared with male students. Sexually harassed females were more likely to report negative emotional effects, including feelings of embarrassment and anger, compared to sexually harassed males.

Findings also included that more than one-third of college students do not tell another person about the harassing incident(s) that they experienced. When they do talk about their sexual harassment victimization, they often do so with a friend. Females are more likely to report sexual harassment to another person than males. Fewer than 10 percent of college students report their harassment to a university official. Reasons for not reporting vary and include embarrassment, their belief that nothing could be done, not knowing who the contact person is in the university, and feelings of guilt about some aspect of their own behavior. The most common reason students fail to report sexual harassment, however, is that they feel that it is not that big a deal.

The AAUW study also found that there is not a consensus among college students about what constitutes sexual harassment. It also found that students often shy away from discussing the issue.

Male Victims of Sexual Harassment

Recent figures have shown that the percentage of sexual harassment claims made by males has been increasing. Figures from the EEOC during the 2009 fiscal year show that males filed 2,094 sexual harassment claims, which constitute 16.4 percent of all claims made. This is double the number of claims made by men during the previous decade and reflects a steady increase of sexual harassment claims made by men over that time period. During the same time period, the total number of sexual harassment claims has declined. The increase in male claims of sexual harassment may reflect an actual increase in the number of males being sexually harassed at work, or it may suggest that they are more likely to report sexual harassment than they were in the past.

The majority of these claims are of male-on-male sexual harassment. While some incidents have involved unwanted sexual advances, many involve sexual comments or horseplay. The nature of some of this behavior has been described as straight men trying to express their "masculinity." In 1998, the EEOC represented a group of male employees from Long Prairie Packing Company (LPPC) who complained that they were victims of repeated sexual harassment (both physical and verbal) by coworkers in the first class-action sexual harassment case that involved male-on-male behavior. A $1.9 million voluntary settlement was agreed upon by the EEOC and the LPPC.

There are some indications that female-to-male sexual harassment complaints are also rising. In 2009, the Regal Entertainment Group paid a male employee $175,000 in damages after he claimed that a female employee groped his crotch repeatedly at work.

Relevant Court Cases

The issue of sexual harassment was first considered by the federal courts in *Williams v. Saxbe* (1976). In this case, sexual harassment was deemed a form of sex discrimination in the workplace under Title VII of the Civil Rights Act of 1964.

In *Meritor Savings Bank v. Vinson* (1986), the Supreme Court decided that a claim of hostile work environment can be considered a form of sex discrimination that may be brought under Title VII of the Civil Rights Act of 1964. The decision meant that quid pro quo incidents were not required to establish sex discrimination. Specifically, the court held that for a sexual harassment claim to be actionable, it must be sufficiently severe or pervasive to alter the conditions of the victim's employment and create an abusive

Male and female members of the U.S. Army attend a "Sex Signals" class presented by civilians who perform skits showing social scenarios of sexual harassment and assault. The army maintains a SHARP (Sexual Harassment/Assault Response Program) resource and informational Website to tackle the problem of sexual harassment and assault in the armed forces.

working environment. Additionally, the fact that sex-related conduct was voluntary is not a defense to a sexual harassment suit brought under Title VII. The court also stated that the prohibition against sexual harassment is not limited to discrimination that causes economic or tangible injury, and that the EEOC guidelines fully support the view that harassment leading to noneconomic injury can violate Title VII.

In *Harris v. Forklift Systems, Inc.* (1993), the Supreme Court ruled that sexual harassment is not required to be psychologically injurious to constitute an abusive work environment. The court stated that Congress intended to prohibit all disparate treatment of men and women in employment practices. Hence, Title VII is violated when a workplace is permeated with discriminatory intimidation and ridicule that is sufficiently pervasive so as to alter the condition of the victim's working environment. Harassing conduct that both objectively and subjectively is so severe and pervasive as to create an abusive environment is required to implicate Title VII protections. According to the court, this level of harassment may be determined by looking at all the circumstances, including the frequency of the conduct, its severity, and whether it interferes with an employee's work performance. Prior to this decision, other courts had been urged to adopt a reasonable woman standard in contrast to a reasonable person standard for sexual harassment cases. This decision explicitly states that the harassment must be objectively abusive to a reasonable person and also subjectively abusive to the victim.

In *Burlington Industries Inc. v. Ellerth* (1998), the court ruled that employers are subject to vicarious liability for a hostile working environment created by a supervisor with authority over a victimized employee. The court acknowledged that Title VII harassment claims may include allegations that employment threats were carried out for declining sexual advances, or if there are no employment consequences, if the work environment becomes hostile and abusive. In this decision, the court attempted to clarify the law surrounding employer liability for harassment. Until 1991, damages were not available to victims of hostile work environment. Rather, only injunctive relief was an option before Title VII was amended.

Liz Marie Marciniak
Neil Guzy
University of Pittsburgh at Greensburg

See Also: 1851 to 1900 Primary Documents; 1981 to 2000 Primary Documents; Bill of Rights; Civil Rights Laws; Gender and Criminal Law.

Further Readings
Burlington Industries Inc. v. Ellerth, 524 U.S. 742 (1998).
Harris v. Forklift Systems, Inc., 510 U.S. 17 (1993).
Hill, Catherine and Elena Silva. *Drawing the Line: Sexual Harassment on Campus*. Washington, DC: American Association of University Women Educational Foundation, 2005.
Karmen, Andrew. *Crime Victims*. Belmont, CA: Wadsworth Cengage, 2010.
Meritor Savings Bank v. Vinson, 477 U.S. 57 (1986).
Roiphe, Katie. *The Morning After: Sex, Fear, and Feminism*. Boston: Little, Brown, 1994.
U.S. Equal Employment Opportunity Commission, "Fact Sheet: Sexual Harassment." http://www.eeoc.gov/index.cfm (Accessed January 2011).
Williams v. Saxbe, 413 F. Supp. 654 (D.C.D.C. 1976).

Shaming and Shunning

The application of shame and shunning as a means to control behaviors that society views as undesirable is not new. Almost every religious and cultural tradition throughout the world has referred to the role that shame can have for controlling behavior. From the first European settlement in Massachusetts to the modern day, criminal justice systems in the United States have utilized the application of shame and shunning as one of the main objectives of punishment.

The concept of shaming has its intellectual roots in the sociological conception of the self that emphasizes the importance that others play in the creation of a person's identity. Shame is an internal emotional response to embarrassing actions, ideas, words, or thoughts. When these embarrassing actions are made public, they threaten to damage a person's value or standing in the community. Shame can be a very effective means of social control, having the ability to both enhance group cohesion and deter unwanted behaviors.

Shaming sanctions in the U.S. criminal justice system are punishments that are directed primarily at publicizing an offender's illegal conduct in a way intended to reinforce the existing social values that disapprove of such behaviors. The primary goal of shaming sanctions is to increase the amount of unpleasant emotions experienced by the offender in the hope of compelling the individual to begin conforming to community norms. Shaming sanctions are explicitly designed to make a public spectacle of the offender's conviction and punishment and to trigger a negative change in the offender's self-concept.

While shaming sanctions can be used to punish crimes of varying seriousness, they have most often been used to sanction minor, first-time offenders. Shaming sanctions were the primary form of punishment during colonial times, but today are most likely to be used as alternative sanctions to jail time, probation, or minor fines when those sanctions are not considered cost-effective or deserved punishments. While traditional sanctions such as incarceration and fines may have secondary shaming effects for an offender, with shaming sanctions, embarrassment and change of self-concept are the principal goals of the punishment. Shaming penalties attempt to mark the defendant publicly as a criminal, whereas that is not the primary goal of sanctions such as incarceration or minor fines. Historians and criminologists have noted the extent to which shaming and shunning sanctions emerge from the public's frustration with conventional punishment options of prison or parole. While there are countless ways that societies have implemented shaming penalties over history and across cultures, these types of penalties can be categorized into three main groups: public exposure, public humiliation, and banishment.

Public Exposure Penalties
The most common form of shaming penalties attempt to expose the offender and his/her

offense to the public. Public exposure penalties often include the literal application of a badge of shame to the offender, allowing the crime to come to the attention of the public, so that the public may in turn respond to the offender with shunning. Probably the best-known example of shaming comes from Nathaniel Hawthorne's 1850 novel *The Scarlet Letter*, which depicts the punishment of its protagonist, Hester Prynne, who is convicted of the crime of adultery in a 17th-century Puritan community and is sentenced to wear a visible scarlet letter "A" on her clothes for the rest of her life.

The Puritans were especially matter-of-fact when it came to methods of public punishment. There is evidence that similar punishments, such as forcing drunkards (habitual drinkers) to sew the letter "D" into their clothing and wear the badge for an entire year, were also commonplace during this time. Among the more severe punishments administered by the early American Puritans was the amputation of ears, slitting of the nostrils, and branding of the face and hands. Repeat property offenders were branded on the cheek or forehead or mutilated, leaving a mark of infamy to expose their criminal histories. Unlike shame letters sewn into a garment, these were permanent reminders to both offender and community of the transgression against society. A less severe and more widely utilized form of public exposure throughout American history has been the use of the dunce cap, especially within the education system. Also referred to as a dunce hat, dunce's cap, or dunce's hat, the dunce cap is a pointed hat, typically made of paper and often marked with a "D" or the word *dunce* and given to schoolchildren to wear as punishment for misbehavior.

More recently, many states have forced sentenced offenders convicted of drunk driving to attach a large bumper sticker or special license plate to their vehicle in an attempt to alert others to their prior undesirable behavior. In Escambia County, Florida, for example, a judge forced those convicted of driving under the influence to attach a red and yellow bumper sticker to their car that read: "How is my driving? Call Toll-Free 1-866-I-SAW-YOU, The Judge wants to know!!!" Historically, one of the main goals of Puritan punishment was to have a church member repent and then return to the congregation. Judges would often force offenders to write formal apologies to newspapers or in front of church members. These variations of public exposure penalties still exist today. In 1988, Champaign, Illinois, Circuit Court Judge Jeffrey Ford required first-time drunken driving offenders who pled guilty to publicly apologize in ads in their hometown newspapers, with their photos included. Apologies to the community often include exposure of the offender's behaviors to the community.

The most prominent example of the public exposure of offenders over the last 20 years has been in regard to those convicted of sexual offenses against children. In 1994, Congress passed the Jacob Wetterling Crimes Against Children and Sexually Violent Offender Registration Act, mandating all states to require convicted sex offenders to register with law enforcement agencies. The first amendment to this act was passed in 1996. Named after Megan Kanka, a 7-year-old girl who was murdered by a convicted sex offender, Megan's Law mandated that all states also develop programs to allow the public to access information about sex offenders who are living in their community.

Public Humiliation

The primary goal of public humiliation penalties is to personally degrade or humiliate the offender. Humiliation penalties are created for the sole purpose of embarrassing and demeaning the offender by forcing him/her to engage in some form of humiliating activity. The belief is that others in the general public will avoid criminal or unwanted behavior simply to avoid the potential of having to experience similar humiliation, and that the offender will experience sufficient shame to not want to repeat the behavior. Embarrassment becomes a formal tactic of punishment rather than an unintentional by-product or outcome. Examples of these types of policies range from the silly and absurd to the brutal and severe.

The use of stocks and the pillory are well documented during the American colonial period. When someone was put into stocks, boards were placed around the legs or the wrists; whereas in the pillory, boards were placed around the arms and neck and fixed to a pole. A key aspect of the pillory and stocks included public exposure. As a result, offenders were often placed in the middle of busy markets in an attempt to expose them to

Hester Prynne, the protagonist of Nathaniel Hawthorne's 1850 novel The Scarlet Letter, *symbolically pictured near the stocks and holding her daughter, the product of an adulterous affair.*

as many members of the community as possible. Crowds were encouraged to ridicule and mock those on display and would often throw mud, rotten food, animal entrails, and excrement. While in the pillory, offenders could receive further punishments such as having their hair cut or heads shaved, as well as repeated corporal punishment such as flagellation, hence the term *whipping post*.

In the United States today, more subtle and less painful forms of the stocks and pillory still exist. While restraints are no longer involved, many offenders are sentenced to remain in public spaces (such as the local courthouse or shopping center) for a determinate length of time with signs describing their offenses. Many shopping malls now display billboard-sized photos of convicted shoplifters. More imaginative sentences attempt to match the humiliating penalty to the nature of the offense. For example, a Louisiana woman convicted of pirating cable television service was told that she would be held in contempt of court if she didn't stop watching cable TV shows for one year. In 1987, Judge Veronica Simmons-McBeth ordered Dr. Milton Avol, a Beverly Hills neurosurgeon convicted of being a slumlord, to spend 30 days in one of his run-down, rat-infested buildings with an electric device strapped to his ankle to assure authorities that he had not left. The case was portrayed in the 1991 Hollywood film *The Super*.

Banishment

One penalty reserved for the most serious crimes in New England until the 18th century was banishment. Banishment was often the last resort to longtime residents faced with patterns of criminality. At that time, the causes of crime were believed to be the result of some supernatural force or spirit. Allowing offenders who had shown evidence that they were "tempted" or "possessed" by these evil forces to remain in the community was only believed to bring further harm to its members. The shunning and condemnation of family members, neighbors, and the community remained, often because of anger over losing a valuable source of labor at a time in history when labor was very scarce. However, that punishment often seemed fleeting, as eventually the challenge of physical survival outside one's protected community would often lead to death. As settlements and communities grew closer together, banishment was less likely to become a death sentence because the ability to travel to another location increased. Today, the effect of banishment on an individual has been greatly reduced. States such as Georgia and Arkansas continue to use banishment for certain crimes such as drug distribution as an alternative to jail time, but their constitutions stipulate that banishment can only be within the state.

As alternatives to incarceration, punishments that incorporate public shaming and shunning remain enduring judicial sanctions in the United States. From colonial America to the current day, the use of shame as a social control mechanism has played a major role in the historical development of the American criminal justice system. Just as the application of shaming as a punishment has evolved over the past 400 years, there should logically be an expectation that it will continue to evolve and adapt to larger social changes such as globalization and innovations in technology such as the development of social networks.

Ryan K. Williams
University of Illinois, Springfield

See Also: Colonial Courts; Cruel and Unusual Punishment; Puritans; Sentencing.

Further Readings
Braithewaite, John. *Crime, Shame and Reintegration.* Cambridge, MA: Cambridge University Press, 1989.
Erikson, Kai T. *Wayward Puritans: A Study in the Sociology of Deviance.* Hoboken, NJ: Wiley, 1966.
Hawthorne, Nathaniel. *The Scarlet Letter.* Boston: Ticknor, Reed & Fields, 1850.

Sheppard, Sam

Sam Sheppard (1923–70) was an osteopathic physician and neurosurgeon turned professional wrestler who was convicted of murdering his pregnant wife Marilyn in 1954. He served 10 years of a life sentence before his conviction was overturned. He was later acquitted in his second trial. Sheppard's case is well known for a variety of reasons. First, it has often been compared to the O. J. Simpson trial due to the carnival feel of its coverage and proceedings. Second, it was one of F. Lee Bailey's first high-profile cases as an appellate defense attorney. It now stands as one of the better known unsolved murder cases in the United States.

On July 4, 1954, in Bay Village, Ohio, Marilyn Sheppard was killed. Sam claimed the killer had attacked him and twice knocked him unconscious. Despite his story, Sheppard was considered the only viable suspect and was arrested and brought to trial in fall 1954. The trial, however, was by no means typical. The prosecuting attorney, John Mahon, was running for a seat on the Cuyahoga County Court of Common Pleas and believed a win in this case would clinch his electoral victory. Newspapers throughout the region ran stories appearing to be biased against Sheppard. *The Cleveland Press*, for example, ran a story with the headline "Why Isn't Sam Sheppard in Jail?"

As the prosecution began making its case, jurors learned that Sheppard allegedly had a three-year-long affair with a nurse named Susan Hayes who worked at the hospital with him. Prosecutors argued that Sheppard's motive for murder was that his wife's pregnancy would force his extramarital affair to end. In his defense, Sheppard called on a neurosurgeon to explain the injuries he had suffered in the attack and describe why they were not possibly simulated or faked. Further, the neurosurgeon explained to jurors that the particular injuries could not be self-inflicted. There was also a lack of blood evidence. Despite the scene having had large amounts of blood, authorities were only able to find transfer bloodstains on Sheppard's watch. Medical evidence indicated that two of his wife's teeth had also been broken. If it had been an injury caused by her being beaten, the pieces would have been found in her mouth; however, the broken pieces were pulled from her mouth, suggesting that she had bitten her attacker. Since Sheppard had no bite marks and the broken teeth were not in his wife's mouth, the defense believed they had shown that the murderer was someone other than Sam Sheppard.

On the stand, Sheppard testified that he was sleeping downstairs when he was awakened by his wife's screams. He explained that after the attack, he had chased a bushy-haired intruder down to the shore of Lake Erie before being knocked unconscious by him a second time. Sheppard's testimony was rambling and seemed as if he were trying to recall a created story rather than reliving horrific events. Jurors did not believe Sheppard's story and found him guilty, and he received a life sentence in December 1954.

Ten years later, Sheppard had a writ of habeas corpus granted by a U.S. district court judge. In *Sheppard v. Maxwell*, the Supreme Court ruled Sheppard had been denied due process and pointed to the "carnival atmosphere" permeating the entire trial. Further, the Supreme Court found that the judge refused to sequester the jury, did not order them to ignore media accounts, and had even gone on the record prior to the trial saying, "Well, he's guilty as hell. There's no question about it." In the retrial, F. Lee Bailey decided that neither Sheppard nor Hayes would testify. The strategy worked, and Sheppard was acquitted.

In the aftermath of the trials, Sheppard attempted a return to practicing medicine, but as he was facing two malpractice suits, he turned instead to writing about his life and professional wrestling. He ultimately became an alcoholic and died of liver failure in 1970. His son, Samuel, who was 7 at the time of his mother's death, launched a civil suit in 1999 alleging his father had been falsely imprisoned and that his estate was owed compensation. After a 10-week trial, however, the jury did not believe Sheppard had met the burden of proof. Sheppard's story and court case have been referred to in literature and on the screen. *The Shawshank Redemption* bears many similarities to the story, and television shows *American Justice*, *Cold Case*, *Law & Order*, and *Notorious* have all aired episodes based to some degree on Sheppard's case.

William J. Miller
Southeast Missouri State University

See Also: Murder, History of; Murders, Unsolved; *Sheppard v. Maxwell*.

Further Readings
Cooper, Cynthia and Samuel Sheppard Reese. *Mockery of Justice*. Lebanon, NH: Northeastern University Press, 1995.
Mason, William D. and Jack P. DeSario. *Dr. Sam Sheppard on Trial: Case Closed*. Kent, OH: Kent State University Press, 2003.

Sheppard v. Maxwell

The case of *Sheppard v. Maxwell*, 384 U.S. 333 (1966), stands for the principle that, in the interests of justice and due process, it is not possible to proceed in an environment where a defendant's right to a fair trial pursuant to the Sixth Amendment shall, in any way, be infringed upon. Extensive public reporting of the crime and the events, through the trial/appellate process, are key aspects of a free press. The Sixth Amendment to the U.S. Constitution provides that "in all criminal prosecutions, the accused shall enjoy the right to a speedy and public trial, by an impartial jury of the State and district wherein the crime shall have been committed." The First Amendment provides that "Congress shall make no law ... abridging the freedom of speech, or the press...." These rights apply equally to the federal government and to the states through the due process provisions of the Fourteenth Amendment and must be protected. Finding the appropriate balance of these rights is never an easy task in a free society.

The Facts
The facts of this case read like a screenplay, perhaps a television show starring David Jansen or a movie starring Harrison Ford; it might even be the basis for a best-selling book that questions whether anyone is really presumed innocent and can receive a fair trial once the various media have taken the sensational facts for a spin. Dr. Sam Sheppard was a bright doctor from a family of doctors, including his father and two brothers. He married his high school sweetheart; they had one child and were expecting another. After several years, they returned to their hometown so that he could join the family medical practice. Sheppard was rumored to have been unfaithful to his wife, and that simply added to his problems on the evening of July 4, 1954.

Sheppard recalled having fallen asleep on the couch but was awakened in response to a call of help from his wife, who was four months pregnant at the time. Upon arriving in his bedroom, he observed his wife fighting with one man but was immediately struck from behind by someone else. When he awoke, he saw his wife and checked her vital signs before checking on his son, who was fine. He heard something on the first floor and then proceeded to follow two individuals toward a nearby lake. As he got close, he recalled being struck again on the back of his head and passing out. By the next month, Sheppard was arrested for his wife's murder; he was tried and convicted by the end of the year. It took 10 years for the court to identify all of the constitutional errors that had taken place during the trial, but the result was that Sheppard received a new trial.

The Right to Freedom of Speech and Freedom of the Press
In its review of the events both outside and inside the courtroom during Sheppard's trial, the

Supreme Court opinion described the atmosphere at the trial as a "carnival." The opinion noted, "The court's fundamental error is compounded by the holding that it lacked power to control the publicity about the trial. From the very inception of the proceedings the judge announced that neither he nor anyone else could restrict prejudicial new accounts." The opinion went on to conclude that the court should have limited publicity and the number of reporters in the courtroom, and limited access to the court as Sheppard's counsel requested. The court should have insulated witnesses and jurors from the press. To further inflame matters, at about the same time this trial, elections were taking place; both the judge and the prosecutor in the case were candidates for judicial office. In exercising its freedom, the press published the names of the prospective jurors.

The Holding
The Supreme Court, in an 8–1 opinion, held the following:

> Due process requires that the accused receive a trial by an impartial jury free from outside influences. Given the pervasiveness of modern communications and the difficulty of effacing prejudicial publicity from the minds of the jurors, the trial courts must take strong measures to ensure that the balance is never weighed against the accused. But where there is a reasonable likelihood that prejudicial news prior to trial will prevent a fair trial, the judge should continue the case until the threat abates, or transfer it to another county not so permeated with publicity.... If publicity during the proceedings threatens the fairness of the trial, a new trial should be ordered.... Since the state trial judge did not fulfill his duty to protect Sheppard from the inherently prejudicial publicity which saturated the community and to control disruptive influences in the courtroom, we must reverse the denial of the habeas petition. (384 U.S. 333, 364)

Conclusion
In 1966, Sheppard was retried for his wife's murder and was acquitted.

The right to a speedy and public trial by an impartial jury is essential in a free society. Our courts do not operate in a Star Chamber. The freedoms of speech and the press are necessary to ensure that the trial process is open and fair. On the other hand, the process is not designed to adversely affect the outcome and jeopardize every defendant's presumption of innocence.

Keith Gregory Logan
Kutztown University

See Also: Bill of Rights; *Estes v. Texas*; Sheppard, Sam.

Further Readings
Grisham, John. *The Innocent Man*. New York: Doubleday, 2006.
Neff, James. *The Wrong Man: The Final Verdict on the Dr. Sam Sheppard Murder Case*. New York: Random House, 2002.

Sheriffs

The sheriff may be the oldest law enforcement office, and its origins can be traced to biblical times. Sheriffs attended the dedication of Nebuchadnezzar's golden image in the Book of Daniel. The Roman *proconsul* and the German *burgermeister* are believed to be the earliest forms of sheriff. Throughout history, wherever laws need enforcing, some form of sheriff can be found in a judicial capacity, law enforcement capacity, administrative capacity, or some combination of all three. Despite its history and the vital role it has played in law enforcement, courts, and corrections, little research has been conducted on the office of sheriff.

English Sheriffs
Before the Norman Conquest (1066), kings appointed county reeves who played numerous roles in the administration of royal law and policy. These were precursors to the modern American sheriff. These men administered policy in certain territories. Maintaining order, arresting and punishing criminals, serving in the military, and collecting taxes were among their duties. It was not uncommon for sheriffs to use their own money to support their offices. After the Norman Conquest,

as the population grew and people organized into larger governmental units, the king appointed shire, as opposed to county, reeves to manage courts, collect taxes, and maintain the peace.

As the result of becoming the king's agent, the sheriff's official power increased. Shire reeves were political appointments, and the candidate had to meet various requirements. In addition to loyalty to the king, he had to own property and reside in the shire he served. As Parliament became more powerful, counties nominated men whom Parliament would then appoint. The appointee took an oath that enumerated his duties, both administrative and legal. Among these duties were collecting taxes, serving writs, keeping the peace, and protecting the lands of the shire.

The Normans abused the English. When King John took the throne in 1199, he also abused his power. Hated by his subjects for a variety of reasons, not the least of which was excessive taxation, the sheriffs and barons revolted. John was forced to sign the Magna Carta, which mentions the office of sheriff nine times. The sheriff's power waxed and waned from 1215 until the 1500s. As local police power grew, the duties of sheriffs, who remained under the control of the Crown, became more administrative. In England today, the office of sheriff is primarily ceremonial, although sheriffs do continue to carry out administrative duties for the court.

American Sheriffs: The Colonies

In what would become the United States, the office of the sheriff evolved in a manner similar to that of its English counterpart. In early colonial history, small communities relied on their members to keep the peace, appointing constables and night watchmen only as necessary. As population grew and counties were formed, sheriffs were appointed by the king, representing both the colonial and the English governments. Duties in the colonies were similar to those in England, with perhaps more emphasis on administration than on law enforcement. The earliest record of a sheriff in the colonies is believed to be William Stone of Virginia, who took office in 1634.

Like English sheriffs, colonial sheriffs were landowners. Because sheriffs were compensated through fees for their work, they tended to focus on those activities that were more lucrative, such as collecting taxes, serving subpoenas, and running the jail. They charged the county for keeping the prisoners, and many even charged the jail inmates for food. Because of the economic opportunities it provided, the office of sheriff was highly sought after. The collection of fees in the colonies made the office of sheriff there more lucrative than it was in England. Additionally, colonial sheriffs did not have the expense of entertaining royal or parliamentary officials like English sheriffs.

Nonetheless, sheriffs had to adapt to the rigors of colonial life. In England, where there were established roads and addresses, it was relatively easy for sheriffs simply to go to someone's address to collect taxes. No such infrastructure existed in the colonies. Sheriffs often waited outside churches to locate the people who owed taxes or to whom they had to serve papers. Since law enforcement duties did not pay nearly as much as administrative duties, it was common for sheriffs to neglect them.

American Sheriffs: The West

During the settlement of the west, sheriffs began to be elected by the people they represented. The western sheriff has a colorful history, including such people as Wyatt Earp, Wild Bill Hickok, and Bat Masterson. In the west, private concerns like banks and railroads hired their own police forces, often private detectives. Sheriffs were hired to keep control of the criminals and cowboys who regularly came to town; consequently, they were often as tough and disreputable as those they were hired to control. In addition, sheriffs had to insure that merchants—the people who ran the saloons, prostitutes, and businesses—continued to make money. Since aggressive law enforcement could drive business away, sheriffs ensured that vice continued, albeit under some measure of control. Because merchants hired the sheriffs, it was not uncommon for sheriffs to practice one or more of the vices on display in town. As a result, many law-abiding citizens often looked down upon sheriffs, equating them with the trouble-making criminals and cowboys.

American Sheriffs: The South

Historically, southern sheriffs were white and male, and they were instrumental in maintaining white supremacy and upholding Jim Crow laws.

During the Civil War period, sheriffs operated with little oversight and ran inept and corrupt administrations. They focused on more lucrative duties and avoided those that paid nothing or might alienate voters.

As major providers of local law enforcement, sheriffs were in a unique position to maintain the status quo. They helped local elites control disorder, such as labor strikes. Sheriffs were also responsible for running local elections and investigating voter fraud. In this position, they were able to suppress the voting of "undesirables," especially African Americans. While they did not take the lead in lynchings, sheriffs seldom did anything to stop them. Likewise, they seldom quelled the vigilantism of the Ku Klux Klan; in fact, many were active members.

Today, white males continue to hold the majority of sheriff's offices, even in counties that are predominately African American. Sheriffs perform three main duties in the contemporary south: countywide law enforcement, jail operation, and acting as the state court officer. It is still a job that is attractive to local male citizens with limited formal education.

There are four reasons why African Americans are underrepresented in the ranks of southern sheriffs: (1) few African Americans have supervisory experience in law enforcement; (2) African Americans in the south have less money than whites, and it is hard to mount a campaign or to attract moneyed supporters; (3) African Americans tend to vote less than whites, or not to be registered to vote; and (4) the stereotype of the white southern sheriff may make the office distasteful to most African Americans

American Sheriffs Today

According to the National Association of Sheriffs, counties in 46 states elect a sheriff. In 41 states, sheriffs are elected to four-year terms; in three states, they are elected to two-year terms; in one state, they are elected to a three-year term; and in another state, they are elected to a six-year term. Forty states conduct sheriff's elections using partisan ballots, while the remaining six use nonpartisan ballots.

In Rhode Island, sheriffs are appointed by the governor. In Hawai'i, sheriffs, along with narcotics enforcement, comprise the law enforcement division of the Department of Public Safety. Although they share a name and some of the duties of mainland sheriffs, their role is more similar to that of police officers. In Connecticut, as a result of an election in 2000, the office of sheriff was eliminated. Deputy sheriffs became state marshals in the state judicial branch. Alaska does not have the office of the sheriff. The county executive appoints the sheriff in Dade County, Florida, and in two counties in Colorado.

One thing that separates the sheriff from the municipal police chief is that he/she is elected, whereas the chief is promoted or appointed. A further distinction is made between the sheriff's office and the police department. Where a department is a subordinate division of city or county government, an office is relatively independent and autonomous; where a department has its power delegated to it by a higher governmental authority, the power of an office is granted to it by the constitution of the state. The sheriff has a public trust and powers conferred on him/her, making him/her answerable to all citizens in the county.

The independence inherent in the elected office of sheriff creates a political personage, one whose concerns extend far beyond merely doing his/her job. Like politicians, sheriffs must raise money and spend a good deal of time campaigning, something that sheriffs argue they do not only during the campaign season but also during the rest of their term. Like politicians, they are beholden to the public as a whole. The public includes numerous constituencies: citizens, courts, the state, political party, police, county officials, and his/her staff. Staff problems may exist for many sheriffs as a result of the divergent duties carried out by the office. Studies have revealed tension between deputies who do law enforcement work and those who work in the jails or courts. It is not uncommon for internal strife to make its way into the public eye.

Other political pressures dealt with by sheriffs include requests to use office funds for various causes, to influence routine legal matters, to provide additional services, and to dispense patronage. The causes that sheriffs are asked to support monetarily tend to be political and charitable, so it is hard to refuse help. However, like any public budget, the sheriff's is limited, meaning that he/she has to weigh the political cost of contributing—or not contributing—to certain causes.

Sheriffs are also asked to use their influence in routine matters. For example, they may be asked to dismiss traffic tickets, increase or decrease the pace of evictions, or provide special treatment for jail inmates.

Those who demand additional services tend to hold a certain amount of political and social power. Sheriffs may find themselves obligated to certain community members to whom they promised political favors, or they may see opportunity in providing such favors to certain citizens. These often take the form of extra patrols, greater visibility, and preferential treatment. Provision of such services may give the impression that the sheriff's office is controlled by special interests. Patronage, which gives the sheriffs the ability to appoint people to jobs in order to gain some advantage, may be used to fill certain positions, but not all positions are filled for political advantage. Sheriffs are often limited by budget constraints and the scarcity of positions that they have to fill. Most are careful to fill such positions with people who are not only politically favorable but who are also capable of doing the job well.

As the only elected law enforcement official in the United States, the sheriff tends to be more open to community influence than hired police officials. In order to be re-elected, the sheriff has to maintain a positive public image. Some believe that this means that sheriffs are involved and invested in community policing to a greater degree than municipal police. Sheriff's offices are also sensitive to new methods of serving the public. Sheriffs have traditionally been responsible for patrolling unincorporated areas in the county. In addition, sheriff's offices, especially those serving populations of 100,000 or more, also provide foot, marine, motorcycle, bicycle, and horse patrol. More than half of the sheriff's offices serving a population of 100,000 or more are responsible for investigating homicides, arsons, drug offenses, and cybercrime. Given the rise in the use of methamphetamine and heroin in rural areas, many have full-time units that deal specifically with drug crimes. Nearly half assign one or more officers to multiagency drug task forces.

Sheriff's departments typically have three functions: road patrol, court-related functions (e.g., courtroom security), and management of the county jail. In 2008, road patrol was the major function, with 59 percent of full-time sworn deputies assigned to it. Operating the jail was next, with 23 percent of deputies assigned to it. Finally, 12 percent of deputies were assigned to court-related operations. The remaining 6 percent were assigned to other duties.

Sheriff vehicles in Monroe County, New York, participate in the 2011 Independence Day parade in Irondequoit, New York. The sheriff's office in Monroe County was established in 1821 at a time of rapid expansion and settlement in western New York. The first sheriff appointed was Brockport merchant James Seymour in 1821. The department now has 1,200 employees.

More than 80 percent of sheriff's offices perform services related to the court. These include serving civil process orders and eviction notices, providing court security, executing arrest warrants, enforcing protection orders, and enforcing orders of child support. More than 60 percent of sheriff's offices operate one or more jails, and more than 80 percent transport inmates from court to jail. Sheriff's offices often play a large role in controlling motor vehicle traffic. More than 70 percent enforce traffic laws, and more than 60 percent perform accident investigations and direct traffic. Sheriffs may also be involved in enforcement of parking and commercial vehicle laws.

The American sheriff today plays an integral role in law enforcement, employing roughly one-fourth of sworn law enforcement personnel and nearly one-half of non-sworn, or civilian, law enforcement personnel. As of 2008, Texas had the largest number of sheriffs' offices (254) followed by Georgia (159), Kentucky (120), Missouri (114), and Kansas (104). As noted earlier, four states do not have sheriff's departments. Duties normally performed by sheriff's departments are dealt with by various state agencies.

Thirteen sheriff's offices employ more than 1,000 full-time sworn personnel. As of 2008, the five largest departments are the Los Angeles County Sheriff's Office, with a total of 9,461; the Cook County (Illinois) Sheriff's Office, with a total of 5,655; the Harris County (Texas) Sheriff's Office, with a total of 2,558; the Riverside County (California) Sheriff's Office, with a total of 2,147; and the San Bernardino County (California) Sheriff's Office, with a total of 1,797.

As of 2008, American sheriffs employed approximately 353,000 people full-time, which included approximately 183,000 sworn officers. Of all sworn law enforcement personnel, about 24 percent were sheriff's deputies. Throughout the country, nearly 60 percent of the sheriff's offices had fewer than 25 sworn personnel, while approximately half of the officers served populations lower than 25,000. As of 2007, 12 percent of sworn full-time officers were females, 19 percent were racial and ethnic minorities, and 8 percent were Hispanic or Latino.

James Geistman
Ohio Northern University

See Also: Community Policing and Relations; Court of Common Pleas; Police, Contemporary.

Further Readings

Brown, Johnny Mack. "Sheriff's Office Versus Office of the Sheriff." *Sheriff* (March/April 1993).

Buckeye State Sheriffs' Association. "History of Ohio Sheriffs." http://www. buckeyesheriffs.org/history.htm (Accessed September 2011).

Hickman, Matthew J. and Brian A. Reaves. *Sheriffs' Offices, 2003*. NCJ 211361. Washington, DC: U.S. Department of Justice, 2006.

Morris, William Alfred. *The Medieval English Sheriff to 1300*. New York: Barnes & Noble, 1968.

Reaves, Brian A. *Census of State and Local Law Enforcement Agencies, 2008*. NCJ 233982. Washington, DC: U.S. Department of Justice, 2011.

Struckhoff, David R. *The American Sheriff*. Joliet, IL: SL Publishing/JRI, 1994.

Sherman Anti-Trust Act of 1890

The aim of the Sherman Anti-Trust Act of 1890 was to ensure that the United States maintained a free and competitive marketplace. The broad principles of interstate commerce had been articulated by the drafters of Article I of the U.S. Constitution, but Congress needed to address how to prevent monopolistic business practices from destroying these ideals.

The federal government after the Civil War had actively encouraged private business growth. But big businesses had then turned to creating trusts that unfairly influenced natural supply and demand market forces. While some states had attempted to slow the growth of trusts, the Sherman Anti-Trust Act was the first federal law enacted to prohibit trusts. On April 8, 1890, the U.S. Senate voted 51–1 to approve the law. The U.S. House of Representatives followed with unanimous approval (242 votes) on June 20, and the bill was signed into law by President Benjamin Harrison on July 2.

The chief architect of the act was Senator John Sherman of Ohio, who at the time served as chair of the Senate Finance Committee and had previously served as secretary of the treasury during the Hayes administration. Since 1890, Congress has passed additional bills to prohibit anticompetitive activities, including the Clayton Act and the Federal Trade Commission Act in 1914 and the Robinson-Patman Act in 1936.

At the turn of the 19th century, trusts were created with the purpose of gaining trade advantages in specific industry sectors. Some of the most famous American business trusts included those connected to the sugar industry, the steel industry, the oil and gas industries, and the tobacco industry. When a trust is formed, the corporate stockholders transfer shares to just a few individuals who then, in the future, act as trustees for the company and its subsidiaries.

These trustees manage all aspects of the business, including price regulation. As a result, it becomes difficult for competitors to enter markets, set their own prices, or acquire raw materials to make their products. When a monopoly dominates the marketplace, producers, manufacturers, and suppliers are more likely to sustain financial losses while the monopoly acquires huge profits. At the height of their power in the United States, business trusts were predatorily capturing both the horizontal and vertical means of production and transportation across most business sectors. Agreements between businesses to restrict trade within a particular sector are described as horizontal practices, whereas agreements among producers and other organizations involved in the trade of the goods or services create a vertical restraint to competition. It is up to the courts, however, to decide whether these arrangements are per se illegal under the Sherman Anti-Trust Act or whether a Rule of Reason test should be applied to determine whether harms resulted directly from unfair competitive practices.

Under the provisions of the act, business trusts that were found to monopolize the market were prohibited. The act made it possible for the U.S. government to bring actions against these trusts, either to break them into smaller parts or to eliminate them altogether. The law provided for fines of $5,000 and up to a year of incarceration for individuals who created trusts, and also created remedies for competitors who sued the trusts. If successful, they could receive treble damages in federal courts.

Challenges and Implications

The law's critics argued that much of the Sherman Anti-Trust Act's language was ill defined. Consequently, it was left to the courts and to the executive branch to narrow its meaning. The first judicial challenge arose in 1895, when the U.S. Supreme Court upheld the law as constitutional but diluted the act's enforcement powers. In *United States v. E. C. Knight Company*, an 8–1 decision, Justice Fuller, writing for the majority, noted that while the American Sugar Refining Company had dominated the manufacturing market for refined sugar, it had not violated the act because the trust had not monopolized the sale or transportation of refined sugar. In 1904, the U.S. Supreme Court decided another significant case applying the act, which resulted in the dissolution of the Northern Securities Company, and in 1911, the Taft administration used the Sherman Anti-Trust Act to dismantle Standard Oil as well as the American Tobacco Company. The law was not used extensively thereafter until the U.S. government brought an action against Microsoft in 1998.

Sections 1 through 7 of the act cover several anticompetitive practices. Section 1 broadly references that no contract, combination, trust, or conspiracy can restrain trade and that there must be proof of a "concerted action" to conduct unfair practices for competitors to claim financial losses. Price-fixing in any form is expressly prohibited by the act. Monopolies are forbidden under the act, but the courts are left to interpret the extent of market power that is monopolized. This may extend to the market share for the product itself as well as the geographic areas in which the product is bought and sold. The act addresses market allocations as a predatory anticompetitive maneuver. The U.S. Supreme Court opinion in *Standard Oil Company of New Jersey* v. *United States* (1911) specifically required that a Rule of Reason be applied when courts examine how markets are divided up by competitors. The act also makes a boycott illegal. If two or more businesses refuse to deal with another company, creating a boycott, this practice is considered anticompetitive. Any form of a tying arrangement, when the trading of one product is dependent on the trading of another, is also considered prohibited under the provisions of the act.

Andrea G. Lange
Washington College

See Also: Antitrust Law; *Standard Oil Company of New Jersey v. United States*.

Further Readings
Bowman, Scott R. *The Modern Corporation and American Political Thought: Law, Power and Ideology*. University Park, PA: Penn State University Press, 1995.
Kirland, Edward C. *A History of American Economic Life*. New York: Appleton-Century Crofts, 1969.
National Archives and Records Administration. "Sherman Anti-Trust Act." http://www.our documents.gov/doc.php?flash=old&doc=51 (Accessed September 2011).
Peritz, Rudolph J. R. *Competition Policy in America, 1888–1992: History, Rhetoric, Law*. London: Oxford University Press, 2001
Posner, Richard A. *Antitrust Law*, 2nd ed. Chicago: University of Chicago Press, 2002.

Simpson, O. J.

Prior to the mid-1990s, Orenthal James (O. J.) Simpson (1947–) was best known for his career as an NFL running back and an actor. After the infamous night of June 12, 1994, Simpson was best known for his suspected involvement in the murder of his ex-wife, Nicole Brown Simpson, and her friend, Ronald Goldman. Although a jury found him not guilty of the murders, he was found liable for the wrongful death of the two victims in a civil trial and ordered to pay $33,500,000 in damages. Simpson and his wife, Nicole, married in 1985, six years after his divorce from his first wife. Simpson was no stranger to the law. He pleaded no contest to a domestic abuse charge against his then separated wife in 1989.

On the night of June 12, 1994, police were called to 875 South Bundy Drive in Brentwood, California, after a white Akita with red, matted fur led two individuals to a house, where they saw what appeared to be a body lying at the bottom of the stairs. They called the police, who discovered the bodies early in the morning, covered with blood and stab wounds. The police tried to reach Simpson, whose son and daughter with Nicole were asleep upstairs in the house, but discovered that he had taken a red-eye flight from Los Angeles to Chicago. Simpson was considered a possible suspect, but without direct evidence linking him to the murders, he was not the immediate prime suspect.

Evidence began piling up against Simpson, including a leather glove that was found at the scene of the crime and had blood on it. DNA tests indicated that the blood on the glove belonged both to Simpson and to the victims. The limo driver who had been hired to drive him to the airport stated that he arrived at the house early and made several unsuccessful attempts to contact Simpson. He saw a man dressed in black enter the house several minutes later, and he finally made contact with him, who claimed to have overslept. A neighbor of Nicole Brown Simpson stated that she saw a man about six feet tall, dressed in black, enter the premises about 20 minutes before Simpson answered the limo driver's call. When he failed to arrive at the police station on June 17, Simpson was declared a fugitive, and a warrant was issued for his arrest. What ensued was a slow-speed chase down the 405 Freeway on June 17, 1994. Once stopped, Simpson was arrested for the murders.

Murder Trial

Simpson's trial, which began January 23, 1995, was nothing short of a media spectacle. Both the defense and the prosecution were comprised of teams of lawyers, presided over by Judge Lance A. Ito. The defense team, often referred to as "The Dream Team," included Robert Shapiro, F. Lee Bailey, Alan Dershowitz, and Johnnie Cochran. Deputy District Attorney Marcia Clark led the prosecution's team, assisted by Christopher Darden.

The defense tried to spin the murders as drug related and called Faye Resnick, a friend of Nicole Brown Simpson, to testify, indicating that drug dealers had murdered Simpson and Goldman in an attempt to scare Resnick into paying off her

In 1990, O. J. Simpson was a popular sports commentator and former professional football player. Here he watches a Thanksgiving Day football game with U.S. troops.

drug debts. Mark Fuhrman, the detective who discovered the leather glove in a pool of blood at the crime scene, also came under serious fire from the defense team. Fuhrman's credibility was strained when the defense questioned him regarding his denial of using a racial epithet.

The prosecution, however, had mountains of evidence against Simpson, including DNA. Several expert witnesses testified concerning blood samples found at the scene. Barry Scheck testified on behalf of the defense, questioning the methods used by the police department when obtaining and preserving evidence. Much of the testimony was technical, and it has been argued that the jury was unable to comprehend the evidence presented. Blood samples found at the scene matched O. J. Simpson, and the blood on the socks found in the main bedroom matched that Nicole Simpson. Blood from both victims was discovered in his Bronco, and a glove matching the one found near the bodies was discovered in his home. The DNA evidence was tested at two separate facilities, and the prosecution argued this was a clear indication of Simpson's guilt. Throughout the investigation, the Los Angeles Police Department committed grievous errors, including not properly preserving the crime scene. This may have planted the seed of reasonable doubt within the jurors' minds, thus influencing their decision at the end of the trial.

The glove was tried on by Simpson in court. Cochran insisted that he wear a latex glove before trying it on, and in front of the jury and TV cameras, Simpson declared that the glove was too small. This public display has been scrutinized since the trial, with critics stating that Simpson had scrunched his hands before putting the glove on, in order to make it impossible to fit. Others insisted that a leather glove that had been soaked in blood would shrink, thus nullifying the entire demonstration.

The jury began its deliberation on October 2, 1995, and was out for only approximately five hours before a verdict. Simpson was found not guilty, a decision that seriously exacerbated already existing racial tensions nationwide. The common assumptions throughout the country regarding his guilt were heavily divided by race. The white assumption of guilt and the black assumption of innocence were only heightened by the verdict. These assumptions heavily indicate the issues within the system as viewed by members of both racial groups. A year later, however, Simpson was found to have contributed to the deaths of Nicole Brown Simpson and Ron Goldman in the civil trial brought against him. Simpson was in trouble once again in 2007, after being arrested for his participation in an armed robbery in Las Vegas. In 2008, he was convicted of armed robbery, kidnapping, and assault charges, and is currently serving a sentence of a minimum of 15 years, and will be eligible for parole after serving at least nine years.

Jeanne Subjack
Sam Houston State University

See Also: Famous Trials; Murder, Contemporary; News Media, Crime in; Trials; Violent Crimes.

Further Readings
Bugliosi, Vincent. *Outrage: The Five Reasons Why O. J. Simpson Got Away With Murder*. New York: W. W. Norton, 1996.
Dunne, Dominick. *Justice: Crimes, Trials, and Punishments*. New York: Three Rivers Press, 2002.
Fuhrman, Mark. *Murder in Brentwood*. New York: Zebra Books, 1997.

Goldman Family, the. *If I Did It: Confessions of the Killer*. New York: Beaufort Books, 2007.

Jones, Thomas L. "O. J. Simpson." http://www.trutv.com/library/crime/notorious_murders/famous/simpson/index_1 (Accessed November 25, 2010).

Sin

The concept of sin is one that today is frequently relegated to questions of theology and religious practice. However, it has also long been recognized by sociologists and historians as a foundational one in the formation of law, social organization, and social responses to deviance and crime.

What is Sin?

In the Judeo-Christian tradition, sin has been understood as an act of transgression against God or other people, as well as an ontological state of being. The former is most clearly epitomized in the Ten Commandments, as well as in the medieval Christian practice of compiling sins according to their severity (i.e., mortal and venial) or typology (i.e., the Seven Deadly Sins). The latter is most clearly epitomized in the Pauline tradition of understanding Adam and Eve's expulsion from the Garden of Eden as the beginning of "original sin," constituting an inherent state of human imperfection.

The Ten Commandments form the foundation of Judeo-Christian understanding of sin as transgression. In the Torah, the Commandments are delivered to Moses by Yahweh on Mt. Sinai and subsequently appear in slightly different forms in the *Shemot* (Exodus) and the *Devarim* (Deuteronomy). The consequences for violations were not listed along with the Commandments but rather interspersed throughout broader Mosaic law in the Torah, and included everything from restitution to death. One consequence not possible was that of eternal condemnation, or "hell." Rather, both the wicked and the righteous descended to *Sheol*, the abode of the dead.

In many respects, early Christians adopted Jewish views on laws and punishments, which was not surprising because many of them were and thought of themselves as Jews. The Apostle Paul, however, differed from many of his contemporaries by arguing that sin was not merely an act but rather a state of being that was inherent in all people. In his Epistle to the Romans (5:12), Paul argued that, "just as sin came into the world through one man, and death came through sin, and so death spread to all because all have sinned." The idea of sins being passed down through generations was not new, but Paul suggested that through Adam's original transgression, all future generations were sinners, regardless of their individual actions. For Paul, the only resolution for this state of original sin was grace, or more specifically, the acceptance of the grace of God as delivered though the suffering and subsequent resurrection of Christ.

In early Christianity however, there was much debate about the eternal consequences of sin. Origen of Alexandria (185–254 C.E.) argued, for example, that it was probable that at some time in the distant future all things would be "restored to the creator," including the souls of the wicked. At the time, in popular Hellenic thought, this was not a radical proposition. Nevertheless, it was one that was later rejected by the church, as well as by theologians such as Augustine of Hippo (354–430 C.E.), who set forth what was to be the most influential understanding of sin for at least 1,500 years. Augustine argued that individual sins, for example, carnal acts, were a result of separation from God in all people as a result of original sin. In other words, sex was not shameful until Adam and Even became "ashamed of their own nakedness" as a result of their eating from the tree of knowledge. The result of this knowledge was subsequently inherent in the human condition itself. People were not merely "sinners," they were "of sin" and thus inclined toward corruption as a result of their "nature."

In this regard, the later practice of monks in the Middle Ages, who frequently categorized and ranked "sins" according to their severity and typology, had an underlying logic. They did not believe they could free themselves from sin as an original state, but they did believe that specific acts of transgression were linked in type and in a gradient fashion that might lead them further astray from recognition of their own imperfect nature. In many respects, the lists of these sins complied by monks in the Middle Ages remain dominant in contemporary views of sin the Seven Deadly Sins, for example. The French historian Philippe Ariès provides an important clue as to why these monks placed such emphasis on their typologies and rankings of sin, and perhaps why these lists have endured to present day. Beginning in the 12th century, argued Ariès, there began a slow shift away from communal views of death and salvation, toward the idea of individual judgment. Prior to this, to be in good standing in the Catholic community was seen as a promise of salvation. Over time, however, depictions of the Book of Life increasingly resembled what Ariès termed a "personal account book" of each person's sins and deeds. To be a member of the communal church was no longer sufficient to ensure salvation; rather, salvation was increasingly seen as requiring faith and good works.

Sociology of Sin

The sociologist Stephen Pfohl has argued that sin, as it has been conceptualized in the Christian tradition, is central to what he terms a "demonic perspective" of social explanations and responses to deviance. This perspective, argues Pfohl, is the oldest of all known social explanations of deviance and views human action as existing within a larger cosmological struggle between good and evil. It was particularly dominant in the Middle Ages, when explanations of deviance were tightly bound to a religious worldview, as well as to the power of the Church, which defined many (but not all) criminal acts as a result of temptation or possession. The Salem witch trials in the late 1600s, for example, paralleled witch trials throughout Britain and continental Europe that viewed the crime of witchcraft as the result of

Sixteenth-century painter Pieter Bruegel the Elder created a work for each of the Seven Deadly Sins, all meant to serve as warnings with their depictions of debauchery and excess. U.S. settlers brought European values with them and prized hard work and frugality in the realms of politics, literature, and art, as well as working, saving, and investing.

temptation by the Devil. As Elliot Currie has noted, however, a primary difference between such trials in Britain and America, and continental Europe, was that the latter employed "trial by ordeal" (torture) as a means of extracting confessions. On the other hand, British and American trials relied on the tradition of English common law, which allowed for jury trials and the right of the accused to confront their accusers. Currie suggests that these differences reflected distinct histories between legal systems, with one consequence being that far fewer witches were tried and executed under the English common law system than in continental Europe.

Currie's argument speaks as well to differences in Protestant and Catholic views regarding the proper role of the church in the administration of criminal law. Even where many witch trials in 16th-century continental Europe were conducted by secular courts, Currie argues that the use of trial by ordeal was largely informed by the use of torture in ecclesiastical courts common throughout various inquisitions. In this vein, the Protestant Reformation set forth more than an irreconcilable theological schism. As the sociologist Max Weber argued, it also set forth, at least in part, the conditions for the historical development of capitalism. Weber proffered that the emphasis placed on original sin by Calvinists in the 16th century led to a theological quandary within their understanding of God as omniscient. If God knew everything, including the outcome of those who would be saved and those who would be damned, then such outcomes were in a sense "predestined."

Weber argued that this quandary of predestination was resolved by the Calvinists through Martin Luther's argument that worldly labor (i.e., work not directed toward charity or the benefit of the church) nevertheless constituted a legitimate "calling" that benefited individuals and society. One no longer had to be involved in higher callings such as the clergy or charity to be doing "God's work." Such works became not a means of achieving salvation but rather an obligation of grace itself, and one's likeliness of being among the elect was thus evidenced in the commitment that individuals demonstrated to work. Yet, the Puritan ethics of frugality and material depravity, argued Weber, led Calvinists to return the material fruits of their labors into further "productive" works, allowing them to amass wealth in a way that did not contradict their evidence of being elect.

This ethic of "working, saving, and investing" was for Weber a prime example of how changes in ideas led to changes in the material structures of society. Capitalism, he argued, emerged most prominently in areas in Europe and the United States where this ethic was dominant. Even where this ethic lost its overt religiosity over two centuries, noted Weber, it retained a core morality that linked material success to attributes of individual character, perhaps nowhere more so than in the United States where the narrative of the "self-made man" has long played a central role in the value placed on hard work and frugality within politics, literature, and art, and social attitudes toward wealth and social welfare.

While Weber's investigation of the Protestant work ethic was rooted in a broad historical investigation of changes in society over time, other sociologists have focused more on the social "functions" of sin. In his work *The Elementary Forms of Religious Life* (1912), Emile Durkheim argued that all societies contain systems of involving people in practices and rituals that lead to a collective sense of belonging, as well as systems of ideas that explain and make sense of the world for people. Durkheim argued that religion has historically been the primary means by which these two systems are linked in a concrete way for individuals, even where the specific forms of these systems exist as a reality sui generis. While earlier societies were characterized more by the sacredness of inanimate objects (totems) and/or ancestral worship, Durkheim argued that even modern forms of morality and law have their basis in religion. To this end, Durkheim suggested elsewhere that morality and deviance were two sides of the same coin, whereby all societies require some level of deviance to maintain a balance between social cohesion and social adaptation.

In a functionalist analysis, sin thus reflects less a uniquely religious explanation of deviance and more a means of explaining this particular form of deviance within systems of collective belonging and making sense of the world. This was an idea explored in Kai Erikson's work *Wayward Puritans* (1967), in which Erikson investigated the "society of saints" in the Puritan Massachusetts Bay

Colony in the 17th century, and found that even in this society of rigid social norms there existed a fairly standard rate of deviance experienced by the community over time. What varied, argued Erikson, were the specific types of deviants that threatened the cohesion and norms of this community: Anne Hutchinson in the 1630s, the Quakers in the 1650s, and the "witches" in the 1690s. These represented different internal or external threats to the social cohesion of the colony, argued Erikson. Yet, even in this relatively rigid society, social norms adapted as a means by which to counter these threats and maintain a sense of social stability.

Sin in America
Erikson's work also speaks to the early centrality of sin as a means of explaining and understanding the social world in early American history. In Puritan colonies such as Massachusetts Bay, sin was inexorably wound to social explanations of and responses to deviance, as in the case of the Salem witch trials. Historically as well, the concept of sin played a central role in the rise of two distinctly different but ultimately intertwining institutions in early America that justified the depravation of liberty as a result or consequence of sin. The first of these is slavery. To the degree that early slavery in the United Stated was justified as means of converting heathens, as it grew, it also saw the conversion of large numbers of slaves. By the 19th century, however, slavery was increasingly justified not as a means of salvation (where many slaves had already been converted), but rather under the "belief" that blacks were the descendants of Ham, the son of Noah, who in Genesis has cursed Ham's son Canaan and his descendants. Although the Bible says nothing about race, it was widely proffered that blacks bore the sin of Ham in the color of their skin.

While the sin of Ham was a primary justification for slavery in the 19th century, the rise of the modern penitentiary system in the northern United States was also rooted in the concept of sin, albeit in a different fashion. Early prisons such as those based on the Auburn and Pennsylvania models in the early 19th century combined hard labor with austere living conditions and solitary confinement as a means to rehabilitate offenders. The use of labor and solitary confinement were vestiges of the monastic tradition, where it was thought that the combination of hard work and religious self-reflection led to spiritual growth. The word *penitentiary* has at its core the idea of "penitence," and the early prisons of the 19th century were seen as places where criminals could be separated from their corrupting environments and learn to lead productive lives. In reality, however, many of these prisons were brutal. Floggings and other tortures were not uncommon, and prisons frequently used prisoners for profitable labor.

Reemergence of Sin
In his work *The Sacred Canopy* (1967), sociologist Peter Berger argued that in the late 19th and 20th centuries much of the Western industrialized world had become secularized. Religion as a predominant means of understanding the world had become less central to people's lives. Berger drew from a variety of sources, in particular Max Weber's idea of the "demystification" of the natural and social worlds. For Weber, Western industrial society had become increasingly characterized by the formal rationalization of social, cultural, and economic life. Highly complex bureaucratic institutions, namely, the state and the modern corporation, had largely replaced the church as predominant forms of social and economic organization.

Berger was not alone in his assessment, and it was widely held among sociologists in the mid-20th century that there was a strong causal link between processes of modernization, such as industrialism and science, and the growth of secularism. This process had not been uniform, nor had it occurred in a linear fashion. The temperance movement, for example, many of whose members viewed alcohol as a sin, was influential in passing the Volstead Act in 1919, which banned the manufacturing, sale, and distribution of alcohol. Throughout the 20th century as well, sin was frequently in the foreground as a justification for laws against homosexuality, interracial marriage, and drugs. Nevertheless, by 1967, Berger had good reason for his thesis. Church attendance had been falling for some time; religion by this point played only a perfunctory role in national politics (although in some regions a much larger role); and in the case of social responses to crime, the predominant approach was a mix of social programs (i.e., the war on poverty) and, for criminal offenders, rehabilitation programs.

By the end of the 20th century, however, Berger's thesis was quite different. The world, he argued, was not becoming less religious, and in many ways over the latter part of the 20th century it had become more so. Most notable was the emergence of fundamentalist Christian movements in Europe, Latin America, Asia, and particularly the United States. Islam had also continued to grow in the Middle East but also in Africa, Asia, Indonesia, and other areas. Berger called this resurgence of religion a type of "counter-secularization," particularly where it involved the rapid growth of fundamentalism in countries such as the United States, even where participation in mainstream Protestant denominations had continued to wane. It was no longer the religious enclaves of modernity that required explication, argued Berger, but rather the secular holdouts.

The significant growth of fundamentalist religious movements in the United States, beginning in the early 1970s, had significant political and social consequences. As the sociologist Robert Wuthnow has argued, the failure of more traditional forms of political conservatism in the late 1960s, which had focused primarily on fiscal restraint and anticommunism, set the stage for the emergence of more grassroots-based evangelical movements that viewed questions of individual morality as legitimate political platforms. Organizations such as Moral Majority and Focus on the Family helped to push questions of "traditional" morality, particularly abortion and homosexuality, to the forefront of politics in the 1980s and early 1990s. With the election of Ronald Reagan, the nation experienced a shift toward conservatism, but in particular, a type of conservatism that brought the concept of sin into the forefront of politics and policy in a way that had not occurred for perhaps a century or more.

In the beginning of the 21st century, the concept of sin continues to play a dominant yet contested role in social understandings of crime and deviance. Debates over the placing of the Ten Commandments in courtrooms and schools, over the protesting of military funerals by the Westboro Baptist Church in Kansas, and over "sins" such as abortion, homosexuality, and the teaching of evolution have become central in American politics. These debates have spilled over more directly as well into questions of social responses to crime. Under George W. Bush, for example, a significant emphasis was placed on "faith-based" initiatives such as the Prison Fellow Ministries as a means of rehabilitating prison inmates, a move criticized by opponents for the use of public funds to proselytize prisoners. More recently, the move toward drug-testing welfare recipients reflects an assumption that those who do not engage in productive work must prove their moral worthiness to receive such benefits, a policy that echoes Weber's causal link between morality and hard work in the Puritan work ethic.

These debates signify a real and sustained shift in American views on the relationship between religion and sin, and crime and deviance. However, the biggest shift has been an increased polarization in American social and political attitudes around the proper role of religion and "sin" in public policy and polity. Each side of these debates sees the other as largely "winning," either in the increasing secularization and immorality of the United States or, conversely, in the increasing influence of fundamentalism and conservative religious morality. In this sense, the "re-emergence" of sin in American politics and society has brought into question what Durkheim identified as structures of belonging and structures of meaning in a way that has not occurred since at least the Great Depression. Even in the face of the most severe economic crises in 70 years, debates surrounding sin and morality remain central to politics and social life in the United States.

William R. Wood
University of Auckland

See Also: Abortion; African Americans; Bible; Capital Punishment; Colonial Courts; History of Crime and Punishment in America: Colonial; Massachusetts; Morality; Puritans; Racism; Religion and Crime, History of; Religion and Crime, Sociology of; Salem Witch Trials; Slavery.

Further Readings
Berger, P. *The Sacred Canopy: Elements of a Sociological Theory of Religion*. New York: Doubleday, 1967.

Currie, Elliot. "Crimes Without Criminals: Witchcraft and Its Control in Renaissance Europe." *Law & Society Review*, v.3/1 (1968).

Durkheim, Emile. *The Elementary Forms of Religious Life*. New York: The Free Press, [1912] 1995.

Erikson, Kai. *Wayward Puritans*. New York: John Wiley, 1967.

Pfohl, Stephen. *Images of Deviance and Social Control: A Sociological History*. New York: McGraw-Hill, 1994.

Weber, Max. *The Protestant Ethic and the Spirit of Capitalism*. London: Unwin, [1905] 1985.

Sing Sing Correctional Facility

Sing Sing is New York's second-oldest continuously occupied state prison. Opened in 1826, the institution still functions as a maximum-security prison. Sing Sing is located near Ossining, New York, and its name is thought to be derived from "Sinck Sinck," the name of a group of Native Americans who originally inhabited the area. Sing Sing was the third New York state prison built, following Newgate (1797–1828) and Auburn (opened 1816).

The prison's construction and early administration were overseen by former Auburn Prison warden and army captain Elam Lynds, who became infamous for his brutality. Operating under the Auburn (or New York) system of penal discipline, inmates were housed separately at night but worked together in factories on the prison grounds. Because inmates spent most of their time working, Sing Sing's cells were initially only seven feet long by three wide and six feet seven inches high. At all times, inmates were forbidden to speak to one another under pain of physical punishment. Moreover, inmates were required to march in lockstep when transported to or from their cells, and failure to maintain military discipline usually resulted in physical punishment. Though Lynds did not design this system, he methodically and brutally enforced it through floggings. Despite his

Sing Sing prison in Ossining, New York, circa 1910. In 1825, 100 convicted criminals were transported from the Auburn Prison to the new site of Sing Sing prison, but no structure stood to house them. Prisoner labor was used to excavate marble from a nearby quarry and construct the prison. Like most post–Civil War American prisons, Sing Sing became overcrowded and cells that were hardly large enough for one inmate (less than 125 square feet) were used for two or three prisoners.

fearsome reputation, Lynds enjoyed the support of some New York legislators because Sing Sing's factory system consistently produced a profit; this was in marked contrast to the prison's ideological rival, Eastern State Penitentiary, which was never profitable. In many ways, the Auburn system was eclipsed by the reformatory movement pioneered by Zebulon Brockway in the 1870s, and the Auburn system's distinctive features (silence, marching in lockstep) slowly disappeared. Unfortunately, Sing Sing also experienced the pervasive overcrowding that affected most American prisons after the Civil War, so cells that were barely large enough to house a single inmate became home to two and sometimes even three, degrading living conditions at the prison.

Reform Attempts

Periodic calls for reform bore fruit in the early 20th century with the benevolent administrations of Thomas Mott Osborne (1914–16) and Lewis Lawes (1920–41). Osborne was a wealthy industrialist and political reformer who was twice elected mayor of Auburn, New York, and was appointed to the New York State Public Services Commission. In 1913, Osborne was appointed to the New York State Commission on Prison Reform; he then had himself incarcerated at Auburn to get a sense of how the prison worked from the inmate perspective. Osborne wrote a book about his experiences, *Within These Walls*, and was named Sing Sing's warden in 1914, after which he instituted sweeping reforms. The best-known and most controversial reform was the Mutual Welfare League, which created an inmate-administered "government" that was given partial responsibility for enacting and enforcing prison regulations. Because of this, Osborne ran afoul of entrenched political interests both inside and outside the prison, and his political enemies engineered Osborne's indictment for perjury, mismanagement of the prison, and engaging in sexual relations with the inmates. Though Osborne was acquitted of these charges and briefly returned to Sing Sing, he resigned shortly thereafter.

Osborne's short tenure at Sing Sing was distressingly common; between 1900 and 1919, the prison had 10 different wardens, each averaging less than two years in office. This all changed in 1920 when Lewis Lawes became Sing Sing's warden. Lawes was in many ways very similar to Osborne: Lawes introduced or expanded Sing Sing's educational and recreational programs as a method of reforming inmates. In addition, Lawes oversaw the construction of several new cellblocks and ancillary buildings in an attempt to transform the aging penitentiary into a modern prison. He encouraged celebrities to visit the prison, many of whom entertained the inmates. Lawes also allowed, and even encouraged, directors to film movies at the prison; some of these included *The Big House* (1930) and *Castle on the Hudson* (1940). There was even a film adaptation of one of Lawes's book, *20,000 Years at Sing Sing* (1932), starring Spencer Tracy.

Despite all of Lawes's attempts at reform, Sing Sing's fearsome reputation (perhaps burnished by the movies he encouraged directors to set at the prison) only grew. In part, this was because the prison was the site of 614 spectacular and gruesome executions. The prison's electric chair was installed in 1891, and by 1916, all of New York's executions took place at Sing Sing. This necessitated a "death house," or a place where inmates waiting to be executed could be segregated from the general population, which only added to the prison's infamy.

Today, Sing Sing continues operation as a maximum-security state prison. In 1983, a massive riot broke out at the prison and 17 guards were held hostage for two days, a testament to the ongoing tensions within Sing Sing. Due to its infamous history of brutality, the prison looms large in the American popular consciousness and has contributed the phrases *up the river* (meaning going to jail) and *the big house* (the prison itself) to the American lexicon. Moreover, the prison is frequently referenced in movies, novels, musicals, and video games, perpetuating its legend.

Paul Kahan
Montgomery County Community College

See Also: Auburn State Prison; Penitentiaries; Pennsylvania System of Reform; Prison Riots.

Further Readings
Brian, Denis. *Sing Sing: The Inside Story of a Notorious Prison*. Amherst, NY: Prometheus Press, 2005.

Cox, Stephen. *The Big House: Image and Reality of the American Prison.* New Haven, CT: Yale University Press, 2009.

Lewis, W. David. *From Newgate to Dannemora: The Rise of the Penitentiary in New York, 1796–1848.* Ithaca, NY: Cornell University Press, 2009.

Sirhan Sirhan

Sirhan Bishara Sirhan is a Palestinian-born assassin who killed Senator Robert F. Kennedy (RFK) on June 5, 1968, in the Ambassador Hotel in Los Angeles following Kennedy's Democratic primary victory in California. Born on March 19, 1944, in Jerusalem to Palestinian Christian parents, Sirhan and his family witnessed the destruction of their homeland from the 1948 Arab-Jewish War. Pivotal to the development of Sirhan's later geopolitical beliefs, his family was forced to leave Jerusalem when Sirhan was 4-years-old, though not before Sirhan witnessed several violent attacks. According to psychiatrists who later evaluated Sirhan after the RFK assassination, these incidents took a toll psychologically that resulted in Sirhan suffering from multiple neuroses as a child, including bed wetting, nail biting, fear of the dark, and insecurity about his body. When he was eight years old, Sirhan witnessed the death of his brother, Munir, who was struck by a runaway army truck. At 12 years old, Sirhan and his family secured the sponsorship of two families from the First Nazarene Church in Pasadena, California, to immigrate to the United States. Although Sirhan was resistant to moving to the United States based on his belief that the United States was aligned with Israel and therefore the enemy of Arabs, his family traveled to New York City in 1957, settling in California soon thereafter.

Struggling to acculturate after settling in Pasadena, Sirhan's father, Bishara, was described by others as physically abusive toward his wife, Mary, and Sirhan. Distraught over the loss of his patriarchal status as his family embraced Western values as well as his difficulty finding adequate employment, Sirhan's father abandoned his family in 1958 and returned to the Middle East, leaving Sirhan without a father and a mother raising him and his four siblings alone. Initially placed two grades below his same-age peers, Sirhan impressed his teachers as polite through junior high school. While Sirhan began to express anti-American sentiments during high school, he became much more vocal in his Arab nationalism and hatred of Jews as a student at Pasadena City College. During this period, Sirhan began attending meetings of the Organization of Arab Students. After earning five F's, however, Sirhan was dismissed from school for poor attendance.

Forced to find employment, Sirhan obtained a variety of odd jobs, including working at several service stations, as an assistant to a gardener, and at several horse tracks. Describing his time working at the Granja Vista del Rio Thoroughbred Horse Farm to NBC News, Sirhan stated that this job was "the most enjoyable experience of my life." Following two horse-riding accidents, however, Sirhan was fired from this job. Disappointed at the demise of his goal of becoming a jockey, Sirhan began drinking, gambling, and experimenting with mysticism. Motivated by his reading, Sirhan applied to join a Rosicrucian order in San Jose, California, and began practicing "white magic," including staring at lit candles to improve his mental powers. After nearly one

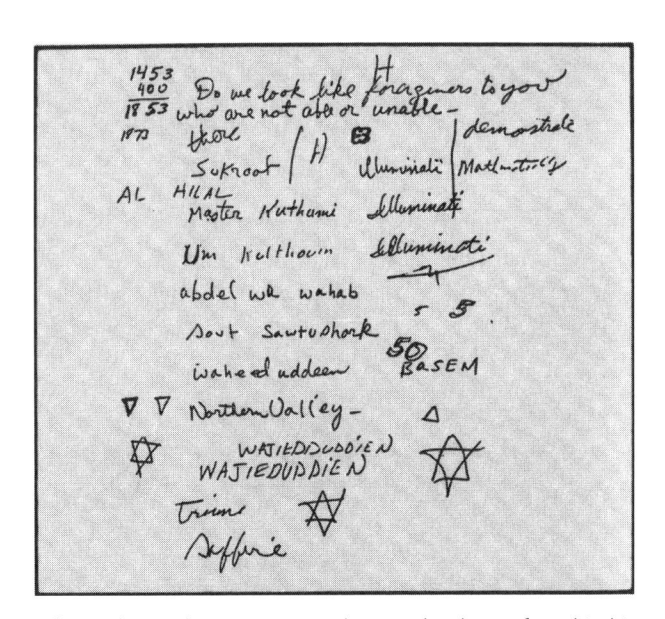

After Sirhan Sirhan was arrested, a notebook was found in his apartment containing diary entries that seemed to focus his anger on Robert Kennedy, who had made campaign promises to send 50 fighter jets to Israel if he were elected president.

year of unemployment, Sirhan's mother became concerned and helped him to secure a job in a health food store. However, Sirhan was fired after less than a year because of an altercation with his boss that culminated in an angry Sirhan airing his grievances against the store owner to a local labor tribunal, to no avail. During this brief period of employment, Sirhan engaged several coworkers in heated debates in which he expressed strong Arab nationalist views. On May 16, 1968, Sirhan watched a CBS documentary, "The Story of Robert Kennedy," on television. Due to RFK's support of Israel, Sirhan wrote, "Robert Kennedy must die..." in his notebook two days later.

Hiding in the pantry of the Ambassador Hotel in Los Angeles on June 5, 1968, following RFK's victory speech after winning the California Democratic primary, Sirhan fired eight shots at RFK and his aides, killing Kennedy and wounding five others. Leading up to his trial, Sirhan underwent extensive psychological and psychiatric evaluation with eight different clinicians. With one exception, all of the psychologists agreed on a diagnosis of paranoid schizophrenia; however, Sirhan refused to introduce a mental disability defense at trial. While a variety of conspiracy theories would surround the case, Sirhan was convicted on April 17, 1969, and sentenced to death on April 23, 1969. Following the California Supreme Court's decision in *California v. Anderson* in 1972, Sirhan's death sentence was commuted to life in prison, where he continues to undergo parole hearings every five years.

Aaron J. Kivisto
Massachusetts General Hospital

See Also: California; *Furman v. Georgia*; Kennedy, Robert F.; Murder, History of; Retributivism.

Further Readings
Ayton, M. *The Forgotten Terrorist: Sirhan Sirhan and the Assassination of Robert F. Kennedy*. Dulles, VA: Potomac Books, 2007.
Meloy, J. R. "Revisiting the Rorschach of Sirhan Sirhan." *Journal of Personality Assessment*, v.58 (1992).
Moldea, D. E. *The Killing of Robert F. Kennedy: An Investigation of Motive, Means, and Opportunity*. New York: W. W. Norton, 1995.

Slave Patrols

Slave patrols were public efforts to regulate slavery. They were part of a broader trend of restrictions placed on slaves and their movements. Slave patrols were initiated in the 16th and 17th centuries in the West Indies by English and Spanish settlers. Patrols grew out of colonial efforts to regulate slavery by creating laws to restrict slaves that required all white colonists to assist in enforcing the resulting slave codes. In South Carolina, for instance, landowners were obligated to punish slaves who wandered onto their property. Slave patrols were charged with questioning wandering slaves, dispersing slave gatherings, searching slave quarters, and patrolling roads between settlements.

In towns and cities, slave patrols usually operated on foot, investigating suspicious gatherings and questionable behavior. After slavery was established in the south, slave patrols were adopted as a way of policing the enslaved population. White southerners were determined to maintain their dominant social position. White citizens were induced to serve on slave patrols through various penalties and inducements such as fines or tax abatements. Substitutes could be hired for those who wished not to perform their turn at patrol service. Many patrollers were nonslaveholders who came to resent their forced duty that largely benefited the elite planter class. The slave patrols evolved from impromptu voluntary vigilante groups to organized institutions staffed by salaried civil servants.

Justification

Slave patrols were established as a reaction to white southerners' pervasive fear that with respect to the potential lawlessness of slaves, including the possibility of an outright rebellion. These fears were partly based on real concerns as slaves were far more numerous than whites in many parts of the south, and there had been instances of slave violence against whites and even of bloody insurrections. For example, in 1739 in Stono, South Carolina, several dozen intoxicated slaves armed with knives and guns set out for Florida, where they would be free; on the way, they slaughtered more than two dozen whites. Other notable acts of insurgency by slaves included the Gabriel Prosser conspiracy of 1800 and Nat Turner's Rebellion in 1831, both of which were in Virginia.

In response to these actions, many restrictions were imposed on slaves across the south. These slave codes included measures, for instance, where a slave could not be off a plantation without a specific pass from the master. Many communities passed laws that required most white males to serve as members of armed patrols; certain professionals were exempt from serving.

Slave patrols were charged with monitoring the activities of slaves. The patrols could stop and question unaccompanied slaves anywhere, and if they could not produce a note from their master or an identification pass, the patrol could seize and hold them. Slave patrols generally functioned as an agent of intimidation to suppress the enslaved populace, as well as free blacks. It became common practice for patrols to beat and sometimes maim blacks, enslaved or free, they encountered, with little fear of repercussion. In effect, the state legitimized violence against slaves through these patrols. Slave patrols searched slave quarters and homes looking not only for runaway slaves but also for weapons, stolen goods, and evidence of literacy such as books, paper, and pens. A patrol returning a runaway slave to a master generally received a bounty.

Organization

Two major models were followed in creating slave patrols. The patrols were sometimes linked with compulsory local militia units intended to protect white settlers from Native Americans, foreign invasion, and other hostile threats. The militia model was used, for example, in South Carolina and Virginia. In other places, such as North Carolina and Texas, county courts were charged with forming local committees that were responsible for creating slave patrols to cover their territory.

In 1704, South Carolina was the first U.S. colony to establish slave patrols. Virginia formed its first slave patrol in 1727. In 1757, the Georgia colonial assembly passed An Act for Establishing and Regulating of Patrols, which required white citizens to serve on patrols of seven or fewer riders to work in districts that were 12 square miles. In 1811, militia officers in the Natchez District in Mississippi were ordered to form patrols in response to a slave uprising in the neighboring parish of St. John Baptist along Lake Pontchartrain, Louisiana, where about 500 slaves had organized and marched toward New Orleans. In 1822, a statute was passed in Mississippi that made each militia captain responsible for maintaining a list of slave patrol detachments of three men each, which were obligated to perform patrol duties once every three weeks. This law was repealed in 1833, when another Mississippi statute granted each Board of County Police the authority to appoint leaders of patrols for each police district. In 1822, another statute in Mississippi authorized slave patrols to kill all dogs owned by slaves. In 1825, Arkansas passed its first regulation establishing slave patrols. In Texas, officials became concerned about the number of slaves escaping to Mexico. In 1846, the Texas legislature directed county courts to form local patrols to cover specific districts. In the antebellum south, every slaveholding state had established slave patrols, principally to prevent slave rebellions.

After passage of the 1850 Fugitive Slave Law, federal commissioners were appointed for every county in the country, charged with responsibility for enforcing the law. Further, U.S. marshals and, if necessary, the U.S. Army, could also be used to return runaway slaves. In 1857, the southern-dominated U.S. Supreme Court under Chief Justice Roger B. Taney handed down the *Dred Scott* decision, which asserted that slaves, and even free blacks, were not citizens and had essentially no rights. The pervasive paranoia on the part of southern whites against slave violence and resistance was fueled by the continued existence of slave patrols. Slave patrols generally came to an end with the cessation of the Civil War. However, the sentiments that led to the formation and maintenance of slave patrols led to the emergence of groups like the Ku Klux Klan during Reconstruction as well as to the evolution of modern policing and, perhaps, also to the tacit acceptance of violence toward African Americans by police.

Victor B. Stolberg
Essex County College

See Also: Buchanan, James (Administration of); *Dred Scott v. Sandford*; Ku Klux Klan; Slavery; Slavery, Law of.

Further Readings

Campbell, Stanley W. *The Slave Catchers: Enforcement of the Fugitive Slave Law, 1850–1860.* Chapel Hill: University of North Carolina Press, 1970.

Hadden, Sally E. *Slave Patrols: Laws and Violence in Virginia and the Carolinas.* Cambridge, MA: Harvard University Press, 2001.

Henry, Howell M. "The Police Control of the Slave in South Carolina." Ph.D. diss., Vanderbilt University, 1914.

Reichel, Philip L. "Southern Slave Patrols as a Transitional Police Type." *American Journal of Police*, v.7/2 (1988).

Slavery

There is a fundamental difference between societies that exist with slavery and those that are based upon it. In the world before about 1450, slavery was not an institution as such; rather, it was simply a part of life. The Narmer Palette, an ancient Egyptian artifact depicting the ascension of Narmer, the first pharaoh of the Old Kingdom, depicts Narmer towering over his conquered foes and either crushing them with a macelike object or driving them before him in chains. Traditional slavery is often represented in this way. This type of slavery persists to the present day in many areas dominated by tribal cultures. Individuals or groups were taken by war parties and then used as personal slaves when the conquering group returned home. In most cases, slaves took part in domestic work and often became part of the family unit they were brought into, raising and caring for children or functioning as housekeepers. In such systems, slaves and other subject classes such as laborers had a porous relationship. Slaves who proved their worth often worked their way into other parts of the lower classes, and in rare cases, went up the social ladder. Systems such as these supported only small slave markets, because of the small-scale nature and limited opportunity for slave acquisition. Because of the nature of records from the earliest periods, it is extremely challenging to arrive at specific numbers or percentages for slave populations.

Early History

Slavery was viewed as a circumstance and as a natural part of life. Aristotle's "great chain of being" was a constructed hierarchy meant to explain the existence of all of the various levels of human society. Traces of this manner of thinking were visible for centuries after Aristotle's time. In his case, the top of the hierarchy was the Athenian citizen, and the slave (anyone not of Greek birth) was at the bottom of the pile. For Aristotle and his contemporaries, slavery was a method of existence that suited certain groups far better than others. For this reason, slaves were normally sought outside one's home territory, because they were seen as more "naturally inclined" for enslavement and less likely to revolt. Many ancient Greek city-states had a significant slave populations. It is estimated that almost all citizen-owned homes had at least one slave in the 5th and 6th centuries B.C.E. in Athens, for example. In the system of many of the city-states, it was possible for a slave to save up the small wage he earned for his work and purchase his freedom. This was reflected particularly in the records of Athens, along with various rules for slave treatment, such as a prohibition on physically striking a slave. In addition, many classifications of slaves existed within Athens: The house slave

A correspondent for Harper's Weekly *in 1860 reported on a slave ship that had been captured by an American steamer with more than 400 illegally imported slaves onboard.*

was a domestic servant, the public slave served as a scribe or keeper of records for the city government, and the freelance slave was essentially independent, but paid his owner a tax. The type of slave most familiar to a contemporary reader is the war slave, a slave taken during a raid or battle. This slave was forced into unskilled labor, such as rowing a ship or undertaking public building projects, and was often chained by the neck to other slaves in a chain-gang arrangement.

Roman slavery was at first similar to traditional forms of slavery. A farmer bought a slave taken during some campaign of warfare, then used him for assistance in farming his land. As the Roman Republic aged and grew in size, slavery took on modern characteristics. The Roman economy was largely based on slaves—they performed a huge number of functions—they farmed, mined, performed unskilled labor, moved trade goods from one locale to another, and in some cases, collected the taxes for municipalities. Although the Romans took slaves from many sources, the main area of collection was Asia Minor, where an estimated 10,000 slaves were moved each day in Delos, the largest of the slave markets. Slaves were employed throughout the empire, but the largest concentrations were in the mining areas—present-day Spain, for example, or the "breadbasket" areas such as Etruria, where they were used in field labor in a way similar to the American and West Indian system of plantation slavery. In urban areas, such as Rome, slaves were put to work in many domestic fields. Female slaves often worked as housekeepers or caretakers for children, and male slaves (often Greeks) were sometimes employed by upper-class families as tutors for their children.

Slaves could be freed for essentially any reason that a master decided. The entire process was to appear before a regional judge and sign a paper of "manumission," which granted freedman status to the slave. Slaves were also often freed at the time of their master's death in a will. Although slaves existed in a non-person status during the Roman Republic, some later emperors took steps to reform slavery in the Roman Empire. Claudius passed a referendum that stated that all abandoned slaves became free; under Nero, slaves gained the right to complain formally against their masters; and Antoninus Pius declared that slaves could not be executed without reason, and if they were, their masters could be tried for murder.

Slavery in the United States

Several aspects of slavery that were present in the ancient world carried forward into and through the ascendency of European imperial powers and their offspring, such as the United States. English colonies, especially those in the Caribbean, had a particular taste for chattel slaves, which were treated as property in the Roman sense, rather than a person who happened to be enslaved, such as in the Greek or traditional Middle Eastern thought processes. Caribbean slavery was used, in one scholar's view, as a testing ground for various crops and farming techniques. Over a period of roughly 50 years in the mid-18th century, the British learned that plantation agriculture with one specific sort of crop was far more conducive to the use of slave labor than a diversified and changing planting schedule, which required slaves to have experience with various crops and, furthermore, gave them access to a variety of tools, which could be used as weapons in uprisings against white masters, for example, the uprising of Toussaint l'Ouverture in the French slave plantation of St. Domingue, which was run in a similar style to a British colony such as Jamaica.

The lessons and methods drawn from Jamaica and Barbados were transplanted almost fully into the American south. Slave labor was not particularly useful in colonies north of Virginia, because the sorts of crops grown were not as labor intensive as those grown from Virginia going south, such as tobacco, and rice (South Carolina), and cotton (Mississippi). Although the British tried several forms of slave labor, including Native American slavery and indentured, contracted servitude, a number of issues made the continuation of such practices almost worthless. Escapes were common among Native American slaves, who knew the lay of the land far better than their masters. Indentured servants had a great deal of social mobility, because they could easily escape their contracted master and go to a different township or colony and have very little issue with assimilation. Furthermore, indentured servants were freed after a time and were legally given a plot of land and a "freedom stipend," which meant that over time, indentured servants took the knowledge they gained while working their master's land and used those techniques to build competitive, albeit much smaller, farms.

The most common and longest-lasting slavery institution in America, particularly the south, was the enslavement of blacks from Africa. Much like Jamaica or Barbados, the southern United States' climate was well suited for growing tobacco, rice, and cotton. Growing and harvesting these crops is very time consuming and in some cases very dangerous to maintain and process. Therefore, African slaves, seen as chattel by those who owned them, were seen as an economic necessity.

Slaves and slavery in the U.S. south were key catalysts for the Civil War. Although not ostensibly a war based on the elimination or retention of slavery as a means of production, overwhelming evidence exists that politicians in both the federal government and state and local governments were concerned about the admission of new states to the Union, which would tip the free slave state balance in favor of either direction. Tensions over slavery erupted first in Kansas, and then in Virginia. John Brown, a radical abolitionist, beheaded several suspected slaveholders in the Kansas Territory and then led a raid with the help of his numerous sons and daughters, along with other radical abolitionists, to assault the National Armory in Harper's Ferry, Virginia. Brown's stated purpose was to bring to light the evil of slavery and to start a war against it; however, present interpretations of these events based on Brown's letters and recorded conversations indicate that he had a desire to become a martyr for abolition.

Effect of the Thirteenth Amendment
Lincoln's 1863 Emancipation Proclamation freed the slaves in "enemy territories" throughout the United States, and so effectively did nothing outside Union-held territory, although at that time, the Union Army had already taken a great deal of the slave south. After the war and reunification of the United States into one legislative body, the Thirteenth Amendment formally abolished chattel slavery in the United States. Regardless, a number of forms of enslavement persist to the present day. Convict slavery, that is, the use of prison convicts as forced, hard laborers with little or no recompense to the inmate in question, was enforced by the wording of the Thirteenth Amendment, which freed all other forms of slaves.

Wording in the document reveals that slavery was completely abolished, except that which was given as a penalty for the commission of a crime. A great deal of scholarship has gone into the level of involvement that these prisoner slaves had in recreating the infrastructure of the American south during Reconstruction following the Civil War. Although a number of former slaves and white abolitionists argued against this practice, court cases such as the 1871 decision handed down in *Ruffkin v. Commonwealth* (Virginia) stated that when a person was placed into criminal custody, all of his rights and his estate likewise were forfeit. This sort of legislation is reminiscent of the Roman slave model, which maintained that a person enslaved was to be treated as a dead person. Because of how the Thirteenth Amendment was worded, Virginia was granted sovereignty on the issue of prisoner treatment, and so the federal government was helpless to effect any change. Key scholars have argued that because of this legislation, the vast majority of the infrastructure of the Reconstruction-era south was rebuilt by prisoner slave labor that was overwhelmingly black. States holding sovereignty on this issue could, and did, create unequal treatment under the law for black and white offenders, which led to a massive disparity in the racial demographics of prisons, and thus prisoner slaves, in the Reconstruction south.

The ability for correctional facilities to "lease" their prisoners to go work for private companies stirred a great deal of controversy at the turn of the 20th century, particularly among labor union leaders who were concerned that unpaid convict labor would overwhelm wage-earning labor because of the lower cost. As early as 1913, legal agitation for the end of prisoner slavery was presented before a number of courts in the United States. Arguments made by a Rhode Island ex-convict in 1913 were similar to views expressed by Adam Smith in 1776's *The Wealth of Nations*—that wage labor was superior to free, and that the convict who volunteered to work would do a far better job than the one forced to work. Furthermore, the point was made that if the state was actually attempting to rehabilitate a prisoner, it should always, without question, be voluntary. The system of convict leasing was abolished in 1928 in Alabama, the last state to allow its practice. Other forms

Africans being auctioned off in front of a crowd of men in the southern United States circa 1861. By the 1800s, slavery was illegal in the United States, but the fact that existing slaves were not freed in the south helped lead to the Civil War.

of forced prison labor continued, though. Chain gangs, for example, were and are a central figure in American prison mythology. Although these have largely fallen out of use in the United States, Alabama attempted to reinstate the practice in the mid-1990s, although it was called off soon after re-establishment because of pressure from various civil liberties groups.

Other Types of Slavery

Sexual slavery was a common practice in the ancient world and remains one to the present day. Although women were heavily trafficked in Greece, Rome, the ancient Middle East, and other areas, the issue came to the forefront for Britons in the late 18th and early 19th centuries. Although there had been concern about the enslavement of whites in the Middle East and north Africa for quite some time, the practice was highly publicized in Elizabeth Marsh's 1769 *The Female Captive*, a narrative of her captivity in Morocco. Marsh's story contained descriptions of not only her captivity but also the seduction that she underwent in the palace of a Moroccan prince. Although in Marsh's account, her captor never actually sexually assaults her, this book opened the door for a variety of increasingly lurid accounts and, as time wore on, concern by a number of moralists and humanitarians to end the trade of sex slaves, particularly in the Middle East. Although the present concern with sex slavery often focuses on southeast Asia and the infamous sex tourism that has become interwoven with Western perceptions of places like Thailand, there remains a sizable population of forced or coerced sex workers in the United States.

Sexual slavery, coerced prostitution, child pornography, and child prostitution were not eliminated by Victorian moralists, however. To the present, it is estimated that some 50,000 sex workers in the United States have been brought in illicitly and engage in any number of sex-related businesses. Strip clubs, street prostitution, massage parlors, and makeshift brothels in bars and other locations make up the base of many of these operations. Often, women, girls, and children are brought into the United States from locations as diverse as Latin America, the former Soviet bloc nations, and southeast Asia and are forced into prostitution stateside. Estimates for the number of people involved in this trade are difficult to ascertain, given the mobility and desired anonymity that is present. Scholars estimate that the number of persons forced into sex slavery or coerced sex work is growing steadily. Trafficking rings run by organized crime groups based in former Soviet countries, particularly Russia, and also in southeast Asia, are thought to be the major source for foreign nationals brought into the United States for these purposes.

Robert W. Watkins
Florida State University

See Also: 1600 to 1776 Primary Documents; 1777 to 1800 Primary Documents; 1801 to 1850 Primary Documents; 1851 to 1900 Primary Documents; African Americans; Slave Patrols; Slavery, Law of; State Slave Codes.

Further Readings

Davis, David Brion. *Inhuman Bondage: The Rise and Fall of Slavery in the New World*. New York: Oxford University Press, 2008.
Drescher, Seymour. *Abolition: A History of Slavery and Antislavery*. Cambridge: Cambridge University Press, 2009.
Foucault, Michel. *Discipline and Punish: The Birth of the Prison*. New York: Vintage, 1995.
Morgan, Edmund S. *American Slavery, American Freedom*. New York: W. W. Norton, 2003.

Slavery, Law of

Laws regulating slavery are as old as slavery itself, and only in the latter half of the 20th century has the world been without widespread legal forms of slavery. American laws of slavery had their origin in Roman law. They came together piecemeal and not systematically. Slavery in the United States involved municipal, state, and federal law. Centuries of Anglo-American common law affected the quotidian lives of slaves across America. Slavery dominated life in the south, and a substantial body of law made slavery functional, institutionalized, and pervasive. The relation of slavery to law is highly complex because slavery implicated many areas of the legal system from criminal law to property law, because it developed over time and in response to changing social conditions, and because it entailed many levels of government from the local to the national. In 1654, John Casor of Northampton County in Virginia, a black man, became the first legally recognized slave in America when his master, Anthony Johnson, a black colonist who had become a free man, prevailed over Casor in a court matter regarding Casor's claim of freedom. The court found that Johnson had a legitimate claim to ownership over and control of Casor. The court decision officially recognized slavery as a valid institution.

Books of history, morals, law, and economics began to address slavery extensively during the 18th century, when Europeans, particularly those in the New World, sought to reconcile the paradox that their society celebrated liberty yet perpetuated slavery. In America, the development of slavery along racial lines was more pronounced than in slave societies in previous eras and regions. In early America, moreover, the institution of slavery retained elements of medieval laws and ethos holding that, as Augustine proclaimed, slaves should be treated as brothers in Christ and that a baptized slave had to be manumitted. But these ideas gradually faded as the American system of slavery hardened during the course of the 18th century and reached the height of its intensity during the 19th century.

Slave Codes

Individual states had their own slave codes that, among other things, defined who qualified as slaves, detailed punishments for assisting escaped slaves, regulated relationships between whites and slaves, prohibited sexual intercourse between different races, and explained the rights of masters over their slaves. Children of slaves followed the condition of their mother into bondage. Laws regulating slavery were mostly consistent at the state level, but they varied from state to state. In 1740, South Carolina became the first state to forbid the education of slaves. Other states followed suit, usually making slave education punishable by fine. Slaves were typically flogged for learning how to read or write. By law, masters could dictate to slaves the type of work slaves were to perform, the amount or kind of clothing slaves could wear, and the rights of property slaves could enjoy.

To varying degrees, slave codes authorized violence as a technique for punishing slaves. Branding and whipping were frequently employed forms of punishment. Other forms included slitting the nose or an ear. Slave codes generally treated slaves as persons in criminal matters but as property in all other matters. Some civil cases, interpreting these slave codes, deemed slaves to have the legal status of a horse or a buggy. The North Carolina case *State v. Mann* notoriously declared that the "power of the master must be absolute to render the submission of the slave perfect." Courts treated slaves differently from time to time and place to place. In *Ford v. Ford*, a Tennessee case, the court wrote, "A slave is not in the condition of a horse or an ox. His liberty is restrained, it is true.... But he is made after the image of the Creator. He has mental capacities, and an immortal principle in his nature, that constitute him equal to his owner but for the accidental position in which fortune has placed him." State laws criminalized black rape of white women but did not criminalize the reverse. In South Carolina, according to that state's Negro Act, the murder of a slave by a white man constituted a misdemeanor only. Criminal trials against slaves were not always held in courtrooms; sometimes, they were held in stores or taverns.

One slave code—the one passed by the Louisiana legislature in 1806—took away slaves' rights to institute any legal action whatsoever. These laws eliminated slaves' previous right to petition the courts for sale away from abusive masters. These same slave codes authorized the criminal prosecution of any individual who mutilated, killed, or severely mistreated a slave. Nevertheless, Louisiana appellate courts rarely heard appeals from criminal trials for cruelty against slaves. If a slave did not prevail in his initial cause of action, he had little recourse available to him.

Property and Criminal Laws

Property and contract law dominated rules about buying and selling slaves. Many if not most slave sales took place at court sales or slave auctions—spectacles meant to degrade and ensure the perpetuation of white supremacy. A slave trader might have been sued for fraud or for breach of warranty for selling a "defective" slave. A slave owner might have sued a hirer or overseer for damaging a slave. Some states criminalized the abuse of leased slaves on the grounds that the hirer or overseer had destroyed or impaired property. Some states designated slaves as freehold property to distinguish slaves from chattel property. Freehold property was property that was not severable from an owner's estate. Cases for fraud or deceit reached the courts when buyers of slaves sued sellers for falsely alleging—often in writing—that purchased slaves had a good character and did not, for example, drink, steal, or run away. Slaves were included in divisions of assets in probate court or for foreclosure of property. Masters could also use slaves to hold liens.

In the courtroom, as elsewhere, slaves were treated differently than whites. Slaves generally could not testify against whites in courts of law because they did not count as people unless they were being punished. This was not always the case. During the period of American history from the Revolutionary War to the 1820s, some courts admitted evidence of slaves in both capital and noncapital cases. A slave's testimony usually was admissible only if two witnesses were present to corroborate the slave's account. Some laws required slaves to take an oath that they were Christians before being allowed to testify. One South Carolina law required preliminary examinations of all potential slave witnesses, after which the judge would decide which evidence would be admissible during trial.

Manumission laws regulated and in some cases restricted the freeing of slaves by their owners. Vermont was the first state to require manumission of slaves within its territory. A typical manumission law might have mandated that owners post bond for each slave he freed. It also might have required owners to petition local courts and to provide notice of manumission. Manumission laws sometimes but not always required manumitted slaves to leave the state in which they had been enslaved. News of slave rebellions, both real and fictional, resulted in stricter manumission laws. Plotting slave rebellions was a prosecutable offense.

Even after the Civil War, all southern states enacted Black Codes, which were regulations maintaining an unofficial, de facto system of slavery. Black Codes replaced slave codes in form and function. Black Codes controlled such activities as migration and labor among former slaves. Although these codes allowed former slaves the right to marry and own property, they also mandated labor contracts, the violation of which entailed criminal penalties involving, among other things, physical labor. Black Codes also prevented blacks from testifying against whites in courts of law.

Federal Laws

The most famous laws about slavery developed at the national rather than at the state level. They involved the admission of new states into the Union, an issue that mobilized proslavery and antislavery activists alike. Promulgated by the Congress of the Confederation, the Northwest Ordinance of 1787, also known as the Freedom Ordinance, created the Northwest Territory and prohibited slavery in that region. The Missouri Compromise of 1820 prohibited slavery in the former Louisiana Territory north of the 36°30' parallel. The compromise did not prohibit slavery in the proposed state of Missouri. The Kansas-Nebraska Act, which created the territories of Kansas and Nebraska, repealed the Missouri Comprise and allowed settlers to those regions to vote to allow or abolish slavery there. Passage of this act resulted in violent border disputes that came to be known as "Bleeding Kansas."

The international slave trade was banned in America according to Article One, Section Nine, Clause One of the U.S. Constitution. This provision was a heated topic during the Philadelphia Convention of 1787, which designed the Constitution to replace the Articles of Confederation.

The Philadelphia Convention also established that three-fifths of the slave population would count for tax and apportionment purposes. Many southerners had wanted to count slaves as full people in order to secure for the southern states a greater power in national affairs.

The Fugitive Slave Act of 1793 was a precursor to the Fugitive Slave Act of 1850. The Fugitive Slave Act of 1793 provided for the return of slaves who had fled slave states for free territory. The Fugitive Slave Act passed by Congress in 1850 required citizens and authorities in non–slave states to return runaway slaves to their masters in slave states. The 1850 act was meant as a compromise between southern slaveholders and northern free-soilers. By making northerners complicit in the institution and perpetuation of slavery, the 1850 act forced northerners to either accept or refuse slavery as a systemic practice.

Dred Scott v. Sandford was probably the most notable U.S. Supreme Court ruling on slavery. Decided in 1857, with southern Chief Justice Roger B. Taney writing for the majority, the opinion maintained that Congress did not have the power to create citizenship for slaves, that free slaves were not citizens as contemplated by the U.S. or Missouri constitutions, that the Missouri Compromise was unconstitutional, and that the right of property in slaves was affirmed in the U.S. Constitution. One of many catalysts for the Civil War, the court's decision denied people of African descent the right to citizenship and constitutional protection. It established that individuals of African descent were not citizens of the United States. In 1873, the Supreme Court declared in the *Slaughter-House Cases* that the Fourteenth Amendment, one of three Civil War amendments, overruled the *Dred Scott* decision.

The Civil War amendments, also known as the Reconstruction amendments, are the three amendments to the U.S. Constitution that, respectively, abolished slavery, guaranteed equal protection and due process to people of all races, and guaranteed voting rights for black men. The Thirteenth

In December 1860, a group of abolitionists, including Frederick Douglass and William Lloyd Garrison, met at Tremont Temple in Boston to commemorate the anniversary of John Brown's execution: Brown was an American revolutionary abolitionist. Some Bostonians took over the proceedings, passed resolutions to condemn John Brown's raid, and expelled the abolitionists.

Amendment passed in the Senate in 1864 and in the House in 1865. It was adopted in December 1865. Section One of the Thirteenth Amendment reads "Neither slavery nor involuntary servitude, except as a punishment for crime whereof the party shall have been duly convicted, shall exist within the United States or any place subject to their jurisdiction." Section Two of the Thirteenth Amendment reads "Congress shall have power to enforce this article by appropriate legislation." The Thirteenth Amendment effectively abolished slavery in America.

Adopted in 1868, the Fourteenth Amendment served as the basis for overturning discriminatory state laws, such as a West Virginia statute prohibiting blacks from serving on juries. The Supreme Court ruled this West Virginia statute unconstitutional in *Strauder v. West Virginia* (1880). The Fourteenth Amendment includes the citizenship clause, the privileges or immunities clause, the due process clause, and the equal protection clause. All of these clauses are important to later Supreme Court decisions based on race. The court relied on the equal protection clause in its decision in *Strauder*. The citizenship clause was deemed to have reversed the *Dred Scott* decision by providing that "[a]ll persons born or naturalized in the United States, and subject to the jurisdiction thereof, are citizens of the United States and of the State wherein they reside." The Fourteenth Amendment effectively secured new rights for former slaves.

The Fifteenth Amendment, ratified in 1870, prohibited both states and the federal government from denying voting rights because of a citizen's race or status as a former slave. Section one of the Fifteenth Amendment reads "The right of citizens of the United States to vote shall not be denied or abridged by the United States or by any State on account of race, color, or previous condition of servitude." Section Two of the Fifteenth Amendment reads "The Congress shall have power to enforce this article by appropriate legislation." The Fifteenth Amendment effectively established voting rights for all male people of color.

The Emancipation Proclamation was law by executive order. Issued by President Abraham Lincoln on January 1, 1863, the Emancipation Proclamation freed all slaves in the states that made up the Confederate States of America. The Emancipation Proclamation did not free any slaves in the border states: Delaware, Maryland, Missouri, and West Virginia. Slavery remained legal in these states until the passage of the Thirteenth Amendment.

Allen Mendenhall
Auburn University

See Also: 1777 to 1800 Primary Documents; 1801 to 1850 Primary Documents; 1851 to 1900 Primary Documents; *Dred Scott v. Sandford*; Fugitive Slave Act of 1850; Race, Class, and Criminal Law; Race-Based Crimes; Racism; Slavery; *Strauder v. West Virginia*; Supreme Court, U.S.

Further Readings

Berlin, Ira. *Many Thousands Gone: The First Two Centuries of Slavery in North America*. Cambridge, MA: Harvard University Press, 1998.

Davis, David Brion. *The Problem of Slavery in Western Culture*. Ithaca, NY: Cornell University Press, 1966.

Finkelman, Paul, ed. *Slavery and the Law*. Lanham, MD: Rowman & Littlefield, 2002.

Goodell, William. *The American Slave Code in Theory and Practice*. New York: American and Foreign Antislavery Society, 1853.

Gross, Ariela. *Double Character: Slavery and Mastery in the Antebellum Southern Courtroom*. Athens: University of Georgia Press, 2006.

Jordan, Winthrop. *White Over Black: American Attitudes Toward the Negro*. Chapel Hill: University of North Carolina Press, 1968.

Morris, Thomas D. *Southern Slavery and the Law, 1619–1860*. Chapel Hill: University of North Carolina Press, 1999.

Oakes, James. *Slavery and Freedom*. New York: Alfred A. Knopf, 1990.

Smith, Susan

Susan Leigh Vaughan Smith was sentenced to life in prison for murdering her two children in 1994. Initially, Smith had claimed that an African American man stole her car and kidnapped her sons. Subsequently, she admitted to drowning her two sons by rolling her car into a lake with the boys trapped inside.

Smith was born on September 26, 1971 as Susan Leigh Vaughan in Union, South Carolina, to Harry and Linda Vaughan. She was the youngest of three children and the couple's only daughter. Her parents divorced when Susan was 7, and five weeks later Harry, age 37, committed suicide. Her mother, Linda, then married Beverly (Bev) Russell, a local businessman. When she was 16, Susan Vaughan reported to the local authorities that she had been molested by her stepfather. No charges were ever filed. In 1991, he married David Smith, whom she met at the supermarket where they both worked. She gave birth to two sons, Michael Daniel Smith (October 10, 1991), and Alexander Tyler Smith (August 5, 1993). The marriage was troubled, with numerous separations and affairs, and divorce papers were filed days before the murders.

On October 25, 1994, Smith knocked on the door of the home of Shirley and Rick McCloud and told them that an African American man had taken her car and her two boys. She said she had stopped at a red light when a man jumped into her car and told her to drive. After driving for a time, she said that he told her to stop and get out of the car. He then drove off with the boys, who she said she could hear crying out for her.

A nine-day nationwide search ensued, with Smith appearing on television to plead for the safe return of her boys. However, Smith subsequently confessed, admitting that she let her 1990 Mazda Protegé roll into nearby John D. Long Lake, drowning her children inside. Her motive for the murder was to enable a relationship with Tom Findlay, the son of her employer. She and Findlay had been having an affair, but Findlay broke it off because he did not want children or to raise someone else's children.

Smith's Trial

Sheriff Howard Wells had been skeptical about Smith's story from the beginning and believed she had killed her own children. They began searching area lakes and ponds, including the lake in which the children were eventually found. Both Susan Smith and her husband took polygraph tests two days after the boys disappeared. The results indicated that Susan Smith was lying when she said she did not know where the boys were. There were no other cars near the intersection where Smith said the carjacking had occurred. This was an important fact, because the traffic light at the intersection would have been triggered by an oncoming vehicle. With no cars in the area, there would have been no reason for her car to be stopped.

On November 3, 1994, David and Susan Smith appeared on *CBS This Morning*, and David voiced his full support of Susan and her story about the abduction. Following this appearance, Smith again met with Sheriff Wells, who challenged her story, explaining to her that the traffic light on Monarch Mills would have stayed green because no other car was in the area. Susan confessed to Wells. She said that she had wanted to kill herself and her children but got out of the car and then rolled it into the lake, drowning her boys. She told the police where the car had floated out before it sank. Divers found the car turned upside down, with the children in their car seats. Also found in the car was the letter Tom Findlay had written to Smith breaking off their relationship. An autopsy of the children concluded that both boys were still alive when the car went underwater.

At trial, the defense offered evidence to try to explain Smith's behavior. They disclosed that she had been molested in her teens by her stepfather, who admitted that he had molested her, and had consensual sex with her as an adult. Her biological father committed suicide when she was 6 years old and she very rarely had a stable home life. At 13, she attempted suicide. She made a second attempt after graduating from high school in 1989. The prosecution countered the defense, asserting that Smith's only concern was her own desires. Her children were in Smith's way: By killing them, she believed that Tom Findlay would resume their relationship.

Smith was found guilty of two counts of murder and was sentenced to 30 years to life in prison. While she has been incarcerated, two corrections officers have been convicted of having sexual intercourse with Smith. In 2001, Alfred Rowe, Jr., was sentenced to five years probation, and Houston Cagle received three months in jail for engaging in sexual intercourse with Smith while she was an inmate at the Women's Correctional Institution in Columbia. She is presently (May 2011) an inmate at the Leath Correctional Institution, located near Greenwood, South Carolina. She will be eligible for parole in 2025. Her ex-husband has sworn to attend every parole hearing to keep Susan Smith in prison for life.

Jeffrey Kraus
Wagner College

See Also: 2001 to 2012 Primary Documents; South Carolina; Women Criminals, Contemporary; Women Criminals, Sociology of; Women in Prison.

Further Readings
Peyser, A. *Mother Love, Deadly Love: The Susan Smith Murders*. New York: HarperCollins, 1995.
Rekers, George. *Susan Smith: Victim or Murderer*. Lakewood, CO: Glenbridge Publishing, 1995.
Russell, Linda and Shirley Stephens. *My Daughter Susan Smith*. Brentwood, TN: Authors' Book Nook, 2000.

Smith Act

The Alien Registration Act of 1940 (Smith Act) was passed as the world stage was set for World War II. Like the Alien Sedition Acts of 1798, the law was intended to protect Americans from "corrupting" foreign political influences (e.g., socialism and communism) and domestic political dissent. The Smith Act accomplished this goal in two main ways: It made it a federal criminal offense to advocate or organize the overthrow of any U.S. government, and it required noncitizen adults to register their occupational status and political beliefs with the federal government. The Smith Act remains on the books today. However, there have been no prosecutions under the law since 1957.

The first Smith Act prosecutions occurred in 1941, when 18 members of the Socialist Workers Party were targeted; it was then used again in 1942 against 28 alleged Nazis. However, the largest number of prosecutions under the law occurred

Benjamin Davis surrounded by supporters as they left the Federal Courthouse in New York. Davis was an African American communist who was represented Harlem on the city council. Davis was a target of the McCarthy investigations and was tried and imprisoned with 11 other Communist Party leaders under the infamous anticommunist Smith Act.

during the beginning of the cold war, when fears that communists were infiltrating American society and the U.S. government inspired government officials to aggressively prosecute members of the Communist Party who resided in the United States. Senator Joseph McCarthy and members of the House Un-American Affairs Committee spearheaded these efforts during the 1950s. During this time period, 131 members of the Communist Party were indicted for advocating the violent overthrow of the U.S. government, 98 of whom were convicted. Use of the act declined in the mid-1950s as McCarthy's influence in the Senate waned.

The first major legal challenge to the Smith Act was in *Dennis v. United States* (1951), a case examined during the height of the Red Scare. Eugene Dennis, an officer of the Communist Party, U.S.A., was indicted under the act for conspiring to overthrow the government. Dennis was found guilty, despite the fact that he had only been making plans to write documents in the future—he had not actually engaged in any actions to overthrow the government. In a 6–2 decision, the court ruled that Dennis's First Amendment rights were trumped by the security needs of the general public. The court drew from *Schenck v. United States* (1919) and concluded that Dennis's actions created a "clear and present danger" for the public. It ruled that while Dennis's actions were unlikely to be successful, the likelihood of success was not required in order to sustain a conviction under the act.

The Supreme Court examined the Smith Act again in *Yates v. United States* (1957), as the Red Scare of the 1950s was coming to a close. The case involved the convictions of 14 Communist Party leaders from California. Oleta Yates and his colleagues were convicted in 1951 of organizing an effort to advocate the violent overthrow of the U.S. government. Yates appealed to the Supreme Court. In a 6–1 decision, the court ruled in favor of Yates. First, the court interpreted important provisions of the Smith Act narrowly. Yates and the others were charged with organizing a conspiracy to overthrow the U.S. government. The court's interpretation of the term *organize* meant that the statute of limitations contained in the Smith Act precluded prosecution for Yates's actions. Second, the court distinguished between two different kinds of advocacy. The first is the advocacy of an idea—a greater overarching philosophy or principle. The First Amendment protects this form of advocacy. The second is advocacy for specific and concrete action, such as advocating the violent overthrow of the government. This form of advocacy is not protected. Yates and his codefendants engaged in the first type of advocacy, general advocacy of a principle. Therefore, their action was protected by the First Amendment. The court found that the evidence in five of the cases was so weak that it dismissed the Smith Act charges against them outright. The cases of Yates and the remaining defendants were returned to the lower courts, where the government, realizing that the Supreme Court's ruling virtually precluded it from continuing the cases, declined to prosecute Yates again. The *Yates* decision effectively ended government prosecutions under the Smith Act.

Darren A. Wheeler
Josh Thompson
Ball State University

See Also: Alien and Sedition Acts of 1798; *Dennis v. United States*; McCarthy, Joseph; *Yates v. United States*.

Further Readings
Belknap, Michael. *Cold War Political Justice: The Smith Act, the Communist Party, and American Civil Liberties.* Contributions in American History. Westport, CT: Greenwood Press, 1977.

Heale, M. J. *American Anti-Communism: Combating the Enemy Within, 1830–1970.* Baltimore, MD: Johns Hopkins University Press, 1990.

Smuggling

Smuggling is the covert transportation of individuals or goods across points of entry in violation of laws and regulations. U.S. government agencies concerned with smuggling include the U.S. Border Patrol, U.S. Coast Guard, U.S. Customs Service, and Drug Enforcement Administration. Smuggled goods include those that are illegal, like drugs, Cuban goods, and some firearms; those that are subject to legal controls, like prescription drugs, most firearms, many plants and animals, and people; and those that are smuggled to evade a tax, like cigarettes.

Points of Entry
There are a number of goods that are smuggled across land borders and ports of entry. These include but are not limited to undocumented immigrants, weapons, drugs, and endangered wildlife. Ports of entry are, in federal law, geographical areas overseen by a port director, where people and goods may enter the country under the supervision of customs and other authorities. For instance, international airports are usually ports of entry, as are major seaports. Some ports of entry may include multiple border crossings; since 2001, there are almost no roads entering the United States without a border inspection station. Unguarded entry points, including overland routes and unguarded shoreline, are of particular importance because it is believed that they are the preferred way of entry for smugglers. While all borders require enforcement and security measures, land borders are of particular importance to the federal government. In terms of resource allocation, land borders tend to receive a larger amount of funding, but securing airports and ports is also significant in matters of national security.

The United States has major ports that respond to a lot of activity on a daily basis. The Los Angeles and Long Beach ports together make up two of the largest port facilities in the world. Slowing down or closing the ports could cost the American economy billions of dollars. A brief lockout in 2002 at ports in the western United States cost the U.S. economy $1 billion a day. Some measures could be taken to increase safety measures at ports.

Land borders are a vital point of entry into the United States. The United States protects approximately 7,000 miles of border with Canada and Mexico. Along the 5,525-mile U.S.–Canada border, there are 84 land points of entry, and a fairly small security presence compared to the southern border. Smuggling is the major issue of concern along the American–Canadian border, with drugs smuggled in both directions, and cigarettes and firearms smuggled in significant numbers from the United States to Canada. In both cases, international crime cartels are involved, as well as local criminal groups. Much of the smuggling passes through Akwesasne, a quasi-sovereign Mohawk territory in which bordering authorities in New York and Ontario have no jurisdiction.

The land border between Mexico and the United States is 1,933 miles across and has 25 points of entry that include land points in California, Arizona, New Mexico, and Texas. For a time in the 1990s, U.S. Army personnel stationed along the Mexican border worked with the border patrol to contribute helicopter support and high technology to attempts to slow the flow of illegal drug smuggling across the border. The attacks of 9/11 also had a tremendous impact on land border security enforcement, though with a focus on security, rather than smuggling.

History of Smuggling
The United States has a long and complex history with smuggling, dating back to colonial times. The colonies under British control were meant to enrich the British Empire, rather than the individual colonies. Using the mercantilism system helped the British Empire to maintain control over goods found in the colonies. The economic philosophy in place was mercantilism. Based on this system, the colonies had many restrictions placed upon them. These included who they could trade with, the ships they could use, and how much they were permitted to manufacture. American colonists were expected to purchase British goods, rather than Spanish or French goods. Americans were expected to pay for the goods they imported as a way to discourage trading. The Navigation Acts and the Molasses Acts were instituted by the British government as a way to restrict colonial trade. One way that colonists were able to defy these restrictions was by smuggling. Smuggling became a way of defying British rule and evading the heavy taxes and regulations imposed upon them. Americans became skilled at avoiding British naval ships. Smuggling became a vital skill for Americans during the Revolutionary War.

Smuggling again became a prominent issue in the United States in the 1920s during Prohibition. Prohibition in the United States lasted from 1920 through 1933. Under Prohibition, it was illegal to purchase, sell, manufacture, and transport alcohol. Rum-running or bootlegging were methods of defying Prohibition. Rum-running became a lucrative business and became a way for organized

Smugglers walking across the Rio Grande from Mexico in 1866 with packs full of contraband on their backs. U.S. customs officers (wearing brimmed hats) can be seen hiding in the bushes on the right. At that time, tobacco was commonly smuggled. Smuggling in the United States dates back to the nation's early years because of strict British control on many goods.

crime to control the distribution of alcohol. Cities like Chicago were faced with an increase in crimes like theft and murder, which were linked to the criminal activities of bootlegging and control over that enterprise by criminals such as Al Capone. An increase in the unpopularity of Prohibition led to the repeal of the Eighteenth Amendment by ratification of the Twenty-First Amendment.

Motivation for Smuggling
Smuggling of other goods, such as wildlife and endangered species, has also dominated U.S. history. A demand for exotic species has led to a lucrative business of smuggling wildlife. As a response to the smuggling of wildlife, CITES (Convention on International Trade in Endangered Species of Wild Fauna and Flora) was established in Washington, D.C., to regulate the movement of exotic species across borders.

Smuggling has also become popular for those attempting to avoid taxes on goods. One example is the purchase of cigarettes from states with low taxes that are smuggled into states that have higher taxes for cigarettes. These cigarettes are then sold for a lesser amount, but still allow a profit. Smuggling also occurs when there is a demand for illegal goods or services or if those goods or services, are heavily taxed. One of example of this is weapons smuggling. In some countries such as Mexico there are strict gun control laws, whereas the United States has lenient gun control laws. Recently, the U.S. Bureau of Alcohol, Tobacco, Firearms and Explosives (ATF) launched Operation Fast and Furious, which entailed purposely allowing firearms to be smuggled from the United States into Mexico. These weapons were supposed to be tracked as part of this operation but the Mexican government was not notified of that intent. This example provides an illustration that smuggling is also enforced by government action against other sovereign nations. There is often a reciprocal relationship between smuggling weapons in exchange for drugs.

In 1973, the Nixon administration established the Drug Enforcement Administration (DEA). The DEA was charged with enforcing federal drug laws and control of drug activity. Since the 1980s, the U.S. government has been waging an unsuccessful War on Drugs. Drugs are trafficked from other countries into the United States across the northern and southern border, as well as through other ports of entry.

Human Smuggling
One of the other lucrative businesses that entail smuggling is human smuggling. Human smuggling has been used in the past to remove individuals from oppressive or dangerous environments. For example, during the times of slavery in the United States, slaves in the south were smuggled to the north though the Underground Railroad and other means. During the Holocaust, Jews were smuggled out of Germany and other territories where they were met with hostility.

Human smuggling has become a booming business because of the increase in border enforcement. The human smuggling business is now just as profitable as drug trafficking. Many individuals who feel incapable of crossing the border on their own turn to human smugglers, without considering the hidden dangers. The people who smuggle them across the border often deceive and victimize women. In many cases, women are smuggled across the border into other countries, and upon their arrival, they are told that they have to pay off their smuggling debt by prostituting themselves for years. In some cases, they are held as prisoners until they have repaid the debt for being smuggled into the United States. Countries around the world have taken action against human smuggling and trafficking organizations by setting up laws and regulations against smuggling operations. One of the steps that the U.S. government has taken to control smuggling operations is focusing on the southwest border, where there is a booming business of smuggling people across the southern border into the United States.

In 2004, in an effort to increase safety around the southwest border, the Department of Homeland Security (DHS) created the Arizona Border Control Initiative (ABCI), which aims at dismantling smuggling and trafficking operations. The ABCI is also supported by Mexican government officials, who have expressed their concerns over immigrant deaths and hope to eliminate human smuggling. ABCI has contributed to the prosecution of 335 individuals facing charges for human smuggling and has been responsible for the seizure of more than $7.2 million from smuggling organizations.

Technological Advances
Those who cross into the United States are required to stop at customs and identify themselves, as well as the items they are bringing with them. Customs agents are required to search the belongings of those who seek entry into the United States as a way to control smuggling. The introduction of new technology has allowed for advances in protecting against illegal goods crossing the border. Some of the ways that technology has played a vital role in eliminating smuggling of goods or people include the use of x-ray machines in vehicles, wiretapping, and other resources.

There are various tools and techniques used to increase control over land borders. One of the most recent tools developed to deter illegal activity around the U.S–Mexico border is the building of a fence along the southern border. Some regions around the southern border already have a 10-foot-high fence in place and funding for additional fencing along the rest of the southern border has recently been approved by Congress. Border patrol agents use an array of tools to apprehend unauthorized people and goods from crossing the border.

In order to complete this mission, border patrol agents use surveillance techniques, follow up on leads, respond to alarms, monitor checkpoints, and conduct anti-smuggling investigations. The surveillance techniques are used to monitor uninhabited deserts, rivers, mountains, and canyons. The border patrol uses electronic sensors to detect people and vehicles that attempt to cross the border illegally. Some of the tools that they use include night-vision scopes, cameras, radar towers, UAVs, vehicles, boats, horses, bicycles, snowmobiles, all-terrain motorcycles, and air surveillance to supervise the border. All of these measures are used to deter and prevent unlawful entry across the border but the effectiveness of these tools has not yet been proven.

Mercedes Valadez
Arizona State University

See Also: 1961 to 1980 Primary Documents; Border Patrol; Drug Enforcement Administration; Immigration Crimes.

Further Readings

Ewing, W. "Money for Nothing: Immigration Enforcement Without Immigration Reform Doesn't Work." http://www.immigrationpolicy.org (Accessed September 2011).

Kamien, D., ed. *The McGraw-Hill Homeland Security Handbook*. New York: McGraw-Hill, 2006.

Snyder, Ruth

An infamous Long Island, New York, murder case from 1927 is reputed to be the inspiration for James M. Cain's works of crime fiction *The Postman Always Rings Twice* (1934) and *Double Indemnity* (first published in serialized form in 1936).

In the early hours of March 20, 1927, 32-year-old Ruth Snyder and her lover, Henry Judd Gray, brutally murdered her 42-year-old husband Albert, a quiet, unsuspecting magazine art editor, as he slept in the family home and as Snyder's 9-year-old daughter Lorraine was asleep in a room across the hall. Gray and Snyder bludgeoned Albert with a sash weight, strangled him using a picture wire tourniquet tightened with a metal pencil, and stuffed chloroform-soaked cloths into his nose and mouth. They then set about ransacking the house and removing items of value to stage the crime scene as a burglary gone wrong. As a finishing touch, Gray tied Ruth up, gagged her, and left her in the hallway where she would claim she had been attacked by two Italian thugs. However, Ruth Snyder's version of events aroused police suspicions from the start, particularly as there was no sign of forced entry to the house and the "stolen" jewelry and fur coat were found under a mattress.

Within days, Snyder had confessed, recanted, and then blamed Gray who admitted his involvement but accused Ruth of being the mastermind. The motive was money. Ruth had persuaded her husband to sign a double indemnity life insurance policy worth nearly $50,000 shortly before the murder. The story of the greedy housewife, her corset salesman lover, and the murder of her husband was a boon for the press. In the 1920s, growing chain newspapers were engaged in a war for increased circulation in which sensationalism and "human interest" stories were published, often at the expense of legitimate news. The tabloid *New York Daily News* was particularly adept at melodrama and the use of photographic features.

Despite protests from their attorneys, Snyder and Gray were prosecuted together and the eagerly anticipated trial began on April 18. Each defendant testified against the other. The trial testimony and proceedings were later reproduced by crime reporter John Kobler, but tabloid and broadsheet newspapers provided daily accounts. In attempting to establish the roles played by each defendant, press and public engaged in a wider gendered discourse about the boundaries of acceptable and disreputable female behavior, wifely loyalty, and respectable motherhood. The picture of Snyder that emerged from the testimony and in the context of the burgeoning field of psychology was of a predatory, sexually aggressive, and therefore abnormal woman who had dominated her cuckold husband. Gray's attorney, William J. Millard, used his summation on May 9, 1927, to characterize Snyder as "a poisonous snake" who had drawn Gray "into her glistening coils, and there was no escape" from her "all-consuming, all-absorbing sexual passion and animal lust, which seemingly was never satisfied." Snyder's attorney countered by describing Gray as a "human anaconda," but this had less impact.

The gravestone of Ruth Snyder (born Ruth Brown) in Woodlawn Cemetery in the Bronx, New York. Snyder and her accomplice murdered her husband and were executed in Sing Sing prison.

The all-male jury deliberated for one hour and 40 minutes before finding both Snyder and Gray guilty of first-degree murder with a sentence of death. Both New York Governor Alfred E. Smith and professional executioner Robert G. Elliott professed anxieties over the prospect of electrocuting a woman, but all appeals failed. Smith refused to grant clemency and Elliott without dissent presided over the third female electrocution in the state. Snyder and Judd were executed minutes apart at Sing Sing prison in upstate New York shortly after 11 P.M. on January 12, 1928. The moment of Snyder's electrocution was captured in an infamous photograph published in the *Daily News*. The image was taken by photographer Tom Howard, using a small camera strapped to his ankle and operated from his pocket.

Vivien Miller
University of Nottingham

See Also: Executions; Murder, History of; New York City; Sing Sing Correctional Facility; Women Criminals, History of.

Further Readings
Elliott, Robert G. and Albert P. Beatty. *Agent of Death: The Memoirs of an Executioner*. New York: E. P. Dutton, 1941.
Kobler, J., ed. *The Trial of Ruth Snyder and Judd Gray*. New York: Doubleday, Doran & Co., 1938.
Margolin, Leslie. *Murderess! The Chilling True Story of the Most Infamous Woman Ever Electrocuted*. New York: Pinnacle Books, 1999.
Ramey, Jessie. "The Bloody Blonde and the Marble Woman: Gender and Power in the Case of Ruth Snyder." *Journal of Social History*, v.37 (2004).

Sodomy

Often referred to as "the infamous crime against nature" and "unmentionable crime," the term *sodomy* refers to an ecclesiastical sin that was codified into secular criminal law in the 16th century. What constitutes sodomy changes over time and reflects the social and cultural sexual mores of the particular time and place. The term *sodomy* has included acts such as bestiality, masturbation, fellatio, cunilingus, and anal sex, as well as referencing sexual acts between both men and women and same-sex partners. In the United States, for example, it changed from a capital offense in the 18th century to a serious felony in the 19th century to an act equated with homosexuality in the 20th century.

Biblical Definition
In its earliest form, sodomy refers to a religious crime and is defined in biblical terms. The crime against nature was the sin of Sodom, the city whose citizens, in an inhospitable moment, assaulted an angel of God and were punished with fire and brimstone, as described in Genesis 19:24. In Leviticus, the third book of the Hebrew Bible that establishes laws, rituals, and codes of behavior, sodomy is described as a man lying with a male as with a woman, and it becomes an abomination to the Israelites punishable by death. Though Jesus never mentions the act, sodomy appears in the New Testament book Romans (1:27), described as a dishonorable passion, condemned by Paul, and punishable by death. Ancient civilizations, such as the Assyrians and the Romans, also adopted laws that banned or restricted homosexual acts.

English Common Law
By the 16th century, most Western nation-states adopted laws outside the biblical tradition. The Bible, however, remained influential on laws governing sexual activity, marriage and family, including sodomy laws. In 1533, King Henry VIII of England introduced the first legislation under English criminal law against sodomy. The Buggery Act of 1533 defined buggery as an "unnatural sexual act against the will of God and man," punishable by hanging. This law and penalty remained intact until 1861. Sodomy's meaning expanded after William Blackstone referred to it as "the infamous crime against nature" in his *Commentaries on the Laws of England*. Lawyers and citizens adopted this vague term, which allowed for some confusion in what constituted sodomy and led to a wide range of rulings.

American Laws
This history directly influenced the legal status of sodomy in the North American British colonies where sodomy, buggery, and bestiality carried

Although the U.S. Supreme Court declared that private, consensual sexual contact was protected by the Fourteenth Amendment's due process protections, sodomy can still be a contentious issue. Here anti–gay rights demonstrators and Christian proselytizers stage a protest during the Proposition 8 debate to recriminalize sodomy at San Francisco's City Hall in 2008.

the death penalty. John Winthrop, the founder of the Massachusetts Bay Colony, reacted to the execution of William Plaine for sodomy by defining sodomy not only as a crime against nature but also an act that threatened the stability of the core social institution of the colony and British society, marriage, and the family.

Throughout the 17th century, colonial governments executed five men. In 1778, Thomas Jefferson attempted to liberalize the sodomy laws in Virginia by authoring a law that would make sodomy punishable by castration. This revision of the Virginia law did not pass the legislature. By the 18th century, colonial governments no longer executed men for sodomitical acts but instead issued severe whippings, burning with a hot iron, or banishment.

Each colony and state adopted its own sodomy law. The state governments' purpose reflected Winthrop's, to protect sexual intercourse as a procreative act to be practiced solely within the legal bonds of marriage. However, enforcement remained sporadic. In the 19th century, *homosexuality*, a term coined by Karoly Kertbeny in 1868, and masturbation fell under the ever-expanding definition of sodomy. After the Civil War in 1865, however, Americans increased their migratory patterns into the cities. Homosexuals, who had been more isolated in rural areas where there was little access to differing opinions on sodomy, found opportunities to form subcultures in urban areas, especially in the arena of intimate male friendships.

Enforcement of sodomy laws increased in the late 19th and early 20th centuries. Two main factors contributed to this increase in sodomy arrests in the nation's cities. First, cities such as Philadelphia and New York expanded their sodomy laws to include explicitly oral sex, with other cities following their lead. Second, urban areas experienced a rise in anti-vice organizations. The most famous of these squads—a mixture of police and zealous middle-class citizens—were the New York Society for the Suppression of Vice, founded by Anthony Comstock in 1873, and the Committee of Fourteen, founded in 1904. These organizations and Comstock, in particular, not only accelerated arrests for sodomy, but also influenced cities to use laws such as vagrancy and morality laws against homosexuals.

Greater Tolerance

By the mid-20th century, sodomy was a felony in every state, with a long prison term or hard labor as punishment. In 1961, however, the Model Penal Code Commission, developed by the American Law Institute, recommended that states remove consensual sodomy from their criminal codes, while maintaining it as a crime to solicit or force sodomy. Illinois was the first state to adopt these recommendations, and by 2002, 36 states had repealed their sodomy laws or their courts had overturned them. State governments also received pressure to decriminalize sodomy from the gay rights movement and to depathologize homosexuality by the American Psychological Association in 1973.

In its 1986 *Bowers v. Hardwick* decision, however, the U.S. Supreme Court held that a right to privacy did not extend to private, consensual homosexual sex. Though states continued to dismantle their state sodomy laws, it was not until *Lawrence v. Texas* (2003) that the court reversed its ruling in *Bowers* and declared that private, consensual sexual contact was protected by the substantive component of the Fourteenth Amendment's due process protections.

Robin C. Henry
Wichita State University

See Also: *Bowers v. Hardwick*; Gender and Criminal Law; *Lawrence v. Texas*.

Further Readings

Boswell, John. *Christianity, Social Tolerance, and Homosexuality: Gay People in Western Europe From the Beginning of the Christian Era to the Fourteenth Century*, 8th ed. Chicago: University of Chicago Press, 2005.

Eskridge, William N., Jr. *Dishonorable Passions: Sodomy Laws in America, 1861–2003*. New York: Viking Press, 2008.

Goldberg, Jonathan, ed. *Reclaiming Sodom*. New York: Routledge, 1994.

South Carolina

One of the original thirteen colonies, South Carolina was also the first to secede from the Union to found the Confederate States of America.

Police and Punishment

In South Carolina's early days, law enforcement duties fell primarily to the town watch and constables. Militias could also be raised by the colonial government when necessary. After statehood, many cities replaced their town watch with a city guard, with expanded duties. Modern police departments evolved out of the city guard and were reorganized during and after Reconstruction.

South Carolinians actively resisted the idea of building a state prison for a surprisingly long time, though it was first proposed in the 18th century. The opposition was predicated on the belief that the availability of a state-run facility, rather than the small-capacity county jails, would encourage judges and juries to issue longer sentences, and that this constituted an inhumane punishment. (Elsewhere, long prison sentences were opposed for the more pragmatic reason that they were a financial burden on the taxpayers who funded the prison; in South Carolina, the argument for humane discipline seems to have been sincere.) It was under a Reconstruction government, with many northerners and their allies serving in the General Assembly, that the legislature finally authorized the construction of a state prison in 1866. Construction was not completed until the 1880s, owing largely to the chaos of the Reconstruction period. Overcrowding quickly became a problem in the South Carolina Penitentiary, and convicts were leased to outside contractors in order to reduce crowding within the prison walls. Chain gangs were also in wide use, using prisoners with short sentences to work as road maintenance crews close to their hometowns.

South Carolina is a capital punishment state. Until 1912, executions by hanging were carried out by the counties. From 1912 to 1990, executions were carried out at the Central Correctional Institution in Columbia; in 1990, the state's death row and execution facilities were relocated to the Capital Punishment Facility in the Broad River Correctional Institution. By law, executions are seen by three media witnesses—one from print media, one from broadcast media, and one from the wire services (the Associated Press)—and up to three witnesses from the victim's family. In cases where there is more than one victim, the number of family members may be restricted because of space constraints. Executions are typically also witnessed by the solicitor or assistant solicitor and the chief law enforcement officer from the county where the murder occurred, a minister, and the inmate's lawyer. Since 1912, the electric chair has been used in executions (replacing hanging); since 1995, the inmate to be executed has been given the choice between the electric chair and lethal injection, a choice to be submitted in writing 14 days before the date of execution.

Since South Carolina began carrying out executions in Columbia in 1912, there have been 282 executions: two women and 280 men, 74 whites and 208 blacks. Before the redrafting of death penalty statutes following the Supreme Court's 1970s decisions, the death penalty could be used in rape and kidnapping cases in addition to murder cases. In 1976, South Carolina's attorney general found that the state's mandatory death penalty for specific circumstances was unconstitutional, and the legislature passed a new death penalty statute in 1977. The new statute has been upheld both by the state supreme court and by the U.S. Supreme Court, in *South Carolina v. Shaw*.

Crime

Racial tensions and racially motivated crimes have been a persistent problem in South Carolina. During Reconstruction, when the federal government imposed a new order on the defeated Confederacy, the Ku Klux Klan was founded in Tennessee as a vigilante group determined to expel Republicans, blacks, northerners, and their allies from the south. The Klan quickly spread through the former Confederate states. Its actions were often carefully orchestrated and politically motivated, and its political assassinations included three South Carolina legislators. When the Klan

Downtown Charleston, South Carolina, as seen from the Cooper River Bridge. The spires of St. Philips church (built in 1860) and St. Michael's church (built between 1751 and 1761) rise in the center. As one of the first states to secede to become the Confederate States of America, South Carolina has experienced persistent racial tension.

refused to dissolve after a federal grand jury determined it was were a terrorist organization, a series of acts empowered the federal government to enforce civil rights provisions. President Grant suspended the writ of habeas corpus and sent federal troops into the nine South Carolina counties where the Klan's presence was the strongest. Hundreds of Klansmen were fined or imprisoned following federal trials.

Following the Klan trials, the Klan declined in power and faded out. It was replaced by new white supremacist paramilitary groups in various parts of the south. In South Carolina, these groups were called the Red Shirts, named for the shirts they wore to identify themselves. Though the various Red Shirt groups shared a cause, there was no centralized organization. In South Carolina, many Red Shirts prominently supported Democratic candidate Wade Hampton in his 1876 and 1878 campaigns for governor and continued the Klan's work of acting as the Democratic Party's paramilitary wing. While the Klan had been secretive, though, the Red Shirts worked fairly openly and were even more politically minded, considering their actions carefully and directing them for maximum progress toward the goal of reestablishing white Democratic rule in South Carolina. They participated in parades and rallies throughout the state, broke up Republican meetings, barred blacks at the polls, and used violence freely. As many as 150 blacks were killed by Red Shirts in South Carolina alone. The Red Shirts are sometimes symbolically revived in the present day, having made an appearance in 2006 at the state capital to protest the observation of Martin Luther King Day.

After Reconstruction, South Carolina established a number of Jim Crow laws aimed to limit the power and rights of blacks, including the establishment of segregation in public places and a law against black guardians having control or custody of white children. New requirements were added for voting eligibility, as well, including an educational requirement and the "eight box law," which required that separate ballot boxes would exist for eight separate offices, and that in order to be counted, a ballot had to be inserted in the correct box—a way of requiring literacy of voters. Democrats also attempted to treat primaries as a private party in order to exclude blacks.

A new Klan, positioning itself as a fraternal organization but with all the violence and hatred of the original, was formed in Georgia in 1915 and again soon spread—not only through the south, but throughout the country. This Klan was dissolved in the World War II years as a result of back taxes. The Klan name was revived by numerous groups throughout the country from the 1950s to the present, none of them with any formal ties to either the first or second Klan. In South Carolina, the Klan's terrorist activities targeted the civil rights movement and activists seeking to end segregation.

South Carolina's crime rate (597.7 violent crimes per 100,000 inhabitants in 2010) is a fair bit higher than the national average (403), mostly because of a large number of aggravated assaults. The rate of aggravated assaults and burglaries has been steadily dropping, however, nearly halving since a 1994 peak, which had been reached after decades of increase. The rates of rape and murder have fallen to close to the national average.

Bill Kte'pi
Independent Scholar

See Also: 1801 to 1850 Primary Documents; 1851 to 1900 Primary Documents; Civil Rights Laws; Ku Klux Klan; North Carolina.

Further Readings
Edgar, Walter. *South Carolina: A History*. Columbia: University of South Carolina Press, 1998.
Foner, Eric. *Reconstruction: America's Unfinished Revolution*. New York: Harper Perennial Modern Classics, 2002.
Williams, Lou Falkner. *The Great South Carolina Ku Klux Klan Trials, 1871–1872*. Atlanta: University of Georgia Press, 1996.

South Dakota

South Dakota was admitted to the union as a state in 1889, when the Dakota Territory was divided into North and South Dakota. Settlement of the area increased following the 1861 establishment of the Dakota Territory, assisted by the

1873 construction of a railway to Yankton and motivated in part by the discovery of gold in the Black Hills.

Police
Early South Dakota law enforcement was handled by federal marshals, private forces hired by business interests, and town officials. County sheriffs had jurisdiction over such large and sparsely populated areas that they were of little help to many small settlements. Constables were often elected officials, and the night watch—which doubled as a fire watch—was often filled by volunteers. In the late 19th and early 20th centuries, modern police departments began to form, staffed by professionals who were trained for the job.

The South Dakota State Penitentiary, built in 1881, began as a territorial prison. Built fairly early in the history of South Dakota settlement, relative to the history of prisons in other states, it was funded with federal appropriations. A number of other facilities were opened in the late 20th and early 21st centuries: the Mike Durfee State Prison, opened on the site of the defunct Springfield campus of the University of South Dakota in 1984 and named for the deputy director of corrections (a former student athlete); the Yankton Minimum Unit, a minimum-security all-male facility opened in the 1970s; the Rapid City Minimum Unit, a minimum-security all-male facility opened in 2004; and the South Dakota Women's Prison, opened in 1997.

Punishment
The town of Deadwood, infamous in Wild West history, was founded in the midst of the Black Hills gold rush. The lawless town was technically an illegal white settlement on Indian land, the whole area having been promised to the Sioux by treaty. The town grew rapidly, reaching a population of 5,000—considerably larger than its modern population—with a Chinatown of several hundred, a brisk opium trade controlled by saloon and brothel owner Al Swearengen, and multiple brothels and gambling dens. The first execution in South Dakota was that of Jack McCall, who killed gunslinger and former lawman Wild Bill Hickok for unknown reasons. Hickok was shot in the back of the head while playing poker, and the hand he held—two pair, aces and eights—has been known as the "dead man's hand" since, an old poker idiom that had previously referred to various hands.

McCall was tried in a Deadwood court and was acquitted; he fled Deadwood to escape lynching by a mob assembled by Hickok's friend Calamity Jane. He made the mistake of bragging about killing Hickok while in Wyoming and was rearrested. Because Deadwood was an illegal settlement, a federal court in the Dakota Territory ruled that the court system there was not legally constituted and that, therefore, retrying McCall would not constitute double jeopardy. He was tried in the Dakota court, found guilty, and hanged on March 1, 1877, a few months after the initial crime.

South Dakota has retained capital punishment since, though it has rarely been used. Between the execution of Jack McCall and the 1972 Supreme Court case, *Furman v. Georgia*, which temporarily suspended death penalty statutes while they were being rewritten, 14 more men were executed. Unlike many jurisdictions, South Dakota has never executed a criminal for a crime other than murder.

Until 1915, hanging was always the method of execution; the death penalty was outlawed in 1915, but when it was reinstated in 1933, the electric chair was introduced as the method of execution. George Sitts, in 1947, was the only person executed in South Dakota by this method. Having escaped from prison while serving a life sentence for the murder of a liquor store clerk during a robbery, Sitts shot and killed Butte County Sheriff Dave Malcolm and Division of Criminal Investigation Special Agent Tom Matthews before being apprehended.

After *Furman*, a new death penalty statute was passed in 1979, defining capital murder—the only crime punishable by death in South Dakota—as first-degree murder with at least one aggravating circumstance (such as the murder of a police officer or a child, the murder of a witness, and other factors used in most states). Juveniles and the mentally unfit are exempted, and the sentence is decided by a jury that chooses between the death penalty (execution by lethal injection) and life without parole. Two men are on South Dakota's death row as of 2011, and Elijah Page was executed for murder in 2007, the first post-*Furman* execution in the state.

The South Dakota State Penitentiary in Sioux Falls, South Dakota, as seen in 2010. The facility was built as a territorial prison and became the state penitentiary when South Dakota was granted statehood in 1889. A large part of the original buildings are still in operation but newer structures have been added. The state's only death row and execution facilities are located here.

Crime

One of the most famous incidents in South Dakota history is the second incident at Wounded Knee, at the Pine Ridge Indian Reservation, from February 27 to May 5, 1973. Tensions had been high between federal authorities and the Sioux reservation, which was run by tribal chairman Dick Wilson, whose opponents saw him as a corrupt dictator supported by his private militia.

The American Indian Movement (AIM) occupied Wounded Knee and demanded that Wilson be removed from office when he evaded impeachment hearings over technicalities. The federal government brought a significant military presence to attempt to force the AIM off the land, including armored personnel carriers, grenade launchers, helicopters, snipers, and .50-caliber machine guns. In the course of the conflict, two AIM activists were killed and a marshal was paralyzed. Charges against AIM leaders Russell Means and Dennis Banks were dismissed as a result of prosecutorial misconduct.

The South Dakota violent crime rate is considerably lower than the national average, at 268.5 violent crimes per 100,000 inhabitants, but has been rising steadily since 2001 (154.4) after fluctuating back and forth between 100 and 200 through the 1970s, 1980s, and 1990s. While the murder rate is low, the rate rape (47.9) is nearly double the national average of 27. Rape and murder both increased by more than 50 percent in 2008 and 2009 but have since returned to their 2006 levels.

Bill Kte'pi
Independent Scholar

See Also: Death Row; Executions; Frontier Crime; Native Americans; North Dakota; Peltier, Leonard; Racism.

Further Readings
Matthiessen, Peter. *In The Spirit of Crazy Horse*. New York: Penguin, 1992.

Sayer, J. *Ghost Dancing the Law: The Wounded Knee Trials*. Cambridge, MA: Harvard University Press, 1997.

Wolff, David A. *Seth Bullock: Black Hills Lawman*. Pierre: South Dakota State Historical Society, 2009.

Spillane, Mickey

Mickey Spillane is a well-known American writer of crime novels. He is best known for his Mike Hammer series of books and he wrote many other crime fiction works. Frank Morrison Spillane, better known as Mickey Spillane, was born on March 9, 1918, in Brooklyn, New York. He was raised in Elizabeth, New Jersey, and attended Erasmus Hall High School, graduating in 1936. After graduating from high school, Spillane briefly attended Kansas State Teachers College at Fort Hays on a football scholarship.

During the Great Depression, he traveled around and held various odd jobs, including summer lifeguarding at Breezy Point, in Queens, Long Island. The day after Pearl Harbor was attacked, Spillane enlisted in the U.S. military; he served in the U.S. Army Air Corps during World War II, becoming a fighter pilot and training air cadets. After the war, he was briefly with the Barnum and Bailey Circus, working as a trampoline artist and knife thrower. Spillane is also reputed to have worked briefly as an undercover operative with the Federal Bureau of Investigation (FBI) to break a narcotics trafficking ring.

Mickey Spillane had three wives. He married his first wife, Mary Ann Pearce, in 1945; they had two sons and two daughters and were divorced in 1962. He married his second wife, Sherri Malinou, a model and nightclub singer, in 1965; they were divorced in 1983. He married Jane Rodgers Johnson, his third wife, in 1983. Mickey Spillane had a long career as a professional writer. At the age of 14, he began professional writing, publishing pieces in the *Elizabeth Daily Journal*. In 1935, he began submitting articles to illustrated magazines. In the 1940s, Spillane wrote for assorted comic books, such as *Batman*, *Captain America*, *Captain Marvel*, and *Superman*. In 1947, he published his first novel, *I, the Jury*, reportedly written in nine days because he needed money to purchase land to build a house for his growing family.

Mickey Spillane's signature character was Mike Hammer, a tough private investigator (P.I.) who reflected the prevailing values of Americans during the cold war. The Mike Hammer series and similar pulp fiction was created for the generation of American men who had served in World War II. These inexpensive paperback books, many of which were crime related and usually sported lurid cover art, revolutionized American reading habits. Mike Hammer was created as a crime-fighting figure who was not afraid to use his two big fists or his .45 handgun, the same gun that had been issued as the service pistol to World War II American infantrymen. Mike Hammer was portrayed as an ardent foe of "Commies" or "Reds"; this character served as a red-blooded opponent to cold war–era enemies, real or imagined, who might try to use subversive tactics to weaken the freedom-loving United States. Mike Hammer did not hesitate to resort to violence, nor did he shy away from sexual encounters. These steamy, violent plots were widely popular with his many avid readers. In fact, more than 225 million copies of his books have been sold internationally.

There were two significant gaps in Spillane's writing career. The first gap began in 1952 after both the release of the sixth novel in his Mike Hammer series, *Kiss Me, Deadly*, and after his conversion to a Jehovah's Witness. His next novel, *The Deep*, another in the Mike Hammer series, was first published in 1961. He published 12 other novels between 1962 and 1973, including five additional Mike Hammer works and four in his new Tiger Mann series. Tiger Mann, a secret agent, was introduced in 1964 with *Day of the Guns*. Spillane then wrote two acclaimed young adult books, *The Day The Sea Rolled Back*, which came out in 1979, and *The Ship That Never Was*, released in 1982. However, there was another hiatus in his crime novel writing that was broken in 1989 with another installment in the Mike Hammer series, *The Killing Man*, which was followed by a few other crime fiction works. In 1995, he received the Edgar Allan Poe Grand Master Award. Mickey

Spillane died of pancreatic cancer on July 17, 2006, in Murrells Inlet, South Carolina, at the age of 88. In 2008, the 13th novel of his Mike Hammer series, *The Goliath Bone*, was completed by Max Allan Collins, Mickey Spillane's literary executor.

Victor B. Stolberg
Essex County College

See Also: Dime Novels, Pulps, Thrillers; Literature and Theater, Crime in.

Further Readings
Collins, Max Allan and James L. Taylor. *One Lonely Knight: Mickey Spillane's Mike Hammer*. Bowling Green, OH: Bowling Green State University Popular Press, 1992.
Van Dover, J. Kenneth. *Murder in the Millions: Erle Stanley Gardner, Mickey Spillane, Ian Fleming*. New York: F. Ungar, 1984.

St. Louis, Missouri

In 2010, *US News and World Report* rated St. Louis to once again be the most dangerous city in America—beating out competitors Detroit, New Orleans, Camden, and Oakland. When considering property crimes, such as vehicle theft and burglary, along with violent crimes, such as robbery, rape, and murder, St. Louis ended up with a crime risk index of 530 based on Federal Bureau of Investigation (FBI) crime data from 2003 to 2009. A crime score of 100 indicates equivalence with the national average. While major crimes are down from recent years, there is still an uneasy feeling for many involved in the city's police force and politics. Officials regularly choose to criticize the rankings of their city, saying that they do not accurately provide data since each city reports data in its own way. As a result, St. Louis could simply be victim to its willingness to report all crimes that occur within the city, county, and surrounding areas.

The criminal history of St. Louis is vast. As early as the mid-1890s, a mafia presence had been established. By 1910, Dominick Giambrone was recognized as the Mafia boss. Throughout Prohibition, Mafia violence dominated the area as seven rival ethnic gangs fought for control of the city. By the time Prohibition was over, the families had come together to work as one cohesive unit as much as possible. Anthony Giordano became St. Louis boss and moved for independence from Kansas City. In 1982, Matthew Trupiano became the new leader of the St. Louis family. A powerful boss, he was a union leader, but would ultimately be convicted of illegal gambling and labor racketeering. Today, there is no known boss of the St. Louis family because the group aims to lie low with regards to state and federal authorities.

Beyond the Mafia influence, St. Louis has suffered from rapid urban growth and decline. Due to its river position, St. Louis was home to significant industrialization and urbanization. With this growth came more citizens and more potential for conflict. The city helped refine uranium to be used in the first atomic bomb, but at the same time, was crippled by severe air pollution as a result of the coal-fired furnaces that were so popular to heat homes throughout the region.

As with the rest of the country, as the economy declined and local manufacturing plants closed their doors, people became unemployed and violence rose sharply. Throughout the 1960s, 1970s, and 1980s, crime rates soared and the city gained its reputation for being a dangerous city—especially East St. Louis. East St. Louis has one of the most violent criminal histories in the country. In 2007, it had a murder rate of 101.9 per 100,000. For comparison's sake, St. Louis rate was 37.2, New Orleans was 37.6, and Detroit was 47.3. Perhaps even more shockingly, the city's rape rate was over 250 per 100,000 in the population.

In 2010, crimes statistics showed a 9.2 percent decline from 2009, marking the lowest overall crime rate for the city since 1967. Scholars have argued over the possible causes. Some have argued that the decline in St. Louis has little to do with crime prevention, but instead merely reflects a drastic decrease in population figures for the city. Consider that in 1970, St. Louis had almost 625,000 citizens, while in 2009, the city had barely over 350,000. Along with population decreases, there is also the unemployment issue. Normally we have witnessed spikes in criminal activity when unemployment increases, yet that has not been the case for St. Louis in the current recession. Some have argued that the decreased popularity of crack cocaine has led to fewer drug-related offenses. While prescription drug abuse and meth have become more prevalent, these drugs are not associated with violent crime like their predecessors. Some policymakers refuse to believe the statistics. As with most cases, individuals that have experienced some type of crime firsthand, in recent memory, will be more skeptical. Many individuals believe that crime is cyclical and that St. Louis is merely hitting a low point from which crime rates will once again continue to rise.

In 2010, the homicide victims were typically African American males between 17 and 40 years old. A vast majority had prior felony arrests and drugs or alcohol in their system. As many would expect in modern St. Louis, around 20 percent were believed to be affiliated with gangs. The St. Louis police have made concentrated efforts to educate citizens—especially at-risk youths—about the crime problem and potential dangers. At the same time, however, high-ranking police officials have regularly explained that they are policemen, not teachers. In an era of budget cuts across the board, there will be less police on patrol, fewer resources available to investigate crimes, and perhaps most importantly, less time for officers to continue working with the youth of St. Louis in an effort to curtail the cycle of violence that is clearly at play in the city.

St. Louis is a city with a deep criminal history. From the Mafia to extreme race wars, the city has long been regarded as violent and dangerous. While the numbers seem to rise and fall annually, St. Louis regularly measures as an area that citizens may rightfully not feel safe at all times. Into the 21st century, the question now becomes what the city can do to start curbing the vicious cycle and its past. Given how drastically different crime rates are in St. Louis (and especially East St. Louis) from state and national averages, the one thing we can clearly see is that this is a city in desperate need of help.

William J. Miller
Southeast Missouri State University

See Also: Crime Prevention; Crime Rates; Urban Police; Urbanization.

Further Readings

Gordon, Colin. *Mapping Decline: St. Louis and the Fate of the American City*. Philadelphia: University of Pennsylvania Press, 2009.

Lumpkins, Charles L. *American Pogrom: The East St. Louis Race Riot and Black Politics*. Athens, OH: Ohio University Press, 2008.

Stamp Act of 1765

After the French-Indian War in 1763, Parliament sought to regain some of its losses from the colonists. Continual warfare, with Native Americans and other countries attempting to usurp British control, left the Crown £123 million in debt. The colonists engaged in warfare 50 percent of the time from 1690 to 1763. George Grenville established his taxation program to counter this growing debt and to make continual defense of the colonies feasible. The three main taxes of his program were the Revenue Act of 1764 (Sugar Act), Currency Act, and Stamp Act. The Stamp Act proved the most controversial because Parliament had never before levied a domestic tax on the colonists. The Stamp Act, seeking to raise defense funds, placed a tax on all paper goods, to be paid in sterling. Local stamp collectors kept 8 percent of the takings. Those hardest hit by this tax were merchants, lawyers, and editors.

The colonists instantly opposed the new tax, with their primary justification stemming from the argument that they paid taxes to their local governments via elected assemblies. Others opposed to the program argued that postwar depression left the colonists short on cash, with inflation growing and customs reforms and currency limits reducing the flow of money into the colonies. The colonists created the Stamp Act Congress to discuss these issues. The Stamp Act Congress set the path for key constitutional issues that later arose in the framing of the national government.

Patrick Henry led the Virginia Assembly in creating its strong statement against the Stamp Act. The six points of this statement proclaimed

The British Stamp Act of 1765, the first direct tax on the American colonies, caused outrage and dissent. Colonists protest by burning Stamp Act papers in Boston.

that (1) Virginians were British citizens, (2) they enjoyed the same liberties as British citizens, (3) self-taxation was a right, (4) they taxed themselves via their own representatives, (5) they denied taxes originating outside the colonies, and (6) anyone who disagreed with these points of order was an enemy of Virginia. Henry used the Virginia Assembly's points as a guide for the Stamp Act Congress, and it proclaimed the same points except it stated that all colonists were British citizens, denied taxes originating outside the colonies, and the final point that those who disagreed were enemies was omitted. The Stamp Act Congress did not use the word *enemy* in its proclamation because, in 1765, the colonists were not ready or even talking about separating themselves from the Crown. The Congress also grappled with the debate on what to do about the Stamp Act: boycott British goods, defy the law and do business without stamps only to face jail or fines, or destroy goods and prevent delivery.

The decision of what to do about the Stamp Act quickly unfolded as the Sons of Liberty and other vigilante groups used mob violence and forceful coercion to prevent the tax from being collected throughout New England. In August 1765, Samuel Adams, leader of the Sons of Liberty, led street demonstrations in Boston. One of these involved an effigy of tax-collector Andrew Oliver. Oliver resigned his post the next day after crowds burned the effigy and officials took no action to appease the public. Twelve days of rioting followed, as the act was to go into effect on November 1.

The growing violence caused the Stamp Act Congress, in October 1765, to declare a boycott of British goods. Local community groups and social networks encouraged and forced the colonists to adhere for fear of social shame. The Crown repealed the Stamp Act in March 1766, but it responded with the Declaratory Act. The Declaratory Act said that Parliament could tax the colonies in any way it deemed fit, and the Crown used this act as a countermeasure to the claim that it could not tax the colonies. Both parties asserted their rights, but the Crown's repeal of the act did little to quell the colonial uprisings. Democratic ideas would flourish throughout the colonies, directly leading to the American Revolution.

Annessa A. Babic
New York Institute of Technology

See Also: American Revolution and Criminal Justice; Tax Crimes; Tea Act of 1773.

Further Readings

Bullion, John L. *A Great and Necessary Measure: George Grenville and the Genesis of the Stamp Act, 1763–1765*. Columbia: University of Missouri Press, 1982.

Haskell, Alexander B. "Defining the Right Side of Virtue: Crowd Narratives, the Newspaper, and the Lee-Mercer Dispute in Rhetorical Perspective." *Early American Studies: An Interdisciplinary Journal*, v.8/1 (2010).

Morgan, Edmund S. and Helen M. Morgan. *The Stamp Act Crisis: Prologue to Revolution*. Chapel Hill: University of North Carolina Press, 1995.

Standard Oil Co. of New Jersey v. United States

Standard Oil Co. of New Jersey v. United States was a 1911 Supreme Court case in which the court held that the Anti-Trust Law of 1890 prohibited all contracts or combinations that constituted an "unreasonable" or "undue" restraint of trade in interstate commerce. Here, the court upheld the decision of the Circuit Court of the United States for the Eastern District of Missouri and found Standard Oil guilty of monopolizing the petroleum industry through a series of anti-competitive actions. The court's remedy was to divide Standard Oil into several competing firms.

The federal government brought an action against Standard Oil under the Sherman Anti-Trust Act. The Sherman Act, sponsored by Republican Senator John Sherman of Ohio, made it illegal to establish or attempt to establish monopolies as part of trade or commerce in the United States. It also prohibited "contracts, combinations, or conspiracies in restraint of trade."

Background

By 1906, when the Justice Department initiated the litigation, Standard Oil had become the dominant oil company in the United States, controlling more than 80 percent of the country's oil production. For products for which they controlled the market, such as kerosene, the company charged exorbitant prices. In cases where they faced competition, the Standard Oil Trust was known to cut its prices to the point where it could drive its competitors out of business or force them to sell out. The company was also known to buy up all the materials needed to make oil barrels, making it difficult for competitors to get their products to the market. When all else failed, it was alleged that Standard Oil hired criminals to physically threaten competitors to drive them out of business.

The company's tactics were brought to light by Ida M. Tarbell, who wrote a series of articles that appeared in *McClure's* magazine between November 1902 and October 1904. Tarbell wrote about the unethical tactics of John D. Rockefeller and the company as it came to dominate the industry. Writing of Rockefeller, Tarbell asserted, "Our national life is on every side distinctly poorer, uglier, meaner, for the kind of influence he exercises." Tarbell's 19 articles were then published in book form as *The History of the Standard Oil Company* (1904). In response to the public outcry, the Federal Commissioner of Corporations began an investigation into Standard Oil. The commissioner's report, released in 1906, found that "the dominant position of the Standard Oil Company in the refining industry was due to unfair practices."

The U.S. Department of Justice, at President Theodore Roosevelt's direction, sued Standard Oil under the Sherman Anti-Trust Act of 1890, charging the company with engaging in anti-competitive practices that resulted in restraint of trade. The government alleged that a conspiracy had "been formed in or about the year 1870 by three of the individual defendants: John D. Rockefeller, William Rockefeller, and Henry M. Flagler," and that this conspiracy had continued. The purpose of this conspiracy was "to restrain the trade and commerce in petroleum, commonly called 'crude oil,' in refined oil, and in the other products of petroleum, among the several States and Territories of the United States and the District of Columbia and with foreign nations, and to monopolize the said commerce."

On June 24, 1907, Judge Franklin Ferriss was appointed special examiner to take the evidence in the case, and his report was filed March 22, 1909. The case was then heard from April 5 to 10, 1909, by four judges on the Circuit Court of the United States for the Eastern District of Missouri. The federal government's case was argued by special prosecutor Frank Kellogg. The circuit court decided for the government, although it did dismiss a number of charges made by the Justice Department because the violations had taken place before the passage of the Sherman Act.

The court found that "the combining of the stocks of various companies in the hands of the Standard Oil Company of New Jersey in 1899 constituted a combination in restraint of trade and also an attempt to monopolize and a monopolization under § 2 of the Anti-Trust Act."

Supreme Court Ruling

Standard Oil appealed to the U.S. Supreme Court, arguing that Congress lacked the authority to enact such legislation under the commerce clause. In making this argument, Standard Oil's attorneys (who included John G. Johnson, described by the *New York Times* in 1917 as "the greatest lawyer in the English-speaking world"), cited the court's decision in *United States v. E. C. Knight*, an 1895 case in which the court held that sugar refining was a form of manufacturing and that manufacturing was a "local activity" that was beyond the reach of congressional power under the commerce clause of the U.S. Constitution. In that case, Chief Justice Melville Fuller wrote, in the majority opinion, "That which belongs to commerce is within the jurisdiction of the United States, but that which does not belong to commerce is within the jurisdiction of the police power of the State." While acknowledging that manufactured goods often cross state lines, he concluded that their affect on commerce is "only incidentally and indirectly," placing such goods beyond congressional regulatory authority.

The government's case was argued before the Supreme Court by Attorney General George W. Wickersham and Special Prosecutor Kellogg. They contended that Congress had the constitutional authority under the commerce clause to enact the Sherman Act. The case was initially argued before the Supreme Court March 14–16, 1910. On April 11, 1910, the court ordered that the case be re-argued, and the case was again before the court on January 12, 13, and 16, 1911.

Ida M. Tarbell, author, journalist, and "muckraker," exposed John D. Rockefeller's business practices in a series of articles published in McClure's *magazine between 1902 and 1904.*

On May 15, 1911, the court upheld the lower court's decision, declaring the Standard Oil Company to be an "unreasonable" monopoly under the Sherman Anti-Trust Act. It ordered breakup of Standard Oil into 34 independent companies with different boards of directors.

In this decision, the court articulated the "rule of reason" as the basis for whether a company has violated the antitrust law. What this meant is that monopolies were not necessarily in violation of the Sherman Act but would be found to have violated the law if they "unreasonably" restrained trade. In the case of Standard Oil, the court concluded that the actions of the company, dating back to the 1880s, constituted unreasonable restraint of trade.

Justice John Marshall Harlan wrote a separate opinion concurring in the result but dissenting from the court's adoption of the rule of reason. He argued that the decision was a departure from prior precedents holding that the Sherman Act banned any contract that restrained trade "directly."

Jeffrey Kraus
Wagner College

See Also: Antitrust Law; Constitution of the United States of America; Supreme Court, U.S.

Further Readings
Granitz, Elizabeth and Benjamin Klein. "Monopolization by 'Raising Rivals' Costs': The Standard Oil Case." *Journal of Law and Economics*, v.39/1 (April 1996).
Hidy, Ralph W., et al. *History of Standard Oil Company*. New York: Arno Press, 1976.
McGee, John S. "Predatory Price Cutting: The Standard Oil (N. J.) Case." *Journal of Law and Economics*, v.1 (October 1958).
Tarbell, Ida M. *The History of the Standard Oil Company*. New York: McClure, Philips, 1905.

State Blue Laws

Blue laws, also known as Sunday closing laws, or simply Sunday laws, were originally established to set aside a day to celebrate or honor particular

God(s) where no government business or private labor was conducted. This practice began with the Roman observance of a day of worship to the sun god and carried over into the Christian faith as an observation of the Sabbath. British colonists brought the practice to the Americas, where it became a lynchpin in the growing American culture. Over time, both businesses and citizens have approached the courts over the legality of blue laws in such areas as their religious validity, workers' rights, and economic feasibility. Changing cultural expectations in the late 20th century have resulted in the repeal of many state blue laws.

The origin of the term *blue laws* is obscured by time and is thought to have been a reference to the blue parchment or blue books the laws were printed on during the early Puritan times. Another possibility is that the term referred to the strict moral standards, meant either descriptively or disparagingly, much in the way that the slang term *bluenose* used to describe someone puritanical or prudish. In either case, the first known written reference of this particular term surfaced in the 1781 *General History of Connecticut* authored by Reverend Samuel Peters.

Historical Context

Historically, blue laws or Sunday laws were not a product of Christianity but were pagan in origin. The Roman Emperor Constantine, with the pronouncement of the Edict of Milan in 313 C.E., gave equal opportunity to many religions, including Christianity. As Sunday was already the designated day of worship, this began Christianity's Sunday observance of the Sabbath.

Blue laws have their roots in the observance of "the Venerable Day of the Sun." Worshipping of the sun was prevalent during this time as the Roman Emperor Constantine was personally inclined to favor Apollo, the sun god (he later converted to Christianity). Sunday was the day set aside for rest from all judicial business as well as trade, excepting for those in agriculture as needed to tend fields or perform tasks needed for immediate health and welfare. This observance was more political than ecumenical and was an attempt to unify the empire to include various religious proclivities. No mention of "the Sabbath," "The Lord's Day," or the Fourth Commandment was made in this edict.

It wasn't until 386 C.E. (when Christianity was becoming more integrated into the politics of the day) that the term *The Lord's Day* was used in an edict set forth by Gratianus, Valentinianus, and Theodosius in which "the Lord's Day" was pronounced as the proper title for the day of the sun. These edicts limited business and labor on this day, and as Christianity gained more power, the laws also came to forbid participation in the theater, horse races, gaming, and other recreational activities.

Sunday laws became more and more specifically Christian in context and design. They required all followers to attend services and denied activities to "heathens" that might result in undesirable behavior (drunkenness and other works of the devil). This also removed temptation for otherwise devout Christians. Sunday laws prevailed throughout Christian Europe. Upon arrival in America, the early colonists fashioned their legal guidelines on the 29th Parliament of King Charles II, who, in 1676, compelled each person over the age of 14 to refrain from all acts on Sunday unless they were works of necessity or charity. Each transgression resulted in a fine of 5 shillings.

Colonial Blue Laws

Many of the original colonists left Europe to seek freedom to practice their own religion; this religious ideology became the legal authority for the New World. Church attendance and worship were compulsory. In order to limit temptation to stray from the word of God or hinder the observance of the Sabbath, colonists were "encouraged" by legal mandates to adhere to stringent religious standards. There was little tolerance for any disobedience. As early as 1610, records show that Virginia required its citizens to attend worship service or suffer a loss of provisions for the first offense, whipping and loss of provisions for the second offense, and the possibility of death for the third offense.

The Puritan settlement at Plymouth strictly observed the sanctity of the Sabbath. In 1650, following the lead of the settlers in Virginia, the General Court forbade the colonists in Plymouth to engage in work on the Sabbath—failure to comply with the decree resulted in a 10-shilling fine or a whipping. Later Plymouth records show a continued refinement of this edict to the extreme. Unnecessary travel on Sunday, gaming or hunting, all manner of labor or sport, and the consumption of alcohol were forbidden. Punishment for any infraction mirrored the perceived severity of the indiscretion ranging from fines, whipping, and confinement in the public stocks to death in extreme cases.

In 1662, the Sunday Excise Law was passed, by which the courts mandated that no wine or liquor could be dispensed on Sunday unless needed to relieve the infirm. Over time, each of the colonies enacted its own versions of the Sunday laws that later would become known simply as "blue laws." All sought to uphold the sanctity of the Sabbath by restricting unnecessary travel, smoking, drinking, gaming or sporting, all manner of labor and, in 1665, expanded the restraints to include people caught sleeping in church. Even Native Americans living within the confines of the colonies did not escape these pious proclamations, as they were prohibited from hunting, playing, or working within the colony grounds. Those found in violation of the law suffered the same fate as the nonobservant colonists.

As the legal apparatus of each of the colonies grew stronger and more structured, the colonists appointed certain men (tithes men) to monitor and enforce the laws and to collect fines for noncompliance on behalf of the towns (church). These men had the authority to search homes where they suspected people were negligent in their devotion and to report their blasphemy to the courts. No one was above the Sunday law edict; even George Washington suffered the ignominious fate of being stopped for unlawful travel on the Sabbath. As the colonies expanded and the reach of the physical church grew strained and people became more involved in life outside the church, they became less enthusiastic about observing the strict Sunday law restrictions. Ecclesiastical groups called for more severe punishments, and the people empowered to enforce the morality implicit in the Sunday laws were given more authority and power to ensure compliance. With greater concern for the survival of the Sunday laws, restrictions increased to the point that children could not play in the streets, funerals were prohibited, and no activity on land or at sea was tolerated. Connecticut enforced the law to such an extent that criminal activity conducted on Sunday resulted in greater punishment; for example, a burglary committed on the Sabbath resulted in the additional punishment of having one's ear cut off.

Evolution of Blue Laws

Rapid urban growth, industrialization, and an increasing immigrant population paralleled an equally rapid rise in crime. Gambling, prostitution, and alcohol were seen as major contributors to the problem. Still, blue laws were not popular with many citizens, were ignored by others, and, coupled with the often meager and untrained police force, resulted in less than diligent enforcement. This presented many opportunities for corruption, especially in the larger, crowded cities where the enforcers could be enticed to "turn a blind eye" to violators. Many of the immigrants concentrated in the larger cities like New York, Boston, and Chicago profited from the saloon, tavern, and brewery business. It didn't help that Sunday was generally the only leisure day for workers, and that the German and Irish cultures promoted the leisurely consumption of alcohol, which often led to noisy celebratory public displays. When police cracked down on enforcing mandatory Sunday tavern closings, many saw this as discriminatory toward the immigrants, and riots ensued. In New York City, riots lasted for three days when taverns in the Little Germany area were pressed into Sunday closings. April 1855 saw Chicago's Lager Beer Riots, which left one dead and many arrested. Similar riots played out in Davenport, Iowa, and Boston, Massachusetts, as German and Irish immigrants tested out their newfound American right to protest.

It wasn't until the late 1800s, more than 200 years after the Puritans, that the first legal complaint about the constitutionality of blue laws appeared before the Supreme Court. In 1885, the Supreme Court ruled on the case of *Soon Hing v. Crowley*, a Chinese public laundry owner arrested for operating his business on Sunday. In response to part of the complaint, the court ruled that the Sunday laws would be upheld, not for any governmental preference to any particular religious observance, but because the laws were essentially good for the laborer. In 1898, the Ohio Supreme Court, in *State v. Powell*, upheld the state's right to prohibit baseball games on Sundays, saying the ban did not violate religious freedom.

Baseball, the all-American pastime, continued to be a blue laws issue as baseball leagues continually appealed the Sunday ban through the early 20th century. In 1917, the managers of the New York Giants and the Cincinnati Reds suffered arrest for staging a game on Sunday in direct violation of the blue laws ban. Because of increasing pressure from the community and business leaders, the New York State legislature lifted the ban on Sunday games but prohibited alcohol sales. This concession illustrated a shift in legal support for enforcing the long-standing blue laws. As consumerism became more a way of life, citizens and businesses largely ignored the blue laws. Even those charged with enforcing the restrictions tended to ignore any indiscretions unless a complaint was registered. Because the Sunday laws resided in the legal realm of the individual states, legal restrictions varied drastically from state to state.

In the late 20th century, four major cases came before the U.S. Supreme Court in 1961, testing the legality of Sunday laws. The most significant of these cases, *McGowan v. Maryland*, received a Supreme Court decision on May 29, 1961. Several employees of a large department store in Anne Arundel County, Maryland, were charged and fined for selling nonexempt items on a Sunday. This violated the county statute that allowed the sale of tobacco, foodstuffs, newspapers, gasoline, and medicines. The complaint was filed based on the establishment clause of the First Amendment and the equal protection and due process clauses of the Fourteenth Amendment, arguing that the law required all persons to comply with specific (Christian) beliefs. Chief Justice Earl Warren stated that even though the laws originally complied with religious doctrine, they have historically become more secular in observance. Acknowledging the secular argument that the laws provided the working people with a day of rest, without which they could be compelled to work with no break, he went on to say the restrictions violated no one's freedom of religion, and the only harm caused was economic in nature.

The second case, *Two Guys From Harrison v. McGinley* (decided May 29, 1961), brought to the courts by a retail establishment in Pennsylvania, claimed discriminatory enforcement of the blue laws as the government's endorsement of a particular religion and as a discriminatory practice. The

A cartoon in a left-wing journal Good Morning, *possibly meant to satirize blue laws that prohibited all labor and business activities on the Christian Sabbath, reads "Hey, take your arm down, don't you know this is Sunday?"*

court upheld its previous decision, stating that the restrictions did not violate religious freedom, and that since the statutes were no longer considered religious in intent, the argument was moot for the establishment of government endorsement of a particular religion.

The Supreme Court went on to provide decisions in two cases filed by Jewish merchants. A group within the Orthodox Jewish faith that included stockholders from the Crown Kosher Super Market, several customers, and a rabbi filed the case *Gallagher v. Crown Kosher Super Market*. Their argument centered on the fact that their religious faith did not allow shopping on the Sabbath (the Jewish Sabbath began on Friday at sundown and lasted until sundown on Saturday). Furthermore, their religion required a diet of kosher foods, and they were only allowed to remain open until 10 A.M. on Sunday. Crown contended that this was not economically feasible and that prior to enforcement of the Sunday closing laws, they had taken in a third of their weekly profits on Sunday alone. They contended that the preponderance of exceptions to Massachusetts' Sunday closing laws, especially those that did not necessarily come under the necessity or charity clauses (these exemptions covered a number of professional sporting events, dancing and concerts of a religious nature, and the sale of desserts and live bait, as well as a number of other business ventures), provided adequate precedent to allow their business to remain open on Sunday to provide kosher food products to their Jewish clientele. Once more, Justice Warren upheld the states' rights, stating that these laws were not in violation of the equal protection clause.

The second case brought before the Supreme Court by Jewish merchants was *Braunfeld v. Brown*. These Orthodox Jewish merchants argued that forcing them to comply with the Sunday closing laws, which required them to close on the day after their Sabbath, unfairly discriminated against their religious faith in favor of their Christian counterparts. The court again pointed out that the purpose of the Sunday closing restrictions was to provide a day of rest for all citizens and felt this intent outweighed any religious injury. Since the blue laws allowed Sunday sales of "necessary" items, a number of state legislatures provided questionable legal interpretations when providing exemptions. Most state blue laws prohibited alcohol sales in general on Sundays, but exceptions could be and were made for New Year's Eve and New Year's Day when the holidays fell on a Sunday. Additionally, while one could not purchase alcohol in an establishment specifically designed for alcohol consumption, alcoholic beverages could accompany a meal in a restaurant. Massachusetts restricted dancing on Sundays, but allowed exemptions for folk and square dancing. Pennsylvania prohibited hunting except for foxes, crows, and coyotes. Virginia also banned Sunday hunting yet made exemptions for hunting raccoons until 2 A.M.

Today, most states have repealed their blue laws as they pertain to retail sales for economic and convenience reasons, and all but 14 states allow Sunday alcohol sales. In addition to alcohol restrictions, some states still ban automobile sales on Sunday, as well as hunting for sport. The punishment for blue law violations are usually small fines, with minimal jail time for more egregious violations. Because of the number of exemptions granted in the past and changing cultural attitudes, a multitude of complaints is normally required for enforcement of current blue laws.

Tina P. Hanson
Jefferson College
Robin Annette Hanson
St. Louis University

See Also: 1941 to 1960 Primary Documents; Drinking and Crime; Puritans; Religion and Crime, History of.

Further Readings
Laband, David N. *Blue Laws: The History, Economics, and Politics of Sunday-Closing Laws.* Lexington, MA: D. C. Heath and Co., 1987.
Lewis, Abram Herbert. *Sunday Legislation.* New York: D. Appleton and Co., 1902.

State Police

When one uses the term *state police* in reference to the United States, the meaning may fall into one of three general categories. These generalized meanings are directly related to the history of the development and functionality of police agencies with statewide authority. The term *state police* may encompass agencies formally named "State Police," agencies that are identified as the primary police force in a state, and agencies that are not the primary police force in a state but nonetheless hold statewide law enforcement jurisdiction.

Formal State Police Units

In the early days of the United States, policing was left to the local jurisdictions, and there were no agencies with statewide police authority. Arguably, one could say that the local officers had the authority to pursue criminals out of their original jurisdiction, but the officers had no authority to patrol outside of their local jurisdiction.

There is great debate over the issue of which agency was the first state police. The Texas Rangers, today a unit of the Texas Department of Public Safety, make the claim on the basis that Stephen F. Austin created the force in 1823, while serving as empresario of the Mexican province of Tejas. There are issues that make the claim weak:

Texas did not attain statehood until 1845; the Texas Rangers largely acted in the role of militia until the Civil War, then lacked funding and support until 1874; it wasn't until the early 1900s that the Texas Rangers began to function as a true law enforcement agency; as in many states, the institution of national Prohibition helped to define the force.

Massachusetts State Police also claim to be the first, identifying 1865 as their founding. This claim also has weaknesses: The agency that was created was known as the State Constabulary and had limited authority, serving mostly in an investigative capacity; this first group went through name changes and worked in relative obscurity until it disappeared completely; the term *state police patrol* was not used by Massachusetts until 1921.

An excellent argument can be made that Pennsylvania State Police have the honor of being the first recognizable state police, if that definition includes a uniformed police with statewide jurisdiction. Founded in 1905, its task was broad in scope, from protecting wildlife to patrolling rural areas, and it became a model for other states in developing their own forces.

Another argument could be made for a state police agency with a short operational span, again in Texas. In 1870, during Reconstruction, the Texas legislature created the Texas State Police, specifically to combat a statewide crime spree. Its creation was innovative in that it was based on the outcome of a crime survey; it actually used the term *state police*; and it employed white, Hispanic, and African American men. The force was unpopular and was dissolved in 1873, largely because of its employment of African Americans. There have been competing claims for and against the work this agency did, but more recent research shows that it was effective in reducing crime in Texas. The state has never assigned the formal name of Texas State Police again.

Only 22 states have an agency with the formal name of "State Police." Of the 27 states east of the Mississippi River, 16 use the formal name of State Police. Only five of those west of the Mississippi River use this as the formal name. Hawai'i is the only state that does not have a state police agency with general authority. Reviewing the history of the agencies reveals that some were created in response to specific criminal activity.

As examples, the Pennsylvania State Police was created in response to the violence of a coal miner strike; the New York State Police was created in response to the murder of a sheriff and the subsequent disorganized manhunt for his killer; and the institution of national Prohibition contributed to the beginning, or reorganization, of many agencies.

The vast majority of those agencies formally known as State Police have evolved from preexisting forces. This conflicts with the common misconception that agencies with the formal name State Police have more authority, or were established earlier than those using other names. Many evolved from agencies created to combat crime, such as the Arkansas State Police, established in 1939, which evolved from the Arkansas Rangers, which was established in 1935; the Delaware State Police, established in 1923, replaced the Highway Traffic Police, established to patrol highways in 1919; and the Kentucky State Police, established in 1948, replaced the Kentucky Highway Patrol, which had been created in 1936.

Primary State Police Agencies

Of the 49 states with agencies having general police authority statewide, but not using the formal name State Police, 19 have the formal name Highway Patrol, and seven use State Patrol; Alaska uses State Troopers. The 49 primary state police agencies commonly use the term *state trooper* to identify their officers, although some use *highway patrolman*.

Using the founding of the Pennsylvania State Police as a benchmark for the first modern state police agency, and recognizing the Alaska State Police as the most recent addition in 1959, we can reasonably observe that the modern primary state police agency developed and spread in a period of only 54 years. As a note, the Alaska State Police underwent a name change in 1967 to become the only state police agency with the official name State Troopers.

Entry-level training within these agencies generally occurs in a formal academy operated by the specific agency. The academies are typically paramilitary and instill in trainees high ideals and standards of conduct. These agencies have typically led advanced in-service training programs and in most states are highly regarded for their professionalism.

Many of the agencies are still evolving, having other specialized state enforcement agencies merged into their organizations. The catalyst for these mergers is usually an attempt to increase professionalization across the spectrum, centralize operations, and save costs. An excellent example is the 1991 Massachusetts Police Consolidation Act, which merged the state police with the metropolitan police, registry police, and Capitol police. Sometimes a merger is initiated to increase the number of troopers without increasing the number of officers employed by the state, which is addressed in the next category.

Becoming a trooper in one of the agencies was once viewed as entering a stable work environment. In recent years, in large part because of taxpayer demands for tighter budgets and the weak economy, some state police agencies have witnessed a reduction of positions. As an example, according to a press release from the Oregon State Police, the agency witnessed a reduction between 1995 and 2008 of more than 30 percent. This situation is aggravated by the fact that for the past two decades, the growth of these agencies has fallen behind that of the general population.

Many of these agencies complain that their ability to recruit qualified candidates is becoming more difficult. Some causes for this include the fact that local agencies have experienced increased benefits and wages, many surpassing those of the state police agencies; many states are increasing the standards for police officers; agencies are becoming better at detecting behaviors that exclude applicants, partially through the increasing use of pre-employment polygraph examinations.

Agencies With Statewide Jurisdiction

Most estimates indicate that there are close to 20,000 law enforcement agencies operating with state authority and funded through state revenues

Massachusetts State Police display a police cruiser, a jet ski, and a state patrol vessel at a 2004 event. Boston is the headquarters for the State Police Marine Section, which has two jet skis, an airboat, a dive boat, and a motor lifeboat. Troopers with tactical weapons are also on patrol in Boston Harbor in support of U.S. Homeland Security.

in the United States. The vast majority of these organizations operating as state police agencies serve a special purpose, sometimes referred to as limited or restricted jurisdiction. This refers to either a restriction of the enforcement authority or the physical limitation of the jurisdictional boundary.

These agencies clearly are modeled on the federal agencies and often have similar purposes. Such agencies include those that monitor and protect wildlife, whatever name is used to describe them, but are commonly referred to as game wardens. In many states, game wardens have full police authority but are encouraged to focus on their official role. In other states, they are restricted to game-related violations.

Other examples may include agencies whose purpose it is to investigate certain felonies or assist local agencies when requested, enforce weight and size limits, enforce tax revenue laws, investigate parents accused of child neglect and abuse, patrol and enforce laws at state institutions and Capitols, and enforce other specific sections of law. Many of these agencies have high levels of specialized training.

In many states, public university campus police are given state police authority within the jurisdictional boundaries of the property associated with the institution. This authority is often extended to include adjoining property and the areas where the officers travel from one facility to another. Even though these agencies may have general policing powers, the jurisdiction within which they operate is special thus they serve in a special purpose policing role.

In recent cases, these agencies have been merged with the primary state police agency. Some have suggested this is a slow trend that will lead to most states having a single state police agency serving multiple purposes. Others argue that it is simply a recurring process, and that the trend will turn at a future point. The latter argument has support from previous attempts by states to consolidate. As an example, in the mid-1970s, Arkansas created a Department of Public Safety and quickly moved several agencies into divisions of what was planned to be a single state enforcement command system. Before the end of the decade, the agency was scrapped, and in ensuing years, a plethora of new state police agencies was created.

When one of these specialized state police agencies merges into the primary one, there are often strained feelings on both sides. The members of the primary agency reject the idea of incorporating the merged organizational members as troopers. The merged members have concerns about being a subclass member of the agency but not a trooper. In fact, the transition most often results in some restrictions being placed on the merged members. These restrictions have ranged from prohibiting promotion to disarming the merged members.

State Police in the Current Era

Writers are fond of noting that the events of September 11, 2001, changed everything. While that phrase is broad in relationship to the role of state police, there have been role changes. This is particularly true of the post–9/11 primary state police agencies, which have had to incorporate antiterrorism considerations into enforcement and response. Many of these agencies have introduced increased tactical response training and created special units to collect and analyze intelligence and monitor reports of suspicious behavior.

Many of these primary state police agencies have a traditional role in providing executive protective services for the state governor and other officials. After the events of 9/11, many of these agencies experienced significant growth in the calls for their assistance in executive protection. This is also true of their assistance in providing security for special events.

Increasingly, these agencies are being called on to enlarge their role in other areas of law enforcement. When state legislators meet, it is seldom to reduce the number of laws on the books. Each state legislative session results in new and refined laws that add to the burden of these agencies. Unfortunately, with these added duties and increasing responsibilities, there is seldom an associated funding stream provided to help the agencies cope with the costs.

In spite of the difficulties they are facing, the primary state police agencies continue to strive for the image of being elite police officers. In turn, many young men and women develop the goal of being a part of their state's primary agency. These state troopers have generally enjoyed a long heritage of being recognized as capable of handling any incident. The trooper attitude and public view have traditionally been supported by these agencies providing training across the wide spectrum of policing. With the increasing roles they now face, the current philosophy is to provide general police training for all troopers and specialized training for specifically chosen ones.

Typically, these primary state police agencies require some term of service in their highway patrol function before a trooper can apply for a specialized unit. These units range across a broad spectrum of specializations from motor carrier enforcement to undercover drug investigation. Thus, the climate is being improved for the merging of the other agencies with state police authority into the primary agency; these agencies bring the specialization with them.

In the immediate future, as states are faced with increasing taxpayer demands for tighter budgets and greater accountability, and as the economy continues to struggle, it is very likely that instances of the merging of state police agencies will increase. In most instances, it only makes sense to merge into the primary agency. The evolution of state policing continues.

Just as the United States is unique in its traditional rejection of a national generalized police force, it is also unique for the way it has embraced the concept of a state police. The 20th century was the "Era of State Police Development"; the 21st century will be era of their refinement.

George R. Franks, Jr.
Stephen F. Austin State University

See Also: Police, Contemporary; Police, History of; Police, Sociology of.

Further Readings
Dulaney, W. Marvin. *Black Police in America.* Indianapolis: Indiana University Press, 1996
Hahn, Harlan and Judson L. Jeffries. *Urban America and Its Police Force: From the Postcolonial Era Through the Turbulent 1960s.* Boulder: University Press of Colorado, 2003.
Johnson, David E. *American Law Enforcement: A History.* Arlington Heights, IL: Forum Press, 1981.
Prassel, Frank R. *The Western Police Officer: A Legacy of Law and Order.* Norman: University of Oklahoma Press, 1972.

State Slave Codes

Between the 1640s and the 1860s, an extensive body of laws was developed in the United States to regulate the institutions of slavery. The earliest codes were Virginia's, passed in 1705. Slave codes were laws enacted in each U.S. state that defined the relationship between slaves and slave owners. These laws codified the permanency of slavery, inherited through the mother, denying slaves all basic rights—citizenship, education, legal marriages, property assembly, and associating with each other. With the explosion of the slave trade between the 16th and 19th centuries, and the widespread establishment of the chattel system—which allowed for ownership of human beings and their descendants—certain laws were needed to allow for more authority and regulation of the slave population.

The fundamental objective of the slaveholding codes was to define slaves as human chattel. Slaves were considered property, and these laws established slaves as tangible personal property or goods. The laws provided that slaves would be treated as goods—sold, transferred, or pawned. These laws were used to codify that slaves had no status as human beings because they were defined as property—a common thread in many state codes. They defined slaves as property that had no power. Slave owners had absolute power over any slaves they owned. Most slave codes outlined which rights a slave did not have versus which rights slaves did have. A common feature among most state slave codes was that slaves did not possess any civil, religious, or political rights as outlined in different variation in the various state codes.

There were an estimated 4 million black Africans and people of African descent in slavery by 1860; these slaves resisted this system of labor exploitation through rebellions, noncompliance, and escaping to Canada and to other non–slave states. Fugitive slave laws were passed in 1793 and 1850 by the U.S. Congress as a means of managing slaves and dealing with the problems slave owners were encountering, particularly with regard to fugitive slaves.

Themes of the State Slave Codes
The various state slave codes outlined the legal relation between master and slave. The statutes

An African American slave family posed in front of the Gaines house in the Virginia area circa 1861. Strict and harsh slave codes were passed in Virginia in 1705 and the rest of the south and the colonies followed suit. Common punishments included maiming, branding, placing slaves in stocks, and receiving 60 lashes for an offense as minor as robbery.

also made provision for punishment; slaves could be punished in any manner, including death, although some state codes did make provision against extreme punishment such as death, maiming, or mutilation. For example, Louisiana's code, passed in 1724, stated that punishment should not mutilate, disfigure, or kill the slave. Florida's code, passed in 1821, had similar provisions. The evidence suggests that these provisions were rarely adhered to. Codes were constantly being revised and tended to get harsher. Codes were also contradictory, as seen in the 1724 Louisiana code that mandated capital punishment for any slave who hit a white person.

The statutes emphasized the domination of slave masters over slaves and the slave as personal chattel with no rights and in the same stead as animals or inanimate properties. This was consistent throughout all the state slave codes. Kentucky's slave code of 1798 defined slaves as property and stipulated that slaves could be passed down only to heirs and not to executors. Virginia's 1705 statute mandated that slaves could be used to pay a master's debts. Slaves were considered personal property, and this was highlighted even in statutes in what eventually came to be known as free states. For example, in the Maryland Act of 1798, slaves were classified as personal property in the same category as furniture, plates, books, working beasts, or animals. This was also seen in the New Jersey slave codes that referred to slaves as property, held with no higher regard than other properties.

South Carolina's slave code deemed slaves to be chattel of their owners to do whatever the owner intended. The objective was to define slaves as possessions, but South Carolina's code, consistent with Virginia's laws, defined slaves as personal chattel. Louisiana's code was even more explicit in what slaves could possess—slaves were permitted to possess or acquire nothing. Not only did Louisiana's slave code outline the relationship between slave and master, it focused on the absolute rights of the slave master or owner. It highlighted not only the power of the master to dispose of a slave as he deemed appropriate but also the master's right to punish the slave. Louisiana's slave code of 1724 stipulated that slaves could be rented and mortgaged as laborers. This provision was popular in other state slave codes as it provided for the prevention of sale of slaves from plantations.

Slave codes were supposed to minimize slave revolts or rebellions. Slaves were forbidden to attend church services unless accompanied by a white person. Slaves were not seen as credible, so they could not testify against any white person in court. Between 1810 and 1860, the slave codes started to include manumission—the freeing of slaves. These statutes restricted the rights of slave owners and made it difficult to free any slaves. Slave owners' ability to free their slaves was limited even if it was outlined in a will. Free blacks were seen as dangerous and might incite other slaves to revolt, thus slaves who were freed were required to leave the state within 30 days.

Another common theme in slave codes defined business relations. Individuals could not engage in business relations with a slave without the consent of the slave owner. Since slaves were viewed as property, they could be used as security for loans, offered as prizes in raffles, and given away as gifts. Education and marriage were also harshly regulated. Education was forbidden for slaves. Anyone found trying to educate a slave faced both fines and imprisonment. Slaves could marry but their marriages were not legally binding. This allowed for slave owners to split families up when selling them.

Most of these codes limited slave movements and gatherings. Slaves could not move freely, nor could they gather without a white person being present or supervising. The physical exploitation and abuse of slaves were also common among various slave codes. Acts such as arson, conspiracy to cause a rebellion, or rape of any white woman were punishable by death. The opposite was not true of the relationship between slaves and whites. Slaves were seen as chattel, thus they could be maimed or killed by owners without any punishment for the owners. However, if someone killed a slave owned by someone else, that person could face a fine because they deprived the owners of their property. White men raping slave women were usually charged with trespassing as a slave woman was viewed only as chattel—property. Although weapons were a common part of life in the colonies, slaves were not permitted to own, keep, or carry guns. Slaves could face between 40 and 60 lashes and had to relinquish the gun as was defined in the codes. Slave codes in many states defined not only the status of slaves but of also free black citizens. This was evident in Alabama slave codes of 1833.

Influential State Slave Codes

The most influential codes were those of Virginia passed in 1705. Virginia's code set the precedent not only throughout the south but throughout the colonies. The 1705 Virginia codes outlined harsh physical punishments and bodily disfigurement. Slaves could have their ears cut off for such things as associating with whites or leaving the plantation without written permission. Common punishments for slaves were maiming and branding. Under the Virginia code, slaves could be placed in stocks and receive 60 lashes for such offenses as robbery. Slaves who were found guilty of murder under this statute were hanged. The slave codes of 1705 eliminated the rights of slaves to bring disputes with their masters before the courts for hearings. Slaves had no means of protection against even the most abusive master.

States that found themselves with a larger black population than white tended to have harsher statutes; this was evident in southern state codes. Alabama, Florida, Louisiana, South Carolina, and Virginia codes are good examples. A 1690 revised South Carolina code outlined harsh punishment for runaway slaves and slaves who hit a white person. Punishments included whippings, slitting the nose, and burning the face with a hot iron. Any slave who was accused of a second offense of hitting a white person could be put to death. Runaway slaves were branded with an "R" on their cheek and had one of their ears cut off. Slaves who ran away two or more times could be castrated (male slaves), have a tendon cut in one leg, or be put to death. South Carolina's 1712 statute provided for the whipping of any slave who left the plantation without written permission.

In 1705, Virginia statutes absolved slave masters of any punishment if they killed a slave during punishment. Some slave statutes extended beyond enslaved persons to other minority members in the population. In 1833, Alabama passed a series of slave codes outlining the punishment for not only educating enslaved individuals but also free blacks, who were referred to as mulatto, Indian, and indentured slaves. The statute provided for fines and whipping on the bare back for anyone who taught slaves or any free person of color to read, write, or spell. Alabama's 1833 statute also punished a slave who wrote for another slave with 50 lashes the first time and 100 lashes to the bare back for every subsequent offense. Any person who wrote for any slave was also subjected to 39 lashes on the bare back, and that person also had to leave the state of Alabama within 30 days.

The District of Columbia codes were viewed as an exception to these harsh southern codes. The District of Columbia was governed by the slave code of Maryland when it was first established in 1800. Slaves in the District of Columbia could hire their services, and these slaves also did not live with their masters. It is important to note that these urban slaves were servants to government elites. Unlike other southern slaves, free blacks were allowed to live in the city and operate schools. By 1850, the sale of slaves within the District of Columbia was outlawed.

Revisions of State Slave Codes

States were constantly revising their codes, and the revised codes usually provided for harsher treatment of the slave population. Florida's slave codes had many revisions influenced by news of uprisings in other locales. Florida lawmakers gave additional power to slave patrols after the Nat Turner Rebellion in 1831. The Florida legislature empowered slave patrols to capture and whip any slave violating the pass laws. Other revisions included the death penalty for anyone accused of inciting slaves to revolt and an automatic verdict of justifiable homicide in the case of any slave killed in the act of revolting. In 1686, South Carolina established a slave status in its code as a freehold property, a higher status than being chattel. Freehold property was attached to a specific estate or plantation and could not be moved or sold from that estate. By 1696, slaves had been degraded to chattel property, provided for in a 1690 revised code that also outlined harsh punishment for the slave population. In 1740, South Carolina again revised its code, passing the Negro Act in response to the Stono slave rebellion of 1739. This act served as a model for Georgia's code of 1755. Under the 1739 Negro Act, slaves had no protection under the law. Murder of a slave by a white person was only punishable by a fine. Slaves could be executed for plotting riots, plotting to run away, or offering any cultural education such as knowledge about poisonous roots and plants. This act controlled all aspects of enslaved population life from what clothes slaves could wear to what fabrics could make these clothes. It also included additional prohibition on learning to read and write, as well as assembling and socializing with one another. Any violations of these laws were subject to flogging.

Denise D. Nation
Winston-Salem State University

See Also: 1801 to 1850 Primary Documents; 1851 to 1900 Primary Documents; African Americans; Civil Rights Act of 1866; Civil Rights Act of 1875; Slavery; Slavery, Law of.

Further Readings
Conlin, J. *The American Past: A Survey of American History to 1877.* Boston: Wadsworth, 2008.
Davis, David Brion. *The Problem of Slavery in the Age of Revolution, 1770–1823.* Oxford: Oxford University Press, 1999.
Goodell, William. *The American Slave Code in Theory & Practice.* New York: American and Foreign Anti-Slavery Society, 1853.
Patterson, Orlando. *Slavery and Social Death: A Comparative Study.* Cambridge, MA: Harvard University Press, 1982.

State v. Heitman

At issue in *State v. Heitman*, 262 Neb. 185 (2001), is whether the police went so far in enticing a man to commit a sexual offense as to entrap him. The case is a significant example of the subjective or predisposition test for entrapment: The entrapment defense was rejected, even though police induced Heitman to commit a crime that otherwise might not have occurred, on the ground, that Heitman was predisposed to commit the crime.

Heitman, 53, approached the drive-up window of a restaurant and gave an envelope with $100 and three condoms to a 14-year-old girl referred to as A. S. The envelope also contained a letter saying how cute the girl was and inviting her to use the money to buy a sexy dress for her lover or to save it for school. It also included Heitman's e-mail address. The girl showed the letter to her manager, who called the police. Detective Steven Henthorn, with A. S.'s consent, posed as A. S. and exchanged e-mails with Heitman, using the name Rodeo Queen. The detective provided opportunities for Heitman to cease contact, but Heitman continued to respond. At one point, Heitman, suspicious, asked Rodeo Queen which color nail polish she wore, and wanted to speak to her on the phone. Henthorn then arranged for A. S. to phone Heitman. In their conversation, A. S., following detective Henthorn's instructions, encouraged Heitman to tell her how he could be sexually creative. After several more e-mail exchanges, Rodeo Queen suggested they finally meet in a motel room. Henthorn then arranged for A. S. to again phone Heitman. During the call, Heitman suggested a "more innocent" place to meet, but A. S. pressed Heitman by saying she'd be going away soon. Heitman agreed, arrived at the motel carrying sexual paraphernalia, and was arrested.

To establish a legal defense of entrapment, the state of Nebraska requires that the government must have induced the crime and that the defendant not be predisposed to commit the crime. This is called a subjective test because it appeals to the state of mind of the defendant and not to whether the police took measures that objectively could induce a normally law-abiding person to commit a crime. On this test, defendants are guilty if they were predisposed to commit the crime even if the police used objectionable methods to induce them—as was arguably the case when Detective Henthorn had a 14-year-old girl engage in sexual banter with Heitman. The subjective test was adopted by the U.S. Supreme Court in *Sorrells v. United States*, 287 U.S. 435 (1932).

The district court sentenced Heitman to 8-12 years in prison for conspiring to sexually penetrate someone under 16 years of age. It held that Heitman was predisposed: He first approached the girl and chose to ignore several opportunities to break off contact. On appeal, the Supreme Court of Nebraska upheld his conviction in a 7–0 decision written by Justice Connolly Wright. The court conceded that there was government inducement: The detective suggested the meeting in the motel and created a sense of urgency; but Heitman was predisposed. Heitman, in his defense, claimed that initially he thought A. S. was 16, but the court noted that mistake as to a victim's age is not a defense to this crime. Heitman also claimed he simply used his e-mails and phone calls to express his fantasies and had no predisposition to have sex with her, but the court held that a reasonable jury could find predisposition.

The predisposition test is sometimes criticized because in using it, the state seems to base punishment on a person's character rather than his present conduct. This may be less a concern in *Heitman*, since the evidence for the defendant's predisposition was not his character as revealed by his past but his making first contact with a 14-year-old girl.

Other courts have allowed an entrapment defense where the defendant was led on or encouraged by undercover agents posing as children. In *United States V. Poehlman*, Judge Kozinsky of the 9th Circuit Court of Appeals reversed the conviction of a man who initiated an online chat with an agent posing as a woman seeking a sexual mentor for her children. That court found that Poehlman was not predisposed to have sex with children; that idea was suggested by the agent.

Mark Tunick
Florida Atlantic University

See Also: Nebraska; Sex Offender Laws; Sex Offenders.

Further Readings
McAdams, Robert. "Political Economy of Entrapment." *Journal of Criminal Law and Criminology*, v.96/1 (2005).
Tunick, Mark. "Entrapment and Retributive Theory." *Retributivism: Essays on Theory and Policy*. New York: Oxford University Press, 2011.

Steenburgh, Sam

Samuel Steenburgh (1833–78) was an African American convicted of the murder of Jacob S. Parker, a white farmer, in Fonda, New York, on November 17, 1877. Shortly before his execution, he confessed to 10 additional murders, which caused great interest in his execution and attracted throngs to witness the event.

Steenburgh's trial was conducted February 26–27, 1878. The prosecution charged that Steenburgh, who knew the victim for more than 20 years, had spent the evening of the murder at a saloon with Parker. Afterward, they entered an area known as Ross' Woods, where Steenburgh struck Parker on the head with a stone and then, to be certain he was dead, crushed Parker's head with a boulder. The motive for the crime was robbery.

Public hanging was the most common method of execution; the first recorded historical mention dates from 1300 C.E. More than 15,000 witnessed Steenburgh's 1878 hanging.

Steenburgh was sentenced to death by hanging. Efforts by Steenburgh's attorney to obtain a new trial based on new evidence were abandoned.

Steenburgh maintained his innocence. However, shortly before his execution, Steenburgh confessed to 11 murders, numerous arsons, robberies, and other crimes. He is also said to have hinted without providing details, that he may have committed other crimes. Steenburgh received $100 from the sheriff and county clerk for his confession, and it was printed in a 22-page pamphlet and sold for 25 cents a copy. More than 5,000 copies were printed.

Steenburgh was executed by hanging in Fonda, New York, on April 19, 1878. According to contemporary newspaper accounts, more than 15,000 people came to the village for the execution, notwithstanding an 1835 law that required executions to take place "within the walls of the prison … or within a yard or enclosure adjoining" (*New York Laws*). The *New York Times* reported that "Two special trains from the east, aggregating 12 cars, and one of 7 cars from the west," brought many of the spectators. Farmers came in from the surrounding countryside. Home and business owners in the vicinity of the prison charged admission for the purpose of witnessing the execution from their roofs, which overlooked the prison. The day of his hanging was declared a public holiday in Fonda and the surrounding area. Following the execution, onlookers were permitted to pass the coffin and view, and even touch, the corpse of the condemned man.

Jeffrey Kraus
Wagner College

See Also: African Americans; Executions; Murder, History of.

Further Readings
1835 N.Y. Laws, ch. 258 § 1.
"Seven Murders Expiated: The Execution of Sam Steenburgh." *New York Times* (April 20, 1878).
Steenburgh, Samuel. *Confession of Samuel Steenburgh, Who Murdered Jacob S. Parker, November 17th, 1877: Executed at Fonda, on Friday, April 19th, 1878* (Making of the Modern Law: Legal Treatises, 1800–1926). London: Gale, 2010.

Strauder v. West Virginia

The 1880 U.S. Supreme Court decision in *Strauder v. West Virginia* looked to the equal protection clause of the Fourteenth Amendment to invalidate a West Virginia policy excluding individuals from serving on juries because of their race. The policy was carried out in a statute limiting jury service to "all white male persons." The case was argued before the Supreme Court on October 21, 1879. It was decided on March 1, 1880. The decision struck down jury exclusion practices common among southern states, which sought to empanel white-only juries despite the provisions of the Civil Rights Act of 1875 that made it a crime to violate the principle that all citizens had a right to serve on both state and federal juries.

The case began when the plaintiff (or defendant, in the initial action in state court) was indicted for first-degree murder in Ohio County, West Virginia, in 1874. The plaintiff was an African American man named Taylor Strauder. Convicted at trial by an all-white jury and sentenced by a white judge, Strauder petitioned to the Supreme Court of Appeals of West Virginia, which affirmed the trial court's decision. Strauder was scheduled to die by hanging.

The case came before the U.S. Supreme Court on a writ of error alleging that West Virginia had denied the plaintiff the rights entitled to him under the Constitution. Because he was not granted a fair trial, the plaintiff had standing to bring his claim alleging a constitutional violation under the due process and equal protection clauses.

Changing the Makeup of Juries

Justice William Strong, a former Republican in the U.S. House of Representatives, a former abolitionist, and an appointee of President Ulysses S. Grant, delivered the opinion of the court. His opinion focused on equal protection rather than on due process. Strong exposed the hypocrisy of a system whereby whites were entitled to juries made up of all whites, while blacks, forced to stand trial before all-white juries, did not enjoy the same entitlement. Strong concluded that the statutory scheme discriminated against blacks and recalled the badges and incidents of slavery. The statutory scheme asserted the inferiority of nonwhites and generated racial prejudice and therefore could not stand. The statutory scheme was ruled unconstitutional because all U.S. citizens, regardless of their race, were deemed to have constitutional rights to criminal trials before juries selected and impaneled in nondiscriminatory ways.

The *Strauder* case represents one of the most prominent antidiscrimination holdings after the Emancipation Proclamation was issued and before the civil rights movement began roughly a century later. The court, liberally construing the Fourteenth Amendment to keep with the putative purposes of the amendment's framers, held that the amendment granted citizenship and the privileges of citizenship to people of color; therefore, states had to ensure the equal protection of the laws to people of color. The West Virginia statute did not ensure the equal protection of the laws to people of color because it denied such individuals the right to serve on juries.

The court also held that Congress, even without an express delegation of power, could protect a right or immunity whether it was created or only guaranteed by the Constitution. According to the court, the Fourteenth Amendment conferred a right or immunity to "the colored race" because it was designed to protect "colored races" when states denied them any rights enjoyed by whites.

The court did not eliminate all forms of discrimination—only discrimination based on race. For instance, the court decision left room for discrimination against nonlandowners. That the decision invalidated exclusion policies based on race did not mean that later attorneys could not impanel all-white juries. Nevertheless, the decision went great lengths toward establishing equal rights for black citizens.

Allen Mendenhall
Auburn University

See Also: Race, Class, and Criminal Law; Racism; Supreme Court, U.S.

Further Readings

Bastress, Robert. *The West Virginia State Constitution: A Reference Guide*. Westport, CT: Greenwood Press, 1995.

Schmidt, Brenno C., Jr. "Juries, Jurisdiction, and Race Discrimination: The Lost Promise of *Strauder v.*

West Virginia." *Texas Law Review*, v.61/1401 (1983).

Strauder v. West Virginia, 100 U.S. 303 (1880).

Stump, Brandon M. "From Reconstruction to Obama: Understanding Black Invisibility, Racism in Appalachia, and the Legal Community's Responsibility to Promote a Dialogue on Race at the WVU College of Law." *West Virginia Law Review*, v.112/1095 (2010).

Strikes

A strike occurs when people simultaneously refuse to work and try to encourage everyone in a workplace to stop working there. Strikes tend to be organized by labor unions, since they provide the social solidarity necessary to persuade people to take action that may be dangerous and certainly expensive for them. Strikers are not paid and unless their union can provide funds, the strike will soon be ended by lack of money and the pressure of feeding a family. It is easier, therefore, for younger and single individuals to mount a strike than older workers who have more personal responsibilities.

Strikes are most commonly organized in response to workplace grievances, including but not limited to desire for higher wages. Other reasons for strikes include concern over health and safety issues, reduction in the number of hours worked, better working conditions, concern over the strategy being pursued by the organization or in support of a political dispute not directly related to the employees at all (this may take the form of a sympathy strike in solidarity with workers elsewhere in the same or a different industry). Historically, one of the goals of the labor movement was to achieve the ability to organize a general strike, in which all workers would strike simultaneously, and the state would be forced to yield to the demands being made. However, antipathy to labor unions in the United States has meant that the level of unionization has always been low by international standards, particularly in the private sector, and that means strikers have been more isolated and hence vulnerable to the force customarily used against them.

A case in which, perhaps as a result of a labor dispute, the owners of a workplace refuse to allow workers onto the premises, is known as a lockout. The opposite occurs when workers occupy a workplace to prevent work taking place or to prevent new employees (sometimes referred to as "scab" workers) to replace the strikers. This is known as a sit-in or workers' occupation.

As labor unions became recognized in American law, restrictions were placed on how and when strikes may be conducted. Generally, an official strike can only be called after a ballot has been held and a majority for strike action reached, as well as other restrictions. Strikes that take place without official union sanction are called wildcat strikes and may follow a spontaneous walkout in response to a new event, which may subsequently become an official strike.

Labor Strikes

Strikes have taken place in the United States almost since settlements were established. The first recorded strike was by Polish crafts workers in 1619 in Jamestown, Virginia. Since then, the number of strikes has waxed and waned in line with overall economic conditions (reaching a peak of more than 4,300 in 1937) and changing in the nature of workers represented. Early strikes tended to affect a comparatively small group of workers, usually skilled, of common ethnicity, and working in close proximity with each other. Just like the Polish crafts workers, they would have been recruited to the New World because they had economically valuable skills that could be transferred to the new economy. However, once relocated, they found in some cases that the terms and conditions of their work were not acceptable, and their personal liberties and rights were constrained in comparison with other people. They called strikes, then, purely for their own benefit and that of their families but had little if any solidarity with any other group of workers. Strikes in these early periods were restricted to those areas that had been settled by Europeans and in the various occupations that were then important to the economy: indentured service, fishing, transportation, and so forth. As the geographical scope of the colonies broadened and the economy became more sophisticated, strikes broke out in different areas and sectors. In the 18th century, for example, they included representatives of river pilots, weavers, construction workers, and tailors. However, these strikes continued to be focused primarily on local issues, with a few exceptions, and had little if any intention of bringing about any meaningful political change.

It was not until the spread of advanced industrialization throughout the country and the entry into the factory age that large numbers of unskilled workers were brought together in a single place with shared working conditions and terms of employment. Such labor unions as existed prior to this were mainly focused on the position of a limited number of skilled workers, almost certainly men. One area of general interest that did arise as an issue of contention was the length of the working day and of the working week. The Boston 10-hour strike of 1832, for example, was portrayed by industrialists as symptomatic of the struggle for overall control of the economy.

The factory age brought a new stage of industrial confrontation and the emergence of inclusive unions. By the time of the year of revolution in 1848, also the year in which the *Communist Manifesto* was also first published, labor unions around the world were beginning to integrate socialist and communist ideas into their thinking, such as the Industrial Workers of the World (IWW) in the United States. Compared to a number of European countries, American labor always had a comparatively limited number of revolutionaries wishing to link strike action with political change. The nature of the country and its geography also lessened the role of revolution; for example, one

African American and Hispanic International Ladies Garment Workers Union members on strike against the Kellwood Company, wearing signs that ask for public support for them to earn more than "poverty wages," circa 1967. In the 1960s, antiunion southern states, the rapid growth of the middle class, and corruption by larger unions hurt American labor unions.

of the principal areas of contention in the years after the Civil War was the railroads. Strikes in the railroad industry tended to be limited to individual occupations (railroad construction, carriage maintenance, or service) and to be characterized by race issues. Black workers were far from welcome in every occupation and tended therefore to crowd into certain jobs. Slavery may have been officially ended by the Civil War but wage slavery still seemed to many to remain firmly in place. The intersection of international economic forces and local labor conditions was seen in the Great Railroad Strike of 1877, which took place amid America's worst economic depression up to that time. This strike led to violence in several states and a violent crackdown by troops, during which dozens were killed.

The encompassing nature of the railroad system was represented by the Pullman Company. Customers were treated to considerable luxury and paid handsomely for the privilege, while the workers waiting on them could scarcely afford to live. Worse, many lived in a Pullman company town and so feared that making any complaint would mean that they lost their homes as well as their livelihoods. In 1894, the company unilaterally reduced salaries by 25 percent while keeping rents at the same level. Facing beggardom, the workers went on strike, and a violent confrontation began. The workers were led by Eugene V. Debs, who called for a national boycott of Pullman cars, and dozens of sympathy strikes began. However, once President Grover Cleveland sent 2,500 armed troops to Chicago to break the strike, the end was inevitable. Government and commerce then colluded to have Debs imprisoned for impeding interstate economic activities, and the Sherman Anti-Trust Act was used to demonstrate that the courts would break labor actions.

In the years following, strikes were conducted nearly always on the basis of limited legality and the threat of violence. Left-wing ideologues were stripped out from the emergent unions of the early 20th century, and the struggle returned to specific, mostly workplace issues, and the concept of widespread worker solidarity fell into abeyance. Strikes were therefore conducted on the basis of limited local resources and often in an atmosphere of public hostility. The resolve needed by family members to continue to support a strike in the face of great economic hardship gave rise to a strand of cultural memory and its productions of music and anecdotes that are of considerable importance in the history of the American people.

Nevertheless, women union leaders and workers led strikes in the garment industry in particular, since factory work in that sector was deemed most suitable for women. The Shirtwaist strike of 1909 was led by female Jewish workers (and largely, therefore, poorly protected migrants) and was known as the Uprising of the 20,000. It provided a notable example of the desire of women to be properly emancipated in society. The strike was settled in 1910, and a year later, the Triangle Shirtwaist Factory fire, which killed 146 workers, highlighted the dangerous working conditions of such women.

Strikebreaking and Rats
Strikebreaking is the attempt to end a particular strike or to reduce the likelihood that a strike will take place through intimidation of union members, attempts to drive union organizers away from companies, blacklisting workers considered to be troublemakers, and a range of other dirty tricks. U.S. authorities have been very willing to tolerate or even encourage the growth in power of employers by permitting the raising of armed mercenary forces to commit strikebreaking acts. As Stephen Norwood put it, labor spies in the country were reminiscent of Czarist secret police tactics and had no counterpart in western Europe: "Labor spies identified union sympathizers and reported them to the employer, undermined confidence in the union by spreading false rumors, and divided the labor force by stirring up ethnic and racial conflict."

The mercenaries hired were overwhelmingly young men, physically strong, and often African Americans, the homeless, or those associated with organized crime. Of course, the state contributed to the strikebreaking process by turning a blind eye to abuses and crimes committed and, in a number of cases, police joined in with strikebreaking, especially on those occasions which further enflamed already existing issues of ethnic conflict. Pinkerton agents, as well as members of Baldwin-Felts, Burns, and other agencies, were paid directly by companies to work on their behalf in order to end strikes. Since such agents could be members of the same communities from which strikers were drawn, enmity could be all the fiercer. The social proximity between strikers and members of the official police and military meant that the loyalties of the latter could be divided. This situation did not really occur in large cities (e.g., Chicago and New York), which were large enough that different neighborhoods had become strangers to one another, but in other cases, out-of-town or out-of-state forces might be introduced to deal with local strikes.

Unions did their best to resist by identifying spies or "rats" and making their names and methods widely known to workers and, where necessary, meeting violence with violence. In contemporary America, popular media customarily portray unions as being dominated by corrupt fat cats primarily interested in their own status and power, and the desire to strike as a means of feathering their own nests. The reality, of course, has throughout history been rather different. The struggle against strikebreakers brought the end to child labor, dangerous workplace conditions, payment of starvation wages, and the absence of freedom of association and collective bargaining. Although there have been some ethical and philanthropic employers in American history, they have been in the minority, and the company town mentality has generally led to freedom-restricting paternalism. When evidence exists of secret proworker agents, such as the Molly Maguires, that evidence depends almost entirely on the testimony of unreliable observers. The Maguires were said to be a secret group of Irish American miners who kidnapped and murdered their enemies, either as part of personal vendettas or in support of striking union workers. Little actual evidence survives either way.

Legislation

Since 1935, strikes have been regulated by the National Labor Relations Act (NLRA), or Wagner Act, which guarantees the right to strike within certain limitations. The act does not apply to railway workers (who are covered by the Railway Labor Act) or to most government-sector employees, agricultural and domestic workers, and some other categories of employees. The NLRA may be used to force strikers to return to work if a court determines that there is a threat to national security. This follows the principle that, in many states, a varying number of state-sector employees are forbidden to strike because of security issues or damage to the state as a whole. This generally includes the police and firefighters and, in some states, teachers in the public sector. When individuals are denied the right to strike but have a grievance they wish to have addressed, they must resort to other methods, mostly based in the workplace, in order to make their feelings known. This includes various types of go-slow or work-to-rule, which generally mean strictly keeping to the letter of any employment contract in order to demonstrate the numerous other tasks that employees are expected to undertake. The Taft-Hartley Act of 1947 (the "slave-labor bill") was introduced as a means of suppressing a range of union activities and free speech in the wake of the labor uprising of 1946 and the pro-Communist sentiment in society at the outset of the cold war.

The bill passed despite President Truman's veto, though the president nevertheless called upon its use on numerous occasions. In public discourse subsequently, anti-union spokespeople have regularly labeled union activity as being Communist in nature and anti-American. No administration has shown much appetite subsequently for opening the political debate required to negotiate a new law covering labor as a whole, although both Ronald Reagan and Jimmy Carter found themselves in conflict with workers undertaking important jobs that administrations wished to bring into the security state category, irrespective of claims from some that they wished to reduce the size of the state. In recent years, attempts to restrict workers' rights further have generally taken place at the state rather than the national level.

Syndicalism

Syndicalism refers to the process of establishing a parallel state organized by labor unions and workers' councils or according to anarchist principles in the case of anarcho-syndicalism. In this case, the strike is generally seen as the precursor to the establishment of the independent state. In the United States, this movement is most closely associated with Big Bill Haywood and the Industrial Workers of the World (IWW) union, also known as the Wobblies. The IWW is particularly

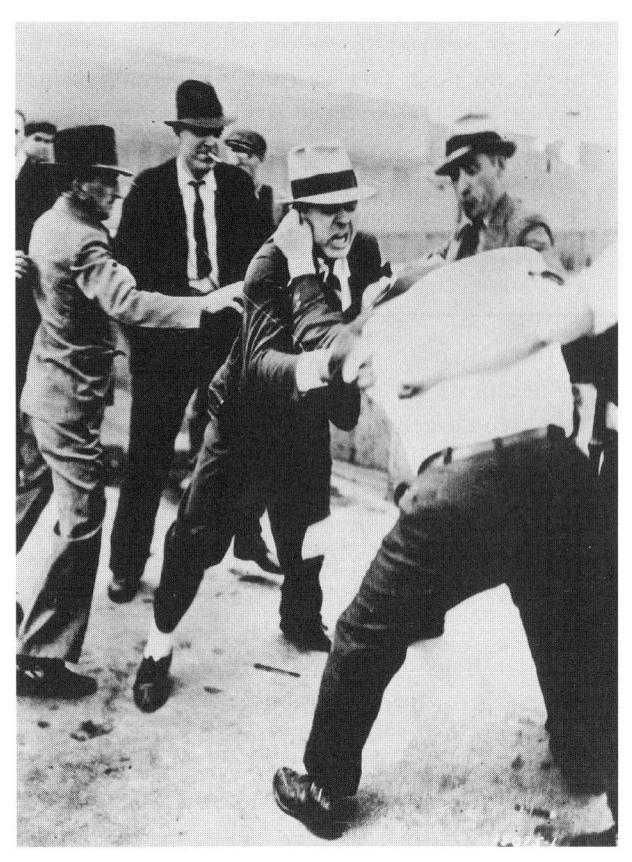

Men striking at Ford Motor Company in a physical altercation in 1937. Strikebreakers could be coworkers or physically imposing mercenaries hired by the company.

influential in American history in that it marked the creation, at least in theory, of a mass organization that would admit workers of all categories and, thereby, cut through the problems that unions had traditionally faced of representing the interests of just one sector of the workforce. Syndicalism was never a major part of American strikes, at least compared to international strike efforts, and although a commune was organized in Goldfield, Nevada (1906), and an occupation took place of the General Electric facility in Schenectady, New York (also in 1906), few expected that these events would lead to revolutionary political change at the national level.

Rent Strikes

Rent strikes occur when people in a neighborhood or other location jointly refuse to pay their rent, relying on the strength of numbers to deter the landlord from having them all evicted. A rent strike can only really be feasible when the people involved are in sufficiently close proximity to offer social solidarity and support when landlords use physical confrontation to intimidate the strikers. Consequently, they occur overwhelmingly in urban settings. Confrontation might also come with representatives of the state because failure to pay for goods or services received is a crime. Rent strikes, like strikes at factories staffed primarily by women, bring a gender distinction to the action. Strikes organized and controlled by women generally have tended to be less violent than those organized by men on both sides, although violence by the state was still used on occasion.

The best-known rent strikes in American history have taken place in New York City. In 1907, a 16-year-old Jewish woman named Pauline Newman, who had worked in factories since age 9, completed a year of action in a city gripped by economic recession by helping to organize thousands of households threatened with eviction because of inability to pay rent. This example sparked decades of tenant action, which eventually resulted in the imposition of rent control in the city. A subsequent generation of protest was led by Jesse Gray, who in 1964, after a decade of tenant organizing, led a rent strike aimed at improving housing conditions. Many carried the rats that infested their buildings in protest at the insanitary conditions. As is often the case with strikes, public sentiment had a significant impact on the result. When the strikers are perceived to have a just cause, politicians in a democratic society will often consent to at least some of their demands.

It is possible to link strikes with other forms of civil disobedience, including tax protests and rioting and looting, although there are clear differences in terms of legality and method. In all cases, those participating in the protest believe that their grievances will not be met through the normal political or negotiating processes available to them.

Prison Strikes

Prison strikes occur when a group of prisoners jointly refrains from working or eating with the purpose of trying to win some concessions from the prison or state authorities. Some prison strikes take place as the result of harsh treatment or conditions while others, benefiting from the wider distribution of information in the modern age, result from the feeling of inequality that arises from working for extremely low wages in industrial activities from which others are making significant profits. Because of the extremely high propensity of American courts to sentence people to jail, this represents a substantial labor force being required to work in conditions of no freedom. Authorities customarily respond to prison strikes with the maximum possible force because any incident of disorder can rapidly spread and be remembered, whereas private-sector operations may be concerned about the loss of their contracts.

Student Strikes

Student strikes occur when a group of students, irrespective of the nature or level of the institution, join together and refuse to participate in the normal programs or activities expected of them. This might occur as part of the desire to change the nature and practices of the educational establishment or in solidarity of another cause. Since students are young and do not immediately lose money by refusing to study, they have often been associated with leading large-scale strikes and political protests, as seen most famously in opposition to the war in Vietnam.

John Walsh
Shinawatra University

See Also: Chicago, Illinois; Civil Disobedience; Prison Riots.

Further Readings
Boren, Mark Edelman. *Student Resistance: A History of the Unruly Subject*. London: Routledge, 2001.
Goldberg, Eve and Linda Evans. *The Prison-Industrial Complex and the Global Economy*. Oakland, CA: PM Press, 2009.
Lawson, Ronald and Stephen E. Barton. "Sex Roles in Social Movements: A Case Study of the Tenant Movement in New York City." *Signs*, v.6/2 (Winter 1980).
Mason, Paul. *Live Working or Die Fighting: How the Working Class Went Global*. London: Vintage Books, 2008.

Milkman, Ruth. *Women, Work, and Protest: A Century of U.S. Women's Labor History*. London: Routledge, 1985.
Norwood, Stephen H. *Strikebreaking and Intimidation: Mercenaries and Masculinity in Twentieth-Century America*. Chapel Hill: University of North Carolina Press, 2002.

Students for a Democratic Society and the Weathermen

The radical student group Students for a Democratic Society (SDS) developed out of the Student League for Industrial Democracy, the youth arm of the League for Industrial Democracy, in 1960. It held its first meeting in Ann Arbor, Michigan, on the campus of the University of Michigan. At that time, it formulated its famous manifesto, the Port Huron Statement, in which the group articulated a critique of U.S. policy and society. Specifically, U.S. domestic and foreign policy were found wanting in that they failed to address the continuing realities of racial discrimination, domination of the economy by big business, and the hegemony of the two-party system. Spending priorities that focused on continuation of the arms race, the threat of nuclear war, and foreign policy were criticized. Reforms suggested included a focus on grassroots citizen involvement and getting workers involved in management of corporations. Other reforms proposed a systematic war on poverty and increasing welfare, and advocated nonviolent civil disobedience in order to foster participatory democracy.

By 1963, the SDS had nine chapters and a highly decentralized organizational structure. The group's first president was Tom Hayden, who became a fixture in radical politics and later was known as a California state senator and as the husband of controversial actress Jane Fonda. When the Berkeley campus of the University of California was paralyzed by the free speech movement in October 1963, it brought radical student movements to the attention of the media, politicians, and other students. By 1965, the now 52 SDS chapters and unaffiliated student peace groups used "teach-ins" and demonstrations to focus public attention on the expanding war in Vietnam. Adopting a proletarian style of dress and demeanor, the group's appearance was not applauded by mainstream and conservative politicians. Local chapters often concerned themselves with campus issues such as expansion into minority neighborhoods, bad food, military presence and recruitment on campus, and seemingly arbitrary university administrative policies. At Louisiana State University, for example, the campus chapter of SDS engaged in helping students evade the draft and picketed a local factory that exploited minority workers.

Other chapters encouraged soldiers to desert or to refuse to fight. The Dow Chemical Company, the makers of various chemicals used in the war effort, became the object of picketing and was a special focus of SDS attention. This sort of activity nationwide drew the ire of politicians and officeholders on the state level. On the federal level, the Federal Bureau of Investigation (FBI) began to direct its counterintelligence program (COINTELPRO) against the SDS. This involved the use of informants and spies, misinformation campaigns, and "dirty tricks," some of which were illegal. That notwithstanding, SDS chapters and SDS-inspired students began to stage sit-ins on campuses nationwide and attempted to draw attention to the inequities of the military draft in 1967. The high point of their activities was a successful march on the Pentagon in October of that year. The following year, SDS leaders, including Columbia University student Mark Rudd, made a trip to Cuba to meet with North Vietnamese and Cuban officials. Most significantly that year, a strike at Columbia University in which the administration building was occupied and trashed drew media attention, much of it negative, to the national organization; its chapter leader Mark Rudd, and the student movement in general.

The Weathermen
The Weather Underground Organization (WUO), founded in 1969, was a dedicated splinter group of the SDS. The goal of this faction was to create a small, covert, elite group that could operate with minimal scrutiny and interference from federal authorities—like Lenin's theoretical construct of the "vanguard of the party" in the early days of the Soviet Union. Another goal was to generate more serious threats to the American capitalist corporate "warfare" state. This group was much more militant and confrontational than the largely disorganized and informer-infected SDS. The name "Weathermen" came from Bob Dylan's song *Subterranean Homesick Blues,* in which the words "You don't need a weatherman to know which way the wind blows" seemed particularly appropriate and visionary to radicalized youth. It became the title of a position paper presented at the SDS Convention, in June 1969. The aim of the Weathermen, which went largely unachieved, was to involve the masses in revolutionary activity; this was to be realized by "bringing the war home."

Accordingly, the members of this faction, living largely underground, commenced a campaign of street actions, jailbreaks, and bombings throughout the 1970s. Many of their activities were aimed at disrupting the efforts of the U.S. government during the Vietnam War. Accordingly, bombings were carried out against the Pentagon, the U.S. Capitol, and the U.S. Department of State. Other

Former Students for a Democratic Society (SDS) National Secretary C. Clark Kissinger with young members of the new SDS at the Left Forum in New York City in 2007.

violent activities were attributed to the Weather Underground but have never been confirmed.

One of the faction's most infamous activities was the Days of Rage street action, carried out in Chicago on October 9, 1969. The motive behind this relatively small but alarming planned riot was to "bring the war home"—to make the American people experience violence as was the norm in Vietnam. During the Days of Rage, a few windows were broken and businesses and cars were vandalized. Police and Weathermen were injured, and numerous arrests were made. A second riot occurred two days later, and more than 100 people were arrested. Several Weather Underground operatives were killed while constructing bombs in Greenwich Village, New York, in 1970. These bombs were supposed to have been used against military targets. After this event, members of the group met and decided to reject the use of more violent methods in order to avoid casualties.

The group dissolved over a variety of personal and ideological issues in the mid-1970s. Federal agencies were unsuccessful in their efforts to capture the members. Many who had been arrested could not be prosecuted because illegal means were used to obtain the evidence against them. Some remained at large until they turned themselves in years, and even decades, later. Some former members are now academics or are involved in community work or social services.

Conclusion
The experience of SDS and Weather Underground radicals of the 1960s and 1970s represents a fugitive and quixotic episode in American history. Their violent rhetoric and activities and disorganized approach alienated potential allies, and the end of the Vietnam War deprived them of their most salient issue. Recent attempts to resurrect the SDS have been met with notable lack of success on college campuses. The American political scene took a decidedly rightward shift, leaving few left-radical groups of any significance on the American scene.

Francis Frederick Hawley
Western Carolina University

See Also: Civil Disobedience; Police, Contemporary; Riots; Strikes; Terrorism.

Further Readings
Ayers, Bill. *Fugitive Days*. Boston: Beacon Press, 2001.
Berger, Dan. *Outlaws in America: The Weather Underground and the Politics of Solidarity*. Oakland, CA: AK Press, 2006.
Sale, Kirkpatrick. *SDS*. New York: Vintage Books, 1974.

Supermax Prisons

Supermax prisons are highly automated institutions, designed to maintain prisoners in long-term solitary confinement, with minimal sensory stimulation. Supermax prisoners spend 23 or more hours per day alone in their cells. Three or four times per week, a prison officer pushes a button in a central control tower, which opens one cell door at a time, allowing each prisoner, in turn, to shower, or go out alone to the caged yard area, usually a concrete area the size of a prison cell, with a roof partially exposed to the sky. Individual supermax cells usually have no windows exposed to natural light and only fluorescent lighting. Supermax prisoners have no physical contact with other human beings. Meals are pushed through small slots in the cell door. No provisions are made for educational or therapeutic programming; visits take place through Plexiglas shields, or by videoconference. During medical appointments, prisoners are locked into upright cages on wheels, often called therapeutic treatment modules.

Supermax prisons, also known as Security Housing Units, Control Units, or Departmental Disciplinary Units, are different from administrative segregation, a correctional term that references shorter-term isolation, of a month or two, within a given prison facility. By contrast, supermaxes are often freestanding facilities, or isolated wings of a given prison, where prisoners are sent for months or years at a time, following an administrative disciplinary process. Correctional administrators assign prisoners to supermaxes after determining that the prisoner presents a threat to institutional security, either because he has broken a prison rule, such as participating in a riot or destroying state property or

The nation's most dangerous criminals, those who are seen as serious physical threats or at high risk for escape, are sent to supermax prisons. At these super-maximum security facilities, they are kept in solitary confinement in darkened cells for more than 22 hours a day and have no access to social contact or environmental stimuli.

because he is identified as a gang leader. (The vast majority of supermax prisoners are men.) Usually, if a prisoner breaks a prison rule, he is sent to a supermax for a fixed period of months or years. On the other hand, if a prisoner is identified as a gang leader, he might be sent to a supermax for an indefinite term. In sum, supermax assignment is an administrative process, independent from both the initial security classification of prisoners entering prison and from the judge-imposed criminal sentence.

Arizona opened the first of these modern supermaxes in 1986 (the Special Management Unit); California opened the second in 1989 (Pelican Bay). In 1994, the Federal Bureau of Prisons opened its supermax (the Administrative Maximum) in Colorado; now almost every state has some form of supermax facility. Estimates of the number of U.S. supermaxes range from 20 to 57. Estimates of the total population of U.S. supermax prisoners range from 5,000 to 100,000. This variation stems from state-based differences in definitions of which conditions constitute supermax confinement.

Supermaxes developed as a way to institutionalize long-term lockdowns, during which prisoners were not allowed to leave their cells for any reason, commonly implemented in U.S. prisons following riots and gang violence in the 1970s. For instance, the maximum-security federal prison in Marion, Illinois, was locked down from 1983 until 1994, when the federal supermax opened. Similarly, California's San Quentin and Folsom State Prisons had certain wings locked down from the mid-1970s until the late 1980s, when California opened its first supermax. In the 1970s and 1980s, federal district courts found many of the conditions in these locked-down, older prison facilities to be unconstitutional.

However, supermax prisons have been more resistant to litigation. According to the U.S. Supreme Court, these institutions are basically constitutional, as long as certain, minimal procedural safeguards are in place: a prisoner must have notice of why he is being placed in a supermax, and he must have some minimal opportunity to respond to the claims against him, either in writing or through some kind of administrative hearing (*Austin v. Wilkinson*). One federal district court recently agreed to hear an Eighth Amendment challenge to supermax prison conditions (*Silverstein v. Federal Bureau of Prisons*); the challenge alleges specifically that the plaintiff's length of confinement (27 years) is so long as to be cruel and unusual. Other lower federal courts have held that severely mentally ill prisoners may not be placed in supermaxes, because long-term solitary confinement might potentially exacerbate pre-existing mental health problems.

International legal bodies are more skeptical of the use of long-term solitary confinement than U.S. courts. In 2010, the European Court of Human Rights refused to extradite two alleged terrorists to the United States until the court further investigated the conditions in the federal supermax in Colorado, where the terrorists were likely to be sentenced to spend the rest of their lives (*Ahmad v. the United Kingdom*). Similarly, in reports on Guantanamo, the United Nations has interpreted the International Covenant on Civil and Political Rights to prohibit the use of long-term solitary confinement for specifically punitive purposes.

Keramet Ann Reiter
University of California, Berkeley

See Also: Arizona; California; Prison Riots; Prisoners' Rights.

Further Readings
Rhodes, Lorna R. *Total Confinement: Madness and Reason in the Maximum Security Prison*. Berkeley: University of California Press, 2004.
Shalev, Sharon. *Supermax: Controlling Risk Through Solitary Confinement*. Portland, OR: Willan Publishing, 2009.

Supreme Court, U.S.

The Supreme Court of the United States is the only court formally established by the U.S. Constitution and is the highest judicial body in the country. In drafting Article III of the Constitution, the founding fathers established the Supreme Court, but they did not make any stipulations regarding its size, membership, or specific authority. Beyond outlining the types of cases that could be considered, the framers did amazingly little to define the function and structure of the country's highest court. Due to the general provisions contained in the Constitution, the court has varied over time in composition, caseload, and influence. The Supreme Court was first implemented by the Judiciary Act of 1789, and it first convened on February 2, 1790, under the guidance of Chief Justice John Jay.

The Supreme Court originally comprised six justices. The Constitution does not specify the size of the Supreme Court, but Article III does authorize Congress to fix the number of justices. In its history, the court has fluctuated from six to 10 members. Since the Judiciary Act of 1869, nine justices have sat on the court. In 1937, President Franklin Roosevelt tried to expand the size of the court. During Roosevelt's first term, the court invalidated many of the New Deal measures intended to strengthen economic recovery during the Great Depression. His plan would have appointed an additional justice for every incumbent justice who attained the age of 70 and a half. These appointments would have continued until the court reached a maximum size of 15 justices. Roosevelt's intention was to pack the court with justices who would uphold New Deal legislation. This plan, known as the "court-packing plan," ultimately failed and hurt Roosevelt politically.

The Supreme Court serves primarily as an appellate court, but does retain original jurisdiction over a small range of cases. The court has both mandatory appellate jurisdiction and discretionary appellate jurisdiction. A case must be reviewed by the Supreme Court if a U.S. District Court invalidates a federal law, if a U.S. Court of Appeals invalidates a state law, or if a state's highest court invalidates a federal law. Most cases heard by the court are discretionary appeals. These cases must be of sufficient national significance and pertain to a question of constitutionality. The court accepts these cases by a writ of certiorari—an order that a higher court issues in order to review the decision and proceedings of a lower court—from the U.S. Court of Appeals and a state's highest court. To accept a case, at least four of the nine justices must grant certiorari. In extremely rare occurrences, the court retains original jurisdiction.

It acts as a trial court if the litigious action is between two or more states, if an ambassador is a party to the action, or if the action is between a state and the federal government.

While some appellate courts sit on panels during the hearing of a case, the justices of the Supreme Court are always "en banc." That is, the full court participates in every case (except cases involving conflicts of interest). After the court hears oral arguments in a given case, the justices retire to their conference room to begin deliberations and conduct a vote. After the vote, the majority opinion is assigned. If the chief justice is in the majority bloc, he can assign the opinion to himself or another justice in the majority bloc. If the chief justice is in the minority bloc, the senior associate justice in the majority bloc will assign the majority opinion. Draft opinions are then circulated among the justices for consideration. Justices typically do not change their vote, but it is during this time that changes in voting will occur. Sometimes the authoring justice may carefully word the opinion in hope of swaying other justices to his/her opinion.

When a vacancy arises on the court, justices are nominated by the president of the United States. The Constitution does not specify qualifications for service; thus, the president may nominate anyone to serve. Traditionally, justices have previously served as lawyers, law professors, and federal appellate court judges. Justices are confirmed with the "advice and consent" (i.e., majority vote) of the U.S. Senate. The Senate Judiciary Committee holds confirmation hearings of all nominees. The nominees are subjected to a vote of both the committee and the full Senate. Under the Constitution, justices are confirmed with life tenure and serve during "good behavior." A justice's tenure terminates only upon death, resignation, retirement, or conviction of impeachment. Only one justice (Samuel Chase in 1805) has ever been impeached by the House of Representatives. He was subsequently acquitted by the Senate.

The 2012 justices of the U.S. Supreme Court, along with the president who made the nomination and the year service began, were as follows:

- Chief Justice John Roberts (George W. Bush, 2005)
- Antonin Scalia (Ronald Reagan, 1986)
- Anthony Kennedy (Ronald Reagan, 1988)
- Clarence Thomas (George H. W. Bush, 1991)
- Ruth Bader Ginsburg (Bill Clinton, 1993)
- Stephen Breyer (Bill Clinton, 1994)
- Samuel Alito (George W. Bush, 2006)
- Sonia Sotomayor (Barack Obama, 2009)
- Elena Kagan (Barack Obama, 2010)

Traditionally, the court is recognized by its chief justice. Subsequently, historical periods of the Supreme Court are named after the presiding chief justice of that time. The earliest courts, under Chief Justices John Jay (1789–95), John Rutledge (1795), and Oliver Ellsworth (1795–1800), heard few cases of national significance. The Supreme Court's first decision was in *West v. Barnes* (1791), a case that originated out of Rhode Island and involved a procedural issue of contract law.

The Marshall Court

Under the leadership of Chief Justice John Marshall (1801–35), the court issued what was perhaps the most important decision in its history. In *Marbury v. Madison* (1803), the court declared itself to be the supreme arbiter of the U.S. Constitution. In his opinion, Marshall wrote, "It is emphatically the province and duty of the judicial department to say what the law is." The court invalidated a section of the Judiciary Act of 1789 on the basis that it violated the Constitution by expanding the original jurisdiction of the Supreme Court. It was the first case in which the court ruled an act of Congress unconstitutional, and it firmly established the doctrine of judicial review. The power of judicial review designates the Supreme Court as the final authority to decide whether or not actions of the president or of the Congress are within the powers granted to them by the Constitution.

The Marshall court made several important rulings giving further substance to the constitutional balance of power between the federal government and the states. In *Martin v. Hunter's Lessee* (1816), the court wrote that it had the authority to correct interpretations of the federal Constitution made by state supreme courts. In *McCulloch v. Maryland* (1819), the court established that states could not tax federal institutions; that decision also upheld the congressional authority to

The front facade of the U.S. Supreme Court building, a national landmark, in Washington, D.C. The court was originally located in the basement of the U.S. Capitol building before construction began on the current structure in 1932. Although not designated by the U.S. Constitution, the Supreme Court can overturn executive actions it deems unlawful or unconstitutional.

create the Second Bank of the United States, even though the authority to do so was not explicitly stated in the Constitution. The court reasoned that because federal laws have supremacy over state laws, the State of Maryland had no right to hinder the bank's operation by trying to tax it. Accordingly, *Marbury*, *Martin*, and *McCulloch* each established and affirmed that the Supreme Court was entrusted with maintaining the consistent and organized development of federal law.

During the tenure of Chief Justice Marshall, the court consistently interpreted the Constitution broadly to ensure the federal government would have the power to become a respected nation. As chief justice, Marshall embodied the majesty and power of the judicial branch of the government as fully as the president stood for the power of the executive branch. The Constitution does not specifically grant the power of judicial review to the court, and President Thomas Jefferson did not agree with Marshall's opinion in *Marbury* because he believed the president should decide whether executive acts were constitutional. The *Marbury* decision established an American tradition and legal system based on the concept of "government under law." Judicial review states that no person (e.g., the president) and no institution (e.g., Congress) may act in violation of the Constitution. The Marshall court also ended the established practice of each judge issuing an individual opinion, a remnant of British tradition. Instead, it began issuing a single majority opinion. Justices in the majority voting bloc may also submit concurring opinions. In nonunanimous decisions, one or more of the justices in the minority bloc will typically write a dissenting opinion.

From Taney to Vinson

Under the leadership of Chief Justice Roger Taney (1836–64), the court made several important rulings. In *Sheldon v. Sill* (1850), the court held that while Congress may not limit the subjects the Supreme Court may hear, it may limit the jurisdiction of lower federal courts to prevent them from hearing cases dealing with certain subjects. The Taney Court is most noted for its ruling in *Dred Scott v. Sandford* (1857)—a case that many argue helped precipitate the Civil War. Taney authored the opinion; he wrote that people of African descent who were imported into the United States and held as slaves (or their descendants, whether or not they were slaves) were not protected by the Constitution and could never be American citizens. The court further ruled that slaves, as chattel or private property, could not be taken away from their owners without due process of law. Though infamously known for the *Scott* case, this court is also remembered for *Charles River Bridge v. Warren* (1837). This decision ruled against legislature-granted monopolies in favor of competition and was a major victory for laissez-faire economics.

During the post–Civil War and Reconstruction eras, many of the Supreme Court's decisions interpreted the new Civil War amendments (Thirteenth, Fourteenth, and Fifteenth Amendments). Under the direction of Salmon Chase (1864–73), Morrison Waite (1874–78), and Melville Fuller (1888–1910), the court also further developed the doctrine of substantive due process. In *Lochner v. New York* (1905), the court held that the liberty to contract was implicit in the due process clause of the Fourteenth Amendment. The case involved a New York law that limited the number of hours that a baker could work per day. The law also limited the number of hours that bakers could work each week. The court ultimately rejected the contention that the law was necessary to protect the well-being of the employees. It concluded that the labor law was an attempt to regulate the terms of employment, and it stated that it amounted to an arbitrary and unreasonable intrusion into the right of the individual to contract.

Another important case during this period was *Plessy v. Ferguson* (1896). Here, the Fuller court upheld the constitutionality of state laws requiring racial segregation in private facilities under the equal protection clause of the Fourteenth Amendment. The decision created the doctrine of "separate but equal." This doctrine was later overturned in 1954. In a major victory for criminal defendants, in *Weeks v. United States* (1914), the court established the exclusionary rule, thus marking the first federal decision to uphold the exclusion of evidence without a proper search warrant in violation of the Fourth Amendment.

During the Charles Hughes (1930–41), Harlan Stone (1941–46), and Fred Vinson courts (1946–53), the Supreme Court gained notoriety for interpreting the Constitution to facilitate President Franklin Roosevelt's New Deal legislation. However, many of these cases were not decided until after Roosevelt's court-packing scheme failed. In *West Coast Hotel Co. v. Parrish* (1937), the court validated the constitutionality of minimum wage legislation in the state of Washington. It further stated that the Constitution permitted the restriction of the right to contract by state law in such cases where the restriction protected the community or the health and safety of employees.

During this era, the court also gave a broader reading to the powers of the federal government. In *Korematsu v. United States* (1944), the court considered the legality of a presidential order that forced Japanese Americans into internment camps during World War II. In the controversial decision, the Supreme Court ruled in favor of the government and upheld the constitutionality of the exclusion order. It held that the need to protect the country against espionage outweighed the defendants' individual rights.

The Warren Court

Under the leadership of Chief Justice Earl Warren (1953–69), the court made many celebrated and controversial rulings. This era in the court's history was known as the "due process revolution" because it expanded the application of the Constitution to civil liberties, most notably for criminal defendants. The Warren court is remembered for extending the Bill of Rights to states, the general principle behind most of its criminal justice decisions. In *Mapp v. Ohio* (1961), the court ruled that evidence obtained in violation of the Fourth Amendment, which protects individuals against "unreasonable searches and seizures," cannot be used in criminal prosecutions in state courts, as well as federal courts. Until this case, the *Weeks* precedent only applied to search and seizure violations committed by federal law enforcement.

In *Miranda v. Arizona* (1966), the Warren court concluded that statements made during a custodial interrogation by a criminal defendant can only be admissible at trial if the prosecution can prove that the defendant was made aware of the right to consult with an attorney before and during police questioning, and of the right against self-incrimination prior to police questioning, and that the defendant understood and voluntarily waived these rights. If a defendant invokes his right to remain silent, the police must immediately cease questioning. This ruling had a major impact on law enforcement practices in the United States. By making the "Miranda rights" a part of routine police procedure, the court ensured that suspects would be informed of their rights. Moreover, in *Gideon v. Wainwright* (1963), the Warren court also concluded that the Constitution grants the right to a court-appointed attorney for criminal defendants unable to afford one.

In a landmark case, *Brown v. Board of Education* (1954), the court reversed *Plessy* by holding that segregation in public schools was unconstitutional. By doing so, it invalidated the long-standing doctrine of "separate but equal." With respect to the separation of church and state, the court held in *Engel v. Vitale* (1962) that public schools cannot administer official prayer sessions, and in *Abington School District v. Schempp* (1963), it ruled that public schools also could not administer mandatory Bible readings. In *Griswold v. Connecticut* (1965), the Supreme Court ruled that the Constitution protects a general right to privacy. The case centered on a Connecticut law that prohibited the use of contraceptives. The Warren court invalidated this law on the basis that it violated married couples' right to marital privacy.

The Burger Court

Since the Warren Court, the Supreme Court has returned to a more conservative political leaning by interpreting the Constitution very narrowly. The court, under the direction of Warren Burger (1969–86), made one of its most controversial rulings in *Roe v. Wade* (1973). In this case, the court struck down outright bans on abortion by holding that the Constitution protected a woman's right to privacy and control over her own body.

The Burger court also reached controversial rulings on affirmative action and campaign finance reform. In *Regents of the University of California v. Bakke* (1978), it wrote that while affirmative action systems are generally constitutional, a quota system based solely on race is unconstitutional. In *Buckley v. Valeo* (1976), the court upheld federal limits on campaign contributions, and it also ruled that spending money to influence elections is considered constitutionally protected free speech.

In another landmark decision, the Supreme Court emphatically stated that it is the ultimate and final authority in determining constitutional questions. In *United States v. Nixon* (1974), a case involving President Richard Nixon and the Watergate scandal, the court ruled that no person, not even the president of the United States, is completely above the law. In a unanimous decision, the court opined that the president cannot claim executive privilege as an excuse in withholding evidence that is pertinent in a criminal trial.

During the Burger court, the American capital punishment system also underwent significant changes. In *Furman v. Georgia* (1972), the court ruled that the arbitrary and capricious implementation of the death penalty was unconstitutional. By making this ruling, the court invalidated the capital punishment sentencing schemes of many states. It ruled that the death penalty was not itself unconstitutional, so several of the states began modifying their sentencing schemes to comply with the *Furman* ruling. In *Gregg v. Georgia* (1976), the court reinstituted capital punishment so long as states followed a system comprising three parts: a bifurcated trial (to determine guilt and sentencing separately), mandatory appellate review, and the inclusion of mitigating as well as aggravating factors. In *Coker v. Georgia* (1977), the court held that capital punishment for the crime of rape was grossly disproportionate and excessive; therefore, it is forbidden by the Eighth Amendment as cruel and unusual punishment.

The Rehnquist Court

The Supreme Court under William Rehnquist (1986–2005) was noted for its revival of the concept of federalism and a strict interpretation of the Constitution's original meaning. It restricted congressional power under the commerce clause in *United States v. Lopez* (1995) for the first time since the New Deal legislation. It also strengthened the power of state sovereign immunity in *Seminole Tribe v. Florida* (1996). The Rehnquist court might be most known for its controversial 5–4 decision in *Bush v. Gore* (2000). Following the 2000 presidential election, the justices split along party lines and effectively ended the electoral recount in Florida, which led to the presidency of George W. Bush. The court concluded that the Florida Supreme Court's system for recounting ballots was in violation of the equal protection clause of the Fourteenth Amendment. The majority decision stated that no alternative method could be implemented within the time limits set by the State of Florida. Three of the justices also maintained that the Florida Supreme Court violated the U.S. Constitution by misinterpreting Florida election law, which had been enacted by the Florida Legislature.

Additionally, the Rehnquist court upheld rights to privacy by decriminalizing private homosexual sex in *Lawrence v. Texas* (2003). It altered the *Roe* framework pertaining to abortion regulations in *Planned Parenthood v. Casey* (1992). It upheld the power of Congress to lengthen copyright terms in *Eldred v. Ashcroft* (2003). It also expanded the government's eminent domain authority in *Kelo v. City of New London* (2005).

The Roberts Court

The John Roberts court (2005–present) was the presiding court in 2012. It has been seen as more conservative than previous courts. *Ayotte v. Planned Parenthood* (2006) was an abortion case in which the court stated that entirely invalidating a parental notification statute was unnecessary if the statute's unconstitutional implementation could be fixed by other judicial actions. The court also limited the scope of *Miranda* by restricting the right to remain silent. In *Berghuis v. Thompkins* (2010), the court ruled that a suspect's silence during a custodial interrogation does not explicitly or implicitly invoke the suspect's right to remain silent under the Fifth Amendment. To invoke one's Miranda rights, one must do so in an unambiguous fashion.

The Roberts court has also decided two important death penalty cases in its brief history. In *Kennedy v. Louisiana* (2008), the court opined that it is unconstitutional to impose capital punishment in nonfatal child rape cases. The court used *Coker* as precedent to determine that the death penalty should only be used in cases involving the death of an individual. Additionally, in a Kentucky case, *Baze v. Rees* (2008), the court ruled that the traditional three-drug lethal injection cocktail (sodium thiopental to induce unconsciousness, pancuronium bromide to cause muscle paralysis and respiratory arrest, and potassium chloride to stop the heart) used for execution is constitutional under the Eighth Amendment.

Other important cases concerning unsettled issues have also been decided by the Roberts Court. In *District of Columbia v. Heller* (2008), it concluded that the Second Amendment guarantees an individual's right to possess a firearm irrespective of militia service. In *Hudson v. Michigan* (2006), it concluded that a violation of the "knock-and-announce" rule by the police during a search does not necessarily infringe on the Fourth Amendment. In *Crawford v. Marion County Election Board* (2008), the court ruled that an Indiana law requiring voters to show photo identification was constitutional. In *Garcetti v. Ceballos* (2006) and *Morse v. Frederick* (2007), the court upheld First Amendment free speech protections by government employees and high school students, respectively. In *Citizens United v. Federal Election Commission* (2010), a campaign finance case, the Roberts Court held that corporate funding of political broadcasts during elections cannot be restricted under the First Amendment.

Christopher Donner
University of South Florida

See Also: 1777 to 1800 Primary Documents; 1801 to 1850 Primary Documents; 1851 to 1900 Primary Documents; 2001 to 2012 Primary Documents; Appellate Courts; Constitution of the United States of America; Due Process.

Future Readings

Bugliosi, Vincent. *The Betrayal of America: How the Supreme Court Undermined the Constitution and Chose Our President*. New York: Avalon Publishing, 2001.

Burns, James. *Packing the Court: The Rise of Judicial Power and the Coming Crisis of the Supreme Court*. New York: Penguin Press, 2009.

Hall, Kermit and James Ely. *Oxford Guide to United States Supreme Court Decisions*. New York: Oxford University Press, 2009.

Lazarus, Edward. *Closed Chambers*. New York: Random House, 1998.

Newton, J. *Justice for All: Earl Warren and the Nation He Made*. New York: Penguin Books, 2006.

Rehnquist, William. *The Supreme Court*. New York: Random House, 2001.

Rosen, Jeffrey. *The Supreme Court: The Personalities and Rivalries That Defined America*. New York: Times Books, 2006.

Schwartz, Bernard. *A History of the Supreme Court*. New York: Oxford University Press, 1993.

Solomon, Burt. *FDR v. the Constitution: The Court-Packing Fight and the Triumph of Democracy*. New York: Walker Publishing, 2009.

Toobin, Jeffrey. *The Nine: Inside the Secret World of the Supreme Court*. New York: Random House, 2007.

Tushnet, Mark. *A Court Divided: The Rehnquist Court and the Future of Constitutional Law*. New York: W. W. Norton, 2005.

Woodward, B., et al. *The Brethren: Inside the Supreme Court*. New York: Simon & Schuster, 1979.

Suspect's Rights

Suspects have rights from the time of engaging in the crime to the point of conviction. The Fourth, Fifth, Sixth, and Fourteenth Amendments are the most common amendments in criminal procedure. These amendments are essential to the idea of due process—a philosophy that assumes the suspect is presumed to be innocent and the state has the burden to prove a defendant's guilt. Through employing due process, the state's prosecution follows applicable case law and rules of evidence. This, in turn, protects private citizens from arbitrary governmental abuses.

Due process can be divided into two main areas: substantive and procedural due process. Substantive law creates, defines, and regulates rights. This allows one to be protected from biased, discriminatory, and unfair law, such as Jim Crow laws, which maintained segregation in the U.S. south before the Civil Rights Act of 1964. In contrast, procedural due process ensures no person will be deprived of freedom without adhering to proper legal procedures. Due process includes proper notice of charges, a formal and unbiased hearing, the right to attorney, to be able to respond to charges, opportunity to confront and cross-examine witnesses and accusers, ability to present one's own witnesses, prohibition against forced self-incrimination, and the right to appeal.

Under due process, there are several amendments that are pertinent to suspect's rights before the commission of a trial. This includes the Fourth Amendment, which guards against unreasonable searches and seizures of a person's home or personal property without a warrant. This warrant is to be issued by a magistrate, a judge-like official, in which the threshold of evidence must reach the probable cause standard. This amendment was produced in response to the abuse of writ of assistance by the British courts before the American Revolution. Warrants are to be limited to the specific information issued by the magistrate's court.

Exclusionary Rule

There are several pivotal Supreme Court cases pertinent to this amendment. One specific area is the exclusionary rule, which provides that evidence obtained in violation of the U.S. Constitution may be excluded at trial. The exclusionary rule was first established with *Weeks v. United States*, 232 U.S. 383 (1914). In this case, Weeks was suspected of using the mail to send lottery tickets, a prohibited gambling. U.S. marshals entered the person's home, without a warrant, and discovered lottery tickets, after a search. These tickets were used as evidence against him in court, in which he was convicted of the unlawful use of the mail. Weeks appealed the case, arguing the officers should have obtained a warrant before search. The appeal was successful with the Supreme Court, whoich overturned the conviction. Weeks was unlikely to be a flight risk, since he was gainfully employed. Additionally, the U.S. marshals had time to obtain the warrant. This ruling became binding to federal law enforcement officials. Some states voluntarily complied with the ruling. An unusual situation developed in which states that did not comply could obtain evidence without going through the more rigorous legal requirements and could provide evidence to federal agents. This was known as the "silver platter doctrine." However, with the cases *Elkins v. United States*, 364 U.S. 206 (1960) and *Mapp v. Ohio*, 367 U.S. 1081 (1961), this was eliminated.

This silver platter doctrine was reinforced through the Supreme Court ruling in *Wolf v. Colorado*, 338 U.S. 25 (1949). Wolf was a physician in Colorado, a nonexclusionary state. He was suspected of performing illegal abortions. The state officers entered his office and seized various documents. There were various violations of procedural law and the warrant had numerous errors. He was convicted. He appealed and wanted to apply the same standards established under *Weeks* to the states, citing the Fourteenth Amendment's equal protection clause. The Supreme Court upheld the conviction and avoided having the states comply with *Weeks*.

With *Mapp v. Ohio*, 367 U.S. 1081 (1961), police in Cleveland, Ohio, believed a suspect was making or possessed bomb-making materials. Police obtained a warrant for Mapp, a female friend. When the police came to the residence, they asked to come in. Mapp refused and suggested the officers obtain a warrant. Mapp called her attorney when the officers left. The attorney arrived at the same time as the officers. The officers arrived waving a piece of paper. Neither Mapp nor the attorney were permitted to review the "warrant." A search of the home produced no bomb materials; however, the police were able to find pencil sketches of what the officers believed to be "pornography." Mapp was then arrested for possessing pornographic materials. The Supreme Court overturned her conviction and it was not known whether what was produced by the police was a warrant. In this case, the exclusionary rule became binding to the states. Thus, any evidence obtained illegally is inadmissible in court, neutralizing the silver platter doctrine.

Also pertinent to the exclusionary rule is the fruit of the poisonous tree doctrine, in which evidence derived from an illegal search or illegal interrogation is inadmissible because of the original illegally obtained evidence. In this case, federal agents illegally seized tax records and produced copies of the books. The Supreme Court ruled permitting derivatives from original illegally obtained evidence was tainted and therefore inadmissible.

This Supreme Court principle was refined with *Wong Sun v. United States*, 371 U.S. 471 (1961). Police searched the area where he lived and found no narcotics on the premises and was subsequently released. Statements, several days later, were provided to Wong Sun and another suspect, but were not signed. Wong Sun and his associate returned to the agents several days later and admitted to the original statement. He and his associate were subsequently convicted based upon charges of transporting and concealing heroin.

Upon appeal, Wong asserted his statements were inadmissible in court because several illegal acts were conducted by the federal agents. The Supreme Court agreed there were a number of illegal procedural actions committed by the federal officers that nullified certain evidence. However, when Wong and his associate came back and admitted to the accuracy of the original statement, this action nullified the taint of the original evidence and it could be utilized against him.

The exclusionary rule has been commonly associated with the Fourth Amendment; however, the exclusionary rule also applies to pretrial

A 2010 protest in Minneapolis, Minnesota, against the Arizona SB 1070 law, which mandates that Arizona officials and law enforcement check for proof of citizenship without defining "reasonable suspicion" or "probable cause."

confrontations in a lineup or photo array. For example, police cannot do anything that persuades the witness to choose the person they prefer, as this would be a violation of due process. The exclusionary rule can be applied to confessions and interrogations that violate the Fifth Amendment against self-incrimination or the Sixth Amendment's right to counsel.

Interrogation
According to the Fifth Amendment, "...shall not be compelled in any criminal case to be a witness against himself." This amendment has precedent in English common law, in which involuntary confessions are not admissible in court. For the past 70 years, the Supreme Court has placed limits on how the police can interrogate suspects. Under *Brown v. Mississippi*, 287 U.S. 278 (1936), physical coercion cannot be utilized to force confessions. In this case, Brown was a suspect of murder. A deputy sheriff hanged him from a tree, let him down, and hanged him up again. He was later tied to a tree and beaten. Several days later he was arrested at his home and taken to jail where he was repeatedly beaten and was told the beatings would continue until he confessed. He confessed and subsequently was found guilty of murder. Upon appeal, he contended he was denied due process under the Fourteenth Amendment. The Supreme Court concurred. Physically coerced confessions and statements are inadmissible.

Neither may a confession be admitted into court if the statement was obtained through psychological coercion. In *Ashcraft v. Tennessee*, 322 U.S. 143 (1944), Ashcraft and another man were suspected of killing Ashcraft's wife. He was interrogated by officers for eight hours and was later interrogated for over 36 hours. During this last period, had he only had a five-minute break and no rest. He appealed, stating his confession was coerced. The court agreed. Thus, psychologically coerced confessions are not voluntary, therefore are not admissible in court.

The paramount Supreme Court case on the issue of interrogation was *Miranda v. Arizona*, 384 U.S. 436 (1966). Miranda was suspected of rape and kidnapping and was arrested. Miranda was not allowed to speak to an attorney nor was he informed of his right to have one. He was interrogated for several hours and eventually confessed to the crime and signed a confession. Upon appeal, Miranda contended he was not advised of his right to an attorney nor of his right to remain silent; therefore, violating due process. The Supreme Court concurred and established the Miranda warning. This decision required that suspects must be advised of certain rights for their confessions to be admitted as evidence. These rights include the right to remain silent, the right to an attorney, and the right to free counsel if the suspect cannot afford one.

Later decisions by the court have refined *Miranda* for a variety of situations. In *Rhode Island v. Innis*, 466 U.S. 291 (1981), the high court ruled that a "spontaneous" statement by a suspect can be admissible in court as long as the responses were not given in response to police questioning or other action that might induce an incriminating response by the suspect. In this case, Innis was suspected of killing a taxi driver. He was presented his Miranda rights, twice; but on both occasions, Innis stated he did not want to speak to the officers and would prefer to have his attorney present. While transporting Innis to the police station, the officers discussed how dangerous it would be if a child discovered a shotgun, since the murder occurred near a school. The suspect, Innis, then showed the police officers where the murder was committed and the location of the shotgun. This evidence was utilized to convict Innis. Upon appeal, Innis contended the evidence was inadmissible, since he asked for an attorney and indicated his desire not to speak to police. The court disagreed because the police were talking to themselves and he interjected into their conversation. This was admissible since the police officers did not question him, nor did they know he would provide self-incriminating response.

Miranda does not have to be delivered in emergency situations as well. This decision was made in *New York v. Quarles*, 467 U.S. 649 (1984). A woman reported she had been raped by an armed man who had run into a supermarket. Police were able to approach Quarles and conduct a pat-down search and found an empty holster. The officers asked where the gun was and he indicated he threw it into some empty cartons. The gun was retrieved by the police and then Quarles was read his Miranda rights. He was convicted of rape. Quarles argued that the initial statement he made should have been excluded because he was not issued his Miranda rights. Upon appeal, Quarles argued the location of the gun should be excluded from evidence because the officers had not told him his rights prior to questioning. The Supreme Court upheld the conviction of Quarles; public safety justified the absence of *Miranda*. This established the public safety exception to the Miranda warning.

A similar ruling was made when police asked routine questions in *Pennsylvania v. Muniz*, 496 U.S. 582 (1990). Muniz was stopped by police on suspicion of drunk driving. Muniz was given a sobriety test but failed it. The suspect stated he failed these tests because he had been drinking. These tests were also given a second time, which were videotaped. Muniz was asked to take a Breathalyzer test, but he refused. He was then read his Miranda rights and admitted he had been drinking and driving. The videotaped evidence was used in court and he was convicted of driving while intoxicated (DWI). However, the Supreme Court upheld the conviction since the questioning before Miranda was routine and the procedures utilized were standard with DWI stops. Thus, police may videotape suspected drunken drivers and ask routine questions, such as age, height, and residence without providing the Miranda warning.

There are other exceptions. With *Illinois v. Perkins*, 496 U.S. 292 (1990), the court concluded that an officer could pose as a fellow inmate and obtain a confession from another inmate without having to provide a Miranda warning. Perkins was held in jail for aggravated battery. An undercover officer entered his cell and Perkins provided information about another crime and a murder. This information was used to convict Perkins of murder. On appeal, Perkins argued the evidence should not have been used in court because he was not read Miranda by the undercover police officer. The Supreme Court stated Miranda is not required when a suspect provides information to people who they do not believe to be undercover officers.

In *Illinois v. Patane*, 542 U.S. 630, (2004) physical evidence derived from information during questioning can be used as evidence in court, even if Miranda was not provided. Police came to Patane's house for violating a restraining order by calling his ex-girlfriend. While he was being arrested, the officers began providing Patane his Miranda rights, at which point the officers ceased reading them. Patane then informed them he had a gun in his house. He was an ex-felon and not permitted to have such a weapon and was prosecuted. Patane contended the gun was found without proper presentation of a Miranda warning. The court ruled that since the testimony was not entered into trial as evidence, the Fifth Amendment had not been violated. Physical evidence obtained through statements in which the suspect was not provided Miranda was permissible, as long as the statements were not forced.

Assistance of Counsel
Under the Sixth Amendment to the Constitution, assistance of counsel is to be provided for proper defense. The Supreme Court has articulated clear standards that are to be adhered to during the interrogation process. This issue was highlighted in the watershed case of *Escobedo v. Illinois*, 378 U.S. 478 (1963). An informant told police Escobedo had committed a murder. Without an arrest warrant, police arrested Escobedo and interrogated him on the way to the police station and at the station. Several times during the interrogation, Escobedo asked to speak to an attorney. His attorney arrived and was denied permission to see Escobedo. Eventually, Escobedo confessed to the murder and was convicted. The Supreme Court overturned the conviction because Escobedo was denied counsel and an accusatory interrogation proceeded, thus violating Escobedo's due process rights. The court stressed that when an investigation switches from investigatory to accusatory, suspects are allowed an attorney and can refrain from speaking.

This ruling was refined in *Edwards v. Arizona*, 451 U.S. 477 (1981). Edwards, through a taped confession by an accomplice, was implicated in a crime. Edwards was provided a Miranda warning. He wanted to strike a deal with the police but he also requested an attorney. At that point, questioning ceased and an attorney was appointed. The following day, two officers came to his cell and provided Miranda rights again. The officers then asked if Edwards would like to talk to them. Edwards initially refused but then requested to hear the taped confession again. After hearing this, Edwards provided incriminating evidence that was used in court and he was subsequently convicted of various crimes. Upon appeal, he sought to suppress the confession. The court agreed, stating that once he requested council, all police questioning should have ceased—even though Miranda had been provided a second time. During the second round of questioning, his attorney was not present. In addition, the officers continued questioning, despite Edwards's desire to have his attorney present. Thus, even if Miranda has been presented twice, police cannot continue interrogation by a suspect represented by an attorney and requests to remain silent. However, if the suspect initiates conversation that may be incriminating, it is permissible to use such statements in court.

The Supreme Court reinforced this ruling with *Minnick v. Mississippi*, 498 U.S. 146 (1990). Two men escaped from a county jail in Mississippi and killed two men while burglarizing a trailer. Minnick was arrested in California on August 22, 1986, by the Lemon Grove police. The Federal Bureau of Investigation (FBI) advised Minnick of his right to remain silent and his right to have an attorney present on Saturday. Minnick began a partial confession but told the agents to "come back Monday" when an appointed attorney would be present. Also on Saturday, Minnick was provided an attorney, who advised he should not say anything to the police. Denham, a deputy sheriff from Mississippi, flew to California and Minnick was told he "had to talk," despite his reluctance. He admitted to one of the murders and was eventually found guilty of two counts of capital murder and sentenced to death. Upon appeal, he moved to suppress the incriminating statements made to Denham and the FBI. The court agreed. Once *Miranda* has been given and an attorney has been appointed, further police questioning cannot continue without an attorney present.

What if a suspect makes an ambiguous statement concerning his attorney? This issue was decided in *Davis v. United States*, 512 U.S. 452 (1994). Davis was an officer of the U.S. Navy who murdered another officer with a pool cue over a $30 pool game debt. Naval investigators read Davis his Miranda rights. During the interrogation, Davis admitted to the murder and made the statement "maybe I should speak to an attorney." The investigators then asked if he wanted one and he stated "no." Thus, the court ruled an ambiguous request for an attorney does not establish that right. Clear and unambiguous requests for counsel must be articulated.

Strip Searching

A recent issue concerning suspect rights has been the issue of strip searching. The Supreme Court granted certiorari and heard arguments in October 2011 concerning this issue. In *Florence v. Board of Chosen Freeholders of the County of Burlington*, 621 F.3d 296 (2010), the Third Circuit considered whether a suspect's Fourth Amendment rights were violated after twice being strip searched for a noncriminal offense and circumstances suggested he was not carrying contraband. In New Jersey, Florence was pulled over and arrested, once it was discovered he had a warrant for not paying a fine, a noncriminal offense in New Jersey. Florence was able to produce a letter stating the fine was paid but an arrest was made by the officer anyway. The suspect was transported to a local jail and was forced to undergo a strip search. A week later, he was transferred to another custodial facility, where he was again strip searched. Florence alleged his Fourth Amendment rights were violated and filed suit under 42 U.S.C. § 1983. Summary judgment was ruled in favor of the defendants by the U.S. District Court for the District of New Jersey, but the Third Circuit of Appeals reversed.

There was no reasonable suspicion for a strip search, Florence has argued, but based on jail policy, every arrestee was subject to strip search. Under *Bell v. Wolfish*, 441 U.S. 520 (1979), the Supreme Court ruled the possibility of innocence should not preclude the performance of searches for the security of the facility. However, *Florence* makes a distinction between minor and major offenders. These matters should be conducted by reviewing each case. Reasonable suspicion, according to the opposing council, was not required because the search was cursory and not invasive. In addition, contraband may be carried by a minor offender as well as by a major offender. Custody officials should determine the appropriateness of action for security. The Supreme Court was due to provide a decision in early 2012.

Conclusion

Suspects rights are essential to due process. As indicated, the Fourth, Fifth, Sixth, and Fourteenth

Amendments are critical to the issue of suspect's rights. This matter has evolved through various Supreme Court rulings during the past decades and will continue to be a pertinent and controversial question in the near and distant future.

J. Michael Botts
Belmont Abbey College
Tina Fernandes Botts
University of North Carolina, Charlotte

See Also: 1941 to 1960 Primary Documents; *Brown v. Mississippi*; *Mapp v. Ohio*; *Miranda v. Arizona*; *Weeks v. United States*; *Wolf v. Colorado*.

Further Readings
Champion, Dean John. *The American Dictionary of Criminal Justice: Key Terms and Major Court Changes*, 3rd ed. Los Angeles: Roxbury Publishing, 2005.
Neubauer, David W. and Henry F. Fradella. *America's Courts and the Criminal Justice System*, 10th ed. Belmont, CA: Wadsworth, 2011.

Sutherland, Edwin

Edwin H. Sutherland (1883–1950) was the third of seven children born in Gibbon, Nebraska to George and Lizzie Sutherland. Edwin Sutherland's father, George, was devoutly religious and somewhat strict but nonetheless had a lasting impression on his son. Sutherland grew up and studied in Ottawa, Kansas, and Grand Island, Nebraska. He received his bachelor of arts from Grand Island College in 1904, and by age 21, he was teaching Greek, history, Latin, and shorthand at Sioux Falls College in South Dakota. After teaching for two years, he left Sioux Falls College to pursue graduate school at the University of Chicago, where he studied sociology and received his doctorate in 1913. While studying under the guidance of Charles Henderson, Albion Small, and W. I. Thomas, Sutherland concentrated on criminal behavior as a social process. However, some scholars argue that Sutherland became disenchanted with the University of Chicago's department of sociology and chose to reroute his efforts toward the department of political economy, studying under Robert Hoxie and James Field. Ultimately, when he completed his studies, Sutherland had earned a Ph.D. in both sociology and political economy and a minor in psychology.

Shortly after receiving his doctorates, Sutherland became a faculty member at William Jewel College (1913–19) in Liberty, Missouri, and later became an assistant professor at the University of Illinois (1919–26), where he published his eminent book *Criminology*. Following the success of his book, Sutherland was offered a promotion at Illinois and later a professorship at the University of Minnesota (1926–29), where he amassed a reputation as one of the country's leading sociological criminologists. Toward the end of his career, Sutherland was briefly employed at the University of Chicago (1930–35) and then the University of Indiana (1935–49), where he was the chairman of the department of sociology. Sutherland eventually had to relinquish his position as department chair due to poor health, but he continued independent research at Indiana. Edwin Sutherland suddenly passed on October 11, 1950, from cerebral hemorrhage.

Influence on Criminology
Although his untimely demise left many in a state of gloom, Edwin Sutherland's academic works continued to profoundly shape the field of criminology. With four major book publications and more than 50 articles, chapters, and book reviews, there is no denying that Sutherland's scholarship left a lasting influence. In his highly influential book *Criminology*, which transcended most criminological thought at the time, Sutherland cultivated a field that was primitive and lacked structure. Straying from the Lombrosian legacy of biological determinism, Sutherland's first edition of *Criminology* avoided the pitfalls of biological theories by emphasizing a sociological perspective; this novel perspective combined W. I. Thomas's attitude/value concept with the sociological concepts of imitation, isolation, mobility, personality, assimilation, and human nature. In later editions, Sutherland included Robert Park and Ernest Burgess's four processes (the economical, the historical, the political, and the cultural). With time and a few revisions, Sutherland's book became the dominant criminology text in the United States.

By his third edition of the book, which was renamed *Principles of Criminology*, Sutherland had successfully developed a theory on crime causation. Relying on the Chicago school theorists Clifford Shaw and Henry McKay, the culture conflict approach, and his own interviews conducted for *The Professional Thief*, Sutherland formulated the theory of differential association. In a series of nine propositions, Sutherland asserted that individuals become delinquent because the excess of definitions favorable to criminal conduct outweighs the definitions unfavorable to breaking the law. Put simply, criminal behavior emerges when one is exposed to individuals (i.e., friends, family) who both engage in criminal conduct and positively reinforce breaking the law. Not only was his concept applied at the individual level, but Sutherland also believed that differential association could explain why individuals at the group level differ in levels of criminal conduct. Ultimately, he viewed crime as a consequence of conflicting values. It should be noted, however, that Sutherland's theory did not go without criticism. A major criticism of differential association is that it does not apply to perpetrators of individual and personal crimes, and that it fails to account for irrational and impulsive criminals.

With his *Principles of Criminology* published and the theory of differential association afloat, Edwin Sutherland quickly became one of the country's leading sociological criminologists. His insight and scholarship continue to influence the field of criminology.

Weston Morrow
Arizona State University
Nicholas C. Athey
Simon Fraser University

See Also: Crime in America, Causes; Criminology; History of Crime and Punishment in America, 1900–1950.

Further Readings

Gaylord, Mark S. and John F. Galliher. *The Criminology of Edwin Sutherland*. New Brunswick, NJ: Transaction Publishers, 1994.

Sutherland, E. and D. Cressey. "A Theory of Differential Association." In *Criminological Theory, Past to Present: Essential Readings,* 3rd ed, F. Cullen and R. Agnew, eds. New York: Oxford University Press, 1992.

Sutherland, Edwin. *Criminology*, 9th ed. Philadelphia: Lippincott, 1974.

Taft, William Howard (Administration of)

William Howard Taft (1857–1930), 27th president of the United States, is the only American to serve both as president and as chief justice of the Supreme Court. He graduated second in his class at Yale University in 1878 and was admitted to the Ohio bar in 1880 after graduating from Cincinnati Law School.

Taft served in a number of public offices before becoming an Ohio superior court judge in 1887. In 1890, President Benjamin Harrison appointed him solicitor general for the U.S. government. In 1892, he was appointed to a seat on the Sixth Circuit Court of Appeals. In 1900, Taft was appointed president of the U. S. Philippines Commission; he was named civil governor of the Philippines on July 4, 1901. In 1904, he was appointed secretary of war.

Presidency

In 1908, Taft was elected president of the United States. An excellent administrator, he was soon faced with difficult political choices. He wanted to continue the Progressive policies of Roosevelt, which included consumer advocates' goals of cutting tariffs. The House passed a tariff bill that lowered rates, but Taft did not exercise enough political pressure on the more conservative Senate to see the bill through. Instead, the Senate effectively rewrote the bill into a tariff bill with even higher rates. As events unfolded, Taft was increasingly less graceful in handling the Progressives, alienating them even more.

Among Taft's legislative accomplishments were the establishment of the Postal Savings Plan and the passage of the Mann-Elkins Act (1910) strengthening the Interstate Commerce Commission and the White-Slave Traffic Act of 1910 (Mann Act). During his term, the Department of Commerce and Labor became two separate departments, the Federal Children's Bureau was established, and Arizona and New Mexico were admitted into the Union. Two constitutional amendments were ratified during his term in office: the Sixteenth Amendment (addressing income tax) and the Seventeenth Amendment (direct election of senators).

Despite his many accomplishments, many Progressives were unhappy with Taft's administration. As the election of 1912 approached, supporters of Teddy Roosevelt called for him to come home from his foreign travels. Roosevelt, disappointed that Taft had not followed his conservation policies as well as his other policies, challenged Taft for the presidential nomination. Roosevelt was able to win support in the states that had direct primary elections, but he failed to win the Republican Party nomination, which went

1745

William Howard Taft was elected president of the United States in 1908. In 1921 he was nominated to be the 10th chief justice of the Supreme Court, where he delivered 253 opinions in his tenure, including upholding Prohibition.

to Taft. Roosevelt then chose to create a factional party to use to run for president. The Progressive Party, popularly known as the Bull Moose Party, was successful in splitting the Republican Party, effectively giving the election to the Democratic Party candidate, Woodrow Wilson.

Supreme Court

Upon leaving the White House, Taft became professor of law at Yale University. He left Yale in 1921 when he was nominated to be the 10th chief justice of the Supreme Court by President Warren G. Harding. The Senate approved the nomination without debate. Taft was able to unite the court and to clear away its large backlog of cases. He delivered 253 opinions in his eight and a half years on the court.

The Taft Court upheld Prohibition, which led to an era of crime during the Roaring Twenties. He issued opinions in a number of criminal justice cases. In 1922 (*Balzac v. Porto Rico*), he wrote in one of the *Insular Cases* that the Fourteenth Amendment did not apply the criminal provisions of the Bill of Rights to overseas territories.

His most important criminal law case was *Carroll v. United States* (1925), which interpreted "reasonable search and seizure" to allow police officers to search a vehicle for alcohol. Also in 1925, Taft wrote *Ex Parte Grossman*. The opinion held that the power of the president to pardon extends to persons jailed or imprisoned for criminal contempt by a court. In *Olmstead v. United States* (1928), Taft wrote for the court that police or federal agents could engage in warrantless wiretapping without violating the Fourth Amendment.

In 1929, Taft persuaded Congress to build a permanent home for the Supreme Court for the first time. Taft saw the designs of architect Cass Gilbert but not the finished building, which was dedicated in 1935. Taft stepped down from the Supreme Court February 3, 1930, as a result of illness and died on March 8 in Washington, D.C.

Andrew J. Waskey
Dalton State College

See Also: 1777 to 1800 Primary Documents; 1941 to 1960 Primary Documents; 1961 to 1980 Primary Documents; Mann Act; Roosevelt, Theodore (Administration of); Supreme Court, U.S.

Further Readings

Anderson, Judith Icke. *William Howard Taft*. New York: W. W. Norton, 1981.
Gould, Lewis L. *The William Howard Taft Presidency*. Lawrence: University Press of Kansas, 2009.
Lurie, Jonathan. *William Howard Taft: The Travails of a Progressive Conservative*. Cambridge, MA: Cambridge University Press, 2011.

Tax Crimes

A tax crime is any form of activity aimed at illegally avoiding paying taxes levied by the state on personal income and a range of other financial transactions. Tax crimes are generally met with a severe response by the authorities, and the threat of a personal or organizational audit helps to deter at least some people from being creative with their tax returns. The notorious gangster Al Capone, for example, was convicted on tax crimes when insufficient evidence could be mustered to prosecute him for his numerous other alleged illegal activities. Personal income tax and corporate tax issues are administered by the Internal Revenue Service (IRS) on the federal level, while other national and some state-level agencies regulate the levying and collection of other forms of taxes.

In addition to financial gain, there are various ideological positions that might persuade people that it is morally acceptable or imperative for them to withhold paying tax of one sort or another. This includes people whose tax protest is aimed at one or more specific policies and the anarchism of some libertarian positions that hold that all taxes are an undue imposition. Irrespective of their ideological position, most people are united in adherence to the romantic view of the Boston Tea Party, at which the call for no taxation without representation became central.

Tax Avoidance and Tax Evasion

It is recognized in American law as well as custom and practice that individuals and organizations are entitled to minimize the amount of tax that they are required to pay. Doing so by means that remain within the law is known as tax avoidance (or mitigation), while resorting to illegal means is known as tax evasion and is a criminal offense. Determining the distinction between avoidance and evasion is a constantly changing undertaking as accountants develop new means of minimizing tax, and tax authorities make rulings concerning which new activities are legal and which are not. New forms of commerce (e.g., e-commerce) emerge that require new national and international norms of regulation, and people will naturally wish to take advantage of them while they remain legal. Since tax codes tend to be very complex and subject to differing interpretations (e.g., when it comes to the classification of expenses as being for personal or business use), the decisions made by authorities are often accompanied by a fair amount of negotiation in the many cases where actions are not clear-cut.

Means of tax avoidance include changing legal status, transferring assets, or making payments to charitable foundations that reduce tax liability. Means of tax evasion include underreporting the value of income and assets, hiding assets, or not declaring money earned by illegal means. The last-named of these is the provision by which suspected criminals may be prosecuted if insufficient evidence exists to mount a case concerning prostitution, illegal gambling, drug dealing, or other illegal activity. Al Capone was successfully prosecuted using this method. When a claim is made that a certain activity is a victimless crime and should, therefore, by legalized, the state can respond that the state itself is the victim because it is deprived of its legal tax income.

Smuggling is also classified as a form of tax evasion in addition to being a crime when goods are imported that are illegal to own, including drugs, weapons, and human trafficking, as well as in the cases in which appropriate inspection or custom fees should be levied. This provides an alternative means of prosecuting suspected criminals when other evidence is not available.

The difference between the amount of money raised by officials from taxation and the amount of money that would be raised if every person reported his/her income fully is known as the "tax gap" and is, by definition, impossible to determine exactly. Efforts were made in the 1970s and 1980s, through the use of the Taxpayer Compliance Measurement Program (TCMP), when the country was struggling to reestablish its economic dynamism amid oil shocks, military defeat, and rising state expenses. The TCMP was considered very intrusive and hence was increasingly unpopular to the extent that it has subsequently been abandoned. Nevertheless, using estimates based on TCMP findings, it has been estimated that the tax gap remains in the hundreds of billions of dollars. Famous Americans who have been jailed for tax evasion include Wesley Snipes, Leona Helmsley, and Henry David Thoreau, one of the first tax resisters, who spent one night in prison.

Transfer Pricing and Corporate Crime

Corporations tend to have many more resources to minimize their tax liabilities and in some cases may be more willing to take chances because responsibility might be spread among many people and the likelihood of avoiding personal punishment is greater. One of the principal ways in which corporations reduce tax, in addition to the constant lobbying of politicians to reduce taxes and regulations, is to ensure that ownership of assets is registered in overseas tax havens. These are countries or territories that offer low or zero rates of taxation, confidentiality of personal or organizational records, and little transparency of the system to outsiders. Many tax havens are to be found in the Caribbean, where otherwise poverty-vulnerable states make themselves open to receiving untraceable amounts of money and associated tourism industry. This is problematic for national governments, which lose income, and also in terms of establishing who owns which company and, thus, has responsibility for its acts.

Despite recent international attempts to force more transparency from tax-haven countries, in efforts stimulated by the 2001 terrorist attacks on the United States and the possibility that terrorism might be combated in this way, little tangible success has been achieved. However, on the domestic front, the desire to force corporations to make proper levels of payment has become popular. Following the 2008 economic recession caused by the underregulated banking industry and reckless and greedy corporate risk taking, the bailout of many companies cost an enormous amount of money that will have to be paid for by the taxpayer; groups such as US Uncut have begun high-profile campaigns arguing that no cuts to public services should be made while corporations fail to pay their taxes. Companies such as Apple, FedEx, and BP are being targeted for use of tax havens, excessive lobbying for corporate tax breaks, and failing to meet their legal or ethical obligations with respect to their impact on society and the environment.

Although there are corporations that are larger and richer than some small countries, and the language of globalization tends to portray them as being so powerful they can effectively ignore governments and their laws, it is still possible for countries to act together to reduce some of the abuses that corporations practice with respect to tax. One notable example of this has been the international effort to bring an end to improper transfer pricing, which has been led by the Organisation for Economic Co-operation and Development (OECD).

Multinational corporations may own assets in a number of different countries, and those countries have varying rates of taxation and other regulatory frameworks. Since corporations can save money by declaring profits in low-tax countries and losses in high-tax countries in which they operate, it was possible to transfer assets at prices that brought about the desired arrangement. This meant that very valuable assets could be transferred for next to nothing or vice versa in order to manipulate the bottom line of each unit in the company. This practice has now been effectively ended by the OECD and international leadership through application of an arm's-length principle that demands the realistic pricing of assets by objective observation.

Tax Protesters

Tax protesters are people who refuse to pay all or part of the taxes levied upon them by the government, primarily in the form of the IRS. Within this category are people who argue that paying any form of tax is wrong and who may be classified as tax resisters. It is practically impossible to determine the extent to which tax resisters are genuinely motivated by ideology rather than simply interested in financial gain.

Tax protesting really began as an important phenomenon in the second half of the 20th century, although probably the first known example was the so-called Whiskey Rebellion in Pennsylvania, which was sparked by the imposition of duties on liquor in 1791 as a means of recouping money spent during the Revolutionary War. This was predictably unpopular and resulted in the deployment of some 12,700 militia by President George Washington to break up the rebellion in 1797. The justification of liquor producers in this rebellion concerned "unjust taxes," and this rhetoric resurfaced after the excise tax was reinstated during the Civil War. Attempts by the Bureau of Internal Revenue to prosecute distillers unwilling to pay the tax were severely hampered by the Whiskey Ring scandal of 1875, in which leading members of the Grant administration were discovered to have looted some $3 million of revenues. However, the fight was taken up by the Bureau of Alcohol, Tobacco, and Firearms (ATF), which continues to pursue mostly cottage industry level producers of moonshine or unlicensed liquor to the present time, mostly in relatively remote mountainous regions of the south.

Intellectual respectability was given to tax resistance in part by Henry David Thoreau, who wrote about it in *On the Duty of Civic Disobedience* in 1849, and political respectability provided by the desire of some rich merchants to avoid import taxes inspired the so-called Boston Tea Party. The Quakers, opposed to all forms of violence, have been protesting against portions of their tax requirements throughout the history of the United States. However, to some extent, it is the spread of mass media that enables people to develop social solidarity in joining tax protests for specific purposes. For example, protests against the Vietnam War brought about a tax protest led by celebrities and intellectuals. In 1964, the singer Joan Baez declared that she would withhold the 60 percent of her tax assessment that she calculated would be used for military activities of which she disapproved. A committee was subsequently established to promote this cause nationally and included notable figures such as Noam Chomsky, Albert Szent-Gyorgi, and Gloria Steinem. It is estimated that 20,000 people nationally participated in this tax withholding. When the state subsequently imposed an additional telephone tax to support the escalating costs of the war, as many as 500,000 people participated in the subsequent tax protest. Similar protests were also made as a result of the increased spending on nuclear weapons, particularly during the Reagan administration. In 1981, notably, Roman Catholic archbishop of Seattle Raymond Hunthausen gained support for his call for people to withhold the 50 percent

The most common tax crimes include failure to file a tax return or requested information, tax evasion, preparing false tax returns, submitting false tax documents. making untrue statements to governmental tax officials, or failing to file currency transaction reports. These popular-culture tax crimes are often portrayed as a contest between the individual and the state, which is a contest that can have only one winner in the long term, most often the state.

of their income tax demands that might be spent on weapons of war. In all cases, the government has responded strongly to tax protesters, understanding that loss of revenue would have a serious impact upon the ability of the state not just to deploy military force but to undertake any of its scheduled activities.

Tax resisters have attempted to use a variety of arguments to justify the decision not to pay their taxes. These have ranged from supposed unconstitutionality of tax demands to the attempted redefinition of income to the claim that only coinage containing a proportion of gold can be counted as real money. Again, the state has rejected all of these arguments and, through the judiciary, branded most of them as "trivial," thereby reducing the need to argue through the merits of such arguments whenever they are put forward. The same approach is used to disallow tax returns that are used as a medium to make additional tax resister protests; such attempts might attract financial penalties. Nevertheless, far-right ideology that denies the legitimacy of government altogether has bloomed in the United States since the latter part of the 20th century and has led to the notion of the tax defier, who is defined according to the TAXDEF Initiative of 2008 as a person who is fundamentally opposed to the state almost to the extent of being considered an enemy.

Tax Amnesty

Since collecting taxes from recalcitrant people can be a lengthy, complex, and expensive business and also serves to criminalize those who are involved, some states have in recent years offered limited tax amnesties to recoup at least some portion of what they are owed. This involves making a time window available for people to repay their back taxes without incurring the late fees or penalties that might otherwise apply. In 2003, for example, Illinois authorities collected a total of $522 million and New York state authorities collected $520 million in back taxes during amnesties, while other states collected rather smaller amounts. Amnesties cannot, by their very nature, be used too frequently or they will provide an incentive to people to delay paying, since the amount they owe will decline in value. Amnesties are also useful in the case of migrant or temporary workers who may not be aware of their tax liabilities in a certain state since education will accompany the marketing of the campaign.

Responsibilities of the Internal Revenue Service

The Internal Revenue Service (IRS) is the branch of the U.S. Treasury that has responsibility for administering the tax code and, hence, leading the fight against the various types of tax crime. The forerunner of the IRS, the Bureau of Internal Revenue, was first established in 1862 when the costs of the Civil War necessitated the first imposition of an income tax. A form of the bureau has been in operation in all years subsequently in which income tax has been in action. Throughout its history, the IRS has been challenged by those who consider it to be unconstitutional or illegitimate and those who consider its choice of subjects for intrusive investigation to be tainted by political interests. It has also faced its share of corruption allegations and abuses, and faces the continual battle to convince people that its actions are in the best interests of society and that the revenue gathered is used in appropriate ways. Unfortunately, the IRS has little actual control over how the money it collects actually is used.

Tax Crimes in Popular Culture

Benjamin Franklin famously observed that the only things inevitable in life are death and taxes, and this inevitability has brought tax crimes into popular culture. Nearly every comedy or drama on television has referred to one or more of its characters struggling to fill out the annual tax return or threatened with a tax audit or weighing the possibility of charging a personal lunch as a business expense. Although subversively portraying people failing to pay tax is beyond the pale apart from the case of obviously criminal characters, cultural productions regularly portray the struggle to minimize tax liability to be a type of game or contest between the individual and the state, which is a contest that has only one winner in the long term.

John Walsh
Shinawatra University

See Also: Capone, Al; Civil Disobedience; Internal Revenue Service; Thoreau, Henry David.

Further Readings

Copeland, Larry. "Tax Amnesty Plans Exceed Expectations." *USA Today*. http://www.usatoday.com/news/nation/2004-01-05-tax-amnesty_x.htm (Accessed September 2011).

Organisation for Economic Co-operation and Development (OECD). *Transfer Pricing Guidelines for Multinational Enterprises and Tax Administrations*. Paris: OECD, 2010.

Slemrod, Joel. "Cheating Ourselves: The Economics of Tax Evasion." *Journal of Economic Perspectives*, v.21/1 (Winter 2007).

Thoreau, Henry David and Michael Meyer. *Walden and Civil Disobedience*. New York: Longman, 2002.

Thorndike, Joseph J. "Reforming the Internal Revenue Service: A Comparative History." *Administrative Law Review*, v.53 (2001).

Zinn, Howard. *The Zinn Reader: Writings on Disobedience and Democracy*. New York: Seven Stories Press, 2009.

Taylor, Zachary (Administration of)

Renowned General Zachary Taylor (1784–1850) served as the 12th president of the United States after his election in 1848, despite his earlier political indifference. Although he was a Whig, his moderate views alienated many party members. He died in office in 1850, just 16 months into his presidency. The biggest crisis of the Taylor administration involved the fate of slavery in the newly acquired Mexican Cession territories that he had helped to gain. Taylor encouraged two of those territories, California and New Mexico, to apply directly for statehood to avoid the need for Congress to legislate slavery's legal status. Although Taylor was a southern slaveholder, he was a staunch unionist and opposed the proposed Fugitive Slave Act that allowed slave catchers to pursue fugitives into free states.

Zachary Taylor was born in Virginia and raised in Kentucky. He was a professional soldier with 40 years' experience in the U.S. Army beginning in 1808; he rose to the rank of brigadier general and earned the nickname "Old Rough and Ready." He was known as an effective but argumentative and undiplomatic military leader. His distinguished service included the War of 1812, the Black Hawk War (1832), the Second Seminole War (1835–42), and the Mexican–American War (1845–48). His service in the latter, his last military campaign, made him a popular national hero and helped carry him to the presidency. He owned a home in Baton Rouge, Louisiana, and a slaveholding plantation in Mississippi.

Taylor returned from the Mexican campaign in 1847 and entered the race for the presidency late in that year, despite having made earlier statements that he would not run if asked. He had previously never even voted, much less run for office. He enjoyed broad popular support because of his status as a war hero. He also appealed to both sections of the country, as northerners supported his strong unionist stance while southerners felt secure in his status as a fellow southerner and slaveholder. Taylor received the Whig Party nomination for the presidential election of 1848, in which he defeated Democratic candidate Lewis Cass.

Moderation and Compromise

Taylor's earlier lack of political interest and experience limited his effectiveness in office and his relations with Congress. Taylor took a moderate position on many political issues and was willing to compromise with opposing politicians, seeking to build a coalition that was not limited by party or sectional loyalties. His moderate views, combined with the fact that he failed to reward loyal Whig Party members with patronage jobs, alienated many. Northern Whigs, known as "Conscience Whigs" for their opposition to slavery, were already alienated by their party's selection of a southern slaveholder for office and his appointment of several southerners to cabinet positions; Taylor also alienated loyal Whigs through his belief that he was above party politics.

The ongoing debate over the expansion of slavery proved to be the Taylor administration's biggest legal challenge. Taylor assumed the presidency as sectional tensions were rising over questions of whether slavery would be allowed into the newly acquired Mexican lands known as the Mexican Cession. Debate also surrounded the question of who should make the decision. Some advocated allowing the territorial governments or Congress to legislate the question while others called for popular sovereignty, a doctrine that would allow the residents of the territory to vote on the issue. Taylor stated that he would not veto the Wilmot Proviso, which would ban the extension of slavery into any part of the Mexican Cession, if Congress approved it. Taylor, however, did not support the abolition of slavery in those southern states where it was already in legal existence.

The question of statehood was active for both California and New Mexico, although the latter was less ready for admission. Taylor encouraged both territories to directly apply to Congress for statehood, knowing that they would likely do so as free states. Such an action would also avoid the necessity for Congress to enact legislation with regard to the slavery question, which would be sure to further inflame already heightened sectional tensions. California voted to enter the Union as a free state where slavery would be legally prohibited.

Southerners were opposed to California's admission because it would upset the balance of power in Congress in favor of the free states, allowing the future possibility of legislation banning slavery throughout the country. Southerners were also angered over Taylor's opposition to Texan claims to all lands east of the Rio Grande River, as Texas allowed slavery. Senator Henry Clay of Kentucky offered a series of acts designed to settle the issues, which became collectively known as the Compromise of 1850. Taylor voiced his opposition to most of the acts, including the harsh Fugitive Slave Act allowing southern slave catchers to pursue fugitive slaves into northern states and territories. His objections have led some historians to conclude that he most likely would have vetoed this and most of the other acts.

The sectional debates over the Mexican Cession and other issues such as tariffs spurred secessionist talk among southern radicals commonly known as "fire-eaters." Taylor was a staunch unionist despite his southern background, declaring secession and disunion to be treasonous offenses punishable by death. Although he was prepared to take a harsh stand against secessionists, he actively sought sectional reconciliation as the more favorable solution to the repression of open rebellion. Zachary Taylor died of cholera in Washington, D.C., on July 9, 1850, just 16 months into his presidency, and was buried near Louisville, Kentucky. He was the last of the Whig presidents, as sectional divisions within the party led to its demise. His successor, Vice President Millard Fillmore, signed the Compromise of 1850 into law.

Marcella Bush Trevino
Barry University

See Also: Fillmore, Millard (Administration of); Fugitive Slave Act of 1850; Slavery, Law of.

Further Readings
Eisenhower, John S. D. *Zachary Taylor*. New York: Times Books, 2008.
Silbey, Joel H. *Party Over Section: The Rough and Ready Presidential Election of 1848*. Lawrence: University Press of Kansas, 2009.
Smith, Elbert B. *The Presidencies of Zachary Taylor & Millard Fillmore*. Lawrence: University Press of Kansas, 1988.

Taylor v. State

Taylor v. State of Mississippi (1943) was a landmark freedom of speech case. The U.S. Supreme Court held in *Taylor* that communications cannot be criminalized by state or federal governments, unless the government can prove that the communication had an evil or sinister intent, advocated or incited subversive action against the government, and presented a clear and present danger. The Mississippi legislature passed the statute under dispute in *Taylor* in 1942, during World War II, when patriotic feelings were heightened. The statute criminalizes communications intended to encourage violence, sabotage, or disloyalty to the state or the national governments, including refusals to salute and otherwise honor the state and federal flags.

Mandatory flag pledges were first instituted by public schools in 1898 during the Spanish–American War. The practice grew during World War I (1914–18). In 1935, Jehovah's Witness schoolchildren began to refuse to participate. Jehovah's Witness students were expelled, and

The Pledge of Allegiance is an expression of loyalty to the flag and the United States. It was composed in 1892 and has been modified four times, with the most recent change in 1954 being to add the words "under God."

Jehovah's Witness teachers were fired by schools across the nation. The U.S. Supreme Court held in *Minersville School District v. Gobitis* (1940) that the First Amendment does not prohibit public schools from requiring students to salute the flag and recite the Pledge of Allegiance. In this case, the students were Jehovah's Witnesses who had declined to salute the flag and recite the pledge on religious grounds. Jehovah's Witnesses suffered increased persecution in the wake of the *Minersville* decision. Mobs attacked Jehovah's Witnesses in 300 communities across the country after the decision was published. Many Jehovah's Witnesses were jailed for proselytizing.

The Mississippi statute under dispute in *Taylor* was part of the response to *Minersville*. Mississippi prosecuted three members of the Jehovah's Witnesses religion for distributing literature alleged to have encouraged Jehovah's Witnesses not to salute the flags of Mississippi and the United States. Taylor, the appellant, had spoken out against the war and against saluting the flag and the government, and had distributed books and pamphlets containing similar arguments. Taylor's co-appellant Betty Benoit had distributed a publication containing a reprint of a newspaper editorial that opposed the U.S. Supreme Court decision holding that public schools could compel Jehovah's Witness students to salute the flag. The editorial also compared flag salutes to a primitive form of idol worship and alleged that flag worship was part of a Catholic conspiracy, possibly imported from France. Taylor's co-appellant Cummings had also distributed literature criticizing mandatory flag salutes.

The *Taylor* defendants moved to quash the indictments, arguing that the statutes violated the First Amendment right to freedom of speech. They were convicted and sentenced to a prison term that would expire at the end of World War II, then still in progress, and which could not exceed 10 years. The U.S. Supreme Court reversed the appellants' conviction. Justice Owen Roberts, writing for the majority, argued that the appellants' speech did not constitute a clear and present danger, and that they were merely expressing "beliefs and opinions concerning domestic measures and trends in national and world affairs. Under our decisions criminal sanctions cannot be imposed for such communication."

In the same year that the court decided in favor of the *Taylor* appellants, it also overturned its *Minersville* decision of only three years previous, in *West Virginia State Board of Education v. Barnette*. In *Jones v. City of Opelika* (1943), the court held that states cannot prohibit distribution of religious literature. The court also decided in favor of Jehovah's Witnesses in several other significant cases that year. Thus the "Jehovah's Witnesses" cases of 1943 helped lay the groundwork for modern religious freedom doctrine.

In subsequent decisions, the court would create a variety of religious exemptions. During the 1940s and 1950s, the court refined its conception of conscientious objectors exempted from wartime service. In *Sherbert v. Verner* (1963), the court agreed that a worker fired for religiously motivated absences from work could qualify for unemployment benefits. In *Wisconsin v. Yoder* (1972), the court exempted Amish parents from mandatory education laws once their children had completed eighth grade. However, beginning with *United States v. Lee* (1982), the court decided against a request for tax exemptions that were based on religious grounds. *Lee* began to reverse the trend, as the court moved away from religious exemptions. Nonetheless, the court's ruling in *Taylor* against the criminalization of unpopular speech remains a fundament of contemporary free speech doctrine.

Thomas F. Brown
Virginia Wesleyan College

See Also: Religion and Crime, History of; Religion and Crime, Sociology of; *Whitney v. California*.

Further Readings
Alley, Robert S. *The Constitution & Religion: Leading Supreme Court Cases on Church and State*. Amherst, NY: Prometheus Books, 1999.
Elias, William A., Jr. "The Jehovah's Witnesses Cases." *Kansas City Law Review*, v.16/140 (1948).
Peters, Shawn Francis. *Judging Jehovah's Witnesses: Religious Persecution and the Dawn of the Rights Revolution*. Lawrence: University Press of Kansas, 2002.

Tea Act of 1773

After the French-Indian War, the British Crown enacted the Proclamation of 1763. This proclamation created a line intended to protect the colonists from Native American attacks and ease the Crown's role of protecting the colonists by prohibiting anyone from crossing over it. It extended from Canada to Georgia, along the crest of the Appalachian Mountains. This act angered the colonists because they felt the Crown no longer trusted them, and by 1773 hostilities intensified. In conjunction with the Proclamation Line, the Crown also instituted the Grenville Taxation Program, which aimed to recover the losses the Crown had incurred while defending the colonists and winning the French-Indian War. Three basic taxes were the Revenue Act (dubbed the Sugar Act as it placed a tax on molasses), the Currency Act (forbidding the issuance of paper money on the colonies), and the Stamp Act (taxing all paper goods).

Almost instantly, the colonists began protesting these new taxes and boycotting British goods. During the next decade, the Crown continually fought the colonists, and one of the most infamous incidents was the Boston Massacre of 1765. With each new tax, the colonists created a new plan for boycott and protest, and the avoidance of tea and coffee hit the Crown particularly hard. The Crown reacted by placing a tax on tea. The Tea Act of 1773 was meant to support the East India Tea Company. The company was nearly bankrupt, as it was a key supplier to the colonies and colonial boycotts prevented sales. The Tea Act removed the tax on tea, but it allowed tea to be sold in the colonies only via its own agents. The act functioned as a default tax. The colonists had been relying on Dutch or homemade teas since the beginning of the Grenville Taxation Program.

In November 1773, the first of three ships arrived at Boston Harbor carrying tea for the East India Tea Company. A standoff immediately ensued, with the *Dartmouth* standing at the center of the controversy. Samuel Adams quickly gathered a crowd—as he had been a key leader for colonial protests—and the militant group the Sons of Liberty joined the masses. Massachusetts Governor Thomas Hutchinson insisted that the tea would be delivered, and he refused to settle for anything else. On December 16, an estimated 8,000 gathered at Boston's Old South Meeting House. The owner of the *Dartmouth* and its captain feared the crowds, and they agreed to return the tea to England. Hutchinson again refused, ordering the blocking of Boston Harbor so that no tea-bearing vessel could leave until all goods had been delivered.

The newly arrived *Beaver* and *Eleanor* waited with the *Dartmouth*. Members of the Sons of Liberty, thinly veiled as Native Americans, headed that night to the harbor to dispose of the tea. The tea was brought up to the hold, dumped overboard, and smashed so that it was ruined. By daybreak, nearly 90,000 pounds of tea was dumped into the harbor, costing the Crown £10,000 or $1.87 million in 2007 currency. Nothing else was damaged or stolen. A padlock was broken in the surge for the tea, and it was anonymously replaced the next day.

A fourth East India Tea Company ship ran ashore in Provincetown, Massachusetts. All 58 tea chests were salvaged and smuggled into Boston via a fishing schooner, but the effects of the Boston Tea Party were still felt. Parliament responded with the Coercive Acts, which closed Boston Harbor, removed the trials of royal officials out of New England, allowed for the quartering of troops in colonists' homes, and extended Quebec's boundaries south. The colonists viewed this act as another token of Britain's distrust of them. The First Continental Congress formed in 1774, establishing the "Declaration of Rights and Grievances" and the Continental Association to prohibit importing British goods. War broke out before the second congress could meet.

Annessa A. Babic
New York Institute of Technology

See Also: 1600 to 1776 Primary Documents; American Revolution and Criminal Justice; Colonial Courts; Tax Crimes.

Further Readings
Bowen, H. V. *Revenue and Reform: The Indian Problem in British Politics, 1757–1773.* Cambridge: Cambridge University Press, 2002.
Carp, Benjamin L. *Defiance of the Patriots: The Boston Tea Party and the Making of America.* New Haven, CT: Yale University Press, 2010.

Technology, Police

Almost from the beginning of American history, the colonists recognized the need for developing some form of policing power in order to maintain order and enforce laws. The first law officers were generally justices of the peace. In 1635, Boston became the first city to use patrol officers to monitor its streets at night. Dutch New York created the Schout, an officer combining the functions of sheriff and justice of the peace, and the rattle watch, a patrol force, in 1651. The first combined day and night patrol was New York's in 1845. The men were armed only with a night stick and were not uniformed until 1853. Technology was limited to providing reliable methods of backup for when assistance was needed. Scholars of the history of American policing identify three major periods during which technology developed: the political era, the professional model era, and the community policing era. In this final era, police technology finally came into its own. A survey conducted by the Police Executive Research Forum in April 2011 revealed that 70 percent of all departments in large cities planned to increase their use of technology over the coming year.

The chief use of police technology has generally been engaging in crime analysis. That analysis may be tactical, involving short-term goals that focus on crime control; strategic, dealing with long-term organizational goals; or problem-specific, identifying and responding to ongoing issues in specific communities. During economic downturns, departments cut back on the number of officers hired, and technology has helped to fill some of the gaps left by decreased manpower. Police departments frequently make use of free forms of modern technology, such as the Nixle alert system or Alert-ID-My Neighborhood, to keep the public up to date on crimes that occur in their neighborhoods. However, most technology is costly and may require training in proper use. It may also call for intensive service and maintenance. Requests for such purchases must be accompanied by explanations of how they can be expected to improve officer safety or enhance job efficiency.

The technology explosion that began in the late 20th century and continued into the 21st century has sometimes overwhelmed police departments, leaving them uncertain of which technology best fits their needs and budgets. To respond to this need, the International Association of Police Chiefs has developed the *Best Practices Guide on Acquisition of New Technology*. The guide has been particularly helpful in assisting small departments with limited budgets. At all levels, police departments are required to justify the need for particular equipment and must be able to explain why certain items should be budgeted and how those items are expected to improve policing. There are approximately 17,000 agencies that make up the highly fragmented police marketplace. Funded by the U.S. Congress, the National Institute of Justice (NIJ) fulfills the role of researching and developing policing technology and making that information available to state and local law enforcement. One of the major accomplishments of NIJ has been to develop soft body armor designed to protect police officers in the course of duty. Current NIJ projects deal with improving the quality and availability of DNA technology and developing technology to allow officers to accurately detect concealed weapons and contraband.

The Political Era

The first phase of police technology, which began in 1840 and continued until 1920, has been identified as the political era. In virtually every large city in the United States, political bosses controlled all official positions, including that of chief of police. While the relationship was mutually beneficial to a large extent, police executives were limited in their ability to make decisions. Technology during this period focused entirely on keeping police officers safe and on making them more effective on the job. In 1850, the Texas Rangers became the first law enforcement entity to use a multi-shot pistol. Around 1854, San Francisco began using systematic photographing technology for identifying criminals. By the late 19th century, police officers were carrying handguns in addition to nightsticks. In New York, for instance, firearms began to be issued to police officers in 1887. Seven years later,

A demonstrator offers a flower to military police at an anti–Vietnam War protest in 1967. Police departments faced many challenges dealing with the growing civil unrest and the counterculture movement during the 1960s.

the city established a School of Police Practice and began requiring regular target practice in 1895. The following year, a .32-caliber double-action Colt revolver with a four-inch barrel became standard issue. By 1901, the weapon of choice was a .38-caliber revolver, and each gun was marked with individual shield numbers to facilitate identification. Albany, New York, became the first city to use the telegraph for police work in 1877. Shortly thereafter, other departments also began using the telegraph to facilitate communication within departments and with outside parties. Washington, D.C., became the first city in the nation to use telephones in policing in 1878, police in Chicago and Detroit first used police call boxes in 1884, and soon the telephone and police call boxes were in use around the country.

Until the early 1890s, American police departments had no reliable way of identifying criminals and tracking their arrest records. European law enforcement had been dealing with the same problem, which was alleviated when ethnologist Alphonse Bertillon (1853–1914) of the Prefecture of Paris Police developed the system that bore his name. The Bertillon system consisted of measurements of particular bony parts of the body that were recorded via photographs of an arrestee standing against a cardboard form. Using this information, along with hair and eye color, arrestees could be grouped into distinct categories for the purpose of identification. The Bertillon system was first used in the United States in 1887 by the Illinois State Penitentiary System. In 1863, French scientist Paul-Jean Coulier (1824–90) developed a method by which latent fingerprints could be permanently transferred to paper by the use of iodine fuming. Because no two are alike, fingerprints proved more reliable than the Bertillon system. Scotland Yard began using fingerprinting as a means of identifying criminals in 1901, and American police departments followed suit. By the end of the 19th century, fingerprinting had become standard practice among American police forces. The first crime lab was established in France in 1910 by Edmund Locard (1877–1966), and it became the model for police departments throughout the world.

Professional Model Era

By the 1920s, efforts were accelerating to remove police departments from political control. The new emphasis was on promoting discipline and equally enforcing the laws. The professional model era began in 1920 and continued for five decades. The most influential figure during this period was August Vollmer (1876–1955), a self-educated expert on police technology who is credited with promoting the use of fingerprinting and handwriting classification systems in the United States. Vollmer was police chief in Berkeley, California, from 1909 to 1931. His innovations set the standards for American police technology. Vollmer established the first evidence training school in the world in 1907. He was the first to use bicycles and motorcycles for patrol officers and later became the first to use automobiles. The crime lab that Vollmer established in Berkeley was the first to use blood, fiber, and soil analysis in solving crimes. In 1921, Berkeley also became the first department to use the lie detector. Not only did Vollmer start the criminal justice program at Berkeley, he also helped to modernize police departments in Los Angeles, Chicago, San Diego, and Dallas. Philadelphia was the first city to use the teletype in its police departments, and Detroit became the first to employ the two-way radio in 1934. In 1932, the Federal Bureau of Investigation (FBI) established its own lab, gaining the reputation of being the most comprehensive crime lab in the world. From the beginning, the FBI lab employed state-of-the-art technology. Radar was introduced in the United States in the 1940s, providing police with the means for tracking the speed of motorists as a means of making roads and highways safer.

During World War II and the postwar years, crime rates began to climb in the United States, doubling between 1940 and 1965. The sweeping changes to the American social structure during the 1960s required police departments to face new challenges when dealing with the developing drug culture and growing civil unrest. A number of riot control technologies were introduced and quickly discarded. The discarded technologies included wooden, rubber, and plastic bullets; tranquillizing dart guns; a volt-shock baton; and strobe lights that caused targets to faint or become ill. Only the TASER, a weapon that released tiny darts containing a 50,000-volt shock, survived. Most police departments still used only the technology that had been developed decades earlier. One exception was New Orleans, where a data processing machine was already in use. In 1958, a former marine invented the side-handled baton, which added versatility and effectiveness to the traditional weapon.

During the presidential campaign of 1964, which followed on the heels of the assassination of President John Kennedy, candidate Barry Goldwater made restoring law and order a cornerstone of his campaign. Goldwater lost the election to incumbent Lyndon Johnson, who established the President's Commission on Law Enforcement and Administration of Justice. In 1967, the commission's report offered 11 recommendations that dealt with police technology. Noting that most police departments were using technology that was several decades old, the commission recommended the use of a 911 system that would allow the entire nation to use a single number to contact police and fire departments during emergencies. AT&T initially attempted to block the 911 system but was eventually forced to come on board. By the mid-1990s, 95 percent of police departments had created 911 systems. Other recommendations of the commission addressed the use of technology in fingerprinting, the allocation of manpower, the implementation of a police call-box system, and the use of comparative studies among police departments. President Johnson also began pressuring Congress to increase funding to state and local law enforcement bodies to the tune of hundreds of millions of dollars. In 1968, Congress passed the Omnibus Crime Control and Safe Streets Act, establishing the Law Enforcement Assistance Administration (LEAA) to manage disbursement and monitoring of federal funds delegated to state and local police agencies.

Community Policing Era

Beginning in the 1970s and continuing into the present, the community policing era of American policing has predictably been the most highly involved in technological advancement. Modern technology allows police departments to work closely with diverse members of the public, and many departments regularly use social networks such as Facebook and Twitter to disperse information quickly when crimes such as child abduction occur. In a 2011 Police Executive Research Forum survey, 86 percent of police departments acknowledged that they use Facebook, Twitter, MySpace,

YouTube, or Nixle alerts to monitor threats and follow leads. Some departments, including those in California, Georgia, Minnesota, New Mexico, and Washington State, have developed their own interactive Websites to maintain ongoing contact with the public and to gather information that helps them to identify theft rings, locate suspects, and track fugitives.

From the beginning of this period, there was a push for the use of computers in policing. Unfortunately, not many police departments had computers in the 1970s. Among those that did, computers were often used only for routine tasks that had previously been done on typewriters or by hand. As police departments became more comfortable with computers, policing capabilities advanced rapidly. The use of databases that compared fingerprints and sophisticated crime mapping software that allowed the police to identify areas in which area crimes occurred or in which they were likely to occur made it possible to enhance performance and improve arrest records. However, few police officers or administrators had received more than basic computer training. By 1990, around half of all police departments had purchased computers, but their use was still somewhat limited because of the lack of software geared toward police work.

By the mid-1990s, computers were coming into common use, and the "information superhighway" was being touted by Vice President Al Gore. A 1996 survey conducted by the Bureau of Justice Statistics revealed that three-fourths of police departments owned computers and were using them in criminal investigations and for crime analysis in addition to depending on them for tasks such as budgeting and manpower allocation. Despite the creation of the Automated Fingerprint Identification System, criminals were still able to slip through the cracks because of fragmentation of the system. The establishment of the FBI's National Crime Information Center, on the other hand, provided dependable nationwide access to databases containing information on fugitives, stolen property, and missing persons.

Over the course of the decade, computer technology became an essential tool of community policing. In New York, for instance, William Bratton developed CompStat, a system of predicting where crimes would occur in order to place police officers in designated areas before crimes took place.

DNA Analysis

The National Institute of Justice (NIJ) has been closely involved in the development of police technology. Working through Community Oriented Policing Services (COPS), NIJ had dispersed approximately $24 billion for technology use at the state, local, and tribal levels by 2009. The NIJ's role has included establishing compliance standards for technological equipment such as mobile and base station transmitters, handheld metal weapons detectors, portable x-ray devices used to disarm bombs, and night vision devices. In 1986, the NIJ began pushing the use of DNA analysis in criminal investigations. Deoxyribonucleic acid, commonly known as DNA, is a highly developed technology that analyzes hereditary materials that are unique to each individual. DNA allows investigators to pinpoint eye color, hair color, height, and bone structure of suspects to substantiate the presence of individuals at particular locations or in connection with specific victims. DNA technology has resulted in the release of numerous individuals who had been falsely convicted of crimes before the technology existed.

DNA is also used to identify victims of crimes and catastrophes when other forms of identification are inadequate. For instance, DNA analysis was an invaluable tool for identifying victims of the terrorist attacks of September 11, 2001. Similarly, the Shoah Project maintains samples of the DNA of victims of the Holocaust to aid them in locating the bodies of missing family members or to put them in touch with lost family members. Both the Olympics Committee and the National Football League (NFL) have used DNA as a means by which official sports memorabilia can be authenticated as a fraud-fighting tool.

Technology currently under development at the NIJ includes an improved weapons detection device that could be concealed under clothing using passive millimeter wave technology, making the current handheld device obsolete. Researchers are also working on a disabling net and launcher system that could ensnare fleeing subjects without the use of firearms, a retractable barrier strip that uses retractable spikes to force drivers of fleeing vehicles to come to a halt, and a siren that uses acoustical energy to prevent a suspect from hearing approaching police cars.

Portable navigation systems are widely used by the general public and police departments alike. Law enforcement teams are using many of the myriad of systems available to keep track of vehicles without endangering themselves or others; one of these systems emits global positioning system (GPS) darts from a launcher mounted on a patrol car.

Global Positioning Systems

Members of the general public often form their perceptions of police technology through sophisticated films such as the James Bond series or from the myriad of police shows that have become a staple of American television. By the early 21st century, many of those fictional technologies had become reality. Some southwestern states are currently trying out a device that shoots a tiny dart equipped with GPS (global positioning system), which is a locating system that employs satellite-based technology. The GPS has been available for general use since the 1980s. Once the device is attached to a fleeing vehicle during a high-speed chase, law enforcement teams are able to keep track of a vehicle without endangering themselves or others. The Star Chase Pursuit Management System emits the GPS darts from a launcher mounted on a patrol car, and a laser pointer provides precision when aiming to keep the dart from going astray. At the same time, a dispatcher is able to monitor the action on a computer screen and to keep officers informed of the suspect's exact location and identify the speed and direction of the targeted vehicle. All the while, the suspect remains completely unaware of being monitored. The device can also be used to track stolen cars or smuggled humans. GPS technologies are also being attached to ankle bracelets to keep track of criminals under house arrest. One of the most advanced tracking systems available is now being tested in Miami, Florida, where federal grant money has allowed law enforcement to use T-Hawk Micro Air Vehicles about the size of a garbage can to engage in intelligence, surveillance, and reconnaissance. GPS systems are also used to track the actions of police officers. In Albuquerque, New Mexico, for instance, patrol officers assigned to targeted high-crime areas are tracked by a computerized system that monitors their presence in the area according to a designated schedule.

Other 21st-Century Innovations
On the west coast, one department is testing a miniature video camera that is mounted on an officer's ear, recording the officer's view of events during traffic stops or crimes in progress. On the east coast, a number of police departments are routinely using cameras to scan license plates of all passing cars in order to track drivers who may have outstanding fines for motor vehicle violations. A routine check of license plates sometimes yields unexpected results. In 2011, a dispatcher in Greenwich, New Jersey, discovered the whereabouts of Anthony D. Saxton, who was wanted for an execution-style murder. Cameras are also used to monitor public places in high-crime areas. Budget cuts that have curtailed the use of updated technology have forced some officers to equip themselves, as is the case in Austin, Texas, where officers are using their own video cameras on the job.

Modern databases and new technologies have provided law enforcement with a wide range of opportunities for identifying and tracking criminals and for predicting where crimes will occur. Most large American cities are now using technology to fight gangs, employing large databases that keep tabs on members, analyze gang behavior, and recover weapons stolen by gangs. Originally designed for commercial use, Google Earth software is being used in police work. In some areas, police use Google maps on a daily basis. Such maps have even been used to locate areas where hidden fields of marijuana are being grown Geographic profiling has been used to draw information from a variety of sources to target suspects. This was used in the Washington, D.C., sniper case in 2002 to track John Allen Muhammad, who, assisted by a minor, killed 10 people chosen at random and critically wounded three others. In Orange County, California, in 2005, police were able to use geographic profiling to locate the perpetrator of more than 200 burglaries. Geographic prediction is also gaining attention. In California, programmers at Santa Clara University have developed software that uses geographic data on past crimes to predict where and when additional crimes will occur. This allows officers to be at the scene before a crime occurs.

Visual technology has also made great strides, and laser cameras have been used to great effect. In 2004 in Redwood City, the California Highway Patrol was able to use evidence from its cameras to disprove that an Acura's brakes had failed before slamming into a Volkswagen Beetle and killing the driver. Laser cameras can accurately pinpoint the distance between one car and another in the case of tailgating citations or during the investigation of accidents. Photographic evidence was also used to convict Roberto Vellanoweth, a prominent member of the California Republican Party, of killing four in an accident while driving under the influence (DUI). Fingerprinting technology has also advanced rapidly. While still on the scene, officers are able to immediately identify criminals by using a handheld device. Even technology used by criminals can occasionally help police to locate them, as in the case of an Orange County thief tracked by dispatchers after his cell phone inadvertently called 911. Cell phones and satellite phones have become important tools for American police departments, and software applications for both are now being designed solely for law enforcement use.

Some of the most important technology used by contemporary police officers is employed in on-site criminal investigations, and such equipment has become entirely portable. Concealed weapons and explosive devices have long posed threats to investigating officers. New handheld x-ray devices are being used to locate such items. Some bomb squads are using robots to hunt down explosives. Special ultra-red flashlights are being used to locate hair, fibers, or body fluids that are invisible to the naked eye. Thermal imaging is widely used to locate missing children or fleeing suspects. Imagers are also used to locate graves or disturbed ground that might indicate the presence of a body or concealed evidence and to locate tire marks on roads. Laser technology makes it possible to analyze the chemical makeup of suspicious substances while officers are still on the scene. Handheld translators allow officers to communicate with non-English-speaking suspects or witnesses without waiting for a human translator to arrive at the scene. As new technologies are developed, existing technologies will become obsolete, and police departments must perforce remain in the vanguard of developing technology.

Elizabeth Rholetter Purdy
Independent Scholar

See Also: Boston, Massachusetts; New Orleans, Louisiana; New York City; Police, Contemporary.

Further Readings
Battles, Kathleen. *Calling All Cars: Radio Dragnets and the Technology of Policing.* Minneapolis: University of Minnesota Press, 2010.
Berg, Nat. "Mapping Where Crimes Are Likely to Occur, Before They Happen." http://www.theatlanticcities.com/technology/2011/10/mapping-where-crimes-are-likely-to-occur-before-they-happen/293 (Accessed October 2011).
Branigan, Steven. *High-Tech Crimes Revealed.* Boston: Addison-Wesley, 2005.
Community Oriented Policing Services. "Technology: Upgraded to 'Must Have.'" http://www.cops.usdoj.gov/Default.asp?Item=2464 (Accessed May 2012).
Foster, Raymond E. "History of Police Technology." http://www.police-technology.net/id59.html (Accessed October 2011).
Kovacich, Gerald L. and Andy Jones. *High-Technology Crime Investigator's Handbook: Establishing and Managing a High-Technology Crime Prevention Program.* Boston: Butterworth-Heinemann/Elsevier, 2006.
Snow, Robert L. *Technology and Law Enforcement: From Gumshoe to Gamma Rays.* Westport, CT: Praeger, 2007.
U.S. Department of Energy. "Human Genome Project Information: DNA Forensics." http://www.ornl.gov/sci/techresources/Human_Genome/elsi/forensics.shtml (Accessed October 2011).

Television, Crime in

Print media, radio, and film provide the precedents for representations of crime in television. In fiction-based television programming, crime plays a key role in creating and increasing drama, though once in a while it becomes part of elevating humor as well. Crime serves as part of the organization in episode plot lines and in generic formulas. More recently, it has become the subject of reality television shows, which comprise a significant and growing part of nonfiction programming. The use of crime within television programming has evolved since the 1950s and 1960s, and overall, its use reflects a combination of general social attitudes, dominant ideologies, and industry motivations, which deal primarily with the bottom line.

By definition, a crime consists of three parts: a perpetrator, an illegal act, and a victim. These three components fall into four different categories of crimes. The first category is interpersonal, which is a crime committed by one person against another, such as a fist fight or some other scuffle. The second category involves the more powerful perpetrator violating the human or civil rights of a less powerful victim. Domestic and gendered violence crimes fall under this category. The third category involves those with less power challenging those with more power. In these instances, the less powerful attempt to undermine or bring down those in power. An example of this category includes a plot against a mob boss by some of his own hit men. The last category consists of victimless crimes, wherein no one's rights get violated. Crimes cover a wide variety of acts, including check forgery, theft, property destruction, personal injury, neglect, prostitution, adultery, civil disturbances, abuse, sexual assault, domestic violence, and murder. These acts carry varying levels of effects on people, from victimless crimes that threaten no one's rights to extremely violent crimes that result in severe injury, permanent injury, or even death.

Representations of the Criminal Justice System

Almost all representations of crime on television involve the criminal justice system in some way. This system includes law enforcement such as police officers and detectives; judiciary personnel such as hired lawyers, public defenders, district attorneys, and judges; and corrections officials such as wardens and guards. Members of this system help determine the perpetrators and their motivations in order to help the victims, figure out the crime's extent, and bring the accused to trial. An enormous number of television shows have represented the system from the police point of view. Other shows focus more on the judicial aspects, including *The Defenders* (1961–65), *The Black Robe* (1949–50), *L.A. Law* (1986–94), *Matlock* (1986–95), and *Perry Mason* (1957–66). These roles later expanded to include other personnel or different facets of the system. *Quincy, M.E.* (1976–83) featured a forensic pathologist who often found foul play during supposedly routine autopsies, and more recent series such as *Crossing Jordan* (2001–07) and *Body of Proof* (2011–) feature a female forensic pathologist who sometimes works with the police to solve crimes and other times investigates situations on her own. More recent shows shift the investigations away from police detective work toward the forensic investigations, particularly the series *CSI: Crime Scene Investigation* (2000–), *CSI: New York* (2004–), and *CSI: Miami* (2002–). In these shows, experts attempt to solve the crime through scientific analyses of hair, fibers, fingerprints, DNA traces, and other means to identify a crime's perpetrator and sometimes the victim. Other shows pair individuals with particular abilities or interests in order to help with criminal investigation, such as a novelist in *Castle* (2009–), a genius forensic anthropologist in *Bones* (2005–), psychics in *Medium* (2005–11) and *The Mentalist* (2008–), and a math professor in *NUMB3RS* (2005–10). While most television representations of the justice system focus on cities or states, some shows expand to include government agencies.

Starring Efrem Zimbalist, Jr., as fictional agent Louis Erskine, *The FBI* (1965–74) included an epilogue mentioning people on the real Federal Bureau of Investigations's (FBI's) Most Wanted List. Other series focusing on the FBI include *Without a Trace* (2002–09) and *Criminal Minds* (2005–). *NCIS: Naval Criminal Investigation Service* (2003–) and *JAG* (1995–05) represented investigation into the realm of military crime. Several shows also bring the criminal justice system into the realms of the paranormal or supernatural, wherein the personnel investigate crimes that involve potential aliens, ghosts, demons, vampires, and others mystical or mythological creatures. Examples include the short-lived *Moonlight* (2007–08), about a vampire detective, and the long-running *The X-Files* (1993–2002), about FBI agents Fox Mulder and Dana Scully, who investigate these crimes of the paranormal and the conspiracies within the government.

How the criminal justice system, perpetrators, victims, and crimes get represented on television shows depends on the social and ideological attitudes of the times. These attitudes have shifted during the decades since television's start and early growth. The 1950s crime dramas largely projected the mentality that criminals held no value in society and needed to be hunted down. *Dragnet* (1951–59) offered one of the first manifestations of this thinking. The 1960s saw multiple social movements, including civil rights, women's rights, and war protests. In that decade, social attitudes toward crimes and their punishments focused more on treatment and rehabilitation of the perpetrators than seeking the fullest punishment possible. In shows from this era, criminals became more humanized, and the explanation for their crimes became sickness, not inherent evil. *The Mod Squad* (1968–73), for example, brought forward the idea that criminals needed pity, not extreme punishment. In the 1970s, the social attitudes moved toward a law-and-order focus, which emphasized rehabilitation less and punishments more. This law-and-order attitude continued into the 1980s and the decades following. The terrorist attacks of September 11, 2001, reinforced this view even further. Aside from a few sanctioned exceptions, television programming about crime often reflects these attitudes and their shifts through their ideologies.

Police Procedurals

The most common representations of crimes, their perpetrators, and their victims appear in police procedural dramas. Even with the wide range of all three components of a crime, the generic formula for the police procedural varies only slightly over the decades. Each episode begins with the revelation of a crime and possible victims. Aspects of the justice system get involved, and representatives of those systems begin to unravel the mysteries behind the crime, which might include the perpetrator, the perpetrator's motivations, the crime's impact, and even other victims. The clues lead the investigators (be they police officers, medical examiners, or other motivated individuals) down a winding path that twists and turns, doubles back, stops, redirects, and finally leads to a conclusion. The drama associated with the investigation emerges through the obstacles that appear toward solving the mystery and thus the crime, bringing the perpetrator to justice, and bringing peace to the victims and their families. Most often, these mysteries get solved, and the perpetrator gets brought to trial and receives punishment. Every once in a while, however, the crimes remain unsolved or perpetrators get away with them in order to maintain viewer interest and to promote entertainment value. Most often, these shows take place in urban areas, such as New York, Chicago, Los Angeles, Las Vegas, and Miami.

The crime plot formula carries with it the connotations of being "real" or "realistic." Part of the connotation comes from crime shows drawing on real cases for their story lines. *Dragnet* (1951–59) relied on actual cases from the Los Angeles Police Department. Other shows were made in cooperation with police departments, such as *Adam-12* (1968–75) with the Los Angeles Police Department. Some shows even were created by police officers, such *Police Story* (1973–78) created by Los Angeles detective sergeant Joseph Wambaugh. More recently, *Law and Order* (1990–2010) claimed its stories often came from the press and were "ripped from the headlines." These relationships with the police and connections to the press help support this connoted realism. Another aspect of this connotation comes from the "gritty" style used to film these shows. Many, such as *Hill Street Blues* (1981–87), relied on a documentary-like style, and aspects of this style include handheld cameras, rapid cutting, and off-screen dialogue. A final aspect of the realism connotation comes from the crime plot formula's consistent and constant repetition. Its formula has become so pervasive that it has assumed mythic proportions.

These police procedures also appear in the ever-growing genre of reality television. Reality shows sometimes prove difficult to define, but their primary distinction from other programming is that they draw on the principles of documentary, particularly in their claims of showing reality. Two general approaches offer the structures for these shows. Vignettes comprise one structure, which uses re-enactments and interviews with victims, the friends and relatives of victims, and law enforcement officials to depict each case. Examples of these types of shows include *America's Most Wanted* (1988–) and *Rescue 911* (1989–96). Ride-alongs comprise the other structure, wherein production crews record the action from inside police cars and from behind police officers while they do their jobs. The long-running *Cops* (1989–) offers the best example of this format. Several of these shows claim connections with law enforcement and thus claim an even greater connection to reality than the fictional shows. The FBI's Public Affairs Office cooperates with the production of *America's Most Wanted*, while local law enforcement officers in the various cities work with the producers of *Cops* on every episode. *Cops* appears dedicated exclusively to crime, but actually is highly constructed with footage created in other cities edited in with others to achieve certain effects. Reality shows prove divisive in that they mobilize people to help or contribute to the perception that television show quality continues to decline.

Crime in Different Genres

While crime procedurals and reality shows provide the primary generic television forum for crime representations, crime appears in a variety of genres. The genre shapes how the crime becomes part of the plot and its narrative tension. Some genres, such as mysteries and westerns, mimic police dramas in their focus on law-and-order justice. Several comedies have focused on crime, including *The Andy Griffith Show* (1960–68), *Barney Miller* (1975–82), and *Night Court* (1984–92). *The Andy Griffith Show* dealt more with small-town life because almost no crime occurred for Sheriff Andy Taylor to solve. Crime's absence allowed the values and ruminations to take center stage in the series. *Barney Miller* took place primarily within the walls of the fictional 12th Precinct in New York's Greenwich Village, and each episode showed not only the officers' lives but also the witnesses, criminals, and other people they brought in as part of investigations. *Night Court* featured multiple cases of petty crimes in each episode, but the laughs generated by the characters' interactions took priority over the crimes themselves. Though some of the crimes on *Night Court*—such as runaways and bomb threats—proved serious, most sought to make audiences laugh more than to scare them. Crimes also appear as part of children's shows, specifically animated ones. For comedic cartoons, such as *Scooby-Doo* (1969–86), crime becomes part of a caper that Scooby and his friends solve, such as finding the lost object or uncovering who stole something. For action-related cartoons, the crimes committed by highly exaggerated criminals become the motivations for the heroes to save individuals or whole populations, such as in *The Justice League of America* or other superhero cartoons adapted from comics, such as Spider-Man, Batman, and Superman. Children's shows in particular support the criminal justice system.

Violent and Victimless Crime in Television
Crime itself, then, serves as more of a plot device than a subject of deep examination with television programming. In terms of fiction programs, interpersonal crimes, violent crimes, and sexual crimes get more focus than other types of crime, primarily for their potential entertainment factor. Crimes get shown, get described, or get presented through a corpse, depending on the type of show. Some crimes get constructed through flashbacks with interviews with witnesses and suspects, some crimes get shown at the opening of the episodes, and procedurals such as *Law & Order* and *CSI* typically begin with a dead body found in part of a crime scene. In those cases, the body represents the crime and the mystery behind it.

Violence becomes a key part of television crimes, particularly in dramas. Violence intersects with crime in four ways: through its overt depiction, through the amount of physical force, through the credibility of its threat, and through the intended

John Walsh of America's Most Wanted *filming a segment for his show in the studio located in the National Museum of Crime and Punishment. This type of reality program takes a vignette approach to its structure, using re-enactments and interviews with victims, the friends and relatives of victims, and law enforcement officials to depict each case.*

harm to people or sometimes property. Ways to consider the levels of violence and crime include the type of act, the act's motivation, its degree of harm, its openness, and its level of reality. While older television shows offered more suggestions of crime and violence, contemporary programs actually show more frequent and graphic violence. Shows such as *Criminal Minds* elevate the level of violence in crimes through depicted scenes of torture, repeated stabbings, and brutal killings. Perpetrators on that show kill entire families, including children, and engage in killing sprees for reasons such as revenge, twisted moral justice, and psychotic breaks. The crime representations also reach deeper into subcultures and alternative cultures, including sexual fetishes, though these fetishes become motivations or explanations as means to heighten the spectacle for the crime.

Fictional prime-time programming tends to avoid victimless, white-collar, and other civil crimes because of their potential lack of entertainment value. These crimes do end up on daytime reality programming, however. Crimes such as property damage, fraud, and other similar conflicts end up on reality justice shows such as *The People's Court* (1981–93, 1997–), *Judge Judy* (1996–), *Texas Justice* (2001–05), *Judge Joe Brown* (1998–), and *Judge Mathis* (1999–). Issues related to marriage and adultery become part of some of these shows, though *Divorce Court* (1957–69, 1985–92, 1999–) addresses them specifically. Other reality shows become part of getting a kind of justice for the partners whose spouses are suspected of committing adultery. *Cheaters* (2000–), for example, followed suspected adulterers and attempted to catch them in the act. These issues also become fodder for the more sensational daytime talk shows such as *Maury* (1991–), *Steve Wilkos* (2007–), and *Jerry Springer* (1991–), which regularly use DNA testing as evidence to prove whose child is whose as part of shouting matches about who cheated on whom.

Representations of Criminals

Aside from the more sympathetic views of criminals in the 1960s and 1970s, perpetrators largely get represented as one-dimensional during the law-and-order eras. At those times, criminals were shown as pathological and were dehumanized. In fiction programming, perpetrators are often men, and unlike criminals in news coverage, are often white. Reality shows follow the news patterns of overrepresenting criminals as African American and Hispanic.

In fiction programming in these eras, criminal representations served to reinforce the ideologies of the criminal justice system, though more recent shows attempt to move beyond that single dimension and create a richer picture. Several shows attempt to show the criminals' points of views. *Law & Order: Criminal Intent* provides selected points of view from the suspects and their victims as the detectives attempt to unravel the mystery. *Criminal Minds* (2005–) specifically offers sequences that reveal the suspects' influences and their actions, though not all episodes portray them in an evil light. Some episodes feature people who experience psychotic breaks that spur them into murdering sprees, such as one graphic novel artist whose pregnant fiancée was killed by a gang; he gets revenge by killing all of them even though he is not aware of what he is doing. HBO's *The Wire* (2002–04, 2006, 2008) offered a series-wide balance in representation of the law's attempts to get wiretaps and the criminals' drug running. Another HBO show, *The Sopranos* (1999–2007), showed a mob family with crime as a way of life, though not as an untroubled one. Instead of the mob family getting shown as one-dimensional, *The Sopranos* offered a more nuanced portrait, with its father seeking psychiatric help, several women playing strong roles, violence pushing boundaries in multiple directions, and an overall ambivalence about violence in general. Instead of providing clear-cut distinctions between protagonists and antagonists, between strength and weakness, *The Sopranos* blurred those boundaries and left them open to question.

Women sometimes become criminals in the drama crime series. Often, their roles as criminals serve as extensions of traditionally feminine roles, such as mothers, nurses, and other caretakers. Mothers assume a "monstrous" dimension in taking their caretaking too far, abusing their children, drugging them, or even killing them. A reality show on the Oxygen channel, *Snapped* (2004–) focused on true crime stories of women murderers and their motivations. The show plays on the uniqueness of women murderers, who represent less than 10 percent of murderers.

Not all shows about crime represent criminals in a negative light. Some shows follow criminals in their activities as well. Some criminals exhibit a type of vigilante justice, stepping in where law enforcement fails, such as *The A-Team* (1983–87). This vigilante justice becomes extreme in *Dexter* (2006–), a Showtime series about a serial killer whose "moral" code allows him to kill only other killers, even though his day job is as a forensic expert in blood spatter. The ambiguity forces some questioning and reconsideration of each side's motivations.

Representations of Victims
Victims of crimes typically include young women and sometimes children. Most crime victims are white. Often, these victims are represented as helpless and defenseless. A key crime against women shown in television programming is rape. Among fiction programs, rape representations started during the 1970s. Most rape stories followed the myths surrounding rape, including an anonymous male, usually an African American, attacker raping a young, defenseless woman attacked in a questionable location. These stories, particularly the earlier ones, engaged in victim blaming, implying that the woman victim was "asking for it." Officers investigating rape cases called into question the victim's profession (such as a prostitute, nude model, or stripper), her clothing, or her location in an attempt to disprove the victim's rape claim. Officers questioned the validity of the claim if she attempted to fight back, and they also believed victims lied about being raped in order to get attention. More recent representations of rape-based crimes, or sex-based crimes, attempt to undo aspects of this myth and show more nuance, including victims other than young women, attackers other than African Americans, victims other than the defenseless, and attackers other than anonymous people. *Law & Order: SVU* offers the primary show in which to see these changes, and Detective Olivia Benson actively challenges these assumptions in her comments and through her investigations. In terms of reality programming, some reality shows such as *America's Most Wanted* also attempt to expand the ideas of women's needs as victims of crimes.

Representations of children and teenagers as victims and perpetrators of crime offer a complicated case for television programming. Child victims often are white, middle-class teenagers. Television docudramas show their stories in both fiction and based-on-a-true-story format. The problems these docudramas address include drinking in *Sarah T: Portrait of a Teen Age Alcoholic* (1975) and runaways who become prostitutes in *Off the Minnesota Strip* (1981) and *Little Ladies of the Night* (1977). In these narratives, the crimes become ways to force broken families to address their issues and work toward resolution. The based-on-true-stories programs attempt to fit this mold even with more complicated cases. Seven-year-old Steven Staynor was kidnapped and held for seven years, during which time he was abused sexually. His story got made into a television movie titled *I Know My First Name Is Steven* (1989), though the formula showed Steven adapting to life back at home in the televised version. On occasion, children become the perpetrators of crime, at least in fiction programming. These shows represent these children as extremes. On the one hand, children commit crimes because they are psychologically or biologically damaged by their parents or other family members through abuse, drugs, or alcohol. On the other hand, less frequently children become killers because they represent pure evil.

Conclusion
Crime-based programming draws audiences, and audiences bring in ratings, which translate into advertisers and money. The television industry makes a significant investment in police procedurals in particular, though it often relies on creators, producers, and executive producers with successful track records of creating such programs for developing new ones. Jack Webb offers the earliest example here with several series, including *Dragnet*, *Adam-12*, and *77 Sunset Strip* (1958–64). Aaron Spelling produced a variety of crime-related series throughout the 1970s and 1980s, including *Starsky and Hutch* (1975–79), *Charlie's Angels* (1976–81), *Hart to Hart* (1979–84), and *T. J. Hooker* (1982–86). Steven Bochco focused on both police and lawyers in his series, including *NYPD Blue* (1993–2005), *L.A. Law*, and the musical *Cop Rock* (1990). The more recent trends in television producers and their programming involve multiple variations or spin-offs from an original series. Dick Wolf took his *Law &*

Order franchise into five variations and several long-running ones, including the original, *Law & Order: Special Victims Unit* (1999–), *Law & Order: Criminal Intent* (2001–), *Law & Order: Trial by Jury* (2005–06), and *Law & Order: Los Angeles* (2010–). These episodes gain new life, audiences, and profits through reruns on basic cable networks, with A&E getting the first syndication rights to the original series in the 1990s and TNT getting them in the early 2000s. In addition to syndication, the show gets adapted for international audiences, with a British version and a Russian version. Episodes also get broadcast globally through satellite television. Producer Jerry Bruckheimer shows how the television industry crosses with the film industry, as he produces both popular film series and television shows, including the *CSI* franchise (which Anthony E. Zuiker created), *Without a Trace*, and *Cold Case* (2003–10). Carol Mendelsohn, one of the few women producing these shows, also serves as an executive producer on the *CSI* franchise. While crime programming continues, these trends toward global programming and franchising move development toward further standardization. Since these shows attempt to appeal to the widest audiences possible, any innovation occurs within the confines of this form, the industry, and social ideas of criminal justice.

Heather McIntosh
Boston College

See Also: Dime Novels, Pulps, Thrillers; Fear of Crime; Film, Crime in; News Media, Crime in.

Further Readings

Cuklanz, Lisa M. and Sujata Moorti. "Television's 'New' Feminism: Prime-Time Representations of Women and Victimization." *Critical Studies in Media Communication*, v.23/4 (October 2006).

Doyle, Aaron. *Arresting Images: Crime and Policing in Front of the Television Camera*. Toronto: University of Toronto Press, 2003.

Humphries, Drew, ed. *Women, Violence, and the Media: Readings in Feminist Criminology*. Lebanon, NH: Northeastern University Press, 2009.

Johnson, Merri Lisa. "Gangster Feminism: The Feminist Cultural Work of HBO's 'The Sopranos.'" *Feminist Studies*, v.33/2 (Summer 2007).

Kohm, Steven A. "The People's Law Versus Judge Judy Justice: Two Models of Law in American Reality-Based Courtroom TV." *Law & Society Review*, v.40/3 (September 2006).

Rapping, Elayne. *Law and Justice as Seen on TV*. New York: New York University Press, 2003.

Rome, Dennis. *Black Demons: The Media's Depiction of the African American Male Criminal Stereotype*. Westport, CT: Praeger, 2004.

van Bauwel, Sofie and Nico Carpenter. *Trans-Reality Television: The Transgression of Reality, Genre, Politics, and Audience*. Lanham, MD: Lexington Books/Rowman & Littlefield, 2010.

Vest, Jason P. *The Wire, Deadwood, Homicide, and NYPD Blue: Violence Is Power*. Westport, CT: Praeger, 2011.

Television, Police in

Police officers have maintained a high-profile presence on television since the earliest days of commercial network broadcasting in the 1940s and 1950s. From police procedurals such as *Dragnet* and *Adam-12* to early 21st century crime dramas such as *The Shield* and *The Wire*, police programs have proven to be among the most durable and popular of all television genres. In their hundreds of iterations, cop shows have sought to depict law enforcement in a "realistic" manner, striving to capture the "true" nature of police work with gritty authenticity. At the same time, cop shows have also tended to emphasize the most visually sensational aspects of police work—gunplay, car chases, physical action, and the like—in order to satisfy the desire of a mass audience to experience the illicit thrills of crime and violence while remaining safely within the parameters of the law.

The long-standing popularity of television cop shows has enabled them to play a pivotal role in shaping the American public's perceptions of the police. Approaching the social problem of crime from the point of view of law enforcement, cop shows have traditionally valorized police officers as heroic guardians of the public welfare, tasked with protecting ordinary citizens from criminals. Television has also familiarized audiences with the minutiae of police work, from the proper technique for handcuffing suspects to the exact language of the Miranda warning ("You have the right to remain silent …"), a staple on nearly all cop shows.

In their more mature incarnations, however, police dramas have explored the most urgent complications attending the role of law enforcement in a democratic society. Cop shows have trained a critical gaze on police authority by depicting corruption and the limits and abuses of police power, as well the substantial personal and emotional costs of working in law enforcement for the officers themselves. As agents of the state, cops have the ability to arrest citizens and compel them to obey commands ("pull over!" "freeze!"), but they are also public servants required to uphold the law as it exists. Police shows frequently figure this relationship as a tension between the institutional constraints of the "system" and the cops' own personal pursuit of justice, presenting police officers as rule-breaking individualists whose own private moral code potentially supersedes their devotion to the law or their tolerance for the bureaucracy of the justice process. In many cases, this intolerance is presented as a justified form of anger against a system hamstrung by regulations that favor criminals over victims.

The American cop show's emphasis on outlaw individualism has, paradoxically, tended to reinforce the conservative political bent of police programs; because cop shows have traditionally seen crime as a problem of law enforcement rather than of social justice, they devote more attention to the contact point between cops and criminals rather than to the underlying social conditions that help to produce crime in the first place. Cop shows have also exhibited evolving social attitudes on race, gender, and authority. Traditionally white and male, police officers on television have diversified significantly over the years, as evidenced by the multiracial ensemble casts of countless TV cop dramas. Because police officers, due in part to television's influence, hold such a prominent position in the American cultural imaginary, the question of who gets to carry a badge and a gun on TV is also, in some sense, the question of who gets to be considered an "American." Thanks to their pervasive presence in U.S. popular culture, television cop shows offer a revealing window into the way that America understands itself and its complex relationship to authority, crime, and justice.

Early Cop Shows

While short-lived crime dramas such as *Stand By for Crime* (1949), *Photocrime* (1949), and *Chicagoland Mystery Players* (1949–50) technically count as television's first cop shows, the most seminal police program of the medium's early years was *Dragnet* (1952–59; 1967–70). Created and produced by actor Jack Webb, who starred as Los Angeles Police Department (LAPD) Sergeant Joe Friday and directed several of the show's episodes, *Dragnet* defined the conventions of the police "procedural" by envisioning police work as a set of routines carried out by detectives committed to preserving establishment values and serving the public good. A typical *Dragnet* episode, shot in semidocumentary style and narrated by Webb in a terse monotone, followed Friday and his partner through the city of Los Angeles as they interrogated suspects and witnesses, pursued leads, and foiled crimes, all within the show's tightly constructed half-hour format. In contrast to earlier radio police serials that tended to emphasize shoot-outs and melodrama, *Dragnet* focused on the details of crime-solving with little action or gunplay; one of Webb's "rules" for the show was that no more than one bullet could be fired every four weeks. "Just the facts, ma'am," Friday's familiar admonition to witnesses, was also an unofficial mantra for the show's no-frills depiction of law enforcement.

Unlike many subsequent cop shows, *Dragnet* also displayed an unshakable faith in the efficacy of the justice system; each episode concluded with a summary of the arrested criminal's successful prosecution and incarceration. The show's positive portrayal of police professionalism made it a virtual promotional vehicle for the real-life LAPD in the Eisenhower era. Not only did *Dragnet* draw many of its story lines from actual LAPD case files, but it also represented the police as moral, rational agents of the law. Webb followed his *Dragnet* success by creating another long-running police procedural, *Adam-12* (1968–75), this time centering on two uniformed patrol officers who cruised the streets of Los Angeles in a black-and-white squad car.

Jack Webb (left) and Harry Morgan from the popular 1950s television program Dragnet. *Webb created and produced the show and starred as no-nonsense Sergeant Joe Friday.*

Though *Dragnet* established an early benchmark for "realism" in televisual depictions of the police, its staid tone and establishment values put it at odds with the social and political transformations taking place in American society in the late 1960s. As U.S. television audiences became increasingly exposed to images of real-life police officers turning dogs and fire hoses on black civil rights demonstrators, predominantly white police forces repressing distressed black communities in northern inner cities, and even America's vexed role as "global policeman" during the cold war and Vietnam, the received notion that the police automatically stood for peace and justice began to seem outmoded and simplistic. In part as a result of these changes, cop shows in the late 1960s and early 1970s began to move away from *Dragnet*'s emphasis on unquestioned white male authority and to absorb, if not wholly endorse, the energies and ideologies of the counterculture.

These changes became apparent in such disparate cop shows as *The Mod Squad* (1968–73), which centered on three former juvenile delinquents— "one black, one white, one blonde"—who worked undercover to fight crime in the southern California "beat scene"; *Ironside* (1967–75), which starred Raymond Burr as a wheelchair-bound ex–San Francisco police detective who combated crime outside the conventional channels of the police department with the help of male and female deputies and an African American bodyguard; and *Hawaii Five-O* (1968–80), a long-running procedural starring Jack Lord as Steve McGarrett, a liberal-minded detective whose Hawai'i state police unit includes both a trusted white deputy and Asian and Polynesian officers. The show's exploitation of Hawai'i's colorful tropical locations, like *The Mod Squad*'s appropriation of the youth culture or *Ironside*'s inclusion of women and people of color on the side of law enforcement, demonstrated how television police shows attempted to leaven traditional police authority with nontraditional elements.

The 1970s

These strategies became increasingly standardized as the cop show genre proliferated in the 1970s, a decade in which over 40 police-themed series hit the airwaves. The sheer abundance of cop shows on TV during this era suggested public ambivalence toward law enforcement. On the one hand, the cop show's ubiquity signaled a reassertion of law and order after the anarchic decade of the 1960s; on the other hand, television cops of the 1970s, though overwhelmingly white and male, tended to be streetwise, ethnically specific individualists who adhered as much to their own personal codes as to the exigencies of law enforcement. Representative examples included *Columbo* (1971–77), which starred Peter Falk as a trench coat–clad LAPD detective whose pose as a polite bumbler masked his skill at solving murders; *Kojak* (1973–78), which featured Greek American actor Telly Savalas as a tough, bald, lollipop-sucking New York police lieutenant whose hardscrabble upbringing gave him special knowledge of the streets; and *Baretta* (1975–78), starring Robert Blake as an Italian American undercover cop who lived in a dilapidated hotel and used his mastery of disguise to infiltrate various criminal organizations.

Perhaps the decade's signature cop show was *Starsky & Hutch* (1975–79), which blended an apparent glorification of police brutality with a tongue-in-cheek emphasis on the homoerotic male bonding between its two odd-couple detective-buddies, Dave Starsky (Paul Michael Glaser) and Ken "Hutch" Hutchinson (David Soul). Taking its cue from movie cops like Dirty Harry and Popeye Doyle, *Starsky & Hutch* depicted its two heroes routinely intimidating, browbeating, and assaulting an array of suspects, often chasing them down in Starsky's tomato-red Gran Torino. The cops' streetwise credibility also hinged on their bond with their loyal black informant, Huggy Bear (Antonio Fargas).

The 1980s

The cop show's tendency toward either cartoonish action or rigid proceduralism made the genre ripe for reinvention by the early 1980s. While *Police Story* (1973–77), an anthology series created by crime novelist and former LAPD officer Joseph Wambaugh, had sought to bring renewed realism to the police drama, the series that best exploited this opportunity was the critically acclaimed *Hill Street Blues* (1981–87). Cocreated by Steven Bochco, *Hill Street Blues* sought to reinvigorate the police drama by taking a humanist, documentary-like approach that balanced procedural elements with a nuanced exploration of the cops' private lives and personal travails. Set in a chaotic police precinct in a crime-ridden section of an unnamed eastern city that seemed to symbolize the decline of America's inner cities during the Reagan era, the show's "tele-vérité" style involved the kind of overlapping dialogue and distracted camerawork characteristic of a Robert Altman film. Moreover, its writers deliberately avoided the cop-show tradition of wrapping up cases neatly at the end of each hour, instead stretching them out across multiple episodes or even leaving them unsolved altogether.

At the heart of the series was the intense but stoic Captain Frank Furillo (Daniel J. Travanti), a recovering alcoholic whose supervision of the dilapidated Hill Street station required him to deal with overworked cops, dangerous criminals, and a tangled city bureaucracy while also coping with a combative ex-wife and carrying on a secret romance with liberal public defender Joyce Davenport (Veronica Hamel). Picturing the police precinct as a quotidian American workplace, each episode began with an early-morning "roll call" in which Sergeant Phil Esterhaus (Michael Conrad) briefed a roomful of weary cops on the day's important cases. Esterhaus's memorable catchphrase, "Let's be careful out there," captured the show's empathy for police officers who, though neither invulnerable action heroes nor robotic civil servants, found themselves on the frontlines of urban chaos. *Hill Street Blues* was also notable for its effort to challenge at least some of the conservative assumptions of the traditional cop show. In addition to its matter-of-fact depiction of a diverse police force that included women and people of color, the show addressed issues of police corruption and tensions between the police and ghettoized minorities.

If *Hill Street Blues* redefined the cop show's commitment to "realism" in a way that would prove hugely influential on later police dramas such as *Law & Order* and *NYPD Blue*, another 1980s cop show, *Miami Vice* (1984–89), sought to move beyond realism altogether by wedding the police drama to the visual and aural innovations of the then-new Music Television (MTV). Executive produced by feature film director Michael Mann and starring Don Johnson and Philip Michael Thomas as undercover vice detectives Sonny Crockett and Ricardo Tubbs, the show reportedly had its genesis as "MTV cops," two words scrawled on the notepad of an NBC entertainment executive.

In addition to a contemporary rock soundtrack, rapid-fire editing, and stylized camera angles that made the cop show akin to a music video, the series also exploited the seedy tropical glamour of Miami in a way that recalled but far surpassed *Hawaii Five-O*'s use of Hawai'i. Crucially, Crockett and Tubbs were "hip" cops, clad in expensive designer clothing and driving flashy cars designed to maximize their undercover image as drug dealers. That the show's two leads were also interracial male buddies—a staple of countless cop shows from *CHiPs* to *Hill Street Blues* to *The Wire*—made the implicit argument that differences in race, background, and culture could be elided through a shared commitment to police work—and, of course, a shared aura of "cool."

Though the show tended to glamorize the various forms of "vice"—drug use, arms dealing, and prostitution—suggested by its title, it also examined the personal cost of prolonged undercover work; in one story line, Crockett sustained a head injury that made him believe that he was his criminal alter-ego. *Miami Vice* was equally notable for its critical, even despairing, attitude toward the Reagan-era "war on drugs," an outlook that later shows, such as *The Wire*, would echo. Numerous episodes ended with Crockett and Tubbs finding their own quest for local justice hamstrung by federal agencies (such as the Federal Bureau of Investigation [FBI] or Drug Enforcement Agency) whose skewed priorities exposed politically motivated U.S. complicity in drug trafficking in Latin America and Southeast Asia.

While *Hill Street Blues* and *Miami Vice* featured female police officers in their ensemble casts, neither show challenged the cop show's essentially masculine point of view. *Cagney and Lacey* (1982–88) was groundbreaking for doing just that; in its depiction of two female New York City police detectives, recovering alcoholic Christine Cagney (Sharon Gless) and married mother of three Mary Beth Lacey (Tyne Daly), the show represented a serious effort to examine the complexities of law enforcement from a female, even feminist, point of view. While women had occupied starring roles in cop shows before—notably Angie Dickinson in *Police Woman* (1974–78) and Teresa Graves in *Get Christie Love!* (1974–75)—those programs tended to treat the female star primarily as a sex object. In contrast, *Cagney & Lacey* presented its female cops as tough, compassionate, and highly competent, and the show melded traditional procedural plots with story lines involving date rape, abortion, domestic abuse, and the workplace sexism of the police precinct.

The show itself was forced to contend with the conservative gender politics of the TV industry. Though actress Meg Foster played Cagney in early episodes, she was replaced by Gless, a "softer" presence on screen, after TV executives noted "lesbian overtones" between Foster and Daly. In pushing past these hurdles and showing women who succeeded in a traditionally male line of work, the series laid important groundwork for later cop shows that featured women in ensemble casts (*NYPD Blue*) or as the stars of their own shows (*The Closer*, 2005–11; and *Saving Grace*, 2007–10).

The 1990s

The innovations in storytelling, style, and gender politics that emerged in TV cop shows of the 1980s were further extended and complicated in the 1990s. Steven Bochco, cocreator of *Hill Street Blues*, teamed with *Hill Street* writer and producer David Milch to create *NYPD Blue* (1993–2005), billed as an "adult" police drama that brought R-rated language, partial nudity, and a renewed sense of gritty urban realism to the genre. Set in Manhattan's lower east side and filmed in a jittery, handheld style, *NYPD Blue* was most notable for its mature, complex handling of the personal drama of cops' lives—variously involving office romance, marriage, infidelity, alcoholism, cancer, and racism—and for interweaving these serial elements with gripping procedural plotting.

The long-running *NYPD Blue* was also notable for its valorization of the Angry White Male cop. In part because of its countless cast changes over 12 seasons, the show's moral core increasingly became the portly, bald, alcoholic, rage-prone Detective Andy Sipowicz (Dennis Franz), who routinely beat up suspects, spouted racist epithets, and derided "perps" who opted to "lawyer up" rather than confess to their crimes. The show arguably excused Sipowicz's compulsive police brutality as the righteous fury of a cop who suffered mightily for the job; though he trampled on the civil rights of his suspects, those suspects were usually shown to be guilty, and Sipowicz was further ennobled by a series Job-like personal trials, including alcoholism, prostate cancer, the murders of his older son and second wife, and the tragic deaths of two of his partners.

The impact of the job on the lives of cops was also a central theme in *Homicide: Life on the Street* (1993–99), another ensemble police drama frequently compared to *NYPD Blue* but which eschewed the latter's soap-opera-like melodrama. Set in inner-city Baltimore and based on former police reporter David Simon's book *Homicide: Life on the Killing Streets* (1991), a gritty nonfiction exposé that detailed 12 months in the life of a Baltimore homicide unit, *Homicide* was a visually stylized, cerebral, character-driven cop show that focused not so much on acts of murder themselves but on the impact of those murders on the detectives who investigated them.

A scene being filmed for Law & Order: Criminal Intent *in November 2007.* Law & Order *premiered in September 1990 and completed its 20th and final season in May 2010, making it the longest-running police show in the history of television. It also tied with* Gunsmoke *for the longest-running prime-time drama series of all time.*

Unlike the flawed-but-valorous cops of *NYPD Blue*, *Homicide*'s detectives were eccentric and chatty, and the show, under the guidance of executive producer Barry Levinson, used cinematic innovations of the French New Wave, including jump cuts, roving handheld camera work, and philosophical dialogue. This approach was particularly evident in the show's acclaimed first-season episode "Three Men and Adena," in which erudite African American detective Frank Pembleton (Andre Braugher) and his white rookie partner Tim Bayliss (Kyle Secor) spend the entire episode trying unsuccessfully to wring a confession out of a suspected child murderer. Perhaps the signature image of the series was the homicide squad's "murder board," a white chart that tracked the progress of the detectives' cases in red marker (for unsolved) and black marker (for solved); the board seemed to symbolize both the fleeting victories and perpetually unfinished nature of urban police work.

As the police drama increasingly became a vehicle for exploring the human costs of both crime and police work, the old-fashioned police procedural reinvented itself as well, as evinced by two crime shows that wrung fresh ideas from technical aspects of the investigative process. *Law & Order* (1990–2010), the longest-running cop show in the history of television, combined the police procedural and the courtroom drama, while *CSI: Crime Scene Investigation* (2000–present) focused on forensic detectives who solved crimes through scientific analysis of physical evidence. That both series became enormously successful "franchises" comprising numerous spin-offs (including *CSI: Miami*, *Law & Order: Special Victims Unit*, and many more) reaffirmed the durability—and profitability—of "stand-alone" episodes in which cops crack cases in under an hour.

Episodes of *Law & Order* were split into two halves: the first tracked the police investigation of a crime, and the second followed the district attorneys' prosecution of that crime. Backgrounding the characters' private lives in favor of ripped-from-the-headlines cases, *Law & Order* nonetheless managed to provide an unusually nuanced view of the antagonistic and symbiotic relationship between cops and district attorneys. While many cop shows portrayed the legal system as inert and attorneys as ethically suspect, *Law & Order* dramatized the intricate chess game that police and lawyers must play in order to convict criminals within the constraints of the legal system. The show's ever-changing cast also suggested the diversification of the cop show genre as a whole: In the series' early days, the cops and lawyers were mostly white and male; in later seasons, African Americans and women took over key roles.

CSI, by contrast, took the police series in a more scientific direction, focusing on forensic "criminalists" who work the night shift at a high-tech crime lab in the Las Vegas Police Department. Instead of familiar cop-show staples such as interrogations, shoot-outs, and car chases, *CSI* immersed viewers in the minutiae of shoe etchings, anal swabs, torn hair follicles, bullet wounds, voice analysis, DNA evidence, and other state-of-the-art techniques that enabled the police to re-create crimes in hypothetical, often gory, flashbacks. While *CSI*'s appeal stemmed in part from its flashy visual style and emphasis on blood and guts, the show's scientific bent also offered viewers a reassuring vision of police work as an exact science in which catching a criminal was often a matter of analyzing evidence correctly. As the unit's brilliant leader, Gil Grissom (William Petersen), admonished his team: "People lie. The evidence doesn't lie." This seductive premise generated what some called the "*CSI* effect," in which real-life families of crime victims expected swifter resolutions to murder investigations and juries required more direct, less circumstantial evidence to convict defendants.

Perhaps the most durable, though least acclaimed, police procedural of this era was *COPS* (1989–present), a so-called "reality" show that used handheld video cameras to track real-life patrol officers on the job. Familiar to American TV audiences for its "Bad Boys" theme song and lowbrow sensibility, *COPS* offered an endless parade of traffic stops, domestic disturbances, and drug arrests in low-income neighborhoods while providing little if any context or social analysis—just the vicarious thrill of watching police apprehend "criminals."

The 2000s

While procedurals such as *COPS*, *CSI*, and *Law & Order* continued to thrive on traditional network television well into the 21st century, two cop shows that appeared on cable in the new century's first decade—*The Shield* (FX, 2002–08) and *The Wire* (HBO, 2002–08)—took the police drama into deeper and darker territory than it had ever been before by offering sociologically grim, dramatically layered examinations of crime and corruption in the urban ghetto. Shot in a grainy, handheld style in some of Los Angeles's grimiest locations, *The Shield* centered on an experimental LAPD "Strike Team" that used illegal methods to combat gangs, drug dealers, and murderers while essentially operating as a gang unto itself. The Strike Team's leader, Vic Mackey, played by the bald, charismatic Michael Chiklis, was the apotheosis of the cop as antihero, far exceeding *NYPD Blue*'s comparatively tame Andy Sipowicz. Dubbed by one TV critic as "Tony Soprano with a badge," Mackey brutalized suspects, planted evidence, stole drugs and money, and, in a shocking act whose consequences rippled throughout the show's seven seasons, shot and killed a member of his own unit.

Like the film *Training Day* (2001), *The Shield* was inspired by the LAPD's Rampart corruption scandal of the late 1990s, and the series arguably glorified, even as it critiqued, the figure of the outlaw cop. That Mackey was a doting father of three ensured audience sympathy, even as his violent acts made him repugnant. By presenting Mackey as an extremely effective but extremely immoral cop, *The Shield* posited corruption as a distasteful but potentially necessary tool for effective crime-fighting. Moreover, *The Shield* showed that Mackey was far from alone in his manipulations; indeed, the series took a pitilessly Hobbesian view of the police as an institution irretrievably shaded by the self-interest of its personnel at all levels.

The Wire's take on the police drama was less sensationalistic but no less unsettling. Created by David Simon and drawn, like *Homicide*, from his years of crime reporting in Baltimore, *The Wire* was equal parts cop show and sociological exposé, examining not just police work but the painful decline of the American inner city. In its first season, the show focused on a single police drug investigation in the blighted housing projects of West Baltimore (the show's title came from the wiretapping technology used to monitor drug dealers) but distinguished itself from cop-show norms by exploring the lives of the dealers and addicts as fully as it did of the police officers. In subsequent seasons, the show's scope expanded to examine labor unions, city politics, public education, and the news media, implicitly arguing that the institution of law enforcement and the war on drugs could not be understood without accounting for the systemic rot in all of these institutions, as well as the human cost facing individuals who live and work within them.

In articulating these critiques, *The Wire* rejected the tidy closure of the police procedural as well as the often ahistorical, decontextualized picture of crime offered in even the most sophisticated police dramas. Moreover, in a genre often prone to glorifying white male heroes (and antiheroes), *The Wire* was notable for featuring perhaps the richest and most varied cast of African American actors in the history of television; its maverick white cop, Jimmy McNulty (Dominic West), was often relegated to the periphery. Perhaps the central theme of *The Wire*'s depiction of law enforcement was the way in which political opportunism and limited resources hamper cops' ability to conduct meaningful long-term investigations; the show revealed how cops are pressured to fudge crime statistics and engage in aggressive street-level arrests that look good in the eyes of the public but actually enable the drug trade to continue unabated and, worse, tend to alienate minority communities. *The Wire*'s bleak position on the drug war was perhaps best expressed by one officer's remark that the "war" on drugs is a misnomer, because "wars end."

Even as *The Wire* characterized police work as an exhausting war of attrition, the television cop show itself appeared to be anything but exhaustible in the early 21st century; indeed, police officers on TV continued to become at once more outlandish and more familiar with each new show. The pay-cable series *Dexter* (2006–present), for example, took the cop-as-antihero concept to a new extreme by focusing on a Miami police "blood-spatter" expert who is secretly a serial killer of serial killers, while *Southland* (2009–present) used cinema-verité techniques to follow flawed patrol officers and detectives through the same sun-bleached LA-noir landscape featured in *Dragnet* and *The Shield*. As these and other cop shows attest, U.S. audiences remain fascinated by the men and women who wear badges, carry guns, and make television their beat.

Andrew Sargent
West Chester University of Pennsylvania

See Also: Film, Crime in; Film, Police in; Literature and Theater, Police in; Television, Crime in.

Further Readings
Buxton, David. *From* The Avengers *to* Miami Vice: *Form and Ideology in Television Series*. New York: Manchester University Press, 1990.
Crew, B. Keith. "Acting Like Cops: The Social Reality of Crime and Law on TV Police Dramas." In *Marginal Conventions: Popular Culture, Mass Media and Social Deviance*, Clinton R. Sanders, ed. Bowling Green, OH: Popular Culture Press, 1990.
Grant, Judith. "Prime Time Crime: Television Portrayals of Law Enforcement." *Journal of American Culture*, v.15/1 (1992).
Inciardi, James A. and Juliet L. Dee. "From the Keystone Cops to *Miami Vice*: Images of Policing in American Popular Culture." *Journal of Popular Culture*, v.21/2 (1987).
Lott, M. Ray. *Police on Screen: Hollywood Cops, Detectives, Marshals, and Rangers*. London: McFarland & Co., 2006.
Siegel, Lee. "Why Cop Shows Are Eternal." In *Not Remotely Controlled: Notes on Television*. New York: Basic Books, 2007.

Television, Punishment in

Compared to the police, there is significantly less television programming devoted to the punishment side of the American criminal justice system. To a large degree, this can be attributed to the fact that punishment in and of itself is not riveting television. If prisons were set up to look like Bentham's panopticon, for example, viewers would simply spend an hour watching the front of cells just as guards do on a daily basis. Further, the most serious form of punishment in the country—the death penalty—is not broadcast publicly. Television writers and producers are consequently left with two options. First, they need to create reality or documentary series that demonstrate to the average television viewer what life in prison is like. Or second, they can create dramatic series that involve punishment and prisons but are not necessarily meant to always accurately depict punishment in the American system.

Scared Straight

In 1979, Arnold Shapiro released a documentary titled *Scared Straight*, which followed a group of juvenile offenders as they entered Rahway State Prison for a three-hour encounter with actual inmates. The convicts would berate, scream at, and attempt to terrify the juveniles in an effort to make them want to avoid prison. It allowed the public to envision the dark side of prison life, and the producers hoped to help the juveniles right their lives before it was too late. In the aftermath of the original documentary, many states began scared straight programs in an attempt to keep young individuals fearful of life in prison and, as a result, less likely to commit criminal acts. Shapiro's initial concept was followed by a second story in 1980, a 10-year follow-up and then a 20-year follow-up. These follow-up episodes showed that most of the individuals from the original documentary were in fact scared straight and went on to live productive lives.

After years of relative dormancy, A&E brought the concept back to television in 2011 with *Beyond Scared Straight*. In each episode, at-risk teenagers are taped as they experience an inmate-run program. Cameras follow them before their arrival, during their time in prison, in its immediate aftermath, and then checks on them a month later to see if there has been any impact. Episodes in the series have shown teens being yelled at, forced into bathroom stalls, pulled out of line into areas away from the cameras, and repeatedly told of how awful life in prison can be. While it may be difficult to watch young individuals in this setting, many of the teen offenders are visibly moved throughout the episode. Campaign for Youth Justice, however, has publicly called for the series to be taken off the airwaves. Likewise, individuals in the Department of Justice have publicly acknowledged they believe the shows to be potentially harmful. They worry that the shows present anecdotal evidence for citizens rather than long-term policy proposals that would better prevent youth offenders. While the experience has the potential to be traumatic for the juveniles (especially those under 10 years old), the scare tactics are typically matched with appropriate counseling components to help alleviate this concern.

A young man in a jail cell shows the reality of life in prison. Crime is a popular theme for television series, but the actual punishment is often ignored or neglected, possibly considered not suitable for television audiences.

Lockup and *Inside American Jail*

Two other documentary series regularly air on TV that show life in prison. Rather than focusing on the impact punishment has on the offenders, these shows instead tend to focus more generally on the prison environment. First, MSNBC airs a series titled *Lockup* (and its related shows *Lockup Raw* and *Lockup Extended Stay*). The original series has now gone through 22 iterations in 22 different facilities across the country. In each episode, the show follows guards and administrators as they go about their workdays, interacting with prisoners and the criminal justice system. Some episodes add a series of interviews with inmates on issues they face in their day-to-day life. For educational purposes, the series does a good job of helping to explain concepts like inmate classifications, expectations of behavior, and modern issues of punishment in America. Viewers are able to understand the structural and procedural differences between low security, high security, and supermax prisons and see how inmate lives differ based on these classifications. They also take steps to show how guards and administrators respond to inmate misbehavior and violence.

Another show that builds on the same format is *Inside American Jail*, which takes a more comprehensive look at punishment by following individuals from booking through incarceration. This show, unlike *Lockup*, does not base entire seasons from the same location but instead bounces from location to location more regularly. Since the show includes the booking process, there is more of a police element and presence than in *Lockup* or *Beyond Scared Straight*. Although this detracts from the consideration of punishment in some respects, it also presents a more holistic approach to the punishment process as it traces each prisoner's full journey through the system. One of its most famous episodes involved the booking of O. J. Simpson into Clark County Jail after his conviction in the stolen goods case. Airing on truTV, this show tends to focus more on the dramatic scenes than on helping viewers to understand the penal system in the United States.

What these three documentary shows collectively demonstrate is how television can use documentaries to introduce the American public to different facets of punitive justice and punishment in the country. In *Beyond Scared Straight*, inmates attempt to prevent juvenile offenders from making the same mistakes that they made by introducing them to life in prison. *Lockup* presents punishment in a different way, by taping one prison for a longer period of time and helping Americans understand the structures and functioning of a penitentiary and the culture of inmates within it. And with *Inside American Jail*, inmates are followed from the moment they are booked through their incarceration. Such an approach offers a different perspective on life as an inmate and how prisoners adapt to their new surroundings.

Law & Order, *Oz*, and *Prison Break*

While the documentaries offer a real glimpse into punishment in America, there have also been numerous dramatic series that show prison in their own way. The least direct example is the *Law & Order* franchise. While none of the *Law & Order* shows deal directly with prison, they do involve numerous scenes in a prison setting and occasional episodes that look at punishments. Regularly, interviews take place with prisoners in prison settings where inmates are shackled or call for guards when they are done talking to prosecutors. Yet, the actual punishment portion of the proceedings is not aired as all episodes end prior to prison. Rather, the show focuses on the investigation and trial and typically ends with the announcement of a verdict or sentencing.

Unlike *Law & Order*, HBO's *Oz* shows a dramatic interpretation of life in a maximum-security penitentiary. Built on the idea that "it's no place like home," Oswald State Correctional Facility is home to Em City, an experimental unit that emphasizes rehabilitation and responsibility as goals of prison rather than punishment. In order to try to ease tensions among different racial and social groups, select numbers of each are brought together in a controlled environment. While the intent is to be lauded, the process is not as clear. The inmates struggle in Em City to fulfill their own needs. Much fighting occurs as different groups and individuals attempt to control the drug trade or inmate factions. Yet, in the violent setting, many inmates—and corrections officers—wish for nothing more than to survive to parole or the next day. Throughout the series, the show demonstrates a clear vision of what prison life would be like in the system created by the writers.

More than anything, *Oz* highlights the role played by different power groups within a prison. Over the course of the show, viewers see the influence of the African American Homeboys, the Muslims, the Wiseguys, the Aryans, the Latinos, the Irish, the gays, the bikers, and a series of unaffiliated individuals that still manage to cause havoc. Mixed in, however, are characters like Tobias Beecher, who comes across as a normal man who happened to make one disastrous mistake—in his case, a fatal drunk-driving accident. The show demonstrates many of the worst elements of prison and seems to focus on the alignments that arise within prison populations over time. Due to its dark nature, some critics have failed to fully discuss and consider the concepts presented and their potential applicability to the actual prison system. A set-up like the one found in Em City has not been attempted in many real-life prisons but carries many potential benefits. If the justice system could bring together groups of individuals that are regularly in conflict outside prison walls and help them see their commonalities, they may be able to better curb group conflict when they are freed. Pragmatically, such an effort is hard to conceive of. After all, it relies on the belief that these groups are truly willing to be rehabilitated and change. Without their buy-in, an Em City system will have no chance at succeeding.

Another prison drama that helps viewers learn about elements of punishment in America is *Prison Break*. The series—which aired on Fox for four seasons—focuses on two brothers. The first has been sentenced to die for a murder he did not commit, and the second intentionally gets himself put into prison to help his brother escape. Lincoln Burrows, who was accused of murdering the vice president's brother, was held at Fox River State Penitentiary. To gain access to help him escape, his brother, Michael Scofield, commits an armed robbery and then pretends to have diabetes to gain access to the prison doctor. Because of his unlimited access to the prison infirmary, he is able to begin thinking of ways to escape. The first season concludes with the escape. Seasons two, three, and four all focus less on the punishment side of criminal justice because the main characters are already out of prison. While the series is clearly fictitious, it does provide interesting ways of viewing punishment in society. Lincoln is shown to have been set up because of his father's poor decisions and is set to be executed as a result. While the idea of prison breaks is fairly far-fetched on television and in movies compared to real life, the process by which Michael gets himself into prison and then fakes health issues to gain access to the prison infirmary does point to potential loopholes in the system.

What the three dramatic series show about punishment is difficult to ascertain. Most of the more famous criminal justice series focus more on forensic science and legal matters than on actual punishment. There are many possible explanations for this. Perhaps punishment is simply not interesting enough to create entire series wrapped around the idea. Or maybe it is difficult to create enough material to have a full series without having less believable plot lines. Another possibility is that punishment in the justice system is just not suited for television. Perhaps it is viewed as inhumane or against viewer's ideals and consequently viewed as not suitable for television audiences. Ultimately, crime is a popular theme for television series, but the aftermath is often ignored or neglected.

Between documentary and drama series on television, the ideas behind punishment in the modern American criminal justice system can be watched by viewers. While documentaries try to demonstrate the reality of prison in the country, even they fall victim in many cases to emphasizing the drama that arises in the system. This is partly because the mundaneness of a regular prison day would likely lose most viewers, but by overexaggerating what happens in prison, nothing but public misconceptions and concerns are added. Many Americans believe what they see on television to be the truth. Whether it is a documentary that focuses too heavily on inmate violence or a dramatic series that shows routine prison abuse, both versions plant a seed in the viewer's head that these depictions are representative of reality. To better educate citizens on punishment in society, it is essential to further refine television depictions of what goes on in our prisons. While great strides have been made to help average citizens who will never see the inside of a prison cell to see what inmates, correction officers, and administrators deal with on a daily basis, there is still much more to do.

William J. Miller
Southeast Missouri State University

See Also: Corrections; Television, Crime in; Television, Police in.

Further Readings
Snauffer, Douglas N. *Crime Television*. New York: Praeger, 2006.
Sparks, Richard. *Television and Drama of Crime: Moral Tales and the Place of Crime in Public Life*. Berkshire, UK: Open University Press, 1992.
Yousman, Bill. *Prime Time Prisons on U.S. TV*. New York: Peter Lang, 2009.

Tennessee

When one thinks of the state of Tennessee, several things may spring to mind: the beautiful Smoky Mountains, several different types of music, the University of Tennessee Volunteers, or a sense of southern hospitality. What one might not think of immediately is the amount of crime Tennessee has; the state's checkered past probably does not factor in. In fact, Tennessee is responsible for several vital changes in the legal system, from the way education is taught to individual rights. Unfortunately, these changes tend to come about as a result of the mistakes people have made or the crimes they have committed.

Police

It was against the threat of night raids from the American Indians, specifically the Cherokee, that the first sheriff's office in Tennessee was established in 1795, still a year away from statehood. These early Tennessee lawmen were expected to handle both civil and criminal matters. When Sir Robert Peel introduced his metropolitan style of policing in 1829 London, America took notice. It was not until after the Civil War, however, that Tennessee developed its metropolitan police force, first in Memphis, and then in Nashville and Chattanooga. The early 20th century brought the automobile and the radio transmitter to policemen all over the world. With these inventions came the transition from foot and horse patrols to automobile and motorcycle. The 1970s wrought further changes, this time in the area of civil rights. Although African American men were first hired as police officers in 1948, it was not until the 1970s that it was an accepted practice. It was also during this decade that women were given patrol duties for the first time. Education was also becoming a primary focus, and although separate cities instituted training curriculums for their officers, it was not until 1966 that the Tennessee Law Enforcement Training Academy opened its doors. The Tennessee Bureau of Criminal Identification, later to be called the Tennessee Bureau of Investigation, was created in 1951. The 1950s and 1960s brought with them the creation of K-9 and Special Weapons and Tactic (SWAT) units, as well. Today, Tennessee is protected by the city police and the sheriff's office, as well as the state highway patrol.

The Ku Klux Klan was started in Tennessee in 1865. Ironically, Tennessee also had areas that were part of the Underground Railroad, where a slave could travel north to freedom.

Crime

Along with the change in the structure of policing has come a change in what is considered criminal. Today, Tennessee concentrates on its small population of gangs and its larger problem of drug manufacturing and trafficking, where methamphetamines are now the main target. At its roots, however, Tennessee was originally infamous for its illegal production and distribution of moonshine, a high-proof liquor distilled from corn. Buford Pusser, the tough-on-crime Tennessee sheriff whose likeness is the basis for the "Walking Tall" franchise, was well known for targeting moonshiners. It was not until 2010 that the practice was officially legalized. The state also practiced slave labor, though it was prohibited in 1784, years before Tennessee was a recognized state. Ironically, Tennessee also has several spots that were part of the Underground Railroad, a path of safe places where a slave could travel north to freedom. Unfortunately, parts of the state have in the past been known for their less than tolerant attitude on civil rights. The original Ku Klux Klan was started in Pulaski, Tennessee, in 1865, and lynching, for instance, occurred well into the 1900s. The lynching of Ed Johnson led to the only criminal trial ever held by the U.S. Supreme Court, in which Sheriff Joseph Shipp, who had arrested Johnson, was found guilty. African Americans were not the only race discriminated against: Red Clay, Tennessee, held one of the largest groups of Cherokee Indians in the United States and the Trail of Tears started there.

This intolerance extended beyond skin color; religion and later, sexuality were also targets for hatred. One of the most famous trials in the history of the United States took place in Dayton, Tennessee, in July 1925. In the spring of that year, the Butler Act was passed by the Tennessee legislature, which made it illegal to teach evolution in public schools. The American Civil Liberties Union (ACLU) offered to pay the legal expenses of anyone willing to challenge that law, and John Scopes, a teacher at the local high school, agreed. The trial drew national publicity, especially with the addition of the two lawyers: for the defense, Clarence Darrow, and for the prosecution, William Jennings Bryan. Because it was being argued theologically, modernism against fundamentalism, the trial soon turned into a circus, literally. Trained chimpanzees even performed on the courthouse lawn. Despite the antics of both sides, Scopes was found guilty and was asked to pay a $100 fine, which was later overturned by the Tennessee Supreme Court on a technicality. The Butler Act was not repealed, however, until 1967. In 2004, the same county where the Scopes trial occurred tried to implement a legal ban on homosexuality and failed.

In 1985, the state also became famous for the landmark decision of the U.S. Supreme Court, *Tennessee v. Garner*. It was held that under the Fourth Amendment, when an officer is pursuing a fleeing suspect, he or she may only use deadly force to prevent escape if the suspect poses a significant threat of death or serious injury to the officer or others. Prior to this law, it was reasonable under the "fleeing felon" common law to shoot the suspect after a warning.

Punishment

Until the 1831 establishment of the Tennessee State Penitentiary House in Nashville, punishment was always public and corporal. Depending on the offense, the punishment could range from being set in the stocks and whipped to hanging and dismemberment. The 1831 penitentiary contained 200 cells, along with a hospital, warden's dwelling, and other structures. This facility was used until 1898, when the Tennessee State Prison was built in Davidson County. In 1930, the first facility for women was built on the grounds of the Tennessee State Prison, and in 1955, the Tennessee Department of Corrections was established. Three years later, a statewide system of juvenile probation became operational. After decades of correctional reform, treatment facilities started appearing in the 1970s; in the 1980s came a more conservative ideology. In 1989, the Riverbend Maximum Security Institution opened in Nashville, and in 1992, the first private prison in Tennessee, established by Corrections Corporation of America, opened its doors.

Brandy B. Henderson
University of South Florida

See Also: Corrections; Courts; Darrow, Clarence; Indian Removal Act; Ku Klux Klan; Lynchings; Race-Based Crimes; Scopes Monkey Trial; Slavery.

Further Readings
Ashmore, Eddie. *Tennessee Lawman: History of the Men and Women Behind the Badge*. Nashville, TN: Turner Publishing, 2006.
Bergeron, Paul H., Jeannette Keith, and Stephen V. Ash. *Tennesseans & Their History*. Knoxville: University of Tennessee Press, 1999.
Tennessee Encyclopedia of History and Culture. http://tennesseeencyclopedia.net (Accessed January 2011).

Terrorism

One of the greatest social, political, and military problems in the modern world is terrorism. It is present around the globe, in both modern developed countries and countries that have not advanced into the technological age. Terrorism is the great fear of most peaceful modern societies, a fact not lost on the leaders and politicians who use it to justify all types of social, political, economic, religious, and even personal agendas. However, defining terrorism is difficult, and it must be realized that terrorism is not just the current (and inaccurate) Western media political portrayals of all terrorists as dirty and ignorant Arabs with beards and burnooses mindlessly reciting the Koran and screaming themselves hoarse for jihad. Terrorism has a long and bloody history in America and highlights the uneasy and frequently contradictory American relationship between its crimes and its politics.

Definition of Terrorism

As a general matter, terrorism can be defined as the threat or the actual use of force or violence aimed at innocent people or noncombatants to attain a political goal by creating a climate of fear or demoralization. This is an admittedly broad definition of terrorism and is arguably open to refinement. But terrorism is not an easy concept to strictly define. The reason for this difficulty is that labeling or defining a threat or an act as terroristic is often a matter of perspective. For example, when a group of people in a society decide to revolt to gain their political independence, they are frequently labeled as terrorists by the then current parties in power. However, to the people who are trying to gain their political freedom, they are viewed as freedom fighters and heroes. A specific example of this contradiction in definition is the situation involving the Contras in the Central American nation of Nicaragua in the 1980s. The Contras were a right-wing revolutionary group who were trying to overthrow the socialist government of Nicaragua. The Reagan administration of the United States supported the Contras and was covertly supplying them with arms. To the established Nicaraguan government, the Contras were terrorists, but to the Contras and the Reagan administration, the Contras were freedom fighters. As is a matter of historical record, the activities of the Reagan administration in the infamous Iran-Contra scandal resulted in numerous indictments, criminal convictions, and subsequent presidential pardons of American officials. Further, Nicaragua took the United States to the World Court over its mining of Nicaragua's harbors, which would qualify as a war crime, where Nicaragua prevailed, but the United States refused to acknowledge the judgment. Thus, it is apparent that it is difficult to objectively determine who is a terrorist and whether certain activities constitute terrorism.

One aspect of terrorism is that it frequently occurs in conjunction with a concurrent or subsequent political revolt. Individual terrorist activities, whether random or coordinated, are usually the precursors to the actual revolution itself. Thus, the concepts of terrorism and revolution cannot be easily separated.

Purposes of Terrorism

Terrorism can involve several purposes or goals. These purposes or goals can include social, political, economic, or religious aspects. There is frequently overlap between these goals. For example, a single terrorist group might use political, economic, and social goals to justify their terroristic activities. Also, religious terrorist groups frequently have political goals that involve the installation of a theocracy as a form of government. The revolt in Iran in 1979, which was preceded by years of demonstrations and terroristic violence and resulted in the overthrow of the shah with the subsequent installation of the Ayatollah Khomeini as the religious and political head of state, is an excellent example of religious and political overlap.

An example of a social goal involving terrorism is the Environmental Liberation Front (ELF), an American terrorist group whose goal is the protection of the environment. Somewhat related to ELF is the Animal Liberation Front (ALF), whose social goal is the protection of animal rights. The Federal Bureau of Investigation (FBI) has ranked ELF and ALF as the most serious domestic terrorism threats to America because of the millions of dollars of property damage they are alleged to have caused. ELF's activities are reported to include the arson and vandalism of buildings that

ELF considers to be environmentally damaging and the staking of trees with nails so that when lumberjacks try to cut those trees down, their chain saws are broken. Through these activities, ELF hopes to advance the social cause of environmentalism. Of course, ELF's activities also have political aspects, but ELF's primary goal appears to be social. ELF apparently does try to avoid harming people and focuses primarily on property destruction.

An obvious example of a religious goal involving terrorism in the modern world is Al Qaeda. Al Qaeda is an extremely well-organized political group and has become international. Al Qaeda is an Islamic group, one of whose goals is the protection and expansion of the Islamic religion and the removal of Western influence from Saudi Arabia. Al Qaeda was led by Osama bin Laden, a Saudi Arabian whose family is extremely wealthy. Al Qaeda is infamous for its use of violence to accomplish its goals and is not hesitant to cause injury to or the death of innocent human beings. The most famous act of terroristic violence committed by Al Qaeda is the destruction of the World Trade Center on September 11, 2001.

An example of a political goal involving terrorism is the Irish Easter Uprising of April 1916 and the subsequent Irish War of Independence, which lasted from 1919 to 1921 and resulted in the creation of the Irish Republic and Northern Ireland, which remained within the British Empire. The Irish Republican Army (IRA) at that time engaged in a guerrilla war of terrorism from 1916 until the war started in 1919. The IRA of that time must be differentiated from the Provisional Irish Republican Army of modern times, which has engaged in numerous acts of terrorism, although in recent years, it has significantly lessened and even ceased—and arguably renounced—its violent terroristic activities. The primary goal of the IRA was the liberation of Ireland from the British Empire.

An example of a purely economic goal involving an extended campaign of terrorism is difficult to find. Most terroristic activities and revolts involve political or religious issues, with economic issues as a corollary issue. However, the Boston Tea Party in 1773 by the American colonists is an excellent example of economic terrorism. In 1767, the British parliament enacted the Townshend Acts, which included a duty on tea imported to the American colonies. The American colonists refused to pay the duty, and a group of American colonists disguised as Indians forced their way onto three British merchant ships in Boston Harbor and dumped all of the cargo of tea into the harbor. In retaliation, the British parliament enacted the Intolerable Acts of 1774, which essentially lit the fuse for the subsequent American Revolution in 1776.

Methods of Terrorism

One of the essential problems with terrorism is that it does not target just the parties who commit the acts that are used to justify the terrorist activities (e.g., torture by police, political oppression by rulers, religious suppression by theologians, economic oppression by oligarchs). It also targets innocent people, in part because those who commit the acts used to justify the terrorism are usually protected by the police, the military, and security services. Further, terrorism's purpose encompasses the terrorism of an entire social group or society, including innocent people. Thus, many terrorists attempt to effect change by terrorizing the general populace in an effort to indirectly force or compel the actual targets of the terrorism (e.g., political rulers, religious leaders, or economic magnates) to act or cease to act.

As previously stated, terrorism involves the threat or the actual use of force or violence to accomplish its goals. Terrorism can be accomplished by various acts, which include threats, extortion, assaults, vandalism to property, arson of property, kidnapping and ransom, and murder and assassination. Thus, terrorism can be considered in light of the degree of violence. The property damage caused by ELF cannot rationally be considered to be on the same level of terrorism as the attacks on the World Trade Center on 9/11, which resulted in the deaths of thousands and the destruction of internationally recognized economic and political symbols: the Twin Towers of the World Trade Center. Moreover, the economic damage caused by the 9/11 attacks was much greater than any ELF attacks.

Terrorists generally cannot effectively operate without weapons. Weapons such as individual firearms are used. Such individual firearms are favored when terrorists are seeking a specific individual for assassination or kidnapping, as they are easily transportable. Explosives are more favored by many terrorists because of the greater amount of harm and damage that can be inflicted by them. For example, a single terrorist with a machine gun can fire into a crowded market and inflict a number of casualties. But that terrorist would likely be swiftly caught and interrogated, hopefully revealing the identity and location of his or her compatriots. In contrast, explosives can be set and detonated later, minimizing the chances of the perpetrators being caught and maximizing the potential harm and damage. Further, as demonstrated so frequently in the Middle East, the use of suicide bombers and explosives is extremely effective. The terror caused by a person willing to sacrifice himself or herself in an explosion for what is believed to be a greater cause while causing the deaths of numerous innocents cannot be underestimated. Further, the fact that the victimized populace will not have any warning of the explosion only heightens the level of fear and terror as a result of it. And there are other methods that raise the level of fear and terror to almost Olympian heights: weapons of mass destruction. Weapons of mass destruction include biological, chemical, and nuclear weapons. The use, or even just the threat of use, of such weapons magnifies the resulting terror to a level that can cripple an entire nation. Thus, obtaining such weapons is the ultimate step for the most committed and unscrupulous terrorists.

Terrorism as a Tool

Regardless of any social, political, philosophical, religious, legal, or ethical arguments that can be made against the employment of terrorism, it cannot be rationally disputed that terrorism works. Many nations have been formed through the use of terrorism and subsequent revolutions. Unfortunately, it is frequently the tool of the fanatic, who cannot employ any logical reason, or the desperate, who have tried to apply reason, logic, and ethics but have been unable to succeed. The examples of terrorism and revolution that have occurred throughout the world that have resulted in the successful attainment of the stated goals are many. The American Revolution and the Irish War of Independence are only two examples. This is not meant to be a blanket acceptance of terrorism or revolution as a legitimate tool of social, political, economic, or religious change. However, it must be acknowledged that the Declaration of Independence of 1776, signed by the founding founders, expressly recognized the right to revolt. The moral conundrum is determining when such an action is justified.

Early Terrorism in America

There have been hundreds if not thousands of incidents of terrorism in the history of the United States. A brief and hopefully representative list of them will be presented to demonstrate the presence of terrorism in America and its strange relationship to crime and politics, especially considering the perhaps arrogant American position that the United States is the leader and ultimate shining example of justice, law, and democracy in the free world.

The United States of America was founded on a series of terroristic acts and a revolution. King George III was the legitimate ruler of the thirteen colonies and the founding fathers displayed episodes of terrorism, such as the tarring and feathering of British tax collectors. They employed violence to accomplish a political goal. It is axiomatic that history is written by the winners of any war, but even American history does not try to hide the role of the colonists as revolutionaries. Indeed, the Declaration of Independence of 1776 specifically recognizes the right to revolt.

In 1841, Thomas Wilson Dorr and many citizens of Rhode Island attempted to change the voting laws, which allowed only landowners to vote under the original state charter. Their legitimate attempts to change the voting laws through the established political process failed, and Dorr and his followers held a Peoples' Convention and adopted a new state constitution, which was subsequently approved by a referendum. The following election found Dorr elected to the governorship under the new constitution; Samuel Ward King was elected governor under the original charter. In what is known as Dorr's Rebellion, Dorr and his supporters unsuccessfully attacked an arsenal; the rebellion failed. However, the limited electorate under the original charter was persuaded of the legitimacy of the cause, and a new state constitution was created. Unfortunately, despite the obvious legitimacy of Dorr's cause, he was tried and convicted of treason to the state, although he was later released. The issue of which state government was valid subsequently came before the U.S. Supreme Court in the case *Luther v. Borden* (1849). The Supreme Court refused to address the issue and held it was a "political question," meaning that it was not for the courts to decide. Interestingly, given the Declaration of Independence and the American Revolution, it would seem that this decision seemed to acknowledge that if there was a rebellion with associated terroristic activities, then the terrorists had better win.

The Civil War, which lasted from 1861 to 1865, was the ultimate political and military act to prevent terrorism against a group of people. The enslavement of the African American people was an extreme form of terrorism directed against a specific group of people for illegitimate social (and economic and political) reasons. Theoretically, with the Emancipation Proclamation and the end of the Civil War, the issue of terrorism against African Americans was over. Reality proved otherwise. Even the enactment of the Thirteenth, Fourteenth, and Fifteenth Amendments and the Civil Rights Act of 1871 did not stop it. Despite all of these attempts to stop it, the Ku Klux Klan formed in the 1860s in the south to terrorize African Americans. Although it died out, the group resurfaced in the 1920s and after World War II in opposition to civil rights and minorities. The Ku Klux Klan has morphed over the years into various modern white supremacist and Aryan Nation organizations, many of them borrowing from the Ku Klux Klan, ultraconservative Christian groups, and the fascism and racial purity theories of Nazi Germany. These organizations continue to engage in extensive terrorist activities to frighten and harm minority groups, especially racial and religious groups.

President Lincoln (in top hat) visiting the battlefield at Antietam, Maryland, on October 3, 1862 during the Civil War, which was the ultimate political and military act to prevent terrorism against a group of people. The slavery issue addressed the question of whether slavery was an anachronistic evil incompatible with American values.

In the 1800s, the political principle of anarchy, that is, society without government, was popular. Famous anarchists included Josiah Warren and Henry David Thoreau, although these proponents were relatively peaceful compared to their subsequent followers. During the late 1800s and the early 1900s, there were a number of violent anarchists operating in America who used bombs, many of them being immigrants from Europe. Coincident with the anarchy movement in the 1800s and the early 1900s was the American labor movement. The cause of the anarchists received much attention when on May 4, 1886, at Haymarket Square in Chicago, a bomb was thrown at police dispersing a labor rally. Eight anarchists, participating in the labor rally, were arrested and convicted of murder even though the police conceded there was no evidence that they had thrown the bomb. Four of the anarchists were executed and one committed suicide in prison. The event was immortalized as the Haymarket massacre and was a rallying point for anarchists and the nascent American labor movement. Anarchists continued to operate in America through the early 1900s, when in the infamous case of Nicola Sacco and Bartolomeo Vanzetti, two Italian immigrant anarchists were executed on August 23, 1927, for an armed robbery, allegedly to obtain funds for more bombings. The case of Sacco and Vanzetti has been a cause célèbre for many years because of the questionable evidence and lack of a fair trial received by Sacco and Vanzetti. After the early 1900s, the anarchist movement and its use of terroristic violence died out, but was reawakened in the 1960s.

Terrorism in Twentieth-Century America
In the late 1800s and the early 1900s, the American labor movement began to form to fight unjust and unfair economic treatment from the corporations and the robber barons. Labor strikes and rallies often turned violent, with the corporations and businesses obtaining the use of military troops and private Pinkerton troops to violently suppress the labor advocates, and the labor advocates responding with violent acts of their own. Despite the widespread violence on both sides, the American labor movement, the socialists, and the communists had great success in forcing through much legislation to address such serious social and economic problems as child labor, the eight-hour workday, minimum wage, workers compensation, and the National Labor Relations Act, which allowed workers to organize and to create labor unions to bargain over conditions of employment and to protect their rights. Interestingly, although the socialists and the communists in America contributed greatly to the enactment of labor laws, they were still considered to be a significant terroristic danger to America, although relatively few were convicted of terroristic crimes when compared to the political hysteria associated with them, as personified by the infamous McCarthy hearings of the 1950s.

During the late 1800s and through the 1930s, the United States participated in the Banana Republic Wars, a number of police actions, occupations, and small wars in a number of countries in Central and South America. The countries that were subject to American military might included Cuba, Panama, Nicaragua, Haiti, Honduras, and the Dominican Republic. Generally, none of these countries had engaged in any acts that warranted invasion, and the overriding reason for the presence of the U.S. military was to protect the economic interests of American sugar companies, fruit companies, and Wall Street banks. These American military actions can only be defined as terroristic in nature, especially as they had no legitimate justification under international law.

In the 1950s and the 1960s, America was very concerned about the revolution in Cuba that resulted in the eventual establishment of a communist government headed by Fidel Castro. Even though the dictatorial Batista government that was overthrown was infamous for its corruption, it received the support of the United States. Even though Cuba had not initiated a war against the United States, America supported, equipped, and financed an invasion of Cuba at the Bay of Pigs by Cuban refugees, which ended disastrously for America, both politically and militarily. Subsequently, the United States engaged in a campaign against Castro and Cuba that included unsuccessful attempts to assassinate him, which can only be considered terroristic. Historically, the activities of the United States and especially the Central Intelligence Agency (CIA) concerning Cuba and the Bay of Pigs brought international criticism for their activities.

The 1960s were a turbulent time for America, socially, politically, and economically. It was the time of the Vietnam War and civil unrest when minorities were seeking equality. Campus unrest was rife. Student protests reached their height when the Ohio National Guard opened fire on student demonstrators at Kent State University in 1970 with live ammunition, killing four students; this event became known as the Kent State massacre. A number of organizations started to engage in violence to protest the social injustice. The Students for a Democratic Society was one of the major organizations trying to effect social change. One of its splinter groups, the Weathermen, started to engage in violent protest and criminal activities that can only be characterized as terroristic. The Black Panthers, a political party that focused on opposing racial injustice for African Americans, were frequently the targets of government attack, but relatively few charges brought against them resulted in convictions. And 1968 was famous for the Democratic National Convention, in which the abuses of the Chicago police against protestors were nationally televised. One official termed the event a police riot. There were many other organizations that fought, both peacefully and violently, for social, political, and economic justice. Despite all of the violence and the associated terrorism, it has been persuasively argued that all of the advancements of the 1960s (e.g., civil rights, racial equality) would not have been achieved without it. The historical effect of the civil unrest and violence of the 1960s on the criminal justice system was enormous. Gun laws were passed. Police training was increased. Formal recognition of civil rights in the criminal justice process was accomplished. Even more important, however, was the social perception of the police. After the 1960s, even some conservatives began to question police activities, and the free pass that police officers and agencies had previously enjoyed was gone.

individual Action and Terrorism
Terrorism as a function of individual action was brought to the forefront in the 1960s with the assassination of John F. Kennedy in 1963 by Lee Harvey Oswald, of Robert F. Kennedy in 1968 by Sirhan Sirhan, and of Martin Luther King, Jr., in 1968 by James Earl Ray. Although each assassination was originally thought to be the act of a lone gunman, subsequent evidence and investigations have cast serious doubt on each of these theories. The historical effect of these assassinations and the subsequent questions raised as to the involvement of the government in them on the criminal justice system and society was incredible. A level of social and political distrust in government and of the criminal justice system entered into the American consciousness.

The pro-life movement in America is an example of domestic terrorism that has divided the nation. The pro-life movement is against abortion and is violently opposed to the U.S. Supreme Court decision in *Roe v. Wade*, which essentially legalized abortion in the United States. The past few decades have seen a number of abortion clinics vandalized and bombed and have seen doctors willing to perform abortions murdered. The ultrareligious, far-right-wing pro-life movement has essentially made heroes of those who committed these terroristic activities.

In 1975, with the American public becoming weary of government corruption, the U.S. Senate formed the Church Committee to investigate the CIA and the FBI. The results were astounding and shocked America. The Church Committee revealed the activities by the CIA and the FBI of not only spying on American citizens but also of being involved in the attempted assassinations of foreign leaders, which can only be termed terroristic in nature. The effect on America and the criminal system was profound. Legal limits were placed on the CIA and the FBI to prevent them from engaging in such activities again.

From the 1970s through the 1990s, America was subject to a series of mail bombings by Ted Kaczynski (the Unabomber), a brilliant but psychologically disturbed individual who espoused an antitechnology political philosophy. Although Kaczynski's effect on the American criminal justice system was negligible, the investigation, arrest, and prosecution of him were extremely costly and time consuming, spanning several decades. However, Kaczynski is illustrative of the ability of a single disturbed individual to be an effective terrorist and that such people exist in free societies such as the United States.

From the 1970s through the 1990s, with distrust of government increasing, a number of militias, independent of either state or federal government, began to form. Many of them were associated with white supremacists and the Aryan Nation, but some of them were based primarily on political beliefs and an expansive interpretation of the Second Amendment to the Constitution. Although there were not a large number of prosecutions for terrorist activities against these militia groups, a number of them were convicted of associated criminal charges such as possession of weapons and explosives. The high-water mark for militia groups in America was the Oklahoma City bombing of 1995, executed by Timothy McVeigh, a militia movement sympathizer. McVeigh used a truck bomb to destroy the Alfred P. Murrah Federal Building; 168 people were killed. McVeigh was arrested, convicted, and executed. Some militia organizations disavowed McVeigh's actions, and the militia movement lost a lot of its support. The effect on the American criminal justice system was immediate. Awareness of domestic terrorism was brought home and defensive measures at government buildings were increased. Numerous laws were passed, including the Anti-Terrorism and Effective Death Penalty Act of 1996. This bombing also brought home to America that terrorism could be homegrown.

In 1993, Muslim extremists attempted to blow up the World Trade Center in New York City. The attempt failed, although six people were killed and more than 1,000 people were injured. The practical effect on America of the 1993 World Trade Center bombing was a clear demonstration that foreign terrorists could strike inside the territory of the United States.

Terrorism in 21st-Century America
The most devastating terrorist attack on American soil was the September 11, 2001, attack on the World Trade Center and the Pentagon by Al Qaeda. Thousands of people were killed, and the World Trade Center was destroyed. Nothing can be said here about it that has not been already stated in other works. It is probably the most influential act of terrorism on American society and the way that America views criminal justice. Essentially, 9/11, despite the previous attempt to destroy the World Trade Center in 1993, was the act of terrorism that destroyed American innocence about the reality of international politics and terrorism. As a result of the 9/11 attack, the USA PATRIOT Act of 2001 and numerous other laws were enacted. The PATRIOT Act, despite its name, provided for a comprehensive reduction of American civil liberties and privacy in exchange for a much greater degree of protection against terrorist attacks. The effect against terrorism of all the restrictions placed on civil liberties has been seriously challenged. Since 9/11, the huge expansion of government power in the criminal justice system over the people has been seriously questioned, especially concerning the activities of the National Security Agency in surveilling the private communications of American citizens. Further, there have been a number of challenges to the government's version of what actually happened at the World Trade Center and how the towers collapsed. However, the most serious result of the terrorism of 9/11 is the ease with which the American people have acquiesced to the curtailment of their civil rights. It was Benjamin Franklin who stated that those who would

View of the World Trade Center after the second tower fell on September 11, 2001. The World Trade Center and the Pentagon were attacked by Al Qaeda, killing thousands.

give up a little liberty for a little security deserve neither and will lose both.

Shortly after 9/11, another terrorist act occurred in America. Anthrax powder was mailed to several Democratic senators and some media outlets. The effect was a national scare about biological terrorism. Initially, there was a huge amount of fear that it was the work of Islamic terrorists. True horror set in when scientific analysis proved that the anthrax originated in America. What was even more frightening was that it was directed only at Democratic senators and not at conservative politicians. FBI investigations focused on one U.S. government scientist who was, with some embarrassment, later cleared. A second U.S. government scientist was then suspected, but he committed suicide. Later revelations indicated that the second scientist might not have been the perpetrator. The anthrax attacks reawakened the fear, raised many decades earlier with the Kennedy and King assassinations, that the American government could have been involved in a terrorist plot against its own people.

Conclusion

Terrorism and revolution work. History demonstrates it. Moreover, domestic terrorism has had some positive effects in America. The labor movement and the civil rights movement probably would not have developed as much as they did, with the concurrent expansion of civil rights and protections to the people as a result of those movements, if they did not involve violence and, by definition, terrorism. History seems to prove the proposition that terrorism works, no matter how distasteful it might be. But the problem is, under what standard can violence and terrorism be considered justified? The U.S. Supreme Court, when it considered Dorr's Rebellion, refused to address the issue and has uniformly refused to recognize the Declaration of Independence as binding legal authority.

Terrorism has a long and bloody history in America, both within its borders involving its own people and outside its borders in actions against other nations. The civil liberties of American citizens generally survived the terrorist threats of the Civil War, the anarchists, the labor movement, the civil rights era, domestic assassinations, and highly questionable foreign interventions and occupations. With the militia movements, domestic terrorism, government abuse, and the threat of terrorism from Al Qaeda, the survival of American society, at least as to its theoretical base of individual liberty according to some authorities, is not only uncertain—it seems unlikely. The powers of government for criminal investigation, individual surveillance, violation of privacy, and criminal conviction of people who might otherwise not have been convicted have been greatly increased. Further, internationally, the United States has developed not only an arrogant sense of superiority concerning the terroristic activities of other nations but a frightening posture of national privilege and willful blindness when it engages in such activities. The final effect of such an attitude on the American society and its standing in the world has yet to be determined, but the universal condemnation of the activities of George W. Bush involving the "war on terror" may provide us with a warning.

Wm. C. Plouffe, Jr.
Independent Scholar

See Also: 1961 to 1980 Primary Documents; 1981 to 2000 Primary Documents; 2001 to 2012 Primary Documents; American Revolution and Criminal Justice; Anarchists; Bush, George W. (Administration of); Chicago Seven/Democratic National Convention of 1968; Civil Disobedience; Homeland Security; Kaczynski, Ted; Kennedy, John F. (Administration of); Kennedy, Robert F.; King, Martin Luther, Jr.; Ku Klux Klan; McVeigh, Timothy; Oklahoma City Bombing; Oswald, Lee Harvey; Ray, James Earl; Sacco and Vanzetti; Sirhan Sirhan; USA PATRIOT Act of 2001.

Further Readings
Dershowitz, Alan. *Why Terrorism Works*. New Haven, CT: Yale University Press, 2002.
Hewitt, Christopher. *Understanding Terrorism in America: From the Klan to Al Qaeda*. London: Routledge, 2003.
Hoffman, Bruce. *Inside Terrorism*. New York: Columbia University Press, 2006.
McKnight, Gerald. *Breach of Trust: How the Warren Commission Failed the Nation and Why*. Lawrence: University Press of Kansas, 2005.
Parry, Albert. *Terrorism From Robespierre to the Weather Underground*. Mineola, NY: Dover, 1976.

Pious, Richard M. *The War on Terrorism and the Rule of Law*. Los Angeles, CA: Roxbury, 2006.

Prados, John, ed. *America Confronts Terrorism*. Lanham, MD: Ivan R. Dee, 2002.

Rasenberger, Jim. *The Brilliant Disaster: JFK, Castro, and America's Doomed Invasion of Cuba's Bay of Pigs*. New York: Scribner, 2011.

Reich, Walter, ed. *Origins of Terrorism*. Baltimore, MD: Johns Hopkins University Press, 1998.

Wright, Stuart. *Patriots, Politics, and the Oklahoma City Bombing*. Cambridge: Cambridge University Press, 2007.

Terry v. Ohio

Terry v. Ohio (1968) revolutionized Fourth Amendment search and seizure law. It is one of the most significant cases that examined the constitutional underpinnings of the officer-citizen dynamic. *Terry* explored the permissible bounds of a seizure and provided a lasting framework to scrutinize the constitutionality of police-citizen encounters. The "*Terry* stop," a by-product of the Supreme Court's decision, represents an exception to the Fourth Amendment's probable cause requirement, which allows for a limited police detention. The *Terry* decision was culturally salient because of its exposition on the "wholesale harassment by certain elements of the police community, of which minority groups, particularly Negroes, frequently complain."

The Case

In *Terry*, a veteran plainclothes Cleveland police detective named McFadden was patrolling downtown Cleveland, Ohio, at approximately 2:30 in the afternoon on October 31, 1963. The detective observed two men, Chilton and Terry, standing on the corner of a commercial street. Officer McFadden had never seen the two men before and could not precisely identify what about the two men caught his attention. Nonetheless, he relied on his 39 years of experience as a police officer—during which he had been regularly assigned to patrol the downtown area for "shoplifters and pickpockets"—to instinctively investigate further.

Officer McFadden assumed an observation post at a storefront entrance approximately 300–400 feet away from the two men. From this perspective, he witnessed the two men engage in a pattern of behavior that consisted of one man standing watch on the corner as the other man paced back and forth across various storefronts, momentarily pausing to stare into one particular store window. The two men regrouped at the corner and conferred. The duo, which was eventually joined by a third man, repeated this process various times. Given his observations of their reconnaissance of the store, the officer suspected the men were "casing a job, a stick-up."

Although he feared the men might be armed with a gun, McFadden approached the group, identified himself as a police officer, and asked for their names. When the men mumbled something following the inquiries, the officer grabbed Terry, spun him around, and patted the outside of his clothing down. In the left breast pocket of Terry's overcoat, the officer felt a pistol. He reached inside the pocket but could not remove the firearm. The officer ordered all three men inside the store, entirely removed Terry's coat, and extracted a .38-caliber revolver. A similar search of Chilton's pocket revealed another revolver.

Both men were arrested and indicted for violating Ohio's concealed firearm statute. They filed pretrial motions to suppress the physical evidence. Because the trial court found the officer had a reasonable suspicion based on his experience, the defendants' motions were denied. Both men were tried and convicted. On appeal, the convictions were affirmed. The U.S. Supreme Court granted certiorari.

Supreme Court Ruling

The Supreme Court identified the issue for decision as one regarding the propriety of the police conduct and the admissibility of the seized evidence. With regard to the validity of the modern-day "stop and frisk," the court delineated a two-pronged analysis. First, in the interest of crime deterrence, the police may briefly detain a citizen if the officer has a reasonable suspicion based on specific and particularized facts that the person is involved, has been involved, or will be involved in criminal activity. Reasonable suspicion is more than a mere hunch or inchoate suspicion. Second, to ensure officer safety during an investigative detention, a limited authority to search the suspect for weapons may be exercised upon the reasonable belief that the person is armed and presently dangerous. The search must be carefully limited to the outer clothing.

The impact of *Terry*'s legitimization of the "stop and frisk" on the racial landscape of urban policing has been long-lasting. The *Terry* opinion recognized that forceful police tactics were often used to harass, humiliate, and dominate African Americans. Ever cognizant of the police-racial tension, the court nevertheless sanctioned street stops or investigatory detentions on less than probable cause. Nearly four decades later, the issue of race is still very much relevant in the police-citizen dynamic. On the one hand, opponents of *Terry* feel that the Supreme Court should have taken a more activist approach in curtailing law enforcement practices to properly protect the liberty and privacy interests of the citizenry. Critics contend the validation of the stop and frisk does not provide sufficient protection for minorities who are most impacted living in urban areas. Specifically, some critics argue the stop and frisk has done more to undermine, rather than safeguard, the privacy interests of African Americans for decades since its inception. One significant flaw noted is the pliable standard of reasonable suspicion the *Terry* court delineated, which affords police officers far too much discretion in carrying out their duties. On the other hand, supporters maintain the *Terry* decision has provided a flexible framework to adapt to an ever-changing political, racial, and societal landscape. The decision, advocates argue, is an ideal compromise between the compelling interest to have law enforcement perform their function and the liberty interests of the citizenry.

Today, law enforcement continues to possess wide latitude in pursuing investigations and ferreting out crime with only the amorphous reasonable suspicion standard to guide or curtail their conduct. Judicial discretion remains the means for ensuring government conduct adheres to, does not trample, and balances the protections inherent in the Fourth Amendment.

Armando Gustavo Hernandez
Independent Scholar

See Also: Cleveland, OH; Constitution of the United States of America; Defendant's Rights; Due Process.

Further Readings
Illinois v. Wardlow, 528 U.S. 119, 120 S. Ct. 673, 145 L.Ed.2d 570 (2000).
Maclin, Tracey. "*Terry v. Ohio*'s Fourth Amendment Legacy: Black Men and Police Discretion." *St. John's Law Review*, v.72 (1998).
Meares, Tracey L. "*Terry* and the Relevance of Politics." *St. John's Law Review*, v.72 (1998).
Ronner, Amy D. "Fleeing While Black: The Fourth Amendment Apartheid." *Columbia Human Rights Law Review*, v.32 (2001).
Terry v. Ohio, 392 U.S. 1, 88 S. Ct. 1868, 20 L.Ed.2d 889 (1968).

Texas

Texas is the second-largest state in the United States in both area (after Alaska) and population (after California). In 2010, the state's population was 25,145,561, a 20.6 percent increase since 2000. The majority of the population is white (70.4 percent) with large minorities of blacks (11.8 percent) and Hispanics (37.6 percent; a Hispanic person can be of any race). Native American tribes lived in the area that is now Texas before (and for some time after) the arrival of Europeans in the 16th century. Texas was colonized by both France and Spain and was also governed by Mexico for part of the early 19th century, and Texas was for 10 years an independent nation (the Republic of Texas) before becoming the 28th U.S. state in 1845. Texas allowed slavery and during the Civil War seceded as part of the Confederacy. On June 19, 1865, federal troops arrived in Texas to restore order and enforce emancipation, a day now celebrated as Juneteenth. Texas was readmitted to the Union in 1870.

Texas had a reputation for lawlessness before the Civil War and became a home to many outlaws and desperados of all types. The initials GTT ("gone to Texas"), chalked on houses by individuals leaving other southern states to indicate they had vacated the properties and left for Texas, came to acquire the metaphorical meaning of fleeing to avoid prosecution for criminal activity, and more generally of embracing a life of crime. The first group of lawmen known as the Texas Rangers was formed in 1835, although some date its history to an unofficial group formed by Stephen F. Austin in 1823. The Texas Rangers played important roles in fighting against Native American and were noted for their role in the Mexican War of 1846–48. After the Civil War, they helped curb lawlessness in the broad ranges of the state and continued battling the Native American tribes. They were also called upon to contend with cattle thieves and to intercept marauders crossing the Rio Grande into Texas. A number of abuses in the early 20th century led to the Rangers, being reorganized in 1919. In the early 20th century, their duties included patrolling the Rio Grande and guarding against cattle rustlers. During Prohibition, they were also charged with intercepting liquor smugglers at the state border. The Ranger budget was slashed during the Depression and in 1933 the force was reduced to 32 men. In 1935, with the establishment of the Texas Department of Public Safety, the Texas Rangers became one of three basic units (the others being the Highway Patrol and Headquarters Division, the latter a crime laboratory and detection center). Today, the Texas Ranger Division (consisting of 144 commissioned officers and 26 support staff) is responsible for leading investigations of major crimes, unsolved and serial crimes, public corruption, officer-involved shooting, and border security.

Conflict about land use in the range areas of Texas in the late 19th century resulted in a number of disputes sometimes referred to as the range wars. One group of disputes was between cattlemen and sheep ranchers when nomadic sheep and cattle herders were also seen as the enemies of the settled ranchers, both because their flocks could spread disease and because the herders often cut fences to allow their herds free passage. In 1881, a law forbidding sheep herding on the open range and requiring quarantine of diseased sheep was passed but not enforced. In 1883, a stronger law was passed requiring a certificate of inspection to prove that sheep were healthy before they could be moved across county lines. A drought in 1883 also heightened tensions between the itinerant and the land-owning cattlemen as the available supply of pasture and water was reduced: More than half of Texas counties reported fence-cutting in that year. In 1884, fence-cutting became a felony and enclosure of public lands a misdemeanor, and this, along with the enforcement of the health inspection law, largely brought the practice of itinerant sheep and cattle herding to an end.

Capital Punishment

Texas used hanging as the means of execution between 1819 and 1923; between 1819 and 1923, the state authorized the use of the electric chair for executions and ordered that all executions take place in Huntsville under the direction of the state. The first offender executed by electrocution was Charles Reynolds, on February 8, 1924; four additional offenders were also executed on that day. From 1923 to 1973, 506 individuals were sentenced to death, all but three of them male and with a racial breakdown of 33.8 percent white, 56.9 percent black, 9.1 percent Hispanic, and 0.2 percent other. In these years, 361 individuals were actually executed, with a racial breakdown of 29.9 percent white, 63.4 percent black, 6.4 percent Hispanic, and 0.3 percent other. After the U.S. Supreme Court declared capital punishment to be cruel and unusual punishment on June 29, 1972, the 52 prisoners on death row or in county jails had their sentences commuted to life sentences by the governor. In 1973, the Texas Penal Code was revised, and this allowed executions to resume in 1974. The first man placed on death row under the new statute was John Devries, who committed suicide before he could be executed.

Although Oklahoma was the first state to legalize lethal injection as a form of capital punishment, Texas was the first to use this method, in 1982 (it has since become the primary method of execution in most states). Texas leads the United States in the number of executions since reinstatement of the death penalty (as of December 2009, 36 U.S. states authorize the death penalty). Between 1982 and 2010, 462 criminals were executed in Texas, of which 46 percent were white, 36.3 percent were black, and 78 percent were Hispanic. As of June 2011, 313 individuals were on death row, of whom 30 percent were white, 38.7 percent were black, 30 percent were Hispanic, and 0.2 percent were other. Ten (3.2 percent) of those on death row in Texas are female, and 23 (7.3 percent) are not

U.S. citizens, the most common non-U.S. nationality being Mexican. Eight categories of murder are eligible for the death penalty in Texas: murder of a public safety officer or firefighter; murder of a correctional employee; murder during a kidnapping, burglary, robbery, aggravated sexual assault, arson, or obstruction and retaliation; murder for remuneration; murder during a prison escape; murder by a state prison inmate also serving a life sentence for murder, kidnapping, aggravated sexual assault, or aggravated robbery; multiple murders; and murder of an individual younger than six.

Reproductive Rights and Sexual Behavior

Texas played a key role in the expansion of abortion rights in the United States because *Roe v. Wade* was originally filed in the U.S. District Court for the Northern District of Texas in 1970. At that time, Texas had strict antiabortion laws, and Norma McCorvey agreed to take part (using the pseudonym Jane Roe) in a lawsuit filed by Linda Coffey and Sarah Weddington requesting that she be allowed to obtain an abortion. The district court declined to grant McCorvey an injunction that would allow her to obtain a legal abortion, and the case was appealed to the U.S. Supreme Court. In 1973 in a 7–2 decision, the U.S. Supreme Court declared that women had a right to privacy that included obtaining a legal abortion, with few restrictions in the first trimester (12 weeks) of pregnancy and increasing restrictions possible in later-term pregnancies. Because this right to privacy was considered fundamental, all state laws restricting it were immediately overturned. However, since 1973, Texas has added a number of conditions that restrict a woman's ability to obtain an abortion: As of January 2001, these include the stipulation that the parent of a minor must be notified and give consent; that public funding may only be used in cases of rape, incest, or life endangerment; and that a woman seeking an abortion must receive counseling designed to discourage her from having the abortion and then must wait 24 hours before it can be performed.

A Texas case also played a pivotal role in the evolution of gay rights in the United States. In 2003, the U.S. Supreme Court, in its decision in *Lawrence v. Texas*, struck down a Texas antisodomy law that prohibited "deviant sexual intercourse" with a person of the same sex. The case involved two adult men, John Geddes Lawrence and Tyron Garner, who were engaging in consensual sex in Lawrence's apartment in Houston. They were arrested by Joseph Quinn, a sheriff's deputy responding to a false report of a domestic disturbance. Lawrence and Garner were charged and convicted of violating the Texas antisodomy law. After a failed appeal to the Texas Supreme Court and a denied review from the Texas Court of Criminal Appeals, the case was appealed to the U.S. Supreme Court. In the 6–3 decision to strike down the Texas law, the justices found that it violated the guarantees of due process and equal protection. However, Texas still has many laws that discriminate against gay and lesbian people, including a 2005 amendment to the state

An antiabortion protester quotes the Bible. Roe v. Wade *was originally filed in Texas, at the time a state with very strict antiabortion laws. The Supreme Court ruled that women had the right to privacy, which included obtaining a legal abortion.*

constitution that bans same-sex marriages and civil unions.

Cameras in the Courtroom

In 1937, the American Bar Association (ABA) recommended prohibition of movie and still cameras in the courtroom, motivated in part by the disruptions caused by photographers during the 1935 trial of Bruno Hauptmann for the kidnapping and murder of the Lindbergh baby (then called "the trial of the century" because of extreme public interest in the case). In 1944, radio broadcasting and still photography were banned from criminal trials in federal court, and in 1962 this was amended to include television broadcasting. Most states followed the ABA recommendation and banned television cameras from the courtroom but a few, including Texas, had no such prohibition.

In 1963, Billy Sol Estes, a financier involved in several schemes, including leasing of nonexistent anhydrous ammonia tanks and fraudulently obtaining federal cotton subsidies, was convicted of fraud totaling more than $24 million and was sentenced to 15 years in prison. However, in June 1965, this conviction was overturned in the U.S. Supreme Court decision in *Estes v. Texas,* which upheld Estes's claim that he had not received a fair trial because of intensive television and radio coverage of his trial (including live broadcasting from the courtroom while the trial was in progress). The court ruled in a 5–4 decision that the right to a fair trial overruled the rights of free speech and a free press, and that the mere presence of cameras was a distraction that could affect testimony and that placed additional burdens on the defendant, witness, and jurors. Estes was retried and convicted.

James Byrd, Jr.

James Byrd, Jr. was an African American resident of Texas killed by three white men (Shawn Berry, Lawrence Brewer, and John King) in Jasper, Texas, on June 7, 1998. Byrd was beaten and chained by his ankles to a pickup truck and dragged for several miles until his head was severed from his body. Berry, Brewer, and King dumped Byrd's body near an African American cemetery, where it was discovered by local authorities who found evidence linking the men to the crime; all three were convicted of murder. The brutality of this crime drew national attention and created the impetus for passage, in 2001, of the James Byrd, Jr. Hate Crimes Act in Texas. This law increased penalties for hate crimes against specified groups, including on the basis of sexual preference, race, color, religion, national origin, ancestry, disability, or sex (a 1993 hate crimes law prohibited violence based on group membership but did not define the protected groups, making prosecution difficult). Byrd's murder, along with that of Matthew Shepard (a gay university student in Wyoming murdered in 1998) also spurred passage of the Matthew Shepard and James Byrd, Jr. Hate Crimes Prevention Act in the U.S. Congress. This act broadened federal hate crimes law to include crimes motivated by the victim's disability, gender identity, sexual orientation, or gender; provided funding for the investigation and prosecution of hate crimes; and ordered the Federal Bureau of Investigation (FBI) to collect statistics on hate crimes motivated by the victim's gender or gender identity.

Current Crime Statistics

Texas has a large number of reported crimes, a fact influenced by the state's large population, but the rate of various crimes per 100,000 population is not remarkable: The murder rate of 5.6 per 100,000 in 2008, for instance, is neither particularly high nor low related to other U.S. states (Louisiana had the highest rate of 12.7 per 100,000 and North Dakota the lowest at 0.9 per 100,000 that year). The rate of major crimes (per 100,000 population) in Texas decreased 2.9 percent between 2007 and 2008, with property crimes decreasing 3.2 percent and violent crimes 0.6 percent. In 2008, 969,807 property crimes were reported in Texas along with 123,621 violent crimes. The property crimes include 230,263 burglaries, 645,133 larceny-thefts, and 85,411 motor vehicle thefts. The violent crimes included 1,373 murders, 8,004 rapes, 37,757 robberies, and 76,487 aggravated assaults. In 2008, 6,363 arson offenses were reported with resultant property damage of more than $128 million. There were total arrests of 1,191,155 in 2008, including the arrest of 134,575 juveniles and 1,056,580 adults. There were 246 hate crimes reported in 2008, a 1.2 percent increase from 2007. The most common motivation reported for hate crimes was racial (53 percent, mainly anti-black), followed by sexual orientation (22.3 percent, mainly anti–male homosexual), ethnicity (14.6 percent, mainly anti-Hispanic), and religion (10.1 percent, mainly anti-Jewish). There were 193,505 domestic violence incidents reported in 2008, with the most common offenses being simple assault (73.3 percent), aggravated assault (14.9 percent), intimidation (8.7 percent), forcible fondling (1 percent), and forcible rape (0.9 percent).

Sarah Boslaugh
Kennesaw State University

See Also: 1851 to 1900 Primary Documents; Capital Punishment; Confidence Games and Frauds; *Estes v. Texas*; *Lawrence v. Texas*; *Roe v. Wade*; Texas Rangers; *Texas v. White*.

Further Readings

Guttmacher Institute. http://www.guttmacher.org (Accessed June 2011).
Hackleman, R. "Texas Hate Crime Law Is Rarely Used: State Lawmaker Wants to Know Why." http://www.kxan.com/dpp/news/local/texas-hate-crime-law-is-rarely-used (Accessed June 2011).
Texas Department of Criminal Justice. "Death Row Facts." http://www.tdcj.state.tx.us/stat/drowfacts.htm (Accessed June 2011).
Texas Department of Public Safety. "Crime in Texas: 2008." http://www.txdps.state.tx.us/director_staff/public_information/2008CIT.pdf (Accessed June 2011).
Texas State Historical Association. "The Handbook of Texas Online." http://www.tshaonline.org (Accessed June 2011).
Texas State Library and Archives Commission. "About Texas." http://www.tsl.state.tx.us (Accessed June 2011).

Texas Rangers

In 1823, Stephen F. Austin hired 10 men to ride the range and protect settlers from Indian attacks. These 10 men, known as range riders, were the first organized police force in Texas and perhaps the first mounted militia in the United States. Texas Ranger history is divided into five distinct eras of protecting the frontier, fighting in revolutions and wars, avoiding abolishment, and formal organization.

History

The Texas Rangers were established for the protection of settlers against Indian raids and attacks by Mexican bandits. Additionally, during this first era, 1823–64, Texas Rangers fought in the Battle of San Jacinto, at the Alamo, and in the Texas Revolution, the Mexican–American War, and the Civil War. The Rangers were inactivated after the Civil War, from 1865 to 1870, while Texas was under military protection. The second era of Texas Ranger history occurred from 1865 to 1900. The Reconstruction Republican government's state police of Texas was abolished in 1873, which led to the reestablishment of the Rangers in 1874 by a Democratic legislature. Collecting taxes, monitoring elections, acting as labor mediators, and protecting prisoners from vigilante mobs were some of the duties of a Ranger during this time. During this era, the Texas Rangers distinguished themselves in the El Paso Salt War of 1877 and in various riots.

The third era, 1900 to 1935, saw increases in the two Ranger units in response to protection needs in west Texas and along the Texas-Mexico border. In an attempt to upgrade the professional conduct of individual rangers through better pay, a 1919 investigation revealed allegations of unprofessional conduct and criminal behaviors. Allegations of prisoner torture, drunkenness, disorderly conduct, and the alleged deaths of numerous Mexicans resulted in limitations in the law enforcement authority of the Texas Rangers. More than 1,000 men were on the force, and many were disreputable. As a result of the investigation, Rangers could not initiate investigations, and involvement came in response to requests from other law enforcement agencies.

The fourth era, 1935–70, was a turning point in Ranger history. By 1935, more than 3,000 individuals had received a Texas Ranger badge, either as the friend of a state official or as an honorary ranger. Rapid urbanization was cause for some to believe the Texas Rangers had outlived their usefulness as protectors of the frontier. Others believed in the modernization of the Texas

The Stephen F. Austin monument in the Texas State Cemetery in Austin, Texas. In 1823, Austin hired a group of elite men to ride horseback on the range, protecting settlers from Native American attacks and keeping the peace in the state. They were the first organized police force known in Texas and perhaps the first mounted militia in the United States.

Ranger legend as a part of Texas history. In 1935, the Texas Rangers, along with the Texas Highway Patrol, came under the responsibility of the newly formed Texas Department of Public Safety. The Texas Department of Public Safety resolved key issues that plagued the Texas Rangers. Standardized employment practices were established in the form of set qualifications and promotions based upon ability instead of favoritism. Formalized training became routine for Texas Rangers.

Formal organization, training, and higher standards did not eliminate the threat of abolishment of the Texas Rangers in the fifth era, 1970–2005. The last attempt to abolish the Texas Rangers failed in 1970.

Law enforcement officials and criminals attested to the respect commanded by the presence of a ranger during investigations. This respect showed the investigative abilities of Texas Rangers had evolved from their legendary status.

Duties

The four basic duties of the contemporary Texas Rangers evolved in the 1970s: (1) using criminal state statutes to enforce the laws for protection of life and property; (2) aiding local law enforcement with order maintenance during riots or insurrections; (3) assisting local law enforcement, prosecutors, and the courts with major criminal investigations and other felonies upon request; and (4) aiding in the capture, arrest, and transport of fugitives and prisoners.

Since 1823, the Texas Rangers have protected the Texas frontier and borders, fought in wars, faced abolishment, and reorganized under the Texas Department of Public Safety. As in the past, today's Texas Rangers are few in number and work independently. The focus of the modern-day ranger is interagency cooperation with local, state, federal, and international law enforcement officials. The 70th legislature in 1987 eliminated the threat of abolishment, and the Texas Rangers became a permanent law enforcement agency. In 1993, an amendment to the 1987 statute established the Texas Rangers as a major division in the Texas Department of Public Safety.

Christine A. Nix
University of Mary Hardin-Baylor

See Also: 1851 to 1900 Primary Documents; Political Policing; State Police; Texas.

Further Readings
Bechtel, H. Kenneth. *State Police in the United States: A Socio-Historical Analysis.* Westport, CT: Greenwood Press, 1995.
Calvert, Robert A., et al. *The History of Texas.* Wheeling, IL: Harlan Davidson, 2002.
Fehrenbach, T. R. *Lone Star: A History of Texas and the Texans.* New York: Macmillan, 1968.
Rigler, Erik T. *A Descriptive Study of the Texas Ranger: Historical Overtones on Minority Attitudes.* Huntsville, TX: Sam Houston State University, 1971.
Texas Rangers. "Rangers Today." http://www.texasranger.org/today/rangerstoday.htm (Accessed May 2011).

Texas v. White

Texas v. White, 74 U.S. 700 (1869) was a post–Civil War case heard by the U.S. Supreme Court on February 5, 8, and 9, 1869, and decided by a 5–3 vote on April 12, 1869. The ruling is significant because the Supreme Court decided that the Union was indestructible and states could not secede. The Supreme Court exercised original jurisdiction in this case based on Article III, Section 2, which states that, "In all Cases affecting Ambassadors, other public Ministers and Consuls, and those in which a State shall be Party, the supreme Court shall have original Jurisdiction." The case was argued by George W. Paschal and R. T. Merrick for the state and Philip Philips, Albert Pike, J. W. Carlisle, and J. W. Moore for the defense.

The case involved a claim by the Reconstruction government of Texas that U.S. bonds that had been owned by the state since 1851 had been illegally sold by the Confederate state government during the Civil War. Ten million dollars in bonds had been transferred to Texas by an act of Congress in 1851 to settle border claims following the annexation of Texas in 1845. These bonds were payable to the state of Texas, or to the bearer, and were redeemable in 1864. The state had sold some of the bonds but was still in possession of about $800,000 in bonds at the time of the state's secession from the Union in 1861.

On January 11, 1862, the state legislature approved the creation of the Military Board of Texas (composed of the governor, state comptroller and state treasurer) to sell or exchange state bonds for the purpose of financing the state's war efforts. In their efforts to finance the war, the military board found that munitions suppliers in Mexico and England preferred receiving the U.S. bonds instead of Confederate bonds.

The Texas state legislature authorized the sale of the remaining bonds. A law requiring that the bonds be endorsed by the governor prior to their sale was repealed.

After becoming aware of the planned sale, the U.S. Treasury published a legal notice in the *New York Tribune* that it would not honor any bonds from Texas unless they were endorsed by Sam Houston, who had resigned as the state's governor on March 18, 1861, because he opposed secession. Despite the treasury's public notice, a brokerage owned by George W. White and John Chiles purchased the remaining bonds from the state. The brokerage then resold the bonds to private investors, some of whom were able to redeem the bonds through the U.S. government. When the treasury became aware of the sale, it refused to redeem bonds presented by White.

The government formed pursuant to the Reconstruction Acts filed a lawsuit on February 15, 1867. The Reconstruction government claimed that the state government that existed during the Confederate era was illegal, that the sale of the bonds to White by the military board was illegal, and that the brokerage's subsequent sale of the bonds to other investors was invalid.

White and Chiles raised the issue of jurisdiction. They contended that Texas was not a state; rather, that it was a territory governed under the Military Reconstruction Act and lacked the ability to bring a suit as a "state." White and Chiles also argued that the sale of the bonds, even if conducted by an illegitimate government, was not in violation of the Constitution. The other defendants in the lawsuit, who had purchased the bonds from the brokerage, claimed that they had purchased bonds on the open market and had no way of knowing that the bonds were invalid.

In deciding the case, the court's majority held that the Union was indestructible and that the Constitution did not permit states to secede from the United States, and that the ordinances of secession, and all the acts of the state legislatures of the Confederate states were "absolutely null." The significance of this holding was that the court rejected the doctrine of state sovereignty.

The court's opinion was written by Chief Justice Salmon Chase. Chase considered Texas' relationship to the Union. He rejected the defendants' claim that Texas was not a state at the time that it filed the suit. He wrote that once Texas entered "an already existing indissoluble political body," it could not secede.

Since Texas could not leave the Union, any actions taken to declare secession or to implement the Ordinance of Secession were null and void. This included "acts in furtherance or support of rebellion against the United States, or intended to defeat the just rights of citizens, and other acts of like nature." Chase wrote that the state's relationship (during the Confederacy era) with White and Chiles was "treasonable and void." He ruled that Texas still retained ownership of the bonds and was entitled to either the return of the bonds or a cash payment from those parties who had successfully redeemed the bonds. As a result of the decision, the proceeds from the transferred bonds were turned over to Paschal, as the Texas representative. He claimed all of the proceeds he collected, $47,325, plus $17,577 for his legal fee. Governor Edmund J. Davis refused the claim and fired Paschal. Paschal then sued and won his case and was allowed to keep his fee.

Jeffrey Kraus
Wagner College

See Also: Constitution of the United States of America; Supreme Court, U.S.; Texas.

Further Readings
Hyman, Harold W. *The Reconstruction Justice of Salmon P. Chase: In Re Turner and Texas v. White.* Lawrence: University Press of Kansas, 1997.
Pierson William Whatley, Jr.. "Texas Versus White." *The Southwestern Historical Quarterly,* v.18/4 (1915).
Waller, John L. *Colossal Hamilton of Texas.* El Paso: Texas Western Press, 1968.

Thaw, Harry K.

The son of a Pittsburgh coal and railroad baron, Harry Thaw is best known as the man who murdered famed New York City architect Stanford White. On a summer evening in 1906, Thaw shot White at Madison Square Garden, a building that White had designed. The motive for Thaw's crime was jealous rage over Evelyn Nesbit, the artist model and chorus girl who once had been White's mistress and whom Thaw had married. This "crime of the century" received extensive newspaper coverage and provided spectators with a window into the lives of the upper class.

Even before he married Nesbit, Harry Thaw had been obsessed with White, whom he both envied and hated. Although he was rumored to be a drug addict, Thaw sought out crusading reformer Anthony Comstock to tell him that White was a debaucher of young girls. Both from Pennsylvania, Thaw and Nesbit met in New York City. Nesbit's widowed and impoverished mother had allowed her beautiful teenage daughter to accept employment as a model. Soon, Nesbit was in demand by painters, illustrators, photographers, and advertisers. She was sketched by illustrator Charles Dana Gibson, becoming a "Gibson Girl," the iconic image of the "New Woman." Then Nesbit was hired as a chorus girl in the Broadway musical *Floradora*.

Nesbit caught the eye of Stanford White. Married and in his 40s, White was known for his larger-than-life personality, his lust for living, and his pursuit of young women. At her husband's trial for White's murder, Nesbit, dressed like a schoolgirl, titillated spectators with her lurid account of her drugged rape by White and their subsequent affair. She told of her first visit to White's apartment in the company of another young woman. Nesbit said she had sat in a "red velvet swing" that White would later have her swing in nude after they became lovers. Determined to have Nesbit for himself, Thaw had begun his courtship by sending her flowers and other gifts under an assumed name. He eventually revealed his identity. He was able to make progress in his courtship when Nesbit needed an emergency appendectomy. Thaw sent a physician to perform the operation. Then, he took Nesbit and her mother abroad to allow Nesbit to recuperate.

When her mother left the two of them alone in Europe, Thaw took Nesbit to an isolated German castle. Revealing the sadism that he reportedly had displayed toward other women, Thaw beat Nesbit with a whip. He questioned her about White until Nesbit told him about the rape that had preceded the affair. Nesbit persuaded Thaw to return to New York. She told White what had happened. But in April 1905, she married Thaw and returned with him to Pittsburgh to live with his mother. On June 25, 1906, Thaw and Nesbit were in New York and spent the evening with friends. White dined with his son, who was home from college. Nesbit glimpsed White in a restaurant. Later that evening, both White and the Thaw party were at the rooftop theater at Madison Square Garden for the premiere of a musical *Mam'zelle Champagne*. As an actor sang "I Could Love a Million Girls," Thaw walked over to White's table. Pulling a revolver from beneath his coat, he shot White three times.

Thaw was arrested at the scene of the crime and taken to jail. His family mounted a public relations campaign aimed at portraying White as the seducer of a young and innocent Nesbit. In one of the three plays the family underwrote the villain was "Stanford Black." The hero, "Harold Daw," gave a speech about "the unwritten law" that allowed a man to defend the honor of his wife. During the trial, Thaw's lead defense attorney, Delphin Delmas, argued that Thaw had killed White while in the grips of "Dementia Americana," that form of temporary insanity that any red-blooded man would have experienced when defending the sanctity of his home and avenging his wife.

The first trial ended in a hung jury. During the next trial, Thaw's defense team settled on an insanity plea (rather than a defense of temporary insanity). Thaw's mother testified about her son's irrational behavior and the mental instability in their family. Committed to Matteawan State Hospital for the Criminally Insane, Thaw escaped to Canada. He was deported and returned to the asylum until his release in 1915. He divorced Nesbit but did not give her the money that his mother was supposed to have promised for her testimony. In 1917, Thaw was accused of horsewhipping a 19-year-old boy. He was recommitted to an asylum and released in 1924. He died of a heart attack in Florida in 1947.

Frankie Y. Bailey
State University of New York, Albany

See Also: Insanity Defense; Murder, History of; Rape, History of; Trials.

Further Readings
Linder, Douglas O. "The Trials of Harry Thaw for the Murder of Stanford White, 2009." http://law2.umkc.edu/facullty/projects/ftrials/thaw/Thawaccount.html (Accessed May 2011).
Lutes, Jean Marie. "Sob Sisterhood Revisited." *American Literary History*, v.15/3 (2003).
Umphrey, Martha Merrill. "The Dialogics of Legal Meaning: Spectacular Trials, the Unwritten Law, and Narratives of Criminal Responsibility." *Law & Society Review*, v.33/2 (1999).
Uruburu, Paula. *American Eve: Evelyn Nesbit, Stanford White—The Birth of the "It" Girl and the Crime of the Century*. New York: Riverhead Books, 2008.

Theories of Crime

Theories of crime are defined in relation to modernity, spanning their development from the Enlightenment to the present, with the advent of postmodernism. Modernity involved the search for natural and human-based explanations and reasons for behavior and actions. Theories of crime became scientific in principle if not in practice.

Approaching behavior and seeking explanations in the human world using logic and/or experience and the reduced reliance on a shared set of morals as the primary factor distinguished modern approaches from premodern ones. Postmodern views stress language as a source of power allowing for the dominance of particular theoretical (and methodological) perspectives at the expense of particular ideas and schools of thought. Even postmodernist thinking would similarly criticize the exclusive use of spiritualistic or metaphysical explanations of crime and deviance behind the dynamics of language and culture. Implicitly or indirectly, most explanations for crime and social control use the instrumental model of rationality as the basic condition of modern societies.

This type of rationality permeates all spheres of modern societies and entails determining the best means to achieve particular ends. While factors may be differently presented in these explanatory models, the means of achieving goals in the form of constraints and facilitators toward crime and social control and the ends motivating individuals and ordering the distribution of conditions are always included. Environmental conditions are the other main aspect of criminological theories that are the source of the origins of both means and ends. In particular, criminological explanations include the notion that means and ends are pertinent to any explanation and criminal and social control behaviors operate through instrumental rationality.

Another relevant fact about many criminological perspectives concerns their focus on urban crime and social control. Modern societies moved toward urban dominance in all respects. Intellectually, socially, economically, and politically, ideas and conditions in urban areas were the motor forces of the historical development and evolution of modern societies. From the lens of urban elites of all types as well as governments, explaining crime included understanding the causes and effects of order derived from criminality. While disorder strongly signifies the political nature of deviance in 19th-century Europe and America, the political nature of criminological theories is closely connected to the notion that all theories of crime and deviance are associated with particular theories of social order and social control. Stephen Pfohl and Dario Melossi converge in emphasizing how theoretical images of deviance and social control correspond historically, spatially, and through disciplines. This includes the notions of theories being partial and non-neutral. Historically, the politics of crime control in any given era synchronized with the predominant social controls utilized in the same time period. Spatial patterns and the distribution of crime and its control are also striking. The geographical nature of a large number of criminological theories supports this particular characterization. The disciplinary bases for many criminological theories is vital to their differences in terms of identification and analysis of the main causes of crimes, their effects on individuals and societies, and what are considered to be the proper social control responses. Classical, biological, psychological, and social-psychological theories all share roots in the disciplines of psychology, biology, sociology, or a combination of two or more of these disciplines.

More recent criminological theories are essentially sociological but borrow from geography, cultural studies, philosophy, and political science. Maintaining order through understanding and controlling crime reflects conflicts within society and the need to shape consensus. The bases of order and crime differed historically with criminological theories. Views of order gained through consensus were evolutionary theories, including premodern theories, biological and psychological theories in the 19th century, and social-psychological theories from the 20th century to the present. Conflict views of order saw order maintained through force, selective enforcement of laws, and oppression. Critical and radical theories fall into these categories, with Marxist, feminist, and labeling variants as examples.

Premodern Theories

Order and morals also have earlier historical precedents. Premodern theories were entirely based on religious explanations of why people committed crime and sin, and the appropriate responses to such behaviors largely involved religious punishments. There was a distinct lack of empirical validation of these theories, and punishments were determined solely by elite leaders to counteract supernatural forces driving crime. Ancient and feudal societies were more homogeneous, punishment more public with strong shaming

Psychological theories of crime can include the perspective that differences in behavior may make some people more likely to commit a criminal act. Personality characteristics and biological factors often contribute to these differences.

components, and enforcement and social controls worked mostly through monarchial and community surveillance and monitoring. Most spiritualistic theories converged in equating crime with sin and worked well with smaller-scale, feudal, and homogeneous societies. While criminological theories became more secular, the influence of religion (to a lesser extent) and morals (to a greater extent) still retained their power to the present. Morality expressed itself in many theories but in different ways, whether through effects on individuals, communities, institutions, or the entire society. In this regard, the transition to modern theories, while considerable and transformative, has not been complete and pure. The closeness of demonological and early positivistic theories in 19th-century Europe is a case in point. Biological and sociological positivists in Europe shared with earlier premodern theories the moral failures of criminals and contrasted criminals with noncriminal members of society. Morality and science were then and remain intertwined with major positivistic theories. Criminological theories may have evolved methodologically, but the ideological trajectories to the present demonstrate strong historical roots.

The decisive transitions to modern criminological theories resulted from major societal changes such as urbanization, industrialization, rapid population growth, and the growth of science and technology toward the end of the 18th century. This time period forward also saw the development of the modern system of government. Heterogeneity in morals, work, and thinking were prominent characteristics of modern societies, and this heterogeneous development was the major context within which modern theoretical perspectives developed and evolved. Modern criminological theories distinguished themselves as using and applying reason to develop a fair, consistent, and reasonable system of crime and punishment. The Age of Reason is a common thread and shared set of contextual forces for most all modern theories of crime. Even those perspectives that deemphasize the rationality of behavior operate and utilize a rational, logical methodology, analytical principles, and data collection in positing the irrationality of criminal behavior or the construction of criminality.

Most notably, the normative and idealistic aspects of these theories were not eliminated due to the use of rational thinking and the scientific method. Theories were prescriptive and reflected varied ideological orientations. Individual defects (and moralizing these failures) have been one prominent ideological strain throughout history (the "nature" part of the nature versus nurture controversy). The other major ideological orientation emphasizes nurture factors, making up the environments influencing crime. Based on the prevailing urban conditions responsible for crime, these theoretical perspectives recommended alternatively utilitarian goals of punishment and rehabilitation, which continue to characterize criminological theories (and associated social control components) to the present. The oscillations of exclusionary and inclusionary social controls are direct evidence of the cyclical nature of criminological theories. During times of societal crises, reestablishing order through the state, community, or other social controls signified the dominance of nature approaches. This included harsher deterrence, more retributive, and incapacitation-focused penal systems. In contrast, inclusionary penal systems in more prosperous times emphasize rehabilitation more than deterrence, the need to reform and change to improve criminals and enhance reintegration, and appreciative perspective of deviants and the forces responsible for their criminality. A combination of deterrence, rehabilitation, retribution, and incapacitation underpinned these perspectives in the past and continue to do so today.

Classical and Positivistic Theories

Early modern criminological theories included classical theories emphasizing free will, rationality, and deterrence that developed toward the end of the 18th century and sociological positivistic ones followed in the early 19th century. Crime prevention was a shared focus of these early theories, whether through an analysis of robbers in mid-18th century England conducted by Henry Felding, or the distribution of property and violent crimes conducted by Lambert A. Quetelet and André M. Guerry in continental Europe in the 19th century. Another element of classical theories was the emphasis on social contract between members of society and governmental institutions. The main roles of the state were to provide security and protection of citizen freedoms in exchange for acceptance of punishment if citizens broke this contract. The rights to punish and use force are integral elements of modern legal and criminal justice systems today. The neoclassical model and more recent rational-choice theories are dominant in social science disciplines consistent with the positivist emphasis on application of scientific methods to validate any study.

Marxist and positivist theories developed almost a century later and dominated from the end of the 19th century and continuing to have influence today. The origins of the criminal class and forces responsible for this class were the distinct questions studied by these perspectives and then moved to related questions about the institutional and organizational aspects of crime and social control. These perspectives developed out of the disciplines of political economy in earlier periods and added the growing subfield of law and society in the 20th century. Developing even later, radical and postmodernist perspectives were influential (not as significantly as the classical and positivist approaches) from the 20th century onward. Not part of mainstream criminology, these perspectives blossomed in the 1960s, a period of significant economic, political, and cultural changes in Europe and North America. Building on detailed studies of modern societies and their social control systems, these theories concentrated on how a significant amount of crime and deviance was directly caused by the actions of social control institutions and actors and powerful groups in society pressuring formal social control agencies to selectively enforce laws.

Three overarching philosophical frameworks with distinct historical evolutions are the main sources of most existing criminological and criminal justice theories today: classical, positivist, and legal (social control) behaviorist. Within these frameworks, there are numerous internal divisions. However, the divisions between and across theories are not absolute. Rather, these theoretical frameworks have considerable overlap and their historical development followed trajectories based on existing conditions of modern society and, particularly, the shared intellectual heritage (including the importance of empirical validation, development and testing of concepts, and collective debates about the validity and utility of theories as well as associated methodologies). Theories are grounded in what is considered commonsense views of criminality and appropriate social control responses. By providing rationalizations to criminal justice policy and practice, theoretical perspectives were consistent and supported visions of crime and social control.

In relation to the extremist tendencies of these broader theoretical frameworks, David Matza noted the tendency to polarize classical and positivist approaches (even by theorists from each camp) and the ensuing overgeneralizations and problems that resulted from these practices. A prominent example is the common practice of stressing the discontinuities between classical and positivist approaches, which is not consistent with the historical record. The classical approach emphasizes human agency and exercise of free will, but also recognizes the positivist focus on external factors on behavior (albeit the particular constraints are different between the two approaches). Similarly, the positivist emphasis on causality and deterministic explanations was easily accommodated with the emphasis on deterrence and free will operating in conjunction whereby external forces influence individual decision making.

Social Control and Environmental Theories
The growth of capitalism and the modern nation-state, along with the development of ideas accompanying the growth of science, were pertinent realities for both these theoretical schools of thought. The political imperative of controlling crime grew with the development of the legal and criminal justice systems in Europe and America. Classicism emphasized the political aspects of crime, and positivism and radicalism jointly centered on the threats to order from growing inequalities in industrial societies. Even radical perspectives are not necessarily incompatible with classical and positivist approaches, as the emphasis remains on understanding the social determinants of criminal behavior from the actions and exercise of power of dominant societal actors. The legal social control behaviorist perspectives, in the same vein, discuss the determinants of choices driving law enforcement and criminality and the relevant environmental conditions that are influential in these choices. The common thread across seemingly divergent perspectives is use of a choice and conditions (environments providing constraints or facilitators for actors) model of criminality and social control with differing emphasis on the choice and conditions aspects behind criminal and social control behavior. Structural approaches focus on environmental conditions, which are the sources for means and ends in different forms in criminological theories. The selection of conditions, means, and ends varies across criminological theories and many perspectives simply assume away either of these components as being uniform or unimportant. For example, many individual positivistic and classical theories simply posit environmental conditions in a static fashion being a fixed set of parameters in their theories. Alternatively, structural theories assume that variations in individual characteristics are unimportant for explaining crime rates.

The classical perspective shares with individualistic-centered positivistic theories the emphasis on attributes of individuals and differences between criminals and noncriminals as being critical to explaining crime and criminality. These include 19th-century biological theories and 20th-century psychological, social-psychological, sociological, and rational-choice theories. These theories are closer to the historically dominant volitional criminological model of modern criminal justice (crime is a product of free choices requiring appropriate responses and environmental factors are ignored in this model). Explaining criminality and the incidence of crime in individuals are the main goals of these approaches. Surprisingly, some radical and postmodernist theories also pay attention to individual-level factors and choices, although extra-individual processes and structural contexts are also stressed. Process-level factors bridge these micro individualistic theories with more macro structural ones.

Structural theories mainly examine the organization of society and environmental conditions as being critical to explaining major crime and social control patterns. These perspectives are radical and positivistic (even combined), emerging in the late 19th century and intensifying in the 20th century. Whether Marxist or Durkheimian versions, these schools of thought coincided with the transformation of societies, the concentration of economic and political power, and the development of mass production and consumption. Based heavily in sociology and political science, these approaches highlight the aggregate distributions of crime and social control within and across societies as products of the arrangements of society in terms of values, status, class, and other related dimensions. Unlike individualistic theories, rates of crime are the main dependent variable. Macro theories remain popular in academic criminology but have been less so with criminal justice practitioners due to their emphasis on the societal origins of crime and social control. From the view of practitioners and policy makers, changing these conditions is extremely difficult and beyond their control. The political economy of crime policy and practice, coupled with the cultural constraints, limit wholesale adoption of macro-structural policies. Crime control policy and practice is heavily skewed toward status quo approaches that warrant traditional individualistic/legal views of crime and traditional individualized social control responses. Criminological history has been covertly a history of competing theories at different levels of analyses. Microtheories have won these historical battles for the most part with some notable exceptions. From the end of the 19th century to the 1960s, critical and radical theories dominated.

Modern Trends

Recent theoretical trends are toward use of integrated and developmental crime theory perspectives. Integrating theories has been proposed as recognition that crime is a result of a combination of multiple factors rather than by unifactorial approaches become prevalent throughout criminological theories. Integration has been impeded by recognition that theories are better suited for explaining specific aspects of crime and do not operate at the same level of analysis. The origins of developmental theories lie with the attention given to career criminals and the need to understand the developmental processes translating crime at younger ages into serious criminality at later stages of criminal career. This trend is consistent with academic criminology being driven by policy and practical concerns. Other, more recent criminological perspectives such as routine activities and environmental criminological theories similarly cater to the needs to understand, explain, and control crime patterns impacting the formal criminal justice apparatus of modern societies. Developmental and integrated theories remain tied to the dominant social control and physical environmental crime theories today, as well as consistent with historical variants of these theories in classical and positivistic forms.

Most of the differences among theoretical perspectives, historically to the present, are overplayed and those promoting the inherent incompatibilities and discontinuities fail to recognize each perspective developed concurrently and involved active exchange and interplay between different theoreticians responding to the same historical conditions of their time. A persistent theme in each criminological perspective involved detailed examination of changing forms of criminality and social control. In early modern classical and positivist theories, serious property and violent crimes were being discovered as following particular trends in society. Vagrancy was treated as a direct threat to capitalism and violence in dense, crowded, and anonymous settings threatened social stability and predictability vital for modern living. Later modern theories, especially those developed in the 20th century, moved to looking at the institutional and technological aspects of crime and social control with specific attention to how socioeconomic diversity posed distinct challenges to understanding and controlling crime. Most changes took a significant amount of time to develop as well as had uneven impacts, which was reflected in the significant overlap between different criminological theories. Most theoretical frameworks and perspectives evolved over long periods of time and were modifications of prior theories to changed historical conditions.

The long historical progression of criminological theories with associated continuities and discontinuities can be better understood through a deprivation and control framework. Most current theories trace their roots back to earlier theories emphasizing individual moral, psychological, and biological deprivations to macro social, economic, political, and cultural deprivations in later theories. Premodern and 19th-century-based theories favored the micro deprivations perspective with emphasis on restoration of formal governmental and community controls or, for the worst criminals, incapacitation or sterilization. Institutions emphasized in these theories include family, peers, community, and socialization ones in general but all of them are linked ultimately to individual deprivations. Modern-day versions of these theories include social control, social disorganization, routine activities, and rational-choice theories.

The other major deprivation and control perspective historically to the present is environment focused. Twentieth-century criminological theories began to focus more on macro social deprivations (or a combination of deprivations particularly micro psychological ones) and penal reform and rehabilitation as the main forms of control. This continued even with more radical and critical theories developed more recently that moved to cultural and political deprivations. The associated controls required for addressing macro deprivations include economic and political investments, emphases on treatment and rehabilitation, and reduced reliance on formal social controls as well as traditional familial and community social controls. Classical, positivistic, and legal behaviorist perspectives of both the micro and macro variety share the need to use particular control types and strategies. While many do not view positivism and critical theories as control-oriented perspectives, these types of theories along with classical ones have promoted the use of particular controls academically and normatively. The history of crime theories and social control can be fruitfully seen as between a history of integration and separation.

The current state of criminological theorizing exhibits theoretical and methodological pluralism. Historically to the present, pluralism has not meant equal influence of each theoretical perspective over time and across space but rather dominance and influence of particular theoretical perspectives during specific time periods and for specific areas. Criminology has become more utilitarian over time and serves the legal and criminal justice systems more directly. Crime has become a prominent political issue and can be used to justify particular ideological and political agendas. The emergence of permanent and extensive criminal justice systems in modern societies has resulted in the favoring and dominance by particular criminological theoretical perspectives. The perspectives favoring family and traditional institutions of social control have stronger currency today than they did 40 years ago.

Sanjay Marwah
Guilford College

See Also: Corruption, Sociology of; Criminology; Morality.

Further Readings
Bernard, Thomas J., Jeffrey B. Snipes, and Alexander L. Gerould. *Vold's Theoretical Criminology*. Oxford: Oxford University Press, 2010.
Melossi. Dario. *Controlling Crime, Controlling Society: Thinking About Crime in Europe and America*. Cambridge: Polity Press, 2008.
Mutchnick, Robert J., Randy Martin, and W. Timothy Austin. *Criminological Thought: Pioneers Past and Present*. Upper Saddle River, NJ: Pearson Education, 2008.
Pfohl, Stephen. *Images of Deviance and Social Control: A Sociological History*. New York: McGraw-Hill, 1994.

Thoreau, Henry David

A renowned transcendentalist writer and radical, Henry David Thoreau was born on July 12, 1817, in Concord, Massachusetts, where he spent most of his life. He is best known for his essay "Resistance to Civil Government" (1849), a provocative assertion of individualism, and the book *Walden; or, Life in the Woods* (1854), a reflection on the spiritual value of simple living. Thoreau started his intellectual career in 1837 after he graduated from Harvard University and returned to Concord. He befriended Ralph Waldo Emerson, a prominent cultural figure, and other well-known writers in Emerson's circle. At his suggestion, Thoreau started to write essays for Emerson's journal *The Dial*.

Walden grew out of Thoreau's personal experience; in the summer of 1845, he constructed a small house by the Walden Pond, on Emerson's

This portrait of Henry David Thoreau is by Benjamin D. Maxham from 1856. There are over 20 volumes of Thoreau's writings in books, articles, essays, journals, and poetry.

property, and lived in it for over two years. His goal was, among other things, to prove the benefits of uncomplicated living. He spent most of his time there observing nature and writing his diary, which served as a basis for *Walden*. The central point of the book can be summed up in the following refrain: "Simplicity, simplicity, simplicity!" Thoreau condemned the increasing sophistication of his age, particularly technological innovations and industrialization, because in his view it undermined individual independence and connection with nature.

Some of Thoreau's comments in *Walden* invite readers today to compare his views to that of Ted Kaczynski, the Unabomber, a Harvard-educated mathematician who gave up his stellar academic career to move to rural Montana, from where he waged a bloody campaign against modern technology. The similarities between Thoreau's and Kaczynski's views, however, are superficial. There is at least one major difference between them—Thoreau was not a proponent of violence.

Thoreau was noted for his political radicalism and support for such controversial figures as John Brown. His essay "Resistance to Civil Government," which was later republished under the more memorable title "Civil Disobedience," offers a provocative argument about man's relation to the state. Thoreau asserted that the value of individual freedom always outweighs the interest of the state. He wholeheartedly believed that it is up to individuals to determine whether they can tolerate the state's power rather than for the state to determine whether it can tolerate individual freedom. In one of the most provocative passages in his essay, he went so far as to declare that governments should not govern at all.

"Resistance to Civil Government," which grew out of Thoreau's lecture "The Rights and Duties of the Individual in Relation to Government," was inspired by Thoreau's brief imprisonment for refusing to pay the poll tax. The episode took place in 1846, at the beginning of the Mexican–American War (1846–48), while Thoreau still lived at Walden Pond. His refusal to pay the tax was prompted by his opposition to the war, which he believed was completely unwarranted. What is more, Thoreau, like many other Americans, was convinced that the war reinforced the institution of slavery in the United States. As an ardent abolitionist, he argued that the government had no right to force him to pay taxes, which could be used to finance the war fought for the benefit of slave owners.

Thoreau was also a vehement opponent of the Fugitive Slave Act (1850), which required northerners to return runaway slaves to their owners. On several occasions, Thoreau flaunted the fact that he aided fugitive slaves. In 1854, he delivered a speech in support of the runaway slave Anthony Burns, whose trial and extradition to the south generated much controversy.

Thoreau's radicalism was even more apparent in his reaction to John Brown's raid on the federal armory at Harpers Ferry, Virginia, in 1859. Brown, a militant and controversial abolitionist, was captured after an unsuccessful attempt to start a slave rebellion in the south. The episode provoked uproar throughout the country. The public opinion, in both the south and the north, was clearly against Brown, who was decried as a fanatic and criminal. Even in the abolitionist circles, his actions were condemned as misguided and even insane. Thoreau was only one of few well-known figures to publicly defend John Brown. Prior to Brown's execution in December of the same year, Thoreau delivered a series of lectures that served as the basis for his essay "A Plea for Captain John Brown" (1860).

Alexander Moudrov
Queens College, City University of New York

See Also: Anarchists; Kaczynski, Ted; Literature and Theater, Crime in; Literature and Theater, Punishment in; Massachusetts.

Further Readings
Harding, Walter R. *The Days of Henry Thoreau: A Biography*. Princeton, NJ: Princeton University Press, 1962.
Richardson, Robert D., Jr. *Henry Thoreau: A Life of the Mind*. Berkeley: University of California Press, 1988.
Thoreau, Henry David. *The Complete Works of Ralph Waldo Emerson & Henry David Thoreau*. Seattle, WA: CreateSpace, 2008.
Thoreau, Henry David. *Walden and Civil Disobedience*. Los Angeles, CA: Empire Books, 2011.

Three Strikes Law

A three strikes law is a criminal provision intended to incapacitate serious, repeat offenders that a number of states passed beginning in the mid-1990s. These initiatives epitomize the selective incapacitation movement (which sought to protect the public from potentially violent and repeat offenders) and the "get tough on crime" movement in general. Although states vary as to which crimes and offenders three strike provisions apply, the penalty for conviction of a third strike offense is typically severe and often results in life imprisonment. States have had habitual offender provisions on the books for many decades. Laws passed under the label of three strikes were generally broader than the older laws, but the three strikes movement was largely symbolic in many states. However, in some states such as California, three strikes provisions significantly expanded existing habitual offender laws and brought about noticeable changes in sentencing practices.

The three strikes movement began in Washington State, which passed the first three strikes law in 1993; other states followed suit and by 1996, almost half of the states and the federal government had passed new legislation under the three strikes banner. Much of the impetus behind the movement came from media attention given to horrendous crimes committed by repeat offenders such as in California, where 12-year-old Polly Klaas was kidnapped and murdered in 1993 by Richard Allen Davis. Davis had an extensive criminal past, and the attention given this tragic crime committed by a repeat offender who had been released from prison caused public outrage that eventually led to the adoption of three strikes in California. Similar high-profile (yet atypical) incidents contributed to a spirit of moral panic, which provided support for various get-tough initiatives, including three strikes.

States differ greatly in how and against whom the laws apply, including how many previous felonies are required to "strike out," what types of crimes are considered strikes, and what happens upon conviction of a third strike. In some states, only serious violent offenses qualify as a strike, but in others a number of crimes are counted as strikes, including property offenses and drug possession. In many states, a third strike brings a life sentence (with or without the possibility of parole, depending on the jurisdiction), while others mandate a long specified sentence enhancement (e.g., 30 years), and still others leave the penalty enhancement to the discretion of the judge. In some states, three strikes laws are actually two strikes laws—offenders convicted of a second qualifying strike offense can be incarcerated for life under the provisions.

Three strikes laws have been criticized for being ineffective at controlling crime, contributing to serious corrections concerns such as prison overcrowding and an aging prison population, and even for increasing homicide rates in jurisdictions that adopt the laws. As for the first concern, studies generally have failed to find any crime-reducing results from three strikes laws. The laws do not appear to deter would-be offenders, and any incapacitating effects are too small to impact overall offending rates. As to the second criticism, the laws may be an unwise use of resources, since third strikes are invoked against older offenders. Criminologists generally agree that criminal offenders eventually age out of crime—that is, as criminals grow older, they tend to desist from serious offending. Three strikes laws may be putting away offenders for life at the time when incapacitation will be least effective: just as they are about to age out of offending. Incarcerating older offenders for decades may also put a strain on corrections budgets since, as these offenders advance in age, their medical care needs become increasingly costly. Finally, studies have found that homicide rates tend to increase in jurisdictions that pass three strikes laws. It is possible that an offender with two strikes is more willing to use violence against victims, potential witnesses, and even police in order to lower the likelihood of being identified, captured, and convicted for a third strike offense.

Rhys Hester
University of South Carolina

See Also: Incapacitation, Theory of; Sentencing; Sentencing: Indeterminate Versus Fixed.

Further Readings
Auerhahn, Kathleen. "Selective Incapacitation, Three Strikes, and the Problem of Aging Prison

Populations: Using Simulation Modeling to See the Future." *Criminology & Public Policy*, v.1/3 (2002).

Clark, John, James Austin, and D. Alan Henry. "'Three Strikes and You're Out': Are Repeat Offender Laws Having Their Anticipated Effects?" *Judicature*, v.81/4 (1998).

Kovandzic, Tomislav V., John J. Sloan III, and Lynne M. Vieraitis. "Unintended Consequences of Politically Popular Sentencing Policy: The Homicide-Promoting Effects of 'Three Strikes' in U.S. Cities (1980–1999)." *Criminology & Public Policy*, v.1/3 (2002).

To Kill a Mockingbird

To Kill a Mockingbird is one of those rare novels that, like *Uncle Tom's Cabin,* was a widely acclaimed work of social criticism that also exposed the injustice in the criminal justice system in America. It gave a realistic and very unflattering portrayal of the criminal courts in America. The book was written by Harper Lee (1926–) and was published in 1960. Lee was awarded the Pulitzer Prize for her work, which became a classic and is today required reading in many schools across the nation. Interestingly, it is the only work to be published by Lee. Lee was born and raised in Alabama. As *To Kill a Mockingbird* is focused on racial injustice, it has been suggested that Lee's work encompasses her own observations and experiences in the south.

During the 1920s and 1930s, it was very difficult for African Americans in the south. It was during this time period in 1931 that the infamous Scottsboro Boys cases were decided. Nine African American boys were arrested in Alabama and charged with the rape of two white girls. The case became a national *cause célèbre*, with numerous trials and appeals involving, among other things, the use of all-white juries. Some of the boys were eventually convicted and sent to prison.

Art Mirrors Life

To Kill a Mockingbird is a story about the arrest and trial of an African American man, Tom Robinson, accused of raping a white girl in the south. The main character is Atticus Finch, a white man and a local attorney in a small southern town. Atticus had two children, a boy named Jem and a girl named Scout. The book employs a literary device of having Scout narrate the events. When Atticus is appointed by the court to defend Tom Robinson, he agrees.

Atticus and his children are repeatedly harassed because of Atticus's acceptance of the case. The town is very angry with Atticus and about the incident. At one point, Atticus barely prevents a lynching of Tom Robinson at the jail. The trial is a classic example of racial injustice in the south during this time period. Scout and Jem watch the trial from the African American balcony, as their father did not want them to attend. Atticus is able to prove that the girl and her father, who is the town drunk, are lying about the incident, and Atticus presents significant evidence to show that Tom Robinson is innocent. Despite the evidence, Tom Robinson is convicted by the all-white jury. Unfortunately, while Atticus is starting an appeal, Tom Robinson is shot while trying to escape from jail.

As a literary technique, Lee presented Scout as an independent observer of the events that transpired surrounding Robinson's arrest, trial, and escape. The technique significantly added to the impact and credibility of the novel, as Scout, being a young girl, would not have and had not developed the racist attitudes that were so prevalent in the south at that time. Further, Scout presented a figure of innocence who was trying to understand the obvious injustice that was occurring. Even Scout, who dearly loved her father, Atticus, had to be told by an elderly African American to rise after the trial when her father was passing. Not even Scout, for all of her love for her father, understood what a great and honorable act Atticus had performed by representing Robinson.

One of the great and terrible ironies of the novel was that Robinson was killed trying to escape after he was convicted. Robinson, to avoid the great injustice of having been convicted for a crime he did not commit, was then visited with the even greater injustice of being killed by trying to save his own life when trying to escape the first injustice.

To Kill a Mockingbird had a significant and long-lasting effect on American society and the criminal justice system. It has been cited as one of the best literary examples of racial injustice in America. As it was published in the 1960s, its effect on subsequent civil rights legislation and judicial decisions has been acknowledged. Moreover, Atticus Finch has been used as an example of what the practice of law is, ethically and ideally, all about. In 1962, the book was made into a critically acclaimed movie starring Gregory Peck. The movie was nominated for numerous Oscars and won three. Despite its acclaim, the book has been subjected to numerous attempts to censor it and remove it from the shelves of public libraries.

Wm. C. Plouffe, Jr.
Independent Scholar

See Also: African Americans; Civil Rights Laws; Literature and Theater, Crime in; Scottsboro Boys Cases.

Further Readings
Johnson, Claudia. *Understanding* To Kill a Mockingbird: *A Student Casebook to Issues, Sources, and Historic Documents*. Westport, CT: Greenwood Press, 1994.
Lee, Harper. *To Kill a Mockingbird*. Philadelphia: J. B. Lippincott and Co, 1960.
Murphy, Mary, ed. *Scout, Atticus, and Boo: A Celebration of Fifty Years of* To Kill a Mockingbird. New York: HarperCollins, 2010.
Noble, Don, ed. *Critical Insights:* To Kill a Mockingbird. Pasadena, CA: Salem Press, 2010.

Tocqueville, Alexis de

Alexis Charles Henri Clerel de Tocqueville (1805–59) was a 19th-century French political theorist, historian, writer, and politician best known for his two-volume study of America, *Democracy in America*. Between May 1831 and February 1832, de Tocqueville and his friend, Gustave de Beaumont, toured the United States to investigate the applicability of the country's two main penal systems (the Pennsylvania system and the New York system) for adoption in the prisons of France; their report *Du système pénitentiare aux Etats-Unis, et de son application en France* (*On the Penitentiary System in the United States and Its Application in France*), published in 1833 in two volumes, strongly recommended that the French government adopt the Pennsylvania system.

De Tocqueville was born in July 1805; his father, Herve Louis Francois Jean Bonaventure Clerel, Comte de Tocqueville, was an officer of King Louis XVI's Constitutional Guard and was later noble prefect under the Bourbon Restoration. At age 25, de Tocqueville entered parliament, representing the Manche department for 21 years. The following year, France's July monarchy commissioned de Tocqueville and Beaumont to visit the United States in order to examine the country's prisons and penitentiaries. This visit, in addition to providing the information for *Du système pénitentiare aux Etats-Unis, et de son application en France*, also resulted in de Tocqueville's famed *De la Démocratie en Amerique* (*Democracy in America*), which was published in 1835. In addition to his observational tour of the United States, de Tocqueville visited England, about which he wrote *Memoir on Pauperism and Algeria*, which inspired his *Travail sur l'Algérie* (*Report on Algeria*). Following the revolution of February 1848, de Tocqueville was elected to France's Constituent Assembly, where he served on the commission that drafted the Constitution of the Second Republic. The following year, he served briefly as minister of foreign affairs but left government in 1851 after opposing Napoleon II's coup. He died in April 1859.

De Tocqueville is considered by scholars to be among the most perceptive observers of American politics and culture, and *Democracy in America* is still widely read today (it has never been out of print). De Tocqueville was particularly impressed by what he considered the relative social equality he found in the United States. Though de Tocqueville was generally enthusiastic about American politics and supported the democratic movement, he observed in the early 1830s (he later called himself "… an old and sincere friend of America"), he was under no illusion about the challenges facing the new nation, including the need to resolve the clear tension between equality, democracy, capitalism, and slavery.

Paul Kahan
Montgomery County Community College

See Also: Eastern State Penitentiary; Pennsylvania System of Reform; Sing Sing Correctional Facility.

Further Readings
Brogan, Hugh. *Alexis de Tocqueville: A Life.* New Haven, CT: Yale University Press, 2008.
Elster, Jon. *Alexis de Tocqueville: the First Social Scientist.* Cambridge, MA: Cambridge University Press, 2009.
Tocqueville, Alexis de. *Democracy in America.* Des Moines, IA: Library of America, 2004.

Torrio, John

Mentor to Al Capone and organizer of what would later grow to become Chicago's "Outfit," Torrio was born near Naples and came to the United States with his parents at the age of 2. Torrio grew up on Manhattan's Lower East Side and soon became the leader of the James Street Boys, part of New York's infamous Five Points Gang. Known as "Terrible Johnny," Torrio, small in stature, had nevertheless acquired a fierce reputation as a tough, cold, and calculating young man, adept with his fists or weapons and able to inflict severe punishment on those who crossed him. After working for a time as a bouncer, Torrio became connected to a brothel/bar in Brooklyn in the early 1910s and soon expanded his criminal activities to include hijacking and drugs. He also became an associate of two other gangsters who would figure prominently later in his life: Frankie Yale, co-owner with Torrio of a bar in Coney Island, and one of their employees, a teenage thug named Al Capone.

Torrio occasionally traveled to Chicago at the behest of prostitution kingpin James (Big Jim; Diamond Jim) Colosimo, to whom Torrio was distantly related through Colosimo's wife. Colosimo, a flashy and ostentatious gangster, had made his fortune by running his wife's prostitution business. He also ran the immensely popular and successful Colosimo's Café, patronized by Chicago's elite society. Because of his lavish lifestyle, Colosimo had begun being harassed by a local Black Hand extortion gang and called on Torrio to help. Torrio led the extortionists into

Dumping wine from barrels to avoid detection in 1921. John Torrio was one of the first gangsters to see the money making potential presented by the new Prohibition law.

an ambush, where his hired guns, led by Yale, had been dispatched to end Colosimo's extortion problem. Staying on in Chicago, Torrio, by this time, was not only soon running Big Jim's criminal enterprise, he was also expanding and building Colosimo's business and soon brought his young protégé, Capone, to Chicago to assist him. Also known as "the Brain" and "the Fox" by this time, as much for his business acumen as for the violence of his younger days in New York, Torrio was quick to spot the moneymaking potential presented by the new Prohibition law, making the manufacture, sale, and distribution of alcohol illegal in the United States. Colosimo, however, was not convinced and, content with his income from the prostitution business and his café, refused to let Torrio enter the bootlegging market. Torrio, for his part, was sure that bootlegging would help him build a criminal empire and once again brought former associate Yale to Chicago, this time to carry out Colosimo's murder.

Torrio's bootlegging idea was a good one, and with Capone as his assistant, was soon bringing in millions of dollars. With his success, however, came competition, and Torrio was soon involved in a struggle to control Chicago's illegal booze market with others, most notably, Dion O'Banion's North Side organization. In 1924, feigning a peace overture, O'Banion double-crossed Torrio in the sale of a brewery, and Torrio decided to have O'Banion killed, touching off a bloody conflict between the rival gangs. In late 1925, in retaliation for their leader's murder, O'Banion's men lay in wait for Torrio as he returned from a shopping trip with his wife. When they left, Torrio's body lay riddled with bullets, but the resilient Torrio was still alive, barely. He fought back and eventually recovered but had enough of the gang lifestyle.

After his recovery, Torrio left Chicago and retired, turning over his entire organization to Capone. The legacy he left behind has been heralded as a solid business organization and criminal enterprise that set Al Capone up as arguably the nation's most notorious gangster, an organization that would endure for decades and would come to be known as "the Outfit," and would influence national, international, and political events in the 1950s and 1960s under the leadership of Sam Giancana. Torrio eventually returned to New York, where, although "retired," he came to be looked upon as somewhat of an elder statesman of the Mafia underworld, his advice sought by Charles "Lucky" Luciano and other top Mafia bosses throughout the years. Torrio died of natural causes in 1957 at the age of 75.

Paul Magro
Ball State University

See Also: Bootlegging; Capone, Al; Chicago, Illinois; Illinois; Italian Americans; Organized Crime, History of; Organized Crime, Sociology of; Prohibition.

Further Readings
Abadinsky, Howard. *Organized Crime*. Belmont, CA: Wadsworth, 2010.
McPhaul, Jack. *Johnny Torrio: First of the Gang Lords*. New Rochelle, NY: Arlington House, 1971.
My Al Capone Museum. http://www.myal caponemuseum.com/index.htm (Accessed December 2010).
Ness, Eliot and Oscar Fraley. *The Untouchables*. New York: Popular Library, 1960.
Roth, Mitchell P. *Organized Crime*. Upper Saddle River, NJ: Pearson Education, 2010.
Sifakis, Carl. *The Mafia Encyclopedia*. New York: Checkmark Books, 1999.

Torture

In the modern world, torture is almost universally condemned by civilized nations and societies as a barbaric practice. Yet even in modern times, torture still occurs, and with much greater frequency than the average person would feel comfortable accepting. Despite the commonly held opinion, at least among Americans, that the United States is the world leader when it comes to freedom, liberty, and individual rights, torture has been and does continue to be practiced in and by the United States of America.

Torture has been used throughout history. The ancient Egyptians used torture against prisoners of war. In ancient Greece, both slaves and prisoners of war were subject to torture, although the Greeks rarely resorted to the torture of free citizens. Torture was also freely used against slaves and foreigners and for treason by the ancient Romans, although it was used for crimes in Rome's later years. During medieval times, torture was institutionalized by the Catholic Church through the infamous Inquisition. Torture was also employed by the medieval lords, who had absolute authority over their subjects. Starting in the 12th century, torture became legitimized in many European nations. Reform movements resulting from the work of such notable intellectuals as the French philosopher and writer Voltaire and the Italian criminologist Cesare Beccaria, who wrote *On Crimes and Punishments*, culminated in the general abolition of torture in the 18th century. Despite this enlightened step, in modern times, torture has once again assumed the mantle of official policy. During the 20th century, torture was an official tool of the German Nazis and the Communists of the Soviet Union. The use of torture, unfortunately, has not been limited to tyrannical states but is also employed by "civilized" nations such as the United States of America, as so sadly illustrated by the scandals of Abu Ghraib prison and Guantanamo Bay.

Today, torture is prohibited by numerous national and international laws and treaties. The primary international treaty on torture is the Convention Against Torture. The United States is a signatory to the convention. Further, the United States prohibits torture as a criminal act under Title 18 U.S.C. §§ 2340, 2340A, and 2340B. The

1810 Torture

United States also defines torture as a war crime under Title 18 U.S.C. § 2441. It is also considered a war crime under international law.

Definitions

Torture is not an easy term to define. Since the scandals of Guantanamo Bay, Abu Ghraib prison, and extraordinary rendition in the United States to other countries so that extreme torture may be inflicted on prisoners that would otherwise not be done in the United States, politicians, academics, and the law have failed to adequately define torture. Indeed, the recent public criticisms of the Bush administration tend to gloss over what constituted torture. In fact, the issue of defining torture became an international political nightmare for the administration of George W. Bush, when memos written by his advisers, including John Yoo and Jay Bybee, provided a very limited definition of torture that allowed physical and psychological abuse of persons just short of death.

The Convention Against Torture defines torture as "any act by which severe pain or suffering, whether physical or mental, is intentionally inflicted on a person for such purposes as obtaining from him or a third person information or a confession, punishing him for an act he or a third person has committed or suspected of having committed, or intimidating or coercing him or a third person, or for any reason based on discrimination of any kind, when such pain or suffering is inflicted by or at the instigation of or with the consent or acquiescence of a public official or other person acting in an official capacity. It does not include pain or suffering only from, inherent to or incidental to lawful sanctions." In the United States, under Title 18 U.S.C. § 2340, it is a crime to commit torture, which is defined as "an

The Salem witch trials were held to prosecute people accused of witchcraft in Massachusetts between 1692 and 1693. Women who were suspected of witchcraft were strapped to a stool over a body of water and dunked until they either confessed or died. If the suspect died, she was found innocent, although it was little consolation.

act committed by a person acting under the color of law specifically intended to inflict serve physical or mental pain or suffering (other than pain or suffering incidental to lawful sanctions) upon another person within his custody or control."

Unfortunately, these definitions do not state what specific acts constitute torture. However, if only specific acts were listed, an unscrupulous and imaginative government official could avoid a criminal charge of torture by simply devising a new method of inflicting pain.

Methods

Some of the better known historical methods of torture include the rack, in which a person was strapped to a table and tied to wheels at both ends, whereupon the victim was stretched until his joints were dislocated; the strappado, in which a person's arms were tied behind his back, and then he was tied to a rope through a pulley attached to the ceiling and then hung until his shoulders were dislocated; the Iron Maiden, which was an iron coffin with spikes in the interior side of the hinged cover, which would be slowly closed on the subject inside; the ripping out of finger- and toenails; the burning of flesh; the blinding of people with hot irons; the attachment and activation of electric cables to a person's genitalia; and the deprivation of food, water, and sleep.

More modern techniques of torture involve waterboarding, the use of high technology to facilitate the infliction of pain listed above, and psychological methods. Two example, of psychological torture were employed by the United States against Islamic prisoners by forcing them to eat pork or by having a female pretend to rub the subject with menstrual blood.

Using waterboarding, which simulates torture, as an example of torture the Bush administration employed it as a lawful interrogation technique, even though most authorities consider it a form of torture. For example, at the end of World War II, Japanese military officers were executed for employing waterboarding and U.S. military personnel, prior to the Bush administration, have been court-martialed and punished for employing it.

Justifications

In recent times, the debate concerning the propriety of torture is whether it is justified in the face of modern threats such as terrorism and the use of weapons of mass destruction. Some people hold the position that torture is justified to prevent possible terrorist attacks. The primary justification for this position is the balancing of the harms done to a few people subjected to torture against the potential harms of hundreds or thousands of people dying from a nuclear, chemical, or biological attack. Most civilized authorities and laws in the modern world take the position that torture is never justified.

One of the major issues concerning torture is extraordinary rendition. This occurs when a nation in which torture is prohibited transfers its prisoners to other countries for interrogation, where the receiving country permits torture. Thus, the renditing country is able to receive all of the "benefits" of having its prisoner tortured to, among other things, reveal needed information without having to be liable for the crime of torture. This rationalization, however, does not account for accomplice liability or conspiracy, which would result in the renditing country being criminally liable. This situation occurred during the Bush administration, which had authorized and employed extraordinary rendition for enemy combatants in the war on terror, resulting in a political firestorm.

As previously stated, American citizens prefer to view their country as a nation that rises above such cruel and inhumane practices as torture. Unfortunately, the history of the United States is replete with examples of institutionalized torture. It is impossible to list every example of torture that has occurred in American history, but a brief chronology of events demonstrates its historical widespread use and acceptance in American society.

The Colonists and Early America

When America was first colonized by English citizens attempting to escape religious persecution in England, many of these new colonists were religious zealots who were very strict in their observance of religious laws. In many of the new colonies, people who broke the law were often subject to punishments or even inquisitorial techniques that would be considered torture today. For example, for minor offenses, violators could be sentenced to the stocks, which were wooden constructs that held the subject in place by locking his/her hands and/or feet in the device, keeping the subject in either a sitting or standing position, sometimes for days. The subject would then be abused by the village populace with insults, mud, stones, or rotten food thrown at him/her until his/her penance was done. For more severe offenses, violators were publicly whipped or flogged, causing serious physical injury.

Torture was not just reserved for the guilty but also for those who were merely suspected of a crime. Women who were suspected of various offenses, such as witchcraft, were strapped to a stool at the end of long pole over a body of water and dunked until they either confessed or died. If the woman died, she was considered innocent. Another method of interrogation was pressing, which was also used to force a suspect to plead to the charges. The suspect was placed between two boards, and rocks were heaped onto the board on top of the suspect until he/she pled, confessed, or died from the pressure. The colonists were also quite effective at psychological torture. The primary example of psychological torture during the early days of America is found in the famous Nathaniel Hawthorne novel, *The Scarlet Letter*. Hester Prynne, a women accused of adultery, was forced to wear a scarlet letter "A" on her chest for the rest of her life in punishment for her crime. Although a novel, *The Scarlet Letter* was illustrative of the social disapproval that the colonists would bring against a person. A number of authorities do not consider such treatment to be torture but more akin to shaming. However, shaming can and does have the same effect as psychological methods of torture. Support for this position is found in modern times when Islamic prisoners were tortured by being forced to eat pork, which would cause no physical harm but would cause serious shame and psychological harm to the victim.

Slavery and Racism

With the advent of slavery in America, torture became a fine art that was employed much more frequently against African American slaves than against the occasional white violator of the law. African Americans were kidnapped from Africa and transported for sale to America in horrible conditions. The men, women, and children were chained below the decks of a ship, frequently without food, water, medical care, or access to sanitary facilities. Many died from the horrible conditions before they ever reached America. Such neglect was worse than what the prisoners at Guantanamo Bay suffered and can only be considered torture.

Once slaves arrived in America to be sold, the torture continued. Families were separated. Slaves who were insubordinate or escaped were beaten, whipped, or flogged. Female slaves were frequently subjected to sexual abuse and rape at the hands of their masters. Slaves were denied basic human rights, both in practice and under the law, at least until the end of the Civil War and the Emancipation Proclamation. But even with their freedom, African Americans continued to be subjected to torture and terrorism.

After the Civil War, the people of the south resented the loss of their slaves, whom they viewed as subhuman. One of the results was the formation of the Ku Klux Klan. The Ku Klux Klan was an organization dedicated to oppressing the African American race and denying them their civil rights. Members dressed in white sheets to hide their identities and kidnapped, beat, and lynch African Americans. Starting in the early 20th century, their universal symbol was a burning cross. Over the years, the Ku Klux Klan waxed and waned several times, in modern times expanding its attention to other minorities and not just African Americans. In modern times, with a major shift in social attitudes and the enactment and enforcement of numerous civil rights laws, the numerous lynchings are no longer practiced by the Ku Klux Klan, but beatings and occasional murders of minorities still occur. Now, minorities have legal recourse, both civil and criminal, against those who would torture or terrorize them.

The Police and the Third Degree

Well-organized police forces did not become widespread until the 1900s. However, police did exist in the United States prior to the turn of the century. These police forces, in both the enforcement of the law and the protection of politicians, frequently employed brutality. The employment of brutality by police forces was usually called the "third degree." The third degree frequently involved being beaten with a rubber hose, placing the suspect under a hot lamp so that the interrogators could not be seen, and questioning the subject for hours on end until he/she confessed. Another method used by the police after the Civil War was the "sweat box." The suspect was placed in an iron box, which often did not even let the prisoner stand. Next to the sweat box, the police would place a stove, fill it with combustible material, light it, and literally cook the suspect until he confessed. Police frequently used black jacks or saps to beat prisoners. A sap was a small leather bag that was filled with lead shot and was used to hit suspects over the head. All of these activities can only be considered torture.

The problem of police brutality was officially recognized as early as 1931, when the Wickersham Commission, an official investigation into the cause of criminal behavior, criticized police torture. But it was not until the 1960s, with the Warren court, that police brutality began to be seriously addressed. Under Title 42 U.S.C. § 1983, victims of police brutality started to bring an ever-increasing number of civil rights lawsuits. The resulting jury verdicts forced police departments to increase training and stop the brutality. However, even these measures have not stopped police torture.

With the advent of modern technology, torture has become more subtle. Using a TASER, which is an electronic device through which a suspect is electrically shocked into submission, police can and occasionally have tortured suspects by continually shocking them. For example, the Rodney King case in California and the Abner Louima case in New York City show that police brutality still occurs.

The CIA and Interrogations
After the end of World War II, the Central Intelligence Agency (CIA) was formed to help keep track of the new nemesis, the Soviet Union, in the ensuing cold war. From 1952 until 1962, the CIA engaged in a massive program to research mind control and developed what was called "no-touch" torture. Essentially, the CIA developed expertise in how to psychologically break a suspect. The CIA researched sensory disorientation, sensory deprivation, and what was termed *self-inflicted pain*. The research was phenomenally successful, employing such techniques as unpredictability, betrayal, false charges, mock executions, and isolation. The method was codified under the title of Kubark Counterintelligence Interrogation and was exported to Latin American and Asian nations for use by their police forces. Even with the no-touch torture technique, America's intelligence agencies began a history of physical and mental torture that was present in Vietnam during the Vietnam War (i.e., the Phoenix Program), in Central America during the 1980s, and in the Middle East since 2001 (i.e., Abu Ghraib and Guantanamo Bay). The recent revelations of the extraordinary rendition program and the secret overseas prisons run by the CIA affirm the continued involvement of the CIA in torture.

The Military and Interrogations
With the close link and operating relationship between America's intelligence and security agencies and special operations units in the U.S. military, such as the Special Forces and military intelligence, the military was frequently involved in and a partner in torture activities. The Phoenix Program during the Vietnam War in the 1960s and the Abu Ghraib and Guantanamo Bay prisons all involved military forces, including military police and military intelligence personnel. Indeed, the revelation of the torture memos of the Bush administration highlight the fact that torture was not only overlooked but was actively encouraged by the highest level of leadership.

Conclusion
It has been generally accepted that the Eighth Amendment's prohibition against cruel and unusual punishment also protected against torture. Further, some authorities hold the position that because some practices were accepted as being appropriate for their time, they did not violate the Eighth Amendment or constitute torture. However, this argument is refuted by the principle that under the Bill of Rights, the society and the protections are subject to growth and refinement. Thus, even though the stocks in colonial times or the shower bath (the equivalent of waterboarding) during the 19th century would have been considered appropriate then, now they are unquestionably considered to constitute torture.

It cannot be reasonably disputed that torture has a long and infamous history in American culture and government. The effect on American society has fostered a significant amount of contempt and disrespect for the government. Even in modern America, many citizens seem to approve of the use of torture, especially in certain limited circumstances. Whether the problem can be adequately addressed remains to be seen.

Wm. C. Plouffe, Jr.
Independent Scholar

See Also: 2001 to 2012 Primary Documents; Ku Klux Klan; Lynchings; Police Abuse; Professionalization of Police; Racism; Salem Witch Trials; Slavery; Wickersham Commission.

Further Readings
Greenberg, K. J., ed. *The Torture Debate in America*. New York: New York University Press, 2006.
Levinson, Sanford, ed. *Torture: A Collection*. New York: Oxford University Press, 2004.
McCoy, Alfred W. *A Question of Torture: CIA Interrogation From the Cold War to the War on Terror*. New York: Henry Holt, 2006.
Nelson, Jill, ed. *Police Brutality*. New York: Norton, 2000.
Roth, Kenneth and Minky Worden, eds. *Torture*. New York: New Press, 2005.
Sims, Patsy. *The Klan*. Lexington: University Press of Kentucky, 1996.

Townshend Acts of 1767

The Townshend Acts of 1767 are a combination of four independent acts passed by the British parliament under Chancellor of the Exchequer Charles Townshend. The acts placed duties on various goods sent to the American colonies and increased colonial dissatisfaction with Great Britain. The duties began in 1767 and were repealed in 1773 after protests by the colonists. In 1767, the British government continued to seek out ways to support the stationing of troops and other government officials in the American colonies. After a change in government from William Pitt to Charles Townshend in 1767, the main emphasis for Townshend was how to raise money for the government. His solution was to add import duties to key items that the colonists would need for day-to-day life. Townshend felt that the colonists would not object to paying import duties for these items if the taxes placed on the items before they left Great Britain were removed.

The first act was the Suspending Act, which was the British government's reaction to the New York Assembly's failure to comply with the Quartering Act of 1765. The citizens of that colony could not afford the expense of building shelter and supplying the army's needs, so the assembly voted against it, leading to the suspension of the assembly. The Revenue Act sought to raise funds using import duties on items that colonists could only acquire from Great Britain because of existing restrictions on imports. Imports affected by this act included lead, paper, glass, and tea. This act was part of Townshend's goal of raising revenue for the government that would be used to pay royal officials stationed in the colonies. The act received opposition from both American colonists and British merchants. From the Americans' point of view, the officials would fall under the influence of the government in England versus the local assemblies who used to pay their salaries. Colonists boycotted the goods, found suppliers who would evade the law, and used this opportunity to begin manufacturing the goods in America. British merchants opposed this act because it encouraged American industry to the detriment of British manufacturers.

In connection with the Revenue Act, the third act created a board of customs commissioners located in Boston to collect the levied duties. The board established a system of inspectors and sought to oversee all American trade. Colonists opposed this new agency and protested by capturing British ships like the *Liberty* and burning ships like the *Gaspee*. Customs officials became so concerned that they asked for British troops to be stationed in Boston, which ultimately led to the 1770 Boston Massacre after a confrontation between British soldiers and American colonists. The fourth act contributed to the first protest about duties on tea. The act removed the taxes on tea on the British mainland and thus it arrived in the colonies without prior taxes. However, the import tax on tea remained. When the acts were repealed in 1770, this act remained in effect as the Tea Act. Colonial protests against this act led to the Boston Tea Party, which forced the repeal of the Tea Act in 1773.

Ultimately, Townshend did not live to see the outcome of the duties that carried his name. He died suddenly in 1767, after a life of poor health. This left the succeeding government to deal with the fallout in the colonies from the taxes. When the British government finally repealed the acts in 1773, it became apparent that the duties did not raise funds for the government. Merchants who produced the goods lost over £700,000—almost three times the amount of revenue collected. The Townshend Acts contributed to colonial protests and conversations about taxation without actual representation. As British subjects, the colonists did not agree with the taxes and actively protested the laws. They took issue with being taxed by act of Parliament to support the stationing of British soldiers in America and to additionally pay for the government officials stationed in the colonies. Ultimately, the Townshend Acts contributed to the decision by the colonists to declare independence.

Theresa S. Hefner-Babb
Lamar University

See Also: 1600 to 1776 Primary Documents; American Revolution and Criminal Justice; Boston, Massachusetts; Tea Act of 1773.

A car wreck caused by drunk driving. The act of operating a motor vehicle while under the influence of alcohol and/or drugs is illegal in all jurisdictions within the United States. Punishment varies widely between and within those states.

Further Readings
Breen, T. H. *The Marketplace of Revolution: How Consumer Politics Shaped American Independence.* New York: Oxford University Press, 2004.
Namier, Sir Lewis and John Brooke. *Charles Townshend.* New York: St. Martin's Press, 1964.
Thomas, Peter D. G. *The Townshend Duties Crisis: The Second Phase of the American Revolution, 1767–1773.* Oxford: Clarendon Press, 1987.

Traffic Crimes

Automobile-related traffic crimes include a range of activities involved with driving or controlling an automobile that have been designated as criminal in themselves or that facilitate or are otherwise related to some form of criminal activity. The most common of these involve speeding, failing to obey safety and maintenance standards, and disobeying traffic signs. Many people believe these offenses to be trivial and even that they should be considered either victimless crimes or not crimes at all. Nevertheless, each of the offenses listed leads to injury and death every day, even if not every incidence of the offense leads to such a negative outcome. Automobiles have been described as inherently dangerous, even deadly weapons in the wrong hands, which require strong laws that are strongly policed in order to make sure that they are used safely. The danger is magnified greatly when the machine is in the hands of a person who is driving under the influence (DUI) of alcohol or narcotics or who is driving while intoxicated (DWI).

Many traffic accidents involving automobiles are not the result of criminal activity but just reflect the difficulties involved in manipulating what are complex and sophisticated machines in a dynamic and busy environment in which other road users might behave in unpredictable or even irrational ways. Generally, other road users (e.g., pedestrians, cyclists, and motorcycle riders) come off worse in any collision with an automobile, and smaller automobiles similarly fare worse when struck by larger ones, bearing in mind also the importance of momentum. While improvements in the safety features of automobiles are in many ways impressive, they cannot protect people entirely, and they provide little help to people outside the automobile. The first person to be killed in America in an automobile accident was H. H. Bliss, in 1899, who was reportedly struck by a horseless carriage while helping a female passenger from a streetcar. Since then, Americans have been introduced to a range of new requirements and legislation as a means of trying to educate people about how to use the roads safely, what kind of insurance is required by law (first introduced in 1925 and then spreading state by state over subsequent decades), and which safety measures are necessary (up to the contemporary focus on child safety seats and the dangers of texting while driving). The rapid increase of automobile ownership and driving culture in the interwar years led to the introduction of most of the initial regimes of laws and safety features. Regulations concerning the way that people use automobiles are continually evolving in light of new technologies and of new forms of understanding of the interactions between the forces involved. However, such regulations appear to many people to be contrary to the American tradition of the open road and the freedom given to an individual and his/her passengers provided by ownership of an automobile. Indeed, the importance of the automobile in daily life is such that driving or riding in one represents the most common encounter with committing or being the victim of a crime in the course of normal living.

Common Driving Offenses

The most common driving offenses include speeding, driving without due care and attention, or disobeying traffic laws relating to maintenance and safety of the automobile. Since a large proportion of these offenses are never identified—or, if the offenses are identified, they are passed off by police without an official charge—it is impossible to know how often they occur or have occurred in the past. In rural areas in the past, the likelihood of meeting any police officers on the road was very low, and in close-knit communities, most minor offenses could be safely overlooked. The situation has become different as technological advances have caused vehicles to be faster and larger, and falling prices have enabled more people to buy automobiles and, hence, increase the volume of traffic on the roads. In suburban and, particularly, urban areas, the volume of traffic means that accidents of various sorts are almost inevitable and the level of police coverage is very high. Police coverage of traffic now extends to the use of computerized systems and helicopters in high-volume areas, and monitoring the automobiles of suspects for more serious crimes via these means has become a new option.

As more roads were built and upgraded to link urban areas and, in comparison with most of the rest of the world, public transport systems outside of large conurbations have been neglected, the demographic nature of people using roads has also changed. Initially, the first automobiles in the United States were slow and expensive machines scarcely capable of competing with horse-drawn carriages and certainly not with the railroad. As time passed, more of the middle and upper classes were drawn into road use and, consequently, also became more likely to be the victims of traffic crime. Broadening automobile ownership resulting from higher incomes in the country as a whole has also broadened the experience of this type of crime. As lower-income people enter the automobile market, most had limited funds, so they would drive secondhand vehicles in need of repair or possibly dangerous to operate. When traffic police have stopped automobile drivers, therefore, they have always had an incentive to stop a larger proportion of young, working-class men than people in any other category.

This custom has persisted as people from ethnic minorities and particularly African Americans have been able to buy and drive their own automobiles. The proportion of young African American men (and young men from some other ethnic groups) stopped and questioned by the police has become a flash point of potential conflict. It was the way in which certain white police officers stopped and questioned Rodney King after a high-speed chase that led to the riots in Los Angeles in 1992 when, despite video records of the police brutally beating King, they were exonerated. In a curious reversal of the race and class issues involved, the famous African American football player O. J. Simpson was involved in a low-speed highway chase when police wished to question him concerning the murder of his estranged wife and one of her friends, and the whole course of events was televised live across the nation, even interrupting coverage of the finals of the National Basketball Association.

Pressure of modern society—especially in the high-volume traffic environments of cities and amid high-value automobiles, some of which represent important status symbols for their owners—has given rise to the phenomenon of road rage. When traffic-related incidents occur, one or more of the protagonists might resort to anger and even violence to try to resolve the subsequent argument. When the perpetrators of such actions are associated with elderly or vulnerable people, the result can appear to be comical because of the indignity, but when young, physically fit, and perhaps armed individuals are involved, the outcome can be very serious. This is particularly the case with respect to urban gang culture, in which the desire to maintain face is of enormous importance and in which the automobile is a direct extension of the status of not just the individual owner but also her or his gang members and, by extension, the territory and perhaps ethnic group from which gang members are primarily drawn. Fear of an armed response has, at least on an anecdotal basis, contributed in some cases to people tolerating outrageous and reckless acts of driving on public roads.

DUI and DWI

Perhaps the most serious and tragic form of traffic crime is when an accident occurs as a result of the responsible person being incapable of operating the machine properly because of intoxication. The intoxication might be caused by alcohol, illegal drugs, or some form of prescribed medication that is not illegal to take. This crime is known as driving under the influence of drugs (DUI) or driving while intoxicated (DWI), which are terms used more or less interchangeably. The exact definition of these crimes varies from state to state but usually a range of potential intoxicants is involved, with a specific amount of the intoxicant in the blood level defined as representing a legal upper limit and a variety of circumstances involved in which guilt may be determined. While once it was the case that only people actually driving a vehicle could be held responsible for what that vehicle did, more recently it has come to be seen that ownership and control of a vehicle while under the influence also means culpability.

There has been quite considerable debate and scientific research concerning the amount of alcohol or other substance that should be present in the blood before an individual can be considered to have broken the law. The limits and the ways in which testing should occur have varied over time and from state to state. The most obvious problem relates to the fact that measuring the amount of alcohol or other substance imbibed as a simple measure does not take into account the fact that individuals range in size, shape, and tolerance. There are also problems concerning the buildup of substances over time and the length of time that should be permitted to have elapsed between the final drink and the use of the automobile.

When DUI offenses result in the death or serious injury of a loved one, the loss felt by survivors appears to be particularly difficult to bear in many cases. If the deceased was the one responsible, then guilt can pass to the relatives who may be damaged psychologically by the events. The damage appears to be worse for those who have lost a loved one because of the illegal DUI offense of another, particularly when the perpetrator receives a sentence that is not held to be commensurate with the severity of the crime. The principle of sentencing is to match the punishment with the nature of the offense and not with the actual outcome of secondary effects of the offense. To some extent, the inclusion of victim statements and similar approaches have been used to try to narrow the gap between the sentence according to principles and the type of sentence believed by the victims to be appropriate.

Reckless Driving

As the number of vehicles on the roads and their size and speed have increased, the possibility of accidents has increased, as has the severity of their outcomes. Notwithstanding improvements in the safety features of automobiles, frequent drivers or passengers face close misses on a quite regular basis. Despite this, people continue to make risk-taking driving decisions because they are able very quickly to forget about past incidents of near misses. The ability to forget within a couple of weeks enables most people to continue driving and even to intensify their level of risk-taking behavior.

The number of people killed internationally on the roads continues to increase because economic growth means that more people are able to afford cars personally. Additionally, the emergence of very small and cheap cars by the Indian manufacturing company Tata has caused the domestic market to expand significantly. The fatalities in such countries are projected to increase considerably, by as much as 147 percent between 2000 and 2020 in the case of India and by 66 percent globally. However, the United States is one of a group of high-income countries in which overall rates are declining because of better policing of road behavior and better safety features. Other countries will join this group when their own level of modernization reaches a certain level. In the United States, road safety came under the administration of the Department of Transportation in 1966.

Clearly, the numbers of collisions and road traffic deaths varies on a state-by-state basis, considering the total size of population, relative number of urban and rural populations, and income and provision of police services. Since so much of the country remains out of immediate police reach, many possible cases of reckless driving are undetected or may be unproven, despite the best effort of forensic scientists and detectives. One of the best-known such examples involved Senator Edward Kennedy, who in 1969 left a party in the company of a young woman, Mary Jo Kopechne, driving his own automobile. He subsequently drove off a bridge, and the car was submerged in water. He was unable to rescue Kopechne and finally left the scene, a crime for which he was subsequently prosecuted. Despite numerous attempts subsequently to come to the truth, uncertainty remains over the nature of which crimes, if any, were committed that night. There are other cases in which individuals, if they have a high profile or have already committed other offenses, claim to be passengers rather than drivers with the collusion of other passengers. The use of closed circuit television cameras and other forms of technology have reduced this problem but there are limits to what might be achieved. An additional problem concerns the distribution of automobiles with significant safety defects, most notably by Toyota but by other companies as well. These models have in a small number of cases contributed to or caused traffic accidents and have led to substantial fines for those corporations involved.

Other Forms of Crime

Some crimes require a means of transportation, and an automobile is the most convenient means of providing that transportation, especially since independent movement is required. Gangsters in the 1920s and 1930s, for example, became associated with the use of limousines and other automobiles as means of transportation for senior figures, to transfer armed individuals as required, and to move prohibited alcoholic products. The automobile as combination transportation device and status symbol has persisted into the age of contemporary drug-dealing and gang activities.

The emergence of mobile or cell phones and other portable personal equipment have made new types of activity illegal or semilegal in nature. This includes distracted driving, which involves taking calls, texting, or otherwise engaging in an activity that significantly detracts from the ability to drive safely. Large numbers of people, especially young people, have, however, come to the conclusion that they are sufficiently skilled as to be able to perform several engrossing activities at the same time.

Traffic Crimes in Popular Culture

American popular culture is replete with the notion of the automobile (or other road vehicle) representing the freedom of the individual, escape from social and state strictures, and the ability of the individual to transcend difficult circumstances in one location. *Easy Rider*, for example, portrays motorcycle riders as outsiders, somewhat romantic in nature but essentially rebellious against the encroaching bourgeois nature of society. The central legends of early American history celebrate the journeys across the prairies to possible future wealth in the face of the hostility of nature and the native peoples, through the medium of the forerunner to the automobile. Away from the trappings of society, according to the myth in any case, the individual (customarily the male leader of a family or social group) is empowered to use all means to protect the vulnerable passengers. Contemporary productions from *Thelma and Louise* to *The Blues Brothers* to *Supernatural* feature iconic cars as the means of bringing about not just a change of location but the ability of the protagonists to meet their goals and affect the external environment. The NASCAR racing circuit has become an important part of the sporting and television worlds but has also become a cultural market of political significance.

The increase in the importance of surveillance as a detective technique for both official police and private detectives meant that they spent more time in their stationary cars waiting for something to happen. This frames a scene familiar to viewers of such programs in which protagonists enact their personal life dramas while waiting for suspected criminals to take some action that makes their job meaningful. In the postapocalyptic genre or productions in which disasters threaten mankind, automobiles become one of the key resources in empowering people to escape a horrible death from radioactivity, zombies, violent neofascists, or other nemeses. Such stories typically portray a world in which any form of act is permitted, whether previously considered legal or illegal, because of the total breakdown of the state and society. In American popular culture, then, very often it is the case that only those in possession of an automobile and a gun are able to navigate the dangerous environment of the world.

John Walsh
Shinawatra University

See Also: Automobile and the Police; Gangs, Contemporary; Simpson, O. J.

Further Readings
Berger, Michael L. *The Automobile in American History and Culture: A Reference Guide*. Westport, CT: Greenwood Press, 2001.
Chapman, Peter and Geoffrey Underwood. "Forgetting Near-Accidents: The Roles of Severity, Culpability and Experience in the Poor Recall of Dangerous Driving Situations." *Applied Cognitive Psychology*, v.14/1 (January 2000).
Kay, Jane Holtz. *Asphalt Nation: How the Automobile Took Over America and How We Can Take It Back*. Berkeley: University of California Press, 1997.
Kopits, Elizabeth and Maureen Cropper. "Traffic Fatalities and Economic Growth." http://www-wds.worldbank.org/external/default/WDSContentServer/WDSP/IB/2003/05/23/000094946_03051404103341/Rendered/PDF/multi0page.pdf (Accessed November 2011).

Training Police

Historically, American law enforcement agencies dedicated little time and few resources to the formalized training of their officers. While some training and education inevitably did occur, much of this training was informal and lacked specificity, coherence, and continuity. In other instances, officers brought formalized military or vocational training with them to the law enforcement profession. However, this training was not directly related to their law enforcement duties or to the practices of the agencies that employed them. As a result, much of the training that officers brought with them to the profession was not directly conducive to policing a civilian population. The widespread belief that formalized training was superfluous and unnecessary continued to characterize early American law enforcement agencies for some time to come. In part, these beliefs were driven by perceptions that police work was an unskilled profession that did not require formalized training. The rampant political corruption that characterized many early American law enforcement agencies contributed to this perception. This corruption crippled many agencies and resulted in an organizational culture that valued avarice and loyalty above all else. As public dissatisfaction with police corruption intensified, tentative efforts to improve hiring and training standards began to take shape. These initial efforts were largely the result of emerging public attitudes and expectations that valued greater professionalism and improved efficacy.

Some of the earliest formalized police training efforts took the form of preservice law enforcement training academies. The earliest of these academies began to appear during the 1800s and early 1900s. These initial training efforts were minimal in prevalence, scope, and duration when compared to contemporary standards and normally involved only nominal levels of instruction in the most rudimentary police duties. Even these modest training efforts did not become the standard for American law enforcement until the middle and later parts of the 20th century. While the efforts were tentative and halting, their importance should not be overlooked, as they helped establish the legitimacy of formalized police training and paved the way for the more ambitious training efforts that followed. Widespread professional acceptance of formalized police training was slow to come, but by the close of the 20th century, police officer training had become an integral part of the law enforcement profession, an accepted standard among police administrators, and an important part of the socialization experience of new law enforcement officers. Further, the scope of the training provided to officers expanded dramatically across time to include a more diverse set of topics like communication skills, community problem solving, and cultural sensitivity.

Reasons for Training

One significant factor that contributed to the growing acceptance of formalized police training was the emergence of the police professionalization movement. The police professionalization movement began during the early 20th century and grew out of larger efforts to reform the criminal justice system. The police professionalization movement resulted in the introduction of substantive reforms that continue to influence the American law enforcement profession. Proponents of this movement believed that the law enforcement system should be reformed in such a way that it would be viewed by the public as a reputable and honorable profession, in much the same manner that the legal or medical professions were viewed. In order to accomplish this objective, the corruption and political influence that characterized early law enforcement agencies needed to be eliminated. While eliminating corruption was certainly important, advocates of professionalization believed that this alone was insufficient; law enforcement agencies also needed to employ highly qualified employees, internalize an efficient managerial structure, integrate technological advances in an attempt to improve outcomes, and create an organizational culture that advocated a proficient and effective response to criminal activity. In order to accomplish each of these objectives, it was necessary for law enforcement agencies to improve the quality of the training that they provided to their employees. The opinions of some of the most respected Progressive reformers associated with the police professionalization movement supported this contention.

August Vollmer was the chief of police of Berkeley, California, and O. W. Wilson was the chief of police of Wichita, Kansas, and Chicago, Illinois. Collectively, Vollmer and Wilson advocated the creation of programs of study related to law enforcement in the American system of higher education and the implementation of improved hiring and training standards for police officers. Given their positions and status, Vollmer and Wilson were able to advance the cause of police professionalization, and in the process, they were able to ensure the greater acceptance of efforts to expand and improve police training.

In more recent times, police training has taken on even greater significance and importance for a variety of reasons. First, political demands for greater accountability have increased during the past several decades. These demands have frequently accompanied high-profile governmental investigations of the American criminal justice system. For example, the National Commission on Law Observance and Enforcement recommended a number of ways in which the American law enforcement profession could be improved. One of the most commonly identified recommendations made by committees of this nature has pertained to the need to increase both the quality and quantity of police training. High-profile incidents of police corruption or brutality are frequently accompanied by public calls for increased professionalism and enhanced personnel standards. One commonly suggested method of achieving both of these objectives is the implementation of more exhaustive education and training requirements for law enforcement officers. The legal system has gradually provided greater civil liability for law enforcement agencies, resulting in an increased potential for financial losses stemming from civil lawsuits. Law enforcement agencies have increasingly

In recent years, police training has taken on greater significance and importance due to political demands for greater accountability and higher requirements for levels of domestic security. High-profile incidents of police corruption or brutality have also resulted in public calls for increased professionalism and enhanced personnel standards.

viewed training as one way that they can protect themselves from the ongoing threat of civil liability. The environment in which policing occurs has become increasingly complicated, and law enforcement duties have taken on greater complexity. This increasing complexity has necessitated the introduction of institutional expectations for a better trained and educated law enforcement officer. For example, community policing philosophies have necessitated the employment of law enforcement officers who have superior communication skills, an ability to relate well to a diverse group of community stakeholders, and the capacity to problem solve and identify innovative ways in which the root causes of crime and neighborhood disorder can be permanently resolved.

Methods of Training

The increased importance of formalized police training has been reflected in the greater amount of time and organizational resources that law enforcement agencies have dedicated to the training of their officers and in the greater variety of training to which those officers are exposed. Early training efforts focused primarily on providing rudimentary vocational skills to new police officers. This training signified a departure from the ways of the past, but it also failed to account for the diverse training needs of law enforcement officers and the way in which training needs changed at various stages of a law enforcement career. This is a significant limitation given that the training needs of new officers with limited amounts of experience are substantively different from the training needs of more experienced officers with multiple years of practical experience in the field. Over time, police training has become more holistic by providing a greater variety of training to law enforcement officers with the intent of better meeting both current and evolving training needs across the entire course of an officer's law enforcement career.

Today, vocational police training is generally divided into one of three broad categories: preservice or academy training, field training or on-the-job training, and in-service or ongoing training. Most law enforcement officers will be exposed to training from each of these three different categories at multiple points throughout the course of their policing careers. Pre-service or academy training refers to that portion of law enforcement training that is meant to prepare law enforcement officers for the duties that they will encounter during the course of their employment. The term *pre-service* is a bit misleading as some states have provisions that allow officers to begin their employment before they have completed a formalized police training academy. This is especially common in locations where the existing system of law enforcement training academies is unable to operate at the capacity necessary to meet the demand of the law enforcement community. Despite some minor geographic variations, this type of training is typically intended to be a prerequisite to employment as a law enforcement officer. Field training or on-the-job training is typically viewed as a continuation or extension of the pre-service or academy training that officers receive. This type of training provides officers with the opportunity to work in the field in a controlled manner under the supervision of a more experienced senior officer. The senior officer is typically referred to as a field training officer and is charged with both the provision of ongoing instruction in the field and the production of evaluation reports regarding the performance of the officers assigned to him/her.

In-service or ongoing training is a mandated requirement for law enforcement officers. In order to maintain their law enforcement certifications and continue their employment, law enforcement officers must acquire a certain number of training hours each year. A failure to secure the required number of training hours could result in the revocation of certification and the inability to maintain employment. While the specific requirements for in-service training vary somewhat from state to state, the purpose and intent of this type of training is generally the same. More specifically, this type of training is mandated in an attempt to ensure that police officers remain up to date on current developments in the field and proficient in the skills and knowledge that are required of them. In addition, many departments use this type of training as an opportunity to update officers on any changes made to existing, policies and procedures and to inform officers of any new initiatives that the department has undertaken. In addition to the formalized types of training that new officers receive, they are also exposed to and influenced by the informal training that they receive from their more seasoned and experienced colleagues.

During the course of their careers, many officers learn that there are both formal and informal ways of getting things done. Informal interactions with colleagues, private conversations, and observational role modeling serve to underscore the importance of informal practices and advance a new, albeit unofficial, dimension to police training. This type of informal training may also contribute to the creation and continuance of the police subculture.

Scope and Delivery

The scope of police training has also changed dramatically during the course of the past several decades. Early training efforts focused almost exclusively on teaching officers the most basic of vocational skills. While officers did need at least some basic instruction of this type, early training efforts did not reflect the true diversity of the police mission or the complexities of the duties undertaken by law enforcement officers. As a result, initial training efforts did not provide new officers with the scope or depth of information that they needed to effectively perform many of the more nuanced aspects of their jobs. As the amount of time devoted to training officers increased, it became possible to integrate new topics alongside those that were already being taught. Training dedicated to patrol tactics and firearms usage began to be supplemented with training regarding problem solving, cultural sensitivity, communication skills, and a number of other topics that had previously been overlooked. Today, police officers are required to go through hundreds of hours of academy and field service training in addition to the mandated number of annual in-service training hours that they must attain.

At the same time that the scope of law enforcement training expanded, the way in which training was provided to officers also began to change. Classroom training has increasingly been supplemented with hands-on training that allows officers to practice new skills under controlled conditions. The intent of this type of training is to provide a realistic training experience for officers in an attempt to ensure that they are prepared for the types of duties that they will face during the course of their employment. This transition process has accelerated recently with the advent of new technologies and their infusion into the realm of law enforcement training. Today, law enforcement officers are able to engage in realistic training simulations of high-risk law enforcement duties, such as pursuit driving or firearms usage, through the use of training simulators that mimic real-world conditions and provide officers with immediate feedback concerning their performance. These new training technologies have the benefit of providing officers with the opportunity to learn about high-risk duties through experience and repetition in a safe environment where mistakes are not irrevocable.

Many officers decide to supplement the vocational training that they receive with additional education and educational credentials that they can attain through the American college and university system. While most law enforcement agencies do not require their employees to have a college degree, some do require prospective law enforcement officers to have either prior law enforcement or military experience or some college credits as a precondition of employment. For officers who lack prior military or law enforcement experience, higher education may become a pragmatic method of securing employment. Even in agencies that do not have any formal educational requirements, many officers have still pursued an advanced education, which has resulted in American law enforcement officers becoming increasingly well-educated over time. This process accelerated dramatically as a result of the Law Enforcement Education Program (LEEP). LEEP was a part of the Law Enforcement Assistance Administration (LEAA), which was established by the Safe Streets Act of 1968. The LEAA was the federal agency that provided assistance and financial resources to local and state law enforcement agencies in an attempt to improve effectiveness and reduce crime. LEEP's purpose was to provide funding for education and training programs. During the course of its existence, LEEP provided funding to colleges and universities for both research and the establishment of criminal justice programs of study. In addition, the program provided funding for law enforcement officers who wished to pursue such a program of study.

Today, the benefits of higher education and the need for educational requirements remain controversial topics. Advocates of higher education requirements argue that a college education improves communication skills, enhances critical thinking aptitude, cultivates a greater appreciation for diverse viewpoints, and ultimately results in improved performance and enhanced police-community relations. Critics of educational requirements counter that there is no definitive proof that educated officers perform better than their noneducated counterparts, that educational requirements can limit both the size and the diversity of applicant pools, and that they can result in increased personnel costs for agencies. Debates of this nature underscore the dynamic and evolving nature of police training and educational practices. This idea is further underscored by the dramatic changes that have taken place in police training and education in the past and the many changes that are expected to continue occurring in the future.

Jason R. Jolicoeur
Cincinnati State Technical and Community College

See Also: National Commission on Law Observance and Enforcement; Professionalization of Police; Reform, Police and Enforcement; Vollmer, August; Wilson, O. W.

Further Readings
Dunham, Roger and Geoffrey Alpert. *Critical Issues in Policing: Contemporary Readings*, 6th ed. Long Grove, IL: Waveland Press, 2010.
Haberfield, Maria. *Critical Issues in Police Training*. Upper Saddle River, NJ: Prentice Hall, 2002.
National Commission on Law Observance and Enforcement. *Report on Lawlessness in Law Enforcement*. Washington, DC: U.S. Government Printing Office, 1931.

Palmiotto, M. and M. Dantzker. *Police and Training Issues*. Upper Saddle River, NJ: Prentice Hall, 2003

Reaves, Brian. *State and Local Law Enforcement Training Academies, 2006*. Washington, DC: U.S. Department of Justice, 2009.

Trials

Criminal trials have been a source of public fascination since the colonial era not only for the lurid details often involve but for the fear and horror they often invoke in the public. In the United States, criminal trials may take place at the federal, state, or municipal level, depending on the statute violated. Felony trials occur at either that state or federal level. The majority of cases are misdemeanor cases that are handled at the municipal level and often by bench trial, but though numerous, such cases rarely evolve into full trials.

Although trials are seen as the normal course for all criminal prosecutions, there are actually relatively few cases that reach the trial stage. It has been estimated that only 10 percent of all cases go to trial across the United States, although this percentage fluctuates by jurisdiction and can be as low as 7 percent. The number of criminal acts that reach trial are far lower because not all crimes are reported, nor are all criminals apprehended, nor are all crimes prosecuted. Among cases that are filed, the primary reason for a case not proceeding to trial is the reaching of a plea bargain between the defendant and prosecutor's office.

Plea Bargains

A plea bargain can be reached at any point in the trial process before the jury has reached a verdict. A plea bargain is technically the defendant's waiving his/her Sixth Amendment right to a jury trial. It is called a "bargain" as the defendant is often enticed to accept the plea by the promise of the ability to plead to a reduced charge or to receive consideration in sentencing. Before a defendant may enter a guilty plea, he/she must be advised by the judge of the nature of the charge to which he/she is pleading in detail; the maximum possible penalty for the offense plus any mandatory minimum penalty; that he/she (the defendant) has the right to plead not guilty; and that by pleading guilty, he/she is waving the right to a trial. Once sentencing has occurred, there are only four possible reasons to revoke a plea agreement: that the plea was not voluntary, that the court that took the plea did not have jurisdiction over the case, that the defendant did not have effective assistance of counsel or counsel misrepresented the plea agreement to him/her; and that either side failed to keep to the terms of the plea bargain.

It has been argued by some commentators that plea bargaining is not only the norm in the American judicial system but that the system would not be able to process all the cases if no one took a plea bargain. There has been criticism of the use of plea bargaining to induce innocent victims to plead guilty rather than risk wrongful conviction. Innocent defendants often are willing to plead guilty if the sentence is for time already served, for probation, or for a duration shorter than it is likely to take for a trial to conclude if they cannot afford bail and thus would be in custody anyway. This has become of particular concern in states with recidivist statutes, as an earlier plea can mean a severe increase in sentencing should the person be convicted of a subsequent felony later in life. Some commentators have called for restrictions to be placed on plea bargaining, including a possible ban on plea bargaining altogether, but this seems unlikely to occur given the system's dependence on plea bargaining to process cases.

Evolution From Common Law

Under modern American law, any defendant who refuses to plea is assumed to have pled innocent, and a trial date is set. Under traditional English common law, this was not the case, and a defendant who stood mute was simply not pleading. This was because of the historical development of the jury trials, which meant that trial by jury was an option but not a requirement for Englishmen. The other options were trial by battle or ordeal. However, the Lateran Council's prohibition of clergy's assistance in ordeals in 1215 removed them as an effective trial procedure, and the use of battle faded over the course of the 14th century, leaving jury trials as the only viable option. If a defendant refused to plea under the common law, they were in effect refusing trial by jury, which meant that there was no way to try them. Under the common law it was beneficial to not enter a plea if you had property or title to pass to descendents as a felony conviction meant that you forfeited all property and titles to the Crown. Some defendants refused to plead out of stubbornness or to preserve their good name from being tarnished by a wrongful conviction and execution they knew was coming anyway. To discourage defendants from refusing to plead, the system of pressing, placing large weights onto the defendant's chest until he/she either agreed to plea or died, developed. This was technically the law in all North American colonies until independence. The most infamous use of this procedure in North America was the pressing death of Giles Corey during the Salem witch trials. It is often erroneously reported the he was pressed to death as a punishment for being a witch, when it was in fact a result of his refusal to enter a plea.

In the colonial era, the colonies implemented English common law trial practices. The primary mode of trial was the "accused speaks" form of trial, in which the defendant was expected to answer the accusations made by prosecution witnesses. It was believed that an innocent person had nothing to hide from the court and that any instruction in the law would come from the judge. This form of trial rested on the lack of defense counsel; indeed, there was a prohibition against defendants receiving legal counsel until the 1720s in England, although some North American colonies did provide for defense counsel beginning in the 17th century. By the mid-18th century, most North American colonies provided for the assistance of counsel, even though they made no provision for providing counsel for indigent defendants.

Early colonial legal systems rested on English criminal procedure, but some did deviate to include more morals-based crimes than the common law. Among the more notorious criminal codes was the call for capital punishment for adultery, children being disobedient or striking their parents, bestiality, sodomy, and witchcraft. Although these acts were criminalized in several New England colonies, capital punishment was rarely implemented. In addition to reduced sentencing for adults, all colonies had provisions for reduced punishment for children and took youth into account in sentencing. Some colonies also provided that foreigners, including Englishman from other colonies, would be granted lenience if they lacked knowledge of the local criminal laws.

Public Interest in Trials

The Salem witch trials were an early form of mass interest in a trial, but more importantly, they helped shape the type of evidence that would be deemed acceptable in a capital trial. Until the Salem trials, spectral evidence, or evidence that could only be sensed (seen, heard, smelled, tasted, or felt) by the victim was admissible to convict a person of witchcraft or sorcery. It was common but not required to have some form of corroborating evidence before a person was convicted of witchcraft. Judge Stoughton, presiding over the Salem trials, dispensed with this requirement and convicted numerous individuals based on spectral evidence alone. This lack of evidence was defended by the minister Cotton Mather, but the subsequent doubt cast on the guilt of the persons convicted in the trials led many, including Mather's own father, Increase Mather, to doubt the validity of spectral evidence alone. The Salem witch trials were the last major witch trials in the North American colonies, although antiwitchcraft statutes remained on the books in some jurisdictions into the 20th century.

The use of criminal law, and thus trials, to advance a moral or political agenda has continued to the present day. In the United States, these attempts have often backfired and created public disdain for those who attempted to criminalize moral or political beliefs. One of the best known of these cases was the Scopes Monkey Trial of 1925. The Tennessee legislature had passed a law making it a crime to teach any theory that man descended from a lower order of being or that contradicted the divine creation of man as described in the Bible at any university or school supported in part or entirely by state funds. Within a few weeks of the law being passed, a group in Dayton, Tennessee, decided to set up a test case to challenge the law. They arranged for a local biology teacher, John Thomas Scopes, to be caught in the act of teaching evolution. This was done, and he was arrested. William Jennings Bryan volunteered to assist the prosecution, and Clarence Darrow was retained to assist the defense. The trial also was one of the rare instances in the history of common law trials that the prosecuting attorney, Bryan, was called as a defense witness. Bryan's testimony proved fatal to the cause of anti-evolution laws but not to the prosecution's case. Scopes was found guilty and was fined $100. The verdict was overturned on appeal, but the law was allowed to remain on the books. While technically a victory for anti-evolutionary politicians, the drubbing that Darrow submitted Bryan to on the literalness of the Bible was broadcast across the country on radio and undermined their long-term goals; it is now legal to teach evolution in all states.

Public fascination with trials can be traced to the colonial era when ministers would preach sermons on the occasion of public executions. These sermons often provided lurid details of the crime, but their primary purpose was to persuade the condemned to repent and to instruct the audience in proper moral behavior. These sermons were often printed for wider distribution. The tradition of printing execution sermons continued into the early republic era. In the 18th century, the genre of true-life crime stories began to emerge in England, although the detective novel would not arise for another century with the publication of Edgar Allen Poe's *The Murders in the Rue Morgue*. The public's fascination for salacious details about criminals and trials continued to be satisfied by dime novels and media coverage in the "penny press," tabloids, and by yellow journalism in the 19th century.

The introduction of radio and television as forms of mass communication revolutionized the speed and depth of media coverage that could be achieved of a single trial. The term *trial of the century* has been applied to numerous trials, but its originator is not entirely certain. The first trial that the term was applied to was the murder trial of Harry Kendall Thaw, accused of killing Stanford White, the renowned architect, for sleeping with his wife, Evelyn Nesbit, before they were married. The two trials that followed were heavily covered by the media, and public attention was captivated by the sensational testimony of Nesbit and Thaw. The jury deadlocked in the first trial, and then Thaw was acquitted using a defense of temporary insanity based on Nesbit confessing to him that she had lost her virginity to White and

Lizzie Borden was tried for killing her father and stepmother with a hatchet in 1892: pictured is the jury from her trial. The murders and the trial became an infamous case, arousing widespread controversy and public debate. Borden was acquitted and no other individual was ever arrested for the murders. The dispute over the identity of the killer continues to the present day.

that he, White, had abused her. Since the Thaw trial, numerous other trials have been termed *trial of the century*, and it is generally used to mean any sensational trial, such as the Leopold and Loeb kidnapping and murder trial in the 1920s, and the 1930s trial of Bruno Richard Hauptmann, convicted and executed for the kidnapping and murder of Charles A. Lindbergh, Jr.

Pretrial Proceedings
As a defendant moves from arrest to trial, there are several steps that are normally undertaken prior to the start of a formal trial. The exact names and order vary from jurisdiction to jurisdiction; however, the following is a rough idea of the pretrial, postarrest process that most criminal defendants go through. The initial appearance, also called arraignment in some states, must take place within 48 hours of arrest, as must some form of hearing to determine if there is probable cause to detain the defendant. During the initial appearance, the judge reads the defendant his/her rights, appoints counsel, and set bail. In some states, this is also the stage at which the defendant will enter a plea (guilty or innocent). In all federal cases, the Fifth Amendment of the Constitution requires that a grand jury hear the prosecution's evidence to determine if there is probable cause to prosecute. The level of evidence required is low, and the defendant has no right to present evidence. In many states, an indicting jury can be used with a simple written statement of facts presented by the district attorney's office, as the Supreme Court determined in *Hurtado v. California* that the Fifth Amendment's requirement for a grand jury is not incorporated to the states. At the preliminary hearing, which can take place several weeks after arrest, both sides are represented by counsel, who present evidence before a judge to see if there is sufficient evidence to go to trial; if there is, then a trial date is set. Initial motions to suppress evidence, change the venue, request discovery, or even dismiss the case are often made at this stage. Some states have a separate taking of the plea that occurs after or during the preliminary hearing rather than at the initial appearance.

Trial by Jury
The traditional method of trial in the United States is trial by jury. The defendant does have a right to waive a jury trial in favor of a bench trial, but this is usually only done if the defendant believes that the jury will be swayed by the emotional nature of the case into deviating from the black-letter law. The Constitution of the United States provides multiple safeguards for a fair trial and gives criminal defendants several rights. However, until after the Civil War, these rights were not applicable to the states. Indeed, it was not until the 20th century that the Supreme Court began to use the Fourteenth Amendment to incorporate the rights guaranteed in the Bill of Rights to the states. The Supreme Court incorporated the jury requirement of the Sixth Amendment in *Duncan v. Louisiana*. The defendant was convicted of a simple misdemeanor battery, with a potential sentence of two years' imprisonment, but was sentenced to only 60 days. The court held that the Sixth Amendment did apply to the states in all cases that would be tried by a jury under federal law. Today, this means that a defendant has a right to trial by jury for all crimes that can lead to more than six months in prison.

The majority of cases involving violation of the right to a jury have revolved around the impartiality, composition, and number of jurors. In *Irvin v. Dowd*, the court held that because eight of the 12 jurors believed the defendant guilty before the start of the trial, a violation of the Sixth Amendment had occurred. In *Apodaca v. Oregon*, the court held that the Constitution does not require a unanimous 12-person jury to convict. In *Taylor v. Louisiana*, the court found that the jury must represent a cross-section of the county, though in the United States, women were not permitted to serve on juries until the 1950s in most states. In *J.E.B. v. Alabama ex rel. T.B.*, the court held that a juror cannot be excluded on the basis of gender.

Presentation of Evidence
The primary part of a trial is the presentation of evidence to prove that the defendant was the perpetrator of the crime. The elements of a crime that need to be proven are actus rea (a voluntary act or culpable omission), mens rea (the state of mind the defendant must have when he/she perform the actus rea), causation (cause-in-fact and proximate), and result. Conversely, the defense presents evidence to prove that one element of the crime was not proven by the prosecution

or that there is a valid defense for commission of the crime. The elements of most crimes have not changed much over the past 300 years, but the methods of detection of criminal acts have improved dramatically over that same period. The burden of proving all elements of the case is on the prosecution. The standard for all felonies in the United States is beyond the reasonable doubt of an average person.

A defense can challenge any element of the crime. Defenses that challenge the actus rea are case-specific as they attempt to show that the defendant did not commit the criminal act or had no duty to act. In common law, there is no duty to aid another person unless you put the person in danger or have a special relationship that creates a duty to aid. If a person enters into a conspiracy to commit a crime, it is not enough to withdraw from the conspiracy; the person must also notify authorities of the conspiracy. Similarly, defenses that attempt to show that there was no causation between the defendant's actions and the resulting criminal act are case-specific. Some well-established defenses have developed regarding the mens rea required for the commission of a crime under the common law.

In establishing his/her defense, a defendant is given wide leeway in presenting his/her case. The complexity of trials has grown dramatically in the past 100 years as more sophisticated scientific techniques have been introduced to detect, investigate, and prosecute criminals. The increased use of scientific techniques has given rise to the use of expert witnesses in criminal trials. An expert witness is a person who, through education or experience, has developed knowledge on a given subject, typically scientific, business, or technical. The witness can only be called to provide testimony that is not common knowledge of the average fact finder or to establish the chain of custody of evidence tested. Today, the most common expert witnesses are crime lab technicians to explain evidence gathered at the scene of a crime, including DNA, fingerprints, and other samples.

Technology and Evidence
The use of fingerprints in the United States began in New York City in 1902. It was initially used as a method to track civil servants but was quickly adapted to criminal detection. Although used in previous convictions, the first case to clearly state that fingerprint evidence was admissible against a criminal defendant was the 1911 *People v. Jennings*, in which the Illinois Supreme Court upheld their use against Thomas Jennings in a case of murder and robbery of Clarence Hiller. Jennings had previously been fingerprinted after a parole violation had led to his temporary reincarceration the previous year; these prints were matched to a set found in the victim's home. An expert was called to testify that in his opinion the prints from the crime scene matched Jennings's. After conviction, Jennings appealed, claiming that fingerprint evidence was inadmissible under the common law, but he lost the appeal. The admissibility of fingerprints was upheld by other states and extended to include palm prints in Nevada in 1918 and footprints in Massachusetts in 1938. Early use of fingerprints was not without its flaws.

The use of deoxyribonucleic acid (DNA) in criminal trials to establish both the identity of victims and perpetrators has become so universally accepted that it is often forgotten that it was only introduced in the 1980s. DNA profiling, pioneered by Alec Jeffreys, is the comparison of a biological sample (e.g., blood, hair) taken at a crime scene for comparison to a sample taken from an individual to link him/her to the crime scene. In *State v. Searles,* the Kansas Supreme Court upheld the admissibility of expert testimony that the blood found in the back of the defendant's truck was the same blood type as the victim's blood and that only a small percentage of the population had that blood type. The defendant had argued that statistical evidence was speculative and therefore was not admissible. The court denied the appeal, holding that statistical evidence based on facts was admissible in felony trials.

The United States Supreme Court has upheld the admissibility of scientific evidence if it derives from a well-recognized scientific principle and the test has been sufficiently established in the scientific community. In *Frye v. United States,* the court upheld the use of the systolic blood pressure test as lie detector test as it had received general acceptance among the scientific community. The standard of general acceptance remained in place until the court overturned it in *Daubert v. Merrell Dow Pharmaceuticals Inc.*, replacing it with a much laxer standard arising from scientific method and pertaining to scientific knowledge. This new standard meant that all scientific evidence was admissible if relevant, reliable, and previously subjected to peer review of the scientific community.

Insanity and Temporary Insanity

One of the early uses of expert witnesses was to prove an insanity defense. With the rise of the view that insanity was a medical condition came the defense that the defendant lacked the competence to know he/she was doing wrong and therefore should be excused from his/her actions. The concept that idiots and lunatics should not be held criminally accountable for their acts was well established in the common law before the 19th century. The related defense of provocation was well established before the 19th century. Provocation is when a person is pushed into temporary loss of control, which is limited to physical assault, mutual combat, or catching a spouse in the act of adultery. But provocation is limited to the crime of murder and only serves to mitigate the murder to voluntary manslaughter, thus making it only a partial defense. In contrast, temporary insanity can be a full defense as it asserts that the defendant lacked the intent to commit the crime.

The standard for determining insanity was established in the English case of Daniel McNaghten, who murdered Edward Drummond, the prime minister's private secretary. The court held that for a defense of insanity to be valid, the defendant had to be laboring under such delusions that he/she could not tell right from wrong. This test was adopted by most U.S. jurisdictions, although a few used broader definitions such as irresistible impulse akin to a wild beast or that mental disease in general could be grounds for acquittal. The first use of the defense of temporary insanity in the United States was made by Daniel Edgar Sickles in 1859. Sickles admitted to killing Phillip Barton Key, then district attorney for the District of Columbia, because he found out that Key was having an affair with his wife. His attorney, Edwin Stanton, argued that Sickles was driven temporarily insane by the graphic confession of the affair given to him by his wife before he murdered Key. The jury accepted the defense and acquitted him of the murder. Sickles went on to become a major general in the army, and his lawyer later became secretary of war.

The temporary insanity defense has given rise to many of the memorable defenses in the lexicon of American trials, including the Twinkie defense, taxicab driver defense, the closely related Matrix defense, and, more recently, the gay panic defense. In 1978, Dan White was charged with the murders of San Francisco Mayor George Mascone and City Supervisor Harvey Milk. During the trial, he asserted the defense of insanity based on depression. Part of the evidence presented by psychiatrist Martin Blinder that White was depressed was his change in diet from health foods to junk foods. The media ran with this depiction and erroneously reported that he was claiming to have been driven insane by the sugar in the foods, which is incorrect as the change in diet was evidence of mental illness, not its cause. White was found guilty of the lesser crime of voluntary manslaughter. A few years later John Hinckley, Jr., attempted to assassinate President Ronald Reagan, wounding him and his press secretary, James Brady. At trial, Hinckley's lawyers argued that the shootings were the result of Hinckley's fixation on Jodie Foster and his belief that if he reenacted part of a movie, he would impress her. The jury found Hinckley not guilty by reason of insanity, and he was committed to a state mental hospital.

A combination of provocation and temporary insanity has arisen in the gay panic defense, which claims that the defendant was provoked into attacking because of homosexual romantic or sexual advances that drove him/her into a state of unusual violence. This defense has been less successful than other insanity defenses. However, it has led to some deadlocked juries in the United States and has been successfully employed in other countries to mitigate murder to voluntary manslaughter.

Sentencing

A defendant has the right to present mitigating factors that would lean toward a lesser sentence. Among the factors that are often taken into account are age, maturity, lack of a previous criminal history, and probability of recidivism. During the sentencing phase, the victim or his/her family is usually granted the right to address the court. The effect of mitigating factors has been limited by the increased use of mandatory minimum sentencing in the last quarter of the 20th century as legislatures sought to remove discretion from trials. As several commentators have noted, the introduction of mandatory sentencing simply transferred discretion from the hands of judges to district attorneys, as the crime with which the defendant is charged or pleads to will have a greater effect on the sentence than mitigating factors presented to the judge or jury.

Conclusion

The core crimes and method of criminal prosecution for felonies in the United States has remained fairly constant since the colonial era. The major changes that have occurred are the increased use of scientific evidence in trials, increased media attention to a select group of trials, and the increase of defendant rights. However, the increased use of plea bargaining and other changes have led some academics to argue that the death of the American trial is imminent as jury trials become more costly and less frequent.

John Felipe Acevedo
University of Chicago

See Also: Colonial Courts; Common Law Origins of Criminal Law; Court of Common Pleas; Court of Oyer and Terminer; Court of Quarter Sessions; Courts; Courts of Indian Offenses; Defendant's Rights; Due Process; Famous Trials; Insanity Defense; Juries; Sentencing.

Further Readings

Cole, Simon A. *Suspect Identities: A History of Fingerprinting and Criminal Identification*. Cambridge, MA: Harvard University Press, 2001.

Gazal-Ayal, Oren. "Partial Ban on Plea Bargain." *Cardozo Law Review*, v.27 (2006).

Heffernan, Liz. *Scientific Evidence: Fingerprints and DNA*. Dublin: First Law Limited, 2006.

LaFave, Wayne R. *Criminal Law*, 5th ed. St. Paul, MN: West Publishing, 2010.

Langbein, J. H. *The Origins of Adversary Criminal Trial*. Oxford: Oxford University Press, 2003.

Leverick, Fiona. *Killing in Self-Defense*. Oxford: Oxford University Press, 2006.

Maeder, Thomas. *Crime and Madness: The Origins and Evolution of the Insanity Defense*. New York: Harper & Row, 1985.

Redmayne, Mike. *Expert Evidence and Criminal Justice*. Oxford: Oxford University Press, 2001.

Truman, Harry S. (Administration of)

President Harry S. Truman (1884–1972) played direct and indirect roles in the understanding of crime and punishment in the United States during his time in the White House. The Truman administration was particularly concerned about youth crime. For example, Attorney General Tom Clark noted as early as 1946 that juvenile crime was on the rise. According to Attorney General Clark, boys under the age of 18 were increasingly arrested for crimes such as homicide, theft, and rape. Because of these concerns, Truman issued a presidential proclamation in 1948 that called for a national conference to address the prevention of juvenile delinquency. The concerns of the 1940s spilled over into the 1950s, a decade that saw numerous news and magazine reports of depravity among the youth. In the minds of many, the budding concerns of the Truman administration seemed to be realized when pop culture embraced the music of Elvis "The Pelvis" Presley and movies such as James Dean's *Rebel Without a Cause*.

Influence in the Law

President Truman nominated Tom Clark, his attorney general, and Sherman Minton to the U.S. Supreme Court; Justice Clark served for nearly 18 years, and Justice Minton for seven. These justices were involved in several noteworthy cases that impacted crime and punishment in the United States. These cases include *United States v. Rabinowitz* (1950), a case in which the Supreme Court ruled that the Fourth Amendment permitted warrantless searches incident to lawful arrest; *Feiner v. New York* (1951), in which the court ruled that speech inciting a riot was not protected by the First Amendment; and *Stack v. Boyle* (1951), which ruled that bail could not be set higher than necessary to ensure the defendant's presence at his or her trial.

Perhaps the case most related to crime and punishment decided by the Supreme Court during the Truman administration was *Wolf v. Colorado* (1949). *Wolf v. Colorado* is a case in which the U.S. Supreme Court incorporated, or made applicable to the states, the protection of the Fourth Amendment's prohibition against unreasonable search

President Harry S. Truman issued a unusually large number of presidential pardons (1,913), many of which were conscientious objectors who refused to fight in World War II.

and seizure. *Wolf* had a widespread legal impact, and the extent of the rule against unreasonable search and seizure is still being determined.

The Truman administration played a major role in these cases beyond the participation of Truman's appointments to the Supreme Court. The Justice Department, in particular the solicitor general, who is a presidential appointee, must decide which cases the federal government will appeal from lower courts and also serves as the U.S. attorney during oral arguments at the Supreme Court. The solicitor general also must decide whether to issue an amicus, or friend of the court, brief detailing the position of the federal government in a particular case. The importance of these briefs should not be understated, as they have impact on which cases the Supreme Court chooses to hear and, potentially, on how the court decides a case.

Civil Rights and Pardons

Truman played a major role in protecting the rights of African Americans while he was president. Isaac Woodward, a veteran of World War II, was beaten and blinded, while wearing his uniform, by police officers in his home state of South Carolina. When President Truman was told of this event, he was furious, and ordered a Justice Department probe. The investigation led to a federal trial of several police officers, all of whom were found not guilty. Although the verdict was a political hit against the Truman administration, the impact of the Isaac Woodward incident perhaps led Truman to later sign Executive Order 9981, which desegregated the armed forces. Truman also formed the President's Commission on Civil Rights, which recommended antilynching laws, and the Truman administration offered an amicus brief in *Shelley v. Kraemer* (1948), a case in which the Supreme Court unanimously deemed housing covenants to be illegal.

Communism was among the biggest fears in American history, and the so-called Red Scare began during the Truman administration. During the Truman administration, there were several key international events that led to fears of communism at home. After World War II ended, the Soviet Union increased it satellite nations in eastern Europe, the pro-United States government in China fell to communist Mao Zedong, and communist North Korean invaded American ally South Korea. At home, the fear of spreading communism led to many actions by Congress and the president. President Truman himself issued Executive Order 9835 requiring the loyalty of any federal worker. Although President Truman was a committed anticommunist, he took issue with the tactics of Senator Joe McCarthy's crusade against communism.

One key to understanding how presidents impact policy, lawmaking, and law enforcement is to understand the unilateral powers of the presidency. One such unilateral power is the constitutional power to pardon. The power to pardon is found in Article II, Section 2 of the Constitution. The pardon is intended to be a check on the judicial branch; a fear of the authors of the Constitution was that a judge might provide a punishment that was not commensurate with the crime the person committed. There are few limits to the president's power to pardon, with impeachment being the lone instance in which a presidential pardon is not allowed. Truman issued 1,913 pardons. This was an unusually large number of pardons. By comparison, President Dwight Eisenhower issued 1,110, President John F. Kennedy issued 472, and President Lyndon Johnson issued 960 pardons. Perhaps the most interesting pardon issued by Truman was one in which he pardoned approximately 1,500 conscientious objectors who had refused to fight in World War II, and also who had refused alternative service to the country. The pardon returned voting rights and other rights of U.S. citizenship, in addition to deleting the conscientious objectors' charges and imprisonment from official records.

Conclusion
In many ways, from the appointment of Supreme Court justices and other federal judges to the issuing of pardons that limited those judges' influence to involvement in expanding civil rights of African Americans to roles played in key anticommunist legislation, Truman and his administration had major impact on the understanding, implementation, and enforcement of key aspects of crime and punishment in the United States.

Tobias T. Gibson
Westminster College

See Also: 1941 to 1960 Primary Documents; Dewey, Thomas; Eisenhower, Dwight D. (Administration of); Roosevelt, Franklin D. (Administration of).

Further Readings
Barnosky, J. "The Violent Years: Responses to Juvenile Crimes in the 1950s." *Polity*, v.38/3 (2006).
Cooper, Phillip J. *By Order of the President: The Use and Abuse of Executive Direct Action*. Lawrence: University Press of Kansas, 2002.
U.S. Department of Justice. "Presidential Clemency Actions by Administration (1945 to present)." http://www.justice.gov/pardon/actions_administration.htm (Accessed January 2011).

Twining v. New Jersey

The Fourteenth Amendment (ratified in 1868), states that "No state shall deprive any person of life, liberty or property without due process of law." It was intended to limit state power to enact laws regulating certain areas of life, and the procedures states use when prosecuting the criminally accused. *Twining v. New Jersey* (1908) raised an issue under the Fourteenth Amendment of procedural fairness in criminal proceedings. In *Twining*, the Supreme Court considered whether the Fifth Amendment's privilege against self-incrimination (which at the time applied only to the federal government) is a procedural guarantee that also applies to criminal proceedings in state courts. The court held that the right against self-incrimination is not part of the meaning of due process found in the Fourteenth Amendment. Rather, it is a nonessential procedural guarantee that is unnecessary to prevent arbitrary abuse of state power. In doing so, the court adopted the doctrine of selective incorporation, an approach that considers on a case-by-case basis whether some provisions of the Bill of Rights also limit the power of the states.

State regulators charged Albert Twining and David Cornell, directors of the Monmouth Trust & Safe Deposit Company, with a misdemeanor for falsifying documents on the financial condition of the bank. At trial, Twining and Cornell refused to take the stand in their own defense. New Jersey law allowed a trial judge to instruct a jury that they could draw the inference of guilt from a defendant's refusal to testify. The judge appeared to do so by stating "... the fact that they stay off the stand, having heard testimony which might be prejudicial to them, without availing themselves of the right to go upon the stand and contradict it, is sometimes a matter of significance." However, the judge later indicated that the jury should not interpret Twining's refusal to testify as prejudicial. Because the Supreme Court determined that the privilege against self-incrimination was a nonfundamental procedural guarantee, it never took up the issue of whether these jury instructions actually impaired Twining's right. Twining was found guilty and sentenced to six and one-half years in prison.

In upholding the New Jersey law, the Supreme Court defined due process in the Fourteenth Amendment as any legal concept or guarantee that is "a fundamental principle of liberty and justice which inheres in the very idea of free government and is the inalienable right of a citizen of such a government." The right against self-incrimination, the court argued, is not part of the meaning of due process based either upon this formulation or upon historical analysis. Rather, while a guarantee against self-incrimination is a useful principle of law, the court determined it is not essential for preventing a state from acting arbitrarily through its courts. States may include the guarantee in their own laws or state constitutions (in 1908, all but Iowa and New Jersey did), but the Fourteenth Amendment does not require this.

The court outlined an organic approach to due process that emphasized historical developments in law, and the norms, traditions, and usages of a people. For example, the Supreme Court explicitly refused to apply the entire Bill of Rights as a limitation on the power of state government, opting instead for selective incorporation. Under the selective incorporation doctrine, the court may apply some of the Bill of Rights to limit the power of the states, "… not because those rights are enumerated in the first eight amendments, but because they are of such a nature that they are included in the conception of due process of law." The court went on to examine the historical evolution of the concept of due process, and to explore the American tradition of rights identified as "fundamental principles of liberty and justice which lie at the base of all our civil and political institutions." Historically, the privilege against self-incrimination was distinct from due process, and thus could not be considered part of the meaning of due process in the Fourteenth Amendment. Furthermore, it is not fundamental to ordered liberty because state courts comply with all constitutionally mandatory procedural due process requirements when they determine that they have jurisdiction, act in conformity to general laws, act upon evidence, provide notice to parties, and provide an opportunity for them to be heard.

The selective incorporation approach in *Twining* typifies the Supreme Court's early 20th century analysis when balancing individual interests against governmental power. For example, in *Twining*, the court stated that nothing is more fundamental than the right of a state to govern in accordance with the wishes of its people. The presumption in favor of the state rarely resulted in the vindication of the individual exercise of liberty. However, by the latter half of the 20th century, societal conceptions of fundamental fairness had changed. In 1964, the Supreme Court overturned *Twining*, holding that the privilege against self-incrimination is part of the due process found in the Fourteenth Amendment.

Hans J. Hacker
Arkansas State University

See Also: Due Process; *Gideon v. Wainwright*; Trials.

Further Readings
Amar, Akhil. *The Bill of Rights: Creation and Reconstruction*. Hartford, CT: Yale University Press, 2000.
Baum, Lawrence. *The Supreme Court*, 10th ed. Washington, DC: CQ Press, 2009.
Legal Information Institute. "*Twining v. State*, 211 U.S. 78 (1908)." http://www.law.cornell.edu/supct/html/historics/USSC_CR_0211_0078_ZS.html (Accessed April 2011).
Twining v. New Jersey, 211 U.S. 78 (1908).
U.S. Supreme Court Center. "*Malloy v. Hogan*, 378 U.S. 1 (1964)." http://supreme.justia.com/us/378/1/case.html (Accessed April 2011).

Tyler, John (Administration of)

Vice President John Tyler (1790–1862) served as the 10th president of the United States, assuming office after the death of President William Henry Harrison. He was the first vice president to ascend to the presidency upon the president's death. In the wake of constitutional silence on the succession issue, Tyler established the precedent of assuming full presidential powers rather than the lesser role of acting president. Tyler was a Democrat turned Whig whose conflicts with Congress led to his use of the presidential veto power. The key event of the Tyler administration was the debate over Texas' admission to the Union as a slave state.

John Tyler's political career began in 1811, when he was elected to the Virginia legislature as a Democrat at the age of 21. He also served as Virginia governor and in the U.S. House of

Representatives and Senate. Tyler's early political career shaped his views and he became known as an advocate of the supremacy of states' rights over the federal government and a strict interpretation of the Constitution. He was a southern slaveholder and opposed federal restrictions on slavery's expansion. He also became known as a political maverick willing to oppose Democratic Party leader Andrew Jackson. Although he was a Democrat, the Whig Party chose Tyler as vice presidential candidate on the ticket with William Henry Harrison in the 1840 presidential election because of his differences with Jacksonian Democrats and his ability to attract southern voters.

The Whig ticket defeated Democratic incumbent Martin Van Buren, but Harrison died one month into his presidency. Tyler assumed the office on April 4, 1841, creating a constitutional crisis, as he was the first vice president to succeed to the presidency upon the president's death. Some politicians argued that he was simply an acting president. Tyler disagreed and assumed the full powers and duties of the office, thereby establishing future precedent, despite critics who nicknamed Tyler "His Accidency." There was no constitutional guidance on succession, which would not be added until the Twenty-Fifth Amendment in 1967.

Tyler's ascension to the presidency led to his rejection by Whigs, who were willing to accommodate his political differences as vice president but not as president. They were also angered over his vetoes of a Whig-supported act to establish a national bank, resulting in the resignation of most of the cabinet members he had inherited from Harrison. He had already alienated the Democrats and thus largely functioned as a political independent. Tyler's divisions with Congress were apparent through his use of the presidential veto power against several key pieces of legislation, including the chartering of the Third Bank of the United States, a tariff he believed violated the principles of an earlier compromise tariff of 1833, and the distribution of public land sale proceeds to the states.

Tyler demonstrated his belief in state sovereignty through his reaction to Dorr's Rebellion in Rhode Island in 1842. The rebellion, led by Thomas Wilson Dorr, sought to implement universal manhood suffrage by force when legal means had failed. Dorr himself traveled to Washington, D.C., and personally petitioned Tyler for his assistance, but Tyler denied the request, as he believed the affair to be a state matter with which the federal government should not interfere. Tyler's administration also ended the lengthy, expensive Second Seminole War (1835–42) in Florida as the U.S. Army stopped its pursuit of the few hundred remaining Seminoles who refused to emigrate west under the Indian Removal Act of 1830.

The most prominent issue facing the Tyler administration was the congressional debate over the annexation of Texas, which had recently won its independence from Mexico. Most northerners opposed annexation, while most southerners supported annexation as Texas allowed slavery. Tyler approved its annexation, which was accomplished just before he left office when Texas entered the Union as a slave state. Tyler had run for reelection in 1844 through his own third party, but withdrew after receiving little support. He remained a defender of states' rights, but also sought to avoid disunion through participation in the Washington Peace Convention of 1861. He supported Virginia's secession when that failed and was elected to the Confederate House of Representatives. John Tyler died on January 18, 1862, in Richmond, Virginia.

Marcella Bush Trevino
Barry University

See Also: Constitution of the United States of America; Indian Removal Act; Slavery, Law of.

Further Readings

Crapol, Edward P. *John Tyler: The Accidental President*. Chapel Hill: University of North Carolina Press, 2006.

Monroe, Dan. *The Republican Vision of John Tyler*. College Station: Texas A&M University Press, 2003.

Walker, Jane C. *John Tyler: A President of Many Firsts*. Granville, OH: McDonald and Woodward Publishing, 2001.

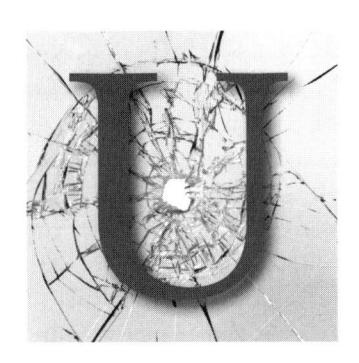

Uniform Crime Reporting Program

Uniform crime reporting refers to a standardized system of offense reporting that allows or mandates that different law enforcement agencies report on the same types of events (such as offenses known to the police or arrests), for the same time periods, using the same offense classifications, and the same rules for counting and classifying offenses.

Uniform Crime Reports

The American history of police reports on crime mirrors the history of American law enforcement in general: Crime reporting is local and of widely varying quality. In order to provide a measure of crime that is comparable across jurisdictions, the International Association of Chiefs of Police (IACP) initiated a uniform crime reporting system in 1927. This became the Uniform Crime Reports (UCR), which are compiled by the Federal Bureau of Investigation (FBI) from information submitted by local and state law enforcement agencies. For most of the last century, Americans have used the Uniform Crime Reports as their measure of the nature and extent of crime.

In his review of the history of crime statistics in America, Michael D. Maltz describes the sequence of events leading up to the creation of the Uniform Crime Reports. In the legislation creating the U.S. Department of Justice in 1870, Congress mandated that the attorney general report annually on federal and state crimes. In the following year, the National Police Association called for police to compile crime statistics. It was not until 1927 that the IACP (the successor organization to the National Police Association) formed a Committee on Uniform Crime Records. The committee included William P. Rutledge, commissioner of the Detroit Police Department, as chairperson, and August Vollmer, who was chief of the Berkeley, California, Police Department.

At its first meeting, the committee formed an advisory committee that included J. Edgar Hoover and W. M. Stuart of the Bureau of the Census. The committee's work led to the publication of *Uniform Crime Reporting* by the IACP in 1929, and police departments around the country began to collect data based on the uniform format. The first monthly reports of offenses known to the police were published by the IACP in 1930. The FBI took over the task of publishing the Uniform Crime Reports later that year. As Maltz observes, any attempt to measure crime confronts three questions: (1) What type of data should be collected? (2) Who should collect the data? and (3) How accurate are the data?

Types of Data

Early advocates of uniform crime statistics favored the use of statistics based on court convictions. But the IACP Committee on Uniform Crime Records favored the view of August Vollmer that reports of "offenses known to the police," either through citizen complaints or through police observation, furnished the best measure of the amount of crime occurring. His view was seconded by pioneering criminologist Thorsten Sellin, who argued that the value of a measure as an indicator of the "criminality" of a jurisdiction decreased as the number of procedures between the criminal event and the report increased. Judicial and correctional statistics, because they exclude crimes in which no offender is identified, underestimate the amount of crime. Further, these statistics are influenced by all the variables that affect judicial and correctional decision making.

A related question concerns which offenses should be included in uniform crime reporting. The IACP committee selected seven offenses: murder (including non-negligent manslaughter), rape, robbery, assault, burglary, larceny, and auto theft). Clayton J. Mosher, Terance D. Miethe, and Dretha M. Phillips note that these crimes are prevalent and widely agreed to be serious offenses and are likely to be reported to the police. These seven offenses are referred to as "Part I Offenses" and "Index Offenses." In 1978, arson was added by an act of Congress as an eighth Part I Offense. The FBI compiles data on the Part I offenses for offenses known to the police and for arrests. For a second set of offenses—Part II offenses—local law enforcement agencies report arrest data to the FBI.

The Part I Offenses have a long history in the common law of crime and capture the main elements of criminal behavior, namely theft and violence. Nonetheless, the index offenses do not include many crimes of great interest to police, policymakers, and the public. Notably, offenses involving possession and dealing in controlled substances are excluded, as are acts of intimate partner violence that do not rise to the level of aggravated assault. Another of the foremost criminologists of the 20th century, Edwin Sutherland, noted that white-collar crimes are also ignored. More broadly, the crimes of the wealthy and powerful (crime in the suites) are neglected compared to the crimes of the working class and poor (crime in the streets).

Collection of Data

Because law enforcement is administered in the United States through thousands of local agencies, there was an obvious need for oversight and administration of data collection at the national level. Although some groups advocated using the Bureau of the Census, the IACP report on Uniform Crime Reporting called for the effort to be housed at the Bureau of Investigation (later the FBI) in the U.S. Department of Justice. This arrangement was implemented in 1930 and has remained in place ever since.

Accuracy of Data

There is no gold standard in the measurement of crime. All crime measures are based on compiling reports from observers with their own biases, including victims, offenders, and police officers. All police statistics, no matter how scrupulously they are collected, can capture only those offenses that citizens report or that the police detect. There is a "dark figure of crime"—offenses that are not reported. Crime analysts generally assume that, with the exception of rape, more serious crimes are more likely to be reported than minor crimes. Therefore, more reliance is placed on murder data from the UCR than other data. Another problem that plagues police measures is "cooking the books." Because crime statistics may be used to measure the effectiveness of the police in reducing crime, there is always the temptation to manipulate the statistics to make crime problems appear less extensive than they really are.

The uniform classification and reporting of offenses under the uniform crime reporting system also leaves room for error. There may be discrepancies between the definitions of offenses in the *UCR Reporting Handbook* and state statute. Further, the rules for counting are complicated in their treatment of attempted crimes, the number of separate offenses to be counted in multiple offense incidents, and the application of the FBI's hierarchy rule, which mandates that when multiple offenses are committed in the same incident, only the most serious offense is to be counted and the rest are to be ignored. For example, in the case of an offender who breaks into a house, steals some credit cards, and rapes one of the occupants, only the rape is counted. Yet another issue is who reports a crime when several different agencies respond to the same call for service.

Many agencies submit incomplete reports to the FBI, omitting data for some time period. The FBI uses imputation procedures to estimate the number of crimes occurring annually in such cases. Researchers have questioned these procedures, which ignore seasonal variations in the number of crimes reported and assume that similar size population units have similar crime rates. The FBI uses several methods to improve data quality, including training and education, tests of the logic of and reasonableness of the data, the soundness of the aggregated statistics, and a quality assurance review process.

Interpreting Crime Statistics

Every year when the Uniform Crime Reports are released, media outlets report that crime has increased or decreased in a local jurisdiction or nationwide. Although the bureau notes

J. Edgar Hoover, the director of the Federal Bureau of Investigation (FBI), and W. M. Stuart headed a committee to create a uniform crime reporting system, which the FBI continues to use. Hoover is pictured in his FBI office in 1940.

that they cannot vouch for the accuracy of such statistics, these disclaimers are usually ignored. For the media and for many politicians, crime as measured by the UCR is actual crime. Mosher, Miethe, and Phillips note that the FBI has done little to discourage this practice. In fact, J. Edgar Hoover used the UCR to bolster his own assertions about trends and causes of serious crime. This practice continues to this day: the press release from the FBI for the 2010 Uniform Crime Reports begins by making assertions about the estimated number of violent crimes and property crimes (and not numbers of offenses known to the police).

In 1958, the FBI began to estimate national crime rates for each of the Part I Offenses and to report indexes of violent crime, property crime, and "total" crime based on the rates of index offenses. The UCR crime rates are crude crime rates that are computed by simply dividing the number of offenses occurring in a calendar year by the estimated population of the jurisdiction, and multiplying this number by 100,000. This yields a rate per 100,000 population. It is described as a crude rate because it is computed for the population as a whole and not for subgroups or other units that are most likely to be affected. For example, the rate of motor vehicle theft is not reported per 100,000 motor vehicles, but per 100,000 persons.

The rates for each offense may be added to create the index offense rates for violent crimes, property crimes, and a total crime rate. Great care must be taken in interpreting these rates, because generally, the more serious a crime is, the less frequently it occurs and the less it contributes to overall crime rates. Thus murder, the most serious of the index offenses, is typically around one tenth of 1 percent of all index crimes, while larceny-theft, the least serious index offense, is about 60 percent of all index crimes. There are more larceny-thefts committed each year than the combined total of all other index offenses. Another issue is the comparison of crime data across time and across jurisdictions. The accuracy of UCR data is plagued by a number of different threats. As a result, attempts to determine whether City A has more crime than City B, or whether crime has increased or decreased over time in City A, must proceed with caution. One method of smoothing out random fluctuation in crime rates is to average them over a three-to-five-year period.

Incident-Based Crime Measures

In 1962, the FBI began collecting data on the characteristics of homicide offenses, victims, and offenders and reporting them in the *Supplementary Homicide Reports*. This was the first example of collecting data based on the characteristics of crime incidents, as opposed to a summary count of offenses such as the Uniform Crime Reports. After extensive review and consultation with the IACP and a number of experts on crime measurement, the FBI and the Bureau of Justice Statistics issued the *Blueprint for the Future of the Uniform Crime Reporting Program* in 1985. The *Blueprint* recommended that law enforcement agencies move to an incident-based reporting system for all offenses. After piloting these ideas in South Carolina, the FBI presented the National Incident-Based Reporting System (NIBRS) in 1988.

NIBRS does not present an aggregated, summary count of offenses like the UCR. Instead, it presents data on characteristics of victims, property targets of offending, offenders, incidents, and offense characteristics. This creates a wealth of offense data that is potentially of great utility, but it also demands that law enforcement agencies have crime information system software and hardware that are up to the task. There are other variables to implementing NIBRS (or similar incident-based systems). Since police officers are not primarily concerned with the completeness of data for research purposes and may not be diligent in completing the detailed reports, missing data is a problem. Mosher, Miethe, and Phillips note that the incentives for the police to go to the trouble and expense of participating in NIBRS are not immediately clear. They also note that, since NIBRS eliminates the hierarchy rule used in the UCR (described above), reporting NIBRS data may make it appear that index offenses have increased dramatically.

Incident-based data is regarded as essential by crime analysts. Crime analysis involves using crime data and other relevant information for the purposes of detecting, analyzing, and responding to crime and related problems. Many police departments have incorporated crime analysis into their strategic and tactical responses to crime. But in addition to the information that NIBRS provides, analysis requires data on locations and their characteristics for purposes of mapping and crafting responses based on making locations less tempting places for crime to occur. As incident-based reporting becomes less cumbersome with technological advances, and as police officers begin to find utility in this approach, it should become more common. Since the change to incident-based systems is voluntary for most law enforcement agencies, the process will take some time.

Jerome McKean
Ball State University

See Also: Common Law Origins of Criminal Law; Crime and Arrest Statistics Analysis; Crime Rates; Federal Bureau of Investigation; Hoover, J. Edgar; International Association of Chiefs of Police.

Further Readings

Federal Bureau of Investigation, "Crime in the United States" http://www.fbi.gov/stats-services/crimestats (Accessed May 2011).

James, N. and Logan Rishard Council. *How Crime in the United States is Measured*. Washington, DC: Congressional Research Service, 2008.

Maltz, Michael. "Crime Statistics: A Historical Perspective." *Crime and Delinquency*, v.23/1 (1977).

Mosher, Clayton J., Terance D. Miethe, and Dretha M. Phillips. *The Mismeasure of Crime*. Thousand Oaks, CA: Sage, 2002.

U.S. Department of Justice. *Blueprint for the Future of the Uniform Crime Reporing Program*. Washington, DC: U.S. Department of Justice, 1985.

United States Attorneys

The 93 U.S attorneys represent the United States in all legal matters in which the United States has an interest. While the United States has interests in both civil and criminal matters, the bulk of the work performed by U.S attorneys involves the prosecution of federal criminal offenses. Created in 1789, the function of U.S. attorneys has not changed significantly. This does not mean the position has remained static. Over time, the position has gained stature, grown in numbers, increased its workload, and lost some independence. As a result, U.S. attorneys have featured in most of the nation's significant legal battles. As the legal representatives of the United States, U.S. attorneys appear before federal district and circuit courts throughout the nation. They represent the government in cases when the government is sued, such as civil rights violations, and they prosecute federal criminal offenses. This latter role generates the most attention and controversy.

History
Created by the Judiciary Act of 1789 by the first Congress, U.S. attorneys were spread among the 13 district courts to represent the government in all legal matters occurring in the respective courts. Congress gave the president the power to appoint each U.S. attorney. The first U.S. attorneys primarily brought civil lawsuits to collect money owed to the United States either by its officers or those who evaded taxes. They were paid on a fee basis, meaning that they could only work for the government on a part-time basis.

While their civil function consumed much of their time, their prosecutorial role garnered the most controversy. U.S. attorneys soon became a means to implement government policy. In 1793, the government proclaimed neutrality when war began between Great Britain and France. To enforce neutrality, U.S. attorneys prosecuted Americans who fought for one side or the other. Five years later, U.S. attorneys prosecuted newspaper writers and a congressman who criticized President John Adams's policies. U.S. attorneys, however, were not merely tools of the president. They exercised independent authority to pursue, or refuse, criminal charges. President Thomas Jefferson imposed an embargo on all foreign trade. Though he had selected all of the U.S. attorneys, not all enforced the embargo as Jefferson wished. Instead, they sided with local merchants who strongly opposed the trade embargo. Despite his efforts, Jefferson could not force cases upon them.

Over time, the U.S. attorney position changed but maintained its original function. The position's independence decreased while it increased in reputation, workload, and numbers. At first, few people wanted to become U.S. attorneys. It was not a lucrative position, and it detracted from private practice. Over time, the position became more prominent. Those who held U.S. attorney positions used them to obtain higher offices or to move to the judiciary. As the position rose in prominence, attorneys with more ability filled the positions, providing the United States with better representation.

Evolution
While the initial workload of U.S. attorneys was burdensome only to their private practices, with the end of the Civil War, the government's legal business increased dramatically. At first, they handled claims for reimbursement from veterans. Soon after, they began enforcing new civil rights laws. These cases proved remarkably difficult for U.S. attorneys. They often lacked the support of the attorney general, the presiding judges, and the members of juries. After that, U.S. attorneys turned to antitrust and national security. Throughout this process, the need for assistants increased. As more assistants were appointed, the power of U.S. attorneys increased.

To check this increasing power, discretionary authority for some crimes began shifting from the U.S. attorneys to the Department of Justice. To cope with the increasing workload and to unify the government's legal positions, Congress created the Justice Department in 1871 and mandated that U.S. attorneys answer to the attorney general. Prior to that point, there had been several executive officials to whom U.S. attorneys answered but these officials lacked significant power. With the creation of the Justice Department, a cabinet-level official controlled all government litigation.

Despite this control, U.S. attorneys still filed criminal cases without oversight from the Justice Department. This led to questionable prosecutorial decisions. For example, during World War I, ambitious U.S. attorneys prosecuted speech-related Espionage Act cases, which was not consistent with the Justice Department's policy regarding such cases. It also led to pretextual prosecutions, prosecutions designed to incapacitate criminals for crimes committed but not prosecutable. The most notorious example of this was the prosecution of Al Capone for tax evasion. Soon after, the Justice Department began issuing directives requiring department approval prior to filing tax charges. Similar directives followed for racketeering and national security–related offenses.

The ever-increasing workload, coupled with westward expansion and population growth, created the need for more U.S. attorneys. New states meant new judicial districts, and as the population increased, districts within states divided. As the number of U.S. attorney positions increased, the president delegated the appointment task to others. Senators began making recommendations to the president regarding whom to appoint.

Expansion and growth also increased the workload, necessitating assistants for the U.S. attorney. The number of assistants was established by the attorney general, and later by the Justice Department. While this gave the administration some measure of control, the U.S. attorney selected the assistant, making the assistant loyal to the U.S. attorney. In most instances, the assistants left office when the U.S. attorney did. This left the government with talented but inexperienced representation. To resolve this problem and to provide more central control, assistant U.S. attorneys were given the same protections as other government employees.

These changes to the U.S. attorney position made federal prosecutors central players in the legal battles that shaped the United States throughout its history. Today, they serve on the front lines of the domestic war against terrorism. Prior generations dealt with problems of organized crime, Soviet espionage, antitrust, civil rights, and slavery. In each instance, the U.S. attorneys represented the government's position, for better or for worse.

Scott Ingram
High Point University

See Also: Adams, John (Administration of); Alien and Sedition Acts of 1798; Antitrust Law; Capone, Al; Espionage Act of 1917; Fugitive Slave Act of 1793; Fugitive Slave Act of 1850; Jefferson, Thomas (Administration of); Judiciary Act of 1789; Justice, Department of; Neutrality Enforcement in 1793–1794; Organized Crime, History of; Washington, George (Administration of).

Further Readings
Baker, Nancy B. *Conflicting Loyalties: Law and Politics in the Attorney General's Office, 1789–1990*. Lawrence: University Press of Kansas, 1992.
Cummings, Homer and Carl McFarland. *Federal Justice: Chapters in the History of Justice and the Federal Executive*. New York: Macmillan, 1937.
Eisenstein, James. *Counsel for the United States: U.S. Attorneys in the Federal System*. Baltimore, MD: Johns Hopkins University Press, 1978.
Richman, Daniel C. and William J. Stuntz. "Al Capone's Revenge: An Essay on the Political Economy of Pretextual Prosecution." *Columbia Law Review*, v.105 (2005).

United States v. Ballard

United States v. Ballard, 322 U.S. 78 (1944), is the Supreme Court case prohibiting the government from inquiring into the truthfulness of a religious belief. Edna and Donald Ballard had been convicted for using the mail system to defraud people by falsely asserting that they had the supernatural power to cure illnesses and disease. Fraud is obtaining property under false pretenses. A majority of the court held that a jury may not inquire into whether the Ballards' beliefs were true, only whether the Ballards sincerely believed their beliefs to be true. Guy Ballard was the founder of the I AM movement, one of several 1930s theosophical movements popular at the time. The I AM movement claimed to have 1 million followers in the United States and may have reached over 3 million people through classes and meetings. It taught that a society of liberated and immortal souls worked to guide the evolution of humanity. St. Germain, Jesus, and George Washington were among these ascended masters. Ballard claimed that he was an embodiment of some of these souls and that he possessed miraculous powers to cure afflictions that medical science could not. Ballard, his wife Edna, and their son Donald solicited contributions through the mail in exchange for the promise of being cured. The Ballards alleged that they had healed hundreds of people.

Several former members of the I AM movement questioned the Ballards' claims. After Guy

A portrait of Guy and Edna Ballard hangs at the Saint Germain Foundation, located in Schaumburg, Illinois, outside Chicago. Saint Germain Foundation is the parent organization for about 300 groups using variations of the name I AM.

Ballard's death, his wife and son were tried and convicted of using the mail to defraud their victims by professing to have the power to cure all illnesses. The government charged that the Ballards "knew well" that they were making false claims and that the beliefs about miraculous healing were themselves false. The defendants had allegedly extracted over $3 million from their followers in their scheme.

The trial judge instructed the jury not to consider the truth or falsity of the Ballards' religious beliefs but only whether they honestly believed they had the powers they claimed. The jury convicted the Ballards on one count of fraud. The government asked the Ninth U.S. Court of Appeals to overturn the judge's instructions and order the trial court to determine whether the Ballards in fact had the power to heal. The Ballards' attorney responded that the government intended to attack the Ballards' religious beliefs, the free exercise of which is protected by the First Amendment. The Ninth Court sided with the government.

In a 5–4 decision, the Supreme Court overruled the Ninth Circuit Court. Justice William Douglas, supported by Justices Hugo Black, Stanley Reed, Frank Murphy, and Wiley Rutledge, held that the judge's instructions were proper. A jury should only decide whether a religious belief is sincerely held. There should be no attempt to determine whether the belief is actually true. The First Amendment's free exercise of religious belief clause prohibits the government from placing religious beliefs on trial. "Men can believe what they cannot prove." Chief Justice Harlan Stone, along with Justices Felix Frankfurter and Owen Roberts, dissented. He argued that the truthfulness of the claims should be considered by the jury. Stone feared that a religious exemption for fraudulent beliefs would turn the "freedom to worship" into the "freedom to procure money by making false statements about one's religious beliefs." Justice Robert Jackson dissented. He believed that the case should have never come to trial because the government must never entwine itself in disputes over the truth or falsity of any religious belief or doctrine.

Neither Edna nor Donald Ballard served time for their conviction. In a second case, *Ballard v. United States*, the Supreme Court overturned the original conviction. The exclusion of women from their jury violated the federal law on jury selection. *United States v. Ballard* established the constitutional doctrine that the sincerity of religious beliefs may be challenged but not the beliefs' truthfulness. The First Amendment's free exercise clause prevents the government from unfairly burdening individuals' constitutional right to the free and unhindered exercise of their faith. Supreme Court rulings in a long line of cases support the right of small and unpopular groups to spread their message The *Ballard* case protects minority religions disfavored by mainstream culture by shielding them from government harassment.

Timothy J. O'Neill
Southwestern University

See Also: Douglas, William O.; Religion and Crime, History of; Religion and Crime, Sociology of.

Further Reading

Ahlstrom, Sidney. *A Religious History of the American People*. New Haven, CT: Yale University Press, 1972.

Noonan, John. *The Lustre of Our Country*. Berkeley: University of California Press, 1998.

United States v. E. C. Knight Company

Enacted in 1890, the Sherman Anti-Trust Act was a federal government effort to combat the increasing monopolization of industries during the latter decades of the 19th century. This effort was impeded by the 1895 U.S. Supreme Court's decision in *E. C. Knight*, which held that under the Constitution, the act could only be used to regulate commercial activities, which the court distinguished from the processes of manufacturing.

When the American Sugar Refining Company purchased stock in four sugar refineries in Philadelphia, it gained almost complete control of the nation's sugar refining business. It was charged with violating the Sherman Act, which made it illegal to engage in any "contract, combination in the form of trust, or otherwise, or conspiracy in restraint of trade or commerce among the several States." The Supreme Court was asked to decide whether this was a constitutional exercise of Congress's power to regulate interstate commerce. Article I, Section 8 of the Constitution states that Congress may "regulate Commerce with foreign nations, and among the several States, and with the Indian Tribes." In an 8–1 decision, the court ruled that the Sherman Act was constitutional, but that it could not be used to restrict the purely manufacturing processes of the sugar refineries. Chief Justice Melville W. Fuller wrote the opinion for the majority of the court.

Emphasizing the need to maintain a distinction between congressional power to regulate interstate commerce and the police power of the states (to regulate for the health, safety, and welfare of their citizens), Fuller reasoned that manufacturing was not a part of commerce. He rejected the government's argument that refined sugar was a "necessary of life" and that the monopolization of its manufacture inevitably affected the commercial relations of "a large part of the population of the United States." Fuller explained that "Commerce succeeds to manufacture, and is not a part of it." He argued that when a company manufactures a product that is intended to be transported across state lines, the manufacturing is not itself a commercial activity. Fuller distinguished between indirect and direct effects on interstate commerce, concluding that manufacturing had only an indirect effect. As such, the manufacturing processes in this case were not commerce and were therefore not subject to the terms of the Sherman Act. They were local activities that could only be regulated by the states.

This approach was emblematic of the formalistic approach to interpreting the Constitution that prevailed in a majority of the court's cases during the late 19th and early 20th centuries. In *Gibbons v. Ogden* (1824), the court concluded that Congress was empowered to "prescribe the rule by which commerce is to be governed." In decisions such as *E. C. Knight*, the court placed significant constraints on this prescription power by adopting a narrow definition of "interstate commerce." In a lengthy dissenting opinion in *E. C. Knight*, Justice John Marshall Harlan argued that the Sherman Act could regulate the sugar manufacturing monopoly because the company was controlling much more than just the manufacture of refined sugar. Adopting the approach of legal realism, which would later dominate the court's decisions, Harlan accounted for the way in which the nation's economy was changing and looked at the economic effects of the sugar trust. He concluded that when "manufacture ends, that which has been manufactured becomes a subject of commerce."

E. C. Knight dealt a blow to efforts to rein in industrial monopolies. However, in *Northern Securities Co. v. United States* (1904), the court held that Congress had the constitutional power to break up a railroad monopoly because at issue was transportation which, unlike manufacturing, was a commercial activity. This demonstrated that the Sherman Act could still be used to achieve some of its original goals. The 1895 decision represented a triumph for the conservative laissez-faire approach to the regulation of business and a strong fidelity to principles of federalism. However, by the 1930s, changes in the court's personnel had brought a new, more liberal majority to the bench, a majority that adopted many of the realist principles of Justice Harlan's *E. C. Knight* dissent.

Helen J. Knowles
Whitman College

See Also: Antitrust Law; *Gibbons* v. *Ogden*; Sherman Anti-Trust Act of 1890.

Further Readings
Gibbons v. Ogden, 22 U.S. 1 (1824).
McCurdy, Charles W. "The Knight Sugar Decision of 1895 and the Modernization of American Corporation Law, 1869–1903." *Business History Review*, v.53/3 (1979).
Northern Securities Co. v. United States, 193 U.S. 197 (1904).
Sherman Anti-Trust Act of 1890, codified at 15 U.S.C. §1.
United States v. E. C. Knight Company, 156 U.S. 1 (1895).

United States v. Hudson and Goodwin

A U.S. Supreme Court case decided by the Marshall Court in 1812, *U.S. v. Hudson and Goodwin* (11 U.S. 32) held that federal courts lack authority to adjudicate common law crimes. Prior to an inferior federal court rendering a criminal conviction, Congress must statutorily declare the activity to be criminal, assign penalties, and extend jurisdiction over the offense to the federal courts. The defendants in the case, Barzillai Hudson and George Goodwin, were charged with having libeled Congress and President Thomas Jefferson by alleging a conspiracy with Napoleon Bonaparte. As libel was a common law crime that had not been codified by Congress, the broadly defined question of law concerned the power of federal courts to exercise common law jurisdiction in criminal cases.

No Punishment Without Law
Writing the majority opinion, Justice William Johnson, Jr., commenced by observing that the Constitution concedes only express limited powers to the federal government and reserves all others to the states. With reference to the judicial branch, the Constitution provides original jurisdiction only to the Supreme Court, and only with regard to particular cases and controversies. All inferior federal courts, along with their respective jurisdictions, depend entirely upon the will of the legislature. By statute, Congress both creates lower federal courts and defines the authority of their operations. To assume otherwise, according to the court, would permit inferior courts to infinitely and unconstitutionally expand their own authority.

Although the case presented an issue of first impression—that is, an original question of law for which no precedent by earlier courts yet existed—the Marshall Court noted a general acquiescence among legal scholars and public opinion in affirmation of the outcome. The decision served as a validation of Republican convictions, which held—in opposition to Federalist views—that the powers of the federal government were strictly limited to the express grants of the Constitution. Republicans thus denied that federal judicial jurisdiction encompassed a federal common law of crimes.

In dicta, the court recognized an exception for ancillary implied powers of the judiciary deemed necessary for the exercise of vested powers. In order to manage proceedings, vindicate authority, and effectuate decrees, the court admitted that federal courts possessed inherent authority to hold litigants in contempt and to enforce court orders. Later decisions expanded this ancillary jurisdiction in order to appoint prosecutors for criminal contempt actions (*Young v. United States ex rel. Vuitton et Fils S.A.*, 481 U.S. 787 [1987]) and to compel payment for misconduct sanctions (*Chambers v. NASCO, Inc.*, 501 U.S. 32 [1991]). Although these implied administrative powers are exercised without direct authorization in statute, the court reiterated that federal courts possess no criminal jurisdiction absent statutory authority.

The Marshall Court ratified within American federal jurisprudence the concept of *nulla poena sine lege* ("no punishment without law"), which prohibits punishment for actions that are not specifically prescribed in law. The principle mirrors the related axiom, *nullum crimen, nulla poena sine praevia lege poenali* ("neither crime nor punishment without previous penal law"), reflected in the Constitution's prohibition against ex post facto laws. These principles required clarification in light of America's recent independence from the English common law system and transition to a constitutional republic of limited federal powers.

Effect on Common Law

Within common law jurisdictions, substantial areas of law are almost entirely defined by the common law rather than legislative statute. An inheritance of immemorial custom, ancient reason, and natural law, the English common law is understood to have been discovered over many centuries as courts developed a corpus of judgments suitable to safeguard English liberty. Judicial decisions therefore serve as legal precedent for new cases, which are resolved by analogical reasoning and the principle of *stare decisis et non quieta movere* ("to stand by decisions and not disturb the undisturbed").

Nearly all U.S. criminal law statutes are codifications of common law crimes and rely heavily upon precedent for clarity and meaning. In order to preserve this common law tradition, some state legislatures have enacted statutes that incorporate the entire common law—insofar as it does not conflict with federal or state statutory law—and thereby permit state courts to continue the common law tradition. Yet the Marshall Court effectively terminated the enforcement of common law crimes at the federal level.

Justin Paulette
Independent Scholar

See Also: Common Law Origins of Criminal Law; Federal Common Law of Crime; Judiciary Act of 1789; Supreme Court, U.S.

Further Readings

Hall, Kermit and James Ely. *The Oxford Guide to United States Supreme Court Decisions*. New York: Oxford University Press, 2009.

Rehnquist, William. *The Supreme Court*. New York: Random House, 2001.

Rowe, Gary D. "The Sound of Silence: *United States v. Hudson & Goodwin,* the Jeffersonian Ascendancy, and the Abolition of Federal Common Law Crimes." *Yale Law Journal*, v.101/4 (1992).

United States v. Nixon

The decision of the U.S. Supreme Court in *United States v. Nixon* (1974), an important landmark in constitutional law, held that even the president of the United States has to comply with requests for evidence from criminal prosecutors.

In this case, President Richard Nixon was attempting to withhold audio recordings of Oval Office conversations that implicated him in a conspiracy to cover up burglaries orchestrated by members of his campaign. The episode as a whole—known as the Watergate scandal—represents one of the worst instances of government corruption and abuse of official power in American history.

United States v. Nixon was the key legal battle in the scandal and led to Nixon's resignation as president. The conflict began with the botched burglary of the Democratic National Committee headquarters in Washington's Watergate complex on June 17, 1972. The burglary was part of a wider effort, financed by supporters of the president and led by members of his administration, to use illegal tactics to gain every advantage in Nixon's bid for re-election. Following the discovery of the break-in, Nixon and his aides used campaign money to bribe the five burglars into silence after they had been tried and convicted.

Under pressure from the press, the president authorized appointment of a special prosecutor to investigate the Watergate break-in. In the course of the investigation, it was revealed that Nixon had maintained an audio recording system in the White House that could confirm allegations of high-level involvement in the crimes. Special prosecutor Archibald Cox subpoenaed the president, asking for these tapes, but the president fired Cox and refused to comply with the subpoena, releasing only edited transcripts of the tapes. Nixon was forced to appoint a replacement

First Lady Pat Nixon kisses Betty Ford while Gerald Ford (left) and President Richard Nixon stand by. The Nixon family was leaving the White house for the last time after Nixon resigned.

special prosecutor, Leon Jaworski, who took the case to the Supreme Court.

Before the court, President Nixon invoked the principle of executive privilege, arguing that the president's conversations with his advisers must remain private in order to ensure frank and open counsel. Nixon argued that this executive privilege was absolute and not subject to judicial review. Further, it was argued, because the special prosecutor was a member of the executive branch (the Department of Justice), this was an intrabranch dispute, and the court's involvement would violate the separation of powers. Because of the intense scrutiny and the importance of the case, the justices strove for a unanimous decision. On July 24, 1974, Chief Justice Warren Burger delivered an 8–0 decision that President Nixon had to comply with a subpoena for copies of the "Watergate tapes." (Justice William Rehnquist, a former official in the Justice Department under Nixon, had recused himself from the case.) In his ruling, Burger rejected the attempt to bar the court's review, even though the dispute occurred between two executive branch officers, citing the court's historic duty to "say what the law is."

Supporting the doctrine of executive privilege for the first time, the court stated that the privilege is "fundamental to the operation of Government." However, the court ruled that Nixon's claim of an absolute privilege went too far. Except in cases of "military, diplomatic, or sensitive national security secrets," the public interest is best served by allowing criminal proceedings to function. The justices ruled that, in order to create a "workable government," the president's "generalized assertion of privilege must yield to the demonstrated, specific need for evidence in a pending criminal trial."

Just three days after the decision was released, the House Judiciary Committee passed articles of impeachment against the president. Complying with the court's judgment, Nixon released the audio recordings. Among the tapes was a "smoking gun," in which the president can be heard agreeing to end the Federal Bureau of Investigation (FBI) investigation into the Watergate burglary. Facing certain conviction in the Senate, Nixon resigned on August 8, 1974. In the wake of the episode, a number of important reforms were aimed at ensuring the powers of oversight and investigation into high-level political corruption. The decision in *United States v. Nixon* remains a major landmark in American law, often taken to represent the principle that no individual or crime is "above the law." While unquestionably a defeat for Nixon, however, some legal commentators have argued that by recognizing even a limited executive privilege, the court in fact helped to expand executive power.

Patrick Schmidt
Joseph Lalli
Macalester College

See Also: 1961 to 1980 Primary Documents; Corruption, History of; Nixon, Richard (Administration of).

Further Readings
Kutler, Stanley L. *The Wars of Watergate*. New York: W. W. Norton, 1992.
Olson, Keith W. *Watergate: The Presidential Scandal That Shook America*. Lawrence: University Press of Kansas, 2003.

Stefoff, Rebecca. *U.S. v. Nixon: The Limits of Presidential Privilege*. New York: Marshall Cavendish Benchmark, 2009.

United States v. One Book Called Ulysses

United States v. One Book Called Ulysses was a 1933 case in which James Joyce's novel *Ulysses* was examined for obscenity. The case originated in the U.S. District Court for the Southern District of New York, where Judge John Woolsey ruled that the novel was not obscene, but protected under the U.S. Constitution as free expression. Woolsey's decision was affirmed by the U.S. Court of Appeals for the Second Circuit. Woolsey's decision helped to encourage the importation and publication of serious literature, even if it contained explicit language or sexual situations.

Novelist James Joyce's most famous novel, *Ulysses*, was published in 1922. The novel was first published in serial installments in the literary magazine *The Little Review* from 1914 to 1921. One of the installments, "Nausicaa Episode," which contained a masturbation scene, was the subject of a complaint to the U.S. district attorney after it shocked a girl of unknown age in New York. Publishers Margaret Caroline Anderson and Jane Heap were fined for publishing the installment, which the court declared seemed "like the work of a disordered mind," and was found to be obscene. Publication of the novel *Ulysses* in the United States was subsequently implicitly banned.

In 1933, Random House, which maintained rights to publish the novel in the United States, arranged for a test case to challenge the informal ban. Random House hoped to publish the novel without fear of prosecution. The publisher made arrangements to import a French edition of the novel into the United States, where it would be seized by the U.S. Customs Service upon its arrival. Initially, U.S. Customs agents neglected to seize the novel, with an official reasoning, "everybody brings that in." Officials were convinced later to confiscate the novel. In spite of declaring it a literary masterpiece, the U.S. attorney found the novel to be obscene and brought charges against the novel under the Tariff Act of 1930, which allowed for the forfeiture and destruction of such imported works.

Random House contested the seizure of *Ulysses* in the U.S. District Court in New York City. The United States asserted that the novel was obscene because it contained sexual and "unparlorlike" language; was blasphemous, particularly in its treatment of the Catholic Church; and openly printed coarse thoughts and desires that were traditionally not shared in public. Such attributes were perceived as a threat to long-held moral, religious, and political beliefs and thereby subversive of the established order. The lawyer for Random House, Morris Ernst, concentrated on downplaying the novel's potentially offensive or subversive elements and emphasized its artistic integrity and literary success.

Trial judge John Woolsey ruled that *Ulysses* was not obscene. He acknowledged the success of the novel and declared that the author was sincere in showing how the minds of his characters worked and what they were thinking. He suggested that eliminating the sexual themes from Joyce's characters would have been an artistic failure. Finally, Judge Woolsey ruled that the novel, when read in its entirety, was not predominantly sexual or lustful. *Ulysses* was not obscene and could be published openly in the United States. Within minutes of the decision, Random House started work on printing the book. One hundred copies were published in 1934 in order to establish official copyrights. This was the first legal publication of *Ulysses* in any English-speaking nation. England did not publish *Ulysses* until 1936.

The U.S. attorney appealed Judge Woolsey's decision to the U.S. Court of Appeals for the Second Circuit, where a three-judge panel affirmed the decision by a 2–1 vote. The trial and appellate court decisions established that a court evaluating obscenity characteristics of a work should consider the entire work, rather than isolated excerpts; its effects on an average, rather than an overly sensitive, person; and its relationship to contemporary community standards. These principles ultimately contributed to the Supreme Court's establishment of obscenity standards. Judge Woolsey's trial court opinion has been reproduced in Random House printings of the novel and is believed to be one of the most widely distributed judicial opinions in history. The opinion continues to be recognized as a perceptive analysis of Joyce's work.

Tiffany Middleton
Independent Scholar

See Also: 1921 to 1940 Primary Documents; Appellate Courts; Obscenity; Obscenity Laws; Pornography.

Further Readings
Ellmann, Richard. *James Joyce*. New York: Oxford University Press, 1982.
Vanderham, Paul. *James Joyce and Censorship: The Trials of* Ulysses. New York: New York University Press, 1998.

Urbanization

Urbanization refers to the process in which people move from rural areas to cities; it also involves the transformation of rural areas into cities. It is a historical as well as contemporary worldwide phenomenon, with criminological, cultural, economic, environmental, and social dimensions and implications.

Although anatomically modern humans originated about 200,000 years ago, cities have existed for fewer than 10,000 years. Social scientists often claim that human history has been marked by three "urban revolutions." The first urban revolution—from around 8000 to 2000 B.C.E.—occurred with the advent of agriculture; animal husbandry, along with the cultivation of plants and fungi for food and other by-products, afforded humans a sedentary lifestyle for the first time. The second urban revolution—from around 1700 to 1950—coincided with the Industrial Revolution; changes in agriculture, manufacturing, mining, transportation, and technology turned cities into loci of commerce, and many people flocked to cities to take advantage of the opportunities provided by the new urban-based economy. The third urban revolution is currently under way and in 2008, for the first time in history, half of the world's population lived in cities. (In comparison, less than 30 percent of the world's population lived in cities in 1950.) Though on a global scale people are increasingly concentrating in cities, the greatest population growth is occurring in cities in developing countries. Demographers predict that by 2025, developing nations will account for 85 percent of the world's population, and that in 2025–50, the percentage of the global population living in cities will rise to 67 percent.

Characteristics of Urban Areas
Cities differ with respect to climate, culture, economic development, and size. Early modern writers on cities such as Germans Max Weber, Georg Simmel, and Oswald Spengler treated the city as a "unitary phenomenon" by contrasting the city with other kinds of social entities. Subsequent writers such as those affiliated with the Chicago School of Sociology at the University of Chicago (sometimes referred to as the "Ecological School"), which emerged in the 1920s and 1930s, took a different approach.

These scholars treated the city as a living organism—they thought of "the city, that is to say, the place and the people, with all the machinery and administrative devices that go

The streets of a 1920s ghetto in Chicago. The social characteristics of urban life have been studied extensively by the Chicago School of Sociology at the University of Chicago.

with them, as organically related"—and endeavored to understand the "ecology" or internal workings of the city by asking questions about the relations between the parts in the city and about the different kinds of experiences people had within the same city at the same time. For example, Louis Wirth, who defined the city as "a relatively large, dense, and permanent settlement of socially heterogeneous individuals," explained that "[u]rbanization no longer denotes merely the process by which persons are attracted to a place called the city and incorporated into its system of life. It refers also to the mode of life which is associated with the growth of cities, and finally to the changes in the direction of modes of life recognized as urban which are apparent among people, wherever they may be, who have come under the spell of the influences which the city exerts by virtue of the power of its institutions and personalities operating through the means of communication and transformation." Wirth suggested that the characteristics of urban life and the differences between cities of various sizes and types could be explained on the basis of three variables—number, density of settlement, and degree of heterogeneity.

According to Wirth, urbanism, as a characteristic mode of life, could be approached empirically from three interrelated perspectives: (1) as a physical structure comprising a population base, a technology, and an ecological order; (2) as a system of social organization involving a characteristic social structure, a series of social institutions, and a typical pattern of social relationships; and (3) as a set of attitudes and ideas, and a constellation of personalities engaging in typical forms of collective behavior and subject to characteristic mechanisms of social control.

Today, scholars of cities and urban areas agree that characterizing an area as "urban" on the basis of size alone is an arbitrary endeavor; what constitutes a city will vary from country to country. Rather, when distinguishing between urban and rural areas, they frequently look to how people make a living. Whereas most people residing in rural areas engage in occupations that involve the cultivation or harvesting of natural resources (e.g., farming, fishing, and logging), most individuals in urban areas hold jobs that are not directly connected with natural resources and thus need to rely on rural areas for food, fibers, and other by-products.

Many contemporary urban ecologists, who employ methods from natural science and the social sciences, take inspiration from their German and, to a larger extent, Chicago predecessors and study urban patterns, processes, and trends in the context of four variables: (1) population (i.e., the number of people in a city and factors that affect this number such as births, deaths, emigration, immigration, and the composition of the city in terms of age, ethnicity, and sex); (2) organization (i.e., the social structure of the city); (3) environment (i.e., its natural environment, such as its proximity to or presence of deserts, forests, mountains, and water bodies, as well as its built environment such as its roads and bridges); and (4) technology (i.e., human inventions that affect the urban environment, such as aqueducts and air conditioning).

Regardless of the approach taken to the study of cities, and regardless of the size, density of settlement, sociopolitical-economic organization, natural and physical environment, or technological features of the city, certain traits are common to urban populations in general. As both the German and Chicago scholars identified, city populations generally possess far greater heterogeneity with respect to ethnicity, race, religion, and socioeconomic status than rural populations. People residing in cities also tend to be younger than those in the hinterlands. While urban and rural areas tend to have different proportions of men and women, cities in developing nations tend to have more men, who migrate to the city in search of employment (leaving the women to remain in rural areas to farm and tend to children), whereas cities in developed countries frequently have a higher ratio of women to men (because women in rural areas often have few employment prospects after graduating from high school and thus move to urban areas in search of economic opportunities).

Criminological Issues

While the Chicago school is distinguished for its ecological approach to understanding the city, it is also renowned for exploring and developing links between environmental factors and crime. But in order to understand the Chicago school's impact on criminological theory, it helps to consider the ways in which Chicago had changed in the years leading up to and during the Chicago school's heyday.

When Chicago was incorporated in 1833, it had a population of just over 4,000. By 1890, this figure had climbed to 1 million and by 1930, Chicago's population had exceeded 3 million—in large part because of immigrants from Europe and African Americans migrating from the south. This influx of people served to transform Chicago from a small frontier trading post to a vibrant city with a wide range of ethnic groups and social worlds.

Building on Robert Park's ideas about the social ecology of the city, Ernest Burgess developed his concentric zone theory, which maintained that modern cities expand radially from their inner-city core in a series of concentric circles. Focusing on Chicago, Burgess identified five main zones. At the center was the central business district, the Loop—a place with low population and high property values. Encircling this downtown area was the "zone in transition"—an area with run-down housing, lots of residential mobility and turnover (due, in part, to immigrant families who would stay until they had secured sufficient funds to move farther from the business district), some business and light manufacturing, and high rates of poverty and disease. The zone in transition was surrounded, in turn, by a zone inhabited by industry workers who had escaped the second zone. The "zone of workingmen's homes" was a residential area containing high-class apartment buildings and single-family dwellings. Beyond the "residential zone" lay the "commuters' zone"—suburban areas.

The Chicago school focused on the zone in transition—a region of great flux where residents developed mostly impersonal relationships with each other and possessed few ties to the community. Such neighborhoods were sometimes described as "socially disorganized," and it was within these urban spaces that the Chicago school sought to understand the city's many social problems, including the causes of crime and delinquency.

Park contended that the best way to identify the causes of crime and delinquency and other social problems was through close observation of the social processes endemic to urban life. To accomplish this goal, the Chicago school developed and employed new research methods, such as participant observation (which anthropologists had been using in their studies of small, autarchic groups with little or no connections to the modern world) and the focused interview—methods that allowed them to "enter the world of the deviant." Such methods were subsequently adopted by Nels Anderson in *The Hobo: The Sociology of the Homeless Man* (1923) and Clifford R. Shaw in *The Jack-Roller: A Delinquent Boy's Own Story* (1930), which provided tremendous insights into two different urban subcultures. These methods continue to be used by criminologists and sociologists interested in studying social action.

Juvenile Delinquency

Clifford R. Shaw and Henry McKay, who worked at the Institute for Social Research in Chicago, were heavily influenced by the Chicago school thinkers. In particular, they believed that Burgess's concentric zone theory might help guide their investigation of juvenile delinquency. Shaw and McKay hypothesized that rates of delinquency would be higher in the socially disorganized inner-city areas. To test this assumption, they analyzed how measures of crime and delinquency (e.g., youth referrals to juvenile court, truancy) were distributed in Burgess's zones of the city. (More specifically, they mapped the addresses of each juvenile delinquent, compiled them, and then computed rates of delinquency by census tract and city zone.)

They found that over time, rates of crime and delinquency were highest in the inner-city zones and became progressively lower as one moved out into the more prosperous zones. They also discovered that rates of crime and delinquency by zone remained relatively the same, irrespective of the neighborhood's ethnic or racial composition. These findings allowed Shaw and McKay to conclude that crime and delinquency were products of sociological factors rather than individual pathology—that characteristics of the zone, not the individuals living in the zone, regulated levels of crime and delinquency. Having established this important position, Shaw and McKay then proceeded to claim that socially disorganized areas perpetuate a phenomenon whereby criminal conventions and delinquent behavior patterns are culturally transmitted—that is, these traditions are passed down through successive generations of boys in much the same way that language is transmitted. In contrast, socially organized communities are those where conventional values are deeply ingrained and where residents can control youths or prevent competing forms of criminal organization such as gangs from emerging.

Aside from serving to dispel the then still popular criminological theories that criminality was a product of innate biological or pathological factors, Shaw and McKay's work proved to be seminal for the development of two main theoretical traditions in criminology: differential association/social learning theory and control theory. Shaw and McKay's contention that social areas have different mixes of criminal and conventional influences—and that exposure to learning about criminal values from fellow neighborhood residents is a key source of crime—proved inspirational for Edwin Sutherland's theory of differential association, which sought to systematize the insights of Shaw and McKay. Shaw and McKay's efforts to tie delinquency to the attenuation of control in inner-city areas would serve as the foundation for early permutations of control theory, such as those developed by Walter Reckless and Albert J. Reiss, Jr.

Although Shaw and McKay's work was subsequently criticized for suggesting that individual action can be explained solely by the larger environment in which the individual resides—and while some have expressed reservations about basing empirical research about juvenile delinquency on official statistics—Shaw and McKay's research—and, more generally, the Chicago school's promulgation of linkages between environmental factors and crime—have had considerable bearing on the development of criminological theory. Today, important researchers such as Robert J. Sampson (who has extended social disorganization theory and who has developed the concept of collective efficacy) as well as Robert J. Bursick, Jr., and Harold G. Grasmick (whose scholarship has investigated the relationship between neighborhood dynamics and criminal events) can trace their roots back

The National Aeronautics and Space Administration (NASA) Earth Observatory captures Brooklyn, New York, from space in 2009. Some patches (dark gray) of green parkland can be seen amid the crowded urban landscape. The two largest ones in the upper left corner are Prospect Park (right) and Greenwood Cemetery, but their relatively small size does little to help the urban heat island effect.

to early thinking on the connections between urbanization and crime, and the work of Shaw and McKay and the Chicago school.

Environmental Issues
Cities present a number of problems for and threats to their natural environments. Urbanization affects land use patterns, frequently destroying or dividing wildlife habitat and consuming natural areas and farmland. The large number and high density of automobiles, commercial businesses, and factories results in emissions of sulfur dioxide, nitrogen oxide, carbon dioxide, particulate matter, mercury, and other toxic heavy metals—air pollution that increases rates of morbidity (especially respiratory illness and cardiovascular disease) and mortality in humans and contributes to a loss of biodiversity. In addition, while soil absorbs rainfall, buildings and paved roads are impervious.

In areas with high levels of precipitation, urban runoff—which is often polluted with animal feces, fertilizers from lawns, garbage, and motor oil—can overwhelm city storm sewage systems, resulting in the release of untreated urban runoff into water bodies. This contaminated water can cause harm to aquatic and human life and can adversely affect ecosystems far downstream. Even cities with low levels of precipitation can experience the negative effects of polluted runoff. Parking lots, streets, and rooftops of buildings absorb solar radiation during the day and radiate heat into the atmosphere at night, making the high-density urban areas significantly warmer than their surrounding rural areas—a phenomenon known as the urban heat island effect. The heated air from the city cools when it rises, causing water vapor to condense into clouds, producing thunderstorms. Such thunderstorms can increase the volume and velocity of runoff, resulting in flooding and property damage, and can alter the biological, chemical, and physical composition of receiving waters, creating an unhealthy environment for aquatic organisms, wildlife, and humans.

While the high concentration of people in urban areas frequently has a harmful effect on the local and surrounding natural environment, urbanization does not necessarily have to result in environmental problems such as air pollution, water pollution, and the loss of wetlands and biological habitats. Compact development, in which tall, multiple-unit residential buildings are in close proximity to jobs, shopping, and eating establishments—which are all connected by public transportation, thereby decreasing dependence on motor vehicles—results in lower amounts of air and water pollution than sprawling cities and preserves surrounding rural areas. Smart growth, which incorporates compact development, mixes land uses (commercial, manufacturing, and residential) to create communities where it is easy for residents to walk or bike from homes to jobs to businesses and entertainment, thereby lessening the need to expand highway systems that carve up open space and farmlands. Such pedestrian-friendly cities are frequently people-friendly, where poor and rich residents may come into greater contact with each other. This can help lessen the social gulf between classes, and such areas often enjoy lower crime rates. Well-planned cities that use land efficiently (e.g., Portland, Oregon) not only can sustain population growth, but by creating or maintaining space for parks and open space, and by decreasing the noise pollution caused by construction and heavy traffic (which can result in physiological and psychological harm), they can be desirable locations to live.

Urbanization Trends
Urbanization has become a worldwide phenomenon. Although the percentage of people living in urban settings compared with rural areas is greater in highly developed countries than in developing countries, urbanization is increasing rapidly in developing countries—and, as a result, most of the world's largest cities are in those countries. According to the United Nations Population Division, most of the world's largest urban agglomerations—cities plus their surrounding suburban areas irrespective of administrative boundaries—are located in developing countries. In 2010, eight of the top 10 urban agglomerations were located in developing countries: Delhi, India; São Paulo, Brazil; Mumbai (Bombay), India; Ciuded de Mexico (Mexico City), Mexico; Shanghai, China; Kolkata (Calcutta), India; Dhaka, Bangladesh; and Karachi, Pakistan. (The other two were the Tokyo-Yokohama-Osaka-Kobe agglomeration in Japan and the New York, New York–Newark, New Jersey agglomeration in the United States.)

In addition, almost 400 cities worldwide have a population of at least 1 million inhabitants—284 of which are located in developing countries. The number of megacities—urban areas with more than 10 million inhabitants—is also growing and is projected to increase from 19 to 26 worldwide by the year 2025; all seven of these new megacities will be in Asia and sub-Saharan Africa.

Future Directions and Considerations

The recent rapid rate of urbanization in developing nations has outpaced the limited capacity of many of those cities to provide basic services to their residents. Many cities—especially those in the developing world—will not (or will continue not to) be able to provide basic services such as adequate housing, clean water, garbage collection, medical care, new schools, police and fire protection, and sewage treatment to their rapidly expanding populations and will face challenges regarding poverty, unemployment, and violence. When cities grow too quickly, competition for land causes real estate prices to rise, which can drive poor residents into crowded squatter neighborhoods, which are frequently marred by crime, disease, and social unrest. In addition, most megacities, including some of the seven new megacities, are located in coastal areas, making them especially vulnerable to rising sea levels—and subsequently, loss of life and property damage—that experts predict will result from global climate change in the 21st century.

By 2070, approximately 150 million individuals will reside in urban areas—primarily in parts of Bangladesh, Burma, China, India, Thailand, and Vietnam—that could be in danger from the effects of global climate change. In order to ensure that urbanization does not conflict with goals for economically, environmentally, and socially sustainable cities in the 21st century, government officials and representatives of the public sector, members of nongovernmental organizations, and those involved with corporations, finance, and industry in the private sector will need to understand the interaction between population growth, energy demand, regional climate, transportation, and water use.

Avi Brisman
Emory University

See Also: Chicago, Illinois; Los Angeles, California; New York City.

Further Readings

Cullen, Francis T. and Robert Agnew. *Criminological Theory: Past to Present*, 4th ed. New York: Oxford University Press, 2011.

Gmelch, George, Robert V. Kemper, and Walter P. Zenner, eds. *Urban Life: Readings in the Anthropology of the City*, 5th ed. Long Grove, IL: Waveland Press, 2009.

Little, K. *Some Aspects of African Urbanization South of the Sahara*. McCaleb Modules in Anthropology. Reading, MA: Addison-Wesley, 1971.

Park, Robert E., et al., eds. *The City: Suggestions for Investigation of Human Behavior in the Urban Environment*. Chicago: University of Chicago Press, 1925.

Raven, Peter H., et al. *Environment*, 7th ed. Hoboken, NJ: John Wiley & Sons, 2010.

Reckless, Walter C. *The Crime Problem*, 3rd ed. New York: Appleton-Century-Crofts, 1961.

Sutherland, Edwin H. and Donald R. Cressey. *Principles of Criminology*, 8th ed. Philadelphia: Lippincott, 1970.

Weeks, Jennifer. "Rapid Urbanization." *CQ Global Researcher*, v.3/4 (April 2009).

USA PATRIOT Act of 2001

The USA PATRIOT Act was signed into law on October 26, 2001. The name of the act stands as an acronym for Uniting and Strengthening America by Providing Appropriate Tools Required to Intercept and Obstruct Terrorism Act of 2001. A young 23-year-old congressional staffer, Chris Cylke, is credited with creating the acronym for the bill. The PATRIOT Act reduced restrictions on law enforcement's ability to search telephone and e-mail communications along with medical, financial, and other records. Foreign intelligence surveillance abilities were expanded inside the United States, the Department of Treasury gained more allowance with restricting transactions, and the detaining and deporting of individuals was broadened. Access to and use of toxins, biological agents, and poisons were further restricted in the act. Most significantly, the act expanded the definition of terrorism to include domestic terrorism. Prior to 2001, domestic terrorism was treated differently within the U.S. justice system. Initially, the act received overwhelming support from Republicans and Democrats in both houses of Congress.

The bill stemmed from the aftermath of the 9/11 attacks on New York City, the Pentagon, and the failed attack on the White House. These attacks, linked to the Middle Eastern terrorist group Al Qaeda, caused holes in American intelligence agencies to surface along with questions on U.S. homeland safety. Since the nature of the attacks stemmed from an Islamist militant group, the initial days of the act's enforcement saw a disproportionate number of Middle Easterners detained and subjected to vigilante violence. Backlash and criticisms of the law primarily center on the indefinite detentions of immigrants or those perceived (even loosely) to have connections to terrorist's fronts. Further abrogations of civil liberties from the act are the allowed searches of homes or businesses without the owner's or occupant's knowledge, allowing the Federal Bureau of Investigation (FBI) to search personal records without a court order, and expanding law enforcement access to records including library and church records.

Restricted Persons Identified

Controversial parts of the act describe restricted persons. According to the confines of the PATRIOT Act, a restricted person is anyone who is under indictment for a crime punishable by a term of a year or more, convicted of a crime punishable by imprisonment for more than a year, a fugitive, an unlawful user of a controlled substance, is unlawfully in the United States, has been committed to any mental institution or deemed mentally unfit, a national of any country believed to be a threat to the United States (primarily Cuba, Iran, Iraq, Libya, North Korea, Sudan, or Syria), or received a dishonorable discharge from the U.S. armed forces.

Information Sharing Between Agencies

Aside from expanding the role of law enforcement personnel, the law also encouraged and enabled the sharing of information between agencies. Lack of information sharing was seen as a primary fault leading to the events of 9/11. Previous legal restrictions preventing sharing of information, usually

President George W. Bush signs PATRIOT Act antiterrorism legislation in 2001. "With my signature, this law will give intelligence and law enforcement officials important new tools to fight a present danger," said the president.

concerning search warrants, right of access, and privacy have been lifted under the PATRIOT Act. Direct effects of this expansion of powers can be seen with the "Virginia Jihad" case. The case centered upon members of the Dar al-Arqum Isalmic Center who trained for terrorist activities in Northern Virginia. Training involved paintball maneuvers and paramilitary training, with eight individuals traveling to Pakistan and Afghanistan for further instruction. These individuals, associated with the extremist Islamic group Lashkar-e-Taiba, are also connected to Al Qaeda. Interagency communication enabled these individuals to be brought to trial, with six pleading guilty and three convicted in March 2004.

Digitally Expanded Search Warrants

In conjunction with enabling agencies to communicate with one another, the act allows law enforcement personnel to use digital technologies to catch suspected criminals. Search warrants can be issued in any area where terrorism activities occurred, even if the event were to appear elsewhere. These warrants cross jurisdictional boundaries, facilitating the process. More so, the law allows law enforcement agencies to monitor computers for suspected terrorist behavior and victims of computer crimes can request law enforcement to assist in tracking hackers. The premise of these later developments stems from previously sanctioned laws allowing burglary victims to invite law enforcement into their homes for the pursuit of a criminal.

Penalties Increased
Finally, the act increased penalties for terrorists and those connected to terrorists. The act prohibits the harboring of terrorists, doing business with terrorists, or facilitating an atmosphere where terrorist activities can occur. More so, acts of hijacking, computer hacking, and money laundering have been added to the list of terrorist offenses. Maximum penalties and conspiracy penalties have been strengthened under the PATRIOT Act. Previously, conspiring to commit terrorist offenses could only be tried under general federal conspiracy laws, which did little if terrorist activities targeted private property. The general conspiracy laws only held five years in prison, but the new laws can imprison a person for life. Terrorist attacks or threats to mass transit and bioterrorists are also included in the law, and the statute of limitations does not apply to terrorist crimes.

Many of the act's provisions were to end December 31, 2005, but supporters of the act pushed to make the law permanent. In July 2005, the Senate passed its reauthorization of the act with significant changes, particularly to those concerning perceived civil liberty violations. The House, on the other hand, passed its reauthorization with little changes to the original language. The two bills faced reconciliation in a conference committee, and Republicans and Democrats argued that civil liberty concerns were not taken into full account. A large share of the civil liberty concerns relate to the detaining of suspected terrorists, targeting of restricted persons, and the removal of need for search warrants. The bill passed Congress in March 2006, and President George W. Bush signed it. Democratic Senator Joseph Biden wrote most of the final legislation.

Annessa A. Babic
New York Institute of Technology

See Also: Civil Rights Laws; Homeland Security; Terrorism.

Further Readings
Baldwin, Fletcher N., Jr. "Money Laundering Countermeasures With Primary Focus Upon Terrorism and the USA PATRIOT Act 2001." *Journal of Money Laundering Control*, v.6/2 (2003).

Collins, Jennifer M. "And the Walls Came Tumbling Down: Sharing Grand Jury Information With the Intelligence Community Under the USA Patriot Act." *Criminal Law Review*, v.39 (2002).

Germain, Regina. "Rushing to Judgment: The Unintended Consequences of the USA PATRIOT Act for Bona Fide Refugees." *Georgetown Immigration Law Journal*, v.16 (2002).

Jeager, Paul T., John Carlo Bertot, and Charles R. McClure. "The Impany of the USA PATRIOT Act on Collection and Analysis of Personal Information Under the Foreign Intelligence Surveillance Act." *Government Information Quarterly*, v.30/3 (2003).

Utah

Admitted to the Union as a state in 1896 on the condition that it outlaw polygamy, Utah is one of only two states in which more than half the population belongs to the same religious denomination—in this case, the Church of Jesus Christ of Latter-day Saints (LDS). Though the Utah region had been explored by the Spanish and by fur traders, the LDS were principally responsible for the area's settlement, large groups of them having relocated to the Salt Lake Valley in the 1840s, 1850s, and 1860s, fleeing religious persecution in the midwest. Utah has sometimes been characterized as a partial theocracy, but this can be misleading; many of its laws were religiously motivated, but this is equally true of laws passed by the Puritans in New England, or blue laws throughout the country.

Crime
Despite that religious heritage and the political power of the LDS Church, prostitution was generally tolerated in Salt Lake City in the territorial and early statehood eras, treated much as it was in other western cities: While there was no openly acknowledged red-light district, prostitution was rarely prosecuted. When it was, it was nearly always the prostitute who was arrested, not the man hiring her—with a set of notable exceptions. In the 1880s, the dispute between the LDS

Church, which then still proclaimed the doctrine of polygamy, and federal authorities and non-Mormons ("gentiles") had become vigorous, and several prominent LDS leaders had been arrested, while others had been forced into hiding. Polygamy was not simply disliked by the LDS's opponents, it was openly despised and condemned as sexually immoral—a condemnation many LDS, who considered that they held themselves to a higher standard of moral conduct than gentiles, could not abide. Brigham Young Hampton, a Salt Lake City bureaucrat, used prostitutes to attempt to entrap federal officials in order to demonstrate that it was the non-Mormon side of the dispute that suffered from immorality—and thus in these cases it was the male client who was arrested for lewd and lascivious conduct, while the prostitute generally went free.

Polygamy was officially condemned by the LDS Church and outlawed by the Utah government as a condition for statehood, a decision that upset many LDS at the time, and forced some polygamists unwilling to give up the practice into hiding, or into secret double lives. Others started separatist denominations, and many Mormon fundamentalist sects persist in Utah and nearby states, some of them integrated into society, others operating their own communities. The official ban on polygamy led to a shift in feelings about prostitution, and in the early 20th century, as many young women became more active in the public sphere than in previous generations—taking jobs or spending more time in public places instead of in the home—middle- and upper-class older women and social reformers worried that this would lead to their descent into prostitution. LDS and gentile reformers worked together in an attempt to eradicate prostitution to prevent this eventuality. Police raided brothels and rooming houses, regulations that had to some degree protected sex workers were abolished, and the law very firmly focused on prostitutes as the cause of prostitution and any attendant ills, while ignoring the role of their clients.

One of the most violent incidents in Utah history was also part of the story of the territorial-era conflict between the LDS settlers and the federal government: the Mountain Meadows massacre in 1857. Nervous about the announcement that President James Buchanan had ordered federal troops into Utah, an LDS militia led by John D. Lee attacked a wagon train of emigrants moving from the Arkansas region to California, which had about 120 members at the point that it reached the Salt Lake City area. Intending to make their attack look like Native American aggression, members of the militia attacked the wagon train for five days while dressed as natives. Following the initial attack, two militiamen approached under a white flag, claimed to have negotiated a treaty, and offered to escort the wagon train safely to Cedar City. When the emigrants accepted the help, the men were separated from the women and children, a signal was given, and the rest of the militia ambushed the group. Only children too young to tell anyone what they had seen were spared. The militiamen were sworn to secrecy, determined to blame the massacre on the local Paiutes.

Investigations both territorial and federal followed, but only Lee was found guilty. Under the Utah Territory's death penalty statute, he was allowed to choose his method of execution: hanging, firing squad, or beheading. Lee was executed by firing squad.

Utah's crime rate is well below the national average. At 212.7 violent crimes per 100,000

An 1850s Mormon, or Church of Jesus Christ of Latter-day Saints (LDS), baptism ceremony. The LDS church holds its followers to high standards of moral conduct, which keeps Utah's crime rate well below the national average.

inhabitants in 2010, it is nearly half that of the United States as a whole. While Utah followed the national trend of a rising crime rate after World War II that eventually peaked in the 1990s before falling again, its overall numbers were never high—even at that peak (334 in 1997), crime was well below the present-day national average. Of course, this also means that, proportionally, crime has not declined in Utah as much as it has elsewhere in the country: The 2010 level is about the same as the 1970s levels, when crime was considered to be climbing rapidly. Most of the decrease in crime has also been in aggravated assaults and robberies; the rape rate of 34 per 100,000 is actually higher than the national rate of 27.5.

Police and Punishment
Apart from local jails, the first prison in Utah was the Utah Territorial Penitentiary, later called the Sugar House Prison, built in the Sugar House neighborhood of Salt Lake City in 1853, during the territorial era. The original prison consisted of 16 small cells dug into the ground, covered with iron bars—a common prison design for the time. Federal marshals assumed control of the prison from 1871 until 1896, when the new state government took control. As Salt Lake City grew, residents inevitably complained about the placement of the prison in their midst, but not until 1951 was a new Utah State Prison built, south of the city in Draper. The old prison was razed and became the site of Sugar House Park and Highland High School. In 1990, the Utah State Prison was joined by the Central Utah Correctional Facility in Gunnison.

While further east, city and town police departments often weren't established until a lengthy period in which the law was kept by elected marshals and part-time constables, the Salt Lake City Police Department was established in 1849, two years after the first settlers arrived. The city was the product of centralized planning, developed with future growth in mind, and the early establishment of a well-organized police department was part of this. The city, after all, was intended to be a Latter-day Saint alternative to the "Babylon" of mainstream America, and the outlawry so common in the frontier was not acceptable to the city fathers.

Utah remains a capital punishment state and was the first (and for a long time the only) state to allow a death row inmate to choose the method of his execution. Upon becoming a state, Utah ended beheading as a method of execution; in the territorial period, it was used because of the LDS concept of blood atonement as taught by Brigham Young. According to the doctrine, murder is so vile a sin that Jesus's sacrifice is not sufficient to atone for it; the perpetrator's blood must be shed on the ground for forgiveness in the afterlife to be possible. Both the firing squad and beheading accomplished this, while hanging did not. No prisoner ever chose beheading.

Utah executed both the last inmate before the nationwide suspension of death penalties resulting from the Supreme Court decision in *Furman v. Georgia* in 1972 and the first inmate after the resumption of death penalties with the Supreme Court decision in *Gregg v. Georgia* in 1976. Lethal injection replaced hanging in 1980, and in 2004, the firing squad was abolished and lethal injection made the only method of execution; however, the law was not retroactive, and the three inmates on death row who had already chosen the firing squad were allowed to retain that choice.

Bill Kte'pi
Independent Scholar

See Also: 2001 to 2012 Primary Documents; Frontier Crime; Religion and Crime, Contemporary; Religion and Crime, History of.

Further Readings
Krakauer, Jon. *Under the Banner of Heaven: A Story of Violent Faith*. New York: Anchor, 2004.
Larson, Stan, ed. *Prisoner for Polygamy: The Memoirs and Letters of Rudger Clawson at the Utah Territorial Penitentiary, 1884–87*. Chicago: University of Illinois Press, 1993.
Nichols, Jeffrey. *Prostitution, Polygamy, and Power: Salt Lake City, 1847–1918*. Chicago: University of Illinois Press, 2008.

Vagrancy

The common law definition of the term *vagrant* refers to an individual who is idle, has no visible means of support, and travels from place to place without working. Historically, individuals found to be in violation of vagrancy statutes were viewed with suspicion and tended to be treated by local communities as beggars or to be viewed as potential criminals. In practice, vagrancy statutes have been used to discourage individuals considered to be undesirable from remaining in a community. Accordingly, the crime of vagrancy is one more of code violation than of harm to person or threat to property as with traditional crime connotations.

English Origins

Vagrancy and vagrancy statutes in the United States have origins in the criminal laws of England that stipulated where laborers could reside, as well as compensation rates. Laborers were prohibited from wandering and could be prosecuted for a criminal violation for doing so. Punishments for being found to be a vagrant included branding, whipping, conscription to military service, and even banishment to English penal colonies in Australia. As the feudal system of England began to break down, the crime of vagrancy was born, as vagrants were commonly runaway serfs. The collapse of the feudal system also prompted various additional peccadilloes, such as begging, drunkenness, and prostitution, which also were generally defined as vagrant activity. Early in the 19th century, the Vagrancy Act of 1824 consolidated existing vagrancy laws toward the goal of removing individuals considered to be undesirable from public view. The act made it a criminal offense to engage in behaviors associated with extreme poverty (e.g., public begging, homelessness) and ascribed homelessness to elective idleness (i.e., that being homeless was a deliberate act), making vagrancy, by definition, a social class–based offense.

In the United States, vagrancy statutes in the American colonies closely followed doctrines established in English common law. In early America (and in contemporary times as well), the primary basis of vagrancy laws was to control criminals as well as those who were deemed by society at large to be undesirable. The largest shift in the formation and implementation of laws between England and America is that in England, vagrancy laws were originally intended to maintain a pool of laborers as the feudal system began to decline, and in America, the original intent was an attempt to control individuals perceived likely to engage in criminal activity. Individuals who were labeled "paupers" or "vagabonds," for example, were excluded from the privileges set forth in the Articles of Confederation. During the Great Depression of the 1930s, some states, most notably California, also used vagrancy laws in an attempt to control the migration of transient workers, not unlike the earlier incorporation of vagrancy law into the post-bellum era, which was focused on the newly freed slave population.

Application of Vagrancy Laws

One of the main criticisms levied against the practice of vagrancy laws centers on observations that various statutes implemented around the country were either vaguely worded or were arbitrarily applied. An examination of magistrate courts in Philadelphia during the early 1950s provides a good example. Due process protections were largely ignored, and magistrates oftentimes decided to discharge or incarcerate individuals charged with being vagrant based on extralegal factors, most notably, personal appearance. Moreover, most were found guilty almost immediately with little or no consideration of the merits of individual cases. On one specific day, 55 cases were heard by a magistrate in a mere 15 minutes. During the examined hearings, four individuals were tried, found guilty, and sentenced in only 17 seconds. While these observations reflect vagrancy law application in only one city, figures from the Uniform Crime Report (UCR) for 1951 suggest that vagrancy laws were adjudicated in a similar manner across the United States. Somewhat telling of how significant and far-reaching vagrancy laws had become, the 1951 UCR figures also reflect that 39 percent of all arrests reported were for charges falling under the heading of vagrancy-type offenses (vagrancy, disorderly conduct, drunkenness, and suspicion).

Enforcement by courts as discussed above appears indicative of how vagrancy statutes were applied in the United States until 1972, when the U.S. Supreme Court issued a ruling in the case of *Papachristou v. Jacksonville*, which ultimately struck down the majority of vagrancy statutes that were then in effect throughout the country. The case originated when several individuals were arrested and charged with various offenses such as prowling by auto, being a vagabond, and loitering. The Supreme Court found in a unanimous decision that vagrancy laws were too vague in wording and that the statutes were enforced in an inconsistent and arbitrary manner. The court also found that the manner in which vagrancy statutes were drafted gave law enforcement officials an unfettered amount of discretion when applying the vagrancy ordinances in place and time. Accordingly, the majority of vagrancy laws in effect in the United States were found to be unconstitutional.

While vagrancy-type statutes remain in effect across the United States, there is a higher burden placed on law enforcement officials to observe some type of prohibited behavior (e.g., public begging, panhandling, or disorderly conduct) before making vagrancy arrests. There is some degree of controversy regarding the impact of vagrancy statutes on the homeless population, and there are also questions concerning the

A homeless veteran panhandling in New York City with a sign that reads "veteran." Controversy exists regarding the vagrancy statutes and the homeless population in New York.

racial profiling of individuals accused of violating vagrancy-type ordinances, especially in the context of gang intervention and suppression.

The underlying related issue of social class conflict continues to lend controversy to socio-legal dialogues on vagrancy. It is important to note that vagrancy determinations are heavily based on the perception of criminal justice system functionaries, often resulting in the law being used as a mechanism of social control. Processes of social control and politics imply that those holding legitimate authority create rules of conduct and designate officials to implement and enforce those rules. This translates into the group that holds the most powerful position in a society is able to codify the values and beliefs that it finds to be the most important into law, and that the powerless will remain so. To present this concept in a more succinct manner, the decision of what is criminal depends heavily upon who formulates, enacts, and enforces the laws, echoing Marxist and related critical theoretical perspectives on social control mechanisms.

Relative to other crimes, very little empirical research has been conducted on vagrancy legislation and its effects. More detailed and scientifically informed future dialogues regarding vagrancy should certainly include the topics of racial profiling; the proper role of government with regard to creating, implementing, and enforcing legislation; and the impact of constitutional restraints upon the criminal justice apparatus. In a very real sense, the seemingly low-level offense of vagrancy speaks directly to issues such as freedom of movement and appropriate law enforcement intervention sans violence, property threat, or moral affront—important considerations inseparable from the democratic ideal.

J. Mitchell Miller
Douglas M. Smith
University of Texas, San Antonio

See Also: 1941 to 1960 Primary Documents; Articles of Confederation; Equality, Concept of; Prostitution, History of.

Further Readings
Chambliss, W. "A Sociological Analysis of the Law of Vagrancy." *Social Problems*, v.12/1 (1964).
Foote, C. "Vagrancy-Type Law and Its Administration." *University of Pennsylvania Law Review*, v.104/5 (1956).
Leigh, L. "Vagrancy and Law Reform." *Modern Law Review*, v.40/1 (1977).
Quinney, R. "Crime in Political Perspective." *American Behavioral Scientist*, v.8/4 (1964).

Vermont

The second-least populous state in the country, Vermont was the first state to join the United States after its formation, having been established as a sovereign republic during the Revolutionary War. One of the only states to have once had a sovereign government, it abolished slavery during its 14-year Republic period and thus became the first state to do so; the state was a strong supporter of nationwide abolition in the 19th century.

Police and Punishment
For 140 years, Vermonters relied on county and town jails for incarceration, and particularly in the colonial era, nonincarcerating methods of punishment were used, like stockades and flogging. The first state prison was built in Windsor and opened in 1809. Made entirely of stone, it was three stories high, with a 170-prisoner capacity (though there were then only 24 convicts), riveted iron doors, and a three-foot-thick prison wall. The legislature appointed five commissioners—Ezra Butler, Samuel Shaw, John Cameron, Josiah Wright, and Elihu Luce—to oversee the prison, an antecedent to the modern Department of Corrections. An additional building for solitary confinement was added to the complex in 1830. Prisoners were put to work making shoes and nails originally, with textile industries later replacing these industries.

The first chartered municipal police department was established in the town of Bennington in 1856, and other towns soon followed. Prior to this, towns relied on town marshals and constables, many of whom were elected; the advent of formal police departments meant the creation of a full-time professional policeman, complete with training; the eventual creation of a police academy toward the end of the century; and certification, uniforms, and officially issued firearms. Law enforcement remained based at the town and county level, with each county electing a sheriff responsible for law enforcement in towns without police departments, until 1947, when the Vermont State Police was formed. A statewide police force had been discussed for over a decade and was strongly supported by the Vermont State Grange, a powerful farmers group, because of the disproportionate distribution of law enforcement in rural areas. But it took the 1946 disappearance of Bennington College student Paula Jean Welden (never solved) to end the last opposition to such a system. The state police headquarters was established in Montpelier, and the uniform was based on that of the Marine Corps. Predominantly white, Vermont has never had serious problems with race relations, but there have been scattered incidents of racial tension and racial violence. In 1968, three weeks after Reverend David Lee Johnson, an African American Baptist minister, moved to Irasburg, shots were fired into his home. The police were reluctant to respond, but eventually arrested a 21-year-old soldier on leave from the army, charging him with breach of the peace, rather than an assault or firearms charge.

Further, Johnson and a white woman staying in his house were arrested on adultery charges, a charge rarely used except when brought by one spouse against another in a divorce case. The woman was given a fine and a suspended sentence and left the state; Johnson received a significantly higher fine and a suspended sentence, and continued to face harassment. A board of inquiry appointed by the governor found that the state police had acted inappropriately toward Johnson both in their investigation of the shooting and their unnecessary adultery investigation (which never succeeded in proving adultery had actually occurred). Johnson relocated to California.

Capital punishment was legal in Vermont until 1965, and 26 people had been executed by hanging and electrocution since the Republic era. Today, only treason remains punishable by death.

The role of county government has diminished since Vermont's early days, and today the 14 counties are responsible only for maintaining a sheriff's office and a courthouse. None except Franklin County continues to operate its own jail, because of simple lack of demand.

Crime

Sparsely populated even relative to its small size—the largest city, Burlington, has fewer than 50,000 people—Vermont has enjoyed a fairly low crime rate. However, this has been punctuated by several high-profile crimes that have commanded national attention.

On the morning of New Year's Eve, 1957, Newbury farmer Orville Gibson disappeared; his body was found in the Connecticut River three months later by the state police, and the case became a national news story. The murder remains officially unsolved, and the reward staked by the state of Vermont unclaimed. The national press at the time described Gibson's death as a vigilante punishment for beating one of his farmhands a week earlier, and the media latched onto the idea of a quaint little Vermont town covering up a murder by one of its own. Two men were arrested for the murder the following year, but both were acquitted, leaving no other known suspects.

In 1966, Paul Lawrence moved to Vermont as a young man after being discharged from the army for behavior problems and took a job with the Burlington Police Department, which did not subject him to a background check—nor did the Vermont State Police when he began working for them. Over the next decade, he was involved in hundreds of arrests, which became increasingly problematic because of inconsistencies in his testimony against defendants and the charges he leveled against them. Before long, several prosecutors refused to prosecute his cases, and in 1974, his own partner began to suspect that Lawrence was regularly fabricating crimes. A sting organized by the Burlington police proved that Lawrence lied about buying drugs from police decoys while acting as an undercover agent. Other lies soon came to light, and the state was soon given no choice but to drop pending charges against defendants accused by Lawrence and to pardon those who had been convicted based on his previous testimony.

Even for a small state, Vermont's crime rate is very low. At 130.2 violent crimes per 100,000 inhabitants in 2010, its crime rate was less than one-third the national average. While many states with a low crime rate still maintain a close-to-average rape rate, Vermont rates well there, too, at 21.1 per 100,000 compared to the national average of 27. Most of the remaining violent crimes are aggravated assaults. Vermont has for the most part bucked the trend—while in most of the country crime rose steadily in the post–World War II decades to reach a 1990s peak before declining, Vermont followed in rising until the 1970s, and has fluctuated back and forth since. Its highest crime rate, 184.2 in 1979, came well before most states' peaks; and in the 1990s, when most of the country was breaking violent crime records, Vermont hit a 20-year low of 96.9. Currently, crime is on a slight decline after an equally slight bump corresponding to the 2008 financial meltdown.

Bill Kte'pi
Independent Scholar

See Also: New Hampshire; News Media, Crime in; State Police.

Further Readings
Duffy, John J., Samuel B. Hand, and Ralph H. Orth, eds. *The Vermont Encyclopedia*. Lebanon, NH: University Press of New England, 2003.
Ginsburg, Philip. *Shadow of Death: The Hunt for a Serial Killer*. New York: Scribner, 1993.
Sherman, Joe. *Fast Lane on a Dirt Road: A Contemporary History of Vermont*. White River Junction, VT: Chelsea Green, 2000.

Vice Commission

Vice commissions emerged during the early 20th century in metropolitan U.S. cities such as Chicago or Louisville as a way to suppress social problems. In New York, the equivalent would be the Bureau of Social Hygiene. The main focus of the vice commissions was prostitution and combating white slave traffic.

The context of the vice commissions was interlinked between sex, drugs, and vice reform. An investigation of prostitution often pointed to the practice of drug use, such as opium, heroin, and cocaine. Progressive reformers viewed prostitution and drug use as part of the new urban vices and felt the need to understand them in a scholarly manner.

The vice commission reports focused on three themes: environmental and systemic explanations of the vices, the larger urban and industrial transformation of the time, and the scientific and medical authority in explaining issues pertaining to sex and drug use. While the discourses surrounding the vice commission were mostly academic and technical, the overarching moral beliefs denounced the impropriety of vices and the culpable agents.

Progressive reformers employed a rigid moral dichotomy on various disconnected and related practices, refusing to see the nuances in the living contexts of the working classes. Behaviors that appeared to deviate from the contemporary norms were condemned. In Philadelphia, for instance, the vice commission decried the direct exchange of sex for money, as well as any sexual practices that they deemed perverted, including homosexual contact, close physical contact or sensuous movements in dancing, and burlesque shows. Proclaiming its role in upholding proper middle-class behavior, the vice commission viewed all related matters through a homogenous lens, aiming to suppress all deviant forms of urban amusement and drawing the line between legitimate and illegitimate conduct.

A close-up view of some vice commissions will show why and how they were formed and their goals. The cases of Chicago and Louisville show the variation in locales and local experiences.

Chicago Vice Commission
On January 31, 1910, the Church Federation organized a meeting at the Central YMCA Building in Chicago to discuss the "social evil problem" in Chicago. The federation was comprised of clergy representing 600 congregations in the city. Dean Sumner read a paper on the topic, and presented a resolution for the mayor of Chicago to appoint a commission to investigate the social evil problems. Members of the commission had to include men and women who were respected and trusted by the public.

The "red-light district" known as Murder Bay at the corner of C Street NW and 13th Street NW, in Washington, D.C., in April 1912. Leaning against the tree at left is a "night messenger" or child laborer who directed customers to brothels. U.S. vice commissions were heavily focused on mitigating prostitution and white slavery.

The resolution proposed that upon the completion of a thorough investigation, measures should be undertaken to provide relief from these conditions. The resolution called for the support of the people of Chicago from all walks of life to execute the suggested plans. Should the city administration be unable to carry out this plan, it was asked that this resolution be made a ballot issue at the next election.

The resolution, having been unanimously adopted, was presented to the mayor by a committee from the Federation of Churches. The committee members were exclusively religious, including Professor Herbert L. Willett at the University of Chicago; Reverend J. A. Vance of the Hyde Park Presbyterian Church; Reverend Smith T. Ford of the Englewood Baptist Church and president of the Church Federation Council; Reverend Frank D. Burhans of the Washington Park Congregational Church and vice president of the Church Federation Council; and Professor Benjamin L. Hobson, Secretary of the McCormick Theological Seminary.

On April 16, 1911, the *New York Times* reported the Chicago Vice Commission (CVC) as the first salaried municipal commission of its kind. The CVC was formed to address to address the social problem of crime and vice, especially prostitution. The CVC provided a thorough review of the current status of the social ills in Chicago and recommendations on how to repress them. The recommended course of immediate action was ongoing and tenacious suppression. The recommendations were in opposition to the European principle of segregation. The CVC was created via the appointment of a morals commission and the establishment of a morals court.

The CVC made other recommendations such as the physical examinations of applicants for marriage license, more equitable pay for girls, removal of the fining system against members of the vice districts, a logical adult probation system, a home for old offenders, monitoring of the employment agencies, laws that evoked public attention to the social ills, women officers in the police force, municipal dance halls, and hotels and homes for working women and girls.

The CVC lists poverty as the most prominent cause of these social ills, alongside the want for basic needs, desire for luxuries, lack of protection for immigrant girls, and insufficient pay for girls. Other causes include the lack of ethical and religious teachings, the influx of seasonal trades for women, unhappy home conditions, reckless and ignorant parents, desertion, want of ease and luxury, and the lure of excitement.

Louisville Vice Commission
Another prominent vice commission was established in Louisville, Kentucky. In its 1915 report, the Louisville Vice Commission (LVC) provided reasons for combating evil, examined its commercialized aspect, and argued why it should be a public concern. The LVC argued that the need to combat social problems was extensive and permeating. First, the LVC stated that commercialized prostitution was cancerous to a community and had detrimental consequences. The commission believed that prostitution affects both the innocent and the guilty, resulting in numerous cases of paralysis, blindness, idiocy, insanity, and unspeakable physical and moral degeneracy. The LVC was also concerned with the degradation of womanhood and the greed and passion of men found in commercialized prostitution.

Like the CVC, the LVC realized that prostitution cannot be eradicated or entirely suppressed. It suggested instead a steady and gradual repression, in tandem with moral and physical education. The LVC believed that there were enough conscientious citizens in Louisville to engage the public conscience and to offer a realistic picture of the city's prostitution problems. The goal was to reach the greatest possible level of control.

The LVC also stated that this battle was for everyone, expressing trust in how each responsible party would act accordingly. While there was an emphasis on the law enforcement agents and regulations, the commission pointed out that the key to a sustainable campaign lay with the citizens. People from all walks of life, from the professional to the religious, from the business sector to the social sphere—all must take initiative to show a progressive attitude toward commercialized vice. There must be a strong sense of uniform and connected opinion among the people and a spirit of hope in succeeding with the task at hand.

The LVC also supposed that every woman sought to be decent and respectable, avoiding unnatural sexual immorality. The commission asserted that it had not encountered a single case in which the "poor, unfortunate creature" was not brought into prostitution through misuse, abuse, or dissipation of indecent men. The LVC argued that it was the degraded men who took advantage of loneliness, the lure of the street, and the economic pressure upon the women.

The LVC also judged that the fulfillment of the need for women to lead a wholesome and respectable life could also help discourage prostitution. The commission pointed out that community attitudes and public view had made it hard for a "fallen woman" to regain her moral strength. Therefore, the commission suggested the formation of an institution for the training, direction, and education of young girls who had been made victims of immorality. Such an effort was believed to have been long neglected and was thought to help the young girls pursue a decent life through trade or other jobs.

It was observed that the order of things had been altered as a result of the technological advances in the 20th century, coupled with the commercialization of entertainment, rapid transportation, the communication industry, and all the convenient and amusing things that had become available.

As the workday became shorter, the time for recreation was expanded. Human interests were commercialized, and the search for pleasure became a focus. The LVC believed that this condition contributed to the decrease of morality among women. Pleasure seeking and commercialization was a two-way street, where the need for pleasure worked to raise the supply for it.

Trangdai Glassey-Tranguyen
Stanford University

See Also: Prostitution, History of; Vice Reformers; Victorian Compromise.

Further Readings
"Report of the Vice Commission, Louisville, Kentucky," 1915. http://faculty.tnstate.edu/tcorse/h2020/report_of_the_vice_commission.htm (Accessed November 2011).
Taylor, Troy. *Murder & Mayhem in Chicago's Vice Districts*. Charleston, SC: History Press, 2009.
Vice Commission of the City of Chicago. "Social Evil in Chicago." http://www.brocku.ca/MeadProject/Vicecommission/SEC_pref.html (Accessed November 2011).

Vice Reformers

Vice laws aimed to control acts that many people engaged in for pleasure and about which the question of who was the "victim" and who the "offender" were often debated. Attempts to enforce existing laws and to enact new legislation occurred within the context of public discourse about the family, gender, sexuality, race/ethnicity, class, and immigration. During the late 19th and early 20th centuries, reform-minded individuals and organizations focused their attention on activities such as prostitution, drug sale and use, gambling, and pornography. Such "vice" activities were often carried out in areas that were known as "red-light districts." In the early 20th century, such areas existed in every major city and many smaller ones. A debate was ongoing regarding what should be done about vice crime. Some, including some police chiefs, acknowledged the existence of these districts, but argued that such activities could never be eliminated. Therefore, they favored continuing to "segregate" gambling houses and brothels (also known as "houses of ill-fame" or "disorderly houses") in designated areas. Others, particularly reformers, favored abolishing the red-light districts and claimed that these flourishing districts were symbolic of police and political corruption. The efforts by reformers to eliminate these vice crime areas involved both direct action and attempts to influence public officials. The individuals who took part in these reform activities ranged from evangelical Christians to professionally trained social workers. Their goals overlapped, but their perceptions of the people involved in vice activities sometimes differed. These reformers who focused on vice crime were active during the Progressive Era when a cross-section of activists was involved in efforts to improve and reform public institutions.

Anthony Comstock

Many of these reformers believed that the weakest and the vulnerable, specifically women and children, needed to be protected. However, the women and children who were perceived as most in need of protection reflected the racial/ethnic and class biases of the reformers. For example, Anthony Comstock, the founder of the New York Society for the Suppression of Vice (1872), was concerned with the distribution of works that he considered pornographic. Of particular concern

Anthony Comstock as pictured in the 1913 book Fighter: Some Impressions of a Lifetime Adventure in Conflict With the Powers of Evil *by Charles Gallaudet Trumbull.*

for him was that these readily available works might fall into the hands of upper-class adolescents who might be tempted by the ads to buy and read the books. Comstock placed much of the blame for these obscene materials on foreigners and immigrants.

Comstock's campaign to suppress what he considered offensive literary works had begun when he arranged to have woman's rights activist Victoria Woodhull arrested on the charge of obscenity. Woodhull had published an article alleging that New York minister Henry Beecher Stowe was involved in an adulterous relationship. Comstock arranged the arrest using an 1865 postal law. He was able to successfully advocate passage of a stronger law suppressing mail circulation of "obscene literature and articles" in 1873. The word "Comstockery" was used to describe the effort to ban or expunge literary works because of their content. In the same vein, "banned in Boston" became a popular description of works that had been banned by the censorship efforts of the New England Society for Suppression of Vice (1878), founded with advice from Comstock.

Committee of Fourteen

In 1905, the Committee of Fourteen, a private anti-vice organization, was founded in New York City. The committee focused its attention on the abolition of hotels that violated the Raines Law. Enacted in 1896, the law forbade the selling of liquor on Sunday. To get around the law, some saloon owners added rooms for rent and applied for a hotel liquor license that allowed Sunday liquor sales. Concerned that these rooms were available to prostitutes and unmarried couples, the Committee of Fourteen worked to have the law amended to require a city inspection of a hotel before a license was issued. The group hired investigators to gather evidence against violators. In 1928, four years before it disbanded, the Committee of Fourteen hired a young black schoolteacher to undertake an investigation of prostitution and other vice activities in Harlem. As a result of this five-month undercover operation, mass arrests were made and cabarets and speakeasies were closed. Future singer Billie Holiday, only 14 years old at the time, was among those arrested in the sweep of alleged prostitutes. The arrests that began with this surveillance report continued over several years, with increasing numbers of black women being arrested and causing the suppression of Harlem nightlife.

Woman's Christian Temperance Union

Another organization, the Woman's Christian Temperance Union (WCTU), was national in its antiliquor efforts. However, the group also created a "department of social purity." This department agitated for revision of sexual consent laws. In conjunction, the WCTU had a "department of rescue" that was charged with saving women from the sex trade. Investigators were sent to the midwest to look into forced prostitution in lumber camps. As did other antivice groups, the WCTU appealed to legislatures for tougher laws.

Chicago Vice Commission

In 1910, after several years of agitation on the part of reformers, the mayor of Chicago appointed the Chicago Vice Commission to investigate the presence of vice crime. Ironically, when the commission's report, *The Social Evil in Chicago*, was released to the public, it was temporarily banned from distribution by the post office because it was alleged to violate the obscenity law. The commission had focused its attention on prostitution ("the social evil") in red-light districts in the city. It found the concentration of vice in or near those areas that were becoming African American (Negro) ghettos. The commission also found that a number of factors contributed to the entry of young women into prostitution, including environment, lack of moral training, the craving for excitement, economic pressures, and the temptations offered by male seducers. The commission made recommendations that included establishing a permanent morals commission and setting up venereal disease wards in the city hospital. The commission also recommended the Chicago Police Department create a morals squad and recruit female police officers to assist with women and children.

Over the next four years, other cities followed the example of Chicago and established vice commissions. These cities included New York City, Philadelphia, Atlanta, Baltimore, Newark, and Louisville. In 1914, in Virginia, the mayors of Richmond and Danville were recognized for their efforts to eradicate the red-light districts in their cities. But by 1917, the local newspaper reported that Danville officials had noticed that several men had purchased houses in the city and women had come to the city, apparently to work in these intended brothels. The city faced the issue of what to do with those women who were found to be infected with venereal diseases. Aside from the health of the women, there was the concern that if released, they might infect their clients.

In the early 20th century, the "social hygiene" movement was under way across the country. Beginning in 1905, the movement aimed to educate young people about the dangers of venereal disease. This movement overlapped with concerns about "white slavery," the sexual trafficking of women. The social hygiene movement reflected the wariness that reformers had felt since the 19th century about the intermingling of young men and women in the city. The "wayward" or "fallen" woman, either promiscuous or a professional prostitute, was seen as the source of contagion, spreading venereal disease to young men. This perception of the fallen woman carried with it stereotypes of poor women, immigrant women, and women of color. In the stereotypes of these women, they were seen as oversexed and diseased as opposed to the virginal and pure white upper-class women. However, reformers such as settlement house founder Jane Addams rejected these wholesale stereotypes, while at the same time expressing concern about the involvement of young working-class women in prostitution. At Hull House, Addams and the other workers offered a variety of programs aimed at helping the women navigate the challenges of their lives in the city.

In the red-light districts, prostitution flourished alongside other activities such as drug sales and gambling. During this era, gambling, alcohol, and drugs were seen as threats to the nuclear family. A man who drank, took drugs, and/or gambled might never marry or might cause his wife and children to go hungry because he had spent his paycheck instead of bringing it home. These vices were also associated in popular culture and law enforcement with groups who were considered outside the mainstream, such as musicians and actors or racial/ethnic minority groups.

Just as those reformers who were concerned about prostitution sometimes invaded brothels to gather information, since the 19th century, antiliquor reformers had favored direct action. Perhaps the most notorious of these direct action reformers was Carrie Nation, who in cartoons was often pictured with the axe she was supposed to wield in saloons. The antiliquor crusade by prohibitionists was an effort by reformers to deny access to alcohol to both present drinkers and young people who would take up the vice. In the 19th century, drinking had become associated not only with the lifestyle of young bachelors in the city but also with "saloon culture." Irish immigrants, who used saloons as sites for political meetings, were identified as drinkers and brawlers by nativists (who favored the native-born over immigrants).

Prohibition
The passage of the Eighteenth Amendment and the enactment of the Volstead Act empowered the federal government to enforce the ban on alcohol and represented the culmination of a decades-long struggle by prohibitionists. However, as the Roaring Twenties demonstrated, passing the legislation was not sufficient to eliminate drinking. In New York and other major cities, people who had not formerly violated the law were now going to speakeasies. In the post–World War I era, the consumption of alcohol became a part of the youth culture of flappers and college men. Moreover, as

Prohibition laws alone did not eliminate drinking. Hooch Hound, a dog trained to detect liquor, sniffs a flask in the back pocket of a man fishing on a pier on the Potomac River in 1922.

the Wickersham Commission found, Prohibition had created a situation in which police officers and public officials were susceptible to bribes by organized crime. In New York City, Chicago, and other major cities, the rise of organized crime during Prohibition provided opportunities for mobsters to move into and solidify their hold over gambling operations. For example, in New York City, mobster "Dutch" Schultz moved into Harlem and took over the numbers rackets formerly operated by African American gangsters.

At the same time, the political machines present in major cities sometimes worked to control the structure of the vice activities. Upstate in Albany, New York, the entrenched Democratic machine resisted the efforts of Jack "Legs" Diamond and other gangsters to establish liquor operations in the city. The lucrative gambling operation in Albany that began as a baseball pool and later spread into neighboring states was allegedly operated by machine politicians rather than gangsters. Protests by reformers and opposing politicians about the harm caused by gambling and related vices had little impact. Investigation and prosecution of the alleged operators of the pool was necessary.

By the 1930s, the various reform movements had died out as Prohibition proved to be unworkable and as society in general experienced the changes of World War I and its aftermath. In part, the war had speeded up the social changes that were already under way. Attitudes about gender, sexuality, race/ethnicity, and even class had been challenged.

Frankie Y. Bailey
State University of New York, Albany

See Also: Chicago, Illinois; Comstock Law; Corruption, History of; Prohibition; Prostitution, History of; Schultz, Dutch; Wickersham Commission.

Further Readings
Anderson, Eric. "Prostitution and Social Justice, 1910–15." *Social Service Review,* v.48/2 (1974).
Beisel, Nicola. "Class, Culture, and Campaigns Against Vice in Three American Cities, 1872–1892." *American Sociological Review,* v.55 (1990).
Fronc, Jennifer. *New York Undercover.* Amherst: University of Massachusetts Press, 2009.
Johnson, Val. "The Moral Aspects of Complex Problems: New York City Electoral Campaigns Against Vice and the Incorporation of Immigrants, 1890–1901." *Journal of American Ethnic History* (2006).
Keire, Mara L. "The Committee of Fourteen and Saloon Reform in New York City, 1905–1920." *Business and Economic History,* v.26/2 (1997).
Robertson, Stephen. "Harlem Undercover: Vice Investigators, Race, and Prostitution, 1910–1930." *Journal of Urban History,* v.35 (2009).

Victim Rights and Restitution

Emphasis upon victim rights and restitution was once a prominent feature of the American criminal justice system. In the 19th century, the state began to replace the role of the victim as the party damaged by criminal acts. Eventually, the victim was reduced in importance to a secondary consideration and little more than a witness in criminal cases. By the latter 20th century, sentiment and public policy began to shift to once again stress the role and rights of victims within the legal process. A range of circumstances acted in combination to facilitate the resurrection of the once prevalent theme of victims rights in the United States: Civil rights activists viewed victims as having inadequate rights and protections within the unbalanced legal system; supporters of law and order and opponents of offender-centric and failed rehabilitative programs sought to redirect attention in support of victims; feminists endeavored to ensure criminal law and police policy properly addressed crimes directed toward women; and legislators and other politicians increasingly lent support to the victims' rights cause, correctly judging the movement to have considerable public support. Proponents of victims' rights have advocated a range of initiatives, including social welfare support of victims, increased victim participation in the criminal justice process, and financial restitution for the losses and suffering incurred by victims.

In the colonial and early Republic periods, victims played key roles in the criminal justice process. Victims or their family and friends were principally responsible for apprehending offenders, at which point victims would hire a private attorney to prosecute, with the goal often being reparations rather than imprisonment. Indigent offenders who could not pay compensation often agreed to perform service to the victim to retire the debt owed. Such arrangements and emphasis upon the role and needs of victims had been typical of many Western societies for centuries. In the 19th century, police forces became increasingly common and began to assume sole responsibility for apprehension. Simultaneously, criminal acts began to be regarded as offenses against society rather than against individual victims. Criminal charges were pursued by professional prosecutors and victim indemnification began to give way to fines that were levied and retained by the government. A broad societal transformation both in policy and perception changed the role of the victim from an integral part of the process to merely initiating reports of incidents and testifying in court on behalf of the state. Within the U.S. criminal justice system, the victim gradually faded in importance and eventually become an afterthought within the system, but this trend would eventually be reversed.

In the 20th century, the reform and rehabilitation of offenders gradually replaced punishment as the primary goal of the criminal justice system. Laws were interpreted and new laws enacted to protect the constitutional rights of those accused or convicted of criminal conduct. Calls for empathy toward offenders became increasingly common in academic and governmental circles, alleging offenders were in fact the victims of poverty, unequal opportunity, untreated mental illness, lack of education, or other societal shortcomings. Rather than being punitive, proponents of offenders' rights argued that incarceration should provide opportunities to better detainees through such means as vocational training or even college educations funded by taxpayers. However, few new laws, governmentally funded programs, or other forms of positive redress existed or were being proposed to assist the victims of crime. Rates of recidivism among offenders remained high and public support for and confidence in rehabilitation eroded, along with sympathy for offenders. In fact, sentiment in favor of safeguarding and adding to the civil liberties of criminal offenders and in favor of allocating large amounts of public funds toward their well-being and rehabilitation began to generate public outcry in the United States. The public and many elected officials began to voice concern that attention had been at least partly misdirected, and that attention, governmental support, and efforts aimed at preserving and expanding rights should also be focused upon the victims of criminal acts. The victim rights movement, including calls for financial restitution for victims, came into existence partly in response to policy trends favoring rights and entitlements for offenders, illustrating the core principle underlying victim rights advocacy, that of balance. If offenders are entitled to a range of rights and services, victims should have guarantees of rights and services that address their unique status and needs.

Significant government action on behalf of crime victims was uncommon prior to the 1970s. Reports of many crimes were often not taken seriously, and victims could be treated dismissively or otherwise inappropriately by authorities. The privacy and security of victims and witnesses was often not guaranteed, inspiring fear of retribution. The bureaucracy of the legal system and the trauma of the criminal proceedings, including unnecessarily aggressive and intrusive cross-examination of victims by the counsel for defendants, was a traumatic experience for many, who regarded their experience with the criminal process as a "secondary victimization." Such experiences contributed to widespread victim dissatisfaction with the criminal justice process. In turn, many victims declined to report crimes, fully cooperate in investigations, or testify in court. Without victims to initiate formal complaints and to support the prosecution process, the criminal justice system was compromised. Reforms related to victims' rights, contributing to victim satisfaction, were a practical step to ensure the continued effective functioning of the criminal justice process.

Victims' Rights and Women's Rights

Another catalyst for the emergence of the victims rights cause was the feminist movement that arose in the 1960s and 1970s. Throughout much of the 20th century, certain crimes that typically involved women as victims were commonly treated dismissively or with lack of sympathy by law enforcement. Victims of domestic violence or sexual assault would often be blamed for their own victimization, discouraged from filing formal complaints against their attackers, or otherwise treated with condescension, contempt, or lack of sensitivity. Women's rights activists played an effective role in improving the experience of women who had been victimized by crime in many ways, including sensitivity training for law enforcement, enactment of numerous laws such as mandatory arrest in spousal abuse cases in many states, and establishment of facilities such as women's crisis centers and assistance hotlines.

Also of practical importance to the victims' rights movement was the increase in the crime rate in the 1960s and 1970s and the concomitant anticrime stance adopted by lawmakers and the general public, which in part manifested in support for victims' rights programs. In 1965, California became the first U.S. state to award public compensation to crime victims. By the 1970s, numerous victim/witness assistance programs had been established across the United States, funded by the Law Enforcement Assistance Administration and organized largely through prosecutors' offices.

The decade was also witness to the country's first sexual assault crisis centers, though initially due to previous negative experiences, not all such centers actively cooperated with police or prosecutors, a situation that would change over time. By the 1970s, domestic and child abuse also began to receive greater attention from both law enforcement and the general public. Perhaps the single most important development of the period was the founding in 1976 of the National Organization for Victim Assistance (NOVA), one of the nation's principal catalysts for awareness and legislative action in support of victims rights.

Marchers display signs in Knoxville, Tennessee, during Slutwalk Knoxville. The anti–sexual violence march was one of numerous worldwide Slutwalk rallies held throughout 2011 to raise awareness for the rights of rape victims and protest against explaining or excusing that a rape was warranted because of any aspect of a woman's appearance.

The 1980s witnessed significant advances, in part reflecting the strong support of the Reagan administration. The first National Victims of Crime Week occurred in 1981. The President's Task Force on the Victims of Crime was established the following year, which was to prove instrumental in issuing policy recommendations and advancing the movement. Many of the task force's recommendations were implemented over time, including the Crime Victims Fund, which has financially supported thousands of separate initiatives and provided funding for state-level programs for victim assistance and compensation. Other recommendations implemented include the Witness Protection Act, which criminalized witness harassment or retaliation, and the Bail Reform Act, which required courts to consider the risk to public safety posed by criminal defendants in bail hearings. Most states have implemented pro-victim laws/policies recommended by the Task Force, and nationally, over 5,000 programs have been established in support of victims' rights and restitution.

The victims' rights movement has varied goals, some of which have proven controversial. The three principal dimensions of victims' rights advocacy are victim satisfaction/services, victim impact, and restitution/compensation. Near universal agreement exists that victim satisfaction should be a goal of society and that crime victims are rightly entitled to a range of quality social welfare support services to assist in their recovery. However, questions remain as to exactly how many victims exist in society, how many need assistance, to what extent their needs are being met, and what types of services are the most appropriate to various circumstances. For example, victims of violent or sexual assault are often severely traumatized and in need of professional services in order to aid in the recovery process. However, universal agreement does not exist as to the type of assistance that is most appropriate for all cases. Many advocate mental health counseling and other assistance but not formal psychiatric treatment for the average victim, as the victim is not mentally ill but undergoing a normal psychological response to a traumatic experience. Although the current situation in terms of victim support services is not ideal, the United States at present does provide a wider range of support services to victims than at any point in its history, and many (though not all) studies indicate far higher levels of victim satisfaction than in decades past.

Victim impact broadly refers to the ability of victimized parties to directly participate in the criminal justice process as related to bringing offenders to justice. Many proponents of victim rights contend that victims have entitlement to direct involvement in each phase of the legal process: pre-trial, trial, and post-trial. An example of pre-trial victim involvement would be granting the victim power of veto with regard to plea bargains. Since the majority of criminal cases in the United States never reach the trial phase due to plea bargaining, the victim veto would be a meaningful step toward empowering victims in the process if they feel the state's offer to the defendant is either too lenient or too harsh. An example of trial participation is a right to provide testimony if so desired. Examples of victim rights in the trial stage include the right to meet with the judge and prosecutor and the possibility of added victim protections from overly aggressive or otherwise inappropriate cross-examination from defense council. Perhaps the best example of a post-trial goal of victim rights advocates is the right to make a victim impact statement in order to convey the extent of harm inflicted to those responsible for sentencing the offender.

Restitution

Another dimension of victims' rights is the issue of restitution. There are two basic types of victim restitution programs: traditional and punitive. Traditional (or simple) restitution involves direct compensation from the offender to the victim for the loss of or damage to property, or physical or emotional injury. Punitive restitution supports compensation while simultaneously seeking to inflict some measure of punishment beyond the direct cost of losses incurred. In a traditional restitution scenario, a victim who had been robbed of $10,000 could expect compensation for that amount plus certain incidentals such as anguish, distress, or lost work time. With punitive restoration, additional compensation would be demanded, going beyond mere reimbursement in making the offender undergo additional penance for criminal acts, addressing society's need for punishment and in so doing possibly act as an additional deterrent beyond simple compensation. In such a scenario, the amount paid in restitution could significantly exceed the amount actually owed to the victim.

Restitution programs can serve multiple purposes, including financial assistance for victims (often regarded as the most important purpose) and alternative or additional means of punishment of offenders. Such programs might also relieve some stress from the overburdened criminal justice and correctional systems and potentially help reduce and/or redirect some public expenditures. Restitution could provide additional incentive for victims to report crimes and assist with prosecutorial efforts. Restitution also forces offenders to accept financial responsibility, and in so doing, ostensibly assume psychological or moral responsibility for their actions.

The latter is a component element of another potentially important aim of restitution, that of offender rehabilitation. Some studies have shown that many perpetrators of serious crimes such as homicide desire to make some form of reparation, though critics note that such sentiment can be insincere and may often be conveyed by offenders to curry favor with parole boards or other authorities. Many behavioralists and penologists contend that by obliging offenders to engage in meaningful work to meet this financial obligation, it could help instill positive work habits, impart ethical understanding/reflection with regard to issues such as reward-punishment outcomes for individual choices, and instill responsibility and alleviate feelings of anger toward and detachment from society, all of which are positive steps in the rehabilitation process.

Presently, 30 states in the United States have mandatory restitution programs. Ordinarily, judges are provided the latitude to overrule mandated restitution provided they can document a justifiable reason for doing so, such as the inability of an indigent offender to pay. All states permit courts to order victim restitution if deemed suitable to the circumstances. Historically, judges tend not to order restitution unless they are obligated to do so by mandates, and considerable variation exists among states as to the amounts awarded and the procedures through which restitution is determined and implemented. Many supporters of victim restitution advocate that the practice become mandatory and that procedural protocols related to restitution be standardized across the country.

Those who do not support court-ordered restitution programs note that victims of crimes have the option of pursuing civil actions against offenders separate from the criminal process. However, a number of problems have historically existed with initiating civil suits against offenders: such legal action costs the victim both time and money that may not be at their disposal; the offender is often never identified or convicted; and civil judgments can be difficult to obtain, certainly when the offender is financially destitute. Proponents of victim restitution note that the first problem can be addressed by making restitution a mandatory part of criminal prosecution and judicial and probationary purview. Many victims' rights advocates contend that all such problems and the necessity of bringing civil actions against criminal offenders can be superseded by implementing programs of state compensation for victims of crime.

Whereas "restitution" or "reparation" refers to payments made by an offender directly to the victim in order to at least partly compensate for the harm inflicted, "compensation" refers to payments made via public funds to victims of crimes. Supporters of public compensation argue that governments should regard assistance to crime victims including compensation for their losses as a standard component of a broad social welfare policy. Also, since the government failed in its duty to protect the victim against crime, compensation by the state is appropriate and necessary. An additional argument of practical importance is that even if restitution is ordered or a civil judgment levied, the government often imprisons criminal offenders, limiting their ability to pay indemnities to victims; therefore, the government should accept the financial responsibility for compensating victims.

Compensation of crime victims from public funds has been implemented as policy in a number of nations including Great Britain. Several U.S. states have also implemented public compensation programs as component elements of their social welfare compensation models, including California, Hawai'i, New York, and Massachusetts. In the United States, compensation plans generally share several characteristics in common:

A young girl photographs posters of Marsy Nicholas during National Crime Victims' Rights Week in 2009. Marsy Nicholas was stalked and killed by her ex-boyfriend in 1983. Marsy's mother was later confronted by the accused murderer, not knowing he had been released on bail. Surviving family members of murder victims had no legal rights before Marsy's Law was passed; courts must now consider the safety of victims and families when setting bail and release conditions.

The state assumes no legal liability for the occurrence of crime but offers compensation as a social policy consideration, compensation is paid from public revenues derived from taxpayers, limits are usually placed upon conditions that justify compensation (e.g., only crimes involving violence and/or physical injury), and eligibility for public compensation often requires victims to demonstrate acute financial need or hardship. Opponents of public compensation contend that such action is not the responsibility of government and that taxpayers bear no responsibility for the acts of criminals and should not be taxed to indemnify the actions of offenders.

Criticisms

Criticism has also been levied against restitution programs. Since poverty and lack of economic opportunity is an underlying factor behind at least much if not most criminal activity, it may be unrealistic to expect many offenders to pay restitution, even if wages are garnished and meager assets are seized. Compounding this practical consideration is the fact that prisoners have limited if any opportunity to earn income. Although prison manufacturing and other forms of labor were common in the United States in the 1800s, in part due to the protests of competing private businesses, numerous federal and state statutes began restricting prison industries in the 20th century and as of today, it would be uncommon for inmates to be able to earn significant wages via prison labor. The inmate jobs that do exist are usually menial, low paying, and ill suited to the goal of victim restitution. One option to assist in the goal of restitution would be advocacy of work-release programs wherein certain offenders could be permitted or even required to maintain outside employment while completing their sentences and probations. Additional options to address the issue of offenders' ability to pay include adjustment of restitution levels based upon financial capability (i.e., offenders with resources pay more, those without resources could still be expected to pay, but a reduced amount reflective of their realistic economic ability); direct arbitration between victims and offenders could be incorporated in the plea bargaining process or some other stage of prosecution or sentencing; and indigent offenders in some instances (e.g., nonviolent offenses) could substitute personal services/labor to the victim or to an institution of the victim's choosing in lieu of payment.

A significant concern with restitution systems is the problematic nature of determining appropriate amounts to award and no single simple model of restitution will be applicable to all offenses and victims. When restitution programs were initially implemented in some parts of the United States, the amounts awarded generally relied upon victims to provide clearly demonstrable evidence of tangible losses of money or property, and the victim's ability to provide detailed estimates of losses remains the most accurate predictor of restitution judgments. In reality, victims do not incur only tangible, measurable losses such as stolen items/funds, lost wages, and medical costs. Victims also experience subjective, less measurable losses, such as psychological trauma, pain, and stress. It has been proposed that typical jury awards in similar cases be used to establish appropriate restitution levels for intangibles such as pain and suffering and that judges should consider both tangible and intangible losses in determining restitution amounts. Victims' cost also varies widely according to the type of crime. For example, petty larceny or simple assaults pose significantly less overall cost to victims than sexual assault.

Numerous additional criticisms have been offered regarding victim restitution. Since crime impacts society in general and combating and prosecuting criminal acts incurs expenses for society at large, many contend that society in general should also receive financial compensation from offenders rather than a single victim. Many proponents of victim restitution cite its effects as an additional deterrent of crime, that is, if crime does not pay, fewer individuals will pursue crime. However, the evidence supporting restitution as an effective deterrent is scant at best. If restitution is tied to plea bargaining, sentencing, or early release, then issues of class, privilege, and egalitarianism are raised. For example, offenders with financial resources could receive reduced or even commuted sentences via their ability to pay restitution, whereas indigent offenders who perpetrated similar crimes could serve significantly longer sentences. The latter shortcoming could be addressed at least in part by adjusting amounts of restitution appropriate to the wealth level of offenders.

Additionally, some studies have revealed that offenders ordered to pay restitution have more difficulty successfully completing probation and were more likely to have probation revoked and to report health or financial problems, undermining the contention that restitution can aid in the process of rehabilitation. One of the strongest criticisms of restitution is opposition to its use as a substitute to traditional punishments. However, most supporters of victim restitution advocate the approach not as a substitute for other punishments, but to be used in conjunction with other forms of correctional justice.

Barry D. Mowell
Broward College

See Also: 1981 to 2000 Primary Documents; 2001 to 2012 Primary Documents; Gender and Criminal Law; Plea; Rehabilitation; Retributivism.

Further Readings

Davis, Robert. *Securing Rights for Victims: A Process Evaluation of the National Crime Victim Law Institute's Victims' Rights Clinics*. Santa Monica, CA: RAND Corporation, 2009.

Tobolowsky, Peggy, et al. *Crime Victim Rights and Remedies*. Durham, NC: Carolina Academic Press, 2009.

Walker, Irvin. *Rights for Victims of Crime: Rebalancing Justice*. Lanham, MD: Rowman & Littlefield, 2010.

Wolhuter, Lorraine, Neil Olley, and David Denham. *Victimology: Victimisation and Victims' Rights*. New York: Routledge-Cavendish, 2008.

Victimless Crime

A victimless crime is one in which, in the perception of perpetrators and observers, no other individual has been harmed. Since no one is harmed by a crime, many people argue that the act should not be considered a crime at all. This includes a variety of sexual activities that contravene some religious texts (e.g., homosexuality) or personal ethical standards (e.g., gambling) or activities people believe they should be allowed to do because criminalizing them is meaningless (e.g., jaywalking). The basis of objection to these claims includes the role of the state as a victim (e.g., through lost revenue) and that some participants do not have the genuine ability to make an informed decision about whether to take part (e.g., prostitution or polygamy). In any case, as society has developed, changing awareness of the threats posed by certain activities and the changing nature of acceptable ethical norms in society have together brought about amendments to the way that such victimless crimes are policed and judged, adding some new categories and removing others.

Prostitution

Prostitution is representative of a group of activities in which it may be argued that since people are involved in the acts voluntarily as part of a commercial transaction, then no one should be considered a victim. Other activities that might be included in this category include pornography, polygamy, and bare-knuckle fighting. Typically, American federal and state governments have permitted prostitution in certain places apart from when pressure has been placed upon them for reasons of morals or public health. In the early history of the United States, prostitution was just as legal and was considered a necessary part of society as it was in the countries from which settlers had originally arrived.

In newly settled colonial societies and in distant frontier settlements, it has generally been accepted throughout history and around the world that prostitution on a casual or organized basis not only services a demand among groups of unmarried men but also provides a means of income of last resort for women without alternatives. Men generally prefer sex workers of a similar ethnicity to themselves, and so, as new waves of migration came to America, men were followed by women destined for one aspect of the sex trade or another. Chinese women, following Chinese men working on building the railroads, were apparently held as items of great interest and were exhibited in peep shows for customers interested in determining whether their genitalia were any different from those of other women.

It was not until the early 20th century that prostitution began to be outlawed in many states, largely in the years leading up to World War I. In this period, a combination of the Woman's Christian Temperance Union, suffragists, and labor unions was actively campaigning for reform of society through moral and aesthetic issues such as reduction in public drunkenness and promotion of family life (hence the ban on prostitution) as well as improvements in workplace safety and conditions. As ever, criminalizing an activity for which demand continues unaffected means the burden of punishment falls on the providers of the service, in this case the sex workers themselves. With the outbreak of human immunodeficiency virus and acquired immune deficiency syndrome (HIV/AIDS), further legislation was introduced in some states to intensify the punishment for sex workers aware of an HIV-positive status. Once their status became illegal, women in the sex work industry lost their opportunity to appeal to the state authorities when abused or threatened, or simply cheated.

There are arguments that sex work is such a demeaning and traumatizing activity that no woman or indeed man can ever truly work in it voluntarily. This seems to contradict empirical evidence that shows at least some sex workers to be reasonably content with their choice of lifestyle given the alternatives open to them. What does seem to be the case is that when the techniques of industrialized capitalism are applied by pimps to their sex workers, increasing productivity by maximizing the number of customers while minimizing costs, then there is little doubt that the sex workers become victims. The same is true of other types of work related to sex, such as acting in pornographic films or exotic dancing. It is possible for workers in these areas to be reasonably well empowered and to control their own means of production, which is their own bodies.

However, there are many cases in which their power is removed from them and their position becomes similar to if not exactly the same as victims of a crime.

The situation of multiple wives in societies such as Mormons, which once accepted the practice, or in an earlier period the brides for sale in frontier settlements, was similar. Depending on the particular circumstances they found, the women might have a tolerable or even comparatively pleasant life, given the alternatives open to them, or they might be very badly treated in the way that continues to happen to disempowered mail order or Internet brides in various countries today. The principle involved is whether the women actually have genuine economic alternatives to explore apart from selling themselves.

Gambling
Gambling is an example of a victimless crime that is based on a sense of personal morality. Religious texts tend not to emphasize restrictions on gambling, although most religious authorities do tend to preach against it because of its impact on families and because of the possibility of addictive or compulsive gambling. However, gambling has long had a relationship with the state in the form of lotteries, which have been used in America since the time of settlement to help fund state government budgets. This has led to tension across the centuries between the authorities and the moral establishment that has resulted in a series of compromises restricting gambling to specific licensed casinos in restricted locations, which can, it is imagined, be easily controlled and regulated. This led to the creation of riverboat casinos operating out of New Orleans and the casinos located on the reservations of some Native Americans as well as the construction of gambling-based conurbations such as Las Vegas and Atlantic City. Despite attempts to control these activities, gambling establishments have continued to be bedeviled by connections with organized crime, money laundering, sex work, and the type of petty crime that is associated with addicted gamblers searching for money to repay debts, not to mention the violence that comes from attempts to regain unpaid debts. On a day-to-day basis for those people who did not live in a gambling-permitted location, neighborhood numbers or underground lotteries or semiformal gambling at horse racing tracks or boxing arenas helped fill in the gap. These activities, too, because of their nature as occasionally illegal and cash-based, have been subject to the same forms of petty crime and possible corruption by bribing police to turn a blind eye.

The argument for legalizing gambling has been effectively won in contemporary America because of the influence of the Internet. This has given access to online gambling markets in sporting contests and has also popularized the online playing of poker for money. State-level attempts to restrict, control, and tax Internet-based activities have so far proven to be less than successful.

Gambling is said to be a victimless crime and is legal in many states in the form of lotteries. However, many experts warn of the potential for addiction and harm to families when the stakes get high enough to bet with borrowed money.

Homosexuality

The same has been true of other activities that are defined by some as being morally or ethically abhorrent based generally on a religious tradition. The most notable example of this is homosexuality or, more specifically, male homosexuality. The consideration of homosexuality focused primarily on the act of sodomy, which was criminalized in early America according to laws that were, as in most countries, largely ignored as long as those involved showed some discretion. It was not until the years following World War II and the onset of the cold war that any form of what was considered to be deviant behavior became stigmatized by the right-wing establishment and its allies in the emergent conservative Christian lobby. This resulted in stricter antisodomy laws, which had been enacted in all states by the 1950s. However, the tide of public opinion turned against this approach and a more tolerant attitude was evident by the 21st century, when most of those laws were removed. Opponents of homosexuality have transferred their hostility to new areas of the law by aiming to prevent gay people from getting married or enjoying other forms of basic rights. This debate continues.

Use of Drugs

Perhaps the area of greatest controversy in the issue of victimless crimes comes with the use of drugs ruled to be illegal. The drugs involved include heroin, cocaine, marijuana, and amphetamines. Each of these has either been legally available in the past or prescribed for various medical conditions or both. From the perspective of the individual, the principal issue concerns the right of the individual to enjoy a product that harms no one else; the argument against drugs on this level is that the drugs are addictive to the extent that an individual cannot make a rational decision to use or to stop using them. Clearly, there is a degree of inconsistency attached to these arguments as there are many products that are legally available and that cause damage to the health of an individual and an attendant cost to society in dealing with the health issues involved: foods promoting obesity, automobiles, and firearms are examples of such products.

Marijuana (or cannabis), in various forms, is the illegal drug most widely used and the most

There is a great deal of controversy as to whether the use of some illegal drugs constitutes victimless crimes, particularly regarding marijuana, which is prescribed to some patients.

contentious in this regard. Cannabis is prescribed by some doctors for conditions such as multiple sclerosis and also to stimulate favorable symptoms in patients who are HIV-positive or receiving treatment for cancer. The drug is also widely used in various spiritual belief systems, and its use has been decriminalized in a number of countries. However, the U.S. judiciary, as a whole, continues to criminalize the use, growth, or distribution of the drug, irrespective of the use to which it might be put. This has led to the prosecution of various individuals who are quite removed from the normal expectations of criminal behavior and has contributed to the public feeling that the banning of some items rather than others is either inconsistent or is subject to the intervention of industry lobbying groups. This feeling is accentuated by the ways in which laws have been framed with respect to specific types of drugs that have usage linked to certain socioeconomic groups: for example, crack cocaine, more likely to be used by black Americans, is prosecuted with much more severity than those forms associated with middle-class white Americans.

Jaywalking
Some activities have been posited as being harmless to others; their practice is claimed to be part of the rights of any American under the freedoms provided by the Constitution. One of the most emblematic of these is jaywalking. This is a term that dates to 1909 and refers to a reckless or irresponsible act by pedestrians in crossing the road. This appears to be an innocent enough activity and not worthy of much consideration, but in fact, the implications of a motorist striking a pedestrian can be very severe for those directly involved and also to the state as a whole. While the psychological costs of such an incident are paid by the families of those involved, the physical costs have to be met at least in part by the state and by society at large in the form of increased insurance fees. There is no act, in fact, in which it is not possible for a person to become a victim in one way or another.

Jaywalking also has both class and racial implications. From the 1930s, the growing importance of the automobile vis-à-vis the pedestrian meant that police customarily sided with the former against the latter. Where once roads were part of the commons and a resource to be used by all, they became enclosed by automobile drivers whose speed and power forced all other would-be road users to stay on the sidewalks apart from occasional regulated periods when they are permitted to cross. Laws were enacted to enshrine the rights of usually wealthy automobile drivers above the rights of the often not-so-wealthy pedestrians. In poor districts of cities, some of the roads of the communities involved have been ruled out of bounds for residents and designated as the property of those passing through. Further, police in urban areas in particular have been accused of using jaywalking legislation as a means of stopping and questioning pedestrians, particularly pedestrians who belong to certain ethnic minority and demographic groups. When it comes to a prosecution for jaywalking, the evidence presented at court will generally be little more than the testimony of one or more officers compared to that of the accused and, despite some checks and balances in the system, this is sufficient to inspire many people to believe that their odds of acquittal are reduced.

The Victim Is the State
In general, the American state has usually been prepared to retain criminal status for any act to which it has been attached, on the basis that the state can be declared as the ultimate victim and that this represents a useful stream of revenue. In the case of speeding or other acts of improper use of an automobile, it has been argued by one or more of the jurisdictions involved that the act itself represents a potential threat to safety and hence a cost to the state, while a fine may at least recoup some of the costs involved in documenting the action. The same approach has been used in the case of smuggling, failing to declare earnings from an illegal source, and any other act that might affect the health of that person or anyone else.

The one great anomaly in this long-term policy and perhaps the greatest failure in contemporary American political action is the so-called war on drugs. This disastrous and simplistic approach has had incalculable costs when an alternative approach could have reduced the harm done by regulating quality and taxing every transaction to pay for the costs incurred.

John Walsh
Shinawatra University

See Also: Abortion; Adultery; Drug Abuse and Addiction, Contemporary; Prostitution, Contemporary.

Further Readings
Fejes, Fred. *Gay Rights and Moral Panic: The Origins of America's Debate on Homosexuality*. Basingstoke, UK: Palgrave Macmillan, 2011.
Grinols, Earl. *Gambling in America*. Cambridge: Cambridge University Press, 2004.

Norton, Peter D. *Fighting Traffic: The Dawn of the Motor Age in the American City.* Cambridge, MA: MIT Press, 2008.

Victorian Compromise

The Victorian age was a time of great contrasts: moralism versus vice, philanthropy versus greediness, wealth versus poverty, and the like. Therefore, Lawrence Friedman, who coined the term, argued that the Victorian Compromise served as a double standard that tolerated sin and vice, so long as they took place in the private sphere, to protect the reputation of respectable men and women who deviated from the official norms.

The religious and philosophical elements of the Victorian Compromise stood in contrast to the Victorian era itself. Evangelicalism, created in the 18th century by John Wesley, focused on moral conduct, emphasizing humanitarian causes and social reforms. Utilitarianism, a theory by Jeremy Bentham, upheld reason as the means to overcome problems, abandoning human and cultural values.

Empiricism, an attack on utilitarianism headed by Charles Dickens and John Stuart Mill, relied on legislation to help men develop their natural talents. As such, education and art had a significant role. Mill also launched a series of reforms to improve the lot of the disadvantaged population, namely, to provide free education, emancipation of women, and trade union organization, among others.

Given the competing realities in the society of the Victorian age, the rigid and nonnegotiable doctrines of the 19th century served to protect reputation. The Victorian Compromise forged a personal zone of privacy, which in turn permitted deviations from the norms. Because of its tolerance of sins, the Victorian Compromise was attacked by the moralists, but in the second half of the 20th century, it had become the norm. The legal and social control over sex, reproduction, gambling, and intimate relationships was normalized. At the core of the Victorian Compromise was the concealing of questionable practices in a fashion accepted by the elite.

An 1854 cartoon describes a Victorian dilemma—"If we lift our skirts, they level their eye-glasses at our ankles." Men of the time did not often see the "titillating" display of an ankle.

Vice in the Private Sphere

The Victorian era was known for its pious moral codes and sense of propriety. Across history, Western societies have experienced intervals of licentiousness and reticence. The Victorian era was the symbol of prudish attitudes and shrouded deeds. In both England and America, strict laws penalized various sexual activities that were reproved, from adultery to sodomy. At the same time, vice was nonetheless tolerated if found in small amounts, discreet, and well controlled. This duality was the essence of the Victorian period. An example of the double standard was the red-light districts, which sprouted up across cities. Brothels, casinos, and other houses of vice developed swiftly in these districts. The law and law enforcement tolerated them as part of normal urban activities.

Blackmail was another aspect of the Victorian Compromise. The blackmail laws acted in favor of elites to protect their public personas, shielding them from threats or extortion by illicit lovers or servants through blackmail. The blackmail statutes had basic principles found in the Victorian Compromise and came about at the same time.

The tolerance of hidden vices and misconduct, furthered by the blackmail statutes, spawned hypocrisy and asserted the view that sins could not be eradicated. While the Victorian Compromise relied on privacy and secrecy to sustain itself, hypocrisy worked to keep the "virtuous, respectable" class on its public pedestal in spite of its deviant indulgences.

The contexts in which the Victorian Compromise emerged deserve close attention. During the Victorian era, the middle class enjoyed their wealth, espoused their social etiquette, and their middle-class values. As such, the word *Victorian* came to denote a set of moral and sexual values. However, the Victorians had ignored the issues affecting the disadvantaged classes of England. The distressed working class faced stifling living conditions in urban slums, health problems, epidemics, and poor working situations. The New Poor Law of 1834 did not help resolve the problems, yet created the workhouse that was so loathed by the poor. Poverty, regardless of the circumstances, was qualified as a crime with penalty. Debtors were imprisoned in appalling conditions. Education also failed, with incompetent teachers who used corporal punishment as a disciplining method.

This coupling of prosperity and progress versus poverty and injustice gave birth to the Victorian Compromise. Other opposing forces included ethical conformism versus corruption, moralism and philanthropy versus money and capitalistic greediness, private life versus public behaviors. To some extent, the values the Victorians promoted indicated their preferred world and were not reflective of the social realities around them. The Victorian Compromise provided a sort of escape for them from social ills in that it allowed for deviance to take place behind closed doors, restraining much of the undesirable acts from flooding the façade of a moralistic society.

Another aspect of the contradiction inherent in the Victorian Compromise had to do with how it prompted theorists and reformers to improve the life of the disadvantaged populations, especially when it comes to public spaces such as hospitals, schools, and prisons. The concern to conduct the public space as respectable must have come from the idea of respectability, which discriminated the middle class from the working class.

Besides economic possessions, manners became the measure of class standing and altered greatly during this time. Queen Victoria had exerted her influences and caused the era to be highly puritanical. Sex became a taboo subject, and sex-related words were purged from daily use or replaced with euphemized terms. Speech and act, therefore, underwent chastening, enabling respectability to be a key concept of the Victorian era.

Trangdai Glassey-Tranguyen
Stanford University

See Also: Adultery; Obscenity; Prostitution, History of; Sin; Sodomy.

Further Readings
Friedman, Lawrence. *Guarding Life's Dark Secrets: Legal and Social Controls Over Reputation, Propriety, and Privacy.* Palo Alto, CA: Stanford University Press, 2007.
Tate, Joshua C. "Gambling, Commodity Speculation, and the 'Victorian Compromise.'" *Yale Journal of Law and the Humanities,* v.19 (2007).

Vigilantism

Vigilantism is the practice of using private methods of obtaining justice and/or enforcing social control when the state is unable or unwilling to do so. A vigilante, in the formal sense of the word, is a member of a vigilance committee. This is a group or organization voluntarily constituted to "take the law into their own hands" in place of the justice system of an incipient, weak, or failed state. Vigilantes often create alternative courts and punishment mechanisms in lieu of those offered by the state. In the American narrative, such punishments included hanging (rarely), and more commonly, forms of public humiliation such as tarring and feathering, "running out of town on a rail," or flogging. Modern forms of quasi-vigilantism in the United States include Internet vigilantism and extreme manifestations of neighborhood protectionism—using protests and pressure to coerce undesirables such as sex offenders into finding other housing arrangements.

Vigilantism is condemned by most legal writers and authorities as it denigrates and further delegitimizes the authority and majesty of the law and the state. It calls into question the very basis of the social contract through individuals collectively taking the state's prerogative unto themselves.

This is why group vigilantism is almost uniformly condemned in fiction and cinema.

The raw-boned hero who takes vengeance as his own province, however, is paradoxically an American icon. Said hero, a cowboy or modern urban dweller in his own "frontier," is forced to exact personal vengeance because legal institutions are not equal to the task of imposing justice. Examples of the former would include *Hang 'em High*, in which Clint Eastwood's character tracks down and kills those who illegally (and imperfectly) lynched him. This theme is frequently encountered in classic Westerns. An example of the latter tendency would be the guy-next-door character played by Charles Bronson, whose family is destroyed by street punks. He embarks on a mission of revenge in the popular *Death Wish* series. The theme of private vengeance as problematic can be traced to Shakespeare and to ancient Greek plays.

Vigilantism in Early American History
The practice of vigilantism has existed in the United States since colonial times but it enjoyed its first florescence in the anarchic period immediately before and during the American Revolution. Generally, most American vigilantism arises from conservative roots. Vigilantism in the south after the revolution stemmed from the need to protect slavery and business interests, such as plantation or cattle interests. In other parts of the country, vigilante impulses generally stemmed from the same conservative, locally oriented mercantile interest. Threats to the existing order were frequently targets; exemplars of the existing order were seldom victims of vigilantes. Such outstanding citizens and male members of rising elites were almost always holding the rope, not dancing on the other end. Victims were frequently members of pariah groups, strangers, slaves, union members and organizers, political outsiders, immigrants, and occasionally, real criminals. The involvement of such conservative elements may seem paradoxical given the critique of the existing order that vigilantism suggests. However, in the absence of an effective state, private justice functions admirably and may even been seen by practitioners as superior to the organs of the state.

The first major manifestation of vigilantism in the nascent United States was "Regulator" violence, which broke out in South Carolina in 1771. Regulators came into conflict with British forces and Crown loyalists before and during the American Revolution. They also punished outlaws and drove them from the colony or state. British authority and institutions were weak, and British taxes and laws were seen as hampering mercantile interests in the hinterlands. In rural Virginia, the situation was much the same, but not nearly as hard fought and bloody. One interesting note is that Judge Lynch of "lynching" notoriety was supposedly a real historical figure who frequently employed public humiliation of British sympathizers to make a point. "Lynching" came to mean an extralegal hanging only after the revolution. As the American state began to assert its authority in the last decade of the 18th century, these movements faded from the scene. The pattern of weak authority leading to vigilante activity and then losing its rationale in the emergence of growing state power occurred repeatedly throughout the next century.

State courts and local law enforcement existed in the frontier in the early 1800s but their authority was very weak. Fantasies of slave revolts or feared outlaw outrages occasioned the creation of vigilance committees. These were not anarchic mobs of toothless bumpkins but usually represented the gentry and rising elites. They often used the local press to post statements of concern and purpose to rationalize and defend their activities. The local press was almost always supportive, and many editors served as vigilantes.

A still from the trailer for the 1956 film The Searchers, *starring John Wayne, who sought revenge for a kidnapped sister. Western films used the setting of the frontier and its unformed system of law and order to explore vigilantism.*

In the south, such committees typically rounded up suspects and any strangers in the area if a slave revolt was feared. Many slaves were hanged in these situations; some were burned alive. Sometimes, however, vigilance committees tried to calm the situation and keep events from getting out of hand. After all, the wholesale hanging of slaves, while seen as a powerful deterrent, was a ruinously expensive experience for the planter aristocracy. Often, flogging a "symbolic enemy" such as an unfortunate New England traveler, or perhaps a few "uppity" slaves, might appease public opinion. In Mississippi in 1835, a minor slave revolt or reputed slave revolt at Beattie's Bluff set off a mass vigilante movement. The famous Murrell conspiracy that same year generated even more hysteria. Purported "land pirates," gangs of murderous thieves, were operating on the Natchez Trace. How much crime they committed and how much was imaginary is anyone's guess. Most problematically, the Murrell gang was alleged to be fomenting a slave revolt. Vigilance committees put a stop to that and in the same year turned their considerable energies to expelling professional gamblers from Vicksburg and Natchez. Even in the presence of state mechanisms to deal with sedition, thievery, and cheating, getting rid of all these problematic enemy deviants through legal means would have been almost impossible. The extralegal methods that vigilantism exemplified allowed for an expeditious resolution when dealing with difficult legal issues and pariah groups. Thus, vigilantism was also seen as a practical way to get things done, both in the absence of an effective state and in the presence of one whose institutions did not offer expeditious-enough resolution of complex social and legal issues.

The Civil War Era to World War I
After the Civil War, various conservative groups such as the Red Shirts, tried to restore the old order by harassing former slaves, scalawags, and carpetbaggers. They were reasonably effective in their efforts and achieved the withdrawal of Union troops in 1877.

Texas was plagued by outlawry and vigilantism at two different periods in time. In the 1830s and 1840s, east Texas was plagued by outlaws and cattle thieves. Vigilantes known as "Regulators" used severe methods to root out escaped slaves, outlaws, and criminals hiding in the border between Texas and Louisiana. So harsh were their methods that "Moderators" arose to counter their reign of terror, and a Moderator/Regulator war broke out. This was only subdued when the nascent Republic of Texas sent in militia to quell the disturbance. The second era of vigilantism was after the Civil War, when vigilante groups arose all over the state to deal with cattle rustlers and outlawry. Many hangings occurred, and reputedly corrupt lawmen were killed in their jails by armed vigilante bands. Finally, the Texas Rangers were called in to settle the violence and bring an end to family feuds. Complicating matters was extreme animosity between ex-Confederates and freed slaves and Republicans. Ambushes and public shootings were common up to the 1890s. Ironically, this era's media promulgated a myth approving of both vigilantism and the actions of the Texas Rangers. This tension between private and public justice was to continue in the American narrative.

The most famous vigilante events in American history took place in California in the 1840s. The gold fields attracted both law-abiding prospectors and outlaws from all over the world. Law enforcement was nonexistent in the gold-producing areas, and crime was dealt with harshly by local vigilance groups and kangaroo courts. San Francisco, with weak and reportedly corrupt political controls, had a serious crime problem. Gangs of criminals were supposedly at large, and formerly respectable citizens turned to crime simply to survive. Isolated from family, friends, and home, and often heavily armed and drunk, prospectors turned violent when hitting the fleshpots of "Bagdad by the Bay." The city was in chaos, if highly biased partisan contemporary accounts are to be credited.

This and Democratic control of local government, of course, were bad for business, and conservative elements created the San Francisco Committee of Vigilance in 1851. They held court and set up patrols. Most criminals they convicted were publicly whipped, and problematic members of a particularly obnoxious Australian gang were transported home, but only a few hangings took place. A second iteration in 1856 was more explicitly political, and harassed Democrats and their supporters. Backed by armed militia, this group evolved into a wing of the Republican Party, and today it is difficult to assess how much of its activities were simply partisan violence and how much actually dealt with real crime and criminals.

New Orleans in the 1850s was an even more chaotic and corrupt political milieu than it is at present. Working-class whites, using the American (Know-Nothing) Party as their vehicle, were in the process of seizing power from the planter elite and for a brief period controlled the mayor's office and the police department. Democrats, in this case a very conservative group, merged with Whigs and staged an abortive coup in 1859 using a vigilance committee as a front. Respectable elements such as future Confederate General Beauregard and U.S. Senator (and political boss) John Slidell were deeply involved with the vigilante movement. Local merchant elites and planters were appalled that white workingmen would have the effrontery to challenge their hegemony, but their ham-fisted coup failed. After the war, vigilance groups tried to enforce white supremacy and even staged armed revolts in 1866 and 1874. Local authorities usually looked the other way when such white supremacist violence from groups like the Ku Klux Klan took place, even as late as the 1960s. Local juries would not convict those who attempted to enforce white racial norms in this period. In 1891, a vigilante group lynched 11 alleged Mafiosi in the parish prison, an event that precipitated a diplomatic frisson between Italy and the United States.

In an atypical departure from the prototypical nongovernmental and state-disavowed manner of operation, occasionally the state sanctions and even uses private vigilante organizations. An example of this rare occurrence is the case of the American Protective League, which operated during World War I. Enjoying the approval of the Bureau of Investigation, the precursor to the Federal Bureau of Investigation (FBI), this group harassed German Americans, socialists, pacifists, and radical unionists. It notably persecuted draft evaders and antiwar activists. Its actions were often undisciplined and uncontrolled, and the group was disavowed by the Department of Justice and disbanded after the war. Another example of private, state-sanctioned vigilantism that can be cited is the American Legion, in Washington State, which took action against the radical International Workers of the World in the postwar period.

Present-Day Quasi-Vigilante Activity and Impulses

During the 1970s, several quasi-vigilante groups emerged out of the crime crises of the urban United States. The most publicized was the Guardian Angels. Founded by Curtis Sliwa in 1979 and known for wearing red berets, the Guardian Angels attempted to deter crime through unarmed patrols and by calling attention to high-crime areas. They were media darlings but were heartily disliked by local police, who saw them as potential gang members or provocateurs. They were not a real vigilante group, as they had almost no support from elites or merchants and have mostly faded from the scene in recent decades.

The most celebrated vigilante case of modern times was that of Bernard Goetz. In 1984, surrounded and feeling threatened by four African American youth on a subway, Goetz shot them at close range. Dubbed the "subway vigilante" by an overstimulated media, Goetz was convicted of a minor weapons violation and faded into obscurity. Again, as he did not work in a group context and was not working in concert with local elites, he cannot be called a true vigilante, though his conduct certainly appealed to impulses for private justice. It was widely perceived that order had broken down, and that Goetz's actions made him a hero in the eyes of many. Others saw him as a maladjusted, dysfunctional advertisement for alienation and ill-conceived celebrity.

Anti-immigrant groups such as the Minuteman Project have often been in the news in the early 21st century. Angry about crime in Mexico and increased immigration, this group has established patrols along the Mexico-U.S. border. Group members, like Tea Partiers, link themselves to the founding fathers and seem unfazed by the knowledge that the founders, in fact, wanted to encourage immigration to build the nation. This group has been accused of far right-wing sympathies by progressives, and significantly, by former members as well. It is not a true vigilante group as it is not supported by local elites; local businesses want access to cheap immigrant labor. Furthermore, the group does not have courts or

The Native American or Know-Nothing party was founded in 1841. In 1854, the party adopted the policy that U.S. citizenship should be granted only after an emigrant had lived in the country for 21 years—thus the symbolism on this flag.

punishment mechanisms; they simply call the U.S. Border Patrol or local law enforcement when they encounter immigrants who have crossed illegally. Still, they articulate widespread and inchoate public frustration with a porous frontier and a dysfunctional immigration system.

Another manifestation of contemporary quasi-vigilantism is Internet or cyber vigilantism. In the largely unguarded and unprotected "frontier" that the Internet represents, law enforcement is ill equipped to deal with the myriad issues that have arisen. Sexual exploitation of minors by pornographers, predators, and pedophiles through the medium of the Internet has led individuals to get involved. Groups have targeted individuals for demonstrations or boycotts. Sexual offenders in group homes find angry groups of neighbors calling for their ouster. The situation is so severe that in some municipalities, ex-offenders simply have nowhere to live because of restrictive existing laws and continuing agitation by these groups.

One media-created group is Perverted Justice, a group that lures unwary would-be lotharios of underage girls and boys, that is, sexual predators, into supposed meetings with people the predators believe to be vulnerable minors. The "children" on the Internet are actually adult members of Perverted Justice. After "grooming" the supposed underage objects of their would-be affection, the predators agree to meet with their correspondents. Upon arriving at a private residence, they are lured into the home with an invitation, a further intimation that something more rewarding than a talk will be forthcoming.

At this point, they are confronted by a reporter, and ultimately arrested by the local police. They are generally tackled unnecessarily and hectored at gunpoint. Attendant public humiliations such as booking and questioning follow and are duly recorded for the network audience. This is obviously very close to entrapment, and few of those arrested are actually charged and convicted with more serious sex crimes. But some members of Perverted Justice have reportedly harassed arrestees at home and work, causing some to lose their jobs. They have also used the Internet to post pictures of the offender, his home, and place of business. Perverted Justice does enjoy support from most in the criminal justice community; who would, after all, advocate for the sexual predator? Some Websites and groups of civil libertarians find these activities unfair, objectionable, and outrageous. A few have pointed out that the dedication of this group seems excessive and more than a bit perverse in its own self-righteousness.

Other Internet-based vigilantism might involve turning the tables on "Nigerian scam" artists by promising to cable them money in some distant or dangerous Nigerian locale. When the con artist arrives at the scene, there is no money, only peril. Some of these vigilantes have been able to obtain and post photos of such scammers in custody or in dangerous situations. Other vigilantes meet in chat rooms and other forums and agree to harass individuals or corporations that they feel are inimical to their goals or interests. In one case, an Internet service provider that had hosted malware sites and other scams was forced off the web by collective activist efforts. People who torment or do not take proper care of their animals have been the special target of Internet-based activists. In South Korea, a woman who failed to pick up her dog's feces on the subway was the target of an intense campaign of Internet vilification. Eventually known as "Dog Poop Girl," she resigned from her university and made a public apology. Companies that have refused to let children use their restrooms have been similarly targeted by Internet vigilantes.

Internet vigilantism is especially notable in China. A cuckolded husband's pitiful postings about his wife's romantic alliance got a strong reaction, and the object of her affection was harassed on the street. Online groups coalesced and, meeting on the street, verbally tormented the lover unrelentingly until he quit his university and hid out in his home. More recently, Internet vigilantes in China have focused on government inefficiency in its reactions to disasters and perceptions about its perceived general corruption.

Vigilante Themes in Drama and Media

It is hard to delve into ancient or Renaissance literature without dealing with themes of private justice, if not true vigilantism. Among the first Greek dramas, Aeschylus's *Oresteia* deals primarily with vengeance and the gods' reactions. Shakespeare deals with similar themes in *Hamlet*, and other playwrights of his age were interested in retributive-oriented plots.

But in American cinema, private vengeance themes ring a responsive chord with the popular mind. Classic Westerns from the 1950s and 1960s, using weak law and order on the frontier as a backdrop, explore private vengeance at length. In *The Searchers*, John Wayne tracks down and kills the Indians who kidnapped his sister, recovers her, and restores order to a disordered post–Civil War Texas. Clint Eastwood seeks private justice in *The Outlaw Josey Wales*, as he does in *Hang 'em High*. John Wayne (again!), in one of his last Westerns, shoots down gunmen in *The Shootist*. *High Noon* and *The Man Who Shot Liberty Valence* also deal with private vengeance versus legal justice; this nexus is an interesting frontier of its own.

Clint Eastwood (again), although seemingly a modern law enforcement agent, is clearly on a series of private missions in the *Dirty Harry* franchise. Certainly, these are popularly viewed as vigilante-type films. In a more nuanced and sensitive portrayal, he becomes positively messianic in *Gran Torino* (2008), in which a vigilante-like everyman saves poor Asian immigrants from a gang of urban thugs.

Women as vigilantes go back to the Greeks, but in modern cinema they include Jodie Foster in *The Brave One* and Ashley Judd in *Double Jeopardy*. More films and television series with women as avenging protagonists include a growing number of police procedurals and standard cop shows.

It is strange that the rich vigilante tradition in America has spawned almost no television drama that deals with this theme. Apart from a random *Bonanza* or *Rawhide* episode from the early 1960s where mistaken identities almost lead Hoss or Clint Eastwood (yet again) to be lynched in some godforsaken one-horse town, the vigilante theme is seldom taken up as a dominant motif. The notable exception to this generalization was the 1957 Western *The Californians*, which took place in gold rush-era San Francisco. The main protagonist was an editor who had mixed feelings about the extralegal proceedings in the city by the bay.

Still, it was a standard shoot-'em-up and did not raise many deep existential or philosophical questions. *Have Gun Will Travel* (1957) featured an erudite hired gun, Paladin, who was both detective and muscle for the downtrodden. His hidden derringer furnished a fitting denouement to many a desperado or plutocrat-employed hired gun. In this respect, it was both contemporary and forerunner to the plethora of detective dramas of the late 1950s, 1960s, and 1970s. A recent, somewhat distorted use of the theme of private vengeance visited on the truly deserving is *Dexter*. This cable network offering concerns a sociopathic CSI expert who systemically tracks down and murders sociopathic murderers. Its popularity raises serious question about the public's ability to distinguish right from wrong: In the show, it is permissible for evil people to use their privileged law enforcement position to hunt down, torture, and murder similarly evil malefactors. Still, it is clearly in the tradition of private vengeance, though technically not truly a vigilante series.

It is evident, then, that much that is labeled as "vigilante" in dramatic content is actually more correctly called "private justice" in terms of motif. Furthermore, it is interesting that private violence is often justified in media, but mob-based vigilantism is almost always subject to strong disapprobation. This reinforces the system but legitimizes the deep anger and alienation felt by many Americans. This tension may produce much more frustration and simplistic thinking about how to deal with crime and complex political issues than many in the media might suppose.

Francis Frederick Hawley
Western Carolina University

See Also: 1901 to 1920 Primary Documents; Ku Klux Klan; New Orleans, Louisiana; San Francisco, California.

Further Readings

Ayers, Edward L. *Vengeance and Justice: Crime and Punishment in the 19th-Century American South.* New York: Oxford University Press, 1984.

Brown, Richard M. *Strain of Violence: Historical Studies of American Violence and Vigilantism.* New York: Oxford University Press, 1975.

Courtwright, D.T. *Violent Land: Single Men and Social Disorder From the Frontier to the Inner City.* Cambridge, MA: Harvard University Press, 1998.

Cutrer, Thomas W. "Southwestern Violence." In *Encyclopedia of Southern Culture,* C. R Wilson and W. Ferris, eds. Chapel Hill: University of North Carolina Press, 1989.

Lane, Roger. *Murder in America: A History.* Columbus: Ohio State University Press, 1997.

Neely, Richard. *Take Back Your Neighborhood.* New York: Donald I. Fine, 1990.

Richards, Leonard. *The California Gold Rush and the Coming of the Civil War.* New York: Knopf, 2007.

Thompson, E. P. *Whigs and Hunters: The Origins of the Black Act.* New York: Pantheon, 1975.

Wyatt-Brown, Bertram. *Southern Honor.* New York: Oxford University Press, 1982.

Violence Against Women Act of 1994

The Violence Against Women Act of 1994 (VAWA) passed the U.S. Congress as Title IV, sec. 40001-40703 of the Violent Crime Control and Law Enforcement Act of 1994 (HR 3355), and President William Clinton signed it as Public Law 103-322. The basics of the law provide $1.6 billion to enhance investigations and prosecutions of violent crimes against women. The bill also aims to increase pre-trial incarceration of those accused, automatic and mandatory restitution for those convicted, and civil redress for cases prosecutors fail to prosecute. The monies were originally allocated for disbursement over six years for improvement in local and state justice systems, shelters, education, and training of court personnel. The bill also provides for paying for sexually transmitted disease tests, statistical records, and protection of battered women and children. The bill stemmed from perceived increases in violence against women and the UN Committee on Women calling for more federal intervention in the protection of women, children, and gender-based attacks.

Advocacy organizations like the National Coalition Against Sexual Violence, National Coalition Against Domestic Violence, and the National Organization for Women supported the bill with great applause. At its passage, VAWA supporters dubbed it the greatest achievement for women's rights in two decades. Senator Joseph Biden's office wrote the bill. Since its original inception, the VAWA has been reauthorized by Congress in 2000 and 2005. The act was up for reauthorization in 2011. The VAWA is a foundational piece of legislation because the U.S. Justice Department has no specific office dealing with violence against women. This legislation enabled the Office on Violence Against Women, in 2000, to begin administering monies to develop federal policy on domestic violence, sexual assault, dating violence, and stalking.

The VAWA first reached Congress in 1990, and testimony from victims and families helped support the legislation. The Clarence Thomas–Anita Hill confirmation hearings and a rise in the number of elected women in 1992 launched the bill's passage. In 1994, the VAWA was voted on as part of the Omnibus Crime Bill, and it was overwhelmingly favored in both houses. The VAWA makes it a felony to cross state lines with the intent to injure, harass, or harm a person's spouse or partner, allows protective orders to cross state lines, and lets victims testify to the threat or level of perceived violence in pre-trial hearings. Finally, the restitution clause of the law provides temporary housing, child-care expenses, lost income, attorney's fee, and other costs associated with the crime to be paid to the victim. While the bill was met with a great amount of applause, it was not without problems. The bill's provision allowed gender-based victims to have a course of action against attackers. In 2000, the U.S. Supreme Court struck down this section of the law in *U.S. v. Morrison*, saying that only the states could provide these rights to victims.

Annessa A. Babic
New York Institute of Technology

See Also: 1981 to 2000 Primary Documents; Rape, Contemporary; Rape, History of; Violent Crimes.

Further Readings
Conyers, John, Jr. "The 2005 Reauthorization of the Violence Against Women Act: Why Congress Acted to Expand Protections to Immigrant Victims." *Violence Against Women*, v.13/5 (2007).
Rutkow, Lainie, et al. "Violence Against Women and the U.S. Supreme Court: Recent Challenges and Opportunities for Advocates and Practitioners." *Violence Against Women*, v.15/10 (2009).
Tomes, Henry. "Research and Policy Directions in Violence: A Developmental Perspective." *Journal of Health Care for the Poor and Underserved*, v.6/2 (1995).
U.S. v. Morrison, 529 U.S. 598, 120 S. Ct. 1740, 146 L. Ed. 2d 658, 68 USLW 4351 (U.S.Va. 2000).

Violent Crimes

Violence has been part of the fabric of American lives since the first settlement in 1607. In colonial America, there were vast distances between settlements, and traveling between them was often difficult and time-consuming. Thus, crimes tended to be concentrated in small areas. Most premature deaths in the colonies were caused by disease or violence, and both were seen as inevitable aspects of life. In this harsh environment, vigilante groups often sought out accused violators and exacted their own brand of justice. Vigilantism was more common in new settlements than in those that were well established. Historians have identified as many as 500 vigilante groups operating in America between the 1760s and 1905. In early America, highwaymen often roamed areas between settlements. While robbery was their goal, violence sometimes occurred. Within each colony, crime was dealt with according to the seriousness of the offense. Common punishments included public embarrassment, branding, physical mutilation, fines, and incarceration. Some colonies adopted capital punishment as a means of dealing with a variety of serious crimes, including suspected witchcraft. In the years following the American Revolution, states began the debate over the death penalty that has been ubiquitous throughout much of American history. Political events and social upheavals have affected crime rates by causing them to decline during wars or soar during times of civil unrest, as was the case during the heydays of the labor and civil rights movements. In the twenty-first century, many Americans had become more afraid of terrorists than strangers wielding guns. The United States continues to be one of the most violent nations in the world, with twice the crime rate of France and four times the crime rate of Canada. While experts do not always agree on the reasons, most explanations focus on the prevalence of guns in the United States and on racial and ethnic relations, social inequities, and the ubiquity of violence in American media. Crime rates have continued to fluctuate. In 2002, the Federal Bureau of Investigation (FBI) reported that there were 1.4 million violent offenses committed in the United States. Breaking them down into categories, those offenses included 16,204 incidents of murder and non-negligent manslaughter; 95,136 incidents of forcible rape; 420,636 incidents of robbery; and 894,348 incidents of aggravated assault. In general, these are the same crimes that besieged colonial Americans, indicating that human nature does not change over time.

Pre-Twentieth-Century Violence
In the late 18th century, political violence was closely interwoven with the fight to win independence from England. During the Boston Massacre in 1770, a crowd of roughnecks began heckling British soldiers. The deaths of the five Americans that resulted from the confrontation were instrumental in the tightening of British control over Boston and in precipitating the colonists into war with the mother country. The Boston Tea Party, which is one of the most told tales of American history, was in large part due to the enlistment of members of Boston's South End mob, which helped to dump the tea in Boston Harbor. The mob continued to engage in violence throughout the revolutionary period. Even Americans

who considered themselves law-abiding were not always above harassing or even tarring and feathering Tory neighbors who refused to forswear allegiance to the British Crown. Slave uprisings also resulted in violence, with the first taking place in New York in 1712. South Carolina was the venue for a second uprising in 1739, and a third took place in New York two years later.

Reliable crime statistics were generally unavailable before 1900; but by the 1840s, some large cities were beginning to report homicide rates. Philadelphia experienced a homicide rate of 3.3 incidents per 100,000/population in 1840. Boston was less violent, reporting an incident rate of 2.1 per 100,000/population. As might be expected, the rate of homicides declined during the Civil War since attention was focused on fighting and sheer survival of the hardships entailed in living in a nation at war with itself. After the war ended in 1865, crime rates began to increase sharply. In the south, the southern resistance to Reconstruction after the assassination of President Abraham Lincoln in 1865 led to an environment in which whites rioted in at least 80 incidents, railing against what was perceived as northern interference. The Ku Klux Klan instigated many of those incidents. After the election of Rutherford B. Hayes in 1876 and the official end of Reconstruction, power reverted to the white majority, and lynching was considered by many to be a legitimate method of dealing with African Americans who refused to stay in the place assigned to them by Jim Crow laws and discriminatory social practices. Between 1882 and 1951, some 3,400 African Americans were lynched. During the peak period of 1891–1901, more than a hundred African Americans were lynched each year.

Riots have been part of the American scene for centuries. The draft riots of 1863 were a result of federal conscription laws that allowed the wealthy to avoid the draft by finding a substitute or paying a fee of $300. While many riots of the late 19th and early 20th centuries dealt with labor disputes, they became increasingly concerned with racial and ethnic tensions. Rioting broke out in Wilmington, North Carolina, in 1898 in response to the restoration of white supremacy. When Atlanta, Georgia, attempted to disenfranchise blacks in 1906, African Americans responded by rioting. Two years later, the alleged rape of a white female by a black man led to riots in Springfield, Illinois. Competition for jobs erupted into rioting in East St. Louis, Missouri, in 1917. Rioting continued into the 20th century, and 1919 became known as "the Red Summer" because of 26 separate riots. The most serious riot occurred in Chicago on August 2 after an African American youth was stoned until he drowned for daring to swim in a Whites Only section of a public swimming area. When it was over, 38 were dead and another 537 had been injured. One thousand people had been rendered homeless. Other riots broke out that summer in Washington, D.C.; Charleston, South Carolina; Knoxville

The Tory's Day of Judgment by E. Tisdale, circa 1795. American colonists prepare to tar and feather a loyalist seated on the ground as another loyalist hangs from a gallows. The loyalists would not abandon their loyalty to the British Crown.

and Nashville, Tennessee; and Omaha, Nebraska. More than a hundred African Americans were killed that summer, and thousands were left homeless. In 1921, another alleged rape ignited riots in Tulsa, Oklahoma. Tensions between whites and Filipinos broke out into riots in 1928 and again in 1930 in California and Washington State.

The Great Depression and World War II ushered in another rash of rioting. In 1935, New York's Harlem was the scene of widespread unemployment and underemployment. When the Depression forced African Americans out of the jobs they had managed to obtain, race riots resulted. A young Puerto Rican boy who had stolen a ten-cent penknife was removed from the store where the crime took place. When an ambulance and hearse arrived at the scene, onlookers assumed he had been murdered by police and began rioting. When it was over, three African Americans had been killed and approximately 60 had been injured. Damages were estimated at $200 million. In 1943, competition for jobs in the automobile industry led to riots in Detroit, and Harlem again saw rioting after a black soldier was shot in the arm for trying to keep police from hitting an African American woman who was being arrested for disorderly conduct. Six people died in the Harlem riot, and another 400 were injured. Some 500 were arrested. That same year, the so-called Zoot Suit Riots broke out in Los Angeles as tensions rose between military men and the Mexican American community, which had become enamored of the broad-shouldered suits with narrow waists worn with balloon pants. After days of rising tensions, the worst rioting occurred on June 7 when 5,000 civilians headed toward the African American community of Watts and the Mexican American community of East Los Angeles. Watts was also the scene of the worst riot in American history in August 1965 when violence broke out after white police officers stopped an African American suspected of driving while intoxicated. The Watts riots lasted for six days and spread outward for 150 blocks. When it was over, 34 had been killed and 1,032 injured. Nearly 4,000 had been arrested. Estimates of property damage varied between $40 million and $100 million.

Violence on the Rise
Violence continued into the 1960s and 1970s in response to the drug scene, 500 race riots, and a score of antiwar protests. It was a period when self-styled political revolutionaries frequently resorted to violence to make their views known. The Ku Klux Klan also launched a second wave of attacks during this period, continuing to promote its creed of white supremacy. Traditional criminal activities also continued to flourish. In 1971, the rate of aggravated assault reached 90.3 per 100,000/population. About a quarter of all fires were caused by arson, which became the second leading cause of death by fire, second only to smoking.

By the mid-1980s, violence was becoming even more common in the United States. It was also spreading its geographical reach, spreading out from traditional areas into the suburbs, and even reaching some rural areas. Nationwide, approximately 20,000 people were being murdered each year. The majority of those victims were young African American males, and homicide became the leading cause of death for young African Americans. Women were also frequent victims of violent crimes, and more than 75,000 rapes were being reported each year. Rape had the highest increase among all serious offenses between 1977 and 1984. Since rape is a vastly underreported crime, the number of actual rapes was assumed to be considerably higher. Another 650,000 women a year were being victimized through serious nonsexual assaults. One in every five females reported being physically abused by a male at least once. Child abuse rates were also soaring. In 1986, the National Committee for Prevention of Child Abuse reported that the results of a 50-state study indicated that at least 2 million incidents of child abuse and neglect had been recorded that year. Throughout the 1980s, approximately 500,000 robberies were reported annually. Automobile thefts and gang wars were also on the rise. Gunshot wounds became the second leading cause of injury mortality in the United States, outranked only by deaths from automobile accidents. National figures on violent crime revealed that between 1986 and 1987, some 66,182 Americans died from firearm injuries. That number was greater than the number of Americans lost in eight and one-half years of fighting in Vietnam.

Much of the increase in violence in the 1980s was a result of the crack cocaine epidemic. Drug traffickers moved into the suburbs, where they found it much easier to sell their products. The move also saved them money and time by cutting down on travel. Initially, police departments outside large cities were totally unprepared for the sharp rise in crime rates. By 1991 national polls revealed that most Americans were afraid to walk in their own neighborhoods after dark. Crime rates peaked that same year at 758.2 per 100,000/population. Although a decline was subsequently under way, violence was still very much in evidence. Experts blamed the rise in violence on increased divisions by race and class and on a declining sense of community throughout American society. Others pointed out that the existence of large shopping centers and community banks continued to provide increased opportunities for crime in the suburbs.

Despite the lack of safety in suburban America, violent crimes continued to be far more likely to occur in inner cities than in any other area. For instance, in the Washington D.C. area in 1992, incidents of violent crimes decreased 4 percent in Maryland's suburbs and 23 percent in Northern Virginia while rising 13 percent in the capital itself. The most vulnerable cities are those that contain impoverished areas where joblessness, dysfunctional families, inadequate schools, and the presence of gangs are a way of life. Most cities have "hot spots" where most crimes take place, leaving other areas of the city relatively safe. In Boston, for instance, violent crimes disproportionately take place in the "Combat Zone" located within Chinatown. Within the Combat Zone, assault and battery is more common than any other crime, fluctuating between 152 and 177 a year. Threats and armed robbery (46 to 113 per year) and rapes and other sexual offenses (25 per year) are also common occurrences. Some 210 to 374 incidents of property damage are reported in the Combat Zone each year.

In 1990, some 1,820,127 violent crimes were reported in the United States at a rate of 729.6 per 100,000/population. The year 1991 represents the peak of criminal activity in America, and there were 1,911,797 violent crimes committed that year at a rate of 758.2 per 100,000/population. In response to the national crisis, government leaders and law enforcement officials responded with a plethora of reforms and initiatives. Violent crime rates followed the general pattern of decline. As the most populated city in the United States, New York City also experienced a crisis with drastic increases in rates of violent crime in 1990 with 2,245 murders. Mayor David Dinkins introduced community policing. His successor, Rudy Giuliani, also made crime fighting a priority issue, and Giuliani is generally given credit for the turnaround in New York's crime statistics. By 1996, the number of murders in New York had declined to 984.

After experiencing an unprecedented level of crime in 1991, it became clear that overall crime rates were beginning to decline in response to improvements in the field of policing, particularly as a result of the rise in community policing that brought law enforcement and local groups together to fight crime. Politicians also responded to rising crime rates by toughening sentencing laws in 26 states. That trend continued in evidence in the early 21st century. Between 1993 and 2004, crime rates fell from 747 per 100,000/population to 463. New York City, Chicago, and Los Angeles reflected this decline. Between 2000 and 2009, the national rate of violent crimes dropped from 506.5 per 100,000/population to 429.4 per 100,000/population.

However, some cities continued to report upsurges. In 2006, three cities reported homicide rates of three times the national average: Detroit, Memphis, and Sumter, South Carolina (a city with a population of less than 40,000). Between 2006 and 2007, homicides in Washington, D.C., rose from 169 to 181. In the first month of January, an 18-year-old female was shot and killed in a D.C. suburb while walking home from school, a 17-year-old male was murdered in a drive-by shooting, and two other shootings left eight young people and one adult dead. In 2008, rates also rose in Atlanta, Baltimore, Dallas, New Orleans, and Miami.

Gun Violence

One of the oldest debates concerning the constitutional rights of Americans involves the Second Amendment, which states that the necessity for maintaining a well-regulated militia establishes the basis for "the right of the people to keep and bear Arms." Proponents of a literal interpretation insist that the right to own guns was intended to apply in perpetuity, while opponents insist that it was only applicable before police departments and the National Guard were established to serve in a protective capacity. The American Rifle Association has one of the most powerful lobbies in the United States and does a noteworthy job of keeping the issue of the right to bear arms before the public. The courts have not always agreed on the constitutionality of gun control, but they continue to uphold the right to bear arms. Washington, D.C., is considered one of the most violent cities in the United States, and officials attempted to deal with that fact by passing a law that made it illegal to own unregistered handguns. Registration was only available from the chief of police for one-year periods. Residents legally possessing a handgun in their home were required to keep the weapon unloaded or disabled with devices such as trigger locks. A police officer who had been denied a permit to keep a weapon in his home challenged the law. The Supreme Court heard *District of Columbia v. Heller* (554 U.S. 570) on appeal from the D.C. district court, which had upheld Heller's argument. The Supreme Court agreed, holding that the statute violated the Second Amendment's protection of the right to bear arms for lawful purposes. Firearms are generally available in every city in the United States. According to the Centers for Disease Control and Prevention, in one single representative year, some 99,000 Americans experienced nonfatal gunshot wounds. Wounds turned out to be fatal for approximately 38,000 Americans. Around half of all gunshot wounds were the result of homicides. The others were due to defensive gun use, accidents, or suicides.

Overall, gun-related violence costs the United States around $100 billion each year. Violence also exacts a heavy cost in human life. In Chicago in 2009, 151 people were killed in a series of incidents within a 10-day period. Between 2006 and 2010, more than 23,000 people were killed along America's southern border in response to drug-related gun violence. Violent crime rates continue to be particularly high among African American youths living in inner cities. In 90 percent of those deaths, guns are the weapon of choice. Law enforcement is generally opposed to the easy accessibility of guns. In 2007, for instance, a survey of police chiefs and sheriffs revealed that more than half of them believed easy availability of guns was a major cause of violent crimes.

Drive-by shootings have become newsworthy events in contemporary America. In a drive-by shooting, shots can be fired from a vehicle before a victim is aware of the shooter's intentions, and the vehicle provides the perpetrator with an instant means of escape. While such crimes are far more likely to occur in gang-ridden urban areas, drive-by shootings can take place anywhere. The most common reasons underlying the crime are gang motivations, retribution for perceived wrongs, and road rage. During the 1990s when a wave of drive-by shootings was terrorizing Americans, analysis of violent crimes indicated that gun violence using a vehicle was far less common than other kinds of crimes involving guns.

In West Oakland, California, it was revealed that perpetrators of violent crimes were 10 times more likely to walk up to a victim and open fire than to shoot them from a vehicle. Similarly, in San Diego, between 1999 and 2003, drive-by shootings accounted for only 10 percent of incidents with gun violence. Since aim is not always accurate when shooting from a vehicle, particularly at night when most of these incidents occur, and since some perpetrators want to scare victims rather than kill them, not all incidents of drive-by shootings are fatal. Additionally, when medical help arrives quickly, fatalities are sometimes averted. A study of drive-by shootings in Los Angeles in 1991 revealed that more than 50 percent sustained nonfatal leg injuries. Some of the cases that have received the most media coverage are those involving innocent victims, particularly children, who became unintended targets. Such was the case with a 20-month-old who was killed in Chicago in 2009 when a rival gang member attempted to kill her father. A study of drive-by shootings in Los Angeles in 1996 revealed that innocent victims were shot in 38 to 59 percent of all incidents.

Youth Violence
While all violent American youths are not in gangs, it is gang members who continue to dominate the scene of youth violence. Modern gangs are also very different than those depicted in the award-winning movie and play of the 1960s, *West Side Story*. Even in the face of falling crime rates, youth violence has continued to plague cities throughout the United States. There are at least a million gang

members in the United States dispersed among 20,000 separate gangs. In 2008, some 24 percent of students reported that there was gang activity in their schools. As might be expected, the largest number (36 percent) was in urban areas, and the smallest gang showing was in rural areas (16 percent). In areas where gang activity is particularly pervasive, youth violence accounts for 80 percent of all crimes. Reasons cited for the phenomenon include easy availability of drugs and guns, peer pressure, violence in media, video gaming, and lack of parental responsibility. According to the Centers for Disease Control and Prevention, homicide is the leading cause of death for African Americans between the ages of 10 and 24, and it is the second leading cause of death for Hispanics in that same age group. In 2008, while walking home from school on Chicago's South Side, Derrion Albert, a 16-year-old honor student, was beaten to death. His murder was caught on a cell phone video. In Seattle, security guards refused to interfere when a girl began beating another in the head. The scene was captured and made available on the Internet. A video available on YouTube showed three teenagers attacking a homeless man just for the fun of it. The following year, in Richmond, California, a high school student was beaten, robbed, and sexually assaulted by a gang outside a homecoming dance.

School violence became a 20th-century phenomenon. Before the 1990s, students were more likely to use harsh words or fists to release anger. Even in worst-case scenarios, weapons were likely to be "brass knuckles," baseball bats, or knives. While these weapons were capable of killing others, most incidents involved inflicting injuries on a single victim. Psychologists have developed a profile of the typical school shooter, identifying him as a young male who feels alienated from his peers, is often fond of violence in video games, movies, television, and the Internet, and has trouble controlling anger. He may have begun to collect weapons, written about violence, or have tortured animals. He is likely to have talked about plans to commit his crimes before they happened, but either no one believed him or they chose not to act. The saga of school shootings began on February 2, 1996, when 14-year-old Barry Loukaitis brought a rifle to school in Moses Lake, Washington, killing a teacher and wounding a classmate. A number of other shootings followed, but the one that forever afterward remains in the mind when the phrase "school shootings" is mentioned is Columbine. The high school is located in Littleton, Colorado, where the shootings occurred on April 20, 1999, when perpetrators Dylan Klebold, 17, and Eric Harris, 18, opened fire with a handgun, a rifle, and two shotguns. When the carnage was over, one teacher and 12 students were dead, another 23 students had been wounded, and the psyches of all Americans had been changed forever. No one would ever again feel entirely safe about sending a child off to school for the day.

Notorious Killers
Each day, approximately 45 people are murdered somewhere in the United States. The category of murder has now been broadened to include partner homicide, murder of children, hate group homicide, mass murder, serial murder, terrorism, sex-related homicide, and children who murder. While most partner homicides continue to be committed by males, the number of females who murder partners has risen. Most of them are involved with males who are either physically abusive or who regularly use drugs and alcohol. Many such women have records of suicide attempts. Hate crimes usually target their victims on the basis of race, ethnicity, religion, or sexual orientation. Some killers are remembered longer than others. They are the ones who have become so famous that books, magazine and newspaper articles, movies, and documentaries have been written or made about them.

The murders that have aroused the most attention are usually child murders, mass murders, serial murders, and celebrity-related murders. Mass murder is defined as one in which at least four people are killed at the same time. Such murders may be the result of gunfire, arson, or bombings. Experts believe that most mass murders are motivated by desire for power, profit, revenge, sex, loyalty, or control. The names of American serial killers have become legendary, and their deeds have continued to fascinate Americans for a variety of reasons. Some of the best-known are John Allen Muhammad, a sniper who terrorized the Washington, D.C. area in 2003; Gary Leon Ridgway, the Green River killer who strangled 48 women in the 1980s and 1990s; Ted Bundy, who murdered 28 women in the western United States in the 1970s; David Berkowitz, better known as the Son of Sam, who killed six people in New York in the 1970s; Jeffrey Dahmer, who raped, murdered, and dismembered in the 1980s; and John Wayne Gacy, a purportedly upstanding citizen of Chicago, who murdered 33 young boys in the 1970s.

Boston is the setting for both a historical and a contemporary murder that caught the public's eye. The first murder involved the Boston Strangler, who began a 19-month killing spree in 1962. Subsequently, convicted rapist Albert De Salvo admitted to being the Strangler. From the beginning, his admission was questioned by experts in criminology, but his guilt was accepted among the general public. Contemporary research suggests that he likely had no connection with the Boston Strangler, leaving the identity of the true murderer unknown. The contemporary murder occurred in 2009 when a clean-cut medical student named Philip Markoff was arrested and charged with the murder of Julissa Brisman, a 26 year-old actress and model. Because he regularly offered his services on the Website Craig's List, the media dubbed Markoff the "Craiglist Killer."

One of the grizzliest murders in American history was committed in California on August 9, 1969, by members of the so-called Manson Family who later testified that they had been ordered to commit murder by leader Charles Manson. The murder victims were Sharon Tate, the actress wife of director Roman Polanski, and four guests at the Polanski home. Tate was eight months pregnant at the time. In all, the Manson Family inflicted 102 stab wounds on their victims and shot one other victim. The following day, the group murdered Leno and Rosemary LaBianca, neighbors of the Polanskis. Some reports of the crime have suggested that the intended victim was not Tate but musician Terry Melcher, the only child of singer-actress Doris Day. All members of the Family were convicted of first-degree murder. Manson's death sentence was reduced to life imprisonment after California's death penalty law was found unconstitutional. The courts have repeatedly denied his applications for parole.

The crime that became the cause célèbre for the last half of the 20th century was the O. J. Simpson case. The media frenzy surrounding all aspects of the case was unparalleled in the United States. Simpson, a former football player and an occasional actor, was a popular public figure even though there had been rumblings of his violent temper. On the evening of June 12, 1994, someone waited near the entrance of the home of Simpson's ex-wife, Nicole Brown Simpson, and viciously murdered her and a visitor, Ron Goldman, when he arrived. Forensic evidence immediately pointed to Simpson's guilt. On June 17, television cameras caught Simpson apparently trying to evade arrest in a white Ford Bronco. All networks showed the Bronco chase, with some going to split screen to keep from cutting away from programs in progress or to offer commentary. Approximately 94 million Americans watched the chase. During the trial, both sides pulled out all the stops. The defense hired experts to help in picking a jury that was most likely to find Simpson innocent and ultimately pulled out what came to be labeled "the race card." On October 2, after less than four hours of deliberation, Simpson was cleared of the murders. Polls indicated that the

Urban areas hold the majority of youth gangs (36 percent), and in those areas with pervasive gang activity, youth violence accounts for 80 percent of all crimes.

majority of Americans still believed in his guilt. This was particularly true of white Americans. In 1997, the families of Nicole Brown Simpson and Ron Goldman were awarded $8.5 million in compensatory damages for the deaths of their daughter and son, and Simpson was ordered to turn over his assets. No one else has ever been arrested in connection with the crime.

Most children who are murdered are killed not by pedophiles but by abusive or mentally ill parents or guardians such as Andrea Yates, the Texas mother who drowned her five children in a bathtub in 2001. Cases of parents cold-bloodedly murdering their children to promote their own self-interest are rarer. That is one reason that Americans were so shocked in 1994 when Susan Smith, the mother of two sons, calmly strapped them into car seats before pushing the car into a lake. She then "escaped" and began to play the role of the frantic mother making pleas for a mythical kidnapper to return her beloved children. In the first years of the 21st century, the case that attracted the most media attention had many similarities to the Smith case. It concerned the death of 2-year-old Caylee Anthony, who disappeared from her home in Orlando, Florida, on June 16, 2008. Her mother Casey did not report the child missing until July 15. During questioning, Anthony repeatedly lied to the police about facts that were easily disproved. Although Anthony was released, evidence continued to build. On October 14, Casey Anthony was charged with her daughter's death. The trial was televised in 2011, becoming a media circus. The jury accepted the arguments of Anthony's lawyer, who insisted that the child died in an accident that was covered up, and exonerated Anthony. Freed from jail on July 17, and besieged by death threats, Anthony went into hiding.

The United States continues to be a nation of violence. Street gangs remain a major threat, and schools and even churches have become frequent scenes of violent rampages. Even though great strides have been made since the late 20th century with the advent of community policing and work being done with imperiled youth, most Americans are still afraid to walk the streets of their own neighborhoods at night.

Elizabeth Rholetter Purdy
Independent Scholar

See Also: 1941 to 1960 Primary Documents; 1981 to 2000 Primary Documents; 2001 to 2012 Primary Documents; Atlanta, Georgia; Boston, Massachusetts; Bundy, Ted; Chicago, Illinois; Gangs, Contemporary; Larceny; Murder, Contemporary; New York City; Organized Crime, Contemporary; Philadelphia, Pennsylvania; Police, Contemporary; Prohibition; Rape, Contemporary; Robbery, Contemporary; School Shootings; Serial and Mass Killers; Smith, Susan; Terrorism; Yates, Andrea.

Further Readings
Ames, M. *Going Postal: Rage, Murder and Rebellion: From Reagan's Workplace to Clinton's Columbine and Beyond*. New York: Skull Press, 2005.
Blumstein, A. et al. *The Crime Drop in America*. New York: Cambridge University Press, 2000.
Elliott, D. S., et al. *Violence in American Schools*. New York: Cambridge University Press, 1998.
Englander, Elizabeth Kandel. *Understanding Violence*, 2nd ed. Mahwah, NJ: Lawrence Erlbaum, 2003.
Geist, Gilbert and Leigh B. Bienen. *Crimes of the Century: From Leopold and Loeb to O. J. Simpson*. Lebanon, NH: Northeastern Press, 1998.
Meloy, Michelle L. and Susan L. Miller. *The Victimization of Women: Law, Policies, and Politics*. New York: Oxford University Press, 2011.
Monkkonen, Eric H. *Crime, Justice, History*. Columbus: Ohio State University Press, 2002.
Pogrebin, Mark R., et al. *Guns, Violence, and Criminal Behavior*. Boulder, CO: Lynne Rienner Publishers, 2009.
Reamer, Frederic G. *Heinous Crime: Cases, Causes, and Consequences*. New York: Columbia University Press, 2005.
Roth, R., et al. "The Historical Violence Database." *Historical Methods*, v.41 (Spring 2008).
Waldrep, C., et al., eds. *Documenting American Violence*. New York: Oxford University Press, 2006.

Virginia

The Commonwealth of Virginia is an east coast state in the south, and was one of the first thirteen colonies. As a Confederate state during the Civil War, it was subject to reorganizing under Reconstruction, which was resisted by vigilante groups like the Ku Klux Klan, which was founded in Tennessee, but quickly spread throughout the south and midwest. The second Klan group was broader in its hatred, targeting immigrants and Catholics, as well as nonwhites. It was also more politically minded: In Virginia, it joined with several other social and activist groups, including the Sons and Daughters of Liberty and a white nativist group called the Junior Order of the United American Mechanics, to lobby the legislature to outlaw teaching evolution or any other science that conflicted with the Bible. This incarnation of the Klan was active, both legally and through illegal graft and corruption in state and local government, and managed to prevent the nomination of Catholic presidential candidate Al Smith at the 1924 Democratic National Convention. It also introduced the use of the burning cross as an intimidation tactic. The Klan's use of cross burning led to statutes in several states against cross-burning; in 2003's *Virginia v. Black*, the U.S. Supreme Court ruled that Virginia's statute and those like it were unconstitutional violations of free speech.

The second Klan formally dissolved in 1944 after being prosecuted for failure to pay federal taxes. This in turn was followed by a variety of Klan-aligned groups in the 1950s to the present, initially in response to the civil rights movement. It seems to have been the postwar Klan groups that first used the Confederate flag—the battle flag of the Confederate Army, strongly associated with the Army of Northern Virginia commanded by Robert E. Lee—as a symbol of white supremacy and racial violence.

Police and Punishment
In the colonial era, Virginia—like most of the country—relied principally on corporal punishment in order to avoid the expense to the taxpayers of long-term incarceration. Even county jails for short-term jail sentences were not initially used and the first prisoners in Jamestown were kept incarcerated in an anchored ship. Europe first began to build penitentiaries as places where criminals would be removed from society and, ideally, reformed. Thomas Jefferson began a campaign to build a Virginia penitentiary after the Revolutionary War, but the idea wasn't taken up by the General Assembly until the turn of the century. The Virginia State Penitentiary opened in 1800; in the next 200 years, the state opened dozens of facilities of various levels of security for men, women, and juveniles. The Department of Corrections, established in 1974, employees some 13,000 people, overseeing more than 30,000 inmates.

The first formal law enforcement in Virginia was the provost marshal in the 1620s, but county sheriffs soon replaced them; the first were influential men chosen from among the colony's richest land owners. Police departments formed early in Virginia, displacing the earlier institutions of the town marshal, night watch, and elected constables. Richmond's police department, established in 1807, was one of the first in the country, preceding even the city jail (built in 1816). By 1840, Richmond had built a second police station, and soon after adopted the practice of appointing officers from the wards in which they would serve. By the turn of the century, Virginia police departments were modernizing: uniforms, call boxes, and officially issued equipment had been introduced, as had professional training and certification; fingerprinting was introduced in 1900, and police dogs and police cars followed in 1905. The Virginia State Police were founded in 1932, originally tasked with the enforcement of highway laws, with duties soon expanding.

Virginia is a capital punishment state. The first execution in what is now the United States took place in Virginia in 1608. Virginia leads the nation in executions, at 1,384 as of 2011. Until 1909, the primary method of execution was hanging, although a female slave was burned to death in 1737, and in 1700, three convicted pirates were gibbeted (hung from chains with their dead bodies displayed as a warning to would-be criminals). In 1909, the electric chair was adopted as the sole means of execution; in 1994, inmates were given the choice between the electric chair and lethal injection. Historically, crimes that could be and were punished by death included rape, arson, burglary, horse theft, and robbery.

After death penalties were interrupted by the 1972 *Furman v. Georgia* Supreme Court decision, Virginia's death penalty statute was rewritten along the lines of Georgia's new law, which was upheld in 1976's *Gregg v. Georgia* Supreme Court ruling. Under the current death penalty statute, only willful, deliberate, premeditated murder with one or more various aggravating factors (e.g., murder committed during various other felonies, murder of special victims like police officers or children) is punishable by death, although Governor Bob McDonnell has supported an expansion of the death penalty to include participants in a homicide who did not themselves commit the murder.

The Supreme Court ruling in *Atkins v. Virginia* (2002) found that an execution of the mentally retarded is a violation of the Eighth Amendment's protection from cruel and unusual punishment. Atkins was an 18-year-old with an IQ of 59, who had abducted an airman from Langley Air Force Base, forced him to withdraw money from his ATM, and killed him. Atkins's codefendant William Jones was given life in prison in exchange for testimony against Atkins. Specifically, the court found that it has not been shown that executing the mentally retarded promotes the goals of retribution and deterrence and thus imposes purposeless pain and suffering. Dissenting justices Antonin Scalia, Clarence Thomas, and Chief Justice William Rehnquist criticized the decision for being based more on the personal feelings of the justices than on the language of the Eighth Amendment, which provided no clear basis for determining what is cruel and unusual. A Virginia jury found in 2005 that Atkins's frequent contact with his lawyers had made him more intelligent, and thus no longer retarded, and eligible to be put to death; however, this proved a moot development when allegations came to light of prosecutorial misconduct in the original trial that rendered Jones's testimony inadmissible. A circuit court judge commuted Atkins's sentence to life in prison, a decision upheld by the Virginia Supreme Court.

Crime

Virginia's crime rate is significantly lower than—nearly half that of—the national average, at 213 violent crimes per 100,000 inhabitants in 2010. Until the late 1960s, Virginia's crime rate was slightly higher than average; since then, it has fallen faster than the national rate. It has fallen steadily since 1995 (when it was 361) and had previously peaked at 380 in 1975.

Virginia's crime rate is significantly lower than the national average (nearly half as low), at 213 violent crimes per 100,000 inhabitants in 2010. Until the late 1960s, Virginia's crime rate was slightly higher than average; since then it has fallen faster than the national rate. It has fallen steadily since 1995 (when it was 361), and had previously peaked at 380 in 1975.

Modern Virginia has seen a surprisingly high number of spree killings. The Virginia Tech massacre, on April 16, 2007, is the deadliest shooting incident by a single gunman in American history, resulting in 32 murders in two separate attacks about two hours apart. Seung-Hui Cho was a senior-year English major with previous mental health problems who had been the subject of a stalking investigation involving two female students, and his attacks prompted the legislature to address the legal loopholes that had allowed him to purchase handguns despite having been ruled mentally unsound by a court. The incident also led to a strengthening of federal gun control laws for the first time in over a decade.

Bill Kte'pi
Independent Scholar

See Also: 1600 to 1776 Primary Documents; 1801 to 1850 Primary Documents; 1921 to 1940 Primary Documents; 1941 to 1960 Primary Documents; Capital Punishment; Executions; Serial and Mass Killers; Washington, D.C.

Further Readings
Agger, Ben and Timothy W. Luke, eds. *There Is a Gunman on Campus: Tragedy and Terror at Virginia Tech*. Lanham, MD: Rowman & Littlefield, 2008.
Heinemann, Ronald, et al. *Old Dominion, New Commonwealth: A History of Virginia 1607–2007*. Charlottesville: University of Virginia Press, 2008.
Horwitz, Sari and Michael Ruane. *Sniper*. New York: Ballantine, 2004.
Roy, L. *No Right to Remain Silent: The Tragedy at Virginia Tech*. New York: Harmony, 2009.

Vollmer, August

August Vollmer (1876–1955) is considered by many to be the father of American police professionalism. The literature on policing credits Vollmer as the primary advocate of modern police reforms. He set the pioneering pathway for other police officers to follow and was on the cutting edge of police work. The son of hardworking immigrants, as a youth, Vollmer was an athlete interested in boxing and swimming. These experiences formed a foundation for discipline, excellence, and a competitive lifestyle. Vollmer strove for excellence his entire life, frequently demonstrating courage and dedication to the field of law enforcement.

A Service Career

Vollmer enlisted in the U.S. Marines and served from 1898 to 1899, fighting in 25 battles. He joined the U. S. Postal Service after his military tour in the Spanish–American War. Vollmer emerged as a local hero in 1904, after he leaped into a runaway freight car and applied the brakes, preventing a collision and the deaths of commuters at the Berkeley Station. His hero status provided the notoriety that eventually led to Vollmer's election in 1905 as the town marshal.

Vollmer was the first chief of police to implement a motorized police patrol and to incorporate the police radio system. Leading the crusade for modernizing American policing, Vollmer and his protégé O. W. Wilson advocated (1) centralized records, (2) organized investigative processes, (3) established communications through the call box system, (4) motorcycle patrol, and (5) marksmanship training for police officers. Vollmer served as a reform chief for the Los Angeles Police Department from 1923 to 1924. During this brief tour of duty on sabbatical leave from his position as chief of police in Berkeley, he became concerned with corruption. After his experiences in Los Angeles, Vollmer opposed the enforcement of vice laws because they encouraged police corruption and disrespect for law enforcement officers.

During his career, Vollmer served as a consultant to many police agencies. Many of his reforms continue to influence American policing. Vollmer authored the famous Wickersham Commission *Report on the Police*, which ultimately served the reform agenda well. Police agencies strove for modern management practices and established higher police entry requirements. Vollmer himself hired women and African American police officers, encouraging their training and professional development.

A Lasting Influence

August Vollmer served as the first chief of police in Berkeley, California, from 1905 to 1932. He eventually became a professor of police administration at the University of California, Berkeley. At Berkeley, Vollmer organized the first university police administration courses. Vollmer was the founder of many of the criminal justice programs that emerged and flourished throughout the 20th century. Among Vollmer's students at the University of California, Berkeley, was O. W. Wilson, who learned to modernize the police department in the Vollmer tradition. Because of Vollmer's teachings, Wilson strived for police modernizations and innovations that included (1) police cars for patrol, (2) mobile two-way radios, (3) the use of the mobile crime laboratory, and (4) academic degrees for police officers. Vollmer also advocated the use of the polygraph, or lie detector, technology.

Vollmer served as an advocate for disadvantaged children. He was concerned for the welfare of alcoholics and people addicted to drugs. He opposed police involvement with drug offenders and supported the federal distribution of habit-forming drugs. Vollmer was criticized for his leniency toward minor offenders and the marginal members of society.

Vollmer's distinguished career unfolded with extraordinary professionalism. He achieved excellence in fields of academia, law enforcement, and military service. On November 4, 1955, Vollmer, suffering from Parkinson's disease and cancer, ended his own life; his legend, legacy, and professional contributions live on wherever policing excels.

Thomas E. Baker
University of Scranton

See Also: Chicago, Illinois; Community Policing and Relations; Wilson, O. W.

Further Readings

Carte, Gene E. and Elaine H. Carte. *Police Reform in the United States: The Era of August Vollmer.* Berkeley: University of California Press, 1975.

Cordner, Gary W. and Kathryn E. Scarborough. *Police Administration,* 7th ed. Cincinnati, OH: Anderson Publishing, 2010.

Swanson, Charles R., Leonard Territo, and Robert W. Taylor. *Police Administration: Structures, Processes, and Behavior,* 7th ed. Upper Saddle River, NJ: Prentice Hall, 2007.

Walker, Samuel and Charles M. Katz. *Policing in America: An Introduction,* 6th ed. New York: McGraw-Hill, 2008.

Volstead Act

The Volstead Act, or the National Prohibition Act, passed October 28, 1919. The act, which functioned as the enforcement arm of the Eighteenth Amendment, also made illegal the production, transport, or sale of any intoxicating liquor. "Intoxicating liquor" was defined as anything containing more than 0.5 percent alcohol by volume. The act was the result of a long-running temperance movement that began in the 19th century. The temperance movement wanted alcohol made illegal on the grounds that it corrupted the morals of those who drank it, ruined lives, and broke up families. By 1916, a total of 19 states had completely outlawed the sale or transport of spirituous liquors.

In 1917, Congress passed the Eighteenth Amendment, which limited the production of alcohol to only those to be used as sacraments (sacramental wine) or intended for medicinal use as anesthetic agents. At the war's end, Wilson's wartime measure was set to expire, which would return the ability to brew beer and ferment wine. However, long-running temperance groups such as the Anti-Saloon League and the Woman's Christian Temperance Union, successfully lobbied Congress, which at that time held a rural, Progressive majority. Wilson, citing an imposition on private freedoms, and a belief that a long-term Prohibition would not solve the problems that its supporters railed against, vetoed the original Volstead Act, which strengthened the Prohibition amendment to outlaw any beverage with more than 0.5 percent alcohol content.

Congressional Progressives took another view. In his book *Why Prohibition?*, Charles Stelzle, a Presbyterian minister, informed that alcohol was the source of everything ailing America in the early 20th century. Medical insurance costs were on the rise, and he blamed the damaging qualities of drinking for a degradation of national health. He argued further that alcohol and the saloon culture were incompatible with a nation's progress. Crime was also on the increase, as was alcohol intake. Recalling the squalor and debauchery that he saw in Victorian London, he made an impressive case that Congress took very seriously. These views shaped the debate that resulted in the 1919 ratification of the Eighteenth Amendment and the quick overturning of Wilson's veto by Congress by a vote of 176–55 on the same day that Wilson vetoed it. The Eighteenth Amendment and the Volstead Act both became effective in early 1920.

A debate in 1924 between Clarence Darrow and John Haynes Holmes exhibits the difference of opinion that was rampant throughout the country on this issue. Darrow represented the detractors of the act, whereas Holmes was in favor of it. Holmes presented the Volstead Act as another sensible law designed to protect the decency of the nation. He referred to the outlawing of opium and the abolition of slavery in the 19th century as acts that limited a person's individual freedom at the cost of protecting the greater part of society. Darrow's rebuttal was that slavery, opium, and whiskey were not in the same category at all, and that the whole thing was a circus. He further noted that Prohibition agents were not particularly "drier" than any other person, which proved, to him, the farcical nature of the law.

To combat bootleggers and enforce the Volstead Act, the government employed 1,520 men in 1920 as Prohibition agents. In 1930, their number was 2,836. These men, operating under the Treasury Department, attempted to stop smuggling and raid warehouses to halt the distillation or transport of the illegal liquors. The agents often employed local police departments, Coast Guard, or immigration agents in order to man raids or attacks on smuggling caravans because of their limited number and low budget. The salary was very low—$1,200–$2,000 in 1920 and $2,300–$2,800 in 1930—and many agents had no prior police or supervisory experience. Success was limited, to say the least. The public support for Prohibition began to wane as World War I faded from immediate memory. As a result, the already poorly staffed and inexperienced Volstead enforcement officers found increasing difficulty in getting leads on warehouses or smuggling rings, and as the 1920s wore on, their position only became more challenging.

Repeal Efforts

Growing economic concerns for state governments in the late 1920s further restricted the budget allowed to Prohibition agents and deepened their frustration and ineffectiveness. An increasingly resentful public did not help matters. The federal government had expected localities to invest in enforcing Prohibition on their own territory, but this rarely happened. Municipalities were as badly off financially as other governments. Smuggling rings and large-scale production continued essentially unabated. As Wilson predicted, the law had failed to do anything except make criminals very wealthy. When Herbert Hoover took over the presidency in 1928, many expected him to make some sort of declaration about Prohibition. He called it a "noble experiment" but other than that, nothing was done to give satisfaction to either side. Hoover was personally in favor of Prohibition and called a committee to report findings. The 11 committee members reported that enforcement attempts were a complete failure, but nonetheless, they believed it was a necessary law.

The 1932 campaign was a hotbed of talk about Prohibition. Hoover steadfastly backed Prohibition, while New York Governor Franklin Delano Roosevelt, the Democratic candidate, ran on a platform of repeal. The essence of Roosevelt's platform was that repeal could be used to tax liquors and beer and raise a great deal of revenue for a national government ailing from the world economic depression. In March 1933, Roosevelt signed the Cullen-Harrison Act, which amended the Volstead Act to allow the manufacture and sale of light wines, and beers of up to 4 percent alcohol by volume. The act became law in April 1933. In December 1933, the Twenty-First Amendment was ratified, and Prohibition was officially repealed.

Robert W. Watkins
Florida State University

See Also: Hoover, Herbert (Administration of); New York; Prohibition; Roosevelt, Franklin D. (Administration of); State Blue Laws; Wilson, Woodrow (Administration of).

Further Readings

Allen, Frederick Lewis. *Only Yesterday: An Informal History of the 1920s.* New York: Harper & Row, 1931.

Clark, Norman H. *Deliver Us From Evil: An Interpretation of Prohibition.* New York: Norton, 1976.

Kyvig, David E. *Repealing National Prohibition.* Kent, OH: Kent State University Press, 2000.

Waco Siege

The Waco siege is one of the most iconic examples of sect-related tragedies in America's history. Those events in 1993 sit alongside those in Jonestown in 1978 (which actually took place in Guyana, but involved the mass suicide of hundreds of American citizens) as the country's most devastating reminders of what can happen when highly charismatic leaders with alternative worldviews are able to exert their influence over followers. On February 28, 1993, members of the Branch Davidian sect made headline news around the world. Led by the highly charismatic David Koresh, the group holed up in the organization's ranch, the Mount Carmel Center close to Waco, Texas. Agents from the Bureau of Alcohol, Tobacco and Firearms (ATF) had attempted to execute a search warrant on the premises; however, the raid was repelled and a standoff ensued. The siege lasted until April 19, when a second attempt to storm the compound led to disaster as the compound was destroyed by fire. At the end of the siege, scores of people lay dead, predominantly sect members, including children and pregnant women, and a number of law enforcement agents. The leader, David Koresh, committed suicide.

The Branch Davidian Seventh Day Adventists is a Protestant sect originating in the 1950s. Vernon Howell, later known as David Koresh, took control of one faction of the sect and eventually seized legal control of the Mount Carmel complex in 1989. Howell was a controversial figure and in the same year released an audiotape in which he claimed that he had received instructions from God compelling him to procreate with women in the sect in order to create a House of David. In 1990, Howell legally changed his name to David Koresh. Koresh exercised a profound influence over group members. Various allegations against the group surfaced, including child abuse and wider concerns for the welfare of the children living in the group. The group consisted of a number of families who had lived with Koresh at the center for a number of years, including some British followers. Another suspicion concerned the stockpiling of illegal arms, which prompted the attention of the ATF and the eventual raid on February 28, 1993. There is conflicting information regarding the exact behavior of the ATF in the period running up to the raid; however, the group was put under surveillance.

On the day of the raid, it has been reported that news of the pending action was inadvertently leaked to Koresh as a reporter in the know asked for directions to Mount Carmel from what turned out to be Koresh's brother-in-law. When officers arrived at Mount Carmel, Koresh and his followers were waiting for them. Exactly how the gunfire was initiated is a matter of dispute, both

ATF agents and sect survivors claiming that the first shots came from the other side. Nonetheless, a fierce battle erupted, with agents attempting to gain access to the compound via a roof. However, agents were eventually pushed back under heavy fire and sustained significant casualties. As ATF agents withdrew, they suffered four dead and a number wounded.

Following the failed raid, a state of siege ensued, with the Federal Bureau of Investigation (FBI) now taking charge. Communications with Koresh were established and negotiations were conducted. Yet, Koresh claimed that he had been instructed by God to stay in the compound. Remarkably, however, the FBI managed to facilitate the release of some children, who under interview claimed to have been sexually and physically abused. Agents stopped water and power supplies into the compound. Koresh released other members of the group, but most remained inside, including some children.

As suspicions grew concerning the possibility that cult members would commit suicide as in Jonestown in 1978, and fears grew for the well-being of children still inside, the FBI prepared for a second assault on Mount Carmel. They were eventually given the go-ahead by Attorney General Janet Reno. This time, the tactics had changed in light of the failed initial assault, and the new approach involved using tear gas to force out occupants. On April 19, armored vehicles punctured holes in the compound to deliver the gas. Several hours after the start of the raid, no members had left the compound. At about midday, fires started in separate parts of the compound; this forced out a small number of people; however, most remained inside. There are conflicting accounts regarding how the fires started. One explanation involves sect members deliberately starting these fires, while another suggests that the armored assault, purposely or not, was responsible. However, a government-sponsored report in 2000 cleared the FBI of responsibility. The remaining occupants died in the fires through smoke inhalation, gun shots, or other means—approximately 76 people died within the compound that day. Koresh is believed to have committed suicide.

Following the siege, those running the operation were criticized, and this has changed how such situations are dealt with. During resultant trials of sect survivors, all sect members were cleared of the most serious charges relating to the deaths of ATF agents; however, some were convicted of lesser charges relating to firearms and voluntary manslaughter. In 2000, a claim against the U.S. government by relatives of sect members was thrown out of court.

Tony Murphy
University of Westminster

See Also: Religion and Crime, History of; Religion and Crime, Sociology of.

Further Readings
Crime & Investigation Network. "The Waco Siege." http://www.crimeandinvestigation.co.uk/crime-files/waco-siege/crime.html (Accessed January 2010).
Samples, Kenneth R. *Prophets of the Apocalypse: David Koresh and Other American Messiahs.* Grand Rapids, MI: Baker Publishing Group, 1994.
Wright, Stuart. *Armageddon in Waco: Critical Perspectives on the Branch Davidian Conflict.* Chicago: University of Chicago Press. 1995.

Walling, George

George Walling (1823–91) was born in Middletown township, Monmouth County, New Jersey. He recounted his paternal heritage as Welsh and his maternal line from Denmark. His father was a small-business owner and had exposed Walling to sea life and minor trades. Through a friend's referral, he joined the police force. Walling was the police chief of New York City from July 1874 until June 1885. Walling earned the reputation of a tough but fair and honest law officer during his years of service.

When he served as captain of the 20th precinct on the Lower West Side of the city, his courageous deeds during the 1863 New York City draft riots prompted his elevation to chief of police. He played a crucial role in helping restore order to a city in crisis during the American Civil War. George Walling was respected during his term, having worked to bring professionalism to the New York police force by severing it from any link to corrupt city politics. Walling was noted among those who helped professionalism in policing make great strides in the latter half of the 19th century. George Walling was known for several law enforcement efforts, one of which was the suppression of the Honeymoon Gang. The Honeymoon Gang was notoriously feared for their brutality among city street gangs in 1853. They assigned members to each corner of Madison Avenue and 29th Street to attack any passerby who looked wealthy. Their terrorism on 29th Street concluded each night with the Honeymooners adjourning at midnight to drink away their gains.

The Honeymoon Gang was so violent that even the gang-aiding Tammany politicians of the crime-laden 1800s refused to protect them. Walling organized the first Strong Arm Squad, in which tough cops beat gang members with vicious force. The Honeymooners dissolved after two weeks.

Ferreting Out Corruption

Walling was also famous for the arrest of the corrupt mayor of New York City, Fernando Wood. Wood was first elected mayor in 1854 and was reelected during a rigged election three years later. The state legislature intervened, shortening his term from two years to one and establishing a metropolitan police force to replace Wood's corrupt municipal police. The governor of New York appointed a board of commissioners to replace a municipal commission to hire police officers. However, Wood maintained that the amending legislation was unconstitutional and did not step down, even when faced with a Supreme Court order.

George Walling was among the lawmen signed on with the new state-created metropolitan police. Fifteen other captains and hundreds of patrolmen chose to side with Wood and the municipal police. Things heated up, and the people of New York were caught in the rivalry of patrolmen from both sides. At the same time, those arrested by one side were often set free by the aldermen or magistrates who were loyal to the opposite side. Gangs took advantage of this situation, and so did criminals from other places.

It was George Walling's personal assignment to arrest Mayor Wood. He entered City Hall alone with the warrant and reached the mayor's office. However, once he made clear his intent to arrest the mayor, the Wood-sympathizing municipal policemen threw him out. Fifteen metropolitan officers joined him later, but they were outnumbered and pushed out. At this time, the board of commissioners brought out the militia, and the 7th Regiment surrounded City Hall. Wood surrendered and was charged with inciting a riot, but was soon released on bail and returned to his office.

As the feud went on throughout 1857 in the summer, disorder rose, with gangs feeding on the chaotic situation. Militia units came to help establish order. The state supreme court decided in the fall against the municipal police, causing the mayor to surrender and the municipal force to be dissolved. The metropolitan board of commissioners was confirmed as legal, commencing the process of rebuilding public trust and order.

In 1861, the American Civil War started, and social unrest was brewing. After the 1863 Conscription Act passed, a bureau was set up to draft those who had not volunteered for the war. Draft offices were unwelcome in New York when they were opened July 11, 1863. In the early morning of July 13, a draft riot started. George Walling, together with the newly formed police force, worked to return order to the city.

George Walling continued to contribute to the keeping of public safety and order over the years. On June 9, 1885, he left his post as superintendent of the New York police force, feeling a great sense of commitment and satisfaction, as he revealed in his out-of-print memoir *Recollections of a New York City Chief of Police*. Walling died on December 31, 1891, in New York.

Trangdai Glassey-Tranguyen
Stanford University

See Also: New York City; Police, History of; Riots.

Further Readings

Ephemeral New York. "How the Honeymoon Gang Terrorized 29th Street." https://ephemeralnewyork.wordpress.com/tag/george-w-walling (Accessed November 2011).

"The Police in New Hands." *New York Times* (June 10, 1885).

Walling, George W. *Recollections of a New York City Chief of Police.* New York: Caxton Book Concern Limited, 1887.

Walnut Street Jail

Walnut Street Jail was one of the most significant and early innovations in prison history. Situated in Philadelphia, Pennsylvania, it was built in 1776, altered in 1790, and demolished in 1835. One of the first jails used for punishment instead of administrative purposes, it incorporated labor and solitary confinement in order to reform its inmates. It was widely copied.

Early in the American Revolution, Pennsylvania created a constitution calling for the reformation of its penal laws. In particular, it was to have fewer capital offenses and punish instead with "houses of correction"; the state, it said, should reform rather than kill. Thus, in 1786, Pennsylvania both reduced its list of capital offenses and inaugurated its first experiment with public labor in the streets of Philadelphia. The experiment with public labor, however, was an unmitigated disaster and came under swift attack from statesman, physician, philanthropist, and reformer Benjamin Rush, among other members of the Philadelphia Society for Alleviating the Miseries of Public Prisons, who also advocated the reformation of existing jail facilities. Rush began calling for a "penitentiary house" that would both reform its occupants and deter those who would hear of the institution. Thus, in 1790, Pennsylvania legislators passed a law changing the punishment of noncapital offenders to solitary confinement at Walnut Street Jail with the hope that it would reform them and deter others.

Walnut Street Jail Opens

The Walnut Street Jail had been taken over as a military prison soon after being built. In the late 1780s, Walnut Street was used to house the

Roughly 15 years after the Walnut Street Jail was built in Philadelphia, Pennsylvania, an addition was made called the penitentiary house. It was a series of small cells designed for individual prisoners, or solitary confinement. Prisoners could not communicate with each other with windows that were high up and louvered to prevent them from looking onto the street.

criminals laboring under the 1786 law when they were not in public. With the passage of the 1790 law, however, it was renovated and its purpose altered. Its new form consisted of large common rooms and workshops, as well as 16 new solitary cells. Unlike true prisons of the 1820s and later, the exterior architecture of the jail was not greatly dissimilar from other colonial architecture like that of a Quaker meeting house or a private home.

The new penal regime began well enough. To prevent the spread of vice to those less criminally inclined, prisoners were housed according to a classification system based on gender, the nature of the criminal (young or old, hardened or cooperative), and the criminal's period of confinement. Revenue from the prison labor helped to maintain the prison and some inmates could use the proceeds once they were free. But the reality of the experiment at Walnut Street never fully conformed to the plan. The "unremitting solitude" imagined by the statute was never actually part of prison management except as a punishment for misbehavior within the prison; those inmates who misbehaved were sent to the solitary cells. Nevertheless, crime rates and the rate of incarceration actually decreased during the first four years of Walnut Street's reformed regime. The jail appeared sufficiently terrifying to citizens. But the "good" days were short-lived, and even these were soon filled with violent episodes and instances of misbehavior.

Overcrowding and Disruptions

In the mid-1790s, the state moved to make Walnut Street Jail an institution for the whole state rather than just for Philadelphia. The jail soon became overcrowded, thus ending its record of a diminishing number of inmates, and embarked on a tangible decline. In June 1798, arson destroyed part of one of the workshops in the prison, preventing inmate labor. In a few months, a yellow fever epidemic broke out in Philadelphia, flooding the prison with more charges and disrupting the meeting schedule of the jail's inspectors. These two events occurring so closely together greatly disrupted the prison order.

The prison population continued to increase between the mid-1790s and 1820, a portion of which included recidivist criminals. Having too many prisoners for the numbers of cells in the aging structure precluded any degree of separation (individually or by group classification) as well as inmate labor, a problem worsened by the loss of workshop space. During the following two decades, complicity of the guards in aiding or overlooking schemes of the inmates, increased numbers of successful and attempted escapes, and disobedience of inmates made prison discipline difficult if not impossible. There were four large riots between 1817 and 1821. As crime and the perception of crime in Philadelphia increased, citizens and reformers blamed Walnut Street's design. Its failure in the 1810s prompted Pennsylvania to adopt its first prisons. Finally, with Eastern State Penitentiary well established, the jail was demolished in 1835.

Model for Future Jails

Walnut Street Jail represented a significant break with the past. Punishment was now private rather than public. Jails were now a place of punishment, reformation, and deterrence instead of temporary confinement for administration purposes. However, Walnut Street was still like colonial jails in that it continued to house those awaiting trial, witnesses, debtors, vagrants, and other miscreants held for administrative and other nonpenal reasons along with convicted offenders held for punishment purposes, and as such was not a true prison. There was also the lack of cellular, solitary confinement as a regular part of the jail's regime. Walnut Street influenced the penal developments in other states, with similar jails adopted in New York, New Jersey, Virginia, Kentucky, Massachusetts, Connecticut, Tennessee, Vermont, New Hampshire, and Maryland by 1810. Moreover, it laid the foundation for the first prisons. When the New York legislature authorized the building of the first prison in the United States in 1816, it looked to the lessons of Walnut Street and the jails that copied it. New York adopted the solitary confinement that Walnut Street employed for only its most hardened offenders but used this punishment only at night. Pennsylvania in 1818 and 1821 also authorized solitary confinement for its inmates at Western and Eastern State Penitentiaries.

Ashley T. Rubin
University of California, Berkeley

See Also: Auburn State Prison; Eastern State Penitentiary; Pennsylvania.

Further Readings
Barnes, Harry Elmer. *The Evolution of Penology in Pennsylvania.* Indianapolis, IN: Bobbs-Merrill Company, 1927.
Meranze, Michael. *Laboratories of Virtue: Punishment, Revolution, and Authority in Philadelphia, 1760–1835.* Chapel Hill: University of North Carolina Press, 1996.
Teeters, Negley K. *The Cradle of the Penitentiary: The Walnut Street Jail at Philadelphia, 1773–1835*, Philadelphia: Pennsylvania Prison Society, 1955.

Wambaugh, Joseph

Joseph Wambaugh is a best-selling American writer known for both his fiction and nonfiction works about police and their work. His characters are portrayed in a gritty, realistic manner that has helped readers develop a sympathetic appreciation for the challenging expectations of modern police.

Joseph Wambaugh was born Joseph Aloysius Wambaugh, Jr., on January 22, 1937, in East Pittsburgh, Pennsylvania. On November 26, 1955, he married Dee Allsup; they had three children. He served in the U.S. Marine Corps from 1954 to 1957. Wambaugh received an A.A. degree from Chaffey College in 1958, a B.A. in 1960, and an M.A. in 1968 from California State College in Los Angeles, California. He served first as patrolman and then as detective sergeant with the Los Angeles Police Department from 1960 to 1974. He wrote his first two novels and his first nonfiction book while serving with the Los Angeles Police Department.

Wambaugh is best known for the empathetic and objective way that he portrays police officers in both his fiction and nonfiction writing. He depicts police officers as real human beings with all their fallibilities. Through his realistic style of writing, he helps his readers acquire a sympathetic understanding of real and imagined officers, even when they make unsavory choices. He does not shy away from showing the violence and profanity often exhibited by police as they strive to protect people who may resent their presence. Many of Wambaugh's characters are referred to by nicknames that are commonly unflattering and, at other times, downright whimsical, but these help to instantly paint an image of the characters for readers.

Wambaugh's first novel, *The New Centurions*, follows three young males as they go through the police academy and on to serving in the streets of Los Angeles, culminating in the tumultuous 1965 Watts riots. These three lead characters are depicted as idealistic cadets who are unwillingly hardened into callous guardians of the social order. While Wambaugh's first novel was about those entering a career as police officers, his second novel, *The Blue Knight* (1972), was about a veteran policeman, "Bumper" Morgan, who was approaching retirement. Wambaugh's next book was nonfiction, *The Onion Field* (1973). In 1975, Wambaugh published his next novel, *The Choirboys*, which initiated his use of shocking incidents and dark humor to stress the psychological stress that modern police must endure. These were followed by 12 other novels and four nonfiction books.

Wambaugh wrote a series of Hollywood works about those serving in the Los Angeles Police Department. The Hollywood series is built around the title character "Hollywood" Nate, a policeman hoping to launch a career in movies, and other recurring characters, such as officers like "Flotsam" and "Jetsam," who are avid surfers, and "Compassionate" Charlie, who is a somewhat lazy night-watch detective. The first installment in this series was *Hollywood Station*, which came out in 2006. In 2008, he published his first sequel, *Hollywood Crows*; this was followed in 2009 with *Hollywood Moon* and this, in turn, by *Hollywood Hills* in 2010.

Always a keen observer, Wambaugh devoted considerable portions of some of his novels to showcasing aspects of the myriad extravagant lifestyles pursued in southern California. In his 1977 novel *The Black Marble*, he satirically discussed dog shows and a then-fading Pasadena milieu. In his 1981 *The Glitter Dome*, it was a reconnoitering of the making of pornographic movies, while his 1983 *The Delta Star* explored some of the

The son of a police officer, Joseph Wambaugh brought this unique familial perspective on police work to his first highly acclaimed novel and has continued to enthrall readers throughout his career.

intrigues involved in scientific research endeavors and the politics behind the Nobel Prize, and his 1985 *The Secrets of Harry Bright* exposed the extravagances of the wealthy of Palm Springs, saturated with alcohol and other drugs. Other locales exploited by Wambaugh include Orange County, California, for his 1990 *The Golden Orange* and San Diego, California, where his 1993 *Finnegan's Wake* and 1996 *Floaters* were set.

In addition to his 14 novels and five nonfiction books, Wambaugh has written a couple of acclaimed screenplays and a couple of teleplays. He has also served as creator and consultant for two television series for NBC-TV, the 1973 to 1977 *Police Story* and the 1977 *The Blue Knight*. Joseph Wambaugh has received numerous awards and honors for both his fiction and nonfiction writing. In 1974, his first nonfiction book, *The Onion Field*, was recognized with the Mystery Writers of America's Edgar Allan Poe Special Award for Non-Fiction. In 1981, he won the Edgar Allan Poe Award for Best Screenplay for *The Black Marble*. In 1989, the International Association of Crime Writers gave him their Rodolfo Walsh Prize for Investigative Journalism for his *Lines and Shadows*. In 2003, his *Fire Lover: A True Story* garnered the Edgar Allan Poe Award for Best Crime Fact Book. In 2004, he was recognized with the Mystery Writers of America Grand Master Award.

Victor B. Stolberg
Essex County College

See Also: Dime Novels, Pulps, Thrillers; Literature and Theater, Crime in.

Further Readings
Smith, Jay Charles. *Joseph Wambaugh and the Jay Smith Case*. Bloomington, IN: Xlibris, 2008.
Van Dover, J. Kenneth. *Centurions, Knights, and Other Cops: The Police Novels of Joseph Wambaugh*. San Bernardino, CA: Brownstone Books, 1995.
Wambaugh, Joseph. *Hollywod Hills: A Novel*. Boston: Little, Brown, 2010.

Warren, Earl

Earl Warren was born on March 19, 1891, in Los Angeles, California. He attended the University of California at Berkeley where he received his bachelors' degree in 1912 and subsequently received his law degree from Boalt Hall in 1914. After serving in the U.S. Army in World War I, Warren worked as the deputy city attorney for the city of Oakland, California, from 1920 to 1925. In 1925, he was appointed to be the district attorney of Alameda County and was re-elected to the position three times. Warren gained a reputation as a tough district attorney who was strongly opposed to corruption.

Japanese American Internment Camps
After his stint as district attorney, Warren was elected to the post of attorney general for the state of California. Warren is known as one of the moving forces behind the Japanese American

internment camps during World War II. Despite the subsequent acknowledgment of this action in American history as one of the most despicable by America, Warren maintained that he thought that, at the time, it was the right thing to do. Several authorities hold the opinion that Warren's subsequent focus on civil and human rights in his later years as the chief justice of the U.S. Supreme Court was strongly influenced by his profound personal regret for his previous actions concerning the Japanese American internment camps.

In 1942, Warren was elected governor of California. Warren was very popular and was re-elected twice. Even though he was a Republican, Warren initiated numerous public works projects similar to those created by Roosevelt during the New Deal. Warren was also instrumental in expanding the University of California and public education. Warren was appointed to the U.S. Supreme Court as chief justice by President Dwight D. Eisenhower and was seated in January 1954. Eisenhower was a conservative Republican and he thought that he was appointing a fellow conservative when he appointed Warren to the bench. Warren's many subsequent liberal rulings prompted Eisenhower to later remark that his appointment of Warren to the U.S. Supreme Court as chief justice was "the biggest damn fool mistake I ever made."

Civil Rights Legislation
Warren wasted little time in asserting an activist judicial perspective based on human and civil rights. The first major decision of what was to be become known as the Warren Court was the now famous decision of *Brown v. Board of Education* (1954). In *Brown*, the Warren Court overruled the long-standing precedent of *Plessy v. Ferguson* that had instituted the doctrine of separate but equal, which had only exacerbated the racial inequality in America. Of prime significance in *Brown* was Warren's ability to forge unanimous decisions. What was considered most notable about Warren was not his intellectual brilliance but his ability to bring the various justices together. This is not to say that Warren was not intelligent—far from it. However, he was not known for his ability as a legal scholar so much as his ability to bring differing perspectives together and form unanimous if not just strong majority opinions.

Warren was probably best-known for his sweeping changes to the law of criminal procedure and the Fourth and Fifth Amendments. It was through the criminal prosecution of African Americans that much of the racism in America found official expression. With the decision in *Mapp v. Ohio* in 1961, the Warren Court made it clear that the constitutional protections of the Fourth Amendment applied equally to all people, regardless of race. It was in *Mapp v. Ohio* that an illegal police search of an African American woman's home and illegal seizure of evidence was invalidated. And, in the famous decision in *Miranda v. Arizona* in 1966, a Hispanic man's criminal conviction was overturned because he did not understand his rights, resulting in the Miranda warning. In the decision in *Gideon v. Wainwright* in 1963, Warren led the U.S. Supreme Court in providing substance to the right to an attorney by requiring free counsel to indigent criminal defendants. Warren's ventures into civil rights engendered much criticism. Much of the criticism was focused in conservative and racist southern groups. Throughout his term in office, there were numerous calls to impeach Warren, none of which ever came to fruition.

Greater Fairness and Interpretation of the Law
However, Warren's fame as a jurist was not focused on just race relations and criminal procedure. The Warren Court was instrumental in bringing greater fairness to the U.S. political system of apportionment of votes. In several decisions, the Warren Court announced the doctrine of "one man, one vote," ending decades of the domination of state legislatures by rural areas over urban areas. The Warren Court also broke new legal ground with the recognition of a constitutional right to privacy in the famous case *Griswold v. Connecticut* in 1963. The Warren Court also continued to engender much criticism by declaring that mandatory school prayer was illegal in the case *Engel v. Vitale* in 1962. The Warren Court also breathed life into the, up to that point, little-used civil rights statute, 42 U.S.C. § 1983, which had been enacted during the time of the Civil War. With the decision in *Monroe v. Pape* in 1961, the Warren Court placed its approval on the employment of 42 U.S.C. § 1983 for individual victims of civil rights violations to pursue civil remedies in federal court.

Earl Warren's legacy was not limited to his work as chief justice of the U.S. Supreme Court. Warren had the unfortunate duty to chair the Warren Commission, which was the appointed body assigned to investigate the assassination of John F. Kennedy in 1963. Warren did not want the position but eventually agreed to accept it. The subsequent Warren Commission Report concluded that the assassination of President Kennedy was the work of a lone assassin, Lee Harvey Oswald. The report was strongly criticized as containing numerous inconsistencies, distortions of evidence, failures to consider evidence, and cover-ups of government involvement. Subsequent studies and books have raised numerous other problems with the investigation and the report, which include missing evidence.

Despite these problems, Earl Warren has been recognized as one of the greatest chief justices of the U.S. Supreme Court in American history. It has even been stated that Chief Justice Earl Warren breathed life into the Bill of Rights and made it much more than a mere form of words. Internationally, Earl Warren and the Warren Court have been recognized as true leaders in human and civil rights.

Wm. C. Plouffe, Jr.
Independent Scholar

See Also: California; Civil Rights Laws; Japanese Americans; Miranda Warnings; *Terry v. Ohio*.

Further Readings
Horwitz, Morton. *The Warren Court and the Pursuit of Justice*. New York: Hill & Wang, 1999.
Newton, Jim. *Justice for All: Earl Warren and the Nation He Made*. New York: Riverhead Trade, 2006.
Schwartz, Bernard, ed. *The Warren Court*. New York: Oxford University Press, 1996.

Washington

A Pacific Northwest state, Washington was admitted to the Union in 1889. More than half of the population lives in the Seattle metropolitan area in the western half of the state; the eastern and central portions of the state are more rural and much more sparsely settled.

The Territorial Government of Washington authorized the creation of a penitentiary in 1883 for incarcerations of longer terms than local jails could be expected to accommodate. The town of Walla Walla was chosen as the site of the new prison, and construction of the brick and concrete facility began in 1886. The prison was candlelit until 1902, when electric lights were installed, and mixed-sex until female prisoners were relocated to the Washington Corrections Center for Women in 1971. From 1892 to 1921, prisoners worked manufacturing sacks; the new popularity of automobiles led to turning the jute mill used for sack manufacture into a license plate factory, and the penitentiary continues to manufacture 2 million license plates a year. Due to prison population increases, the late 20th century saw numerous other facilities built as well: the Larch Corrections Center (Yacolt, 1956), the Washington Corrections Center (Shelton, 1964), the Washington Corrections Center for Women (Gig Harbor, 1971), the Clallam Bay Corrections Center (Clallam Bay, 1985), the Airway Heights Corrections Center (Airway Heights, 1992), and the Stafford Creek Corrections Center (Aberdeen, 2000). The newest correctional facility is the Mission Creek Corrections Center for Women, built in Belfair in 2005, with a capacity of 305, bringing the statewide female inmate capacity to 1000.

Early Washington law enforcement was handled by federal marshals (until statehood) and town marshals. Seattle replaced its town marshal with the Seattle Police Department in 1886, soon creating a modern professional police force. The state police agency, the Washington State Patrol (WSP), began as the Highway Patrol in 1921, consisting of six patrolmen on motorcycles; it was reorganized as the WSP in 1933.

Washington's early history was marked by numerous incidents of anti-Chinese violence, similar to those in Oregon and Wyoming. The earliest major incident was an attack on sleeping Chinese hop pickers in Squak Valley (now Issaquah) in September 1885, resulting in three dead and three wounded. The details are unclear except that local white men were angry that hop farms had hired Chinese laborers—who would work more

A 2011 voter initiative in Washington ended state liquor stores, closing this location. Underage drinkers often find it easier to buy liquor from an independent seller as opposed to a state store clerk who makes no financial gain on sales.

cheaply—because of the low market price for hops, and retaliated violently. The attackers were acquitted. A month later, the Knights of Labor—the most important labor organization in the country at the time—stirred up anti-Chinese sentiment in Tacoma over the same issues (Chinese labor being cheap enough to make it difficult for whites to compete), and a mob of whites—led by the mayor and the police department—forced the residents of Tacoma's Chinatown out of the city, marching them to the rail station and onto a Portland-bound train. Continued efforts by the Knights of Labor led to another riot in Seattle the following year, as whites rounded up Seattle Chinese and tried to force them onto ships that would transport them elsewhere. In Seattle, the police at least attempted to defend the Chinese but were outnumbered. Martial law was declared in the city and federal troops moved in to protect the Chinese. Restitution was paid by the U.S. Congress to the Chinese government, but not to the actual victims.

Washington's most famous criminal is Gary Ridgway, better known as the Green River Killer, a serial killer who murdered at least 71 women—and possibly many more—from 1982 to at least 1998. His first five victims were found in the Green River, giving him his name. As a child, Ridgway had been troubled and was tested with a low IQ (82). As a teenager he stabbed a 6-year-old boy, who survived the attack. He was in his 30s when he began murdering women in the Seattle and Tacoma area, and in court statements he said he had killed enough that he had lost track of the numbers. Some were prostitutes or runaways, and his practice was to pick up a woman for sex and to strangle her from behind during or after sex. In some cases he returned to the corpses to have sex with them later. The Green River Task Force interviewed incarcerated serial killer Ted Bundy several times, hoping to shed light on their profile of the Green River Killer, with little luck. Ridgway was identified as a suspect as early as 1983 but passed a polygraph test, and no evidence was found sufficient for conviction. DNA evidence eventually led to his arrest in 2001, and he plea-bargained a life sentence in exchange for his full confession and information about the location of the remains of his victims.

Washington voters approved Initiative 593 in 1993, making it the first state with a "three strikes" law. Washington is a capital punishment state and has carried out 110 executions since its territorial era, predominantly by hanging. The death penalty was abolished twice—in 1913 (revived in 1919) and in 1975 (reinstated the same year). The current form of the law dates to 1981, the 1975 statute having been rewritten twice to correct problems of constitutionality. Since 1996, inmates have been allowed to choose between lethal injection or hanging. Washington is the only state with an active gallows, though no inmate has chosen it since lethal injection was introduced. Since 2010 Washington's lethal injection has been conducted with a single-drug protocol using sodium thiopental, although the 2011 expiration of extant supplies of the drug following the manufacturer's discontinuation of it will force the state to change its protocol.

Under the 1981 law, the death penalty may be used for treason or for first-degree murder aggravated by one or more of several factors (including murder comitted during the commission of a felony, contract killings, and murder of a police officer). Most of the aggravating factors that qualify a murder for the death penalty are the same as in other capital punishment states, but Washington also allows several less common aggravating factors: murder of a reporter with the intent of obstructing the reporting of a story, murder of someone who held a restraining order against the murderer, and murder committed in order to obtain or advance position in a gang or other criminal organization. The last factor reflects Washington's growing concerns with gang violence and the specter of initiation killings.

Gang representation in Washington is substantially the same as that of nearby Oregon, with the largest gangs being chapters of the Texas-based Bandidos Motorcycle Club, the Oregon-based Brother Speed Motorcycle Club and Free Souls Motorcycle Club, the Boston-based Friends Stand United, and the California-based Gypsy Joker Motorcycle Club and Hells Angels. Motorcycle gangs are largely responsible for the traffic and sometimes manufacture of methamphetamine in Washington.

The violent crime rate in Washington, 313.8 crimes per 100,000 inhabitants in 2010, is substantially lower than the national average and has been falling steadily since a 1992 peak of 534. As in most of the country, crime climbed steadily in the decades leading up to that peak. In Washington, it grew especially quickly in the late 1960s (nearly doubling from 1966 to 1969) and from 1973 to 1975. The rape rate of 38.1 per 100,000 inhabitants is significantly higher than the national rate of 27 but has fallen from its 1992 high of 72.

Bill Kte'pi
Independent Scholar

See Also: Chinese Americans; Chinese Exclusion Act of 1882; Oregon.

Further Readings
Daniels, Roger. *Asian America: Chinese and Japanese in the United States Since 1850.* Seattle: University of Washington Press, 1990.
Guillen, Tomas. *Serial Killers: Issues Explored Through the Green River Murders.* Upper Saddle River, NJ: Prentice Hall, 2006.
Morehead, Pennie. *Green River Serial Killer: Biography of an Unsuspecting Wife.* Wellesley, MA: Brandon Books, 2007.

Washington, D.C.

The U.S. capital is a metropolitan region like no other. For the average American, Washington, D.C., houses the infrastructures sustaining the federal government, and the city represents one of the most revered symbols of national power. Though the city has been the center stage of much of American history, the district government is also, like metropolitan regions throughout the country, immensely preoccupied with providing adequate services, including public safety.

This means that while different federal agencies attempt to protect elected officials from terrorism and other subversive activities, much of the success and popularity of local representatives is measured to a great extent by how well these officials pursue policies to control the crime rate. Judging from published statistics, the metropolitan police and other law enforcement responsible for deterring crime have succeeded considerably in recent years, for while the general population continues to rise, practically all recorded categories of criminal offenses have actually decreased. In fact, in 2009, the crime rate per 100,000 reached levels not seen in Washington since 1968.

However, there is more to this issue than the mere variations in the crime trend indicate. A careful examination of the social history of crime in the city reveals three considerations deserving further study. The first is the extent to which the distribution of crime historically has fluctuated in characteristically similar patterns to other municipalities around the nation and whether a careful mapping of the city's crime confirms at least some of the conclusions proposed by recent structural criminologists and sociologists.

The second observation relates to whether the recent influx of immigrant families and, concomitantly, the changing social fabric in the city have had some or no effect on the crime rate. Another area deserving further research is the degree to which the juxtaposition of the local and national character, function, and cosmology of the city has impacted the crime rate in the district.

Washington, D.C., according to the latest census data, has a population of just over 500,000 permanent residents. Blacks continue to constitute the majority of residents with 54 percent of the overall district population, followed by whites with 41 percent and Hispanics with 9 percent. Some 13 percent of all residents in 2009 were born overseas. The median household income of $58,553 places the city well above the national average, but a sizable portion of the district's residents (17 percent in 2008) also live below the poverty line. Finally, the Metropolitan Policy Program at the Brookings Institution (2010) ranks the Washington metro region the highest in educational attainment in the nation, with close to half (47 percent) of its residents age 25 and over holding at least a bachelor's degree in 1990 and 2008. Similarly, the number of those holding a college degree topped 39 percent in 2009 in Washington, D.C., alone.

Background
Crime in the nation's capital often spills over from the ideological, racial, and economic battles that define American history. The growth of the crime rate during the early 1900s resulted primarily from the racial tensions of the epoch. The rise of extremist nationalism exacerbated racial tensions in the city, as was primarily characterized by the 1925 Ku Klux Klan march in Washington, which is said to have attracted close to 500,000 followers. During the Great Depression, the social tensions brought about by unemployment and the frequent confrontations among organized labor, anarchists, Bolshevik sympathizers, and New Deal enthusiasts mainly accounted for the violence and property deterioration.

During the upheavals of the 1960s, social tensions erupted again, contributing to a surge in the crime rate that resulted in the doubling of the crime index per 100,000 between 1966 and 1969. In particular, the aftermath of the 1968 riots, brought about by the assassinations of Martin Luther King, Jr., and Robert F. Kennedy, still resonates in the city as one of the most regrettable series of events in the history of its urban dwellings.

The growth of such conventions of social control as the police department and correctional institutions also reflect the uneven trajectory of crime. The creation of the Metropolitan Police Department dates back to the summer of 1861, when its personnel did not exceed 200 officers. To accommodate the growth and professionalization of the department, a training school was established in 1930. However, by 2007, the D.C. police department had grown to more than 4,000 enlisted and civilian personnel. The Three Prisons Act of 1891 established three penitentiaries to service the district. After a brief reorganization in 1907, the Bureau of Prisons was established under the Justice Department in 1930. By the end of the decade, the correction agency consisted of 14 facilities housing more than 13,000 inmates. Ten years later, the agency grew to 24 facilities and more than 24,000 recruits. When the 1990s came around, the inmate population topped 130,000 and the number of correctional employees was close to 20,000. This latest jump was directly attributed to the increased rate of convictions as a result of the war on drugs.

Mapping Crime
Oscillations in the crime rate in Washington, D.C., have been conditioned by structural and exogenous factors. Among the former, perhaps the most important is the racial divide in the city as illustrated by current levels of residential segregation. In fact, to talk about the crime rate in D.C. is a misnomer, for there is a very strong correlation between the character of neighborhoods, social isolation, dispersion of low-income households, and crime. To take one startling illustration, according to recent data reported by the Metropolitan Police Department, in Precinct 2 of the district, which is mostly white and affluent, there were 16 homicides reported from 2001 through 2009. On the other hand, in Precinct 7, one of the least affluent and most isolated, the police reported 496 homicides, 31 times more than in Precinct 2, during the same years.

Another feature is how the racial and class disparities in the city relate to the type of crime committed in its neighborhoods. Paradoxically, while the number of thefts reported in Precinct 7 ranged from 903 to 1,279 between 2001 and 2009, Precinct 2 reported almost three times that amount, from 2,027 to 4,398, during those years. The point that should be made clear with this comparison is

Soldiers stand guard on a Washington, D.C., street after the assassination of Martin Luther King, Jr. Rioting destroyed many buildings and social tensions erupted during the aftermath of his death, as well as the tragic death of Robert F. Kennedy, both considered the most regrettable series of events in the history of the city.

that more violent crimes tend to cluster in poor and working-class neighborhoods, whereas more affluent neighborhoods experience the break-ins and other less violent offenses. In this sense, the evidence from the district is not very different from the national trend. One of the reasons for this particular finding is that most violent crimes are interracial and interethnic, while the victims of robberies are more often than not class based. This observation may seem inconsequential but there is enough evidence from other cities to overwhelmingly corroborate this conclusion.

Moreover, data compiled by the Urban Institute and the Washington, D.C., Local Initiative Support Corporation (LISC) reveal an additional possible explanation for the dispersion of crime in D.C. Ward 7, which dominates most of Precinct 7, which is overwhelmingly black and poor. From 2005 through 2009, blacks accounted for 96 percent of the residents and whites and Hispanics for just 1.5 and 1.8 percent, respectively. In addition, the poverty rate amounted to 26 percent and the unemployment rate was twice the city's average, reaching 19 percent. Ward 3, on the other hand, is 5.3 percent black, 7.8 percent Hispanic, and predominantly white (78 percent). Its poverty rate was 7 percent and the unemployment was 3.4 percent. This data, therefore, seems to support most of the tenets and conclusions proposed by contemporary cultural and structural criminologists; along with the high dispersion of income and residential segregation, distressed areas also experience social distance and isolation. The sociology and criminology literature is emphatic about how, in socially isolated distressed communities, residents develop a particular code of the street as a conforming mechanism to gain respect and survive in inner-city neighborhoods. This culture, which tends to informally reproduce itself through generations and socialization, distrusts institutional mediating regimes, in particular, those sponsored by or involving law enforcement, adhering instead to popular norms of conflict mediation that condone violence and other forms of deviant behavior.

When one adds the effects of exogenous factors to these structural conditions, the effects on crime are evident. In the case of D.C., one the most transcending factors determining crime has been the influx of drug trafficking into and around the city. The Office of National Drug Control Policy (ONDCP) summarizes the impact of drug-related crimes in communities as follows: "Drugs are related to crime in multiple ways. Most directly, it is a crime to use, possess, manufacture, or distribute drugs classified as having a potential for abuse (such as cocaine, heroin, marijuana, and amphetamines). Drugs are also related to crime through the effects they have on the user's behavior and by generating violence and other illegal activity in connection with drug trafficking."

In Washington, the complex relationship between drugs and crime is evident when one considers the number of Drug Enforcement Administration (DEA) drug-related arrests in the city between 2004 and 2007. In 2004, the DEA made 170 arrests, according to the ONDCP, and the same year the number of homicides reached 198. As the number of DEA arrests decreased in 2005 and 2006, so did the number of homicides, but in 2007, when the number of DEA arrests jumped to 41, the homicides also swelled to 12.

Drug crimes have also been impacted by the proliferation of youth gangs as they fight for turf to become distributors themselves. To make matters worse, there is ample evidence to ponder the significance of the transnational dimensions of drug trafficking. Mexican cartels, for instance, are known to have contracted local gangs to take advantage of their extensive networks and keen local knowledge that enables them to distribute and sell cocaine in multiple cities throughout the United States. In Washington in particular, the estimates are that in 2009, the 130 criminal gangs and crews operating in the district were responsible for as many as 60 percent of the city's homicides.

The Impact of Migration on Crime

Another point deserving close attention is the extent to which migration flows contributed to the amount of crime in the city. This issue has been, and continues to be, a point of contention among sociologists and criminologists. In recent years, the district has become increasingly diverse and multicultural. For instance, it is now well documented that the number of blacks residing in Washington is down by roughly 4 percent while the number of foreign-born residents has continued to soar since the 2000 census. Some, like Harvard professor Robert J. Sampson, have concluded that between 1990 and 2004, the rise of immigration did not impact the homicide rate across the nation in any meaningful way. In addition, Sampson demonstrates that some immigrant groups, notably Mexican Americans, have a significantly lower rate of violence compared to whites and blacks. Proponents of a different position have argued forcefully that when it comes to migration and crime, findings should be inferred from reported crime incidence with some reservations. The rate of violence among immigrants is actually much higher, and instances usually go underreported because of the lack of trust immigrants usually demonstrate toward law enforcement agencies and personnel for fear of deportation.

Data from Washington tends to partially corroborate Sampson's findings, although immigrant youths are generally overrepresented in the criminal justice system. From 1980 when migrants began to settle in the city in significant numbers to 2009, the total number of violent crimes decreased by 676 citywide while the Hispanic population alone rose by 14 percent. Reasons for this inverse relationship may include the imminent fear of deportation among offenders, the sustained levels of economic opportunities in the region, or the close-knit supporting ties one finds among immigrant communities. Admittedly, other factors unrelated to migration might also have contributed to this downward trend because the city has become more gentrified since 1980, the unemployment rate consistently scores below the national average, and the metropolitan police have successfully adapted policing tactics to embrace community policing, more efficient intra- and interagency coordination, and multiple innovative problem-solving initiatives. All of these factors usually contribute positively to the reduction of violence. However, the fact remains that the presence of immigrants has not significantly undermined the efficacy of these deterrence strategies.

When one examines more specific neighborhoods, the picture changes a bit from the citywide perspective. In the cluster of Adams Morgan, Columbia Heights, Mt. Pleasant, Pleasant Heights, and Park View, where most first- and second-generation immigrants reside, the reported crime per 1,000 people more than doubled from 15 in 2000 to 46 in 2009. When one takes into account the demographic diversity in these neighborhoods along with how well integrated the community is with the rest of the city, the social isolation arguments become less persuasive. It seems that other structural conditions such as the relatively low levels of educational attainment and high concentration of deprivation and despair provide more feasible causal explanations to account for the phenomenon of violence.

The Culture
One of the unique features of Washington, D.C., is its juxtaposition of identities between the symbolic power associated with serving as the nation's capital and simultaneously as the home for families with deep roots in the area. As any Washingtonian would likely corroborate, the possibility of forging a distinct Washingtonian identity is severely impaired by the transient culture of many city residents and the amount of transplanted dwellers who settle in Washington every year to seek professional opportunities. And yet the neighborhoods that embrace norms associated with hope, prosperity, achievements, and other positive attitudes tend to support a sense of ownership, of belonging, and are more likely to sustain an affable social character and order.

To what extent, however, these norms contribute to crime prevention is open to speculation. In 1938, urban sociologist Louis Wirth asserted that such intrinsic urban conditions as population density and heterogeneity multiply opportunities for diverse social interactions, reducing allegiance to a single group and compromising the effectiveness of the various mechanisms of social control more homogeneous populations usually assert. Perhaps for this reason, the uniqueness of the district's character as the nation's capital has made the city more susceptible to instances and situations when political discontent and frustration translates voice into violence. Thus, Washington experienced a steady increase in violent and property crimes during the aftermath of the 1968 urban riots than at any other time in its recent history. During years of urban neglect and depopulation, the damage caused by the upheavals of the late 1960s left the city in despair. It was not until 1998 when a new generation of elected officials firmed their control over city hall and instituted incentives for working professionals to move back into the city that the overall rate of violence began to recede and Washington experienced a renaissance of sorts.

Conclusion
In short, this brief social history of crime in Washington, D.C., reveals numerous lessons worthy of serious reflection. First, the evidence calls us to reconsider some of the tenets of the social isolation perspective. The evidence from the city seems to suggest that structural conditions possess equally if not more plausible explanatory power than culture when it comes to explaining violent crimes. Second, the impact of migration also needs to be carefully reexamined. Third, to what extent the role of identity, place, and diminishing social control influence the propensity for crime should certainly be of interest to scholars and students alike. But perhaps the finding that must resonate is that when it comes to analyzing crime, the city as a social unit of analysis needs to be disaggregated by race, class, and ethnicity.

Enrique S. Pumar
Catholic University of America

See Also: Drug Enforcement Administration; Gangs, Contemporary; Ku Klux Klan; Urbanization.

Further Readings
Brookings Institution Metropolitan Policy Program. *State of Metropolitan America*. Washington, DC: Brookings Institution, 2010.

Fontaine, Jocelyn, Joshua Markman, and Carey Nadeau. *Promising Practices of the District of Columbia Metropolitan Police Department*. Washington, DC: Urban Institute/Brookings Institution, 2010.

Office of National Drug Control Policy. http://www
.whitehousedrugpolicy.gov/publications/factsht/
crime/index.html (Accessed April 2011).

Pumar, Enrique S., ed. *The Hispanic Presence in the Washington DC Metropolitan Region. Studies of Migrant and Urban Development.* Bingley, UK: Emerald Books, 2012.

Sampson, Robert J. "Rethinking Crime and Immigration." *Context*, v.7 (2008).

Washington City Paper. "DC Street Gang on the Rise."http://www.washingtoncitypaper.com/blogs/
citydesk/2009/06/15/dc-street-gangs-on-the-rise
-report-says (Accessed April 2011).

Washington, George (Administration of)

The first president of the United States, George Washington (1732–99) was called the "Father of His Country" for leading the victory over Britain in the American Revolutionary War. Washington was born in Westmoreland County, Virginia, the eldest son of Augustine Washington and his second wife, Mary Ball Washington. Washington's father died in 1743, and the younger Washington, then 11, went to live with his half-brother, Lawrence. Washington did not attend college but developed excellent handwriting, became a skilled and prolific writer, and was good in mathematics, which suited his interest in surveying, through studying on his own.

By the age of 17, Washington was managing a successful career as a surveyor and bought unclaimed land to establish himself as a member of the aristocracy. When his brother died in 1752 from tuberculosis, Washington inherited the Mount Vernon estate, obtained Lawrence Washington's place in the Virginia militia, and received a major's commission.

Military Service

Washington first gained public recognition in 1753, when the rivalry between the British and French over control of the Ohio Valley erupted into the French and Indian War (1754–62). As adjutant in one of Virginia's four military districts,

When George Washington assumed office, his first acts established federal judiciary policy, including the Judiciary Act of 1789, which set up a six-member Supreme Court.

he was dispatched by Governor Robert Dinwiddie in October 1753 to warn the French against further encroachment on territory claimed by the British. In delivering the message, he learned that the French were organizing further advances. Commissioned a lieutenant colonel in 1754, Washington was sent to reinforce a post that was under construction at the junction of the Allegheny and Monongahela rivers, where he fought the first skirmishes of the French and Indian War. Disappointed by his capture and defeat by the French at Fort Necessity in July 3, 1754, Washington resigned his commission near the end of that year. Both Britain and France escalated military actions and sent troops to North America in 1755 and formally declared war in 1756.

In 1755, Washington returned to the frontier as the senior American aide to British General Edward Braddock, who had been sent by the king of England to drive the French from the contested Ohio Country. In Braddock's ill-fated expedition, his army was defeated by the French and their Indian allies in the battle of the Monongahela River. Washington was able to rally the broken survivors of the British and Virginia troops to an organized retreat and safety. At age 23, he was promoted to colonel and commander in chief of the Virginia militia to defend the frontier. In 1758, the British finally took the abandoned forks of the Ohio, with Washington as commander of one of the three brigades headed by General John Forbes. He thereafter resigned his commission and returned to Mount Vernon.

In 1759, Washington married Martha Dandridge Custis, a wealthy young widow with two small children. From 1759 to the start of the American Revolution, he was a farmer, member of the House of Burgesses (1759–74), and leader of Virginia opposition to the British colonial policy. He served as a delegate to the Continental Congress (1774–75). Britain, in an effort to pay for the French and Indian War, taxed the American colonists without representation, angering them. The colonists revolted and dumped precious tea into Boston Harbor, called the Boston Tea Party. In 1775, the Continental Congress organized for defense and commissioned Washington as the commander in chief of the colonial army. In 1776, the colonists declared their independence from Britain, and the Revolutionary War began.

Presidency
After many bloody battles, Washington's army defeated the British in 1781 with some help from the French, and America became independent. In 1787, Washington presided over the Constitutional Convention, during which the written U.S. Constitution delineated a representative form of government. The Constitution was ratified in 1788 and went into effect in 1789. Washington was unanimously elected president in 1789 and again in 1792.

Washington's administration was challenged by violent resistance and uprising from a 1791 excise tax on whiskey, commonly known as the Whiskey Rebellion, or the Whiskey Insurrection. Protesters of the tax, mostly western farmers, used violence and intimidation to prevent officials from collecting it. In July 1794, more than 500 armed Pennsylvanians criminally terrorized and attacked the home of tax inspector General John Neville. In response, Washington's administration sent negotiators and militia forces to control the violence. That action gave credibility to the administration for its capability and willingness to suppress violent assault and resistance to its laws. Washington's administration set a precedent of valuing democracy and the will of the people for decision making. Washington is viewed as one of the greatest presidents to ever serve. His legacy includes the naming of the capital, Washington, D.C., numerous ships, the state of Washington, and hundreds of schools. His portrait is on the $1 bill.

Felix O. Chima
Prairie View A&M University

See Also: 1777 to 1800 Primary Documents; Constitution of the United States of America; Declaration of Independence; Tea Act of 1773; Washington, D.C.

Further Readings
Ellis, Joseph. *His Excellency: George Washington*. New York: Alfred A. Knopf, 2004.
Higginbotham, Don, ed. *George Washington Reconsidered*. Charlottesville: University of Virginia Press, 2001.
Hoth, David and Carol Edel, eds. *The Papers of George Washington: Presidential Series Volume 16*. Charlottesville: University of Virginia Press, 2011.

Watergate

In the evening on June 17, 1972, at the Watergate Hotel in Washington, D.C., because of the alertness of a security guard, five men were arrested for burglary inside the Democratic National Committee's office. These otherwise unremarkable arrests would launch a criminal investigation and prosecution and a political scandal that would have serious political and legal repercussions in the American criminal justice system and American society.

Arrest and Investigation
Richard Nixon was seeking reelection to the office of president of the United States. The national committee of the political party of the president was

active in seeking the reelection. The five men who were arrested were James W. McCord, Jr., Virgilio Gonzalez, Bernard Barker, Eugenio Martinez, and Frank Sturgis. E. Howard Hunt, Jr. and G. Gordon Liddy were later indicted for their activities in support of the burglary and the wiretapping. The men were attempting to gain information to support the reelection of President Nixon.

The subsequent investigation showed a financial link between the men and their crimes with the Committee to Re-Elect the President (ironically known as CREEP). Thousands of dollars had been funneled to the men through the Republican political apparatus. Initially, John Mitchell, the former attorney general of the United States, and Nixon denied any knowledge of or involvement with the Watergate incident. On October 10, 1972, the Federal Bureau of Investigation (FBI) reported that the Watergate burglary was part of a huge organization of political espionage and sabotage in support of the reelection campaign of President Nixon. Despite the revelations, President Nixon was reelected.

The interior of the Watergate Hotel complex. Richard Nixon's second term as president of the United States saw an Arab oil embargo, his vice president's resignation, and the Watergate scandal—the main reason for Nixon's resignation in 1974.

However, two *Washington Post* reporters, Bob Woodward and Carl Bernstein, initiated an intensive investigation into the conspiracy. Through the use of a then-confidential informant known as "Deep Throat" (who many years later was revealed as a high-level FBI official), they were able to discover that the conspiracy led deeply into the FBI, the Central Intelligence Agency (CIA), the Justice Department, and the White House. Attempts at damage control by White House aides H. R. Haldeman and John Ehrlichman were unsuccessful.

The U.S. Senate created a committee chaired by Sam Ervin to investigate the matter. Subpoenas were issued. Initially, the White House resisted the subpoenas. However, White House attorney John Dean became a star witness against the conspirators, and Alexander Butterfield revealed that there was a tape recording system in the White House that recorded the president's conversations. One of the taped conversations between Nixon and John Dean established that Nixon was not only aware of the cover-up but that he was an active participant. This tape would not be revealed for some time.

White House Tapes

At that point, Archibald Cox, the special prosecutor appointed to investigate the matter, subpoenaed the White House tapes. The White House ordered Cox to drop the subpoena and he refused. The president then went through several Justice Department officials in an attempt to find someone willing to fire Cox. Robert Bork was appointed acting attorney general and he subsequently agreed to do it. The forced resignations of various Justice Department officials and the firing of Cox were dubbed the "Saturday Night Massacre." Numerous charges of wrongdoing were raised against Nixon and he subsequently stated to the press that "I am not a crook." Nixon then appointed another special prosecutor, Leon Jaworski, to continue the investigation. Jaworski also subpoenaed the tapes. Nixon refused and only produced transcripts with large portions redacted.

The issue went to the courts and ultimately was presented to the U.S. Supreme Court. President Nixon argued that he should not have to produce the tapes under the principle of executive privilege. Finally, on July 24, 1974, in the case *Untied States v. Nixon*, the U.S. Supreme Court rejected the argument of executive privilege and ordered

President Nixon to produce the tapes. On July 30, 1974, President Nixon turned the tapes over to the special prosecutor. As a result of the cover-up, indictments were issued against a number of White House staff, including Haldeman, Ehrlichman, Mitchell, and Charles Colson. John Dean and Jeb Stuart Magruder had already pled guilty. Numerous other officials were indicted and convicted.

Resignation

The political pressure on President Nixon was enormous. On July 27 through July 30, 1974, the House Judiciary Committee voted to recommend impeachment of President Nixon. Then, on August 5, 1974, the June 23, 1972, tape of President Nixon and Haldeman organizing a cover-up of the Watergate burglary using the CIA was released. After the release of this tape, Congressmen on the House Judiciary Committee who had previously voted against the impeachment of President Nixon changed their minds. On August 8, 1974, President Richard Nixon resigned from the office of president. Gerald Ford succeeded him. The political effects of the Watergate scandal were enormous. The Republican Party was severely damaged and many credit the election of Jimmy Carter to the next term as president as one of the results. Politically, politicians were almost universally branded as crooks and the phrase "I am not a crook" became a national joke.

From a historical context concerning the criminal justice system, the Watergate scandal gave substance to the principle that no man is above the law, not even the president. In one sense, it allowed popular America to think that the criminal justice system worked. However, that belief was challenged when President Gerald Ford, before any charges were ever brought against Richard Nixon, pardoned him. Ford endured a significant amount of criticism but held firm on the grounds that the nation had to heal and that the prosecution and possible conviction of Nixon would harm the nation. Some authorities hold the position that Ford was not elected to the presidency because of his pardon of Nixon. One principle of criminal law that the Watergate scandal established is that executive privilege is limited and cannot be used to cover up criminal behavior. However, that principle has been seriously undermined by the administration of George W. Bush from 2000 to 2008 with revelations of such executive activities as torture, secret rendition, and secret surveillance of American citizenry. If nothing else, the Watergate scandal serves as a historical illustration and a warning as to how far politicians will go—even to the point of criminal behavior and cover up—to maintain personal political power.

Wm. C. Plouffe, Jr.
Independent Scholar

See Also: 1961 to 1980 Primary Documents; Nixon, Richard (Administration of); Political Crimes, History of; *United States v. Nixon*.

Further Readings

Bernstein, Carl and Bob Woodward. *All the President's Men.* New York: Simon & Schuster, 1974.

Bernstein, Carl and Bob Woodward. *The Final Days.* New York: Simon & Schuster, 1976.

Dash, Samuel. *Chief Counsel: Inside the Ervin Committee—The Untold Story of Watergate.* New York: Random House, 1976.

Sirica, John J. *To Set the Record Straight: The Break-in, The Tapes, The Conspirators, The Pardon.* New York: W. W. Norton, 1979.

Weathermen, The

See Students for a Democratic Society and the Weathermen.

Webb v. United States

Webb v. United States was decided by the U.S. Supreme Court in 1919. The decision held that prescriptions of narcotic drugs for the sole purpose of maintenance treatment were not permissible. This was because such prescriptions were not interpreted to be within the discretion of physicians and thus not privileged under the Harrison Narcotics Tax Act. This act was a U.S. federal law that taxed and regulated the production and delivery of opiate drugs. The act was proposed by

New York Representative Francis Harrison, and it was approved by the U.S. Congress on December 14, 1914.

The case was accepted on certiorari from the Sixth Circuit Court of Appeals. It was argued before the Supreme Court on January 16, 1919, and was decided on March 3, 1919. The case ended in a 5–4 split decision, with Justice William Day writing the majority opinion. He was joined in the majority by Justices Oliver Wendell Holmes, Mahlon Pitney, Louis Brandeis, and John Clarke. Chief Justice Edward White wrote a dissenting opinion and was joined by Justices Joseph McKenna, Willis Van Devanter, and James McReynolds.

The case involved Webb, a physician and Goldbaum, a pharmacist. They were both convicted and sentenced in the U.S. District Court for the Western District of Tennessee on a charge of conspiracy to violate the Harrison Narcotic Tax Act. Webb wrote prescriptions for morphine that was furnished by Goldbaum to habitual cocaine users for addiction maintenance, not in an attempt to cure the patients' cocaine habit. In *Webb*, the court interpreted part of the act to mean that physicians could prescribe narcotics to patients in the course of normal medical treatment but not for the maintenance treatment of drug addicts.

During the 1800s, opiates and cocaine were generally unregulated drugs in the United States. However, beginning in the early part of the 20th century, cocaine began to be linked to crime. Some journalists claimed that cocaine use caused African Americans to rape and assault Caucasian women, and that Chinese immigrants were to blame for importing opium into the country. In 1908, President Theodore Roosevelt appointed Dr. Hamilton Wright as the first U.S. opium commissioner. In 1911, Dr. Wright stated that the United States consumed the most addictive drugs per capita, and that opiates were the most harmful drugs known at the time. The act is partly concerned with the marketing and taxation of opiates.

However, a clause applying to doctors allowed distribution "in the course of his professional practice only." This clause was interpreted to mean that a doctor could not prescribe opiates to an addict, since addiction was not considered a disease. A number of doctors, including Webb, were arrested and convicted under this law.

In *United States v. Doremus* (1919), the U.S. Supreme Court ruled that the act was constitutional. After upholding the constitutionality of the act, the *Webb* decision focused on a case that specifically pertained to the act. In *Webb*, the main question before the court was this: If a practicing physician issues a prescription for morphine to a habitual user, not being issued in the course of professional treatment for the attempted cure of the habit, but being issued for the purpose of providing the user with morphine sufficient to keep him comfortable by maintaining his customary use, is such an order justified under the act? The court's majority answered in the negative, meaning that opiate prescriptions for maintenance treatment were not a permissible exception under the law.

In 1925, the act's applicability in prosecuting doctors who prescribed narcotics to addicts was successfully challenged in *Linder v. United States*. Dr. Charles Linder was arrested and convicted of prescribing opiates to addicts, which was in violation of the Harrison Act. Linder appealed, and the court unanimously overturned his conviction. Justice McReynolds wrote the majority opinion, which stated that the federal government had overstepped its authority, had no power to regulate medical practice, and that the Harrison Act could not be used to prosecute doctors who prescribed narcotics to drug addicts. Much of the act's current authority has been superseded by the Controlled Substances Act of 1970.

Christopher M. Donner
University of South Florida

See Also: Drug Abuse and Addiction, History of; Narcotics Laws; Supreme Court, U.S.

Future Readings
Hall, Kermit and James Ely. *The Oxford Guide to United States Supreme Court Decisions*. New York: Oxford University Press, 2009.
Rowe, Thomas. *Federal Narcotic Laws and the War on Drugs: Money Down a Rat Hole*. New York: Routledge, 2006.
Schwartz, Bernard. *A History of the Supreme Court*. New York: Oxford University Press, 1993.

Weeks v. United States

Weeks v. United States was a monumental case decided by the U.S. Supreme Court in 1914. Prior to *Weeks*, it was common for American courts to accept evidence without scrutinizing the means by which such evidence was procured. *Weeks* set forth the exclusionary rule, which dictated decades of case law upholding the protection against unreasonable searches and seizures. Specifically, the case dealt with the safeguards of the Fourth Amendment to the U.S. Constitution, which provides "The right of the people to be secure in their persons, houses, papers, and effects against unreasonable searches and seizures, shall not be violated, and no warrants shall issue but upon probable cause, supported by oath or affirmation, and particularly describe the place to be searched and the persons or things to be seized." At its inception, *Weeks* was "not viewed as a means to achieve police conformity with law or indeed as a means to anything ... [but] [i]t was viewed as an expression of the Fourth Amendment itself."

Without an arrest warrant, the Kansas City Police Department arrested Fremont Weeks. Similarly, without a search warrant or consent, several other police officers went to Weeks's home and after "being told by a neighbor where the key was kept, found it and entered the house." After searching his room, the officers took certain papers and articles into custody and later turned them over to the U.S. marshal. Later the same day, the police officers returned with the marshal. Without a search warrant, the marshal searched Weeks's room and took custody of letters and envelopes that were found in a drawer.

Unlawful Search and Seizure
Weeks filed a pretrial motion for return of the seized property, arguing that his rights under the U.S. and Missouri constitutions had been violated. Specifically, the petition urged the court to order the return of his property because it was taken "without warrant or authority to do so" and that such property was "being unlawfully and improperly held" by the district attorney, marshal, and clerk of the court. Despite the initial violation of his rights occasioned by the police seizure of his belongings, Weeks argued that the district attorney's attempted use of the unlawfully obtained evidence at trial would constitute an independent violation, unless the court returned his property. The trial court entered an order requiring the return of Weeks's materials, which were not pertinent to the charges against him, but denied the petition generally as to materials that were, or could potentially be, pertinent.

Weeks renewed his request for the seized property at the beginning of the trial before any evidence had been introduced. Yet again, the petition was denied. As each item was introduced into evidence, Weeks contemporaneously objected and argued that the materials had been obtained without a search warrant and by breaking into his home in violation of the Fourth Amendment to the U.S. Constitution. The trial court overruled the objections. On appeal, Weeks advocated for reversal of his conviction because of the prejudicial error consisting of the trial court's denial of his petition and admission of the unlawfully seized materials at trial.

The government relied primarily on the decision of *Adams v. New York* (1904). Utilizing the *Adams* holding, the government argued that because the evidence was in the court's physical control, it was competent evidence, and the court should not inquire into method used to acquire it. The Supreme Court found little merit in the government's argument and found the facts in *Adams* were in stark contrast with those present in Weeks's case. Specifically, the challenged evidence in *Adams* was recovered incidentally during the execution of a valid search warrant.

The court engaged in a historical analysis, which thoroughly examined centuries of American and English laws and customs, beginning with the 15th-century adage that a man's home is his castle and that it shall not be invaded by general authority. The court explained that the Fourth Amendment was intended to "forever secure" against unreasonable searches and seizures as was evidenced by the founding fathers having placed it in the Bill of Rights. Ultimately, the court found that the taking and holding of Weeks's items was a direct violation of his Fourth Amendment rights, further characterizing the violation as a "manifest neglect" or an "open defiance" of the proscriptions of the Constitution. The act of maintaining custody of the items and then later allowing their introduction as evidence at trial was deemed prejudicial error. Accordingly, Weeks's conviction was reversed. The applicability of the *Weeks* holding was binding on federal courts only since the decision preceded the incorporation of various provisions of the Bill of Rights via the Fourteenth Amendment by decades.

Armando Gustavo Hernandez
Independent Scholar

See Also: Bill of Rights; Constitution of the United States of America; Defendant's Rights.

Further Readings
Adams v. New York, 192 U.S. 585, 24 S. Ct. 372, 48 L.Ed. 575 (1904).
Hirsch, Milton. "Big Bill Haywood's Revenge: The Original Intent of the Exclusionary Rule." *St. Thomas Law Review*, v.22/35 (2009).
Weeks v. United States, 232 U.S. 383, 34 S. Ct. 341, 58 L.Ed. 652 (1914).

West Virginia

West Virginia originated as part of Virginia, one of the thirteen colonies, and seceded from Virginia in 1863 in order to break away from the Confederacy and rejoin the Union. From its conflicted beginning, crime, police, and punishment have had important roles to play in the development of the state.

Police and Punishment

At the time of West Virginia's secession, county sheriffs and town police departments were the extant forms of law enforcement. The West Virginia State Police was founded in 1919 in response to the mine wars and was the fourth statewide police agency formed in the United States. Secession from Virginia left West Virginia with a shortage of prisons, and the legislature's initial preference was to use existing county jails and send prisoners to facilities in other states when necessary. A prison escape turned public opinion in favor of a state prison, and the West Virginia

Matewan, West Virginia, is protected by a floodwall and is located along the Tug Fork River. Matewan played a major role in the historic mine wars in the early 20th century.

State Penitentiary began construction in 1867, finishing in 1876. The facility was based on the Northern Illinois Penitentiary at Joliet, and prison labor was used to construct the North Wagon Gate and two cellblock areas. A four-story tower provided housing for the warden and his family, and a separate space for female inmates. Once the prison was opened in 1876, prison labor was used to build secondary facilities and workshops for prison industries, including a paint shop, wagon shop, brickyard, hospital, and carpentry shop. The prison remained in use for more than a century but was decommissioned in 1986, after several decades of repeated riots and escapes, when the West Virginia Supreme Court ruled that the cells were small enough to constitute cruel and unusual punishment. Since then, inmates have been kept primarily in the Mount Olive Correctional Complex in Fayette County.

West Virginia abolished the death penalty in 1965. It had been a capital punishment state as part of Virginia and remained one for a century after its secession, as well as retaining Virginia's statute allowing the death penalty in rape cases. Hanging was used as the method of execution until 1949, when West Virginia became the last state to adopt the electric chair.

Crime
Coal mining has long been key to West Virginia's industry and economy, and the state was the site of historic "mine wars" in the early 20th century. The first such war, from 1912 to 1913, transpired in the southern part of the state between Paint Creek and Cabin Creek and led to at least 100 and maybe several hundred deaths. It began with a coal miner strike in April 1912. There were 96 coal mines in the region that employed 7,500 miners; the 41 mines on Paint Creek were unionized, though the Paint Creek miners were paid less than other unionized miners in the area. When the Paint Creek union negotiated a new contract and demanded that their pay be raised, the mine owners refused. When the Paint Creek miners began a labor strike, the Cabin Creek miners decided to join them, demanding that they be unionized under similar terms. The United Mine Workers Union pledged its full support and financing, and the strike lasted a month without violence—until mine operators hired the Baldwin-Felts Detective Agency as strikebreakers. The agency sent 300 armed guards, and the ensuing siege saw 50 deaths by gunfire and other violence, while many more starved to death while under siege.

The Baldwin-Felts agency was employed again by the mine owners in Matewan when a dispute arose with the local miners who were attempting to unionize in 1921. This culminated in the Battle of Blair Mountain, fought from August 25 to September 2, 1921, between 15,000 coal miners and an army of Baldwin-Felts agents and police. More than 1 million rounds were fired, and the army was ordered to intervene. In the end, 985 miners were indicted for treason, murder, conspiracy to murder, and accessory to murder. The southern part of the state wasn't able to fully unionize until 1935.

Crime in West Virginia is lower than the average rate, though significantly higher than in neighboring Virginia, at 314.6 violent crimes per 100,000 inhabitants in 2010. While crime in West Virginia peaked in the 1990s (350 in 1999) as it did in much of the country before gradually falling, it has been on the rise again since 2005. The recent increase reflects a rise in aggravated assaults, which have increased almost 50 percent since 2002; rape and robbery have actually declined somewhat in recent years.

The most serious recent violent crime in West Virginia was the 2003 sniper attacks, which resulted in three deaths. Reminiscent of the Beltway sniper attacks in the Washington, D.C., area in the previous year, the 2003 sniper fired a single shot (apparently from a .22-caliber rifle) at victims stopped at stores or gas stations late at night. Two of the three victims had drug connections. A fourth person was shot twice in the chest five months later, and it wasn't clear if this was a victim of the same sniper. In 2011, a suspect was arrested for the murder of one of the victims; as of this writing, the investigation continues.

Bill Kte'pi
Independent Scholar

See Also: State Police; Strikes; Virginia.

Further Readings
Lewis, Ronald L. *Transforming the Appalachian Countryside: Railroads, Deforestation, and Social Change in West Virginia, 1880–1920*. Chapel Hill: University of North Carolina Press, 1998.
Savage, Jon. *Thunder in the Mountains: The West Virginia Mine War, 1920–21*. Pittsburgh, PA: University of Pittsburgh Press, 1990.
Williams, John A. *West Virginia: A History*. Morgantown: West Virginia University Press, 2003.

White-Collar Crime, Contemporary

The first use of the term *white-collar crime* was in 1939. Sociologist Edwin Hardin Sutherland (1883–1950) used it in a speech given to the American Sociological Society. He coined the term in order to refute the claims of those criminologists, social workers, and others who claimed that crime was the work of poor, disadvantaged young men from broken homes, or those from psychopathic or sociopath conditions. In contrast, Sutherland stated that people in business or in public positions of authority or in nonprofit organizations could commit crimes. The more sophisticated in society could and do engage in a number of practices or behaviors that are criminal acts against the peace of society and just not simply civil wrongs.

Sutherland defined white-collar crimes as crimes committed by people who are respectable, with high social status in the course of their occupations. In his last major book, *White Collar Crime* (1949), he argued that street crimes such as robbery and murder were less damaging to society than white-collar crimes. Yet, there were relatively few white-collar criminals in prison. Sutherland succeeded in focusing attention upon crime committed by prominent people and large corporate enterprises. Other definitions of white-collar crime have since been offered. Today, definitions of white-collar crime refer to the offense rather than to the social status of the offender. An example of a modern definition of white-collar crime was used in the 1983 annual report of the attorney general of the United States. It focuses on the acts of people who try to avoid payment obligations or financial losses or who take money, property, services, business advantages, or professional advantage, engaging in a form of robbery that is nonviolent and deceptive.

White-collar crimes often go unreported or unprosecuted because of the threat to the reputations of institutions such as banks, churches, or charities. The effect of reporting the crimes would be to weaken public confidence in these trusted institutions. Because of the damage to reputations and the broad nature of white-collar crimes, it is difficult to gather statistics on these kinds of offenses. One agency that gathers statistics on white-collar crimes is the Federal Bureau of Statistics, which collects statistics on fraud, counterfeiting and forgery, and embezzlement.

The people who commit white-collar crimes violate their positions of trust in business, industry, the professions, civic organizations, or the government. White-collar criminals may be bankers, business people, doctors, lawyers, computer experts, or others in socially responsible positions.

Because the number of deceptive practices that can be performed is so large, there is no set list of crimes that can be categorized as white collar. Historically, the courts have taken a broad view of crimes that can be categorized as white-collar crimes. The courts have included crimes such as mail fraud, wire fraud, conspiracy, racketeering, bribery, false statements, obstruction of justice, tax crimes, forgery, money laundering, bank fraud, false statements, securities fraud, and computer, environmental, health, and antitrust violations. Prosecution of white-collar criminals took a major step forward when the famous gangster, Al Capone, was convicted for tax evasion.

Since 2000, there have been numerous cases of white-collar crimes, but a drop in prosecutions occurred during the administration of George W. Bush. The drop was because of the redeployment of Justice Department assets to terrorism and illegal immigrant investigations. One area in which white-collar crimes rose was crimes that involved official corruption or political corruption, up 15 percent. Some of these cases involved notorious examples of adultery, prostitution, homosexual propositioning of young staffers, tweeting lewd pictures, extortion, and bribery.

Illegal Prescription Drugs and File Swapping

A category of white-collar crime that is frequently overlooked because the offenses are not usually prosecuted is the illegal importation of prescription drugs from pharmacies in Mexico and Canada. Thousands of senior citizens have purchased these drugs through the Internet. The amount is usually a 90-day supply for personal consumption. The need and the amount do not matter because such importation is a violation of federal law. To date, few if any prosecutions of senior citizens who have imported more affordable prescriptions have been made. Prior to 2006, small quantities of drugs were seized. Since then, the policy has been changed to one of supervision due to political pressure over the high price of American-made prescription drugs.

Another category of offense rarely prosecuted is downloading music and file swapping of entertainment over the Internet. It is a widespread practice. However, it is illegal and could result in prosecution. The justice department is unlikely to prosecute millions of teenagers and college students for file swapping, but it is a nonviolent crime that involves deceptive practices. To prosecute such cases would raise a huge political uproar. So, such prosecutions are unlikely to occur on a mass scale. Only egregious cases are likely at the insistence of the recording industry or other media industries leaders. The costs to the industries are in the billions of dollars in losses, but the loss of public support could be even greater if the public does not support prosecutions of senior citizens, teenagers, or children.

Critics have denounced the refusal to prosecute an elderly grandmother for illegally importing medications while prosecuting an unknown accountant involved in a cover-up of financial malfeasance. They claim that the refusal to prosecute reveals the class warfare nature of white-collar crime prosecutions. The whole concept of white-collar crime is a sociological concept. White-collar crime prosecution seeks to punish the wealthy, powerful, or famous while ignoring others who have a low social status. The current practice is to prosecute on the basis of economic activity regardless of class or ethnic distinctions. The reality is a little more class oriented than some would like to admit.

Enron, Worldcom, Tyco, and Adelphia

There have been a number of famous white-collar criminal cases in recent years. In the 1990s, the deregulation of energy resources and the rising cost of energy put firms such as Enron into an excellent position for dynamic growth. Enron was deemed an energy giant at the beginning of the 2000s, until it was revealed that it was engaging in illegal accounting practices. Its manipulation of its financial records was aided by the Arthur Andersen accounting firm, one of the "Big Five." The Enron white-collar crimes were massive, cost billions, and ruined many people.

Jeffrey Skilling, Enron president and chief executive officer (CEO), along with a staff he assembled, hid billions of dollars of debt through fraudulent financial reporting, accounting loopholes, and the use of special-purpose entities. Andrew Fastow, chief operating officer (COO), fooled the board of directors into believing that Enron's accounting practices were sound. Accountants with Arthur Anderson were important players in the conspiracy. When the true financial condition of Enron was revealed, its stock became virtually worthless. Securities and Exchange Commission (SEC) investigations led to Skilling's being sent to prison for a 24-year, four-month sentence. Andrew Fastow was given six years in prison. Kenneth Lay, the company's CEO and chairman from 1985 to 2002, died of a heart attack before he was sentenced. The accounting firm of Arthur Andersen, the nation's leading firm, collapsed. The Sarbanes-Oxley Act of 2002 was adopted to increase the criminal penalties for falsifying corporate financial information.

After Enron's collapse, Worldcom became the next scandal. It was a company created by CEO Bernard Ebbers. In the great telecom expansion of the 1990s, he built an enormous company. However, in 2000, there as a downturn in the telecommunications business. To protect the value of the company's stock, Ebbers used deceptive accounting methods in order to trick investors into believing the company was in sound financial health. In truth, there was an underreporting of $3.8 billion, which eventually led to the company's bankruptcy. Ebbers was sent to prison for 25 years for conspiracy and fraud.

Executives stealing from a company seemed to reach new heights when Tyco CEO Dennis Kozlowski and former chief financial officer (CFO) Mark Swarts were found to have stolen over $150 million from the company. Two million dollars was spent for a birthday party in Sardinia for Kozlowski's wife. Both were convicted and given prison terms of at least eight years and four months. Another manipulation involved the Adelphia Company. In 2002, it was the fifth-largest cable provider in the United States. In 2003, it generated $3.6 billion in revenue; however, the figure was fraudulent. Adelphia's founder, John Rigas was given 15 years in prison and his son Timothy Rigas, the company's CEO, was given 20 years in prison for embezzling the company's funds for personal use. The company was sold to Comcast and Time Warner in 2006.

Healthcare Fraud and Martha Stewart

Credit card fraud, bankruptcy fraud, telemarketing fraud, embezzlement, money laundering, and home-repair fraud are also types of white-collar crime. Many white-collar crimes are carried out though the Internet via unsolicited e-mails. In an effort to prevent this type of fraud, Congress passed the Controlling Assault of Non-Solicited Pornography and Marketing Act in 2003. Acts such as knowingly failing to list assets in a bankruptcy filing or the unauthorized use of a credit card are white-collar crimes. Healthcare fraud is a white-collar crime usually treated with severity. In 2001, Robert R. Courtney, a Kansas City pharmacist, was convicted of healthcare fraud for adulterating chemotherapy drugs. He was sentenced to 17 to 30 years in prison.

All of his property was forfeited and he was compelled to disclose the full range of his wrongdoing and those of his associates. Even greater healthcare fraud was committed by HealthSouth. It was revealed in 2002 that its leader, Richard Scrushy, had engaged in deceptive billing practices that had defrauded Medicare and other federal healthcare providers. Scrushy was not convicted, but the company paid $325 million in restitution to Medicare.

The advances in technology in computers have created stock fraud opportunities. If a stock offering deliberately withholds information, those responsible for bringing the shares to the market are committing a white-collar crime. Insider trading is also a form of white-collar crime. Insider trading is a white-collar crime that may receive less punishment. In December 2001, Martha Stewart, famous television homemaker-hostess, engaged in a stock trade of 3,900 shares of ImClone stock worth $250,000 that she owned. The transaction was based on the advice of her stock adviser, Peter Bacanovic. The advice gave her what amounted to inside information, affecting the value of stock she held. She was not convicted of insider trading. During the course of the investigation, she lied to a

Before it was discovered in 2008 that Enron had managed to hide billions of dollars of debt by using fraudulent financial reporting, accounting loopholes, and special-purpose entities, it was thought of as an energy giant. Enron maintained this glittering headquarters complex in Houston, Texas, and claimed revenues of almost $101 billion in 2000.

federal investigator, which is a crime. She was convicted of obstruction of justice for lying to government agents in a 2004 case involving sale of her ImClone stock following insider information. She was subsequently sent to federal prison and was fined. Peter Bacanovic, her stock broker, received a similar sentence.

Jack Abramoff and Bernie Madoff

The Jack Abramoff lobbying scandal was a case of political corruption. In the Abramoff case, a number of scandals emerged that involved politicians and the mob. In 2006, he pled guilty to fraud, conspiracy, and tax evasion. He had attempted to cheat Indian casino interests out of $85 million. He also used a fake wire transfer in order to get a $600 million loan in order to purchase SunCruz Casinos. The deal led to the murder of the former owner Konstantinon "Gus" Boulis. For his involvement in politically directed bribery, Abramoff was sent to prison.

In 2007, the housing bubble began to collapse as it was discovered that subprime lending had been based in many cases upon fraudulent housing pricing assessments, fraudulent lending to unqualified borrowers, and to other manipulations. Many of these activities were white-collar crimes that were not prosecuted. The resulting damage from the sale of securities based on the loans caused global losses. In New York, it was discovered that Bernard Lawrence "Bernie" Madoff, a well-known financier and former chairman of the NASDAQ Stock Market, had been running a Ponzi scheme and committing the largest white-collar crime in history. The losses from his financial manipulations were estimated to total about $50 billion. In 2009, he pled guilty to 11 federal crimes, including theft from an employee benefit plan. He was given 150 years on prison and ordered to pay $170 billion in restitution. His son, Mark, and three other people working in his business committed suicide.

The bursting of the housing bubble in 2008 not only exposed Bernie Madoff, but it also brought to light many deceptive practices in the housing industry. These included appraisers who submitted false appraisals for the value of a house; subprime lending practices that included loans to people who were completely unqualified; the development of financial instruments by Wall Street brokerage houses that were not sound because they included bundles of billions of dollars of subprime loans, and many other dubious practices. Countrywide, a real estate loan company, was almost destroyed in the financial crisis. It was found to be engaged in lending to politicians at very advantageous rates to gain political influence. Industrial or economic espionage is of growing significance as a white-collar crime. If successful, foreign agents may cause the loss of billions of dollars for companies that have invested huge sums in product research and development. With their industrial or trade secrets stolen, companies will be put at a competitive disadvantage and may not survive.

Andrew J. Waskey
Dalton State College

See Also: 2001 to 2012 Primary Documents; Enron; Madoff, Bernard; White-Collar Crime, History of; White-Collar Crime, Sociology of.

Further Readings

Bazle, Tom. D. *Investigating White-Collar Crime*. Upper Saddle River, NJ: Prentice Hall, 2007.

Benson, Michael. *White-Collar Crime: An Opportunity Perspective*. London: Taylor & Francis, 2009.

Dodge, Mary. *Women and White-Collar Crime*. Upper Saddle River, NJ: Prentice Hall, 2008.

Ermann, M. D., and R. J. Lundman. *Corporate and Governmental Deviance: Problems of Organizational Behavior in Contemporary Society*. New York: Oxford University Press, 2002.

Friedrichs, David O. *Trusted Criminals: White-Collar Crime in Contemporary Society*. Stamford, CT: Thomson Wadsworth, 2009.

Geis, Gilbert. *White-Collar Crime: Offenses in Business, Politics, and the Professions*. New York: Simon & Schuster Adult Publishing, 1994.

Gottschalk, Petter. *White-Collar Crime: Detection, Prevention and Strategy in Business Enterprises*. St. Leonards, Australia: Universal-Publishers.com, 2010.

Podgor, Ellen S. and Jerold H. Israel. *White-Collar Crime in a Nutshell*. St. Paul, MN: West Group, 1997.

Wand, Kelly. *White-Collar Crime*. Farmington Hills, MI: Gale Cengage Learning, 2009.

Weisburd, David. *Crimes of the Middle Classes: White-Collar Offenders in the Federal Courts.* New Haven, CT: Yale University Press, 1991.

Young, Mitchell. *White-Collar Crime.* Farmington Hills, MI: Cengage Gale, 2009.

White-Collar Crime, History of

The words *crime* and *criminal* inevitably conjure up images of street prowlers bent on stealing, raping, and even occasionally murdering innocent citizens. In the popular mind, these individuals share similar idiosyncrasies: born to lower-class families, physically foreboding and aggressive, vicious and remorseless, often addicted to drugs, uneducated but cunning, and animated by an uncontrollable lust for transgression. To some extent, this stereotypical description of the bogeyman is perpetuated by the media on a daily basis. Less covered, however, is another form of illegal behavior with an unfortunately larger scope and more deleterious impact on American society than street crime. Interestingly, this type of deviant act is not committed by financially precarious or antisocial persons. On the contrary, what makes it so special is the occupational prestige of its perpetrators.

First coined in 1939 by sociologist Edwin Sutherland during a speech given to the American Sociological Society, the term *white-collar crime* was subsequently defined as any "crime committed by a person of respectability and high social status in the course of his occupation." Within the academy, this provocative conceptualization of criminals wearing the proverbial white collar—a symbol of professional success as opposed to working-class employees' blue collar—created a scientific divide: While some maintained that burglary, armed robbery, sexual assault, and murder (i.e., illicit activities generally associated with disadvantaged neighborhoods) were the "real" crimes, others were impressed by Sutherland's argument that large-scale fraud was not only more socially harmful but also, because of the culprit's profile and respectability, had better chances of going unreported and/or unpunished.

Over the years, the term has grown to encompass a multitude of illegal activities ranging from petty scams and swindles to political corruption and even state crime (e.g., war profiteering). Much activity may be observed either among individuals (e.g., employee theft, consumer fraud, Ponzi schemes) or within corporations (e.g., antitrust violation, labor exploitation, environmental crime). Given the myriad categories of activities falling under the white-collar crime umbrella, drawing a list of every act ever passed to regulate and sanction it is an impossible task. More useful is an examination of some of the most important cases and subsequent legal measures that have delineated the nature and impact of white-collar crime to the present day.

Fraud

Fraud is arguably one of the most common forms of white-collar crime. It can be defined as a deceptive practice by individuals or entities entrusted with money or property that they appropriate for their own use and benefit, resulting in financial losses for the other party during apparently legitimate business transactions. Fraudulent acts typically include employee theft (ranging from a clerk's embezzlement to a CEO's plunder) or consumer fraud (e.g., identity theft, telephone and mail solicitations, Internet fraud, consumer investment, credit card, financial and securities fraud), but also bankruptcy, illegal payments, money laundering, bribery, kickbacks, and other forms of corruption, including income tax evasion or counterfeiting.

It is important to note that although the academic definition of white-collar crime is fairly recent, historical records show that legal actions against what would now be considered cases of fraud were taken as early as the 15th century. The 1473 Carrier's case was a landmark in the history of elite deviance. For the first time, a clear distinction was made between theft and the conversion of initially lawfully possessed goods for personal profit. The defendant, an English carrier, had been hired by a Flemish merchant to carry bales of wool to Southampton but eventually took them to a different location for his own gain. The carrier was arrested and charged with larceny (i.e., theft), a felony. The problem was that according to the common law, he could not technically be found guilty of theft since the bales were already in his possession and were not actually stolen from the merchant. Nevertheless, the chancellor opined that although the case did not break common law statutes, it was still infringing on the laws of nature. Consequently, the defendant was found guilty. The case marked a precedent in the annals of English law. Unlike ever before, a court came to investigate, define, and criminalize embezzlement. In some respects, it paved the way for the future sanctioning of various white-collar crimes in the United States.

Throughout the American Civil War, the Union and Confederate armies were plagued by fraud. Notoriously unethical contractors took advantage of both parties' dire needs by selling them unhealthy horses, flawed guns and ammunition, and rotten provisions. Congress took action against such unprincipled activities by passing the 1863 False Claims Act (also known as the Lincoln Act). Nevertheless, during the Reconstruction era after the Civil War, the presidency of Ulysses S. Grant was marked by a succession of white-collar crimes, such as Black Friday, September 24, 1869, when an attempt by speculators Jay Gould and James Fisk (both linked to Grant) to corner the gold market and drive up its price caused a national panic, resulting in massive financial losses); the 1871 Emma Silver mine scandal, in which promoters Senator William M. Stewart of Nevada and James E. Lyon attempted to sell phony mine stock to British investors; or the 1875 Whiskey Ring, where a group of distillers and public officials defrauded the federal government of liquor taxes. Ironically, President Grant came to experience fraud himself when the Wall Street brokerage firm owned by his son and Ferdinand Ward (a dishonest speculator known as "the young Napoleon of finance") crashed in 1884, leaving Grant—who had invested large amounts of money in it—ruined.

Fraud, however, was not the main type of illegal behavior associated with economic transactions. In fact, dishonest practices flourished during the Industrial Revolution, with corporations creating monopolies and raising prices capriciously, which was easily done given the lack of penal definitions prohibiting those acts. Nevertheless, things changed with the creation and strict enforcement of antitrust laws.

Antitrust Violation

A trust can be defined as an illegal group of commercial enterprises in which the stock is controlled by a central board of trustees, which makes it possible for them to minimize production costs, fluctuate prices, and most importantly, get rid of competition, a symbolic and—according to the 18th-century economist and capitalist enthusiast Adam Smith—healthy component in any liberal economy. 1890 saw the passing of the Sherman Anti-Trust Act, a cornerstone in the history of competition laws. The act was christened after John Sherman, then chairman of the Senate Finance Committee and secretary of the treasury under President Rutherford B. Hayes. Sherman intended to use the constitutional power of Congress to regulate interstate commerce. Passed by the Senate by a vote of 51–1 on April 8, 1890, and by the House by a unanimous vote of 242–0 on June 20, 1890, the Sherman Anti-Trust Act was subsequently signed into law by President Benjamin Harrison on July 2 of the same year. Still, a substantial problem lay ahead: Because the bill was not clear in the terms it used (e.g., *trust*, *monopoly*), it remained open to interpretation and thus vulnerable to loopholes. Not surprisingly, the Supreme Court overturned the Sherman Act in *United States v. E. C. Knight Company* (1895). Accused of constituting a control trade, the defendant (the American Sugar Refining Company) was found not guilty even though it controlled an outstanding 98 percent of all sugar refining in the United States.

It took the hard work and determination of several journalists to reveal more such monopolistic policies. Lincoln Steffens, Ida Tarbell, David Graham Phillips, Ray Stannard Baker, Samuel Hopkins Adams, and Upton Sinclair proceeded to expose business abuses and corruption in politics. Although he lauded the group's efforts, President Theodore Roosevelt nonetheless disapproved of their unsubtle methods in a 1906 speech, nicknaming them "muckrakers" in reference to a character from John Bunyan's *Pilgrim's Progress* who was only interested in raking the filth. Regardless of the lack of propriety of their investigative processes, the muckrakers laid the path for a more serious scrutiny of white-collar crime, culminating in the 1914 Clayton Antitrust Act, which made the Sherman Anti-Trust Act stricter by fixing a certain number of loopholes. The act was especially effective in uncovering the infamous Teapot Dome scandal (1927), a massive fraud and corruption case dealing with the conservation of U.S. public oil resources. Albert Fall, then secretary of the interior and a personal friend of President Warren G. Harding, was convicted for corruption. The investigation revealed that Fall had accepted bribes of $400,000 in cash and gifts from oil executive Harry Sinclair in exchange for leases to drill for oil at Teapot Dome, Wyoming, and from Edward Doheny, another tycoon who had expressed interest in oil reserves at Elk Hills, California.

Because of the position and influence of the parties involved, the ensuing lawsuit created great sensation and sent shock waves along the corridors of power in America. Not surprisingly, the most important pieces of white-collar crime legislation during the 20th century sought to increase the depth and scope of their authority. With the rapid growth and influence of the U.S. stock market, new opportunities for fraud flourished. By the early 20th century, millions of dollars worth of stocks were traded on the market. As a result, stock market manipulation became a substantial problem.

Stock Market Manipulation
Originally passed to regulate the secondary trading of securities (e.g., stocks, bonds), the Securities Exchange Act of 1934 was really meant to crack down on stock market manipulation. One example of such manipulation is insider trading, which can be defined as a fraudulent act by individuals entrusted with confidential information about important events who use such knowledge to make a profit or avoid losses on the stock market at the expense of those buying or selling their stock without the advantage of such nonpublic information. Notorious instances of insider trading include the cases of Ivan Boesky and Martha Stewart. Another form of stock market manipulation is what is known as a Ponzi scheme. This type of scam was named after Charles Ponzi, who convinced thousands of New England residents to place their money into a fraudulent postage stamp speculation scheme back in the 1920s. The fraud consisted in having people buy international reply coupons, which could then be redeemed for return postage from the recipient's nation at a much higher price. Ponzi promised his investors that he would double their investment in 90 days. The credibility of the plan was such that Ponzi managed to do so in only 45 days, which in turn attracted even more investors. The problem was that Ponzi had not bought the coupons, but only promised that he would, and early investors were actually paid with later investors' money. Ponzi was charged with 86 counts of mail fraud, tried and sentenced to five years in federal prison, then tried again on state charges in Massachusetts.

More recently, the Ponzi scheme by the nonexecutive chairman of the NASDAQ stock market Bernard Madoff cost investors an astounding $50 billion. Nevertheless, this colossal figure pales in comparison with the total cost of corporate crime (i.e., the "organized" version of white-collar crime), which undeniably represents a higher financial burden on society than does street crime. Controlling for inflation, the current cost of corporate crime to the United States may be around $500 billion, that is, between 20 and 25 times the cost of street crime. Importantly, this figure does not even include the combined costs of private sector corporate crime with fraud and government spending abuse.

The magnitude of the problem is such that even the Racketeer Influence and Corrupt Organizations (RICO) Act originally passed by Congress in 1970 to crackdown on organized crime was subsequently extended to apparently respectable corporate officials, particularly syndicate leaders suspected of ordering or assisting others in committing a large variety of offenses ranging from gambling and extortion to murder. In fact, RICO is very rarely applied to the Mafia *per se* and is mostly used against individuals, businesses, political protest groups, and terrorist organizations. The legal definition of racketeering includes unlawful activities such as embezzlement of union funds, bribery, money laundering, and other types of fraud. Not only did RICO facilitate the prosecution of corrupt organizations, it also allowed the seizure of the property of the accused (e.g., drugs, cars, mansions). A further novelty of RICO was the recovery of triple damages. That is, those found guilty would be ordered to pay a monetary compensation worth three times the amount of actual damages. Famous cases in which RICO was applied include the Hells Angels Motorcycle Club, Catholic sex abuses, the Key West Police Department, Major League Baseball, and pro-life activists, as well as various fraud cases, which testifies to the wide array of applicability of the act. Such versatility is necessary, considering the myriad forms white-collar crime can take.

Medical Fraud

In a society that relies so heavily on drugs and surgical procedures, illegal behaviors are inevitably bound to extend to the medical arena. Consumer healthcare fraud includes filing claims for non-received services or medications, forging or altering bills or receipts, or using someone else's coverage or insurance card. Medical fraud encompasses such illegal activities as accepting kickbacks, billing for unperformed services, falsifying diagnoses to justify unnecessary surgeries, upcoding (i.e., billing for a more expensive service than the one that was actually performed), unbundling (i.e., billing every stage of the same procedure as separate procedures), waiving patient copays or deductibles and overbilling the insurance carrier, or billing more than the copay amount for services prepaid by the benefit plan. Since its creation in 1965, Medicaid has been plagued by such fraud. Congress responded by enacting the Medicare-Medicaid Anti-Fraud and Abuse Amendments of 1977. Over the years, though, medical fraud has continued to be reported in general and psychiatric hospitals, ambulance services, laboratories, pharmacies, and nursing homes. Further, besides being financially detrimental to victims, healthcare fraud and abuse are particularly notorious for their impact on human life. Pharmaceutical companies and physicians have been shown to deliberately endanger human lives by releasing or prescribing dangerous drugs or inducing patients into unnecessary surgeries. The literature on white-collar crime is rife with examples of Hippocratic Oath violations, starting with the infamous Fen/Phen drug case, in which the injurious effects of a supposedly harmless anti-obesity medication were silenced until they had caused the death of more than 100 people. Another similar scandal was the thalidomide prescription disaster, in which a sleeping pill/tranquilizer caused 8,000 babies to be born deformed. Less reported examples of medical crimes include the countless numbers of health complications related to unnecessary—yet highly lucrative—silicone breast implant surgeries or Viagra prescriptions.

Thus, the claim that white-collar crimes are victimless—in the sense that those abuses are committed for the sole purpose of maximizing profits and do not physically endanger people—is unwarranted. For example, street crime is less costly to society in terms of loss of human life than is corporate crime. The empirical evidence supporting this claim is abundant. Despite legislation such as the 1970 Occupational Safety and Health Act meant to protect employee health and safety in the workplace, research shows that between 9,000 and 11,000 people die from preventable work-related accidents every year. Further, workplace

The New York Stock Exchange in Lower Manhattan in New York City. The Securities Exchange Act of 1934 was meant to crack down on stock market manipulation, like insider trading—one of the most costly forms of white-collar crime.

A young girl works in a Georgia cotton mill. President Franklin D. Roosevelt signed the Fair Labor Standards Act in 1938 and effectively put an end to child labor nationwide.

killings caused by exposure to toxins claim the lives of 50,000–70,000 workers. In fact, the total number of workplace deaths because of violation of law has been estimated to be as high as 59,000 and perhaps closer to 100,000 per year, compared to the 24,330 homicides reported by the Federal Bureau of Investigation (FBI) when homicide rates peaked in 1990.

Environmental Crime
The popular enthusiasm that resulted from advanced manufacturing processes in industrial societies rapidly gave way to growing concerns regarding the harmful impact on the air, water, and land. Such concerns were addressed by important pieces of legislation such as the 1906 Pure Food and Drug Act, which was directed at protecting consumers from dubious ingredients in patent medicines and adulteration of food with chemicals or inorganic material like sand. Legislation also included the 1956 Federal Water Pollution Control Act, the 1970 Clean Air Act, and 1976 Toxic Substances Control Act, which provided the U.S. Environmental Protection Agency (EPA) with authority to require accurate recording and testing of chemical and other hazardous substances from industrial companies. All too often, however, corporations would rather reach an out-of-court settlement with environmentally induced diseases or workplace manslaughter victims and their families, instead of investing in safety-conscious work environments. Man-made disasters such as the 1984 Union Carbide poisonous gas leak in Bhopal, India (which caused 558,125 injuries, including 38,478 temporary partial and nearly 4,000 severely and permanently disabling injuries), could have been avoided, but bribing officials and paying plaintiffs proven more cost-effective than prioritizing safety regulations in the workplace.

An important case in the history of physically harmful white-collar crimes was the 1972 Ford Pinto scandal, in which the car manufacturer giant Ford avoided a sentence for criminal homicide by paying millions of dollars in compensatory and punitive damages after its refusal to redesign a defective fuel tank on the Pinto model led to several deaths by burning in rear-end collisions. Such choice was the result of a risk/benefit calculation based on the National Highway Traffic Safety Administration's estimate for the dollar value of human life. Ford's decision to prioritize profit over public safety set a precedent in American understanding of illegal corporate behavior. Already impacted by the 1965 Federal Cigarette Labeling and Advertising Act and the 1971 Cigarette Advertizing Broadcast Ban, defendant tobacco companies accused of lying to their clients regarding the dangers associated with smoking are also notorious for settling out of court. Further, filing for bankruptcy is yet another, albeit last-resort, alternative to avoid paying claimants. Such was the case for the Johns-Manville Company, which was found guilty of lying to its employees about the link between asbestos (a silicate mineral then commonly used as a building material) and the fatal lung disease asbestosis. The passing of important pieces of legislature such as the 1972 Consumer Product Safety Act and the 1986 Pure Food and

Drug Act also helped legally define, uncover, and penalize physically harmful corporate practices. As a result of these laws, large industrial corporations are regularly found guilty of dangerous chemical exposure, both in manufactured foods and products (e.g., lead in toys) as well as in hazardous waste dumping, particularly in the vicinity of ethnic minorities with very limited legal recourse.

Labor Exploitation

Following the Great Depression, President Franklin D. Roosevelt signed the 1938 Fair Labor Standards Act, which effectively ended child labor nationwide. The act also sought to regulate adult working conditions by requiring employers to pay covered employees at least the federal minimum wage and overtime pay of one and one-half times the regular rate of pay. Nevertheless, and albeit provocative, the claim that modern slavery still exists in 21st-century America holds some truth. While exposure to information regarding the ghastly working conditions in U.S. company–owned southeast Asian sweatshops may be disconcerting to many, learning about the existence of domestic slavery among foreign workers on American soil is surely more difficult to accept. Still, Berkeley's Human Rights Center and the Washington D.C.–based antislavery group Free the Slaves have evidenced illegal practices in more than 90 American cities, ranging from prostitution and sex services to forced labor.

Violation of Antidiscrimination Laws

The conflicted relationship between gender and power is also inherent in sexual harassment and employment discrimination cases. Consequently, any violation of antidiscrimination laws (e.g., sexual harassment, racial and gender discrimination in the workplace) by an employer is ipso facto considered a form of white-collar crime. Because historically the U.S. economic system was modeled by and for affluent European males, disparities in opportunities at the racial, socioeconomic, and particularly gender levels abound, both in the streets and within the corporate world itself. A substantial body of literature has evidenced unfair salary differentials between men and women, as well as the lack of representation of ethnic minorities at the top executive positions, and this is in clear violation of the 1980 Equal Employment Opportunity Commission and affirmative action laws. In the age of globalization, some criminologists are calling for an even broader reconceptualization of the white-collar crime construct that would include a wider array of political deviant acts such as state and war crime, terrorist financing, and illegal invasion of sovereign nations. This proposition may have arisen from the fact that laypeople and social scientists alike tend to limit white-collar crime to petty frauds committed by unscrupulous but relatively modest employees (i.e., bank tellers) when in fact the worst, most socially harmful acts are perpetrated by high-ranking individuals or groups aware of their power and influence and confident in their legal immunity.

Cedric Michel
University of South Florida

See Also: 2001 to 2012 Primary Documents; Corruption, Contemporary; Madoff, Bernard; Pure Food and Drug Act of 1906; Sutherland, Edwin.

Further Readings

Brasch, Walter. *Muckrakers and the American Social Conscience.* Lanham, MD: University Press of America, 1990.

Hall, Jerome. *Theft, Law and Society.* New York: Bobbs-Merrill Company Inc., 1952.

Lynch, Michael and Raymond Michalowski. *Primer in Radical Criminology,* 4th ed. Monsey, NY: Criminal Justice Press, 2006.

Sutherland, Edwin. *White Collar Crime.* New York: Holt, Rinehart and Winston, 1949.

White-Collar Crime, Sociology of

Sociologists study the social causes and consequences of human behavior. In reference to crime, sociologists aim to analyze the nature, cause, and control of criminal activity. White-collar crimes create widespread and dramatic social harm exceeding that of street crimes like homicide and robbery.

What Is White-Collar Crime?

The term *white-collar crime* was first introduced in 1939 by Edwin Sutherland in an address to the American Sociological Association. Sutherland defined white-collar crime as "a crime committed by a person of respectability and high social status in the course of his occupation," reflecting Sutherland's desire to move academics' and society's focus beyond lower-class criminals. Emphasizing the high social status and occupational prestige of offenders in his definition of white-collar crime, Sutherland advanced criminological theory by drawing attention to deficits in poverty-driven theories of criminal behavior and how the opportunities for learning and engaging in criminal behavior vary across social and economic groupings.

Sutherland's landmark study of 980 law violations over 40 years by the 70 largest corporations of the early 1900s established that white-collar crimes like price-fixing, copyright infringement, or unfair labor practices were pervasive and committed early and often, with many corporations having multiple violations. These illegal practices often were committed early in the organization's history, contributing to the organization's success. Sutherland's working definition of white-collar crime included violations that were criminal (harmful to the public to be handled by law enforcement), civil (private damages to be settled among the parties), and regulatory (violations of government agency standards like the Environmental Protection Agency [EPA], the Occupational Safety and Health Administration [OSHA], or the Securities and Exchange Commission [SEC]). Criminal infractions made up only 16 percent of the incidents, but 60 percent of the corporations had at least one criminal conviction. Sutherland favored this expansive definition of white-collar crime and focused on the offender's status because even civil and regulatory violations inflict social harms and white-collar offenders are particularly unlikely to be criminally processed due to their high status.

Since Sutherland firmly established the study of white-collar crime in sociology, its definition has been greatly debated among scholars and enforcement agencies. Variations in the definition stem from the debate over whether the term should be offender- or offense-based. Both approaches have implications for what is considered white-collar crime and who are considered offenders. Offender-based approaches focus on occupational crimes that take place during the course of one's legitimate occupation and emphasize the high social status, power, and respectability of the actor. Offense-based definitions explore the modus operandi of how a particular crime is committed, regardless of the social status of the offender. In 1970, the Department of Justice proposed an offense-based definition, emphasizing crimes committed by nonphysical means that utilize deceit to gain personal or business advantage. This approach would include unemployed confidence men and low-rank employees as white-collar criminals along with politically powerful elites. By the 1980s, focus had shifted toward crimes committed within organizations, primarily corporations and government, with an emphasis on high-status employed individuals or groups and the organizational cultures and structures that facilitate or impede offending.

Types of White-Collar Crime

The majority of white-collar offenses typically share three common characteristics. First, white-collar crimes occur because individuals tend to have legitimate access to the location where the crime was committed. Second, the illegal actions of the offender have a superficial appearance of legitimacy. Third, white-collar crimes involve spatial separation between victims and offenders. These crimes tend to be comprised of complex and elaborate behaviors over periods of time, so researchers have tended to organize the offenses into several overarching categories.

Some of the most recognizable forms of white-collar crime fall under the realm of corporate fraud. These offenses are perpetrated within organizations and involve groups of offenders in collusion, or conspiring together. The majority of corporate fraud offenses that are studied include antitrust violations, securities fraud, tax fraud, bribery, credit fraud, false claims, mail fraud, and embezzlement. Often, the monetary sums that are involved with these types of crimes are large and require the use of organizational resources to commit.

Corporate violence is another major category of white-collar crime involving multiple offenders

A white-collar criminal is fingerprinted by a police officer. White-collar offenses range from various types of fraud to embezzlement to environmental and public safety offenses.

and organizational resources. Unlike corporate fraud, corporate violence involves organizations that produce and market products or services with knowledge that they are unsafe and may potentially injure or kill a consumer. Examples of this type of white-collar crime include the production of defective vehicles such as the Ford Pinto, cover-ups that result in health risks to the public as with the link between asbestos and cancer, and facilities with unsafe working conditions resulting in the harm or illness of workers.

Fraudulent activity by individuals in health and medical professions is another form of white-collar crime that also has the potential to directly endanger human life. Criminal activities in this category include administering unnecessary procedures or medications, directing patients to specific pharmacies, diverting prescription drugs for nonmedical use, insurance fraud, and filing false insurance claims. These types of crimes are estimated to cost the public billions of dollars and thousands of lives each year. The increasing number of medical procedures that individuals receive in their lifetime suggests that the opportunity for such crimes to occur is growing.

Similar to white-collar crime, environmental crime has no commonly agreed-upon definition because of the wide and diverse nature of the offenses. Simply put, environmental crimes are acts that violate statutes meant to protect the environment. Committed by both organizations and individuals, they are extremely difficult to detect because of their nature and lack of directly identifiable victims. The system of enforcement of environmental regulations is continually negotiated, increasing the difficulty of uncovering and pursuing offenders. Hazardous-waste violations and fraudulent activities such as fabricating or falsifying data submitted to regulatory agencies are two primary types of offenses. Environmental offenses also include international smuggling of harmful toxins, improper training and handling of pesticides and other chemicals, and trafficking in endangered species. Environmental violations by organizations are often uncovered through self-reports, inspections by regulatory enforcement agencies, whistle blowing, or when accidents occur.

Instances of lower-level fraud, forgery, and embezzlement are common among employees and nonemployees and typically do not involve organizational resources or collusion. Such offenses typically include when a bank teller or accountant embezzles from his/her workplace for individual gain. Credit card and welfare frauds do not require employment, allowing more individuals the opportunities to offend, and tend not to involve large amounts of money. As such, it is debatable whether these offenses are properly considered white-collar crime.

Computers have played major roles in traditional white-collar crimes such as embezzlement; however, recently, they have enabled entirely new methods of crime. The illegal reproduction of digital materials and hacking are several of the most common computer white-collar crimes. Fraudulently obtaining personal and/or financial information via computers is a growing concern, but much of this information continues to be gained through conventional methods such as theft from a trash receptacle. Unlike corporate crime and many forms of environmental crime, computer crimes do not require the use of organizational resources or the assistance of others and are less likely to impact large groups of people. Regardless, recent estimates suggest that nearly 80 percent of computer crimes are committed by employees within an organization, the majority of which go unreported to authorities.

Studying White-Collar Crime

Determining the extent of white-collar crime remains challenging. Due to their incongruence with societal views of typical criminals, many white-collar offenders are never prosecuted and first-time offenders are treated with leniency due to their status. Additionally, political pressures impact the types of regulations that organizations must adhere to and the enforcement of those regulations. The result is that officials tend to focus their efforts on crimes committed by groups who lack power, such as youth or lower classes whose crimes are more easily uncovered and fall into more common categories of criminal activity.

A primary factor inhibiting the availability of systematic data on white-collar crime is that many violations take place over time. In such situations, it becomes necessary to determine whether an actual violation occurred, and if so, whether to count each specific instance as an individual violation or one continuous violation. These issues make data collection of offenses exceedingly problematic. Primary sources of data on criminal activities, including the Federal Bureau of Investigation's (FBI's) Uniform Crime Report (UCR), the National Crime Victimization Survey (NCVS), and self-report surveys are extremely valuable to researchers; however, these sources contain little to no information pertaining to corporate or occupational crimes. Criminal justice agencies and professional associations, with

The Federal Bureau of Investigation has broken down the white-collar crime of telemarketing into five categories: charity room (falsely collecting money for charity), prize room (callers send a fee to collect an alleged prize won), product room (purchased product is worth less than claimed or was never delivered), recovery room (fraud victims told they can recover their money by paying a fee), and rip and tear: scammers taking as much fraud money as possible and leaving town.

few exceptions, do not keep statistics of occupational crimes, and when violations do occur, most employers rely on unofficial sanctions, such as termination. Also, law enforcement is often the responsibility of state and federal regulatory agencies instead of criminal justice agencies.

Despite a lack of systematic data and funding, sociologists continue to study white-collar crime by performing qualitative case studies of regulatory agencies and/or organizations in addition to studying violations or victimizations of specific offenses such as embezzlement. From these studies, demographic information of both offenders and victims has been derived. Although the applicability of these studies is unknown, together they comprise the most comprehensive data sources available for addressing white-collar crime.

Opportunity influences who is able to commit white-collar crimes. Most white-collar crimes occur in the context of organizations, so factors such as the structure of the labor market determine which individuals will be in a position to offend. Overall, women and minorities are still less likely to hold senior-level positions, which restricts their ability to commit highly profitable white-collar offenses requiring high occupational status and accompanying resources. Crimes of fraud and embezzlement are less likely to require the offender to have a high occupational status or access to specialized resources, resulting in a greater opportunity for females and nonwhites to offend.

Using an offense-based definition of white-collar crime that includes antitrust violations, bribery, embezzlement, and various forms of fraud, previous research has shown that the majority of white-collar offenders are employed, middle-aged white males with at least a high school education. However, the demographics vary slightly depending on the particular offense. Most individuals who commit antitrust violations, securities fraud, tax evasion, and bribery tend to be middle-aged white males with medium to high incomes and at least a high school diploma. If one considers individuals who commit crimes of fraud and embezzlement to be white-collar offenders, they tend to be younger in age, have lower incomes and educational levels than those committing other white-collar offenses, and are also more likely to be nonwhite or female.

Victims of White-Collar Crime

Sutherland's emphasis on crimes involving organizations and corporations directs attention to how victimization is often diffuse and hidden, making the identification of victimization patterns difficult. In some instances, individuals may not be aware of their victimization, as with certain types of identity fraud, and in many instances, victims choose not to report the crime to police. To complicate matters, sometimes entire organizations or groups (e.g., consumers, workers, or the public) are targets of white-collar crime. Overall, the lack of systematic data and difficulty in detection means very little is known about white-collar crime victims. Criminologists agree, however, that personal fraud victimization is common and that the financial and social costs of serious white-collar crime far outpace those of street crime.

Sociological Theories of White-Collar Crime

Sociologists are concerned with and theorize about the factors that cause individuals and organizations to break the law. Rational choice theory has been used to explain white-collar crime based on its assumption that all actors are self-interested and make calculated decisions about whether to engage in criminal behavior by estimating the costs and benefits. Rational choice theory suggests that perceptions of the certainty and severity of punishment and other characteristics of the criminal event like potential profit affect the likelihood of offending. However, sociologists have identified other social influences besides an individual's perceived risk and potential reward that increase the likelihood of committing a white-collar crime, such as being presented with opportunities for offending and having the requisite motivation and know-how to capitalize on those opportunities.

Sutherland's differential association theory suggests that criminal behavior is learned from others who define the behavior favorably. In the organizational context, individuals are socialized to accept certain attitudes and behaviors that may be contrary to the law but that over time become viewed as acceptable and even necessary business practices. Deviant organizational cultures often do not promote obedience to the law and can persist over time because the informal norms remain, despite changes in written policies, procedures, or personnel. As behaviors and attitudes pass from one cohort of executives and employees to the next, illegal practices become known as "business as usual." Besides organizational norms, a consistently important factor is opportunity. Opportunities to engage in illegitimate practices vary depending on the individual's social position, as well as the organizational structure, type of organization, and the regulatory structures that govern the rules for organizational behavior. Organizations that utilize complex procedures or that have elaborate vertical and horizontal hierarchies provide increased opportunities for offending due in part to the increased difficulty of discerning a violation.

Anomie theory explores America's overemphasis on material success and individual achievement coupled with its lesser emphasis on using legitimate means to achieve success. Such pressures to achieve success influence both organizational and individual behavior; those who are less able to achieve success through legitimate means sometimes look to alternative and possibly illegitimate means. Success is often measured in comparison with others in similar life situations. Relative deprivation, and an increased propensity to offend, may develop when one perceives similar others as being unfairly advantaged. Thus, some wealthy individuals are likely to participate in criminal behavior because they compare themselves to others whose wealth exceeds their own and accept illegal means as permissible to gain ground. An integrated theory of white-collar crime incorporates crucial elements of several sociological theories, including differential association, anomie, and others to better understand causes of white-collar crime. This perspective emphasizes the important roles of opportunity, motivation, and rationalization of criminal behavior. Motivations originate from cultures of competition and are spread through organizational and occupational subcultures. White-collar crime is more likely to occur when actors who have learned motivations and techniques come across attractive opportunities.

Jennifer Schwartz
Joseph Kremer
Washington State University

See Also: 2001 to 2012 Primary Documents; Crime in America, Distribution; Crime in America, Types; Enron; White-Collar Crime, Contemporary; White-Collar Crime, History of.

Further Readings
Benson, Michael L. and Sally S. Simpson. *White-Collar Crime: An Opportunity Perspective*. New York: Routledge, 2009.
Braithwaite, J. "White-Collar Crime." *Annual Review of Sociology*, v.11 (1985).
Coleman, J. W. "Toward an Integrated Theory of White-Collar Crime." *American Journal of Sociology*, v.93 (1987).
Daly, K. "Gender and Varieties of White-Collar Crime." *Criminology*, v.26 (1989).
Sutherland, Edwin. *White Collar Crime*. New York: Holt, Rinehart and Winston, 1949.

Whitney v. California

In *Whitney v. California* (1927), the U.S. Supreme Court upheld restrictions on free speech and association. During the early 20th century, the court struggled to define the constitutional limits of free speech. The court developed two competing tests for the constitutionality of government restrictions on speech. In *Patterson v. Colorado* (1907), the court established the "bad tendency" test. Under this test, the state did not have to prove that any illegal action resulted from the speech but merely demonstrate that the speech might have a tendency to cause illegal activity. In *Schenck v. United States* (1919), Oliver Holmes, writing for the majority, established the "clear and present danger" test for government restrictions on speech. Under this more rigorous test, unprotected speech must be likely to incite an imminent and substantive harm. However, in subsequent cases, the court continued to apply the looser bad tendency test instead.

Under dispute in *Whitney v. California* was the constitutionality of California's Criminal Syndicalism Act, which criminalized participation in organizations that advocated political or industrial reform by means of sabotage, terrorism, or other illegal means. Between 1917 and 1920, more than 20 states passed criminal syndicalism statutes. States prosecuted and convicted people who did not actually engage in violence but who merely advocated radical social change or who joined an organization devoted to radical social change. These laws were used to curb free speech and union organizing. The laws effectively criminalized membership in radical unionist organizations, such as the Industrial Workers of the World (IWW), and criminalized speech in support of such organizations and their goals.

In 1925, California convicted and jailed Charlotte Anita Whitney—who was former U.S. Supreme Court Justice Stephen Field's niece—for helping to organize the Communist Labor Party (CLP). The state held that the CLP advocated violent revolution. Whitney argued that violence was not the purpose for which she and the other organizers had created the CLP. Whitney argued that California's Criminal Syndicalism Act violated her First Amendment right to free speech. She lost in the lower courts. The *Whitney* majority denied her First Amendment claims, ruling that states may punish speech "tending to incite to crime." Another issue was whether or not California's Criminal Syndicalism Act violated the Fourteenth Amendment guarantee of due process and equal protection. The court unanimously found for California.

Whitney was notable for the minority concurring opinion signed by Justices Louis Brandeis and Oliver Holmes and authored by Brandeis. Brandeis and Holmes concurred on the Fourteenth Amendment issue, but Brandeis argued against the bad tendency test and for the clear and present danger test, asserting that "Fear of serious injury cannot alone justify suppression of free speech and assembly." Brandeis's opinion in *Whitney* eventually became the foundation of modern free speech doctrine, although this did not occur immediately. In 1937, 10 years after *Whitney*, the court ruled in *DeJonge v. Oregon* that the First Amendment protects the right to participate in a peaceful meeting of an organization that advocates criminal syndicalism. However, in *Dennis v. United States* (1951), the court again applied the bad tendency test, upholding a conviction for teaching from books written by communists. In *Yates v. United States* (1957), the court overturned convictions of U.S. Communist Party officials, this time using the clear and present danger test.

In 1969, the court \ overturned *Whitney* with its *Brandenburg v. Ohio* decision. *Brandenburg* struck down Ohio's criminal syndicalism statute and established a new test for permissible speech, which distinguishes between mere advocacy of violent or illegal behavior—which is protected under the First Amendment—and incitement to such behavior, which is not protected. Under *Brandenburg*, unprotected speech deliberately creates a strong likelihood of imminent danger—a restatement of the clear and present danger rule.

Thomas F. Brown
Virginia Wesleyan College

See Also: Alien and Sedition Acts of 1798; *Brandenburg v. Ohio*; Due Process; Sedition Act of 1918.

Further Readings
Bhagwat, Ashutosh. "The Story of *Whitney v. California*: The Power of Ideas." In *Constitutional Law Stories*, Michael C. Dorf, ed. New York: Foundation Press, 2004.
Blasi, Vincent. "The First Amendment & the Ideal of Civic Courage: The Brandeis Opinion in *Whitney v. California*." *William & Mary Law Review*, v.29/653 (1988).
Collins, Ronald K. L. and David Skover. "Curious Concurrence: Justice Brandeis' Vote in *Whitney v. California*." *Supreme Court Review*, v.333 (2005).
Dee, Juliet. "*Whitney v. California*." In *Free Speech on Trial*, Richard A. Parker, ed. Tuscaloosa: University of Alabama Press, 2003.
Whitney v. California, 274 U.S. 357 (1927).

Wickersham, George

George Woodward Wickersham, lawyer, Republican Party leader, attorney general of the United States, and chairman of the National Commission on Law Observance and Enforcement, was born in Pittsburgh, Pennsylvania. He was the son of businessman Samuel Morris Wickersham and Elizabeth Cox. Following the death of his parents when he was young, he was raised by his maternal grandparents in Philadelphia. His childhood home was frequented by the city's social elite. His grandfather founded what was to become the

Philadelphia stock exchange. Wickersham studied civil engineering at Lehigh University. There, he met a leading Republican politician named Matthew Quay; Wickersham became Quay's private secretary and a student of law in the office of a prominent attorney named Robert McGrath. Wickersham enrolled in the University of Pennsylvania Law School in 1879, graduated a year later, and was admitted to the state's bar in 1880. He practiced law for two years in Philadelphia, where he met and married Mildred Wendell in 1883. That same year, he moved to New York and joined the firm of Strong and Cadwalader. He was aggressive and quickly gained status in the firm, making partner in four years. He continued to work at this law firm for the rest of his life, except for several interludes of public service.

Wickersham's legal reputation increased rapidly during the time of President William McKinley's and Theodore Roosevelt's administrations. His partners in the law firm included Henry W. Taft, brother of the secretary of war and future president. Specializing in bankruptcies and corporate reorganizations, his clients included major transportation and manufacturing companies. This allowed him to socialize with important leaders. When William Howard Taft became president in 1909, he appointed Wickersham to be his attorney general. A centerpiece of Wickersham's administration as attorney general was enforcement of the Sherman Anti-Trust Law. This law prevented the combination of entities that could potentially harm competition between businesses, such as monopolies or cartels. Wickersham commanded respect and engendered fear for his readiness to prosecute any corporation for attempting to monopolize an industry. During Taft's administration, Wickersham brought almost twice as many Sherman Act prosecutions in four years as Roosevelt had filed in eight years, a total of 89, including indictments against U.S. Steel, Standard Oil, International Harvester, Alcoa Aluminum, and Burroughs Adding Machine. This unprecedented use of the Sherman Act alienated sectors of big business and was thought to have helped contribute to Taft's defeat in the 1912 presidential election.

After Taft's defeat, Wickersham returned to private practice in New York but always kept a close watch on state, national, and international affairs. Between 1912 and 1929, he served on the commission for the reorganization of New York's state government created by Governor Alfred E. Smith. The outbreak of World War I and the debate about the nation's future role in world affairs brought Wickersham back into national politics. Aligning himself with the internationalist wing of the Republican Party, Wickersham backed the United States' participation in the League of Nations and supported the Allied cause. He continued to advocate a strong internationalist position for the country during the next decade.

Wickersham made his final contribution to public affairs at the age of 71, when he accepted the chairmanship of the National Commission on Law Observance and Enforcement, which later became known as the Wickersham Commission. This commission operated 1929–31. The commission produced 14 book-length reports, each dealing with a different topic of crime and justice. It was the 14th report that perhaps made the largest impact and became a catalyst for reforms involving new accountability for the police. This report addressed problems in police administration and called for more professionalization and proper training of officers. The Wickersham Commission gave a strong endorsement to the sociological approach to the study of crime, noting limitations of psychological and other approaches. In the years between the McKinley administration and the Great Depression, Wickersham made notable contributions to American law and politics in commercial law, enforcement of the Sherman Anti-Trust Act, international law, and criminal justice. A heart attack took his life in 1936 at the age of 78. He was buried in Rockside Cemetery in Englewood, New Jersey.

Kyle A. Burgason
University of Arkansas at Little Rock

See Also: National Commission on Law Observance and Enforcement; Police, Sociology of; Taft, William Howard (Administration of).

Further Readings

Gould, Lewis L. *The William Howard Taft Presidency.* Lawrence: University Press of Kansas, 2009.

Hall, Kermit, Samuel Walker, and Randoplh Boehm. *Records of the Wickersham Commission on Law*

Observance and Enforcement. Bethesda, MD: University Publications of America, 1997.

Parrish, Michael E. "Wickersham, George Woodward." American National Biography Online, 2000. http://www.anb/articles/06/06-00706.html (Accessed December 2010).

Wickersham Commission

In May 1929, President Herbert Hoover established the National Commission on Law Observance and Enforcement, or the Wickersham Commission, to investigate the state of law and order in the United States. The bipartisan commission included 11 notable political and academic figures, among them Attorney General George Wickersham (chairperson); Dean of the Harvard Law School Roscoe Pound; Secretary of War Newton Baker; and the leader of the Chicago Crime Commission, Frank Loesch. Other members included Henry Anderson, Ada Comstock, William Grubb, William Kenyon, Kenneth Mackintosh, and Paul McCormick. The Wickersham Commission's findings were published in 14 reports and released to the public in January 1931. Topics covered in these reports include Prohibition (Reports 1 and 2); criminal statistics (Report 3); prosecution and the federal courts (Reports 4, 7, and 8); deportation and crime among the foreign born (Reports 5 and 10); child offenders and the causes of juvenile delinquency (Report 6 and 13); penal institutions, probation, and parole (Report 9); lawlessness in law enforcement and policing (Reports 11 and 14); and the cost of crime (Report 12). A 15th report on the Mooney-Billings case was submitted to the commission, but not published as part of the original reports.

Prohibition

In 1920, the U.S. Congress passed the Eighteenth Amendment, making it illegal to manufacture, sell, or transport intoxicating liquors in the United States. Prohibition was highly controversial, and nearly $100,000 of the funds used to investigate it was donated by private groups. The commission's findings on the issue overshadowed criminal justice issues raised in remaining commission reports. The report is divided into three sections: a lengthy discussion of liquor enforcement, a brief list of conclusions, and individual statements from each commissioner. The report highlighted the significant challenges faced by law enforcement agencies seeking to shut down bootlegging (smuggling of liquor) and speakeasy (illegal nightclub) operations. Challenges of Prohibition enforcement included corruption among public officials, waning public support, and the profitability of alcohol. Four of the commissioners recommended maintaining the Eighteenth Amendment; the remaining advocated alterations or the outright repeal of Prohibition. In his statement to Congress on the commission's report, Hoover discouraged repeal and stated that Prohibition enforcement was improving. Prohibition was repealed by the Twenty-First Amendment in 1933.

Cost and Measurement of Crime

The commission's report on the costs of crime is the lengthiest report. The commission states that comprehensive data on the costs of crime are insufficient, but it does draw some conclusions about federal, state, and local government spending on crime, as well as the toll of crime on private industry and the general public. The greatest costs for the federal government are enforcement of laws against alcohol, narcotics, and motor vehicle theft. The majority of state funds are spent on correctional institutions and parole agencies, while the greatest cost for local jurisdictions is policing. The commission recommends an increased focus on organized crime, such as fraud, organized extortion, and an overhauling of criminal codes to remove ineffectual or unenforceable laws. In the early part of the 20th century, national and state-level measurement of crime and criminal justice system responses were inconsistent and unreliable. No U.S. state compiled crime statistics, one state (Massachusetts) compiled arrests statistics, 23 states compiled trial court statistics, and seven states compiled adult probation statistics. State and federal prison and jail statistics had been collected by the federal Bureau of Census since 1923. The commission makes recommendations for the federal government to undertake research to determine appropriate state statues for crime data collection and, upon adoption of such legislation by the states, for creating a centralized federal location where state data can be submitted and then disseminated.

Prosecution and Courts
Three concerns about prosecution are discussed by the commission: prosecutorial susceptibility to political influence and whims, inadequate selection and oversight of prosecutors, and lack of suitable safeguards for suspect interrogation. Research on the federal courts concentrates on the District of Connecticut federal court and is incomplete at the time of publication.

Immigration and the Foreign Born
The commission states that the treatment of both legal and undocumented immigrants is unconstitutional, tyrannical, and oppressive. The commission recommends better-qualified immigration inspectors, increased transparency in legal processes, decentralization of immigration enforcement, the creation of an independent review board, and increased border enforcement. Like its report on Prohibition, the commission's report on crime and the foreign born is controversial. The first quarter of the report is devoted to tracing patterns in American public opinion on crime and the foreign born and describing successive waves of anti-immigrant sentiments in the country. The general conclusion of the remaining sections of the report is that the popular view that the foreign born commit more crime than the native born is overstated, if not altogether incorrect.

Child Offenders and the Causes of Delinquency
The commission's report on child offenders focuses on how young offenders are processed in the federal justice system. The report calls for the federal government to refrain from processing child offenders, except in cases where state juvenile justice systems are inadequate. Emphasis is placed on treating young offenders as distinct from adults and for punishments of juveniles to stress education and supervision rather than retribution. The commission's report on the causes of juvenile delinquency emphasizes the role of social disorganization as opposed to individual characteristics as the cause of delinquency. Causes of social disorganization include unregulated industrial growth in cities, nonexistent or weak community or neighborhood organizations, and high residential turnover. No specific recommendations are made based on this report.

Penal Institutions, Probation, and Parole
This report was highly critical of American prisons. They are described as antiquated, overcrowded, inefficient, and incapable of meeting the objectives of reformation of the criminal and protection of society. Prison staff is described as unprofessional and overworked. Report authors advise against the building of new maximum-security prisons; for improving the health and sanitary conditions of existing facilities; for more humane disciplinary practices; for the reform of indeterminate-sentencing practices; and for improved processes to select, compensate, and train prison personnel.

They also argue for equitable prison work programs (and the elimination of prison contract labor) and for the provision of educational opportunities for prisoners. With regard to probation and parole, the commission argues for the establishment of well-compensated, central parole boards in each state; for the increase in competent parole and probation officers and the decrease of these officers' caseloads; and for the broadening of probation as a viable alternative to prison for sentenced offenders.

Policing
Investigations into the state of American policing were compiled by August Vollmer, a respected academic and police administrator. The commission highlights numerous problems with law enforcement. Police leadership is described as incompetent, unduly influenced by local politicians and criminal figures, and vulnerable to changing political whims—the average tenure for local police chiefs was less than four years. Rank-and-file officers are criticized as being untrained, uneducated, inefficient, overwhelmed, and corrupt. Policing organizations are described as having out-of-date communications systems and ineffective law enforcement tools. The commission makes several recommendations to improve policing, including insulating police agencies from the corrupting influence of politics, improving training and pay of officers, improving policing equipment and recordkeeping, and expanding state-level law enforcement agencies. Report authors

also emphasize a need for increasing the ethnic and racial diversity of local police forces. The focus of the report on lawlessness in law enforcement is on the "third degree," or the infliction of physical or mental suffering to obtain information about a crime. Researchers conclude that use of the third degree by police officers is widespread and includes activities such as verbal and physical threats, beating with the hands or with objects, protracted questioning, and illegal detention. The practice was primarily used against suspects, though in some cases it was also used against witnesses. Victims of the third degree were most frequently young (under the age of 25), black, and poor. No specific recommendations are included in this section of the report.

Mooney-Billings Case

This report was the third federal investigation into the Mooney-Billings case. Though submitted to the commission in 1931, it was not published until a reprinting of the commission's reports in 1968. The report examines the investigation and legal proceedings of labor rights advocates Thomas Mooney and Warren Billings. Both men were indicted and convicted of first-degree murder for exploding a bomb along the route of the Preparedness Parade in San Francisco on July 22, 1916. Billings was sentenced to life imprisonment, while Mooney was sentenced to death. Researchers pinpoint the problematic handling of the Mooney-Billings case from investigation to appeal, including ignoring of evidence pointing to other suspects; illegal methods of arrest, detention, and search; questionable methods of identification; use of unreliable, coached, and even perjured testimony by prosecutorial witnesses; deliberate attempts to provoke public prejudice against the defendants; and the use of propaganda to prevent the release of Mooney and Billings after evidence of illegal investigation and prosecution practices were revealed. Both Mooney and Billings were eventually pardoned by the California governor in the late 1930s.

Impact of the Wickersham Commission

Though the commission had issued the most comprehensive study of the American criminal justice system to date, its findings were overshadowed by popular debates on Prohibition and by the social and economic turmoil caused by the Great Depression. Many of the challenges of crime and the problems with the U.S. criminal justice system discussed by the Wickersham Commission were echoed in President Lyndon Johnson's 1967 Crime Commission on Law Enforcement and the Administration of Justice report, *The Challenges of Crime in a Free Society*.

Elyshia D. Aseltine
Lycoming College

See Also: Corruption, History of; Deportation; Police Abuse; Prohibition.

Further Readings
DrugText.org. "Wickersham Commission Report." http://www.drugtext.org/Table/Wickersham-Commission-Report (Accessed January 2012).
Wickersham Commission. *U.S. National Commission on Law Observance and Enforcement*. Upper Saddle River, NJ: Patterson Smith, 1968.

Wilson, James Q.

Professor, political scientist, and public policy expert James Q. Wilson has served on the faculty of several institutions, including Harvard, Pepperdine, the University of California, Los Angeles (UCLA), and most recently Boston College. Among the country's most eminent scholars in his field, Wilson has authored numerous articles and authored or coauthored more than 12 books addressing various aspects of government, social issues, and public administration. He is the former president of the American Political Science Association (APSA) and has received numerous awards in recognition of his contributions to scholarship, including the Presidential Medal of Freedom, the APSA Lifetime Achievement Award, and honorary degrees from six universities, including Harvard. Wilson has held prominent leadership roles on a variety of federal commissions, beginning with his appointment to the White House Task Force on Crime in 1966, followed by service on the National Commission on Drug Use Prevention in the Nixon administration, the attorney general's Task Force on Violent

Crime in the Reagan administration, and a member of the president's Foreign Intelligence Advisory Board from 1985 to 1991.

Causes of Crime

Among other issues addressed by Wilson in his research and writing is the relationship between crime and public policy. He has authored or coauthored several books on crime and related (societal morality/ethics) issues including *Thinking About Crime*, *Crime: Public Policies for Crime Control* with Joan Petersilia, and *Crime & Human Nature: The Definitive Study of the Causes of Crime* with Richard Herrnstein. Additionally, he has contributed a range of articles to the scholarly literature addressing public policy and crime. He is perhaps best known in criminology and sociology circles and for his innovative "broken windows" theory of urban decay and community decline.

In a March 1982 article published in *Atlantic Monthly*, "Broken Windows: The Police and Neighborhood Safety," Wilson and coauthor George Kelling outline their rationale as to how small-scale physical problems and petty crime can lead to the deterioration of the stability and safety of neighborhoods. If within a neighborhood small problems such as broken windows, or street lamps, or the presence of graffiti are dealt with swiftly and decisively, it reflects that residents care for their community and are proactive in response to problems that arise, including petty criminal acts. It reflects pride aesthetically and otherwise in the area and may signal willingness on the part of the community to actively monitor their area and contact the police or other appropriate governmental agencies swiftly as needed.

Broken Windows Theory

Conversely, broken windows theory holds that if a broken window, abandoned vehicle, or graffiti is left unreported and unresolved, it conveys that members of the community are less concerned and perhaps less prone to report problems in the community to local authorities. Such lack of concern for smaller problems can lead to escalation, as perpetrators may commit bolder and more frequent acts if they sense the community is apathetic about such occurrences and that there will be no consequences. What was a single damaged window or street lamp may escalate to widespread vandalism.

A single abandoned car being cannibalized for parts as it sits in the street can lead to other more serious property crimes such as burglaries. Tolerating some small-scale, localized loitering on the part of teenagers or transients can allow escalation to the point that the area becomes a focal point for gangs, drug users, or panhandlers. The physical condition of the area can decline rapidly, with buildings and property in disrepair, public utilities destroyed, and litter increasingly commonplace. As the community begins to deteriorate, law-abiding citizens out of safety concerns or a sense of helplessness may be increasingly less prone to intervene. Residents and perhaps businesses as well may begin to move out of the area, replaced by more lawless elements that potentially see the area as more tolerant of their activities, which further speeds the decline.

To avoid falling victim to such a vicious cycle of crime and urban decay, the theory contends that proactive responses must be implemented from the onset. In a prompt manner, broken or damaged windows, doors, or other physical infrastructure should be repaired. Abandoned items and litter should be removed. Aesthetic concerns should be addressed, such as repainting tagged fences or walls. Public areas such as streets, sidewalks, and bus stops should be properly maintained. Also, petty criminal acts such as loitering, panhandling, truancy, and disorderly conduct should be swiftly addressed by law enforcement and other appropriate agencies.

Theory in Action

Broken windows theory can serve as a geographical predictor of the potential for the development of problems, including increased crime in areas exhibiting early symptoms. Numerous studies have shown the validity of the theory in real-world conditions, including a much-publicized study of crime-prone neighborhoods of Lowell, Massachusetts, that exhibited marked reduction in crime stemming from a commitment by the city to implement the ideas espoused by this theory: cleaning up trash, bringing buildings up to code, repairing street lights and other damaged utilities, and ticketing loiterers and other offenders. Many law enforcement agencies and local governments have embraced the concept, along with the broader idea of pre-emptive approaches to policing and neighborhood well-being. Historically, policing has been more reactive, in that officers would respond to occurrences only after the fact. However, if the onset of problems in communities can be predicted by certain physical or social indicators, as broken windows theory contends, the more severe problems can be averted via prompt positive action on the part of local authorities.

Wilson and Kelling's theory is not without its critics. Many scholars have noted that a complex range of other variables will collectively be more important in determining crime rates and urban decline. An example of the latter would be the socioeconomic makeup of a community and the financial stability of its residents and businesses, and correspondingly, the ability of the community's services to effectively meet the needs of infrastructure maintenance and repair and other demands.

Barry D. Mowell
Broward College

See Also: Crime in America, Causes; Crime Prevention; Urbanization.

Further Readings

Kelling, George and Catherine Coles. *Fixing Broken Windows: Restoring Order and Reducing Crime in Our Communities*. New York: Free Press, 1998.

Kelling, George and James Wilson. "Broken Windows Theory: The Police and Neighborhood Safety." *Atlantic Monthly* (March 1982).

Wilson, James and Richard Herrnstein. *Crime and Human Nature: The Definitive Study of the Causes of Crime*. New York: Free Press, 1998.

Wilson, O. W.

Orlando Winfield Wilson (1900–72) was an advocate of modern policing. He was born in South Dakota on May 15, 1900, which placed him at a pivotal point in American policing. Early in his career, O. W. Wilson attended the University of California, Berkeley, and graduated with a degree in criminology. He was a student of August Vollmer, the chief of police in Berkeley, California, who was considered by many to be the father of modern law enforcement.

Early in his career, Wilson served as a police officer in the Berkeley, California, Police Department, a position that helped him finance his university tuition. An educated police officer with a university degree offered enlightened insight and had an exceptional law enforcement credential during that era. During the mid-1920s, Wilson gained his first law enforcement field executive experience as the Fullerton, California, chief of police, a term that lasted two years.

Wilson eventually became a professor at the University of California, Berkeley, leading the crusade to modernize American police work. He advocated the use of many of the same modern innovations as August Vollmer: centralized records, investigative process organization, communications through the call box system, motorcycle patrol, and marksmanship training for police officers.

After his tenure in academia, Wilson rejoined active duty with the Wichita, Kansas, Police Department in 1928 and served until 1939. Again, he modernized the police department in the Vollmer tradition and required a college degree for employment. He strove for police modernizations and innovations that included police cars for patrol, mobile two-way radios, and the use of the mobile crime laboratory. In addition, Wilson taught at Harvard University during the 1930s at the Harvard Bureau for Street Traffic Research.

Military and Academic Service

World War II changed national priorities and swept many young Americans into the crisis. Wilson joined the war effort with considerable energy and imagination. During the war, he served as provost marshal, the equivalent of a civilian chief of police. At the end of the war, many soldiers departed immediately; however, Wilson stayed on until 1947 as a consultant to German police agencies and other police forces in Europe to contribute to their reorganization and stability for peacekeeping functions. Wilson's four years of eminent military service included the posts of chief of the Supreme Headquarters of the Allied Expeditionary Force (SHAEF) in England and director of public safety in Germany, and two decorations, the Bronze Star and the Legion of

Merit. He eventually retired as a full U.S. Army colonel in the military police branch.

After World War II, Wilson became the dean of the School of Criminology at Berkeley, California, for a decade during the 1950s. His concepts served as the foundation for American policing. He increased efficiency by emphasizing the application of scientific management principles. His textbook on police administration, written while he served as professor, became a bestseller. Wilson's management and leadership strategies served as policing doctrine in the United States. He advocated the importance of crime analysis long before it became the current policing strategy.

Chicago and Beyond

The 1960s saw the Chicago Police Department hurled into turmoil and racial controversy. Mayor Richard J. Daley, in the midst of a corruption scandal, sought Wilson's help. His appointment to police commissioner served as a primary method for Wilson to conduct a nationwide search for a new superintendent of the Chicago Police Department. The search committee and the mayor eventually decided that Wilson himself was the best candidate, and he accepted the appointment in March 1960.

Wilson's administrative approach facilitated the reorganization of the entire Chicago Police Department. The first step was to move the superintendent's office from city hall to police headquarters. Wilson's hands-on approach to management and corruption reform was a challenge for any leader. Central to Wilson's reform was the establishment of a nonpartisan police board to assist with governance. Higher standards for recruiting and hiring police officers were the first priority. The new police board also assisted in supervising graft, corruption, and police discipline procedures. Superintendent Wilson restructured police boundaries and beats without considering the political ramifications. He was on the frontier of improving the communications system, recordkeeping systems, and even computer software. He eliminated many of the foot patrols in favor of the more mobile response of patrol cars to improve response time. Wilson favored single-officer patrol cars.

Wilson was quick to recognize the source of racial tension in Chicago, and he instituted many political reforms in response. He tried to improve police community relations with the African American community. Wilson hired African Americans and sought their promotion through the ranks of the police department. Moreover, he demanded police restraint and good judgment in race relations. Morale improved in the Chicago Police Department under Wilson's leadership. He made a significant contribution that restored the public image until his retirement in 1967. His contributions in Chicago are legendary; his influence remains a reform model for police administrators across the nation. Wilson's firm guidance and leadership made a significant contribution to the field of law enforcement.

Unfortunately, Wilson's effective leadership did not lead to continued easing of racial conflict and political turmoil after his retirement. By 1968, police officers were poorly deployed and supervised throughout Chicago. Officers initiated attacks on demonstrators, reporters, and unwitting pedestrians. The adverse publicity from the Democratic National Convention in August 1968 reverberated around the world.

O. W. Wilson's distinguished career unfolded with extraordinary distinction in three fields: academia, law enforcement, and military. His influence and writing in the United States and Europe placed him in a category of his own that has been unmatched since. Wilson's career continues through his writing as the force in the field of law enforcement. Orlando Winfield Wilson, a legend in his field, died on October 18, 1972.

Thomas E. Baker
University of Scranton

See Also: Chicago, Illinois; Community Policing and Relations; Vollmer, August.

Further Readings

Baker, T. E. *Effective Police Leadership: Moving Beyond Management*, 3rd ed. New York: Looseleaf Publications Law, 2010.

Cordner, Gary W. and Kathryn E. Scarborough. *Police Administration*, 7th ed. Cincinnati, OH: Anderson Publishing, 2010.

Fyfe, James J., Jack R. Green, William F. Walsh, and O. W. Wilson. *Police Administration*. New York: McGraw-Hill, 1996.

Wilson, Woodrow (Administration of)

Thomas Woodrow Wilson (1856–1924), the 28th president of the United States, was a leader of the Progressive movement and won the Nobel Peace Prize in 1919. He was born in Staunton, Virginia, the third of four children of Reverend Dr. Joseph Ruggles Wilson and Jessie Janet Woodrow. Both of his parents were predominantly of Scottish heritage. Although Wilson was raised in an educated household, he was over 10 years of age before he learned to read, a difficulty that may have indicated dyslexia. In 1873, he attended Davidson College in North Carolina for one year, then transferred to Princeton University, where he graduated with a baccalaureate degree in 1879.

Wilson attended the University of Virginia law school in 1879, but his frail health caused him to withdraw. He continued his studies at home in Wilmington, North Carolina. In 1882, he practiced law in Atlanta, Georgia. He entered Johns Hopkins University graduate school in 1883, and three years later earned a doctorate in history and political science. Before becoming a professor of jurisprudence and political economy at Princeton in 1890, he lectured at Cornell University from 1886 to 1887, served as professor at Bryn Mawr College from 1885 to 1888, and was a professor of history at Wesleyan University from 1888 to 1890. Wilson was appointed president of Princeton University in 1902 and served until 1910.

His first marriage was in 1885, to Ellen Louise Axson, the daughter of a minister from Rome, Georgia. They had three daughters: Margaret Wilson (1886–1944), Jessie Wilson (1887–1933), and Eleanor Wilson (1889–1967). Ellen Wilson died in 1914, and Wilson married Edith Gait in 1915. In 1910, Wilson ran for governor of New Jersey. He focused his campaign on his independence from machine politics, with the promise that if elected, he would not yield to party elites. He was elected governor in 1911 and served in that post until 1913, when he became president.

As governor, Wilson successfully pushed for reforms, until the Republicans won control of both houses in 1912. He sought and received the nomination for president by the Democratic Party, with Thomas Marshall as his vice president.

A monument to President Thomas Woodrow Wilson stands in Poznan, Poland. Wilson had a vision of a world where freedom, justice, and peace could flourish.

Wilson won the presidential election of 1912, took office in March 1913, and set about instituting many reforms, including the changing of the tariff, the revising of the banking system, the monitoring of monopolies and fraudulent advertising, and the prohibiting of unfair business practices. During his two terms, he passed major domestic legislation such as improving safety conditions in factories and mines, giving women the right to vote, and ending child labor.

World War I and Beyond

While Wilson was successful in most of his domestic agenda, he spent 1914 through early 1917 attempting to keep the United States out of World War I. He maintained a neutral approach until 1917. Following the sinking of the British ship *Lusitania*, which killed 120 Americans, and after German submarines began sinking unarmed American merchant vessels, the United States entered the war. After the war, he used his famous Fourteen Points address to introduce the vision of a world in which freedom, justice, and peace could flourish.

Foreign influences that affected Wilson's administration included the first Red Scare, from 1919 to 1920, which began following the Russian Revolution of 1917, and the patriotic years of World War I. Fear of the Communist Party, labor union advocacy activities, and strikes were associated with crimes against society, conspiracies against the government, and plots of the Communist establishment. The U.S. political and economic establishments were targeted for terrorist bombings by political radicals, and eight bombs simultaneously exploded in eight cities on June 2, 1919. Thousands of resident aliens were arrested and deported. From 1919 to 1920, laws prohibiting violent protests in demanding and achieving social change were enacted by several states. These criminal syndicalism laws supported aggressive investigation by police, jailing, and deportation of the accused or persons suspected of being either Communist or left-wing.

Wilson's administration was also challenged by crime and criminal activities of the Prohibition era. The prohibition of alcohol began in 1920, with the passage of the Eighteenth Amendment, and ended in 1933. Corruption and criminality were rampant during this time. Businesses dealing in alcohol were commonly raided, and many bar owners bribed police officers to ignore them or to notify them of raids. Law enforcement had difficulty controlling individuals who either wanted to drink or intended to profit from the sale of alcohol. The mob and other gangs held control of the majority of the illegal liquor trafficking.

Despite Wilson's expressed view of a world of freedom and justice, his administration was dangerous to the civil rights of African Americans. He maintained the well-established Jim Crow system of segregation, which restricted African American employment in the federal government.

Felix O. Chima
Prairie View A&M University

See Also: History of Crime and Punishment in America: 1900–1950; New Jersey; Prohibition.

Further Readings
Lawrence, David. *The True Story of Woodrow Wilson.* New York: George H. Doran Co., 1924.
Link, Arthur. *Woodrow Wilson and a Revolutionary World, 1913–1921.* Chapel Hill: University of North Carolina Press, 1982.
Pestritto, Ronald J. *Woodrow Wilson and the Roots of Modern Liberalism.* Lanham, MD: Rowman & Littlefield, 2005.

Wisconsin

Located in the midwest, Wisconsin is the 30th of the United States, admitted to the Union in 1848. Home to more than 5.8 million residents, Wisconsin is bordered by Minnesota and Iowa to the west, Illinois to the south, the Upper Peninsula of Michigan and Lake Superior to the north, and Lake Michigan to the east. Wisconsin encompasses urban areas such as its largest city, Milwaukee, and its capital, Madison, as well as many smaller communities and farms. Wisconsin's history of crime, police, and punishment buttresses its dual nature as a cradle of progressive policies and as a deeply traditional breeding ground for law-and-order procedures. The state courts are organized into circuit courts, appellate courts, and the Wisconsin Supreme Court. The Wisconsin state legislature was an early opponent of capital punishment, and its criminal laws have tended to be progressive in that they have stressed rehabilitation rather than punishment. Although a mid-sized state, Wisconsin has experienced several serial killers in its history. The Wisconsin State Patrol polices the highways, and county sheriffs and local constabulary provide other safety services.

The Wisconsin Supreme Court was established in 1841, five years after Wisconsin became a separate territory and seven years before it became a state, and is the highest appellate court in the state. The court comprises seven justices, who are elected for 10-year terms as a result of statewide, nonpartisan elections. If a vacancy occurs on the court, the Wisconsin governor may appoint a justice to fill the vacancy, but that justice must stand for election in the first year no other justice's term expires. The chief justice of the Wisconsin Supreme Court is that body's longest-serving justice, although that individual may decline the position. The Wisconsin Supreme Court has a long history as an independent and activist group. During the 1850s, for example, the Wisconsin Supreme Court battled the federal judicial system regarding the U.S. district court's ability to enforce the Fugitive Slave Act. The matter was resolved in *Ableman v. Booth* (1859), which held that state courts may not issue rulings that contradict the decisions of federal courts. Since 1977, the Wisconsin Supreme Court has been assisted in appellate matters by the Wisconsin Court of Appeals, which exists primarily to correct errors that occurred at the trial level. The Wisconsin Circuit Courts are the primary trial venues in the state and hear and decide a wide variety of issues, including cases involving juvenile delinquency, traffic matters, and criminal law.

There are 69 circuits, 66 of which serve individual counties, and three of which serve two counties each (Buffalo/Pepin, Florence/Forest, and Shawano/Menominee). Circuit courts have personal jurisdiction over defendants in criminal cases if the defendant violates a Wisconsin law while in the state, or commits an act out-of-state that contributes to a crime the consequences of which occur in Wisconsin.

State highways are policed by the Wisconsin State Patrol, which, with slightly more than 500 sworn members, has a smaller per capita force than many other jurisdictions. County sheriff's offices are responsible for patrolling rural areas of Wisconsin, as well as towns and villages that are too small for their own independent police forces. All of Wisconsin's approximately 190 cities have their own independent police forces.

Corrections

Although the death penalty was included in the Wisconsin Territory's initial constitution of 1838, efforts immediately began to repeal its use. A bill to abolish the death penalty passed the Wisconsin Territorial Assembly in 1847 but failed to pass the senate. During the period in which Wisconsin was a territory, 1836–48, at least seven defendants were executed, although several of these executions were carried out pursuant to military or Indian law. After Wisconsin became a state in 1848, only one execution was carried out, that of John McCaffary in 1851. McCaffary's execution revived the move to abolish the death penalty in Wisconsin, which was accomplished in 1853. Since that time, no criminal defendant has been executed in Wisconsin. Efforts to reinstate the death penalty have been made from time to time, usually in response to current events. This occurred in 1866 when Wisconsin supporters of the execution of former Confederate President Jefferson Davis advocated such a move and when a bill was introduced asking for reinstatement in 1937, shortly after the kidnapping of Charles Lindbergh's baby. During the height of Wisconsin Senator Joseph McCarthy's influence during the 1950s, his supporters also unsuccessfully pushed to have the death penalty reinstated. In 2006, an advisory referendum showed that 55 percent of Wisconsin voters favored restoring capital punishment, but the Wisconsin legislature did not take action to do so at that time. Despite not having a death penalty, Wisconsin's per capita murder rate is below the national average. Wisconsin also faces less violent crime per capita than many other states. In 2009, for example, Wisconsin crime statistics reported 14,533 violent crimes, which included 144 murders or manslaughters, 1,108 forcible rapes, 4,850 robberies, and 8,431 aggravated assaults.

The Wisconsin Department of Corrections, an agency of the executive branch of state government, operates 20 adult and five juvenile facilities across the state, with the Waupun State Prison being the first such institution when it opened in 1851. Wisconsin correctional centers have traditionally attempted to balance protecting public safety with providing inmates with the necessary skills and insights into their past criminal behaviors to ensure a crime-free life upon their release. To that end, Wisconsin correctional centers have long offered programming that provides inmates with basic education, alcohol and drug counseling, work experience, and work release privileges. Wisconsin eliminated black-and-white striped prison uniforms in 1868, initiated the first prison newspaper in 1886, allowed parole of prisoners who were rehabilitated in 1907, opened the State Prison for Women in Taycheedah in 1932, and became the first state to treat sex offenders in 1952. Over the past few decades, however, Wisconsin's prison population has increased substantially. In 1981, the average daily prison population in Wisconsin was 3,821, but it tripled during the 1990s and totaled 23,987 by 2011. Much of this increase was a result of convictions related to drug violations. During the mid-1990s, Wisconsin led the nation in housing prisoners out of state, but by building a prison every two years had ceased doing this by 2005. The Wisconsin Department of Corrections estimates that by 2020, Wisconsin will have more than 26,675 individuals incarcerated.

Serial Killers

Despite its progressive attitude toward criminal justice, Wisconsin has been home to two of the grisliest serial murderers in U.S. history. Edward "Ed" Gein, from Plainfield, was a murderer and body snatcher who murdered at least two individuals and exhumed other corpses from a nearby graveyard in order to fashion keepsakes from their bones and skin. Author Robert Bloch, a Milwaukee native, based his novel *Psycho* (1959) upon Gein's story, which Alfred Hitchcock turned into his 1960 film of the same name. Between 1978 and 1991, Jeffrey Dahmer murdered 17 men and boys in and around Milwaukee. Many of Dahmer's victims were of African American or Asian descent, and and delay in his arrest caused criticism of police officers.

Stephen T. Schroth
Jason A. Helfer
Lynn N. Mueller
Knox College

See Also: 1901 to 1920 Primary Documents; *Ableman v. Booth*; Capital Punishment; Constitution of the United States of America; Dahmer, Jeffrey; McCarthy, Joseph.

Further Readings

Davis, Donald A. *The Jeffrey Dahmer Story: An American Nightmare.* New York: St. Martin's Press, 1991.

Derleth, A. *Wisconsin Murders: An Enquiry Into Mayhem and Homicide in the Midwest.* Sauk Prairie, WI: Mycroft & Moran, 1968.

Stevens, D. J., ed. *Policing and Community Partnerships.* Upper Saddle River, NJ: Prentice Hall, 2001.

Witness Testimony

On November 28, 1976, Robert Wood, a Dallas, Texas, police officer, was shot and killed while making a routine traffic stop. Whenever a police officer is murdered on duty, there is great pressure to find the murderer; consequently, the search for Officer Wood's killer was intense. Despite substantial evidence that the murder was committed by David Harris, a 16-year-old with a history of criminal behavior who had bragged to his friends about killing a police officer the day of the murder, the police pursued another suspect, Randall Adams, a 27-year-old man who had recently come to Dallas looking for employment.

The day before the murder, Harris picked up Adams, whose car had run out of gas, as Adams walked along the highway with an empty gas can. Harris and Adams hit it off; the two spent the day and part of the evening together. Harris dropped Adams off before midnight on November 27, 1976, at the motel where Adams was staying with his brother. A few hours later, Harris had the fatal encounter with Officer Wood. Having been informed that Harris had bragged to friends that he had shot and killed a police officer, the police brought Harris in for questioning. Harris admitted to being present at the time of the killing, but stated that a hitchhiker he had picked up the day before, Randall Adams, was the killer. Based on Harris's statement, Adams was arrested and charged with the murder of Robert Wood.

At trial, three eyewitnesses testified that they saw Adams in the car at the scene of the fatal shooting. Despite serious questions about the truthfulness of the eyewitnesses, Adams was convicted and was sentenced to death. It was later determined that the testimony of two of the eyewitnesses was false, given in exchange for a favorable disposition of charges pending against them. Adams remained in prison for 12 years, once coming within three days of his scheduled execution. His story was the subject of a documentary, *The Thin Blue Line,* which revealed substantial flaws in the murder investigation and the evidence presented by the prosecution at trial. As a result, lawyers for Randall Adams were able to have his conviction overturned. Twelve years after the murder, David Harris, who had been convicted and sentenced to death for a second murder, confessed to having murdered Wood.

Under American criminal law, the prosecution must prove guilt beyond a reasonable doubt. This heavy burden reflects the importance placed on liberty by the U.S. Constitution. Eyewitness testimony makes meeting this burden easier. Jurors tend to find this form of evidence exceedingly persuasive. Indeed, the vast majority of cases that include eyewitness testimony result in convictions, including cases where the testimony of an eyewitness is the only evidence presented of the defendant's guilt.

Accuracy of Eyewitness Accounts
For centuries, the accuracy of testimony by an eyewitness has been challenged using common sense and logic. However, the multitude of factors that could compromise memory was not known. The persuasiveness of eyewitness reports comes from a common misconception that memory, similar to a recording, is an exact representation of what the eyewitness perceived. A substantial body of empirical research has documented that this assumption is incorrect. Two of the best-known researchers who have studied the accuracy of reports from eyewitnesses are psychologists Steven Penrod and Elizabeth Loftus. Their research findings are consistent with the exoneration, based on DNA testing, of hundreds of people who were wrongly convicted, as almost half of these wrongful convictions were based on eyewitness testimony.

Research by cognitive psychologists, neuropsychologists, and neuroscientists reveals that memory is a complex, active process that is vulnerable to a number of internal and external factors. Memory can be meaningfully conceptualized as a three-phase process, consisting of encoding, retention, and retrieval. Encoding is the input phase of memory. This phase includes focusing on, and paying attention to, some concept, item, experience, person, or event; processing it; and storing it in short-term memory. The second phase of the memory process is storage, in which the information that was encoded into short-term memory is moved to long-term memory. The last phase of the memory process is retrieval. When asked to recall a certain event, the individual must retrieve, from all the memories that person has stored in long-term memory, the one specific memory requested. In order for a memory to be retrievable, it has to have been stored in such a way that it can be identified as the correct memory. Any factor that interferes with one or more phases of memory processing compromises the ability to recall a memory accurately. What is remembered is vulnerable to both witness and situational characteristics that may make the memory unreliable or irretrievable. Witness characteristics that may compromise the accuracy of recall include, but are not limited to, visual, auditory, or other sensory acuity; intelligence; education; emotional state; mental status; general health; capacity for attention and concentration; desire to give the police what the witness believes the police want; differences between the race and/or ethnicity of the witness and the perpetrator; and use of medication or drugs.

Factors Affecting Accuracy
Police cannot choose witnesses; they have to work with whoever happens to have witnessed the crime. However, they do have control over some factors such as police interrogation and investigative practices, which can contaminate the memory of an eyewitness. For example, research has shown that the way an interview, lineup, or photo array is conducted can affect the information provided by the witness, potentially leading to the prosecution of an innocent person. Police may inadvertently, or sometimes intentionally, provide the victim or witness with misleading information. This typically occurs when someone is interrogated using leading questions or statements that provide false information. This information may be incorporated into the memory of the victim or witness, leading witnesses to unknowingly change their memories and testify based on this false memory.

Stress affects the quality of individual performance. Studies have found that the effect of

At right, a witness being questioned in court. Research in eyewitness testimony is a field with broad implications, with some researchers finding that visual reports are unreliable.

stress on performance is predictable. This predictable pattern is known as the Yerkes-Dodson law. This law states that performance is best at moderate levels of stress. At very low levels of stress, performance suffers from lack of motivation or lack of focus. At very high levels of stress, performance suffers because the nervous system is overwhelmed, and the ability to exert control over performance is limited. Applying this to eyewitness memory, the Yerkes-Dodson law predicts that an individual's ability to remember an event varies as a function of the amount of stress associated with the incident. For example, witnessing a crime that does not involve violence, aggression, or threat to safety usually produces a low to moderate level of stress. Extreme stress is usually associated with witnessing crimes of violence, aggression, force, or if the witness is threatened. This is counterintuitive; the common belief is that someone will remember dramatic events better than less dramatic events because the drama of the event is riveting, making that person pay careful attention. For example, murder is a high-stress crime. The general belief is that someone who witnesses a murder will have every detail of that event seared into his or her memory. In reality, the opposite happens. The witness's anxiety level is extremely high, interfering with the encoding and retention phases of the memory process.

Related to this is the "weapon effect." When a weapon is used in a crime, the level of stress for the witness is extremely high. When the witness is the victim of the crime, the level of stress exceeds that of a "mere" witness. When a person is threatened with a weapon, that person's primary focus is on the weapon; characteristics that identify the perpetrator may be ignored or only peripherally noted. Since the focus is not on the perpetrator but on the weapon, the victim may have a very poor memory of the perpetrator's appearance.

Another factor that affects the ability to recall a particular event is the duration of the event. The longer an event lasts, the greater the likelihood that the witness will remember the event, and remember it accurately. Although a victim or witness may have experienced the crime as occurring over a long time, most crimes are over relatively quickly. Given the rapidity with which crimes are completed, most victims and witnesses only have a very short period of time, sometimes mere seconds, to observe and encode information about the perpetrator. Counterintuitively, the victim or witness to a crime may not remember many details about the crime, due, in part, to the brief period during which the crime occurred.

Race and Memory

Cross-racial identification constitutes another source of misidentification. Research has found that members of one racial or ethnic group have greater difficulty correctly identifying a person from another racial or ethnic group than they do identifying a member of their own ethnic or racial group. The most likely explanation for this is the lack of experience members of one racial or ethnic group have with members of other racial or ethnic groups. With increased interaction, the high incidence of cross-racial misidentification diminishes.

Witness expectations may result in false memories. The human brain has evolved to respond rapidly when danger is present. One method to decrease response time to threats is to respond before a full analysis of the reality of the threat can be completed. Responding based on biases allows for a rapid response, one that is likely to be beneficial, despite resulting in many false positives (responding to a stimulus as if it were a threat, when the stimulus did not pose a threat). What may have been adaptive at an earlier point of human development may now be harmful, as it can distort what is perceived and recalled.

Witness expectations combine with racial prejudice, as people tend to recall what they think should have happened, based on their prejudice, rather than what actually occurred. This occurs most often when the person has some doubt about what actually occurred in an incident or crime. For example, in one study, participants were quickly shown a picture of a white male robbing a black male in the subway. After viewing the picture, each participant was asked to describe in writing the picture he or she had just seen. The majority of the research participants incorrectly recalled that the black male was the assailant rather than the victim.

The passage of time can decrease the accuracy of what is recalled. Memory of an event, or any material that is committed to memory, tends to deteriorate over time. The greater the length of time between the occurrence of the crime and the testimony of the witness at trial, the greater the likelihood that the witness's recall of the event will be inaccurate. In some cases, the time between the crime and the trial of the accused can be over one year. Most people can state, for example, what they did last weekend; these same people would have great difficulty stating what they did a year ago. The longer the delay between the victim's or witness's statement and the crime or the statement and the trial of the accused, the greater the likelihood that person's memory of the events has deteriorated.

Wrongful Convictions

There have been numerous cases of wrongful convictions, many of which were based in large part on inaccurate eyewitness identification and testimony. In some cases, eyewitness testimony was the only direct evidence that the defendant was guilty. Stories abound of people wrongfully incarcerated for years before being vindicated. These stories are supported by statistics that confirm the incidents of wrongful incarceration. The work of the Innocence Project has brought to light the number of people wrongfully sentenced to death, only to be exonerated by DNA evidence. It is unknown how many people serving time in prison or sentenced to death are in fact innocent. The exact number of wrongfully convicted inmates serving time, sentenced to death, or executed may never be known. What is clear is that, based on the known incidents of wrongful conviction, there are many more than have been identified.

It is in no one's interest to punish the innocent. Convicting and incarcerating the wrong person deprives that person of part of his or her life, a loss for which that person can never be fully compensated. In addition to the irretrievable lost time, the wrongfully incarcerated suffer the humiliation, danger, and physical and psychological harm that are part of the prison experience. Justice also is denied to the victim of the crime, as the actual perpetrator goes unpunished and is free to harm another person.

There has been a growing awareness of the reality of false convictions and the injustice this causes for the one falsely convicted, the victim, and society. False conviction also sullies the reputation of the criminal justice system and raises questions about whether this system actually serves justice. In order to decrease the probability of wrongful convictions based on inaccurate eyewitness testimony, guidelines have been developed. Two major groups have written guidelines for eyewitness testimony: the Technical Working Group for Eyewitness Evidence of the National Institutes of Justice, and the American Psychology and Law Society of the American Psychological Association. They both are based on social science research and reach similar conclusions.

The recommendations from the Technical Working Group for Eyewitness Evidence of the National Institutes of Justice involve the use of photo arrays, specific interview techniques, and bias-reducing techniques in lineups. Photos of previously arrested subjects may be shown to a witness to help the police identify the perpetrator for purposes of arrest. It is recommended that the photos be arranged in a manner that does not bias the witness toward selecting a particular person. For example, photos should be separated into groups with similar characteristics, such as type of photo, age, race, and hair color and style. The goal of an interview is to gather accurate information. The accuracy of this information is jeopardized when the interviewer asks leading questions or makes other types of suggestions indicating the desired answer. It is recommended that the interviewer begin the interview with open-ended questions, ones that do not suggest an answer and that encourage the interviewee to tell what was witnessed in the his/her own words. The witness should be told not to guess what happened but to report only what he/she can remember. In a lineup, the witness views a group of suspects, as well as some people known to be innocent, and is asked to identify the perpetrator. In order for this process to result in an accurate identification, care must be taken to design the lineup in such a way that it does not suggest who should be chosen. The people used in the lineup should be sufficiently similar so the suspect does not stand out. Specific recommendations include (1) instructing the witness that the perpetrator might not be included in the lineup, (2) instructing everyone other than the witness not to do or say anything that identifies the suspect, (3) having everyone in the lineup do the same actions.

The American Psychology/Law Society (AP/LS) published *Eyewitness Identification Procedures:*

Recommendations for Lineups and Photo Spreads. AP/LS stated that its guidelines "represent(ed) an emerging consensus among eyewitness scientists as to key elements that such a set of procedures must entail." This group also has specific recommendations for the way photo arrays and lineups should be designed. Double-blind procedures should be used in lineups or photo arrays. In a double-blind procedure, the person who administers/conducts the lineup or photo spread should not be aware of which person is the suspect. This procedure is analogous to the scientific protocol used in drug testing. It ensures that whoever conducts the identification procedure does not inadvertently lead the witness to select a particular person. The witness should be instructed that the person who committed the offense might not be in the lineup or photo array. This lets the witness know that he/she should not feel that he/she must identify someone in the lineup as the perpetrator. The lineup or photo array must be designed so the suspect does not stand out from the group.

For example, every person used should share similar physical characteristics and dress. Jurors tend to give excess weight to the witness's confidence that the person identified is the real culprit. Feedback from those conducting the identification process may make the witness more confident in his/her selection than he/she was at the time the witness made the selection. Therefore, it is recommended that prior to any feedback from the police, a statement should be taken from the eyewitness at the time of the identification as to his or her confidence that the identified person is the actual culprit. These recommendations are designed to prevent or minimize the likelihood that the beliefs of the police will affect the testimony of the eyewitness. While the police cannot prevent the numerous other causes of inaccurate memory, they can ensure that they do not serve as a source of contamination.

Conclusion

Eyewitness testimony has been shown to be exceedingly persuasive to jurors. It is generally assumed that eyewitnesses provide the best evidence about who committed the crime. Research has shown that eyewitness testimony is often inaccurate, despite the confidence the witness reports having about what he or she recalls. The common belief that memory is analogous to recording an event has been shown to be incorrect. Memory is an active, constructive process that is vulnerable to a variety of factors that can modify or create memories, such that what a witness believes he or she can recall did not happen as he or she remembers it, or did not happen at all. Although there is no way to prevent uncontrollable factors such as victim and environmental characteristics that can contaminate the memory process, it is possible to make systemic changes to prevent or minimize the likelihood that police investigative procedures corrupt or compromise the ability of eyewitnesses to report accurately what he/she observed.

Allen J. Brown
Anna Maria College

See Also: 1801 to 1850 Primary Documents; 1901 to 1920 Primary Documents; 1961 to 1980 Primary Documents; 1981 to 2000 Primary Documents; Courts; Executions; Trials.

Further Readings

Douglass, A. B., et al. "Does Post-Identification Feedback Affect Evaluations of Eyewitness Testimony and Identification Procedures?" *Law and Human Behavior*, v.34/4 (2009).

Gould, L., et al. "Reforming the Use of Eyewitness Testimony." *Oklahoma City University Law Review*, v.35 (2010).

Martire, K. A. and R. I. Kemp. "The Impact of Eyewitness Expert Evidence and Judicial Instruction on Juror Ability to Evaluate Eyewitness Testimony." *Law and Human Behavior*, v.33/1 (2009).

Pozzulo, J. D. and J. L. Dempsey. "Witness Factors and Their Influence on Jurors' Perceptions and Verdicts." *Criminal Justice and Behavior*, v.36/9 (2009).

Wise, R. A., et al. "How to Analyze the Accuracy of Eyewitness Testimony in a Criminal Case." *Connecticut Law Review*, v.42/2 (2009).

Wolf v. Colorado

Wolf v. Colorado (1949) is a case in which the U.S. Supreme Court incorporated, or made applicable to the states, the protection of the Fourth

Amendment's prohibition against unreasonable search and seizure. The case began when a Colorado physician, Julius A. Wolf, was thought to be providing abortions illegally. However, the police were unable to gather conclusive evidence of the alleged activity. Therefore, local police, in an effort to find the evidence necessary to arrest and convict Dr. Wolf, absconded with his appointment book. After investigating the names in the book, police were able to gather the evidence they sought. Wolf was convicted in his criminal trial, and the conviction was upheld by the Colorado Supreme Court.

Upon issuing a writ of certiorari, the legal question facing the Supreme Court was whether or not the exclusionary rule, or the withholding of evidence that was gathered in violation of the Fourth Amendment, was applicable at the state level. Importantly, the Supreme Court, in *Weeks v. United States* (1914), had created the exclusionary rule to prevent illegally gathered evidence to be used in court. According to the court in *Weeks*, if evidence gathered illegally was used in criminal trials, then there is, in effect, no protection from illegal searches and seizures. However, the *Weeks* case dealt solely with federal agents in federal courts. In *Wolf*, the Supreme Court was to decide if this protection was to be made applicable to the states, as Wolf's attorney argued it should be.

Writing for a 6–3 majority of the court, Justice Felix Frankfurter argued that the Fourth Amendment's protection against illegal search and seizure should be incorporated by the states, as it was considered a fundamental right. However, the exclusionary rule, as but one method of protecting against illegal search and seizures, was not a fundamental right, and therefore would not be incorporated. Using evidence gathered from several global jurisdictions and every state, Justice Frankfurter noted that many states had rejected the exclusionary rule in the wake of the *Weeks* decision. However, that did not mean that these states welcomed illegal searches by their police officers. According to Frankfurter, the police departments could punish officers who participated in such activities. Moreover, Frankfurter opined that public opinion could protect against unreasonable actions of local police departments.

Importantly, Justice Hugo Black concurred with the majority opinion, in that he felt that the exclusionary rule was a court-mandated remedy that could be overturned by Congress if it desired to do so. However, Black, using his understanding of legislative history, also felt that the Fourteenth Amendment was designed to incorporate the Fourth Amendment and the other amendments in the Bill of Rights, in its entirety, to the states. Black's view was largely defunct due to the Supreme Court's refusal, in several cases, to incorporate the Bill of Rights en masse. *Wolf* was altered somewhat in *Rochin v. California* (1952), a case in which the court ruled that if an illegal search was conducted in a shocking manner, then the evidence gathered could be excluded from trial. Much of *Wolf*'s holding was overturned in 1961 in *Mapp v. Ohio*, in which the Supreme Court, under the leadership of Chief Justice Earl Warren, incorporated the exclusionary rule to the states.

Wolf is an important case for understanding the evolution of the Supreme Court's view of protections of the criminally accused found in the Bill of Rights. Although it incorporated the Fourth Amendment's prohibition of illegal searches and seizures to the states, it fell short of mandating remedies in instances in which police violated the prohibition. *Wolf* did serve an intermediate role between the creation of the exclusionary rule in *Weeks* and its incorporation in *Mapp*. In that regard, it is an illustrative example of the Supreme Court's tendency to avoid major legal changes.

Tobias T. Gibson
Westminster College

See Also: *Hurtado v. California*; *Mapp v. Ohio*; *Weeks v. United States*.

Further Readings
del Carmen, Rolando V. *Criminal Procedure: Law and Practice.* Belmont, CA: Wadsworth, 2009.
Epstein, Lee and Thomas G. Walker. *Constitutional Law for a Changing America: Rights, Liberties, and Justice*, 5th ed. Washington, DC: CQ Press, 2004.
Rehnquist, William H. *The Supreme Court.* New York: Knopf, 2001.
Wolf v. Colorado, 338 U.S. 25 (1949).

Women Criminals, Contemporary

Women's criminal behavior has only become a focus for criminologists and criminal justice officials since the 1970s. The social constructions of gender have guided the examination and treatment of the genders when responding to their criminal behavior. Earlier history uncovers the belief that women were above the lures of criminal behavior, and hence they had been ignored, while men were defined as possessing criminal tendencies. As a result, people know more about and respond more harshly to male criminal behavior. However, as social constructions change to encompass women as criminals, criminological theories and criminal justice responses have changed accordingly.

Historical Context

Historically, women were viewed to be passive, weak, sometimes naïve and gullible, but always possessing a higher morality than men. On the other hand, men were viewed to be aggressive, strong, competitive, and risk takers. Crime is something that is supposedly only committed by the aggressive and physically stronger individuals of society. How can an individual overpower a victim if he or she is weaker? As a result, women as the weaker sex were given the role of the victim. If she committed a crime, it was believed that there was something very unwomanly about her, something aggressive and masculine.

In the 1970s, society experienced a paradigm shift in how it understood female criminal behavior. It was argued that as a consequence of the Women's Rights Movement and the passage of Title VII of the Civil Rights Act in 1972, female criminal behavior would increase, reflecting that of males. This was known as the liberation hypothesis. Scholars hypothesized that once women had been liberated and gained access to the workforce, they would have freer movements in society that would mimic male behavior, including criminal behavior. Many believed that female access to the workforce would result in more competitive, risk-taking, and aggressive behavior that is often present among criminals. The result was a shift in how society handled female criminal behavior, more than a change in the behavior itself.

Changing Patterns in Criminal Activity and Justice Response

The main sources for understanding criminal behavior in the United States are the annual Uniform Crime Reports (UCR) released by the Federal Bureau of Investigation (FBI) and the National Crime Victimization Survey (NCVS) released annually by the Bureau of Justice Statistics. The UCR provides arrest data for a number of violent and nonviolent crimes nationwide, while the NCVS provides victimization from a large sample of the U.S. population. These statistics provide annual numbers, percentages, and rates, as well as crime trends over time. An examination of these statistics reveals that since the 1970s, arrests of females have increased substantially. In fact, from 1987 to 1998, the arrests of adult women for violent crimes increased by 80 percent. Additionally, arrests for males between 1997 and 2007 decreased by 7 percent, but increased for females by 4 percent.

Many have argued that the criminal behaviors of females, decades later, now mimic those of males. NCVS data, on the other hand, reveal that reported victimizations do not identify females as the offenders at such an increasing rate. As a result, many have argued that the statistics are more of a reflection of social reaction and tough-on-crime ideologies than of increased criminal behavior. Statistics also reveal that increased arrests involve crimes of forgery, possession of stolen property, and simple assault. By the mid-2000s, females represented 18 percent of all violent crime arrests. NCVS data reveal that females represent 11 percent of robbery offenders, 14 percent of aggravated assault offenders, and 23 percent of simple assault offenders.

Research reveals that major changes in women's crime took place between 1960 and 1991, though increases between 1980 and 1991 were small. Social factors that influenced these changes included the various social movements of the 1960s and 1970s, the drug epidemic and resulting war on drugs, and improved law enforcement technology. Social constructs changed to recognize women as potential criminals and brought about increased arrests. Research shows that females are most likely to commit nonviolent crimes and to commit minor crimes when violence is a factor. The most dramatic increase, however, has been in female drug offending.

Female Criminal Activity

By 2007, women represented 18 percent of individuals arrested for drug offenses. Women are more likely to be convicted for drug possession, while men are more likely to be convicted for drug dealing. UCR statistics reveal that between 2000 and 2009, the arrests of women for drug abuse violations increased by 12.5 percent, while the increase for males was 4.6 percent. Black women are three times more likely to be incarcerated for drug offenses than white women. Additionally, many men and women are arrested and prosecuted for other crimes that are drug related. One third of all women incarcerated in state prisons report that they committed their offenses in order to obtain money for drugs. Violence, robbery, and prostitution are crimes commonly committed in order to support drug habits. In fact, almost half of all incarcerated women require drug treatment.

Women's inroads into the illegal drug market are not the same as men. Just as gender inequality exists within the legitimate workforce, it also exists within the illegal drug market. Women make less money than men in the illegal distribution of drugs. Furthermore, women are more likely to procure their drugs through sexual transactions. Other research shows that women tend to play support roles in drug dealing, such as a girlfriend, spouse, or parent to a male primary drug offender.

In order to fully understand female criminality, race/ethnicity must also be examined. Race and ethnicity limit legitimate and illegitimate opportunities, making crime potentially attractive, but at the same time hard to accomplish. However, racial and ethnic minorities are more likely to be labeled criminal, are more likely to be arrested and convicted, and are more likely to be incarcerated. This discrimination tends to distort statistics and impedes the ability to gain a true understanding of criminal behavior. Research reveals that women of color are more likely to commit aggravated and other assaults, burglary, forgery, other thefts, drug violations, and prostitution. White women are more likely to use and possess drugs, and commit fraud, liquor law violations, drunkenness, and driving under the influence (DUI). Latina women are more likely to commit public order crimes, property offenses, and violent crime (in that order).

Women are more likely to commit property and vice offenses (prostitution and drug crimes) and minor violent crimes. Minor thefts are gender-related; that is, they are more likely to be committed by women. While males are still more likely to commit crimes of theft, female criminality in this crime type is growing. UCR data reveal that between 2000 and 2009, arrests of women for larceny-theft increased by 37.3 percent and by 32.4 percent for motor vehicle theft. Many argue that this, and other property and drugs crimes, is the result of the feminization of poverty (the increase of women and children living in poverty today). Females engage in large amounts of shoplifting, but males still dominate in this criminal activity. Between 2000 and 2009, arrests for women for buying, receiving, and possessing stolen property increased by almost 7 percent, while arrests for males decreased by 16 percent.

Female inroads into white-collar crime can be linked, to a point, to the liberation hypothesis. The increase of women in white-collar positions in the last decades is followed by an increase in opportunities to engage in these crimes. However, women still largely represent lower-level employees, and so their crime is more often petty. Women are more likely to work alone when committing a white-collar crime and report a family need. Official statistics reveal that between 2000 and 2009, arrests of females decreased by 28.8 percent for forgery and counterfeiting, 38.7 percent for fraud, and 3.8 percent for embezzlement.

Robbery and burglary are much more likely to be committed by males. Women represent 12 percent of robbery offenders and 15 percent of burglary offenders. One-third of female robbers act alone or with another woman, and financial need (usually for drugs) and peer pressure are the primary motivators for committing these crimes. Two-fifths of all women arrested for robbery were previously arrested for an offense as a juvenile. Female burglars are much more likely to work with others, are more likely to report a drug addiction, and report less contact with the criminal justice system.

Males represent 81 percent of individuals arrested for violent crimes, but females only represent 10 percent of those arrested for murder and 1 percent of those arrested for forcible rape. Further, women are more likely to kill their husbands, lovers, or pimps. Between 1972 and 2002, 10 percent of homicides involved females killing males and 2 percent involved females killing other females. Thirty-five percent of female homicides involved killing intimate partners, while 65 percent of males killed their intimate partners. Compared to males, females represented 38 percent of infanticide offenders (the killing of an infant). And female murderers killed multiple victims in less than 10 percent of all homicides.

Overall, violent crime arrests for women between 2000 and 2009 increased by 0.1 percent. Juvenile females arrested for violent crimes decreased by 17 percent. During this same time, property crime arrests for females increased by 33 percent, but increased by only 0.1 percent for female juveniles. The questions pondered in the last four decades are whether female criminal behavior is increasing, whether females are increasingly violent, and whether or not females are becoming as violent as males. Comparing statistics from the UCR and the NCVS reveals that female violent and property crime is increasing, but only slightly. This conclusion recognizes that the increase is more likely a result of criminal justice official responses than of increased criminality. However, there is irrefutable evidence that women are not becoming as violent as men.

Evolving Debates and Solutions

In addition to the debate on whether female criminal behavior will soon reflect male criminal behavior, society has debated why females commit crime. Criminologists have worked on explaining criminal behavior in the United States since the 1930s. However, these theorists have been guilty of the generalizability problem. Criminological theories historically have been developed by men to explain male behavior. They examined the behaviors of males and then generalized their conclusions to males and females. It was not until the 1970s that theorists started to bring women into the equation. However, with the disparate and sometimes discriminatory behaviors of criminal justice officials and policies, it is hard to determine the causes of crime.

Early theories explained female criminality as a biological deficiency, while others explained it as a mental deficiency. Today, biology and mental deficiencies are mixed to explain that social structures cause criminal behavior. When examining nonviolent offenses such as theft, fraud, drug abuse violations, and prostitution, officials and the larger society are comfortable in claiming that women are just doing what women choose or may be driven to do. However, when women commit crimes believed to be male behavior, it is harder to explain the causes.

If women are thought of and socialized to be passive nurturers and weak, then what causes them to commit such heinous crimes? Experts often explain extreme forms of violence by women as a result of mental instability. The female serial killer or serial rapist is a rare event; however, there are documented cases of such instances. As with the male serial killer, this is often explained as an extreme mental deficiency. Like the male serial rapist, these female criminals

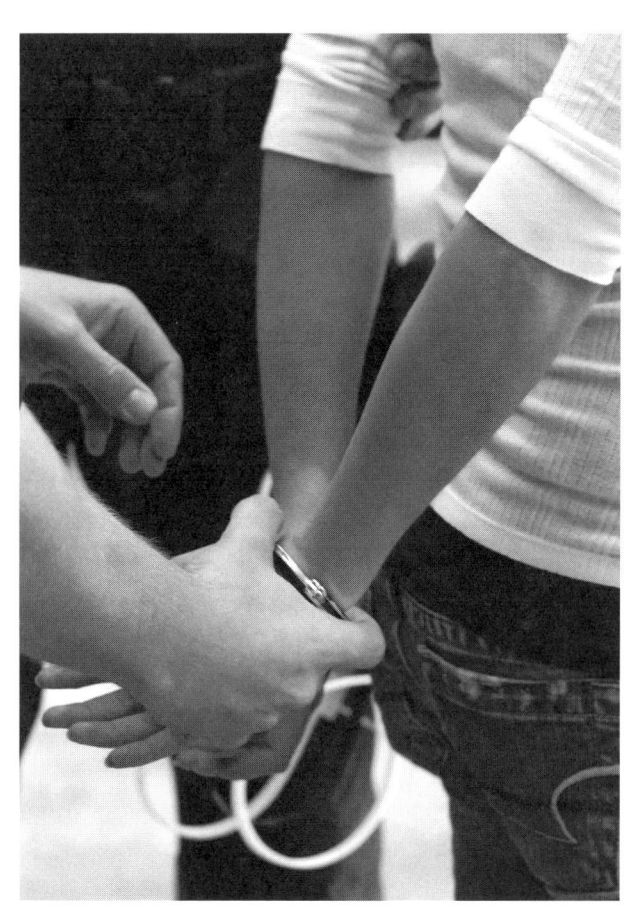

Women represent 12 percent of robbery cases, 15 percent of burglaries, and 10 percent of those arrested for murder. Only 1 percent of forcible rape arrests are women.

are more likely to be tagged as evil and partly mentally unstable, as with Rosemary West and Karla Homolka. Brutal serial rapists/murderers among females are uncommon; however, female child molesters are not. These females are defined as having evil intentions, but as also being mentally unstable enough to sexually assault a child instead of desiring to nurture the child. Many of these convicted sex offenders were teachers, babysitters, or service providers. They were engaged in women's work but committing men's crime. The research has yet to uncover why women who tend to be socialized to be nurturers can turn to destroying the lives of children.

In other instances of female violence, society has focused on the female who murders her spouse or children. As with Andrea Yates, who drowned her five children, or Susan Smith, who drowned her two boys, officials tend to focus on the mental instability of women who kill their children. Andrea Yates, like many women who commit infanticide, was said to be suffering an extreme case of postpartum depression. On the other hand, Susan Smith's crimes were explained by post-traumatic stress disorder (PTSD), a severe psychological distress that follows traumatic events, such as victimization, and can result in destructive actions, both internal and external.

Some cases have been explained with a controversial disorder known as Munchausen syndrome by proxy. In this case, offenders (overwhelmingly women) are said to seek attention to the point of medically abusing their children. Offenders report frequent child illness or injury requiring multiple doctors' visits, medications, and sometimes surgeries. Munchausen syndrome by proxy is a very controversial diagnosis, as many in society claim that mothers are being wrongfully accused of child abuse. Nevertheless, women have been convicted of child abuse and child murder based on this diagnosis.

Women who kill tend to kill the men in their lives. Research shows that almost three-quarters of these women report having experienced abuse at the hands of the men they killed. Research has claimed that severely battered women may experience PTSD and as a result may kill as the only perceived option to survive the abuse. This has been termed "battered woman syndrome" and has been occasionally successfully used as a legal defense in courts since the mid-1980s. While the diagnosis is still controversial as an appropriate legal defense to murder, states have increasingly allowed this type of evidence.

There is still much to learn about female offending. Theories continue to be male-focused and guilty of the generalizability approach. However, with the growing focus on women's issues, this problem is slowly being corrected. Since most crimes tend to be committed by males, criminal justice agencies tend to put most of their resources in apprehending, trying, and convicting male offenders. Most money in corrections tends to be put toward confining and correcting male criminal behavior. Female offending, however, is a problem and in some crime categories is increasing. As a result, there need to be greater criminal justice efforts placed toward understanding and responding to these crimes.

Venessa Garcia
Kean University

See Also: Courts; Domestic Violence, Contemporary; Gender and Criminal Law; Insanity Defense.

Further Readings
Belknap, Joanne. *The Invisible Woman: Gender, Crime, and Justice*, 3rd ed. Belmont, CA: Thomson Wadsworth, 2007.
Chesney-Lind, Meda and Lisa J. Pasko. *The Female Offender: Girls, Women, and Crime*, 2nd ed. London: Sage, 2004.
van Wormer, Katherine Stuart and Clemens Bartollas. *Women and the Criminal Justice System*, 3rd ed. Upper Saddle River, NJ: Prentice Hall, 2011.

Women Criminals, History of

Historically, female criminality has centered on women's sexuality, their mental capacity, and their status as property of men. A study of the history of women criminals uncovers societal constructs of womanhood, femininity, family, and work. In addition to ideologies of gender and family, women criminals must be understood within ideologies of race, class, age, and immigration. Analyses reveal that societies codify their constructs and ideologies within their legal systems. Hence, the ideologies of women's role in society have dictated their status as criminals.

Early Legal Traditions
One can trace the roots of current gender and family ideologies in the United States to the Code of Hammurabi (ca. 1780 B.C.E.), in which women were legally defined as the possession of men passed from father to husband. A woman's role was to provide healthy male heirs in order to continue her husband's family line, and her activities were highly regulated in terms of their property value to men. The Code of Hammurabi criminalized the bad wife, to include undisciplined and adulterous women. The code allowed the husband to send his adulterous wife away or to enslave her. The wife could legally deny the claim of adultery; however, if she could not prove her case, she could face execution by drowning. Many claim that it was the Code of Hammurabi that codified honor killings of females deemed criminal as adulterers.

Under Roman law and the early Christian doctrine, women's behaviors were strictly proscribed. Acts of drug use, use of magic, disobedience, and adultery were grounds for physical chastisement by a husband and for divorce. Under the Christian doctrine, all women carried the sins of Eve. In order to ensure that women maintained morality, the church stressed that they should be closely watched, have their speech and dress regulated, and be beaten when necessary. These early religious and legal codes created gender ideologies that defined women as inherently promiscuous and sinful and required corporal punishment as good for the soul of women. Christian Roman Emperor Constantine the Great was the first emperor to execute his wife in 298 B.C.E. Constantine the Great had his wife scalded to death in a cauldron of slow-boiling water because he suspected her of adultery. While the Christian church later tempered the violence placed on women when it was deemed to be extreme, these religious ideologies were codified within the legal system and later adopted by the English and the American colonies.

Early Female Crime in the United States
Colonial America, which lasted from the 1600s to the 1770s, adopted gender and family ideologies from European legal and religious practices. Woman's place was defined as belonging in the home. A woman was still deemed to carry the sins of Eve and so had to be controlled through her father and her husband. She was legally defined as their property and could be beaten for her offenses. Typically, as in Europe, the crimes of women consisted of fornication, bastardy, disorderly conduct, drunkenness, vagrancy, petty thievery, and prostitution. Serious violent and property crimes were committed by women but with less frequency than by men. For the most part, society was more concerned with the morals of women than the morals of men.

Early colonization of the American and Australian colonies saw a shortage of women and resulted in two common statuses for women: indentured servant and landowner. The first common status of indentured servant resulted in an attempt to increase the numbers of women in the colonies. English and European systems of law sent female (and male) convicts to the colonies in an agreement to serve 7–14 years of indentured servitude in place of being hanged. The latent consequence to women was that it became commonplace to send female offenders for first-time, nonviolent crimes.

The most common crimes committed by female indentured servants were petty theft and prostitution. These women worked in the colonies as servants, maids, or laundresses for masters who paid little and often abused them. Because of the profitability of sending women to the colonies, it was not uncommon for women to be snatched off the streets and forced onto ships bound for the New World. Historical accounts reveal that the conditions were so poor on the transport ships and the systematic rape of the women so horrendous that the survival rate was one in three.

Once these women arrived in the colonies, conditions were so poor, they often turned to theft and prostitution in order to survive. Hence, the criminality of women can be directly linked to their economic conditions. Yet the colonists held the same ideologies as the Europeans. They believed that the young, female, poor, and (later) immigrant were inherently immoral and needed

A sustained campaign to eliminate prostitution did not develop until the later 1800s. William Hogarth's depiction of Harlot's Progress *(1731) shows Molly arriving in London, with Colonel Francis Charteris and Handy Jack leering in the background. In the foreground, a doting madam prepares her before sending her to the waiting customer.*

stronger social controls. As a result, justice placed greater enforcement and harsher sanctions on most of these individuals.

The second common status the early female colonist held was landowner. In 1630, in order to correct the shortage of women, colonies passed laws that gave "maid lots" or ownership of land to unmarried women to serve as dowries to their future husbands. By the 1640s, laws also allowed husbands to will their property to their wives upon their death. Fathers without sons could also deed their property to their daughters. However, again, the property served as dowries for future husbands. As a result, initially it was common for women to own land. However, by 1650, in many areas women outnumbered men, and focus returned to women's morality and their place within the home. Adultery was a major focus regarding the criminality of women since inheritance laws were a major concern. Additionally, it was a crime for women to run away from their husbands, even if escaping abuse. Some also claim that the desire for land was the primary drive of colonial witch hunts.

Witch Hunts

The most famous witch hunts in the United States are the Salem witch trials of 1692. However, a historical analysis can trace witch hunts throughout history. Particularly, the fear of witches in the United States can be traced to medieval Roman and Greek Catholic fear of demons and witches. History documents massive witch hunts by the dominant Catholic Church and its rejection of Greek and Roman religions as paganism, heresy, and demon worship.

The dominance of male leaders in the Catholic Church in the 12th century changed the status of women in religion and society overall. Many of these so-called pagan religions honored and worshipped women and used plants in their spiritual rituals. Women who were influential among pagans suffered torture, mass burnings, and executions. While those accused of heresy and witchcraft were both male and female, more than 80 percent of people executed for witchcraft in Europe were poor rural women. Additionally, these women tended to be midwives, healers, unruly, and political dissenters. Historians have found that millions were executed.

The fear of witches was brought to the American colonies. However, as historians have explained, many of these witch hunts were the product of land greed. For example, it was found that many of the women accused in the Salem witch trials were accused by neighbors who coveted their lands. Many of the accused were female, single or widowed, land or business owners. In Salem, being accused was often followed by shoddy trials that allowed spectral evidence seen only by the accusers. Most of the accusers were young girls of the power- and land-hungry Putnam family. Additionally, many of the accused were midwives who were accused of witchcraft because of their healing powers. In all, 19 people were hanged (14 women) for the crime of witchcraft in Salem, Massachusetts, and many people died in prison. When the mass hysteria ended, more than 100 people were still being held in prison. The Salem witch trials lasted approximately six months and were only stopped when Governor Sir William Phips's wife was accused. It was at this point that the governor claimed the situation to be a farce and pardoned those people who were still incarcerated. The actual number of accused witches in colonial America is disputed; however, it is claimed that between 1620 and 1725, there were 344 accused witches in New England, and that 267 of the accused were women.

Women's Alcohol Consumption as Criminal

In Europe, Britain's gin craze (1720s to 1740s) helped to define female and poor people's alcohol and drug use as problematic to the integrity of a growing urbanized society. Gin, but not beer, was blamed for immorality, crime, and fertility and maternal problems. The Gin Act of 1751 identified the young, illiterate, uneducated, poor, and female dreads of society as less moral and more dangerous to society, especially when consuming gin. Within the United States, Victorian ideologies were more commonly adopted by white, middle-class families and were not readily identified among nonwhite, working-class, and immigrant women. However, Victorian ideologies held powerful influence with U.S. legal policies and liquor license practices. Regardless, as researchers have uncovered, the morality of poor, immigrant, and racial and ethnic minority women was defined as more questionable than was the morality of white, wealthy women. This resulted in disparate treatment within the justice system.

Unlike the witch craze in colonial America, the colonists did not demonize alcohol consumption among women. The focus on female alcohol consumption was criminalized by Prohibitionists (most being women) during the Victorian era (1837–1901). During the Victorian era and with the onset of capitalism, ideologies of womanhood changed drastically. The idea that women belonged in the home, that they were pure, delicate, and possessed a higher morality, became identified as the cult of domesticity. However, the Christian doctrine still had dominance in holding women responsible for the sins of Eve. Thus, women were simultaneously more moral than men and had a greater potential for corruption. As a result, it was believed that women who indulged in alcohol created dysfunctional families, became sexually promiscuous, were possibly prostitutes, and were easily corrupted in other manners. In effect, they were "fallen women." Victorian era progressives criminalized women who did not successfully play the role of the good woman in society (i.e., drunkards, unmarried women, landowners, poor women, promiscuous women, immigrants, and racial and ethnic minorities). Legal proscriptions for women's use of alcohol and drugs sought to minimize the sins of women.

During the Progressive Era (1890s–1920s), temperance reflected protection of women from the harms of alcohol. Temperance advocates and feminists sought to protect women from drunken husbands, while Progressives sought to protect women from society, but also from themselves. The Progressives influenced the passing of many access-limiting laws. Starting in the 1860s, many state laws precluded women from working in establishments that served alcohol. By 1949, 10 states prohibited this activity. The 1890s, however, witnessed the most criminalized activity. Starting at this time, it became criminal to sell alcohol to women for the purpose of drinking in public places. These laws also criminalized women who bought alcohol for these purposes. Later, laws were expanded to include selling and buying anywhere for consumption, even in the home.

Much of the language of the law focused on the sexual promiscuity and the harm to the family that intoxicated women caused. However, married women could not be criminally prosecuted since, until the 1920s, women were legal extensions of their husbands. As a result, husbands were legally responsible for their wives' crimes, unless they could prove that that they did not coerce their wives' actions or that they attempted to restrain their wives. It was not until the 1970s that the states moved to actively remove these laws from their criminal codes.

Following the Progressive Era and the repeal of Prohibition, drunkenness in the 1930s was still one of the three crimes that women were most likely to be arrested for (13 percent each for drunkenness, prostitution, and larceny). Drunkenness accounted for 19 percent of all male arrests during this same time. In fact, arrests for drunkenness were much more common than were arrests for liquor law violations and driving while intoxicated. The 1950s represented a very conservative time within U.S. history, with a focus on family values and fear of communism. Between 1952 and 1957, 35.7 percent of all female arrests were for the crime of drunkenness (49 percent for males); however, by the mid-1960s, 7 percent of female arrests were for drunkenness, compared to 40 percent for males.

Public concern for drunkenness decreased by the 1980s. Today, of all drug and alcohol arrests, drunkenness represents the smallest number of arrests; however, by 2000, females were twice as likely to be arrested for drunkenness as were males (12 percent and 6 percent, respectively). Currently, there is an upswing of police focus on female alcohol-related crimes. Male arrests for drunkenness, driving while intoxicated, and liquor law violations between 2000 and 2009 have substantially decreased (minus 9 percent, minus 11 percent, and minus 22 percent, respectively), while female arrests for this time period have substantially increased (plus 18 percent, plus 32 percent, and plus 2 percent, respectively).

Wars on Drugs

The U.S. war on drugs may be examined from different angles. Colonial America did not place as great a focus on drugs as it did on alcohol. However, in the hunt for witches and in the medical field's pursuit to dominate even household healthcare, women's use of drugs for midwifery and healing purposes was often defined as witchcraft at worst, or as dangerous and untrained at best. Even so, until midwifery and community healers were all but eliminated, drug manufacturers often appealed to female colonists to purchase their drugs, as most rural communities did not employ full-time doctors.

The use of narcotics was also not uncommon among colonial- and Victorian-era women. A common drug used within society was opium. It was not uncommon for women to frequent opium dens and to engage in public drug use. Opium was one of the most common drugs prescribed by doctors, usually for illnesses considered to be women's ailments. Cocaine and marijuana were also commonly used for medicinal purposes. By the late 1800s, cocaine began to be used for recreational purposes. In each of these instances, white, wealthy women (and men) were more likely to use these drugs because they could afford them. Historians describe that many narcotics users were not considered to be addicts and dysfunctional within society.

The idea of addiction was not applied to drug use until the mid-1800s and was first defined as a social problem in the late 1800s. Along with temperance activists, "anti-opiumists" emerged in the mid-1800s with claims of the destructions of opium to the moral fabric of society. Initial focus concerned the criminal and immoral nature of the Chinese as opium smokers. The Opium War (1840–42) in Europe extended to practices and policies within the United States and resulted in government regulation of opium trade, production, and smoking. However, drug manufacturing (including opium, cocaine, and marijuana) for medicinal purposes by Western countries was not a focus. Hence, there was an accepted and even increased use of narcotics within tonics, potions, and pills, especially among the female members of society. Many claim that the Victorian ideology of temperance pushed women to secretly use opium, while men were able to engage in public drinking.

By the early 1900s, the fears of the dangers of women's independence were brought to focus again. The ideology of the day was that drugs were the cause of sexual deviance in women who frequented dance halls and speakeasies, worked as actresses and chorus girls, and dressed in unacceptable attire. Further, society feared the mixing of the races and of white female drug users being seduced by black men. By 1937, the criminalization of marijuana overnight drastically increased the number of female (and male) criminals in the country. In the 1930s, 3 percent of female arrests were for narcotics, while only 0.7 percent of male arrests were for narcotics. Today, marijuana continues to make up the majority of drug arrests in the United States.

The 1950s did not experience as strong a concern with drugs as it did with alcohol; however, the 1960s backlash to the youth counterculture's wide use of drugs resulted in another wave of drug arrests. By the 1970s, 7 percent of all female arrests were for narcotics, while 8 percent of all male arrests were for narcotics. In 1979, one in 10 women were sent to prison for a drug offense. By the late 1990s, this figure was one in three women. Although males are far more likely to be arrested for drug offenses and are far more likely to self-report a greater use of drugs, society's demonization of female drug offenders resulted in an increase in female drug arrests between 2000 and 2009 that was three times higher than the increase in male drug arrests. Records also show that women are more likely to be arrested for possession of drugs, while men are more likely to be arrested for the illegally selling drugs.

Gender-Specific Crimes

Males are more likely to engage in alcohol and drug crimes, violent crimes, and serious and minor property crimes (except embezzlement in the 2000s). Females, on the other hand, are more likely to engage in and be arrested and convicted for prostitution and running away. These are known as gender-specific crimes. Historically, society's focus has been on the sexual behaviors of females and the evils of sexual promiscuity. Prostitution increased during the Civil War and reformers focused on eliminating it completely. In 1870 St. Louis, Missouri, passed a law known as the Social Evil Ordinance, which required the Board of Health to regulate prostitution. This law was similar to England's 1860s Contagious Diseases Act. Common beliefs held that prostitutes were evil women with venereal diseases and that good men such as soldiers needed to be protected. However, moral reformers defeated this regulatory approach in both the United States and England.

Between the 1890s and the early 1900s many states passed laws, later declared unconstitutional or highly problematic, that attempted to regulate, limit, or confine prostitution. However, the strongest concern for prostitution occurred between 1910 and 1914. While much of the earlier concern focused on contagious diseases and overall health, this period focused on what was claimed to be the moral debauchery of prostitution. The result is the continued focus on female prostitutes and not on their male clients. As a gender-specific crime, women dominate this field of illegal sex work and arrests and prosecutions reflect this. Arrest rates steadily remain well over 50 female arrests per 100,000 persons and well under 50 male arrests per 100,000 persons. The debate with prostitution in the United States today is whether prostitutes are victims or criminals. From colonial times through present times, prostitutes have predominantly been females with little economic means for survival. From stranded indentured servants to today's teenage runaways and human traffic victims, prostitutes have often found themselves turning to sex work as a means of obtaining food, clothes, and shelter, not as a means to obtain drugs or sexual gratification.

On the other end of gender-specific crimes are violent crimes. Criminological research has focused on the violent crimes of men because they are the most frequent offenders. Male arrest rates for homicide are eight times higher than female arrests. Felony assault arrests are 13 times higher for males. Gender ideologies tend to identify males as the predators of society. As a result, unless the female was considered to be a "fallen woman," or she was uneducated, poor, a racial/ethnic minority, or an immigrant, she was given the benefit of the doubt. Lizzie Borden was accused and tried, though found not guilty, for violently killing her parents with an axe in 1893. Because Borden was a wealthy white woman in the Victorian era, this was a shocking affair. There was even a children's rhyme written for the crime. Aileen Wuornos was a female serial killer tried and executed in the early 2000s for shooting male clients she picked up as a prostitute on the Florida highways. These women were accused of very violent murders. However, historically, women have been identified as quiet killers whose choice of weapon is poison.

Since the time of midwifery, women have had easy access to poisons and medicines. As a result, we have seen many cases in which women have killed the individuals placed in their care with poison. Referring to them as "angels of death," history has documented many cases of female nurses, caretakers, and midwives who have killed for money or out of a distorted sense of mercy. Amy Archer-Gilligan, known as Sister Amy, was found guilty of smothering or poisoning six of her patients and one husband while operating an elderly care facility between 1911 and 1916. In the 1930s, Anna Marie Hahn was executed for the poisoning murders of three elderly benefactors. The 1980s case of Genene Jones revealed that she murdered several babies while working as a nurse at a hospital. In 1996, Kristen Gilbert was convicted of four murders and two attempted murders while nursing patients at a veterans' hospital. In 2002, nurse Vickie Dawn Jackson was convicted of four murders.

The second most commonly identified female serial killing is referred to as the "black widow." This is the female who, like the black widow spider, kills her husband after using him for his money and possessions. Famous black widows in the United States include Belle Sorrenson Gunness (1908), Nanny Doss (1965), Janie Gibbs (1967), Betty Lou Beets (1985), Blanche Moore (1990), Elfriede "Sugar" Blauensteiner (1996), Judi Buenoano (1998), and, most recently, Betty Neumar and Helen Golay (2008), and Olga Rutterschmidt (2008). There is no shortage of violent female criminals. However, as statistics show, violence is much more commonly committed by males.

A common misperception is that fraud and embezzlement (minor property crimes) are female gender-specific crimes. Society has linked this to the fact that females experience higher rates of arrests for these crimes than for most other crimes (except for prostitution and running away). Their arrests represent between 30 and 40 percent. Considering the trends of arrests, female arrests for larceny have increased substantially every decade. Between 1965 and 2000, female arrests for larceny doubled from a rate of 100 female arrests per 100,000 persons to 292 female arrests per 100,000 persons. On the other hand, male arrests increased slightly less from 321 male arrests per 100,000 persons in 1965 to 583 male arrests per 100,000 persons. While the increase in arrests over time is greater for females, males still commit twice as many larceny-theft crimes. Similarly, in 1965, male arrests for embezzlement represented 15 arrests per 100,000 persons, while female arrests represented three arrests per 100,000. By 2009, female arrests for embezzlement surpassed male arrests by 42 arrests.

Women's criminal activities have predominantly reflected society's concern with their sexual activity and morality. While there are violent female offenders, female arrests for homicide have steadily decreased. Currently, there is not a gender convergence (a decrease in the gap between male and female offending) in the most serious violent crimes. There is, however, a small gender convergence of minor property crimes. This is significant knowledge because throughout

Lizzie Borden, left, was accused of violently killing her parents with an axe in 1893. Amy Archer-Gilligan, right, known as Sister Amy, was found guilty of killing seven people in her care.

history, many of the poor turn to these crimes, and to prostitution, out of economic necessity. However, women have continued to suffer greater economic strain than men, yet have not turned to crime as frequently. Many argue that tighter social controls on women have worked to keep them in line.

With the changing ideologies and women's increasing independence, this is predicted to change. A vigilant watch should reveal the answers to this debate.

Venessa Garcia
Kean University

See Also: 1921 to 1940 Primary Documents; Borden, Lizzie; Drug Abuse and Addiction, History of; Embezzlement; Gender and Criminal Law; Larceny; Prostitution, Contemporary; Race, Class, and Criminal Law; Racism; Salem Witch Trials; Violent Crimes; Wuornos, Aileen.

Further Readings
Boyd, Susan C. *From Witches to Crack Moms: Women, Drug Law, and Policy*. Durham, NC: Carolina Academic Press, 2004.
Horne, Charles F. "Ancient History Sourcebook: Code of Hammurabi, c. 1780 BCE." http://www.fordham.edu/halsall/ancient/hamcode.html#horne (Accessed June 2011).
Merlo, Alida V. and Jocelyn M. Pollock. *Women, Law, and Social Control*. Boston: Allyn & Bacon, 2006.
Nicolaides, Becky M. "The State's 'Sharp Line Between the Sexes': Women, Alcohol and the Law in the United States, 1850–1980." *Addiction*, v.91/8 (1996).
Pavlac, Brian. *Witch Hunts in the Western World: Persecution and Punishment From the Inquisition Through the Salem Trials*. Westport, CT: Greenwood Press, 2009.
Steffensmeir, Darrell J. and Jennifer Schwartz. "Trends in Female Criminality: Is Crime Still a Man's World?" In *The Crime Justice System and Women: Offenders, Prisoners, Victims and Workers*, 3rd ed, Rafel Price, Barbara and Natalie J. Sokoloff, eds. New York: McGraw-Hill, 2004.
Wilson, Lori L. *The Salem Witch Trials: How History Was Invented*. Minneapolis, MN: Lerner Publications, 1997.

Women Criminals, Sociology of

Examining theories of why women commit crimes in the United States reveals some remarkable changes over time, although some schools of thought have been perpetuated throughout the centuries. As research has revealed more about why women commit crimes, theories have progressed from the supernatural and biological realm to consider gender roles and socioeconomics.

The genesis of thought about women criminals in the United States has its roots in European history. In classical Greece and Rome and medieval Europe, when a primary function of women was to produce heirs, adulterous women could be executed, as their adultery threatened the legitimacy of the heirs. In 17th-century England, unmarried mothers were imprisoned, and by the end of the century, mothers of several illegitimate children and homeless women were being sent to the American colonies. It was not an option for married women to leave a husband who was violent or who did not provide for the family. Women who begged and stole for sustenance were imprisoned. Therefore, punishment was a form of social control, and women criminals were largely seen as "fallen women" and shunned.

Colonial Theories
In colonial times, although many women criminals were shipped to the colonies, others were arrested for crimes of vagrancy, morals, or theft. Starting in the 17th century in Europe, women were thought be dangerous sources of temptation and depravity. During these times of strict moral codes, criminal women were seen as more dangerous than criminal men, as they threatened the natural order and authority. The witch hunts occurring in Europe spilled over into New England during this time period.

In Salem, the conservative Puritan community, dominated by Calvinist ideas, forbade celebrating holidays, dancing, music, and other forms of paganism. Tension existed between the town of Salem and the village of Salem over property and churches, and there were serious family rivalries, all of which created a ripe atmosphere for violence. In this context of strife, the people of Salem banded together to punish deviant women—witches—whose nonconformist, seemingly odd, or independent behaviors deviated from the strict moral codes of the time. Women at this time were not seen as frail and were punished in the same way as men. They were arrested, subjected to corporal punishment, incarcerated, or executed. Such practices ended by the early 1700s.

Emile Durkheim, a French sociologist who wrote during the late 19th century and early 20th century, posed theories that have been used to elucidate the history of beliefs about women criminals. Durkheim saw religion as a source of shared moral values and solidarity, a force that binds people together with a common conscience. Violations of these norms or shared values pose a threat to society and usually lead to punishment. This idea echoes the beliefs about societies' reactions to women criminals starting from the early Greeks and Romans, who executed women for adultery, through the genesis of the "fallen woman" and beyond. It is very clearly seen in the Salem witch hunts, during which time women were punished for straying from the strict Puritan moral codes. Durkheim also posited the idea of anomie, which refers to the lack of sufficient normative regulation during times of rapid social change. The solidarity that usually holds society together is challenged by the rapid pace of change, and people become estranged from the groups and norms that hold society together. The United States has been characterized by such rapid growth and constant changes. The 19th century, especially the period leading up to and following the Civil War, saw a great growth in technology, including the advent of the steamship and the railroad, and could be characterized as such a time in history.

Nineteenth-Century Theories

During the 1800s, until the Civil War, women continued to be arrested for moral crimes and for theft, and by the middle of the century, they were more likely to be incarcerated. This coincided with a shift in the thinking about women and femininity during the Victorian era, in which women were seen as more fragile than men. The growing rate of incarceration between 1815 and 1860 can be also linked to such changes as urbanization and the rise in urban police forces and moral reformers. Both men and women were increasingly arrested for drunkenness and vagrancy. However, since stricter moral codes existed for women, they were more likely to be convicted of such crimes.

There were fewer jobs for women, and the wages for women were lower, so many women resorted to prostitution to support themselves and their families. During times of war, the problems increased, as women often had few, if any, options while their husbands were away. After the first offense, women were often seen as outcasts and entered a life of chronic criminality. Although men would consort with such women

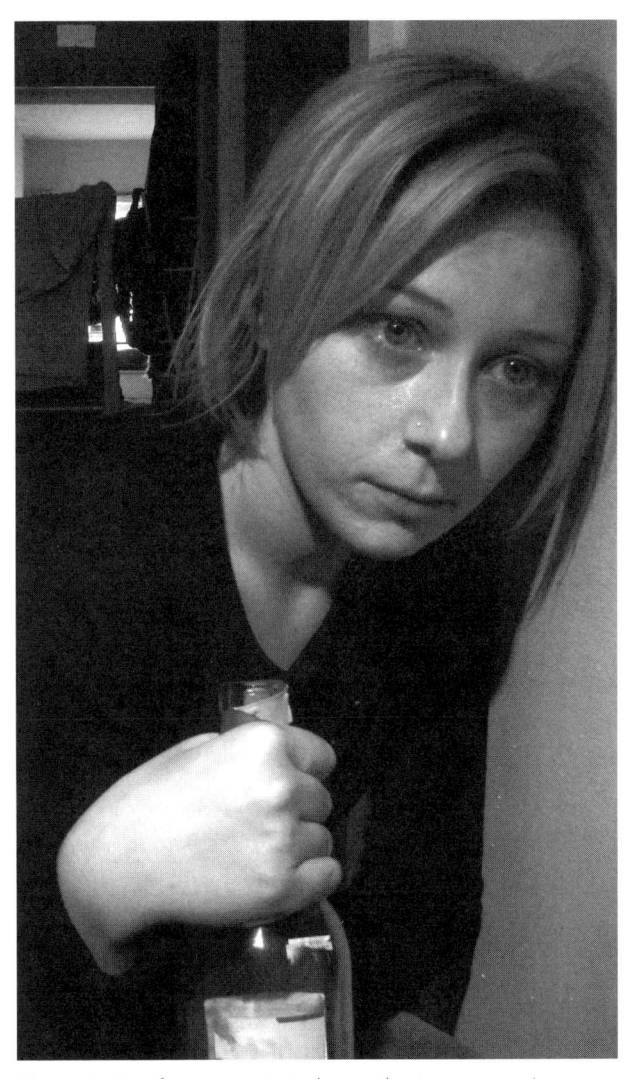

The majority of women criminals are also trauma survivors, reporting higher rates of substance abuse, having been abused as children, and psychiatric diagnoses.

prostitutes, men would openly not associate with or hire "fallen women," or even one suspected of questionable behavior, thus leaving women stigmatized and unable to support themselves by legal means. Once so labeled and incarcerated, women were taught to be "more feminine" and perform female duties such as cooking and cleaning. However, once released from prison and back in society, they continued to be ostracized and had limited options for taking care of themselves. During this period, single women and racial minorities were overrepresented among women criminals.

Prostitution, one of the most prevalent crimes committed by women, rose at the end of the 1800s. Women who became prostitutes were largely in their late teens and 20s. They were often illiterate, disgraced, homeless, and saw few other options. Many immigrant women, who came to the New World hoping for a better life, were forced into prostitution by the lack of opportunities they found upon arrival. Urbanization and the economic prosperity that accompanied the industrial age increased the demand for prostitutes. The irony of prostitution, then and now, is that despite societies' moral objections, prostitutes were in demand by successful men, who, conscious of their reputations, would not interact with such women in other settings.

Starting in 1853, William Sanger conducted one of the earliest sociological studies on prostitution in New York City. Sanger had police interview 2,000 women incarcerated in a hospital for those with venereal disease. The result was his book *The History of Prostitution*, a large statistical study that surprised many with its findings. The median age of the women interviewed was 15, and most women were immigrants who were unskilled. However, about half of the women came from families of elite or of skilled workers. Although most had been deserted by men, or were single mothers or widows, about a quarter of the women reported that they were attracted to the easy money. Other causes cited were drinking, bad company, and being seduced on immigrant ships. That some women cited that it was a choice to make easy money surprised reformers. However, at this time, there were not many job options for women that paid well. Sanger estimated that the average life expectancy of prostitutes was four years after starting to work, and that one-half of prostitutes had a sexually transmitted disease.

Early theories of women's crime also focused on biological causes. Cesare Lombroso and William Ferrero published *The Female Offender* in 1895, which put forth the idea of the "born criminal." Lombroso and Ferrero posited that criminality is a biologically determined masculine trait. Therefore, women who were criminals must be less evolved, prone to deviant behavior, and therefore incapable of being reformed. Lombroso and Ferrero theorized that, because of their biologically defective nature, female criminals were a lot more evil than male criminals. They even ascribed certain primitive physical features to them, including skull abnormalities, darker features, more hair, and shorter stature. They dismissed any ideas that society played any part in the criminality of women. These theories helped to further marginalize women who had been convicted of crimes and were reminiscent of the "whore/Madonna" duality of the times: Good women are submissive and know their place, and bad women step out of the prescribed boundaries and must be evil.

By the end of the 19th century, reformers who focused on women criminals had rejected such theories and began to look at other correlates such as poverty and lack of education. They espoused the idea of preventive training and training in prisons that prepared women to be self-reliant upon release, but prisons still focused on discipline, and women who had committed any crimes were still shunned upon release or given such low-paying jobs that they were unable to support themselves. Although female reformers had moved past such prejudicial notions of biological predetermination, society as a whole had not.

Twentieth-Century Theories

Well into the 20th century, theorists perpetuated biological and sexist theories of female criminality. W. I. Thomas, in his works *Sex and Society* (1907) and *The Unadjusted Girl* (1923), acknowledged that society did play a role in women's criminality, but he did not acknowledge that society played a role in lack of opportunities for women. Thomas's theories featured psychological needs to give and receive love, which led to promiscuity. Judge Marcus Kavanaugh, author of *The Criminal and His Allies* (1928), stated that women criminals were more evil than men, and that all male criminals were influenced by at least one criminal woman. In general, his views on women were very biased. Among other beliefs he held during his career, Kavanaugh held that women's having the right to vote had damaged the natural order by compromising gender roles.

In 1951, Otto Pollak wrote *The Criminality of Women*. In his book, he theorized that women were as prone to crime as men, but that they were better at hiding their crimes because they are more cunning. Therefore, his theory encompassed both biological and sociological underpinnings of women and crime. Pollak believed that women were naturally deceitful, as evidenced by their ability to hide both their menstruation and orgasms. He did not believe that societal constraints and gender roles dictated that women play a passive role in sex. Pollak also believed that women used their innate cunning to obtain leniency in the criminal justice system. According to his theories, women committed as many crimes as men but the statistics were flawed because of this leniency.

Research in the 20th century has spawned other theories as to why women commit crime. Women reformers began exploring the causes of female criminality. They rejected the Social Darwinism of Lombroso and others and began to look at sociological factors, focusing on environmental sources of crime. Their research, which was conducted in women's prisons, led to a shift away from the notion of "fallen woman," although that notion is still invoked by some even in modern times. Their research revealed that such environmental factors as lack of education, poverty, and limited job opportunities for women were reasons that women committed crimes. They advocated less incarceration and more preventive services, which would give women the resources to support themselves by legal means.

Although Social Darwinist theories of women's criminality are still in existence, other theories have emerged, some similar to the ideas of the reformers of the early 20th century. As rates of crime by women have increased over the past few decades, researchers have developed new theories. Freda Adler's masculinity thesis equates criminality with being "masculinized." This theory posits that as women have taken on roles traditionally limited to men, they have also adopted such male behaviors as aggression. It has its root in the early concept of the "fallen woman" in which women were punished for stepping outside traditional roles.

The opportunity thesis holds that as the employment patterns of men and women become similar, their patterns of criminality become similar because they have the same access to opportunities to commit crimes. Opponents of this theory point out that women's opportunities and socialization are still very different, and that the crime statistics do not uphold this theory. The marginalization thesis asserts the opposite of the opportunity thesis, that women commit crimes because of their lack of opportunities. It posits that jobs available to women often do not significantly improve their economic situation, so crime is necessary to improve their economic situation. Critics of this theory state that if this was true, crime would decrease as women's access to jobs increased, but this has not been the case. The chivalry thesis suggests that the women's movement bears some responsibility for the increase in women being convicted for crimes. It asserts that in the past, women received leniency for crimes. However, once they began campaigning for equal rights, the courts began to treat them as equals to men in terms of sentencing.

Feminist pathways theory posits that the pathways for women into the criminal justice system are different than those for men. Women offenders are much more likely to follow a path into criminal behavior that begins with childhood victimization, followed by mental health problems and substance abuse. Research indicates that women prisoners are more likely to have diagnosed mental health problems, report higher rates of childhood sexual abuse, and have higher rates of substance abuse problems than either incarcerated men or nonincarcerated women. Childhood stress created by adverse events is linked to psychological disorders such as substance abuse, depression, suicide attempts, and significant health problems. Childhood trauma is also linked to a higher probability of smoking, unintended pregnancies, sexually transmitted diseases, intimate partner violence, fetal death, and poor life quality related to health conditions. Further, these studies show that as the number of events increase, so does the risk for these adverse outcomes and behaviors, including committing crimes.

Pathways models have become richer in their complexity over time. For instance, Beth Richie described six pathways that lead battered African American women into illegal activities. She also stresses the interaction between illegal activities and such contextual factors as personal history, cultural values, and economic circumstances. She posits six paths that combine in different ways and includes such variables such as poverty, drug use, sex work, battering, sexual abuse, and murder for survival. Each specifically defines a unique pathway into illegal activity for differing groups of African American women who have been battered. Current feminist psychological theory urges researchers and clinicians to look at multiple social contexts for women's mental and physical health issues. These ideas support the pathways models, which see these undesirable contexts (poverty, violence, lack of education) as leading to crime.

Corrections and Women

The treatment of women in prison has mirrored the thinking of the times. Prior to the beginning of the 19th century, corporal and capital punishment were the primary forms of crime deterrents in the United States. However, in the early 1800s, changes in economic and social institutions prompted the increasing use of prisons as means of punishing and reforming the characters of criminals. Differing ideas of reform included discipline, isolation, and religious study aimed at converting criminals into penitent citizens. Some institutions focused on turning inmates into productive citizens. However, the activities were gender stereotyped. The men were taught to be laborers who contribute to the growing economy. Women, however, were taught to be "better women."

Dealing with women presented unique problems. There was no room for women to be isolated, and they could not take part in the training that men received. Women criminals were thought to be more depraved than men as they had defied their feminine nature and were seen as a threat to societal order. This distain led to the idea that they were beyond salvation, so they were largely ignored. However, they were subject to sexual abuse in the penitentiaries. Consequently, 19th-century prisons did little, by design, to reform women.

In 1815, Elizabeth Fry began a prison reform movement in England that spread to the United States by the 1820s. Starting with Quakers in Philadelphia, the reform movement grew throughout the country, working for the spiritual redemption of fallen women. By the 1890s, as more prisons for women came into being (the first women's prison opened in 1873), the voluntary reform movement had become a vocation, and women reformers became politically active. Such early feminists as Susan B. Anthony helped refocus attention on the economic plight of women criminals, away from the idea of the "fallen woman."

Early women's prisons—"feminine prisons"—focused on reformation rather than punishment. Their retraining included domesticity, prayer, and education, and some tried to provide job training that was appropriate for women, including domestic servitude. However, women were not seen as fit for labor. In Massachusetts, women became part of an indentured servant program, working for pay upon release from prison in homes under the supervision of housewives.

By the turn of the century, reformers began questioning the mainstream ideas about the causes of female criminality and supported research on the economic causes of crime. Most notably, Frances Kellor's research became the foundation of theory on the economic factors, discrediting theories on biological determinism. Feminists argued that finding occupations for women would help keep women from such crimes as prostitution, while opposing forces still claimed that putting women in men's occupations would lead to more crime. Research during that time showed that most women in prison were from poor families, had little education, and needed to work to support themselves, often in low-paying and tedious jobs.

By the 1920s, the economic and social theories of women's crime became generally accepted. This prompted new entities, including preventive services and probation for women. However, at the same time, changes were made inside the prisons. Increased focus was placed on education and vocational training (including clerical work), recreational training, and outdoor work in gardens on the prison grounds. The prison took on more of a campus format, with cottages replacing dormitories. Unfortunately, this system did not adequately prepare women to be self-sufficient. Prisons became overcrowded and were ill equipped to handle issues of physical and mental health, and they still were built around gender stereotypes.

By the 1920s, treatment of women in prison began to change, and in 1927, the first federal prison for women opened. The "softer" practice of the "feminine" prisons was replaced with an increased emphasis on social control. Strict enforcement of prostitution laws led to imprisonment of more prostitutes, who were seen as bad for social order. Prison started to develop into the prisons of the modern era.

Crime patterns in the 20th and 21st centuries are remarkably consistent with historical patterns. Crime rates for women have continued to rise, as have incarceration rates. Women have continued to be arrested for property offenses such as larceny, fraud, prostitution, and assault against their children or spouse. There has been an increase in substance-related and violent crimes committed by women over the past few decades.

Contemporary Theories
Today, although more modern theories have moved away from labeling women who commit crimes as innately deviant and much more is understood about why women commit crimes, women criminals are still largely shunned. Those in prison, locked away from our society, are unnoticed by the majority of the people in the United States. Behind bars, they are not in control of their lives. Every hour is scheduled for them, and access to important aspects of life such as food, exercise, contact with family, medical and psychological care, reading materials, and personal belongings are regulated. Although there have been advances in programming for women, there is still much room for improvement. Among female inmates, minorities are overrepresented. Research suggests that 40 percent or more are single mothers who are separated from their children upon incarceration. Women in prison often to do not have a high school diploma and are from lower socioeconomic groups. Once in prison, there are not enough places in needed educational or treatment programs for all who need them, and the vocational programming tends to be gender-stereotyped (food services, clerical), and therefore, women are not much better prepared to support their families than when they entered prison.

The majority of women in prison are also trauma survivors and victims of violent crimes who come from economically deprived, oppressive backgrounds. They report higher rates of substance abuse, abuse as children, and psychiatric diagnoses than incarcerated men or nonincarcerated women. Women in prison are likely to have experienced one or more types of trauma as a child or as an adult (or both), and research has shown rates as high as 80 percent for women having experienced at least one type of sexual or physical abuse.

Incarcerated women who have been diagnosed with mental health problems are likely to fight and have rules violations in prison, and are more likely to have committed violent crimes than those incarcerated women who do not have mental health problems. They are also less likely to have been employed before incarceration or to have lived with both parents, and they report higher rates of abuse, homelessness, having parents with substance abuse problems, having family members in prison, living in foster care or other agencies, and receiving public aid.

Women in prison suffer the same health issues as other women but with a higher frequency and greater severity. Incarcerated women have chronic health conditions, sexual and reproductive health issues, and health issues related to substance abuse and mental health issues. Some research suggests that the overrepresentation of minorities and women of lower socioeconomic status who have less access to healthcare or are less likely to access it contributes to this issue. During incarceration, women cannot easily access healthcare, and services in prisons are limited. Overall, incarcerated women are less healthy than men (incarcerated and nonincarcerated) and nonincarcerated women. They experience high rates of infectious diseases, respiratory conditions, digestive conditions, headaches, ear infections, musculoskeletal diseases, skin diseases, and genitourinary disorders. Substance abuse and sex work also leads to sexually transmitted diseases, including human immunodeficiency virus (HIV).

Conclusion

Theories about why women commit crimes have changed over the centuries, and research has led to a much greater understanding of women's criminality. The crimes that women commit and the treatment that they receive have been somewhat consistent for more than a century. Women's crimes continue to be economic in nature, fueled by lack of education and opportunities. Modern research has also revealed that women's crime follows a pathway that starts with violence and abuse and leads to prison. The needs of women today echo those of the early reformers, who called for better job opportunities for women and more preventive services.

Prisons continue to be overcrowded and gender stereotyped and do not adequately prepare women to be self-sufficient upon release. Prison programming has benefited from the research of those who have helped develop assessment and programming that are uniquely suited to women's needs. However, overall, much change is still needed.

Susan Marcus-Mendoza
University of Oklahoma

See Also: 1921 to 1940 Primary Documents; Gender and Criminal Law; Women Criminals, Contemporary; Women Criminals, History of; Women in Prison.

Further Readings

Belknap, Joanne. *The Invisible Woman: Gender, Crime and Justice*, 2nd ed. Belmont, CA: Wadsworth Group, 2001.

Freedman, Estelle B. *Their Sisters' Keepers*. Ann Arbor: University of Michigan Press, 1981.

Rafter, Nicole Hahn. *Partial Justice: Women in State Prisons, 1800–1935*. Lebanon, NH: Northeastern University Press, 1985.

Sanger, William. *The History of Prostitution: Its Extent, Causes and Effects Throughout the World*. New York: Medical Publishing, 1921.

Simon, Rita J. and Heather Ahn-Redding. *The Crimes Women Commit, the Punishments They Receive*, 3rd ed. Lexington, MA: Lexington Books, 2005.

Zaplin, Ruth. *Female Offenders: Critical Perspectives and Effective Interventions*. Sudbury, MA: Jones & Bartlett, 2008.

Women in Prison

Women have always been considered an afterthought in prisons. When women have been taken into account, it has been in gendered ways where race and class have been structurally interwoven to shape women's prisons and their experiences in prison. Women have always been a small part of the prison system, averaging between 4 and 8.7 percent. However, in the 20th and 21st centuries, their rate of increase has outpaced men since the tremendous growth of incarceration beginning in the 1970s. New draconian drug laws intensified along with net-widening (the redefinition of certain behaviors as crimes (e.g., pushing a child in a fight) along with traditional crimes for which women always have been imprisoned (e.g., bad checks, petty larceny, prostitution). Race and class are equally as important as gender in understanding women's incarceration. In the 19th and early 20th centuries, poor white women were incarcerated in reformatories for their sexual activity, while poor black women post-slavery were imprisoned just like men in prisons for punishment, not reformation. With the jump in women's incarceration in the 1970s and 1980s, however, it has been poor women of color (black, Latina, and Native American) who are overrepresented in prisons today, with a very recent small drop due to new drugs (like methamphetamines) that have slightly increased white women's (and men's) incarceration.

History

In the United States, prisons as we know them have been in existence for the past 200 years. From the early 1800s, women were incarcerated in attics of the very buildings where men were being held and thus subject to the most egregious neglect and abuse by men—as well as by other women. Women defined as criminals were seen as impure, abnormal, a threat to the social order, and worse than incarcerated men. During the 19th century, white middle-class women reformers argued for separate state facilities for women prisoners; so by 1920, at least 20 states had developed female-only reformatories with the objective not to punish women so much as to focus on more feminine education and spiritual guidance that could rehabilitate them. Today, each state in the United States has at least one prison for women; the states with the largest prison populations (e.g., California, New York, and Texas) have considerably more.

Both masculine environments (wings of male prisons where black women were still incarcerated) and feminine reformatories (rural single-sex facilities with dormitories and no external walls where poor and working class white women were kept) existed up until the 1950s. Poor white women in the early reformatories of the late 1800s and early 1900s were being trained to work in newly emerging middle-class reformers' homes as domestic workers. They were being trained to be "ladies"—because so many of them were incarcerated for nonmarital sexual activity, which was not necessarily against the law but was against the newly emerging middle class norms for women. By the 1990s, when women were increasingly incarcerated due to "tough on crime laws" and nonviolent drug offenses, many women's prisons underwent remodeling that reflected the security and punishment of male facilities. Black and Latina women were increasingly being incarcerated in these more "masculine" facilities. Moreover, during the 20th century, some of the prison training programs for women shifted from domestic labor to more nontraditional industrial and skilled jobs, though most remained sex stereotyped even in industrial and skilled training. Today, while there may be a greater variety of programs in some women's prisons, they are often fewer in number and of much poorer quality than in men's prisons.

Contemporary Picture

In 1980, there were fewer than 12,500 women in state and federal prisons. Today, over 200,000 women are in prison, with an additional 100,000 in jail. Add to that the over 800,000 women on probation and parole. Combining these figures yields a shocking result: Today, more than one million women are under the control of the criminal justice system.

The reality of this growth, however, is that there is a differential impact by race as to which groups of women end up in prison. African American women are two times more likely (142 per 100,000 African American women) than Latinas (74/100,000 Latinas) and three times more likely than white women (50/100,000 white women)

Incarceration of immigrants after 9/11 has grown significantly. Most have not committed a crime but have violated civil codes and are awaiting decisions regarding deportation.

to be incarcerated. Women in prison are among the most oppressed and vulnerable populations in the United States. They are typically young, poor, head of household, with limited education, mothers of young children, not infrequently homeless, have serious long-term substance abuse problems, are in poor physical and mental health, and are the victims of childhood physical and sexual abuse with continued abuse in adult life. While far too many men in prison have also been abused in their youth, this abuse generally does not continue into adulthood.

Most women are taken into custody today for the same kinds of crimes for which women have always been arrested: nonviolent larceny-theft, forgery, fraud, and prostitution—with the critical addition since the 1980s of drug possession and sales. Only a minuscule percent of women are arrested for violent crime (and less than 0.1

percent of men as well); and while more than half of all men are imprisoned for violent crime, this is true for less than one-third of all women. Even when women commit violent offenses, gender and abuse play an important role.

Thus, of women convicted of murder or manslaughter, a large proportion of that small number killed husbands or boyfriends who repeatedly and violently abused them. While intimate partner homicide accounts for just 4 percent of all the murders of men by their female partners, a full one-third of all murders of women are by their husbands or male partners. Further, while murder of wives decreased 25 percent over a 30-year period recently, murder of husbands decreased three times as much (by 75 percent). Two of the most common explanations proffered are (1) increased services available for abused women and their children, and (2) women's greater ability to get a divorce and greater access to jobs and wages. Finally, women's incarceration for violent offenses tends to be of a much less serious nature than those of men (e.g., pushing or shoving) and often, too, the behaviors have only recently been defined as "offenses." For example, laws enacted to protect battered women have resulted in the victim being arrested along with the batterer because the police officers do not know whom to arrest. This is called "boot strapping" or "net widening" and brings more women into prison for lower levels of all types of crimes, and especially violent crimes.

Overall, women's incarceration for drug offenses increased between the 1970s and 2000s from one in 10 of all women prisoners to almost two in five. In the federal prison system, two out of three women are in prison for drug offenses. Moreover, it is not all women but mostly women of color (primarily black and secondarily Latina) who are incarcerated on drug charges. Women are much more likely to be given mandatory minimum sentences—and for much smaller amounts of drugs—such as crack, which until recently carried a punishment 100 times harsher than powder cocaine, a drug more typically the drug of choice among the white and upper-middle-class population. In 2010, this was changed to 18 times greater. Women, lower down in the drug hierarchy, are far less likely to have information that they can exchange for a lower sentence. Thus, a case can be made that the war on drugs has been a war on poor black and Latina women, who now comprise about 50 percent of the women's prison population, despite the fact that they represent only 25 percent of the general female population in the United States. In some states like New York, almost nine out of 10 women in prison for drugs are black and Latina. In short, what has changed are criminal justice policies, not the criminality of women, to explain much of the increase in women's incarceration.

With the expansion of detention and incarceration of immigrants after 9/11, there has been a mushrooming of the prison industrial complex and the privatization of immigrants' imprisonment. More than 32,000 undocumented immigrants are held by the federal government, while 1.6 million undocumented immigrants are held in some stage of immigration proceedings. In 2005, immigrants were no longer released on their own recognizance, and a massive building program by private prisons to detain them commenced. Because the federal government has not built more prisons, despite its immigrant detention centers filled to capacity, this has left a huge gap for private prisons to not only build prisons using government funds but also to treat immigrants as if they were criminals. Most detained immigrants have not committed a crime. They have violated civil, not criminal codes; yet they are treated like hardened criminals. This is equally true for women and children, as well as for whole families awaiting a decision about their legal status and deportation. While the majority of immigrants are incarcerated in county jails, private companies are paid to run many of these jails.

Experiences of Women in Prison

Drugs/Trauma/Mental Health: Drug arrests have led to the largest increase of women in prison in the last four decades. Women in prison have histories of higher levels of drug/alcohol use and abuse than men in prison, are more likely to have used drugs/alcohol when they were committing a crime or at time of arrest, and commit more crimes to support their habits. Despite their greater drug problems than men, drug programs are fewer and less effective in women's than men's prisons because they all too often have not addressed the specific and interrelated gendered/raced/classed needs of women. The most common types of drug treatment for women in prison are 12-step programs like Alcoholics Anonymous and Narcotics Anonymous, which vary greatly in structure and content, do not take into account women's point of entry in the addiction process when they enter prison, and do not have a culturally appropriate gender-specific approach to understanding incarcerated women's use and abuse of drugs/alcohol. Feminist scholars have focused on developing a gender-responsive integrated model for the treatment of addiction of women in the criminal justice system. First is the need to identify the theory of addiction being used; second is to use a theory of women's psychological development that understands how women learn, grow, and heal; and third is to understand how a theory of trauma (both sexual and physical, both childhood and adult) must be expanded to include structural racism, the experience of violence in its many forms, and the stigma, stress, and abusiveness of incarceration itself.

Gender-responsive treatment involves the creation of an environment (including staff and programs) that reflects the lives of the women and responds to their strengths and difficulties. Six aspects of such a program include (1) acknowledgement that gender makes a difference; (2) creation of an environment based on safety, respect, and dignity; (3) program development based on relationships that promote healthy connections between staff and participants, and to children, family, and community; (4) addressing substance abuse, trauma, physical and mental health issues through comprehensive, culturally relevant services and supervision; (5) providing women with opportunities to improve their socioeconomic circumstances; and (6) establishing a system of community supervision and re-entry with comprehensive, collaborative services. Most recently, the need to understand the disadvantaged socioeconomic structure and barriers to education, employment, housing, treatment, family reunification, gender/race/class-responsive resources, and other institutions of the communities to which women will return is seen as equally important as the programs themselves in prison.

Women In Prison Are Mothers: Approximately 1.7 million minor children in the United States have a parent in prison. Almost two-thirds of all women in prison are parents of children under age 18. Black children are 7.5 times more likely, while Latina/o children are more than 2.5 times more likely than white children to have a parent in prison. Nine out of 10 male prisoners rely on the child's mother for care while they are incarcerated; only 37 percent of women rely on the child's father when they are incarcerated. Instead, most female prisoners rely on the children's maternal grandmothers and other female relatives. Between 6 and 10 percent of women in prison are pregnant on any given day. All too often, women are still shackled when they are giving birth and the babies are taken away within 24–48 hours.

Parenting programs in women's prisons range from classes on parenting to nurseries where women can live with their infants until a certain age—typically not more than one year or 18 months. Until the 1950s, nurseries in women's prisons were not uncommon. Today, there are only nine prison nurseries in operation or in planning stages in the United States. While some prisons have specialized visitation programs for mothers and children, such visitations are uncommon for a variety of reasons: prisons are too far from children's residences, inadequate finances to get them there, and mothers and/or caretakers experience shame and embarrassment if they expose children to a mother in prison.

Prisoner Reentry and Collateral Consequences
Restrictive crime policies place impossible burdens on marginalized women leaving prison and on the communities to which they return. Financial penalties—including fines, fees, costs, surcharges, forfeitures, assessments, reimbursements, and restitutions—may be imposed on many people in prison. Though little recognized, these penalties form serious impediments to women's successful reintegration into the community. In addition, the vast majority of all ex-offenders cannot vote, although some can once they have finished their parole or probation. But women convicted of felony drug offenses are subjected to a host of additional restrictions that exacerbate their already vulnerable social status.

Implications of Incarceration for Drug Offenders: Laws at both state and federal levels require public housing facilities to deny residence to convicted felons, including drug offenders. As a result, women leaving prison with limited financial means may be forced to seek alternative forms of shelter. Yet, subsidized housing may be one of the very few options open to them. This means women may not reside with their families who live in public housing facilities, as entire families can be evicted for providing housing to ex-offenders, especially those convicted of drug offenses. Public housing facilities are disproportionately located in poor, urban communities of color; thus, women returning to these communities feel the disparate impact of public housing bans. This places women with felony drug convictions at increased risk of homelessness and other substandard housing options, including returning to an abusive partner.

The Felony Drug Provision (FDP) of the 1996 Welfare Reform Act permanently bans receipt of cash assistance and food stamps for anyone convicted of a drug felony. While states can opt out of the FDP, only eight have done so; 22 enforce the ban in full and 20 states in part. Largely due to race- and gender-based socioeconomic inequalities making them highly susceptible to poverty and thus overrepresented in the welfare system, black and Latina mothers are disproportionately disadvantaged by this lifetime welfare ban. People with felony convictions also are banned from certain employment sectors. Typically, former offenders are restricted from civil service and working as beauticians and nurses, in child care and education, and as home healthcare workers, all jobs that are heavily black and female. Thus, for black women, these employment restrictions are particularly harsh given race-based employment segregation that denies them jobs based on their race and criminal history, no matter how minor.

Victim service agencies may refuse treatment and resources to women with criminal convictions. Sometimes, funding requirements forbid service provision to ex-offenders. Denial of victim services is especially problematic for women of color, as well as poor white and immigrant women, who are at greater risk of intimate partner abuse than majority-group counterparts. These policies are particularly harmful to black women who have some of the highest victimization rates for rape, intimate partner abuse, and murder in the country. Lack of access to victim services for poor black and Latina women exacerbates the intensity of poverty, segregation, and isolation within poor black and Latina communities to which formerly incarcerated drug offenders typically return.

Implications of Incarceration for Higher Education of Women Returning to Their Home Communities: Only 5 percent of all prisoners in the United States today participate in postsecondary education, the vast majority not in college classes. Only about 15 percent of college program providers are four-year public colleges, while the remaining 85 percent of programs are provided by community colleges. Education, and even more so college education, in prison appears to be the best predictor of decreased recidivism, greater probabilities for enhanced problem-solving skills, greater opportunities for steady employment and safety on the outside, as well as safer and more manageable conditions inside prisons. However, over the last two decades—with "tough on crime" laws and the elimination of Pell grants for prisoners in the 1990s—state funding of prisons nationally grew at six times the rate of state spending on higher education.

While correctional education reduces recidivism and improves employment for ex-offenders, this is best achieved along with an integrated set of services that meet the woman's needs once she is back home, such as drug counseling and development of work skills, and health and sobriety support and insurance for women and their children. When back in their home communities, despite women's greater challenges due to low levels of pre-incarceration employment, high levels of abuse in their lives, and inadequate healthcare, college education for women in prison has even greater potential benefits for women when they leave prison.

In addition, there is a multiplier effect for women, since they are much more likely than fathers coming out of prison to be living with their children and acting as a role model for them. However, a prison record can act as a real barrier to obtaining and continuing much-needed college work. Being able to begin that college education in prison is a major stepping-stone for some women to continue their education once back in the community.

Colleges and universities in the community today increasingly are including criminal history background checks in admissions processes. Exclusionary policies against ex-offenders have been used, despite the reality that almost no evidence exists showing criminal histories of college applicants are relevant to increasing crime on campus. Crime on campus is more likely committed by students without criminal records, leaving campuses less safe and more racially divided, given the special requirements for former prisoners. Because far larger numbers of African Americans and other people of color are incarcerated, these policies impact people coming out of prison in racially discriminatory ways.

Because of the race, class, and gendered disadvantages for poor marginalized women of color and poor white women, an even greater hurdle occurs for these women coming out of prison and trying to make a better life for themselves and their children. Along with the barriers to higher education for women coming out of prison, research has shown that for women specifically, a criminal record has a negative impact on employment opportunities, and the barriers resulting from them lead especially African American women to being heavily targeted in their pursuit of employment.

The communities to which most marginalized women return after prison are in very poor conditions as well. Most poor women of color leaving jail and prison return to a small number of communities in inner cities with the very same structurally debilitating conditions they left upon entering prison: disenfranchised communities with limited economic, social, and political resources. Affordable housing, jobs, healthcare, child care, and educational opportunities are limited at best, and seriously limited community resources are further inhibited by the women's inadequate education and criminal records. The women face multiple, competing demands as they simultaneously try to regain custody of minor children, juggle childcare, search for housing and employment, try to enroll in educational and substance abuse treatment programs, and keep in contact with their parole officer. Many of these demands are conditions of their release.

In short, the criminal justice system is dealing with social problems at the very end of the causal system. Prevention, both in the community and in prisons, can provide comprehensive resources for culturally competent, antiracist and feminist drug treatment, education, job training, healthcare, domestic violence and sexual abuse programs, as well as transitional services back into the community for women (and men) leaving prison. Next, it is important within communities to provide economic empowerment of residents, decent affordable housing, shelter and nonshelter approaches for battered and sexually abused women, safe affordable child care, and safe neighborhoods and infrastructures that can transform poor, racially segregated neighborhoods.

In addition, it is important to focus on eliminating tough on crime policies, to decriminalize drugs, and to provide alternatives to incarceration in communities outside the prison. Further, women leaving prison will be better served by ending prohibitions on people after they have served their time, including welfare, housing, jobs, voting, child custody, and food stamps. Finally, they need training, resources, and hope, both inside and outside prison. The problems facing women in prison, and before they get there, must include an understanding of these broader structural issues in addition to the lives and experiences of individual women who get entrapped within the criminal justice system.

Natalie J. Sokoloff
John Jay College of Criminal Justice

See Also: Gender and Criminal Law; National Organization for Women; Women Criminals, Contemporary; Women Criminals, History of; Women Criminals, Sociology of; Wuornos, Aileen.

Further Readings
Allard, Patricia. *Life Sentences: Denying Welfare Benefits to Women Convicted of Drug Offenses*. Washington, DC: The Sentencing Project, 2002.
Britton, Dana. "Penology in America: Men's and Women's Prisons as Gendered Projects." In *At Work in the Iron Cage*. New York: New York University Press, 2003.
Bush-Baskette, Stephanie. "The War on Drugs as a War on Black Women." In *Crime Control and Women: Feminist Implications of Criminal Justice*

Policy, Susan L. Miller, ed. Thousand Oaks, CA: Sage, 1998.

Covington, Stephanie. "Women in Prison: Approaches in the Treatment of Our Most Invisible Population." 1998. http://www.stephaniecovington.com/pdfs/15.pdf (Accessed May 2011).

Glaze, Lauren and Laura Maruschak. *Parents in Prison and Their Minor Children*. Bureau of Justice Statistics Special Report. NCJ 222984 (2008, Revised 3/30/2010). http://bjs.ojp.usdoj.gov/content/pub/pdf/pptmc.pdf (Accessed April 2011).

Price, Barbara Raffel and Natalie J. Sokoloff, eds. *The Criminal Justice System and Women: Offenders, Prisoners, Victims, and Workers*. New York: Mc-Graw-Hill, 2004.

Wuornos, Aileen

Dubbed by newspapers as "the nation's first lesbian serial killer," the "lesbian whose hatred of men caused her to murder again and again," and the "Damsel of Death," Aileen "Lee" Wuornos murdered and robbed seven white, middle-aged men in north and central Florida during a period of 13 months in 1989 and 1990.

At this time Wuornos, a prostitute of nearly 20 years, was a so-called exit-to-exit hooker who picked up customers along interstate highways. Prosecutors later argued that she posed as a damsel in distress and used the promise of sex to lure her victims to secluded areas. As the number of murder victims increased—and it became clear that a serial killer was responsible—police were under intense media and political pressure to find the perpetrator.

Following state and national appeals to locate the victims' cars, Wuornos was arrested in January 1991 outside a biker bar called the Last Resort in Daytona Beach. Within a matter of days, she had confessed to the murders to her former lover Tyra Moore, who was assisting the police in return for immunity from prosecution. Wuornos was tried for only one murder, that of Richard Mallory, a 51-year-old Clearwater electronic technician whose body was found near Daytona Beach. Wuornos claimed initially that she had acted in self-defense when her customers became violent or raped her. In January 1992, a jury took just two hours to return a verdict of guilty and then to vote unanimously for the death penalty. Wuornos pled no contest to five other murders and received life sentences for each. The body of one male victim, Peter Siems, was never found, and so Wuornos was not charged with his murder.

Born in 1956, Wuornos was originally from Michigan but had moved to Florida in the mid-1970s. Information on her troubled childhood and teenage years was reported in great detail during her trial. It was also presented as mitigating evidence in her unsuccessful appeals to the state and U.S. Supreme Courts to overturn the death sentence. This included a father whom she never knew who was a convicted child molester and who later committed suicide in prison. Wuornos was a victim of child rape and sexual violence, and she had given birth to a son at age 15, but was pressured into giving him up for adoption. She also had a long history of alcohol and drug addiction, mental health problems, and previous convictions for assault and robbery.

After nearly 10 years on Florida's death row, in July 2001, Wuornos appeared in court and "volunteered" to die, or opted not to make any further appeals against her convictions or death sentence. These actions disturbed Capital Collateral and other anti–death penalty groups in Florida, but in April 2002, the Florida Supreme Court ruled unanimously that Wuornos was mentally competent to fire her attorneys, stop her appeals, and accept her death sentence.

On October 9, 2002, 46-year-old Wuornos became the first woman in Florida to be executed by lethal injection, and the tenth woman to be executed in the United States since the reinstatement of capital punishment in 1976. The *St. Petersburg Times* concluded, "The best thing that Wuornos ever did for humanity was to volunteer to leave it."

Wuornos's life history, her sexual orientation and relationship with Moore, and her abrasive personality and verbal outbursts in court, as well as contemporary fascination with the serial killer, ensured that she captivated the popular imagination. She was the subject of several books, two movies—*Overkill: The Aileen Wuornos Story* and

Monster (starring Charlize Theron, who received several awards, including an Oscar for her performance)—documentaries, and an opera.

Vivien Miller
University of Nottingham

See Also: Executions; Florida; Serial and Mass Killers; Women Criminals, Contemporary.

Further Readings

Miller, Vivien. "'The Last Vestige of Institutionalized Sexism?': Paternalism, Equal Rights and the Death Penalty in Twentieth and Twenty-First Century Sunbelt America: The Case for Florida." *Journal of American Studies*, v.38 (2004).

O'Shea, Kathleen A. *Women and the Death Penalty in the United States, 1900–1998*. Westport, CT: Praeger, 1999.

Reynolds, Michael. *Dead Ends: The Pursuit, Conviction and Execution of Female Serial Killer Aileen Wuornos, the Damsel of Death*. London: St. Martin's True Crime, 2004.

Wuornos, Aileen. *Monster: My True Story*. London: John Blake Publishing, 2006.

Wyoming

The least populous state in the country, Wyoming was admitted to the Union in 1890. An often iconoclastic state, it was the first to extend the right to vote to women—having done so while still a territory in 1869 and subsequently guaranteeing the right in its state constitution. Even in its territorial days, when the area was reputed for its outlaws and frequent violence, Wyoming appointed the first female court bailiff and the first female justice of the peace.

The most famous of those outlaws congregated at Hole in the Wall in northern Wyoming in the Big Horn Mountains. The Hole in the Wall gangs included Butch Cassidy's Wild Bunch (no relation to the Wild Bunch in Missouri years earlier), which operated around the turn of the century. Butch Cassidy (born Robert LeRoy Parker) had alternated between ranching work and crime since his teen years and assembled the Hole in the Wall Gang in the 1890s after his release from prison following a sentence for stealing horses and operating a protection racket. Other members of the gang included Harvey "Kid Curry" Logan, Ben Kilpatrick, "News" Carver, Harry Tracy, the Sundance Kid, and Cassidy's best friend, Elzy Lay.

In its day, and in dime novels for a long time thereafter, the Wild Bunch was described as a nonviolent gang, with newspapers and writers parroting the gang's claim that they abstained from killing. The pacifist boast was incorrect; while victims of their robberies were rarely killed, most of the gang had killed lawmen who pursued them, and Kid Curry alone killed nine lawmen during his stint with the gang. One of the Bunch's most notorious jobs was the robbing of a Union Pacific train near Wilcox on June 2, 1889, during which they wore masks made from napkins taken from a Harvey House restaurant, a job that netted about $50,000.

Lay was wounded and captured after a New Mexico train robbery Cassidy wasn't part of, and the Sundance Kid replaced him as Cassidy's primary partner. Teenager Henry Longabaugh had been imprisoned in 1887 for stealing a gun, horse, and saddle from a ranch in Sundance and took the name Sundance Kid while in jail. Like Cassidy, his criminal activities came between periods as a ranch hand and cowboy. Famous for his quick draw—a skill that dime-novel characters often possessed but that only a handful of real-life gunslingers ever made use of—Sundance is one of the few members of the Wild Bunch not known to have killed anyone while with the gang. Cassidy and Sundance eventually fled to Bolivia while pursued by Pinkerton agents hired by the railroad companies.

Crime, Police, and Punishment

Early Wyoming law enforcement was the province of federal marshals and county sheriffs. The county sheriffs remained an important law enforcement institution after statehood and into the present, helping to provide law enforcement services to rural areas that cannot support a large or advanced police department. The oldest city police departments in Wyoming were established during the territorial era, such as Cheyenne's, established in 1867. Police departments, unlike earlier constables or night watchmen, were staffed by full-time employees who were not elected, a professional class that coincided with the professionalization of fire departments and other industries.

The federal government built the Wyoming Territorial Penitentiary in 1873, in Laramie. It was decommissioned at the turn of the century and is today operated as a museum. It was replaced by the first Wyoming State Penitentiary, authorized in 1888 and opened in 1901, shortly after statehood, in the city of Rawlins. The Wyoming State Penitentiary closed in 1981 and was renamed the Wyoming Frontier Prison, a tourist attraction.

The end of the 19th century was also marked by anti-Chinese violence in Wyoming, some of it stirred up by the Knights of Labor. Anti-Chinese sentiment was at least superficially concerned with economics; Chinese immigrants would work more cheaply than whites would, and companies—sometimes as a matter of policy, sometimes because of economic problems of their own—began to hire Chinese labor instead of white labor, especially as more Chinese workers became available.

The number of Chinese miners working more cheaply than unionized white miners angered the Knights of Labor—the most important labor organization of the decade—who in several states and territories incited whites to attempt to expel the Chinese from their settlements. In Wyoming, this led to the Rock Springs massacre of September 2, 1885, in which at least 28 Chinese miners were killed in a riot.

Wyoming is a capital punishment state, its current death penalty statute dating to 1977, when Supreme Court decisions had forced death penalty laws to be rewritten. Defendants in first-degree murder trials with one or more of 11 aggravating factors (e.g., the shooting of a police officer) may face death or life in prison without parole, at the discretion of the jury. Lethal injection has been the sole method of execution under the current statute, the gas chamber and hanging having preceded it.

The violent crime rate in Wyoming, 195.9 crimes per 100,000 inhabitants in 2010, is less than half that of the national average, and falling. Crime peaked in 1981, much earlier than in most of the country, at 430, and has fluctuated since; crime has generally been falling since 1992, with minor upticks every few years. The 2010 levels are the lowest since 1974.

Bill Kte'pi
Independent Scholar

See Also: Chinese Americans; Executions; Oregon; Washington.

Further Readings
Davis, John W. *Goodbye, Judge Lynch*. Norman: University of Oklahoma Press, 2006.
Hufsmith, George W. *The Wyoming Lynching of Cattle Kate*. Cheyenne, WY: High Plains Press, 1993.
Wilson, R. Michael. *Outlaw Tales of Wyoming: True Stories of the Cowboy State's Most Infamous Crooks, Culprits, and Cutthroats*. Two Dot, MT: TwoDot, 2008.

Xenophobia

Xenophobia, the hatred or fear of strangers or foreign persons—or of anything else, for that matter, that is strange or foreign—is common around the globe. Through various time periods, people or ideas that were "foreign" have been alternately embraced and shunned. These shifts in public thought are often tied to changing political parties, international conflicts, or economic conditions. In American history, these things have contributed to outbreaks of xenophobic behavior, but the United States, as a nation full of immigrants, has also seen such activity as the reaction to waves of immigrant arrival. These periods of immigration have always heavily favored one ethnic group or another, and almost always have resulted in a public outcry against individuals from the migrating group, which was then followed by a reaction by the migrant group against the pre-existing population. Scholars have argued that the prevalence of racially and ethnically self-segregated neighborhoods can be traced to these push and pull factors.

Early American Xenophobia

In early American history, xenophobic behavior was the result of tensions between social classes rather than racial groups. The white landowners were constantly in need of a steady labor source, and in the 17th century particularly, slave labor was not widely available in many of the colonies, or the agricultural produce was not particularly attuned to a system of mass slave labor. Throughout the colonies, indentured servants, who voluntarily signed onto a period of labor in exchange for passage to the colonies and a small stipend upon completion of the term, made up a great deal of the labor population in this earliest period. Alongside them, the British attempted to use incarcerated criminals or native slaves, but the indentured servant was by far the most productive and least disruptive labor source. However, as indentured servant contracts expired and servants began to compete with their former masters, a sort of class conflict based on vast cultural differences between the laboring and planter classes began to crop up. These tensions increased over time and sometimes resulted in armed engagements. These xenophobic attitudes are apparent in the shift away from indentured servitude and toward slave labor in the latter part of the 17th century and into the early 18th century.

The first legislation that directly referenced a control on immigration was the 1790 Naturalization Act. Although passed in the young republic with reference to gaining citizenship, the act accurately portrays the level of xenophobic thought and fear that was with the ruling class and the politicians of the time. Because of racial and class tensions that had steadily grown over the 18th century, the 1790 act refused citizenship to any person who was not a "free white." However, not even all groups known as "white" were particularly welcome. In the years before his death, Benjamin Franklin, who had supported the 1790 act, spoke out publicly and in print against the legalization of German immigration. He was convinced that the two cultures were simply too different—and possessed of a different "characteristic spirit" to ever get along—and proposed limitations or complete prohibition on their legal immigration. This, of course, did not happen, and today German Americans are the most populous of the European-based immigrant communities in the United States, with an estimate of some 4 million persons settled.

Irish and Chinese Immigrants
In the 19th century, young America was the premier destination for immigrants. The opportunities for personal advancement and new beginnings often coincided with challenges in Europe and Asia to lead large groups to American shores. In many cases, these immigration waves were almost immediately followed by a local backlash wherever the populations began to settle. The two most powerful xenophobic reactions against these waves of immigration focused on the Irish in the 1850s and the Chinese in the 1870s.

After a period of incredible tension and anger in Ireland, which culminated in the 1848 potato blight and resultant famine, large numbers of Irish left for America. Economic conditions at home were dire, and there was little to indicate that conditions were going to change in the near future, if at all. Because of these difficulties, along with the growth of urban centers in America, which meant more economic opportunity, large numbers of Irish immigrated to the United States throughout the 1840s and 1850s. These people normally took up very low-paying menial jobs in urbanized areas, particularly New York City and the surrounding metropolis. Although the jobs they took were low paying and not desirable, there was a considerable backlash against the Irish initially because of anti-Catholic sentiment that had fomented for some time. A political party of the time, the Know-Nothing, or American Party, focused on anti-Irish sentiment in the lead-up to the elections of 1852 and 1854. This nativist group typified the anti-Irish xenophobia of the time by calling for a limit or prohibition on Irish immigration, most importantly from the Catholic parts of the isle. Tensions erupted between the groups in 1857 when a group of Know-Nothing Party supporters arrived in Baltimore to try to control a polling location. A group including people from several well-known area Irish gangs such as the Plug Uglies began to riot, and a detachment of U.S. Marines was summoned to put down the brawl.

The Chinese began to immigrate to the United States in small numbers well before the 19th century; however, the largest influx of immigrants came following the conclusion of the Opium Wars between the British and Chinese. The end of these trade wars also marked a period of closeness between the American and Chinese governments. The 1868 Burlingame-Seward Treaty established formal friendly relations and guaranteed China "most favored nation" status. As a result, huge numbers of Chinese immigrants began to pour into the Americas, although the majority of them began in the western United States. As with Ireland, there were far more economic opportunities in mid-19th-century America than in China. American employers, eager for inexpensive Chinese labor, sometimes sent agents to employment agencies in China to find workers. These people, who could not pay their own way, were given a "credit-ticket," which paid their way to the United States and then repaid the ticket cost by way of garnished wages.

Initially, the Chinese immigrants were overwhelmingly males who hoped to come to America, save as much money as possible, send as much back to China as possible, and then return to China. As time went on, relatively more women and children began to immigrate. However, because of high costs of living and low wages, Chinese women often turned to prostitution to increase family income. The connection between Chinese women and prostitution was made as early as the 1860s by moralists and others who decried the Chinese as decadent and a danger to society in the United States. In 1882, the first race-specific immigration act was passed. The Chinese Exclusion Act forbade "skilled and unskilled laborers and Chinese employed in mining" from entering the United States. The act was initially supposed to last 10 years, but was renewed in 1892 and then again in 1902, when the 10-year renewal was removed and the law was made permanent. It was only repealed in 1943 with the Magnuson Act.

Xenophobic Legislation

American xenophobia has taken a number of forms. However, the most damaging and long-lasting has been legislation aimed at restricting or eliminating immigration. The earliest example of xenophobic legislation was the 1798 Alien and Sedition Acts, which gave immigration officials the right to question entering immigrants on their backgrounds and motivations for relocating. The Page Act of 1875 was the first legislation to be enacted that specifically limited immigration. This non-group-specific act prohibited the entry of any person deemed "undesirable" into the country. In this case, "undesirable" referred to anyone coming from Asia to perform contract labor or prostitution, or those who were considered to be criminals in their country of origin. This was followed in 1882 by the much more specific and pointed Chinese Exclusion Act, which specifically forbade Chinese from entering the United States except in rare cases.

Following the renewal of the Chinese Exclusion Act, a law passed in 1903 that was the result of a growing American fear of labor movements and anarchists who were gaining popularity and prestige in Europe at the time. Officially, this act allowed those who described themselves as or were suspected to be anarchists to be denied entry. Provisions in the act allowed the deportation of immigrants who were legally admitted and then later found to be some sort of undesirable, or those who entered illegally and were later caught. This sort of ideological xenophobia was extended in 1906 with the passage of the Naturalization Act of 1906. Further restrictions were placed upon Asian immigration in the 1917 Barred Zone Act, which heavily limited immigrants from the parts of Asia that were still allowed as of that time. The final immigration restriction act of this period came in 1921. The Emergency Quota Act of 1921 limited annual immigration to 3 percent of whatever the population was of the group in question as of the 1910 census. As many groups had not begun to move in earnest to American shores before that time, it was restrictive for some, but less restrictive for ethnic groups that had been in the country for some time, such as the Irish and Germans.

Since the 1920s, xenophobic immigration laws have loosened somewhat. Although a new wave of restrictive immigration legislation is being considered in Arizona and other states, prohibitions have dropped off and regulations all around have been lessened in severity. The Chinese Exclusion Act was finally formally repealed with the 1943 Magnuson Act, and Asian immigration as a whole was liberalized a great deal with the Immigration and Nationality Act of 1952, which abolished specific racial and ethnic restrictions while maintaining a quota system. This act broke immigrants into three groups: Those with special skills or who were relatives of U.S. citizens were admitted without question. Average immigrants fell under the quota system; and for the first time, refugees were considered "immigrants" rather than persons seeking asylum.

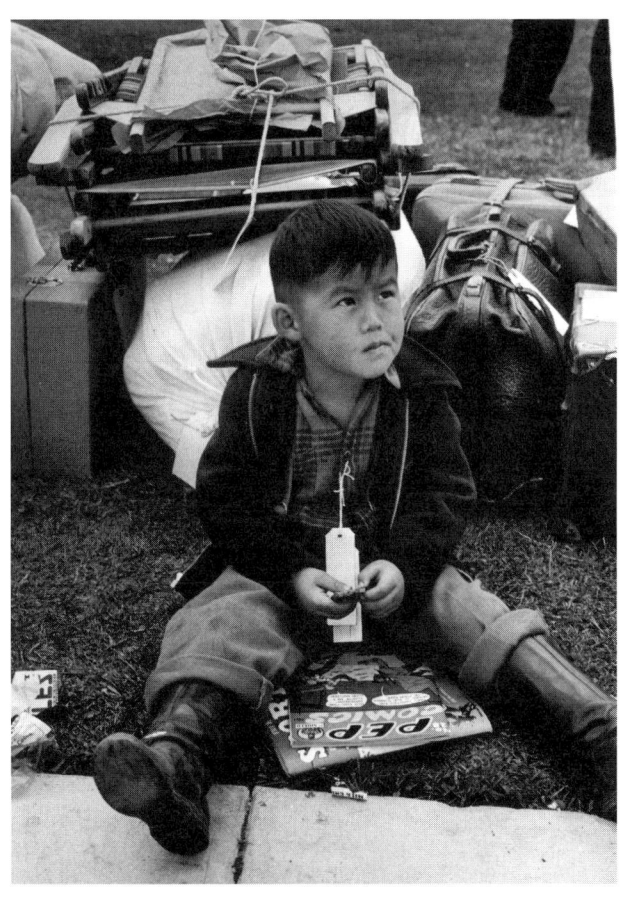

A young Japanese boy is "tagged for evacuation" in Salinas, California, in 1942, his family's belongings behind him. Japanese Americans were sent to internment camps following the attacks on Pearl Harbor, a clear example of xenophobia.

Xenophobic Actions

American xenophobia's more aggressive and shorter-term appearance is likewise multifaceted. From the Know-Nothing nativist party of the 1850s, xenophobic lynching and political agitation became the calling card of the Ku Klux Klan in the years immediately following the American Civil War. In the group's first incarnation, their hostility was pointed at the supporters of Lincoln's Republican Party as well as newly freed slaves and other free people of color within the United States. However, as the self-appointed defenders of American "purity," they focused on any particular group that seemed threatening at the time. Although the organized nationwide Klan fell apart soon thereafter, Jews and Catholics remained popular targets of white supremacists. The 1915 revival of the Klan saw an increased focus on anti-foreign xenophobia, particularly against Jews, Germans, and Irish, although the Klan still targeted blacks. Following World War I, Klan attention turned to communism and other ideologies found to be threatening.

The most famous directed xenophobic action by the U.S. government was the establishment of internment camps for Japanese Americans from 1942 following the Pearl Harbor attacks until the resolution of World War II. Executive Order 9066 was enacted by Franklin Roosevelt after anti-Japanese tensions and fears of full-scale invasion of the United States reached a high point in early 1942. A long-standing part of the Alien and Sedition Acts was the alien enemies clause, that stated that any person belonging originally to a state which was at war with the United States could be questioned and detained. During World War II, German, Italian, and Japanese Americans were required to register any change of address with the Federal Bureau of Investigation (FBI) and were restricted from entering a large number of areas on threat of arrest. Although any of these groups were under threat of detention, the widest-scale effort was the internment of Japanese Americans. A number of organizations—the U.S. military, the Department of Justice, and the War Relocation Authority—were responsible for the maintenance of these camps, which at the height of their use held as many as 120,000 people.

From the early 1980s, Hispanic immigrants have been targeted as the newest wave of "illegals." The "cocaine boom" period of the early 1980s resulted in large amounts of narcotics shipped to ports in Florida from many Latin American countries, particularly Cuba. Since that time, a number of efforts have been made to reduce or eliminate the number of Mexican and other Hispanic persons coming into the United States. During the George W. Bush administration, a plan to construct massive blockade walls began. but has largely been abandoned because of prohibitive costs. However, border patrol efforts, particularly in the southwest United States, Texas, New Mexico, California, and Arizona, were increased a great deal during that time and remain strong.

The current controversy in this area is the attempt by Maricopa County, Arizona, Sheriff Joe Arpaio to require all persons who "appear" to be illegal immigrants to carry documentation of legality with them, because they may be legally stopped by police and asked to show visas or passports.

Since the Al Qaeda attacks of September 11, 2001, a great deal of xenophobic fear has been turned on the Muslim population of America. A number of murders, beatings, and a great deal of harassment have been leveled at this population in a way reminiscent of the attacks on Japanese Americans following Pearl Harbor. Most recently, the construction of a Muslim community center at the site of the attack was the source of a great deal of controversy before the imam in charge of constructing the center bowed out, as of summer 2011, in favor of finding a different spot in the face of public outcry.

Robert W. Watkins
Florida State University

See Also: African Americans; Arpaio, Joseph M.; Chinese Americans; German Americans; Irish Americans; Japanese Americans.

Further Readings
Caldwell, Wilber W. *American Narcissism*. New York: Algora Publishing, 2006.
Knobel, Dale T. and Bruno Knobel. *America for the American: The Nativist Movement in the United States*. New York: Macmillan, 2006.
Robinson, Greg. *By Order of the President: FDR and the Internment of Japanese Americans*. Cambridge, MA: Harvard University Press, 2003.

Yates, Andrea

Andrea Kennedy was born on July 2, 1964, to a middle-class family. Intelligent and athletic, she captained the swim team, was an officer in the National Honor Society, and graduated valedictorian of Milby High School in 1982. She graduated the University of Texas School of Nursing in 1986 and held a postoperative nursing position from 1986 until 1994. She gained international attention in 2001 when she drowned her five children, becoming an early case in the national debate over postpartum depression.

Andrea met Russell Yates, a computer designer for the National Aeronautics and Space Administration (NASA), in 1989; they married in 1993. Between 1994 and 2000, Andrea gave birth to five children and had one miscarriage. For a time, they lived in a 38-foot trailer in which Andrea home-schooled the children; she also cared for her father suffering from Alzheimer's. Mental health symptoms emerged after Noah's birth in February 1994. Her postpartum disorder included mood fluctuations and violent hallucinations. After John's birth in December 1995, Andrea became reclusive, abandoning running and swimming. Paul's birth followed in September 1997, Luke's in February 1999. During this time, Michael Woroniecki, an itinerant minister, influenced Andrea with his sermons that exhorted Eve's sin as the reason "bad" mothers raised evil and damned children.

Events spiraled downward in 1999. On June 16, Andrea attempted suicide. Hospital psychiatrists diagnosed her with severe depressive disorder, yet released her a week later for insurance reasons; they prescribed Zoloft, which she did not take. Her depression morphed into hallucinations, self-mutilation, and a refusal to nurse Luke. In July, she again attempted suicide. In a private care facility, Andrea remained catatonic for 10 days. Haldol improved her condition, but doctors warned Russell and Andrea that another birth could ignite psychotic episodes. Andrea's family insisted that Russell buy a home rather than return to the trailer. Andrea stabilized: She resumed home schooling, cooked, sewed, and began swimming. Russell believed Andrea was strong enough to stop the medication to become pregnant. Mary was born in November 2000. Andrea remained stable until her father died in March 2001.

By spring 2001, psychotic episodes returned. She rebuffed food, recommenced self-mutilation, refused to nurse Mary, and frantically turned to religion. In March, she entered Devereux Texas Treatment Center and resumed Haldol, but a new psychiatrist deemed her not psychotic; he halted Haldol and discharged her. She returned to Devereux in May; the same psychiatrist released her after 10 days and recommended a psychological consult. Two days later, she drowned her children in her bathtub. In her taped confession, she claimed she had raised the children badly; killing them had saved them from Satan. In her 2002 trial, the prosecutor charged her with capital murder and asked for the death penalty. The jury listened to her confession and deemed her cold and methodical; they found her guilty, but rejected the death penalty for life imprisonment.

Yates's lawyers appealed. In November 2005, the Texas Supreme Court overturned the verdict because of false testimony by Dr. Park Dietz, the prosecutor's psychiatric witness: He testified that Yates had viewed a *Law & Order* episode in which a mother drowned her children in her bathtub but pleaded insanity to avoid jail; no such episode existed. In Yates's retrial in July 2006, she pled not guilty by reason of insanity; the jury agreed. She eventually moved to a low-security facility for the mentally ill. Russell, who had divorced Yates in 2005, supported this verdict. Reaction to Yates has been harsh. The press resorted to traditional gender notions: Infanticide is the antithesis of woman as nurturer. While some Americans sympathized with her, they had trouble believing she was insane when committing the acts because she appeared cool and rational in the aftermath. As late as 2010, *Newsweek* listed Yates as the third most mesmerizing crime of the decade, titling the entry "The Horror of Andrea Yates." Yet, psychiatrics have used the case to draw attention to discrepancies between American and European law. Most Western countries provide probation and mandate psychiatric treatment, not murder charges and death penalties. Advances in neuroscience have allowed psychiatrists to understand how mental illness affects brain function, but public understanding has not kept pace with new knowledge, leading the public to demand justice for victims at the expense of criminals who are also victims of their own mental illnesses.

Simone M. Caron
Wake Forest University

See Also: Gender and Criminal Law; Infanticide; Insanity Defense; Smith, Susan; Television, Crime in; Women Criminals, Contemporary.

Further Readings
Denno, Deborah W. "Who is Andrea Yates? A Short Story about Insanity." *Duke Journal of Gender Law and Policy*, v.10 (2003).
Miller, Lisa. "The Horror of Andrea Yates." *Newsweek*. 2010. http://2010.newsweek.com/top-10/mesmerizing-crime-stories/horror-of-andrea-yates.html (Accessed December 2011).

Yates v. United States

In 1940, Congress passed the Smith Act, making it a crime to advocate the overthrow of any U.S. government or organize in an attempt to do so. The act was a wartime measure primarily targeting Nazi, socialist, communist, and other unpopular political groups in the United States. In *Yates v. United States*, 354 U.S. 298, (1957), the U.S. Supreme Court was asked to determine whether the Smith Act's provisions on antigovernment advocacy were consistent with the First Amendment to the U.S. Constitution. In the 6–1 ruling for Yates and his codefendants, the court interpreted a number of the act's provisions in a manner that effectively put an end to all prosecutions under the Smith Act.

Oleta Yates was a Communist Party leader from California. In 1951, he and 13 of his colleagues were prosecuted for violating the Smith Act by organizing an attempt to overthrow the government. Prosecutors had no difficulty establishing that Yates and the other defendants were advocates of Marxist-Leninism. They were found guilty and sentenced to five years in prison. Yates and the others appealed their convictions, arguing that the Smith Act violated their First Amendment rights.

The U.S. Supreme Court heard the *Yates* case in 1957. Interpreting the Smith Act narrowly, the court found in favor of Yates. Writing for the majority, Justice John Marshall Harlan focused on two key terms found in the Smith Act: "organize" and "advocate." The majority determined that "organize" referred only to the actual founding of a group, not its ongoing daily operations. Since the Communist Political Association (CPA) disbanded and reformed into the Communist Party of the United States in 1945, the defendants' CPA activities were the only ones that could be considered "organizing." Unfortunately for the government, these actions fell outside the Smith Act's three-year statute of limitations and were therefore not subject to prosecution.

The second question, the meaning of the term "advocate," was equally challenging but had far greater First Amendment implications. The court determined that there are two different types of advocacy in which individuals and organizations may engage. These are advocacy of an idea and advocacy of an action. While the defendants often spoke about the need to radically change the U.S. government, they never advocated specific actions that would result in the overthrow of the government. Merely advocating a principle—even an illegal one such as overthrowing the U.S. government—the court held, was constitutionally protected by the First Amendment. However, advocating specific actions toward illegal ends, such as the overthrow of the U.S. government, was not protected by the Constitution.

The court's interpretation of "advocate" significantly reduced the reach of the Smith Act. While the act had been in place, simply discussing the theories about the overthrow of the U.S. government could be deemed advocacy, which severely restricted the flow of ideas. The *Yates* ruling allowed the views of those seeking radical change in the U.S. government to be exchanged and even championed, but required that they be expressed in principle only. If the person advocating the overthrow of the government began trying to put the ideas to action, the person could still face prosecution under the Smith Act.

Because the evidence from Yates's trial only demonstrated advocacy of an idea, additional evidence would be required for a conviction. The court overturned Yates's conviction and ordered a new trial. The court also found that the evidence against five of Yates's codefendants was so weak that it ordered their acquittal outright. Given the court's interpretation of the Smith Act, prosecutors declined to try Yates a second time.

Justices Hugo Black and William O. Douglas partially dissented from the court's decision, arguing that Smith Act prosecutions were inconsistent with the principles of the First Amendment because they punished individuals for simply holding and expressing unpopular political beliefs. Justice Tom C. Clark would have upheld all the convictions as he read the term *organize* to include the defendants' actions. Justices William J. Brennan and Charles E. Whittaker did not hear or contribute to the decisions of the case.

Darren A. Wheeler
Josh Thompson
Ball State University

See Also: *Dennis v. United States*; McCarthy, Joseph; Smith Act.

Further Readings

Belknap, Michael. *Cold War Political Justice: The Smith Act, the Communist Party, and American Civil Liberties (Contributions in American History)*. Westport, CT: Greenwood Press, 1977.

Heale, M. J. *American Anti-Communism: Combating the Enemy Within, 1930–1970*. Baltimore, MD: Johns Hopkins University Press, 1990.

Somerville, J. "Law, Logic, and Revolution: The Smith Act Decisions." *Western Political Quarterly*, v.14 (1961).

Zeisel, Hans

One of leading figures in the quantitative study of law and society, Hans Zeisel was a data analyst and a committed scholar who employed statistical evidence to demonstrate various positions on law-related issues. He was noted for systematic research on the jury system, capital punishment, court delay, and the House Un-American Activities Committee (a committee investigating Communist activity and anti-American propaganda).

Born in 1905 in the city of Kadaň, Bohemia (Czech Republic), Zeisel was taken as an infant to Vienna, Austria. He studied law and political science at the University of Vienna, earning a doctoral degree. He practiced law and was a researcher at the Austrian Wirtschaftspsychologische Forschungsstelle (Research Center for Psychology and Economics).

There he carried out, together with Marie Jahoda and Paul Lazarsfeld, his first noted study, *Die Arbeitslosen von Marienthal* (1933) (Unemployment in Marienthal), which investigated the detrimental effects that unemployment had on the psychological state of the unemployed. In the time of the *Anschluss* (the annexation of Austria to the German Third Reich) in 1938, Zeisel, who had just married Eva Striker, a Hungarian designer of ceramics, immigrated with his wife to New York. There he began a rich career in research and lecturing. In New York, he taught economics and statistics at the University of New York and worked with the Bureau of Applied Social Research at Columbia University. Zeisel also worked for the market and media industry, most notably for McCann-Erickson, Inc., and served as consultant for the War Department, the Justice Department, and the American Bar Association.

In 1947, he published his first influential text on statistics titled *Say It With Figures*, which presented Zeisel's methodology for empirical study into various areas of human affairs. Soon after, he joined the University of Chicago Law School and led, with Harry Kalven, several research projects funded by the Ford Foundation. Of these studies, one was published in 1959 under the title *Delay in the Court*, which addressed the congestion and delay in cases brought before the Supreme Court of New York County and discussed various solutions.

Another was *The American Jury* (1966), which examined how often the jury disagreed with the judge, the direction of that disagreement, and the reasons for it. In 1983, Zeisel published *The Limits of Law Enforcement*, which argued that society should cease its exclusive reliance on law enforcement for the reduction of crime and pay more attention to youth education and early life guidance.

Zeisel's fruitful academic career produced numerous articles, most notably discussing the pros and cons of jury size, possible remedies for court delays, and the crime-reducing effect of monthly monetary allowances for ex-convicts. Zeisel believed in abolishing the death penalty, which he argued was hardly a deterrent, was race-biased, and relied on uncontrolled variations of each case that rendered it impossible to be impartial in imposing the death penalty. Zeisel received a number of awards for his work, most notably from the American Association for Public Opinion Research in 1967 and the American Sociological Association in 1992. In collaboration with David Kaye, Zeisel compiled many of his contributions on legal statistics discussing topics such as DNA profiling, composition and selection of juries, unconstitutional flaws in the House Un-American Activities Committee interrogation, trademark cases Zeisel was involved in, epidemiologic studies, and more. This work was published after Zeisel's death in 1997, under the title *Prove It With Figures: Empirical Methods in Law and Litigation*. Zeisel loved sports. He played tennis and swam on a regular basis and was known for his passion for baseball and the Chicago Cubs. Hans Zeisel died of cancer at his Chicago home in 1992.

Nahel N. Asfour
University of Vienna

See Also: Capital Punishment; Crime Prevention; Deterrence, Theory of; Juries.

Further Readings

Kalven, Harry and Hans Zeisel. "The American Jury and the Death Penalty." *University of Chicago Law Review*, v.33 (1965).

Sills, David. "In Memoriam: Hans Zeisel 1905–1992" *Public Opinion Quarterly*, v.56/4 (1992).

Zeisel, Hans. "The Deterrent Effect of the Death Penalty: Facts v. Faiths." *Supreme Court Review* (1976).

Zeisel, Hans. "Race Bias in the Administration of the Death Penalty: The Florida Experience." *Harvard Law Review*, v.95 (1981).

Zeisel, Hans and David Kaye. *Prove It With Figures: Empirical Methods in Law and Litigation*. New York: Springer, 1997.

Zodiac Killer

The Zodiac Killer is one of the most notorious unidentified murderers of all time. Perhaps the only greater unsolved mystery is that of Jack the Ripper. The Zodiac was active in the city of San Francisco from 1966 to 1970. The first possible victim of the Zodiac was Cheri Jo Bates, an 18-year-old who was brutally murdered outside a public library on October 30, 1966. She and the Zodiac conversed in a dark alley for over an hour and a half before she was killed as a result of 10 knife wounds. On November 29, Zodiac sent his first confession to the police, warning them to publish it or he would kill again. This was followed by another missive on May 29, 1967, this time sent to both the police and Bates's father. The police at the time were working on the assumption that she had known her killer, until the similarities of murders committed by the Bay Side or Zodiac Killer were later brought to their attention. There is still some debate as to whether he actually was responsible for Bates's death.

Meanwhile, he had been busy in the San Francisco Bay area. On December 20, 1968, around 10 p.m., he shot and killed David Faraday and Betty Lou Jensen while they were parked off Lake Herman Road. Six months later, shortly after 12 a.m. on Saturday, July 5, 1969, Darlene Ferrin and Michael Mageau were shot as they sat in Ferrin's car in the parking lot of the Blue Rock Springs Golf Course. However, Mageau survived. The Zodiac called in the murder himself, including the weapon he used and the fact that he had "killed those kids last year, too." On July 31, the Zodiac sent letters to the *San Francisco Examiner*, *San Francisco Chronicle*, and *Vallejo Times-Herald*. He also sent each newspaper one-third of a cryptogram, to be published on each of their front pages by August 1; he again promised a murder spree if his request was not met.

The next attack came on September 27, off the western shore of Lake Berryessa. This night, the Zodiac stabbed Bryan Hartnell six times and Cecilia Shephard 10 times with a double-edged knife while wearing ceremonial garb. He wrote the names and dates of his previous attacks on Hartnell's Volkswagen and, again, called the police. Unbeknownst to him, Hartnell was alive and, along with several others who had seen the

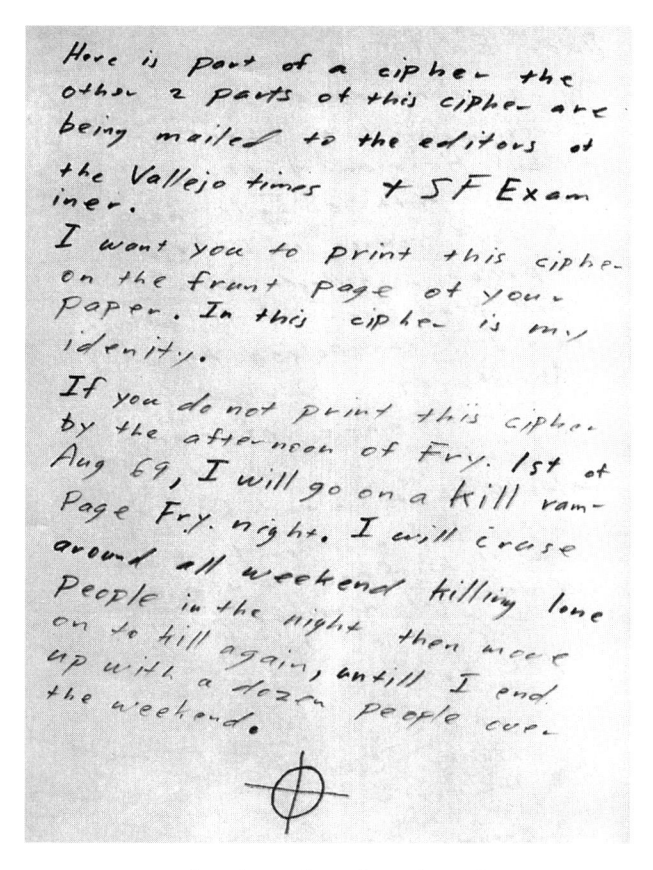

In August 1969, three letters from the Zodiac Killer were sent to the Vallejo Times-Herald, *the* San Francisco Chronicle, *and the* San Francisco Examiner, *demanding that they be printed on the front page of each paper or he would kill again.*

Zodiac that day, was able to give the police a description of a clean-cut man, about 200 lbs., 5'8" to 6', with dark hair. On October 11, the Zodiac shot a cabbie at point-blank range, cut off a piece of his shirt and soaked it in blood, and left. Witnesses watched him do it and called the police. This time, along with his letter of admission and a piece of the cabbie's shirt, the Zodiac sent several taunts to the newspapers about the inadequacies of the police and a card begging for help against the "thing inside him" to famed personal injury lawyer Melvin Belli, though nothing ever came of the latter.

On the evening of March 2, 1970, Kathleen Johns was driving with her infant when a car came up alongside her. A man leaned out the window, telling her that her wheel was loose. She pulled over, and he actually loosened the bolts, causing her tire to come off when she drove away. He offered her a lift to a service station, and she took it. After she became wary of his intentions, she jumped out of his car at a stop sign, clutching her baby to her chest, managing to successfully escape. This was the last time anyone ever saw the Zodiac, though he would continue writing the police letters for several years, intermittently; the San Francisco police have discounted any letters arriving after 1974 as being from the Zodiac. Perhaps one of the most shocking factors about this case is the sheer amount of forensic evidence— over 38 prints—which police collected from the crime scenes and letters. Somehow, even after getting DNA samples from 2,500 men, they were unable to match a single print to anyone, most frustratingly not to their number one Zodiac suspect: Arthur Leigh Allen.

Brandy B. Henderson
University of South Florida

See Also: Murder, History of; Murders, Unsolved; Serial and Mass Killers.

Further Readings
Crime Library. "The Zodiac Killer." http://www.trutv.com/library/crime/serial_killers/notorious/zodiac/river_1.html (Accessed December 2010).
Graysmith, Robert. *Zodiac.* New York: St. Martin's Press, 1976.
Hickey, Eric. *Serial Murderers and Their Victims.* Belmont, CA: Wadsworth, 2010.